Making Open Development Inclusive

Making Open Development Inclusive

Lessons from IDRC Research

Edited by Matthew L. Smith and Ruhiya Kristine Seward

Foreword by Robin Mansell

The MIT Press
Cambridge, Massachusetts
London, England

International Development Research Centre
Ottawa • Amman • Dakar • Montevideo • Nairobi • New Delhi

Published by the MIT Press

A copublication with
International Development Research Centre
PO Box 8500
Ottawa, ON K1G 3H9
Canada
www.idrc.ca / info@idrc.ca

The research presented in this publication was carried out with the financial assistance of Canada's International Development Research Centre. The views expressed herein do not necessarily represent those of IDRC or its Board of Governors.

ISBN: 978-1-55250-595-3 (IDRC e-book)

This book was set in Stone Serif and Stone Sans by Westchester Publishing Services. Printed and bound in the United States of America.

Library of Congress Cataloging-in-Publication Data

Names: Smith, Matthew L., editor. | Seward, Ruhiya Kristine, editor.
Title: Making open development inclusive : lessons from IDRC research / edited by
    Matthew L. Smith and Ruhiya Kristine Seward ; foreword by Robin Mansell.
Description: Cambridge, Massachusetts : The MIT Press, 2020. | Series: International development
    research centre series | Includes bibliographical references and index.
Identifiers: LCCN 2019044368 | ISBN 9780262539111 (paperback)
Subjects: LCSH: Economic development—International cooperation. | Gender mainstreaming. |
    Human rights.
Classification: LCC HC79.E5 M3426 2020 | DDC 338.9—dc23 LC record available at
    https://lccn.loc.gov/2019044368

10 9 8 7 6 5 4 3 2 1

Contents

Preface

This book represents roughly ten years of work on open development in the Global South at the International Development Research Centre (IDRC). The seeds for this work were planted around 2008, when the IDRC program area devoted to information and communication technologies for development (ICT4D) noticed a significant trend emerging in the field concerning openness. The working hypothesis at the time was that open systems related to data, science, innovation, and education could amplify and transform social activities in ways that would radically alter the impacts of ICTs on development.

To better understand the phenomenon, IDRC launched a call for papers in early 2009 to generate critical discussions about the potential of openness in and for development. That call resulted in a volume published in 2013, *Open Development: Networked Innovations in International Development*. That book was the first comprehensive treatment of the matter. However, given the limited amount of research on the subject at the time, it was more about potential and possibilities than realities on the ground.

The last decade of funding research for development focused on openness in various domains has helped to fill this empirical gap—and has been incredibly fruitful in terms of surfacing the realities as to how and in what contexts openness supports development. We believe that there are constructive lessons to draw from these years of research, and we have tried to do so in this volume.

We are hopeful that lessons from this research can be used to improve the production, distribution, and use of open resources in ways that facilitate and challenge people to look beyond their own positions and perspectives.

Acknowledgments

This volume has relied on the dedication and support (and patience) of many people. We would like to thank everyone who contributed to the development of this manuscript—all the authors who have patiently waited while we found the time to bring their parts of the manuscript to completion—as well as the reviewers and International Development Research Centre (IDRC) colleagues who have provided great feedback. Special thanks to Laurent Elder, who leads our team at IDRC and keeps the vision for inclusive development alive, to Cheryl Chan, who really helped us in countless ways during the final stretch of putting the manuscript together, and to Nola Haddadian for shepherding this whole volume through to publishing.

Ruhiya would like to thank Matthew for all the debates and discussions, and for asking her to be involved in this synthesis project. Although finding the time to delve into the material and write while being a program officer at IDRC has been challenging, it has also been incredibly fulfilling to learn so much from our partners' work over the past decade of programming, and to brainstorm new ideas for openness and open practices in development. The collaboration has been enriching and gratifying. She would also like to thank her partner, Dominique, for his support, understanding, and love. Thank you for being a good sounding board and for offering new perspectives. This book is dedicated to you, Dominique.

Matthew would like to thank his father, who was ahead of the curve on openness and is always an amazing sounding board. While Matthew dedicated *Open Development: Networked Innovations in International Development* to his twin daughters, Isadora and Elena, born during the making of the book, this one will be dedicated to his son, Lucas, born a few years later, who is growing up in a world where collaboration and cooperation are needed more than ever to solve our increasingly urgent global challenges. I hope we do, for your and everyone's sake, Lucas.

Foreword

The *Human Development Report 1999* by the United Nations Development Programme (UNDP) asserts that "global markets, global technology, global ideas, and global solidarity can enrich the lives of people everywhere. The challenge is to ensure that the benefits are shared equitably and that this increasing interdependence works for people—not just for profits." The challenge then, as today, is to ensure that governance arrangements consistent with these ambitions are in place. Using a working definition of open development as "the strategic application of open production, open distribution, and/or open consumption of knowledge (often via the digital ecosystem) in the pursuit of advancing human development" (chapter 2), the contributors to this volume foreground the crucial importance of knowledge resources within any development process. Open knowledge resources are understood as those that are shared publicly at no cost for their production, distribution, and/or consumption.

Over more than a decade (since 2009), Canada's International Development Research Centre (IDRC) has sponsored research examining how openness fares in practice. In this volume, the contributors find that "open development" is a very helpful and flexible concept. It signals a wide variety of institutional arrangements and practices that can, in many instances, be consistent with enriching people's lives and livelihoods. Openness is treated as a means toward that end for the Global South, not as a goal in itself. The contributors acknowledge that even when efforts are made to secure open access to data, information, and knowledge, or when projects aimed at enabling inclusive development are labeled as "open," a complex array of power relationships can yield outcomes that may not always be consistent with the goal of inclusive development. This can be the case for initiatives as disparate as open government, open health data, open science, and open innovation in a commercial setting. As Hess and Ostrom (2007, 13) have observed, there are many ways of instantiating an open commons, and the "outcomes of the interactions of people and resources can be positive or negative or somewhere in between."

Castells (1998, 359) observed that "there is an extraordinary gap between our technological overdevelopment and our social underdevelopment." He went on to argue that prevailing interests, values, institutions, and systems of representation often limit collective creativity and generate destructive confrontation. Resistance to opening up data or information resources in a particular country, the presence of conflicting values, such as between openness and the right to privacy, and the use of digital technologies to secure openness in a way that excludes those who cannot access or use the technologies are just some of the factors that can lead to open development not being associated with positive outcomes.

The contributors to this volume are especially sensitive to the potentially asymmetrical power relations that can be reinforced when concepts like open development and their associated practices migrate from the Global North to the Global South, with the risk that they exacerbate existing inequalities and injustices. The contributors seek evidence of whether the sociotechnical and cultural environments are changing in ways that are responsive to the needs and aspirations of people in their local contexts. They offer refreshing insights into the practices that have provided grounds for optimism, as well as for concern, when open development initiatives have been introduced. They present evidence-based challenges to practices that operate through top-down authority and that privilege the private ownership and control of data and information.

The chapters offer a rich panorama of illustrations of the institutions and practices that have promoted bottom-up development. By focusing on practices in the Global South, it becomes clear that initiatives designated as "open," such as some government services, are actually characterized by implementation strategies that exclude as a result of lack of consultation with local people. Open development projects can be exclusionary if they admit only informants and trainees as beneficiaries, with the risk that potential benefits accrue to the already advantaged. The empirical cases emphasize that the governance rules and practices that influence how open development initiatives are designed and implemented are what matter. They demonstrate convincingly that it is crucial to understand these in order to assess whether open development initiatives are addressing development challenges in an inclusive way.

The benefit of a flexible definition of open development is that it allows investigation of the provision of goods and services through nonmarket relations, but also through the commercial market. In addition to research on public-sector and voluntary open development applications, this volume builds a bridge between the literature on openness in the context of commons-based modes of organization for education, governance, or data and the substantial body of research on open innovation and open science. It does so in a way that is sensitive to the potential for various forms of exclusion or repression and to the need to recall that means are needed to ensure that investment is attracted to encourage innovation, often leading to hybrid open and closed institutional arrangements (Mansell 2013).

Questions are raised throughout about the practice of open development, not just about claims to openness and inclusiveness. Whether in relation to gender and inclusion or to open initiatives such as Wikipedia or OpenStreetMap (OSM), it is acknowledged that ostensibly open development initiatives embrace biases associated with power asymmetries, and that the representation of interests is never neutral. The empirical accounts show that absolute "openness" is a chimera. Of greater importance are commitments to values consistent with enriching people's lives and the realization that openness is always situated and conditioned upon the broader context that enables knowledge production, circulation, and application.

This volume offers a very timely tour of practices associated with governing open development at the global, country, and application levels. Its empirically grounded and critical contributions provide an array of perspectives rooted in a variety of disciplines. At the intersection of commons-based research, the role of digital technologies in development, and the challenges of institutionalizing trust and fairness in innovative commercial enterprise, the contributors recognize the persistent tension between those seeking to control data, information, and knowledge and those seeking an open knowledge environment—an environment that makes it more likely that prevailing hegemonies will be challenged effectively.

The outcomes of open development initiatives ultimately depend on choices on the part of stakeholders concerning which values and strategies toward knowledge resources should be favored. As Chambers (2017, xiv) puts it, "we will always need to go on learning how to know better, and through knowing better, doing better." In the case of open development strategies and practices, this volume paves the way for future research agendas that are needed to ensure a scaling-up of forms of openness that will benefit the excluded and disadvantaged. This is one way of ensuring that investment in open development in the Global South succeeds in "doing good" rather than simply "looking good" (Enghel and Noske-Turner 2018).

Robin Mansell
Department of Media and Communications
London School of Economics and Political Science

References

Castells, Manuel. 1998. *The Information Age: Economy, Society, and Culture—Volume III—End of Millennium*. Oxford, UK: Blackwell Publishers.

Chambers, Robert. 2017. *Can We Know Better? Reflections for Development*. London: Practical Action Publishing.

Enghel, Florencia, and Noske-Turner, Jessica, eds. 2018. *Communication in International Development: Doing Good or Looking Good?* New York: Routledge.

Hess, Charlotte, and Elinor Ostrom, eds. 2007. *Understanding Knowledge as a Commons: From Theory to Practice*. Cambridge, MA: MIT Press.

Mansell, Robin. 2013. "Employing Crowdsourced Information Resources: Managing the Information Commons." *International Journal of the Commons* 7 (2): 255–277.

United Nations Development Programme (UNDP). 1999. *Human Development Report 1999*. New York: Oxford University Press. http://hdr.undp.org/en/content/human-development-report-1999.

1 Introduction: Governing Openness in an Unequal World

Matthew L. Smith and Ruhiya Kristine Seward

Introduction

This book is about the practices of openness in international development, and how they serve (or do not serve) inclusive development goals. It builds on and extends the theory articulated in the 2013 book *Open Development: Networked Innovations in International Development,* by deepening the understanding of how the design and deployment of *openness in practice* affects inclusion. When that book was written, open development was a relatively new phenomenon, with limited empirical research. As such, it aimed to document open development activities and their theoretical potential role in social change. Since then, a proliferation of openness practices and concomitant research have emerged, which makes this area ripe for deeper analysis.

This volume represents a synthesis of the research on open development that Canada's International Development Research Centre (IDRC) has been supporting since 2009. Each chapter delves into different aspects of how openness functions in practice in a wide range of contexts and environments. The authors use a variety of approaches to explore the relationship between openness and inclusive development, and, in some cases, critique or problematize its connections to human development. The aim is to present empirically informed critical perspectives and constructive lessons drawn from the research to inform and improve open development practice to ensure that it fulfills its inclusive promise.

This chapter lays out the central question driving the book: what is the connection between open development practices and inclusion (in its manifold political and socioeconomic forms) in the Global South? It starts with a brief discussion of what we mean by openness, inclusion, and development, and how these concepts interconnect. It then problematizes openness and inclusive development by unpacking inequalities in the Global South—the primary research context in this book—and discusses instances when openness has led to inclusive development outcomes and when it has not. Finally, the chapter connects openness and governance of the knowledge commons, which are important to the open development puzzle overall and to the analysis in this book.

Openness, Inclusion, and Development

Openness, inclusion, and development are tricky concepts to unpack and to understand. The term "openness" has multiple meanings and interpretations, associated as it is with a verb (to open), a noun (openness), and an adjective (an open door). And, of late, a wide range of online content and social practices have coopted the term to give ideas, platforms, and applications a veneer of availability or transparency. Indeed, "open" is increasingly associated with nearly anything available on the Internet.

Inclusion and development are similarly contested concepts. In the contexts in which IDRC works, "to include" and "to develop" (or "Who is included?" and "What is development?") are normative statements (and questions) that are built on assumptions about optimizing the good for the greatest number, and on goals of supporting human beings in their quest to achieve their highest aspirations. Yet unpacking inclusion and development into calculable, knowable, empirical notions is not an easy task. As goals—or rather, *pillars*—both seem to be a function of unique experience and positionality. For example, indicators such as gross domestic product (GDP) show something about a context in which people are living, but they do not speak to genuine happiness or well-being (which, at least for some, development and inclusion are meant to support).

You can imagine, then, that combining ill-defined concepts to describe open development might cause confusion, and, in our experience, it has. Indeed, some argue that a singular definition is undesirable and ultimately hypocritical, as it *closes* off other alternatives (Davies et al. 2013). Fortunately, complete agreement on a singular definition is not essential in order for learning to occur. But to help bridge at least some of these communication gaps, we have focused on a definition of "open" as it *exists in practice* (which is spelled out in detail in chapter 2) so there can be clarity about *the actual practices* under discussion. We might not all agree with the use (or not) of the word "open," but we can point to an activity happening in the world as signifying an open practice. We have found this to be a fruitful approach.

In contrast to our attempts to achieve some clarity with the concepts of open and openness, we have allowed for flexibility around the meaning of and perspectives on development and inclusion across the contributions in this volume. As Global North authors, schooled in the social sciences in Europe and North America, we hold our own views on what constitutes development and inclusion. In this volume, we have tried our best not to impose our definitions, in order to allow the volume's authors freedom in defining the territory according to their contexts. Thus, the meaning and expression of inclusion (who is included) and development (how and for what/whom) are determined by each of the authors of this volume, who themselves are drawing on diverse perspectives and practices in a variety of domains.

Now that we have successfully muddled the issue, let us explore what "open development" means. A few examples help set the stage and point to a tentative definition.

Example: Open Educational Resources in Afghanistan

More children are enrolled in school in Afghanistan now than in any other time in the country's history. Yet teachers there struggle to find materials appropriate for their classrooms that are available in the three languages taught in Afghan public schools: Dari, Pashto, and English. Openly licensed learning materials are changing this, making new and relevant content available in Afghanistan through an online portal, Darakht-e Danesh.[1] These learning resources can be adapted and adopted to fit the various curricula and contexts. They enable teachers to download, repurpose, print, copy, and use the materials—as well as to contribute their own content—and to engage students in new ways of learning.

Example: Open Data in Burkina Faso

Supporting free and transparent elections in a country transitioning from single-party rule poses many challenges. Perhaps the most critical concerns for democracy are instilling trust in the electoral process and preventing prolonged uncertainty about the results. Burkina Faso's Commission Électorale Nationale Indépendante (CENI) confronted these challenges when administering the country's election in November 2015. Ensuring political buy-in for the processing and publication of verified election results was one concern that CENI could address by collaborating with the Burkina Open Data Initiative[2] and the Open Data Institute.[3] The resulting Open Elections project supported CENI with a web application that enabled citizens to access election results instantly as they were validated on Election Day. This improved the flow and accessibility of election information such that, just over 24 hours after the polls closed, results were announced, and accepted, by all candidates. The Burkina Faso experience of using open-data tools, skills, and technologies during the election illustrates the potential of sharing data to augment transparency and credibility during moments of political transition.

Example: Open Science in Lebanon

Rural water supplies—negatively affected by pollution and the dumping of waste and hazardous chemicals—are a crucial concern for many communities in Lebanon. And the people living near these water sources are arguably the best positioned to monitor supplies and alert municipal representatives when there are issues. So communities across Lebanon, in partnership with the American University of Beirut–Nature Conservation Center (AUB-NCC), are using crowdsourced citizen data to monitor water supplies, reduce untreated wastewater, and improve recycling and reuse methods. Village committees meet with chemists, engineers, and community development specialists from the AUB-NCC to learn how to test water supplies and exchange information on water-quality issues. Citizen scientists conduct experiments with low-cost monitoring toolkits and generate their own data on the quality of water supplies. Water committees then organize meetings to disseminate and discuss their findings with the community at large, and follow up with municipal and local legal authorities to find ways of improving water quality with new, affordable technologies. In one village, the project has even led to a permanent water-testing lab overseen by the water committee. Supported by the findings from citizen scientists and grassroot-level collaborations, the AUB-NCC is helping communities generate remedial solutions and reach out to local decision-makers, companies, investors, and other communities across Lebanon to improve water supplies.[4]

These three examples—all research case studies featured in this book—demonstrate how the open production, distribution, and use of knowledge resources can support broader human development objectives. Innovations in openness, from open government to open science, are often characterized by their potential benefit to society in many arenas of social activity and organization. Indeed, openness can affect any domain where information and knowledge contribute to social change—data, policymaking, budgets, education and educational resources, science, research data, software, and innovation, to name only a few.[5]

This book documents many examples of these activities and provides numerous cases of openness practices that contribute to achieving inclusive development aims. While open development covers a wide range of activities emerging from theoretically and practically diverse origins, at its core are questions of institutional governance in the production and sharing of knowledge resources to achieve development aims. We discuss the origin and definition of open development more thoroughly in chapter 2 of this volume.

While open development has different historical roots, the diverse practices that it implies are typically inspired by a value system that recognizes openness as a good thing. This stems from the view that open practices can offer cost-effective means of tackling pressing problems of inequity and inequality. Open educational resources (OER), for instance, offer new and virtually cost-free (to the user) resources for learning that can be adapted to local contexts, although there may be associated access costs for users, such as those for connectivity and data to access the resources. Similarly, the transparency and accountability afforded by open governance resources, like open data or open budgets, can be leveraged to uncover not only the existence of socioeconomic inequality, but also the political and economic root causes.

Openness innovations do not just potentially affect development outcomes, though. They also bring into question, rearrange, or even overturn basic assumptions about how to go about development work in practice and who should play what roles (Smith and Reilly 2013). For example, the ability to tap into collective intelligence has brought into question the predominance of the role of experts in many situations, such as when teachers take advantage of the freedom associated with OER to engage students in the creation of course content by drawing on each student's own experiences and knowledge. Similarly, the emergence of crowdfunding and crowdlending for development-related activities like building schools or roads and supporting young entrepreneurs in rural communities challenges what was once primarily the ambit of more traditional bilateral development agencies from the Global North.

More significantly, perhaps, open development creates a space for a reboot of development theory and practice itself. Open development innovations provide novel institutional arrangements in the production and distribution of knowledge and creative works that challenge the dominant development paradigm of a market-led information society (Benkler 2006; Reilly and Smith 2013; Mansell 2013). As Mansell explains, "The 'open' or commons-led alternative imaginaries are characterized by some form of 'digital resistance' to the universal model of the information society. This usually involves some form of countervailing power, a privileging of co-operation and collaboration over competition, and innovative forms of networked collaboration often by dispersed communities" (2013, 11).

Open Development in an Unequal World

The links between openness, inclusion, and development are not always straightforward or direct. The capabilities required to access and engage in open activities vary greatly across people and populations. These differential capabilities across the world are a function of a myriad of social and individual factors, such as infrastructure for mobile phone and Internet access, affordability of pricing structures, education levels, cultural attitudes toward women and girls, and more.

To understand the research and analysis presented in this book, it is imperative to situate the work within the time and context in which it all took place (from about 2009 to 2018) and the overall trends in international development during this period. There was a major recession that affected the world's economy (and led to disruptive austerity measures in Europe) after the financial crisis in 2008. Antigovernment protests in Tunisia in 2011 sparked a wave of political (and then repressive) action across North Africa and the Middle East, which in turn ushered in a war in Syria and the rise of the Islamic State of Iraq and Syria (ISIS), both online and on the ground. We have also seen an increase around the world in nationalism and authoritarianism and a turn away from the principles of international collaboration and cooperation. This includes movements away from earlier commitments to openness, such as Tanzania, Hungary, and Turkey withdrawing from the Open Government Partnership; the 2016 election of a US president who has undermined the open government approach of his predecessor; and the election of numerous leaders in the Global South for whom transparency, accountability, dissent, equitable development, and gender equality are not a priority, or even a part of their governance model.

These global shifts have been accompanied by the diffusion of new online communication and networking tools and platforms, particularly the increasing use of mobile technologies and social media applications. Yet the surge in user-generated content on self-styled web platforms and pages that marked earlier manifestations of the Internet have been increasingly scooped up by online data behemoths like Google and Facebook. Though the wider availability of broadband and mobile connectivity globally has provided billions of people with new communication channels and lowered historical barriers to entry in the information and communication marketplace, new users are now increasingly flocking to a narrowing number of online platforms run by only a few companies. As we see in chapter 5, in some instances, these platforms play a significant role in the potential for shared content to be discovered and used.

Indeed, the reliance on popular platforms like Facebook as the de facto digital public sphere and source for news in many countries is further limiting the possibility for genuine engagement. In contrast to the democratization of the public sphere promised by the decentralized Internet architecture, the existence of a few highly used platforms has centralized the flow of information for many individuals. This results in a high concentration of information power that can then be leveraged by new machine-learning techniques for highly targeted "precision propaganda" campaigns (Ghosh and Scott 2018, 5; Smith and Neupane 2018). This is particularly concerning in countries where ethnic or other tensions already exist. For instance, there are cases where misinformation spread through Facebook contributed to inciting violence in South Sudan, and a viral WhatsApp message provoked retaliatory lynchings in eastern India (Roose 2017).

There are now daily examples in the news of how misinformation is impacting people and political systems. This threat will likely only deepen with the development of artificial intelligence techniques that allow the creation of compellingly realistic fake video and audio files of speeches (*Economist* 2017). This proliferation of freely shared news content as a key means of spreading misinformation and propaganda poses a legitimate threat to democracy (Persily 2017).

Along with this, the ever-increasing amount of data being generated from our online activities is having a broad and often not well understood impact on our rights online—particularly for our privacy and security. The massive increase in online activity and available user data is exponentially increasing surveillance capabilities—not only for state actors from the intelligence communities, but also for private corporations, hackers, and other rogue or non-state actors. This concurrent expansion of surveillance capabilities knows almost no state boundaries and is almost completely unregulated. Although not always well understood by the average user, these kinds of issues have a chilling effect on free expression and undermine trust in online systems over time.

Enduring issues for the bottom billion persist as well. There is, for example, worsening inequality and inequity that persist between and within countries, among rural and urban populations, between women and men, and amid historically marginalized groups, such as Indigenous and ethnic minority populations. Research from the United Nations Development Programme (UNDP) and from the World Bank shows that inequality is rising within countries, and absolute inequality, as measured by the Gini coefficient, has increased dramatically in the past forty years (UNDP 2016, 30–31).[6] Recently, this increase has become even more dramatic, massively disadvantaging the poorest: "Since 2000, 50 percent of the increase in global wealth benefited only the wealthiest one percent of the world's population. Conversely, the poorest 50 percent of the world's population received only one percent of the increase" (UNDP 2016, 31).

Similarly, access to the benefits of the digital revolution remains radically uneven. Despite the rapid spread of mobile devices and broadband Internet around the world, nearly 2 billion people still do not use mobile phones, even though 7 billion people (or 95 percent of the global population) live in areas covered by a cellular network (ITU 2016). And nearly 4 billion people are not using the Internet at all, constituting 53 percent of the global population (ITU 2016). International Telecommunications Union (ITU) data show that "3.9 billion people remain cut-off from the vast resources available on the Internet, despite falling prices for ICT services" (ITU 2016). Only 15 percent of the world can access high-speed Internet (UNDP 2016, 31).

All of this means that even as broadband infrastructure, especially mobile broadband, has become more available in rural areas, last mile challenges,[7] the cost of handsets, and

access to bandwidth continue even now to confine broadband usage to wealthier segments of the population. Considering these figures in relation to the digital gender gap,
women have far less access to the Internet than men in many, if not most, parts of the
world. Globally, the difference is 44.9 percent for women versus 51.1 percent for men;
but in developing countries, it is 37.4 percent for women versus 45 percent for men (ITU
2016, 3).[8]

In sum, open development activities are happening in a challenging climate. There
is a recent slight trend where countries are actively rejecting the principles of openness, as well as an increase in the risks of engaging online, particularly in the political
sphere. Genuine engaged participation among the poorest and least connected in the
public sphere, both online and on the ground, remains limited. Most digital engagement still requires reliable access to the Internet, use of computers or smartphones, and
expendable income to pay for data access. Sometimes these differences are referred to
as "digital poverty" rather than the "digital divide." The divide has been described as
a lack of access to and full use of the information and communications allowed by the
technology tools caused not just by deficient connectivity, but also by lack of demand,
often related to inadequate income, and lower capacity, due to literacy or skill deficits
(Barrantes 2007; also see chapter 9).

Openness = Less Equality?

Given that the contributions of technology to social change are a function of a myriad
of contextual factors, it could be that innovations in openness are contributing to
and exacerbating existing inequalities. Indeed, some research on openness has uncovered examples where it has led to less, rather than more, equitable outcomes in a broad
range of openness activities.

For example, in the area of open data, Rumbul (2015) looked into who engages with
open government data projects seeking to increase public engagement and participation in Kenya and South Africa, and found disparities among users and nonusers along
gendered and educational lines. Across the projects she examined, around 70 percent of
users were male and a majority of users were educated (Rumbul 2015, 13). Indeed, both
open government and open data seem to require tempered or deconstructed optimism,
and both are currently suffering somewhat from the shift in global politics and political alignments that displace transparency and accountability from the main agenda.
A key research finding in the Open Data Barometer (2017) is that the overall readiness
of governments to adopt and implement open data initiatives has been regressing. It is
also the case that government transparency in some contexts might undermine good

governance (Lessig 2009; Bannister and Connolly 2011). For example, open data can be biased, contributing to misinterpretation and misuse (Zuiderwijk and Janssen 2014), and openness around more sensitive types of data can lead to violations of the right to privacy (Martin and Bonina 2013). Moreover, open government initiatives are sometimes coopted to serve a deregulation agenda that generally benefits the private sector and wealthier echelons of society. Jo Bates noted, "As the most vulnerable in society are facing substantial public spending cuts, the OGD [open government data] model risks being interpreted as, and potentially becoming, little more than a corporate subsidy" (2012).

Along similar lines, in a synthesis of citizen-voice crowdsourcing initiatives, Peixoto and Fox (2016) found only seven (out of twenty-three) initiatives resulted in a high degree of governmental responsiveness. When analyzing whose voices were being collected, they found that those most in need were usually underrepresented (Peixoto and Fox 2016, 19)—perhaps due in part to the enduring digital poverty of those communities.

Other research shows that openness practices, such as peer collaboration, are incredibly challenging in low-resource settings (Berdou 2017). In this volume, Graham and De Sabbata (chapter 5) explore the data from online peer production platforms such as Wikipedia and find that use and participation are gendered and deeply unequal geographically (see also Graham and Hogan 2013). Similarly, a study of a microwork platform in Latin America, as discussed in chapter 14 of this volume, found a skewed distribution, where a very small number of freelancers ended up getting the most jobs. Furthermore, full participation on such platforms is not possible without access to computers with the appropriate software—something that is limited in low-resource settings.

Research on the use of MOOCs found that their users tend to have both higher socioeconomic status and more formal education. One study in the United States found that users of sixty-eight MOOCs offered by Harvard University and the Massachusetts Institute of Technology (MIT) "tended to live in more-affluent and better educated neighborhoods than the average US resident" (Hansen and Reich 2015, 1245). The researchers conclude that while such digital learning innovations might raise all boats, it could also lead to an increasing divergence in educational outcomes between low– and high–socioeconomic status groups. Christensen et al. (2013) similarly found that MOOC participants, particularly in middle-income countries like Brazil, Russia, India, China, and South Africa (aka the BRICS) and in other lower-income countries as well, are more likely to be employed, highly educated, and male.

The sharing of open access scholarly journal articles can also generate adverse dynamics that further marginalize academics and research from across the Global South (see chapter 6). One mechanism for this is the increasing dependence on only a few platforms for distribution and discovery of online knowledge resources, which can lead to de facto monopolization and closure through algorithms that systematically favor some results over others. Until larger systemic issues are tackled, such as how metrics like the journal impact factor create bias by placing institutional pressure on authors to publish in particular journals (e.g., tenure predicated on publishing in top-impact journals) and journal editors' choices of what is an acceptably relevant article to publish (i.e., those articles that will be cited), these inequalities will most likely persist despite the emergence of open access (Chan and Gray 2013; Okune et al. 2016).

The fear, then, is that openness could be reinforcing the effect of accumulative advantage where the rich get richer, also known as the "Matthew Effect" (Merton 1968). This is not a surprising development (Gurstein 2011; Toyama 2011), particularly given current levels of inequality and the rise of reactionary authoritarianism, but it is nevertheless a challenge to open development optimism and the hypothesis that it is a force for inclusive development.

On the other hand, there is research that suggests there is room for hope for the openness hypothesis. Snijder (2013) found that over 70 percent of online usage data—from a set of 137 open access academic books—came from developing countries. This provides evidence that researchers from developing countries seek out and benefit from free academic books. Garrido et al. (2016) looked at the use and perceptions of MOOCs in Colombia, the Philippines, and South Africa and found that 80 percent of users come from low- and middle-income populations, and 80 percent have only basic or intermediate information technology skills. Furthermore, they found that women are more likely than men to complete a MOOC or obtain certification. Similarly, research on a teacher-training MOOC developed by Peking University in China found that 60 percent of participants came from the less-developed regions of China (Wang et al. 2018). Furthermore, Maitland and Obeysekare (2015) found that development-focused MOOCs can contribute to building students' social capital even beyond learning gains. And, of course, there are more examples outside of education, some of which can be found in this book.

Policy and Practice Dynamics in Openness

From the research discussed in this book, we can identify three openness-related policy and practice dynamics that contribute to the unequal distribution of benefits flowing from openness in Global South contexts.

First, concerted efforts have not yet been made consistently to overcome constraints and promote effective use. Theories of (and advocacy for) openness have focused on the production and distribution (i.e., the supply) of open content, while largely ignoring, or underresourcing, the use (i.e., the demand for) of the content. The goal for many, but certainly not all, openness projects is to make digital content open, full stop—often for legitimate reasons. Furthermore, openness initiatives have mainly avoided the more contentious power relationships or have met with resistance when doing so. While we see a trend toward more ecosystemic and bottom-up approaches (some evidenced in this book), the literature produced thus far can teach us a lot about how to produce and share, but not as much about how to engage and support effective use.

Second, Global North values are embedded. Openness movements and a plurality of the openness innovations have come out of North America and Europe. In some cases, these innovations are funded by philanthropic foundations, and, in the Global South context, by international and bilateral aid agencies. This is especially true in areas such as open government data, open access, and OER. One consequence has been the emergence of openness best practices, underlying theories, and supporting technologies that implicitly contain the values and assumptions of these contexts, and that at times conflict with the realities of developing-country contexts. When this happens, these best practices can steamroll possibilities for important local adaptations.

Third, openness policy lags practice. As with many emergent technosocial innovations, it takes a while for policy to catch up. Many governments have begun to support openness at the national and international level, such as through OER policies or by joining the Open Government Partnership. Some countries, such as Uruguay, have been first movers in this space (Brazil at one time was also a first mover, but is looking less so at the end of 2019). However, the general trend is that governments have not yet figured out how to leverage the possibilities of openness to improve governance, education, health, and other development outcomes. Where there are well-intentioned policies, they are often not backed up by meaningful implementation, rendering the policies themselves irrelevant. And, in some circumstances, some open policies are short lived, undermined by policy reversals, lax implementation, underresourcing, and problems with institutionalization.

The point of this section is not to argue that openness leads directly to greater inequality—not at all. Neither is its purpose to present a wholly gloomy picture about openness activities in international development. Its point, rather, is to understand what happens in situations where openness has led to unequal outcomes, and to find alternate ways that practices and tools can be harnessed to allow openness to achieve its full potential. This is one of the aims of this book.

As is clear from this discussion, the relationship between openness, development, and inclusion is not straightforward. Open development innovations always have a form and a place, and it is the diversity of these forms and places that results in a wide range of outcomes. The chapters in this book explore a broad variety of experiences of openness in developing-country contexts, across many domains and while uncovering a multitude of outcomes. This knowledge helps to deepen our understanding of the relationship between openness practices, their contexts, and development. It is from this contextualized learning that we can move to more applicable and generalizable lessons for practice and policy. We try to draw out such lessons in the concluding chapter of this book.

Indeed, the imperative for understanding and improving practices of openness is growing. If we view openness within its historical context, it can be understood both through a range of ideas about openness (such as open government) and through theories of development in the twentieth century (such as participatory development). These historical roots are important to understand because even as openness has grown in prominence globally, so has openwashing (Thorne 2009) and counternarratives that appear to close or partition knowledge.[9]

As previously discussed, some innovations in openness afforded by the Internet—for instance, open government data and open access to scholarly publishing—are under some threat by new institutional arrangements and reactionary politics. Indeed the actual closing of open data and open government initiatives, as well as the ending of net neutrality in the United States in 2018, could signal troublesome trends for open development. Boyle's (2003, 2008) predictions from over a decade ago (i.e., that we are headed toward a second enclosure movement rather than more openness) seem worryingly prescient thus far. We can see this happening on a technical level with the emergence of non-web-based applications and in the consolidation of online content by a handful of dominant providers. Now is the moment when policymakers and civil society need to work together to decide what our knowledge commons should and need to be, for the future, to support human potential and innovation.

So while the proliferation of open development innovation could be creating a moment of renewal for development theory and how the work of development is undertaken practically through the day-to-day work of policymaking and research, this moment will not necessarily last. The opportunity could fade if practitioners cannot harness it and make the alternative imaginary a feasible and tangible reality. This involves, in part, countering forces that are threatened by open practices and those people, places, and institutions that seek to maintain their privileged positions. In particular, the inclusivity inherent in the promise of open development must be realized to stir up and improve on the practices for which open development provides enhanced alternatives—like participatory practices or open government. Failing to leverage openness to facilitate inclusive change could translate into a closing of the alternative imaginaries that make open development so compelling.

Governing Open Development for Inclusion

Harnessing open development for inclusive development can be thought of as an issue of institutional governance in the production and sharing of knowledge resources to achieve equitable, inclusive development outcomes. In the same way that communities govern the knowledge commons (Frischmann et al. 2014), they also govern openness (knowledge governance is discussed in more detail in chapters 2 and 3 of this volume). This governance happens at four levels.

First, at a global level, the formal mechanisms of governance for the knowledge commons globally are embedded in relationships among and between states such as bilateral and multilateral trade-agreements. Currently, the trend is toward enclosing (i.e., commodifying) the commons through pushing for increasingly strict intellectual property (IP) regulation within global or regional trade agreements (de Beer and Ogua-manam 2013).

Second, at the national level, governance happens via the state and the market. This level includes IP; telecommunications policy; the current offering of Internet and mobile services; laws around censorship and freedom of expression, surveillance and privacy, and access to knowledge (Internet rights); and various facets of culture, socio-economics, and politics.

Third, at the provincial/state, municipal, and institutional levels, as well as via specific institutions where open development applications reside, there is often some level of autonomy in decision-making and policy direction that affects the shape and nature of openness. For example, some states and provinces might have specific open data or OER policies, and institutions such as specific universities might have an open access policy and a bespoke position on IP rights.

Fourth, there is governance at the level of the application. An application can be hyperlocal or global in scale and scope, depending on the open activity and the underlying technology that facilitates it. This includes a variety of elements that shape the possibilities and nature of human participation, such as the underlying technology and human interface; the related norms, values, and roles of the online community; and the substance and form of data, information, and knowledge. Several specific openness applications are discussed in this book, such as citizen-sourcing applications and collaborative platforms for creating and sharing OER.

The first three levels—the global, national, and state/institutional—can be thought of as the ecosystem within which open development applications, the fourth level, exist. All four levels, however, interact and affect the particular outcomes of the applications and the relative equity of their benefits.

Structure of the Book

This volume has three sections which cover defining open development, governing the open development ecosystem, and governing open development applications.

Part I, "Defining Open Development," has two chapters that provide empirically informed theoretical underpinnings to the concept of open development. While the two chapters present different perspectives on how to frame open development, they agree that the production, distribution, and consumption of knowledge are the defining components.

Following that introductory material, the bulk of the book focuses on synthesizing lessons across research at either the ecosystem or application level. Part II, "Governing the Open Development Ecosystem," has six chapters that examine issues and outcomes at the state and global level. These issues include the inequality of access and use of open knowledge resources, infrastructure (both technological and in terms of knowledge access), and economic and social policy.

Part III, "Governing Open Development Applications," includes a series of in-depth treatments of interventions in specific domains of development, including governance, education, science, and informal innovation.

The concluding chapter summarizes and synthesizes the key takeaways from the book and looks forward to new issues emerging around the governance of the knowledge commons for development.

One cluster of issues that we do not cover in this book are those around openness in relation to privacy—such as issues of surveillance, data governance, and security/safety in relation to digital rights. We do have researchers from our portfolio of projects who work on these issues, but time constraints made the production of a chapter difficult. It is a rich and understudied territory, and we look forward to exploring it more in the future.

We hope that you enjoy the book.

Notes

1. For more on the Darakht-e Danesh library, see Oates (2017).

2. See more about the Burkina Faso Data Portal at http://burkinafaso.opendataforafrica.org/.

3. An open data platform, Open Data Burkina Faso (http://data.gov.bf/), with fifty open data sets, was launched by Burkina Faso's national information and communication technology agency, Agence Nationale de Promotion des TIC (ANPTIC), in June 2014. For more on the case study, see Scott (2016).

4. For more about this case study, see Talhouk et al. (2019).

5. Other areas include open government and data, open legislation, open education and educational resources, open science and research data, open-source software, and open innovation.

6. The Gini coefficient or index is a measure of inequality that shows the income or wealth distribution of a nation's residents. See the Organisation of Economic Co-operation and Development's definition of the coefficient (https://stats.oecd.org/glossary/detail.asp?ID=4842).

7. The last mile challenge refers to the final leg of a telecommunications network meant to deliver services (telephone, internet, or television via cable for instance), often to underserved, remote areas that are not always economically viable because the cost of delivering the service is higher than the anticipated income. For a more thorough explanation, see the "Last Mile" entry on Wikipedia (https://en.wikipedia.org/wiki/Last_mile).

8. The context is more complicated than these figures indicate, though. For instance, household survey data from twelve African countries from 2011 to 2012 and 2007 to 2008 suggest that mobile ownership and Internet use are determined by users' income, education, and location, but *not* gender. See Khan (2016).

9. Thorne (2009) defines openwashing as: "to spin a product or company as open, although it is not. Derived from 'greenwashing.'" Openwashing extends beyond the private sector to the public and not-for-profit sectors as well.

References

Bannister, Frank, and Regina Connolly. 2011. "The Trouble with Transparency: A Critical Review of Openness in e-Government." *Policy & Internet* 3 (1): 1–30.

Barrantes, Roxana. 2007. "Analysis of ICT Demand: What Is Digital Poverty and How to Measure It?" In *Digital Poverty: Latin American and Caribbean Perspectives,* ed. Hernan Galperin and Judith Mariscal, 29–54. Ottawa: IDRC. https://idl-bnc-idrc.dspacedirect.org/handle/10625/29762.

Bates, Jo. 2012. "'This Is What Modern Deregulation Looks Like': Co-optation and Contestation in the Shaping of the UK's Open Government Data Initiative." *Journal of Community Informatics* 8 (2). http://ci-journal.net/index.php/ciej/article/view/845/916.

Benkler, Yochai. 2006. *The Wealth of Networks: How Social Production Transforms Markets and Freedom.* New Haven, CT: Yale University Press.

Berdou, Evangelia. 2017. "Open Development in Poor Communities: Opportunities, Tensions, and Dilemmas." *Information Technologies & International Development* 13:18–32.

Boyle, James. 2003. "The Second Enclosure Movement and the Construction of the Public Domain." *Duke Law Journal* 66:33–74. https://law.duke.edu/pd/papers/boyle.pdf.

Boyle, James. 2008. *The Public Domain: Enclosing the Commons of the Mind.* New Haven, CT: Yale University Press.

Burkina Faso Data Portal. n.d. "Burkina Faso: Data at a Glance." http://burkinafaso.opendataforafrica.org/.

Chan, Leslie, and Eve Gray. 2013. "Centering the Knowledge Peripheries through Open Access: Implications for Future Research and Discourse on Knowledge for Development." In *Open Development: Networked Innovations in International Development,* ed. Matthew L. Smith and Katherine

M. A. Reilly, 197–222. Cambridge, MA/Ottawa: MIT Press/IDRC. https://www.idrc.ca/en/book
/open-development-networked-innovations-international-development.

Christensen, Gayle, Andrew Steinmetz, Brandon Alcorn, Amy Bennett, Deirdre Woods, and Eze-
kiel J. Emanuel. 2013. "The MOOC Phenomenon: Who Takes Massive Open Online Courses and
Why?" November 6, *SSRN*. http://papers.ssrn.com/sol3/papers.cfm?abstract_id=2350964.

Davies, Tim, ed., Duncan Edwards, Linda Raftree, Mika Välitalo, Pernilla Näsfors, Sarah Johns, Claudia
Schwegmann, and Matthew L. Smith. 2013. "Exploring Open Development." In *The Open Book*, ed.
Kaitlyn Braybrooke, Jussi Nissilä, and Timo Vuorikivi, 45–61. London: Finnish Institute in London.

De Beer, Jeremy, and Chidi Oguamanam. 2013. "Open Minds: Lessons from Nigeria on Intellectual
Property, Innovation, and Development." In *Open Development: Networked Innovations in International Development*, ed. Matthew L. Smith and Katherine M. A. Reilly, 249–272. Cambridge, MA/
Ottawa: MIT Press/IDRC. https://www.idrc.ca/en/book/open-development-networked-innovations
-international-development.

The Economist. 2017. "Fake News: You Ain't Seen Nothing Yet." July 1; https://www.economist
.com/news/science-and-technology/21724370-generating-convincing-audio-and-video-fake
-events-fake-news-you-aint-seen.

Frischmann, Brett M., Michael J. Madison, and Katherine J. Strandburg. 2014. "Governing Knowledge Commons." In *Governing Knowledge Commons*, ed, Brett M. Frischmann, Michael J. Madison,
and Katherine J. Strandburg, 1–43. New York: Oxford University Press.

Garrido, Maria, Lucas Koepke, Scott Andersen, Andres F. Mena, Mayette Macapagal, and Lorenzo
Dalvit. 2016. *The Advancing of MOOC Usage for Development Initiative: An Examination of MOOC
Usage for Professional Workforce Development Outcomes in Colombia, the Philippines, and South Africa*.
Seattle: Technology and Social Change Group, University of Washington.

Ghosh, Dipayan, and Ben Scott. 2018. *Digital Deceit: The Technologies behind Precision Propaganda
on the Internet*. Washington, DC: New America Public Interest Technology Team. https://www
.newamerica.org/public-interest-technology/policy-papers/digitaldeceit/.

Graham, Mark, and Bernie Hogan. 2013. *Uneven Openness Barriers to MENA Representation on Wikipedia: Final Technical Report*. Ottawa: IDRC. http://hdl.handle.net/10625/53449.

Gurstein, Michael. 2011. "Open Data: Empowering the Empowered or Effective Data Use for
Everyone?" *First Monday* 16 (2). http://www.uic.edu/htbin/cgiwrap/bin/ojs/index.php/fm/article
/view/3316/2764.

Hansen, John D., and Justin Reich. 2015. "Democratizing Education? Examining Access and
Usage Patterns in Massive Open Online Courses." *Science* 350 (6265): 1245–1247; http://science
.sciencemag.org/content/350/6265/1245.full.

International Telecommunications Union. 2016. *Measuring the Information Society*. Vols. 1 and
2. Geneva, Switzerland: Author. https://www.itu.int/en/ITUD/Statistics/Documents/publications
/misr2016/MISR2016-w4.pdf and the press release: https://www.itu.int/en/mediacentre/Pages/2016
-PR30.aspx.

Khan, Safia. 2016. "Taking the Microscope to ICT Gender Gaps in Africa." *CPRSouth (Communication Policy Research South) Conference. Inclusive Innovation,* Session 6, Zanzibar, Tanzania, September. http://www.cprsouth.org/wp-content/uploads/2016/09/CPRsouth-2016_PP83_Khan.pdf.

Lessig, Lawrence. 2009. "Against Transparency." *New Republic* October 9. https://newrepublic.com/article/70097/against-transparency.

Maitland, Carleen, and Eric Obeysekare. 2015. "The Creation of Capital through an ICT-Based Learning Program: A Case Study of MOOC Camp." In *Proceedings of the Seventh International Conference on Information and Communication Technologies and Development—ICTD '15*, 1–10. Singapore: ACM Press; https://doi.org/10.1145/2737856.2738024.

Mansell, Robin. 2013. "Introduction: Imagining the Internet: Open, Closed, or in Between." In *Enabling Openness: The Future of the Information Society in Latin America and the Caribbean*, ed. Bruce Girard and Fernando Perini, 9–20. Montevideo, Uruguay/Ottawa: Fundación Comunica/IDRC. https://idl-bnc-idrc.dspacedirect.org/bitstream/handle/10625/52195/IDL-52195.pdf?sequence=1&isAllowed=y.

Martin, Aaron K., and Carla M. Bonina. 2013. "Open Government and Citizen Identities: Promise, Peril, and Policy." In *Open Development: Networked Innovations in International Development*, ed. by Michael L. Smith and Katherine M. A. Reilly, 223–248. Cambridge, MA/Ottawa: MIT Press/IDRC. https://www.idrc.ca/en/book/open-development-networked-innovations-international-development.

Merton, Robert K. 1968. "The Matthew Effect in Science." *Science* 159 (3810): 56–63. http://www.garfield.library.upenn.edu/merton/matthew1.pdf.

Oates, Lauryn, Letha K. Goger, Jamshid Hashimi, and Mubaraka Farahmand. 2017. "An Early Stage Impact Study of Localised OER in Afghanistan." In *Adoption and Impact of OER in the Global South*, ed. Cheryl Hodgkinson-Williams and Patricia B. Arinto, 549–573. Cape Town/Ottawa: African Minds/IDRC; Cape Town, South Africa: Research on Open Educational Resources for Development. https://www.idrc.ca/en/book/adoption-and-impact-oer-global-south.

Okune, Angela, Becky Hillyer, Denisse Albornoz, Nanjira Sambuli, and Leslie Chan. 2016. "Tackling Inequities in Global Scientific Power Structures." *African Technopolitan* 4 (1): 128–131. https://tspace.library.utoronto.ca/bitstream/1807/71107/1/Tackling%20Inequities%20in%20Global%20Scientific%20Power%20Structures.pdf.

Open Data Barometer. 2017. *Global Report*. 4th ed. Washington, DC: World Wide Web Foundation. https://opendatabarometer.org/?_year=2017&indicator=ODB.

Open Data Burkina Faso. n.d. "Home Page". http://data.gov.bf/.

Open Data Institute. n.d. "Home Page". http://theodi.org/.

Ortiz, Isabel, Sara Burke, Mohamed Berrada, and Hernan C. Saenz. 2013. *World Protests 2006–2013*. Working Paper No. 274. New York: Initiative for Policy Dialogue; Washington, DC: Friedrich-Ebert-Stiftung. http://policydialogue.org/publications/working-papers/world-protests-2006-2013/.

Peixoto, Tiago, and Jonathan Fox. 2016. *When Does ICT-Enabled Citizen Voice Lead to Government Responsiveness?* World Development Report 2016 Background Paper, World Bank. https://openknowledge.worldbank.org/handle/10986/23650.

Persily, Nathaniel. 2017. "Can Democracy Survive the Internet?" *Journal of Democracy* 28 (2): 63–76.

Reilly, Katherine M. A., and Matthew L. Smith. 2013. "The Emergence of Open Development in a Network Society." In *Open Development: Networked Innovations in International Development*, ed. Matthew L. Smith and Katherine M. A. Reilly, 15–50. Cambridge, MA/Ottawa: MIT Press/IDRC. https://www.idrc.ca/en/book/open-development-networked-innovations-international-development.

Roose, Kevin. 2017. "Forget Washington. Facebook's Problems Abroad Are Far More Disturbing." *The New York Times*, October 29. https://www.nytimes.com/2017/10/29/business/facebook-misinformation-abroad.html.

Rumbul, Rebecca. 2015. *Who Benefits from Civic Technology? Demographic and Public Attitudes Research into the Users of Civic Technologies*. London: mySociety. https://www.mysociety.org/files/2015/10/demographics-report.pdf.

Scott, Anna. 2016. "Case Study: Burkina Faso's Open Elections." London: Open Data Institute; https://theodi.org/case-study-burkina-fasos-open-elections.

Smith, Matthew L., and Sujaya Neupane. 2018. "Artificial Intelligence and Human Development: Toward a Research Agenda." Ottawa: IDRC. https://www.idrc.ca/en/book/open-development-networked-innovations-international-development.

Smith, Matthew L., and Katherine M. A. Reilly, eds. 2013. *Open Development: Networked Innovations in International Development*. Cambridge, MA/Ottawa: MIT Press/IDRC. https://idl-bnc-idrc.dspacedirect.org/bitstream/handle/10625/52348/IDL-52348.pdf?sequence=1&isAllowed=y.

Snijder, R. 2013. "Do Developing Countries Profit from Free Books? Discovery and Online Usage in Developed and Developing Countries Compared." *Journal of Electronic Publishing* 16(1). https://quod.lib.umich.edu/j/jep/3336451.0016.103?view=text;rgn=main.

Talhouk, Salma N., Rima Baalbaki, Serine Haydar, Wassim Kays, Sammy Kayed, Mahmoud Al-Hindi, and Najat A. Saliba. 2019. "Contextualizing Openness: A Case Study in Water Quality Testing in Lebanon." In Contextualizing Openness: Situating Open Science, ed. Leslie Chan, Angela Okune, Rebecca Hillyer, Denisse Albornoz, and Alejandro Posada, 107–121. Ottawa: University of Ottawa Press/IDRC. https://www.idrc.ca/en/book/contextualizing-openness-situating-open-science.

Thorne, Michelle. 2009. "Openwashing," March 14. http://michellethorne.cc/2009/03/openwashing/.

Toyama, Kentaro. 2011. "Technology as Amplifier in International Development." In *Proceedings of the 2011 iConference: Inspiration, Integrity, and Intrepedity*. Seattle, February 8–11, 75–82. New York: ACM Press. http://dl.acm.org/citation.cfm?id=1940772.

United Nations Development Programme (UNDP) (ed.). 2016. *Human Development for Everyone*. New York: Author. http://hdr.undp.org/sites/default/files/2016_human_development_report.pdf.

Wang, Q., B. Chen, Y. Fan, and G. Zhang. 2018. *MOOCs as an Alternative for Teacher Professional Development: Examining Learner Persistence in One Chinese MOOC.* Quezon City, Philippines: Foundation for Information Technology Education and Development. http://dl4d.org/wp-content/uploads/2018/05/China-MOOC.pdf

Zuiderwijk, Anneke, and Marijn Janssen. 2014. "The Negative Effects of Open Government Data—Investigating the Dark Side of Open Data." *Proceedings of the 15th Annual International Conference on Digital Government Research,* Aguascalientes, Mexico, June 18–21, 147–152. New York: ACM Press. https://dl.acm.org/citation.cfm?doid=2612733.2612761.

I Defining Open Development

2 Updating Open Development: Open Practices in Inclusive Development

Matthew L. Smith and Ruhiya Kristine Seward

Introduction

Given that the intention of this book is both to synthesize and to draw practical lessons from a wide variety of *open development* activities, definitional clarity is helpful to allow some generalization and cross-domain learning. The aim of this chapter is to provide a deeper understanding of open development and present a clearer definition of the concept for use in research. In refining our understanding, the definition that we offer is derived from years of research and theory building. It provides a basis for synthesis across cases and domains explored in this book (e.g., comparing lessons from open educational resources (OER) with lessons from open government data). It also focuses more succinctly on the digital knowledge commons as a core theoretical underpinning of open development, a focus that emerged from researchers in various fields adopting this perspective. It also represents a turn away from a technology and network-centric definition.

The chapter starts with a discussion of the term *open development*, its evolution, and a refined definition. It provides a brief overview of key research fields, movements, and concepts that inform openness in general and open development in particular. The contributing schools of thought are useful to foreground, as they offer insights into the influences and practices of open development. We then draw on these schools of thought to refine and operationalize our definition of openness further, with a focus on openness as *praxis*, which is about bringing theory into action.[1] We conclude with a few thoughts on open development and its relationship to other fields of inquiry.

(Re)defining Open Development

When the International Development Research Centre (IDRC) started exploring research and field building on open practices in different domains, the field itself was undefined. While there was an emerging interest in the potential of openness across many domains, such as data, educational practices, science, knowledge, and access to scholarly publishing, evidence for a link between openness and development was weak or nonexistent. There was also no consensus around what openness meant.

One of the earliest attempts to define open development took an inductive approach, selecting and extracting common features from a wide range of activities labeled as *open*. The intention was to develop an inclusive, umbrella-like definition under which the myriad of specific openness activities would fit. The resulting definition of *openness* was "shorthand for information-networked activities that have, relatively speaking, more information that is freely accessible and/or modifiable and more people who can actively participate and/or collaborate" (Smith, Elder, and Emdon 2011, iii). This definition highlighted two key elements: openness of content and openness to people.[2] While this definition included a wide variety of openness activities, it was also vague and proved tricky to operationalize from a research perspective.

This was followed by a more thorough treatment of open development, which framed openness as "networked models predicated on digital network technologies" (Smith and Reilly 2013, 3). These are models that "draw on the power of human cooperation and contain some combinations of … sharing ideas and knowledge; the ability to reuse, revise, and repurpose content; increasing transparency of processes; expanding participation; and collaborative production" (Smith and Reilly 2013, 3).

Since charting out this early territory, we have learned a lot from the experiences and struggles of the open development researchers whom IDRC has supported over the years. This experience has helped us to clarify and provide more nuance to the definition. Perhaps the greatest struggle comes from defining *open*. There is much debate regarding the meaning of this word, with multiple definitions being adopted across various domains and contexts. This is hardly surprising, given the relatively rapid proliferation of the use of the term and the multiple possible interpretations (Pomerantz and Peak 2016). The end result, as we detail later in this chapter, is that often these theoretical definitions of *open* do not match the reality of openness in practice, and the lack of a common definition inhibits the transferability of lessons learned.

Most openness research relies on definitions from the literature from within a specific domain or discipline of research (as discussed in chapter 3 of this volume). For instance, *open* in terms of educational resources is defined in a particular way among educators, which is different from what *open* means to the open government data community. Moreover, researchers referenced throughout this book found that domain-specific definitions did not always resonate with the reality of openness in Global South contexts. For example, there are cases where governments intended to share their data openly, but their efforts did not match the strict definition required by open data theorists. There are also cases where educators shared educational resources openly without a particular intellectual property license required by the widely accepted OER definition. This mismatch between definition and the reality that the researchers uncovered was a common theme emerging from many country contexts and domains of action. To exclude examples from nonconforming initiatives around the Global South would greatly limit our understanding of the reality of how openness plays out on the ground in countries where, for example, strong copyright institutions or cultures are not the norm.

Another common feature is that domain-specific definitions also tend to define *open* as digital content with specific features (such as an appropriate copyleft intellectual property license). We found that this emphasis distracted researchers from issues that we find to be more relevant to the overall success of an open initiative. Typically, the focus on the openness of digital content led to interventions dominated by a supply-side approach, largely ignoring and eschewing responsibility for whether the knowledge resource is part of a change process or not.

Furthermore, conceptualizing openness in terms of digital content with particular attributes makes impact evaluation challenging. Does it make sense to talk about the impact of data that is open, in terms of copyright, if it sits on a website that is never used? The upshot is that we found that researchers who adopted a content-specific definition of *open* struggled to assess or evaluate the impact of openness interventions. Perhaps, not surprisingly, there is little by the way of impact or outcome research in the area of open development thus far (Bentley and Chib 2016).

A key takeaway from these experiences is that digital content does not have an impact on its own; impacts emerge only through the production, sharing, and use of content. This influenced the theorizing of openness presented here that focuses not on digital content, but rather on the particular practices of producing, sharing, and using knowledge resources.

Finally, a further problem of using domain-specific definitions is that they make potentially informative comparisons across openness domains difficult, if not impossible. For example, even though they both share an *open* label, the definitions of OER and open government data are different, and comparing them is to compare apples and oranges. Ideally, we would like to be able to learn and share lessons, where possible, from experiences and research across domains, and, in so doing, be able to avoid making the same mistakes many times over. This will accelerate improvements in open development overall.

Drawing from these challenges and from the research found in this book, we update the definition of open development as follows: *Open development is the strategic application of open production, open distribution, and/or open consumption of knowledge (often via the digital ecosystem) in the pursuit of advancing human development.*

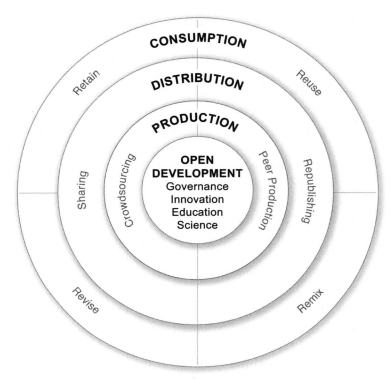

Figure 2.1
Open development as it plays out (such as in education, science, and governance) consists of the practices of producing (crowdsourcing and peer production), distributing (sharing and republishing), and using (retaining, reusing, revising, and remixing) digital or analog resources.

There is a lot to unpack in this definition (illustrated in figure 2.1), including what we mean by "open production," "open distribution," and "open consumption," which we cover in this chapter. This definition offers several clear advantages. It provides both an abstract, crosscutting approach that can be made more specific to accommodate different openness activities and contexts. Furthermore, the greater specificity of the definition through its focus on open practices helps to address the research challenges highlighted previously.

Before unpacking the history and the iteration of the definition, we offer a few observations to help clarify and provide a contrast to past thinking.

First, the definition is agnostic as to the nature of development itself, although it tends toward a normative, or politically progressive, understanding of human development, in that the concern is about expanding human capabilities. It also generally refers to openness within international development contexts. This is consistent with earlier definitions (e.g., Reilly and Smith 2013, 32). One could imagine taking a more ideological position, whereby the definition of what constitutes development—particularly around political and socioeconomic considerations—shapes the contours of the open development definition. However, the focus here is more on the connection of openness to development and how to best engage in open activities to advance development aims, where development itself is defined by the goals of the activities.

Second, this definition places a greater focus on knowledge resources.[3] The first definition of *openness* focused on information-networked activities, or "digital openness" stemming in part from the history of information and communication technologies for development (ICT4D) and literature on the network society (see chapter 2 in Reilly and Smith, 2013). This new definition foregrounds knowledge resources rather than the digital networks that make the production, distribution, and use of these resources possible. In so doing, this definition opens up the possibilities for integrating models of openness that are not driven by technologies. As mentioned, this change of perspective was influenced by IDRC-supported research on open development (see, for example, chapters 3, 6, 10, 12, and 13 in this volume).

Therefore, third, the definition no longer refers exclusively to digitally enabled openness. As the research over the past decade has shown, there are many, typically local, open development activities in developing countries that extend a digitally open initiative through analog means, meaning that not all open development processes are necessarily digital. For example, open budget transparency initiatives sometimes involve holding community meetings and distributing posters about government service delivery in health centers and schools. Indeed, one might argue that in some contexts, local analog (offline) transparency initiatives tend to prove more effective than large-scale national, digital open data based ones. See chapter 3 for further arguments against requiring a link between openness and digital.

At the same time, the benefits of lowered transaction costs and massively increased reach of digitally enabled (typically Internet-based) open activities have propelled the rapid increase in interest in openness since the advent of open-source software. Just as the printing press was a boon for the transmission of selective kinds of knowledge, the ease of replicating and distributing digital content through the Internet has greatly expanded the potential reach of the knowledge itself, including in analog forms.

Fourth, this definition shifts the undergirding theoretical emphasis away from (digital) information networks and the network society and grounds it in the vision of the knowledge society. This is not to suggest that networks are not critical features of today's society, nor that seeing the world through a network society lens is not useful for analyzing open development initiatives (see, e.g., chapter 10 of this volume). Rather, this shift emphasizes a society where learning, training, and participation are core activities (Mansell and Tremblay 2013) and inclusive production, distribution, and consumption of knowledge play a key role in supporting these activities. It is the movement toward elements of social change that interest us. Thus, open development, while for the most part predicated on digital information networks, contributes to social change through innovations of *open* production, distribution, and consumption of *knowledge* resources. As de Beer writes in chapter 3 of this volume, "the tension between control over and access to knowledge is a—perhaps *the*—unifying thread in open development." This has implications not just for the literature that informs open development, but for policy as well, particularly with respect to intellectual property rights (see chapter 6 of this volume).

Finally, the new definition is also much more specific about *open praxis*—bringing theory into action—manifesting as processes and practices. As detailed next, there are three open social processes: production, distribution, and use. The *action*-orientation implied in open praxis ties directly into participation and broad-based engagement, and thus into inclusion—the focus of this book. We have found that this focus on praxis, and these specific open social processes, helps to improve clarity and accuracy when engaging in research and enables comparative research through a common theoretical framing. It also makes for easier identification of other relevant literature that may refer to similar practices but use different terms. Finally, it connects openness with use and, therefore, improves understanding of potential pathways from openness to development outcomes (Smith and Seward 2017). We explore some implications of this approach in more detail later in this chapter.

Contributing Schools of Thought

To understand open development, it is helpful to understand the historical context from which the variety of new openness innovations has emerged. The working definition of *open development* offered in this chapter draws heavily from across these contributing schools of thought and provides an overarching theoretical framework to bring different schools of thought into conversation with each other. One hope for this approach is that it can engender a more interdisciplinary and fruitful path forward for open development, which is already a multidisciplinary field of inquiry.

These are not meant to be comprehensive discussions, but merely distillations or highlights of common recurring themes in open development literature. In many ways, these main contributing schools of thought can be seen as part of the open

Table 2.1
Open development contributing schools of thought.

School of thought	Contributions
Open government	Freedom of information Transparency for accountability
Participatory development and ICTs	Participation as agency Participation as shorthand for inclusion Technology facilitating agency/new participatory processes
Commons-based peer production	Open-source software Open (copyleft) licensing User freedoms: reuse, remix, repurpose, republish
Open innovation	Chesbrough and crowdsourcing von Hippel: User-centered, *free* innovation
Access to knowledge	Right to knowledge Knowledge as key to justice, freedom, and economic development
Knowledge commons	Community governance (creation/sharing) of shared knowledge resources
ICT4D	Connection between ICTs and social change Importance of local context Multiple approaches to development

development literature. This discussion is also useful for pointing readers to other relevant literature that may not always be immediately associated with open development.

Open Government

According to scholars, *open government* emerged as a recognizable term in the 1950s, largely due to journalists and newspaper editors in the United States demanding greater transparency in government decision-making after World War II.[4] One of the first uses appeared in the foreword of a report in 1953 (Cross 1953) about people's right to access public records and proceedings (Yu and Robinson 2012, 185).[5] This seminal report became a foundation for journalists in the United States and the freedom of information movement more broadly. From 1953 on, open government began to resonate more widely as a principle for government transparency and accountability. In 1955, the US Congress created a subcommittee on government information where the main counsel for the committee used the term in an article on public information to convey the need for government accountability.[6] These works on open government in the 1950s helped generate greater public scrutiny and interest in holding governments accountable and also helped to spark far-reaching legislation like the US Freedom of Information Act (FOIA) of 1966 (5 U.S.C. § 552).

Inspired in part by the digital innovation of open-source software (more on this next), open government got a reboot in the twenty-first century. This new iteration, not unlike the 1950s version, is generally undergirded by a similar idea—that democratic governments and governance processes should be open to public scrutiny, characterized by similar themes of transparency and accountability. However, the twenty-first-century version also foregrounds citizen participation and collaboration, acknowledging the importance of giving people (not just journalists) a voice in policymaking and decision-making.[7] In some sectors, open government also serves as a platform for public-sector modernization, in order to foster greater coherence in government activities, and promote more effective public oversight of governance processes. There is also a focus on open standards and open data as a means of sparking innovation and economic growth.

Yet the relationship between open government and open data generates some debate. Perhaps it is one of the ongoing tensions within democracies, or in systems of governance that aim to be more participatory, that real transparency and accountability over high-level decision-making that really matters are often lost. Open government data initiatives can promote the *perception* of transparency and accountability by releasing certain kinds of public data sets, but, ultimately, if the data sets have no real bearing on power and economic relations, then substantive changes to governance (and the promises of greater transparency and accountability) are forgotten. Because discussions around open data often fill the debate space in open governance, a hazy distinction remains between the politics of open government and the technologies used for open data (Yu and Robinson 2012, 181).

Participatory Development and ICTs

Similar to how open government emerged to encourage citizen engagement with governance processes, participatory development emerged and gained momentum by trying to upend human development processes and make them more receptive to local beneficiary populations and less captured by Western donor-driven priorities.[8] And like open government, participatory development (broadly considered) was also renewed in the twenty-first century by innovative communication networking tools.

Philosophically, theories of participatory development coalesced out of critiques of post–World War II modernization ideas that elevated Western institutions and values above the values of then-colonized, so-called *underdeveloped* populations. This imposition of institutional superiority only intensified with the decolonization processes

in the twenty years following the war. While the modernization approach to development was a top-down, high-debt-inducing infrastructure and institutional development process, participatory development prioritized bottom-up, grassroots development
processes that considered the value of unique cultural situations and environments.[9]
Couched in postcolonial, emancipatory narratives, participatory development advocates a role reversal, whereby subordinated subjects take back power from dominant
decision-makers and institutions. In the 1990s, participatory approaches to decision-
making in development became popular, and, over time, branched out into a broad
range of practices, from participatory rural appraisal, to participatory evaluation, to
participatory budgeting.[10]

Yet because participation, like the concept of open, has both a theory and a practice
component, it can also be captured for purposes other than empowerment and transformation. The mainstreaming of participation in development, for instance, meant
that simple consultations and participation in project implementation were framed in
emancipatory language but were often just mechanisms for gaining approval from subjects in development initiatives planned elsewhere (Huesca 2002). What participatory
development offers mainstream development now is the discursive and programmatic
focus on inclusion and pro-poor development; it also indicates that the principles of
development for the poorest and the marginalized remain the norm. Yet relying on
broad categories like *inclusion* and *marginalization* to stand in for development that
prioritizes the poor conveys a much more policy-oriented (even top-down) thinking
and moves the conversation away from the individual agency inherent in participatory methodologies. Fundamentally, the idea that development should be inverted to
serve not educated practitioners, but rather vulnerable recipients elsewhere, remains a
perennial tension in development work.

Participatory development, like open government, was repurposed with the mass
diffusion of information and communication technologies (ICTs). Mobiles and social
media platforms associated with the interactivity of new iterations of the World Wide
Web seemed perfect for the renewal of the idea that people needed to be at the center
of their development—the "participatory potential of new connectivity" according to
Chambers (2010, 28–29). And importantly, these new tools brought agency back into
the development conversation. As noted by Chambers (2010, 29), "With Web 2.0 for
dev, and its cornucopia of potentials through email, Internet, video conferencing, participatory GIS [geographic information system], mobile phones, SMS [short message
service], blogging, Twitter and beyond, a whole new domain of participatory interaction has opened up. … The explosion of activity is based on open source technology and
philosophy and participatory approaches, with continuous and multiplying volunteer

contributions from within and outside. ... It illustrates the runaway empowering potentials of new combinations of technology and volunteer commitment, energy and creativity. We are in a new space."

Today, information and communication networks are continuing to change and upend how international development is conducted. About a decade ago, this was coined "development 2.0" (Quaggiotto and Wielezynski 2007; Thompson 2008; Heeks 2010a), though the extent of change continues to unfold in a multitude of positive—and negative—ways. Every new technology application designed to foster engagement and participation often brings with it a range of other, sometimes pernicious, issues. One increasing concern, for instance, is around data and the data exhaust from all the activities performed online, which affects human rights online (or digital rights), such as the right to privacy and the right to security. But the tools offered by mobile and web connectivity are still expanding possibilities for the participation envisioned by early enthusiasts for these methodologies.

Commons-Based Peer Production

The first, and perhaps most recognized, example of commons-based peer production is the open-source software production model. Open-source software is significant as a pioneering approach and inspiration for the emergence of most other open development initiatives, such as open access to scholarly publishing, OER, open government (Mizukami and Lemos 2008), and even the ICT-based participatory development methodologies highlighted earlier in this chapter. Understanding what made the open-source software production model possible is essential, therefore, to understanding open development.

Open-source software has two important, influential features. The first is the collaborative production model that leveraged the interconnectivity provided by the Internet with the knowledge, skills, and time of volunteer programmers and the sharing of source code. This new form of collaborative production enabled the development of high-quality software products by groups operating outside of public- and private-sector firms, and without the need for large infusions of capital.

The second element is the development of copyleft intellectual property licenses, which made the open-source software production model legally possible. A *copyleft* license uses the legalities of copyright to make it legal to freely share the software while providing, rather than restricting, user freedoms. For software, this was embodied in the following four freedoms. The first is the freedom to run the program as you wish, for any purpose. The second is the freedom to study how the program works and to change it as you like. Access to the source code is a precondition for this freedom. The third is the freedom to redistribute copies of the original program so that others can benefit from it. The fourth is the freedom to distribute copies of your modified version to others. By doing this, you can give the whole community a chance to benefit from your changes.

Together, collaborative production and copyleft intellectual property licenses formed what was later termed "commons-based peer production" (Benkler 2002). The commons-based peer production model has since evolved into a panoply of variations, including the well-known Wikipedia (Fuster Morell, Martinez, and Maldonado 2014). The movement from software to other knowledge production activities was also enabled by the development of a new copyleft licensing system via Creative Commons (CC). CC licenses provide different degrees of freedom regarding the potential use of the knowledge resource, such as to retain, reuse, revise, remix, and redistribute (Wiley 2014). These freedoms and their centrality to most interpretations of openness are discussed in more detail in the following sections.

Open Innovation

Open innovation is another significant and influential school of thought (particularly in innovation management), with a rich and growing tradition (Huizingh 2011). There are two main subfields of open innovation: the collaborative, user-centered innovation of von Hippel and the firm-centric approach championed by Chesbrough. The democratized innovation of von Hippel (2005) focuses on the ability of firms to adopt user-centered, free innovations. These innovations are "developed by consumers at private cost," and the innovations are not protected by intellectual property rights (von Hippel 2017, 1). This model is in contrast to the traditional innovation model, where innovations are developed by firms in a closed manner, using patents and copyrights. In this way, von Hippel's notion of open innovation is similar to Benkler's idea of commons-based peer production in its reliance on open resources and the ability of users to use and reuse them to fit their purposes.

By contrast, Chesbrough's open innovation suggests that firms no longer need all requisite research and development resources in-house. This is driven by the idea that "valuable ideas can come from inside or outside the company and can go to market from inside or outside the company as well" (Chesbrough 2006, 43). While the original definition has been updated over time to reflect both pecuniary and nonpecuniary knowledge flows (West et al. 2014), the basic idea of knowledge purposefully flowing in and out of a firm is the same. The term *open* in this open innovation is employed to describe the firm and its relationship to knowledge resources.

One way that firms are able to attract purposive inflows of knowledge is through *crowdsourcing*, a term coined in 2006 (in contrast to *outsourcing*) to describe how firms can tap into huge pools of digitally connected cheap laborers (i.e., the *crowd*) from anywhere around the world (Howe 2006). Crowdsourcing involves a central entity (individual or organization) enlisting the services of any number of people through an open call, typically through an Internet-based platform (Estelles-Arolas and González-Ladrón-de-Guevara 2012). "Crowdsourcing involves participants who are invited to contribute to highly specific and predetermined tasks, whose completion requires little effort" (Berdou 2017, 19). Key to crowdsourcing is its hierarchical and centrally managed nature, in terms of both governance and technical architecture (de Rosnay and Musiani 2016).

Some definitions of crowdsourcing have also been applied to commons-based peer production models (Mansell 2013; de Rosnay and Musiani 2016). While both models involve collaborative efforts to produce knowledge resources, we follow Benkler, Shaw, and Hill (2015) and Mansell (2013) and make a distinction between crowdsourcing and commons-based peer production models. We do this for two main reasons. First, the model of governance is quite different, as commons-based peer production is not necessarily centrally managed and hierarchical. Second, they differ in their use (or not) of commons-based information resources. Crowdsourcing initiatives do not, by definition, include sharing of the resulting crowdsourced data or knowledge products. Of course, the management of a crowdsourcing initiative *can* choose to share the results if desired. In the international development space, the sharing of the crowdsourced data is common as part of a larger change strategy, such as for awareness raising and advocacy. See chapter 14 for examples and analysis of some crowdsourcing for development activities.

While crowdsourcing here is under the ambit of open development, other elements of Chesbrough's highly influential conception of open innovation sit uneasily within the current open development literature. This is in large part because *open* in Chesbrough's open innovation does not adopt the commons-based approach that is found at the core of most open activities. In contrast to leveraging sharing and the freedoms afforded by copyleft licenses, open innovation, as per Chesbrough, typically requires strong intellectual property rights over knowledge resources to enable firms to extract rents from subsequent innovations. How insights from Chesbrough's firm-centric perspective might further inform open development is discussed in greater length in chapter 3 of this volume.

Access to Knowledge

As with other influential schools of thought in open development, the access to knowledge (A2K) movement supports knowledge generation and sharing that prioritizes benefits to the many over the exclusive rights of a few. Although it remains highly contested territory, according to Shaver (2007, 4–6), there are essentially three basic ideas driving the A2K movement: (1) knowledge is a resource; (2) accessibility is important; and (3) governments are endowed with the means to facilitate access to knowledge and its diffusion. To explain further, this means that first, knowledge is an important resource for human well-being because it accelerates human development and innovation. In turn, the ease or difficulty of gaining access to existing knowledge is thus a significant factor in how quickly innovations can be leveraged and adopted. This includes both a concern over the cost of access, which determines how, when, and whether people can access new knowledge. It also conveys an inherent normative concern for equity, in that everyone should be able to benefit from advances in knowledge. Lastly, knowledge is public, or a *common* good, and thus falls under the purview of governments as the collective holder of public goods, in the context of the social compact between states and citizen/stakeholders. This suggests that governments have the political capital necessary to see through regulation and investment that support more equitable access to knowledge resources. See chapter 7 in this volume for more on the relationship between knowledge, public goods, and social policy.

The A2K movement emerged in the early years of the new millennium in response to what appeared to be the increasing enclosure of knowledge resources through Northern-led intellectual property regimes that were becoming "broader (covering more kinds of information), deeper (giving rights holders greater powers), and more punitive (imposing greater penalties on infringers)" (Kapczynski 2010, 24).[11] This has made intellectual property law "a central battleground in the struggles over the structure and spoils of the contemporary economy" by regulating information production strategies, appropriating value from that information in the marketplace, and also by trying to regulate everything "from how we are able to learn, think, and create together to how and whether we have access to the medicines and food that we need to live" (Kapczynski 2010, 24).

It has become so significant because knowledge resources have become increasingly important for the organization of human society in the twenty-first century—undergirding economic innovation, scientific advancement, and even ethical and human development. As such, the uneven distribution of knowledge stands to have an even larger impact on how societies function, how they cohere, how they grow, and how humans within those societies flourish (Castells 2000). Thus, knowledge and its generation are not only critical to human development but access to knowledge is grounded in basic human rights, in Article 27 of the Universal Declaration of Human Rights (United Nations 1948).[12] For this reason, one of the primary concerns of the A2K movement is to ensure that knowledge resides in the commons as a public resource, not a private one.

Knowledge Commons

The A2K movement, as previously noted, highlights both the importance that knowledge plays in the development of societies and individuals and new agreements for equalizing knowledge access. For the A2K movement, openness innovations represent new ways that more flexible intellectual property contributes to knowledge being produced, circulated, and consumed to advance development. Put in other terms, openness innovations are new forms of governance of the knowledge commons.

The concept of the knowledge commons has its roots in the *traditional* commons as developed by Ostrom and Ostrom (1977), an interdisciplinary study of shared natural resources, such as fish stocks, water bodies, and the air (Hess and Ostrom 2007, 4). The governance arrangements of the commons exist to overcome problems thought to be intrinsic to shared natural resource commons, such as free riding and over harvesting.

The knowledge commons focuses on knowledge resources rather than natural resources. In this literature, knowledge is defined quite broadly as "all intelligible ideas, information, and data in whatever form in which it is expressed or obtained" (Hess and Ostrom 2007, 7). Through examples, Hess and Ostrom (2007, 7–8) suggest that "[k]nowledge … refers to all types of understanding gained through experience or study, whether Indigenous, scientific, scholarly, or otherwise nonacademic. It also includes creative works, such as music and the visual and theatrical arts."

The knowledge commons, then, is "shorthand for the institutionalized community governance of the sharing and, in some cases, creation, of information, science, knowledge, data, and other types of intellectual and cultural resources" (Frischmen et al. 2014, 3). It is important to note that in this case, *knowledge commons* does not refer to knowledge resources, but rather to institutional arrangements (i.e., the governance) of those knowledge resources. These governance arrangements can reside at many levels, local, global, or "somewhere in between" (Hess and Ostrom 2007, 9).

It is these institutional arrangements governing the knowledge commons that allow for "overcoming various social dilemmas associated with sharing and producing information, innovation, and creative works" (Frischmann, Madison, and Strandburg 2014, 1). Note that these social dilemmas are not the same challenges for natural resource commons of free riding and over harvesting. Rather, these threats include "commodification or enclosure, pollution and degradation, and nonsustainability" (Hess and Ostrom 2007, 5). These are clearly the challenges to open innovations. Furthermore, the governance of the knowledge commons also typically comes with a normative goal: maximizing access, equity, and sustainability (Pearson and Stacey 2017).

Information and Communication Technologies for Development

The final contributing school of thought is ICT4D, a field that began in the middle of the 1980s as an offshoot of the information systems discipline (Heeks 2008; Walsham 2017). Information systems is not a technical field, but rather consists of the study of ICTs in society, "positioned between management studies and applied computing," and draws on many reference disciplines (Avgerou, Ciborra, and Land 2004, 1). ICT4D furthers this multidisciplinary approach, focusing research on ICTs and social change in developing countries across a range of domains such as governance, health, education, business, and agriculture (Elder et al. 2013; Gomez 2013).

A key characteristic of the ICT4D literature is the focus on understanding how ICTs connect to socioeconomic development (Avgerou 2010; Heeks 2010b; Madon 2000; Walsham and Sahay 2006). Central to this research agenda is nuancing the relationship of technologies to social change, countering the allure of grand promises of technologically driven change to view ICTs as enablers of change embedded in social contexts and enacted through the individual agency of users (Friederici, Ojanperä, and Graham 2017; Schech 2002). Decades of studies have explored the roles and interaction of contextual factors such as levels of telecommunications diffusion, the institutional environment, socioeconomic status, and ICT skills, among others, in shaping any resultant social change and benefits related to technologies (see, e.g., Alderete 2017; Barrantes and Vargas 2016). Indeed, a corollary contribution of the ICT4D literature is illuminating the significance, role, and diversity of developing country contexts where information systems are being implemented (Avgerou 2008; Walsham 2017). In particular, this literature explores the importance of embracing both contextual sensitivity and diversity (Walsham 2001).

Open development as a potential field of research and practice emerged for some as an offshoot of the ICT4D field (see Smith and Elder 2010; Smith et al. 2011). As mentioned previously, openness was seen as a set of new social organizational models made possible with ICTs (Smith and Reilly 2013). The current definition offered in this chapter, however, is broader than these earlier definitions as it draws more heavily on the contributions and insights of the other schools of thought discussed in this chapter.

Openness as Praxis

Having explored the origins of openness, we now describe in more detail its meaning within open development. In this section, we discuss the specifics of open as a process of producing, distributing, or consuming open knowledge resources (i.e., open production, open distribution, and open consumption of knowledge resources).

First, by knowledge resources, we are broadly incorporating the ideas behind the knowledge commons which includes "all intelligible ideas, information, and data in whatever form in which it is expressed or obtained" (Hess and Ostrom 2007, 7–8). As discussed previously, for the most part, the open development cases in this book represent knowledge in a digital form, although digital representation is not a necessary condition to fit within our consideration of open development.

The term *open knowledge resources,* then, refers to knowledge resources that are publicly shared at *no cost.* This content may or may not be legally in the public domain or openly licensed. This definition is in contrast to other definitions that require resources to be in the public domain or openly licensed (see, e.g., Open Knowledge International's collaboratively developed "Open Definition"[13]). However, our definition allows us to capture the reality that much of the research in this book uncovered; for users of knowledge resources in many developing countries, the line between free, illegal, and open is often blurred at best (Smith 2014; Smith and Seward 2017). Thus, rather than excluding these activities, we choose to include them within the scope of our understanding of open development. Note that this is an analytical position rather than a normative one. We are not saying that illegally downloaded and shared resources are either good or bad, but rather that, as the research shows, the normative stance depends on both the context and one's particular perspective.

The second definitional component is comprised of three processes of *open production, open distribution,* and *open consumption* of knowledge resources (see table 2.2). First, *open production* processes are knowledge production processes that take advantage of collective intelligence (Bollier 2007). In particular, the two most common knowledge production models in open development are crowdsourcing and peer production. Second, *open distribution,* which is also known as *sharing and republishing,* is the practice of making knowledge resources publicly available, which are typically (but not solely) accessed via an Internet-based platform. In other words, it is the sharing of open knowledge resources. Open distribution can have many purposes, such as contributing to the knowledge commons, achieving communications goals, or instigating behavior change, to name a few. It is useful to note that we consider transparency to be sharing with the purpose of accountability.

Third, *open consumption* refers to the set of uses of knowledge resources afforded by the fact that they are shared open knowledge resources. Typically, the affordances are mostly thought to be a function of different legal and technical configurations of content, but they are subject to social influences as well. One typology for open consumption practices, the 5 Rs (retain, reuse, revise, remix, and redistribution), comes out of the OER literature (Wiley 2014). Hodgkinson-Williams (2015) has extended and

Table 2.2

The three open processes, with their associated practices and key characteristics.

Open process	Practice	Key characteristics	Examples
Open production	Peer production	Decentralized governance Nondiscriminatory Voluntary contributions Free to participate	Open-source software production, Wikipedia, open legislation
	Crowdsourcing	Centralized governance Nondiscriminatory Voluntary contributions Free to participate	Open innovation, citizen science, Ushahidi, ICT-enabled citizen voice
Open distribution	Sharing, republishing	Nondiscriminatory Nonproprietary Typically via platform	Open government data portal, OER Portal (e.g., Khan Academy), open access journals
Open consumption	Retain, reuse, revise, remix	Freedoms to use Free (no cost)	Translating educational materials, taking a massive open online course (MOOC), intermediary visualizing open government data

Source: Smith and Seward (2017).

clarified this typology by providing a more concrete operationalization of the 5 Rs, applying it to OER (see table 2.3). For more on OER, see chapter 12.

There are a few important caveats regarding the interpretation of *open* that we use here.

First, these processes are open when they have two characteristics: they are free (no cost) and there is no exclusion criterion (nondiscrimination) for participation in these processes (Smith and Seward 2017). These are *theoretical* characteristics. As the many cases in this book will illustrate, while there may be no fee charged to use openly shared knowledge resources or to engage in open production processes, there is always some cost to doing so, be it related to time or financing or connectivity costs. Similarly, there is a requisite level of access and skills, among other things, required to engage in an open practice. These issues are perhaps even more relevant in some Global South contexts, where Internet connections may be more expensive relative to income, and many may not have the requisite skills to engage. See chapter 9 for a more in-depth look at some of these factors.

Second, it is perhaps more accurate to say that the nondiscriminatory nature of some openness practices is bound to a particular community or geography. For example, HarassMap, an online crowdsourcing platform that collects incidents of sexual

Table 2.3
Types of reusability in OER.

Types of reusability	Ways of reusing an OER	Operationalization
Reuse	Use *as is* or copy verbatim	**Copy:** Make a copy of the original
Revise	Edit, modify, adapt, and improve the OER so it better meets your needs by reauthoring, contextualizing, redesigning, summarizing, versioning, repurposing, translating, personalizing, resequencing the content	**Contextualize:** Changing content or adding new information in order to assign meaning, make sense through examples and scenarios **Redesign:** Converting a content from one form to another, presenting pre-existing content into a different delivery format **Summarize:** Reducing the content by selecting the essential ideas **Repurpose:** Reusing for a different purpose or alter to make more suited for a different learning goals or outcome **Version:** Implementing specific changes to update the resource or adapt it for different scenario. **Translate:** Restating content from one language into another **Personalize:** Aggregating tools to match individual progress and performance **Resequence:** Changing the order or sequence of the materials
Remix	Combine the original or revised content with other open content to create something new	**Decompose:** Separating content in different sections, break out content down into parts. **Remix:** Connecting the content with new media, interactive interfaces or different components **Reassemble:** Integrating the content with other content in order to develop a module or new unit
Retain	Make, own, keep and control (curate) copies of the content	**Save:** Make and save a copy
Redistribute	Share the original OER or your new version with others	**Share:** Share the original OER or your new version

Source: Hodgkinson-Williams (2015).

harassment, is restricted to inputs from Egypt. Bailur and Sharif examine HarassMap and other crowdsourcing activities in chapter 14.

Third, this definition does not cover *all* contemporary uses of the term *open,* as some have only one or none of what we call the key characteristics of no cost and nondiscrimination (see table 2.4). For example, in chapter 8, Gillwald discusses open access broadband policy. This is a form of competition policy to promote access to telecommunications infrastructure, rather than something that directly involves knowledge resources. Similarly, open access in telecommunications policy and regulation typically has two principles: price transparency and nondiscrimination. Therefore, while the price of information is made transparent, there is a fee to participate. This use of open as nondiscriminatory but with a fee to participate also can be found elsewhere. For example, open universities around the world follow the same general model: they are open to anyone to attend, but with associated student fees (Agbu et al. 2016).

In a slightly different vein, open WiFi (also known as *free public WiFi;* see chapter 8), offered by some municipalities as an approach to tackling digital inequality, provides nondiscriminatory, no-cost access to the Internet (a large and complex knowledge resource) (Geerdts et al. 2016). Thus, one could argue that it is a form of open distribution of the Internet as a whole, not of any specific knowledge resource.

While recognizing the potential diversity of meanings and interpretations of the terms *open (openness)* and *development,* we opted for the working definition that we have given in this chapter. Note that the definition provided in this book is intended to be neither definitive nor final. The research here highlights a diversity of meanings and interpretations of the terms *open* and *development* across contexts—a point that we attempted to incorporate into our working definition. Most of the research discussed

Table 2.4
The free and nondiscrimination characteristics of different open practices.

	Free to use/participate (no cost)	Nondiscrimination (anyone can use/participate)
Shared OER	✓	✓
Shared open government data	✓	✓
Commons-based peer production	✓	✓
Crowdsourcing	✓	✓
Open universities	✕	✓
Open broadband policy	✕	✓
Open access in telecommunications policy and regulation	✕	✓
Open WiFi	✓	✓

in this volume does not employ the definition explicitly—although some chapters do (e.g., chapters 7, 8, and 9). However, the particular component practices of open (peer production, crowdsourcing, sharing, and reuse) form the main set of vocabulary that authors use when synthesizing the open development research.

Making this definition explicit helps us to more precisely delimit the contribution that this book makes to knowledge and development practice. Understanding the distinctions highlighted here allows us to understand if and how we can learn lessons across activities. It also makes it clear when open or openness has different referents, making comparisons more challenging or even impossible. This is particularly useful for those uses of open that fall slightly outside the definition focused on knowledge resources (such as the work on open broadband policy and open WiFi discussed in chapter 8, or open innovation in chapter 3).

Conclusion

We recognize that the definition of *open development* that we have offered is just one of many potential definitions. We anticipate that the definition will evolve further with time and more research. We also note that our definition is controversial for some—particularly with respect to including freely, but not legally, shared knowledge resources. For the purposes of this book, however, we believe the definition that we give here works to satisfy two important goals: first enabling comparative research that, second, respects the diversity of research contexts. In particular, the focus on openness as social praxis provides a set of practices in a framework for facilitating openness research and comparing across cases and domains (Smith and Seward 2017).

As discussed, this refined formulation of open development emerged in interaction with the research on openness in Global South contexts that IDRC supported over the last decade. Over time, we learned a lot about researching openness and applied these lessons to our definition.

One thing that we have found during the course of this research is that it is generally a better communication strategy to replace the term *open* with a more specific openness practice whenever possible. This specificity helps to avoid potential miscommunications based on alternative interpretations of the term *open*. This is one of the benefits of focusing on the specific practices of peer production, crowdsourcing, sharing, and reuse. These are more readily understandable concepts that do not carry the baggage of multiple interpretations and meanings that accompany the term *open*.

Second, this definition also responds to the diversity of contexts where research is taking place. Domain-specific definitions typically take on a universalistic, best practice character. We have found that these kinds of definitions sit uncomfortably with the reality of openness as it is carried out and experienced on the ground, as discussed here. Many chapters in this book attest to this disjuncture. In contrast, a focus on practices provides an abstract enough concept to capture variation across contexts without overly prescribing the attributes of the knowledge resource or specifics of the practice. For example, sharing can take many forms, and factors such as intellectual property, document format, the nature of sharing tools, and the subject of content do not determine whether you share, but rather shape the contours and outcomes of the sharing in practice. It is precisely these contours that we need to understand to promote effective sharing, rather than adhering to a predetermined, acontextual—and too often ideological—notion of what it should be. This may not be the most effective approach for advocacy, but we believe that it is useful as a critical research perspective to drive improvements and we hope, ultimately inclusive development outcomes.

Overall, the intention of this chapter is to help scope the contours and contributions of the research in this book. Definitions matter in research, and poor definitions lead to poor research. Open development research has suffered this fate at times. In the course of supporting the research in this book, we have found that the definition offered in this chapter provides a clear and highly practical framework for engaging in open development research. That said, we expect there will be those who take issue with the definition. It is our hope that, whether you agree or disagree with our perspective, you will still find illuminating and useful material in this book to take with you on your open development journey.

Notes

1. *Praxis,* in the context of this book, signifies the instantiation of theory through processes and activities. Through its orientation to action, open praxis picks up the philosophical threads of participation and social engagement, which in turn align with the broader constructs of open development and the underpinning schools of thought. However, note that praxis has a long philosophical history, and it is not the intention of this book to try to engage in the full spectrum of debate on this subject.

2. Note that *open development* is also more narrowly used to mean open international aid—that is, the sharing of data about international aid activities (e.g., Linders 2013). We consider open international aid one specific instantiation of a broader definition of *open development.*

3. *Knowledge,* as discussed later in this chapter, is "all intelligible ideas, information, and data in whatever form in which it is expressed or obtained" (Hess and Ostrom 2007, 7).

4. Most scholars trace the earliest uses of the term *open government* to papers originating in the United States, though apparently the kingdom of Sweden produced what may have been the first "freedom of information act" in 1766, to disseminate government records (see Manninen 2006).

5. The report, *The People's Right to Know: Legal Access to Public Records and Proceedings,* was written by a newspaper attorney, Harold Cross, and commissioned by the American Society of Newspaper Editors. According to Yu and Robinson (2012), the foreword to the report offered one of the earliest known uses of the term *open government* when it discussed Cross's work, saying that he had "written with full understanding of the public stake in open government" (Yu and Robinson 2012, 185).

6. The Special Subcommittee on Government Information, known as the Moss Committee, helped bring the FOIA to fruition a decade later, in 1966. Wallace Parks was the main counsel for the Moss Committee, and his paper "The Open Government Principle: Applying the Right to Know under the Constitution" was published posthumously in 1957; it became a critical piece of the movement for greater accountability and transparency of government. See also Yu and Robinson (2012, 185–86).

7. The Open Government Declaration of the Open Government Partnership, an initiative launched globally in part with the support of US president Barack Obama in 2011, was one cornerstone of the new open government movement. The declaration can be found here: https://www.opengovpartnership.org/open-government-declaration. For anyone concerned about open government (in the United States at least), the removal of the open government portal on the White House website in January 2017 is a disconcerting example of the potential direction of open government at present.

8. These priorities were framed for many years as the "Washington Consensus" for the way that development aid was tied to structural adjustment policies that prioritized neoliberal economic models over state-driven forms of development.

9. On one end of development theory, there are the modernization theorists, who focus on the role of the state and the top-down transfer of Western institutions and values to develop the so-called *underdeveloped* in the postcolonial era (Rostow 1960). Much early participatory-oriented development discourse emerged out of critiques of these notions of development, from dependency theory to discursive political/social theories of language and power (Escobar 1984, 1992, 1995a, 1995b, 1999; Fanon 1961; Foucault 1982; Frank 1966, 1967; Hopkins and Wallerstein, 1982; Spivak 1988; Said 1978; Wallerstein 1976, 1984). Participatory discourse is grounded in bottom-up, people-centered, inclusive narratives that were developed over the twentieth century by scholars in a range of disciplines, from critical anthropology to critical social theory. One of the early, primary figures was Paulo Freire (1970, 1973), who advocated for participation of people in authentic development as active subjects who could, through consciousness raising, help bring about a transfer of power. Note that this is in no way meant to be a full treatment of the subject of participatory development.

10. Robert Chambers from the Institute for Development Studies in Sussex, England, gives a fairly thorough exploration of the range of participatory methods that emerged over the past thirty years. He outlines a range of applications, from community radio to video, which have helped bolster participation. See Chambers (2010).

11. The A2K movement is supported by numerous global compacts, declarations, and agreements, including the Open Access Declaration in Budapest in 2002 (http://www.budapestopenaccessinitiative

.org/read); and the Berlin Declaration on Open Access to Knowledge in the Sciences and Humanities in 2003 (https://openaccess.mpg.de/Berlin-Declaration), which laid out the principles of justice, freedom, and economic development, particularly in relation to academic publishing. In addition, there is the Geneva Declaration on the Future of the World Intellectual Property Organization (2004), and the Open Educational Resources Declaration in Paris (2012) is also considered significant piece of the movement. See https://unesdoc.unesco.org/ark:/48223/pf0000246687.

12. Access to knowledge and science is protected by Article 27 of the Universal Declaration of Human Rights, which also balances the right of access with the right to protection of moral and material interests: "(1) Everyone has the right freely to participate in the cultural life of the community, to enjoy the arts and to share in scientific advancement and its benefits. (2) Everyone has the right to the protection of the moral and material interests resulting from any scientific, literary or artistic production of which he is the author."

13. See Open Knowledge International (n.d.).

References

Agbu, Jane-frances O., Fred Mulder, Fred De Vries, Vincent Tenebe, and Abel Caine. 2016. "The Best of Two Open Worlds at the National Open University of Nigeria." *Open Praxis* 8 (2): 111–121. https://doi.org/10.5944/openpraxis.8.2.279.

Alderete, Maria V. 2017. "Examining the ICT Access Effect on Socioeconomic Development: The Moderating Role of ICT Use and Skills." *Information Technology for Development* 23 (1): 42–58.

Avgerou, Chrisanthi. 2008. "Information Systems in Developing Countries: A Critical Research Review." *Journal of Information Technology* 23 (3): 133–146.

Avgerou, Chrisanthi. 2010. "Discourses on ICT and Development." *Information Technologies & International Development* 6 (3): 1–18.

Avgerou, Chrisanthi, Claudio Ciborra, and Frank Land. 2004. "Introduction." In *The Social Study of Information and Communication Technology: Innovation, Actors, and Contexts*, ed. Chrisanthi Avgerou, Claudio Ciborra, and Frank Land, 1–14. Oxford: Oxford University Press.

Barrantes, Roxana, and Eduardo Vargas. 2016. "Inequalities in the Appropriation of Digital Spaces in Metropolitan Areas of Latin America." In *ICTD '16 Proceedings of the Eighth International Conference on Information and Communication Technologies and Development*. Ann Arbor, MI: ACM. https://doi.org/10.1145/2909609.2909613.

Benkler, Yochai. 2002. "Coase's Penguin, or, Linux and 'The Nature of the Firm.'" *Yale Law Journal* 112 (3): 369–446.

Benkler, Yochai, Aaron Shaw, and Benjamin Mako Hill. 2015. "Peer Production: A Form of Collective Intelligence." In *Handbook of Collective Intelligence*, ed. Thomas Malone and Michael Bernstein, 175–203. Cambridge: MIT Press.

Bentley, Caitlin M., and Arul Chib. 2016. "The Impact of Open Development Initiatives in Lower-and Middle Income Countries: A Review of the Literature." *Electronic Journal of Information Systems in Developing Countries* 74 (1): 1–20.

Berdou, Evangelia. 2017. "Open Development in Poor Communities: Opportunities, Tensions, and Dilemmas." *Information Technologies & International Development* 13:18–32. http://itidjournal .org/index.php/itid/article/viewFile/1429/568.

Berlin Declaration on Open Access to Knowledge in the Sciences and Humanities. 2003. October 22, 2003. https://openaccess.mpg.de/Berlin-Declaration.

Bollier, David. 2007. "The Rise of Collective Intelligence: Decentralized Co-Creation of Value as a New Paradigm of Commerce and Culture." In *A Report of the Sixteenth Annual Aspen Institute Roundtable on Information Technology*. Washington, DC: Aspen Institute. http://dlc.dlib.indiana .edu/dlc/handle/10535/4728.

Castells, Manuel. 2000. *The Rise of the Network Society*, 2nd ed. Oxford: Blackwell.

Chambers, Robert. 2010. *Paradigms, Poverty and Adaptive Pluralism*. IDS Working Paper No. 344. July. Brighton, UK: Institute of Development Studies, University of Sussex. http://onlinelibrary .wiley.com/doi/10.1111/j.2040-0209.2010.00344_2.x/pdf.

Chesbrough, Henry. 2006. *Open Innovation: The New Imperative for Creating and Profiting from Technology*. Boston: Harvard Business School Press.

Cross, Harold. 1953. *The People's Right to Know*. New York: University of Columbia Press.

De Rosnay, Melanie Dulong de, and Francesca Musiani. 2016. "Towards a (De)centralization-Based Typology of Peer Production." *TripleC: Communication, Capitalism & Critique. Open Access Journal for a Global Sustainable Information Society* 14 (1): 189–207.

Elder, Laurent, Heloise Emdon, Richard Fuchs, and Ben Petrazzini, eds. 2013. *Connecting ICTs to Development: The IDRC Experience*. London/Ottawa: Anthem Press/IDRC. https://www.idrc.ca/en /book/connecting-icts-development-idrc-experience.

Escobar, Arturo. 1984. "Discourse and Power in Development: Michel Foucault and the Relevance of His Work to the Third World." *Alternatives X* (Winter 1984–85): 377–400.

Escobar, Arturo. 1992. "Culture, Economics, and Politics in Latin American Social Movements Theory and Research." In *The Making of Social Movements in Latin America: Identity, Strategy and Democracy*, ed. Arturo Escobar and Sonia E. Alvarez, 62–88. Boulder, CO: Westview Press.

Escobar, Arturo. 1995a. *Encountering Development: The Making and the Unmaking of the Third World*. Princeton, NJ: Princeton University Press.

Escobar, Arturo. 1995b. "Imagining a Post-Development Era." In *Power of Development*, ed. Jonathan Crush, 211–227. London: Routledge.

Estelles-Arolas, Enrique, Fernando González-Ladrón-de-Guevara. 2012. "Towards and Integrated Crowdsourcing Definition." *Journal of Information Science* 38 (2): 189–200.

Fanon, Frantz. Les Damnés de la Terre. Paris: François Maspero, 1961. Published in English as *The Wretched of the Earth*, 1965. Trans. Constance Farrington. New York: Grove Press.

Foucault, Michel. 1982. *The Subject and Power*. Chicago: University of Chicago Press.

Frank, Andre G. 1966. *The Development of Underdevelopment*. New York: Monthly Review Press.

Frank, Andre G. 1967. *Capitalism and Underdevelopment in Latin America*. New York: Monthly Review Press.

Freire, Paulo. 1970. *Pedagogy of the Oppressed*. New York: Herder and Herder.

Freire, Paulo. 1973. *Education for Critical Consciousness*. New York: Seabury Press.

Friederici, Nicolas, Sanna Ojanperä, and Mark Graham. 2017. "The Impact of Connectivity in Africa: Grand Visions and the Mirage of Inclusive Digital Development." *Electronic Journal of Information Systems in Developing Countries* 79 (2): 1–20. http://onlinelibrary.wiley.com/doi/10.1002/j .1681-4835.2017.tb00578.x/pdf.

Frischmann, Brett M., Michael J. Madison, and Katherine J. Strandburg, eds. 2014. *Governing Knowledge Commons*. Oxford: Oxford University Press.

Fuster Morell, Mayo, Rubén Martinez, and Jorge L. S. Maldonado. 2014. "Mapping the Common-Based Peer Production: A Crowd-sourcing Experiment." Presented at the *The Internet, Politics & Policy Conference*, Oxford Internet Institute, University of Oxford. http://blogs.oii.ox.ac.uk/ipp -conference/2014/programme-2014/track-a-harnessing-the-crowd/design-i/mayo-fuster-morell -ruben-mart%c3%adnez-jorge.html.

Geerdts, Christopher, Alison Gillwald, Enrico Calandro, Chenai Chair, Mpho Moyo, and Broc Rademan. 2016. *Developing Smart Public Wi-Fi in South Africa*. Cape Town, South Africa: Research ICT Africa. https://www.researchictafrica.net/publications/Other_publications/2016_Public_Wi -Fi_Policy_Paper_-_Developing_Smart_Public_Wi-Fi_in_South_Africa.pdf.

Geneva Declaration on the Future of the World Intellectual Property Organization. 2004. September 29, 2004. https://www.opensocietyfoundations.org/sites/default/files/wipo_declaration_0.pdf.

Gomez, Ricardo. 2013. "The Changing Field of ICTD: Growth and Maturation of the Field, 2000–2010." *Electronic Journal of Information Systems in Developing Countries* 58(1).

Heeks, Richard. 2008. "ICT4D 2.0: The Next Phase of Applying ICT for International Development." *Computer* 41 (6): 26–33.

Heeks, Richard. 2010a. "Development 2.0: Transformative ICT-Enabled Development Models and Impacts." *Communications of the ACM* 53 (4): 22–24.

Heeks, R. 2010b. "Do Information and Communication Technologies (ICTs) Contribute to Development?" *Journal of International Development* 22 (5): 625–640.

Hess, Charlotte, and Elinor Ostrom. 2007. "Introduction: An Overview of the Knowledge Commons." In *Understanding Knowledge as a Commons: From Theory to Practice*, ed. Charlotte Hess and Elinor Ostrom, 3–26. Cambridge, MA: MIT Press.

Hodgkinson-Williams, Cheryl. 2015. "Grappling with the Concepts of 'Impact' and 'Openness' in Relation to OER: Current Developments in the ROER4D Project." Presented at Open Education Global 2015, Banff, Canada, April.

Hopkins, Terence K., and Immanuel Wallerstein. 1982. *World-Systems Analysis: Theory and Methodology (Explorations in the World Economy)*. Beverly Hills: SAGE Publications.

Howe, Jeff. 2006. "The Rise of Crowdsourcing." *Wired* 14 (6): 1–4. https://www.wired.com/2006/06/crowds/.

Huesca, Robert. 2002. "Tracing the History of Participatory Communication Approaches to Development: A Critical Appraisal." In *Tracing the History of Participatory Communication Approaches to Development: A Critical Appraisal*, ed. Jan Servaes, 180–198. Paris: UNESCO. http://old.unesco.kz/publications/ci/hq/Approaches%20Development%20Communication/CHP8.PDF.

Huizingh, Eelko K. R. E. 2011. "Open Innovation: State of the Art and Future Perspectives." *Technovation* 31 (1): 2–9. https://doi.org/10.1016/j.technovation.2010.10.002.

Kapczynski, Amy. 2010. "Access to Knowledge: A Conceptual Genealogy." In *Access to Knowledge in the Age of Intellectual Property*, ed. Gaëlle Krikorian and Amy Kapczynski, 17–56. New York: Zone Books. https://www.opensocietyfoundations.org/sites/default/files/age-of-intellectual-property-20101110.pdf.

Linders, Dennis. 2013. "Towards Open Development: Leveraging Open Data to Improve the Planning and Coordination of International Aid." *Government Information Quarterly* 30 (4): 426–434.

Madon, Shirin. 2000. "The Internet and Socio-economic Development: Exploring the Interaction." *Information Technology & People* 13 (2): 85–101.

Manninen, Juha. 2006. "Anders Chydenius and the Origins of World's First Freedom of Information Act." In *The World's First Freedom of Information Act: Anders Chydenius' Legacy Today*, ed. Juha Mustonen, 18–53. Kokkola, Finland: Anders Chydenius Foundation.

Mansell, Robin. 2013. "Employing Digital Crowdsourced Information Resources: Managing the Emerging Information Commons." *International Journal of the Commons* 7 (2): 255–277.

Mansell, Robin, and Gaëten Tremblay. 2013. *Renewing the Knowledge Societies Vision for Peace and Sustainable Development*. Paris: UNESCO.

Mizukami, Pedro N., and Ronaldo Lemos. 2008. "From Free Software to Free Culture: The Emergence of Open Business." In *Access to Knowledge in Brazil: New Research on Intellectual Property, Innovation and Development*, ed. Lea Shaver, 25–66. New York: Information Society Project.

Open Educational Resources Declaration in Paris. 2012. World Open Educational Resources (OER) Congress. Paris. June 2012. Paris: UNESCO. http://www.unesco.org/new/fileadmin/MULTIMEDIA/HQ/CI/CI/pdf/Events/English_Paris_OER_Declaration.pdf.

Open Government Partnership. 2018. "Open Government Declaration." https://www.opengovpartnership.org/open-government-declaration.

Open Knowledge International. n.d. "Open Definition 2.1." http://opendefinition.org/od/2.1/en/.

Ostrom, Elinor, and Vincent Ostrom. 1977. "Public Goods and Public Choices." In *Alternatives for Delivering Public Services: Towards Improved Performance,* ed. E. Savas, 7–49. Boulder, CO: Westview Press.

Parks, Wallace. 1957. "The Open Government Principle: Applying the Right to Know under the Constitution." *George Washington Law Review* 26 (1): 1–22.

Pearson, Sarah H., and Paul Stacey, eds. 2017. *Made with Creative Commons*. Copenhagen: Crtl+Alt+Delete Books.

Pomerantz, Jeffrey, and Robin Peek. 2016. "Fifty Shades of Open." *First Monday* 21 (5), May 2. http://www.ojphi.org/ojs/index.php/fm/article/view/6360.

Quaggiotto, Guilio, and Pierre Wielezynski. 2007. "Development 2.0: A New Paradigm for the Non-profit Sector?" *FreePint Newsletter* No. 230. May 24. http://web.freepint.com/go/newsletter /230#feature.

Reilly, Katherine M. A., and Matthew L. Smith. 2013. "The Emergence of Open Development in a Network Society." In *Open Development: Networked Innovations in International Development*, ed. Matthew L. Smith and Katherine M. A. Reilly, 15–50. Cambridge, MA/Ottawa: MIT Press/ IDRC. https://www.idrc.ca/en/book/open-development-networked-innovations-international -development.

Rostow, W. W. 1960. *The Stages of Economic Growth: A Non-Communist Manifesto*. Cambridge: Cambridge University Press.

Said, Edward. 1978. *Orientalism*. New York: Pantheon.

Schech, Susanne. 2002. "Wired for Change: The Links between ICTs and Development Discourses." *Journal of International Development* 14 (1): 13–23. https://doi.org/10.1002/jid.870.

Shaver, Lea. 2007. "Defining and Measuring Access to Knowledge: Towards an A2K Index." *Yale Law School Faculty Scholarship Series*. Paper 22. http://digitalcommons.law.yale.edu/cgi /viewcontent.cgi?article=1021&context=fss_papers.

Smith, Matthew L. 2014. "Being Open in ICT4D." November 19. Available at *SSRN* 2526515. http://papers.ssrn.com/sol3/papers.cfm?abstract_id=2526515.

Smith, Matthew L., and Laurent Elder. 2010. "Open ICT Ecosystems Transforming the Developing World." *Information Technologies & International Development* 6 (1): 65–71.

Smith, Matthew L., Laurent Elder, and Heloise Emdon. 2011. "Open Development: A New Theory for ICT4D." *Information Technologies & International Development* 7(1): iii–ix. http://itidjournal.org /itid/article/viewFile/692/290.

Smith, Matthew L., and Katherine M. A. Reilly. 2013. "Introduction." In *Open Development: Networked Innovations in International Development*, ed. Matthew L. Smith and Katherine M. A. Reilly,

1–14. Cambridge, MA/Ottawa: MIT Press/IDRC. https://www.idrc.ca/en/book/open-development-networked-innovations-international-development.

Smith, Matthew L., and Ruhiya Seward. 2017. "Openness as Social Praxis." *First Monday* 22 (4), April 3.

Spivak, Gayatri C. 1988. "Can the Subaltern Speak?" In *Marxism and the Interpretation of Culture*, ed. Cary Nelson and Lawrence Grossberg, 271–313. London: Macmillan. http://abahlali.org/files/Can_the_subaltern_speak.pdf.

Thompson, Mark. 2008. "ICT and Development Studies: Towards Development 2.0." *Journal of International Development* 20 (6): 821–835.

United Nations. 1948. *Universal Declaration of Human Rights*. December. Paris: United Nations. http://www.un.org/en/universal-declaration-human-rights/.

Von Hippel, Eric. 2005. *Democratizing Innovation*. Cambridge: MIT Press. http://web.mit.edu/evhippel/www/books/DI/DemocInn.pdf.

Von Hippel, Eric. 2017. *Free Innovation: How Citizens Create and Share Innovations*. Cambridge: MIT Press. https://evhippel.mit.edu/books/.

Wallerstein, Immanuel. 1976. "The Modern World-System." In *Capitalist Agriculture and the Origins of the European World-Economy in the Sixteenth Century*, ed. Immaneul Wallerstein, 229–233. New York/London: Academic Press. https://thebasebk.org/wp-content/uploads/2013/08/The-Modern-World-System.pdf.

Wallerstein, Immanuel. 1984. *The Politics of the World-Economy: The States, the Movements and the Civilizations*. Cambridge: Cambridge University Press.

Walsham, Geoff. 2001. *Making a World of Difference: IT in a Global Context*. New York: Wiley.

Walsham, Geoff. 2017. "ICT4D Research: Reflections on History and Future Agenda." *Information Technology for Development* 23 (1): 18–41.

Walsham, Geoff, and Sundeep Sahay. 2006. "Research on Information Systems in Developing Countries: Current Landscape and Future Prospects." *Information Technology for Development* 12 (1): 7–24. https://pdfs.semanticscholar.org/7158/db5dfcec87fcf6d52edb8780fbeb4996359c.pdf.

West, Joel, Ammon Salter, Wim Vanhaverbeke, and Henry Chesbrough. 2014. "Open Innovation: The Next Decade." *Research Policy* 43 (5): 805–811.

Wiley, David. 2014. "Clarifying the 5th R." *Iterating Towards Openness* (blog). https://opencontent.org/blog/archives/3251.

Yu, Harlan and David G. Robinson. 2012. "The New Ambiguity of 'Open Government.'" 59 *UCLA Law Review Discourse* 178. http://www.uclalawreview.org/pdf/discourse/59-11.pdf.

3 Open Innovation in Development: Integrating Theory and Practice across Open Science, Open Access, and Open Data

Jeremy de Beer

Introduction

We know that innovation—the implementation and diffusion of new products, processes, business methods, or organizational strategies (OECD 2005, 46)—is a driver of development. Over seventy-five years of solid research proves that innovation creates jobs, generates wealth, and produces benefits for society as a whole (Arrow 1962; Marshall 1920; Rostow 1960). Innovation also has the potential to enhance individual freedom and improve people's capability to lead longer, healthier, and happier lives.

However, ensuring that the socioeconomic benefits of innovation are not concentrated among society's elites but rather are shared inclusively by all people is a significant challenge. The crucial importance of research on *inclusive* innovation has been recognized, although much work remains to be done (IDRC 2011). While the leader on inclusive innovation in recent years has been the Organisation for Economic Co-operation and Development (OECD) (OECD 2015), a number of scholars have begun to lead in the field (Altenburg 2009; Heeks, Foster, and Nugroho 2014).

Can open innovation be inclusive? Can it help unlock access to knowledge or contribute to more just, equitable, and inclusive societies? Perhaps. But, as this chapter argues, much work still must be done to align the central concept of openness applied to the phenomena of both innovation and development.

This chapter exposes and criticizes the failure of most existing research on information and communication technologies (ICTs) and open development to integrate the theories and practices of open innovation. It uses the method of meta-analysis to challenge assumptions and build an understanding of innovation across the domains of open science, open access, and open data. It brings critical insights from literature in the disciplines of law, economics, management, and public policy to bear on this problem. Finally, it considers the advantages and limitations of using the theoretical lens of open innovation to shed light on open development.

Open innovation is a useful lens for looking at open development, as the chapter concludes. Open science, open education, and open data are distinct areas where open development theories have been tested and explored. Open science, open education, and open data are also applications of open innovation models in practice. A common denominator across these various areas/applications of both open innovation and open development is the concept of access to *knowledge*. Open science, open education, and open data are all areas where knowledge flows are essential for innovation, and therefore development.

Extending Open Development Theory

Among those interested in development, open innovation is often misunderstood. It is conflated with concepts like open source, copyleft, or crowdsourcing. While such concepts may be examples of open innovation practices, the core principles of open development and open innovation are not necessarily aligned. This ambiguity and misinterpretation are emblematic of broader problems with overuse of the word *open*, which a recent review showed is associated with dozens of different terms (Pomerantz and Peek 2016). Better understanding of the relationship between open innovation and development will help grow open development beyond its roots in ICTs, in both theory and practice.

First, in theory, anchoring the concept of open development in ICTs specifically, as opposed to innovation systems more broadly, limits its potential to explain models of openness driven by socioeconomic as well as (or instead of) technological factors. A more integrated theory has wider explanatory potential and creates greater possibilities for impact.

Second, in practice, our understanding of what *open* means for development is fragmented across science, education, software, data, and other domains, despite the fact that innovation happens in all those contexts. Moreover, the focus on legal and economic formality in much existing research on these topics ignores the informality of innovation practices throughout the developing world. A more crosscutting analysis offers technologically agnostic, universally applicable, and sector-neutral insights into the concept of open development.

(Open) Innovation for Development

This section of the chapter extends the theoretical framework for open development beyond its roots in ICTs, and frames openness within the broader context of innovation management strategies and policy systems. After pushing the theory of open development beyond information and communication technologies for development (ICT4D) to innovation systems, it may be possible to take the concept much further. Open development, for example, could critically influence fields such as information systems (Myers and Klein 2011). Once untethered from the sole domain of ICTs, open development could even shape mainstream development discourse in the way of other breakthroughs by authors such as Sen (1999) and Nussbaum (2011). Theoretical growth may start, however, with the far more modest move from ICTs to innovation.

Reilly and McMahon suggest that there is consensus emerging from open development research about what *open* means: "Open resources are defined as those which are accessible, digital, affordable, locatable, timely, sharable, and appropriately licensed. In addition, they need to be presented in a format that allows for their reuse and modification" (2015, 74). However, we know that digital resources are not accessible to many people given the levels of connectivity around the world, so conditioning open on being both accessible *and* digital does not work.

If access is about more than mere connectivity, then the temptation to characterize *open development* as being a theory formulated for ICTs, or a phenomenon driven necessarily by ICTs, creates limitations. Chapters 1 and 2 of this volume acknowledge the constraints of previous conceptualizations of open development. An early framing of open development introduced it as a set of possibilities to catalyze change through ICTs (Smith, Elder, and Emdon 2011). Smith and Reilly, leaders in the field, further suggest the idea behind open development is "harnessing the increased penetration of information and communications technologies to create new organizational forms that improve the lives of people" (2013, 4). In their foundational chapter defining open models of development, they positioned open development as an outgrowth of literature on the information society and the subsequent work on ICTs as a tool for development, so-called ICT4D (Reilly and Smith 2013). Then, in explaining the history of open models, they begin with open-source software and trace the evolution of openness from that starting point.

One possible direction is to focus on "ICT-enabled open practices" and ground theory–building in those practices (Smith 2014, sec. 1). Yet it is also possible to invert the analytical framework. ICTs may be less the tool driving social and economic reorganization than a vehicle through which social and economic changes are easily visible to community outsiders. For this, the foundational social elements, rather than technological elements, are the true drivers of information networking for innovation (de Beer and Armstrong 2015, 62).

This inverted perspective explicitly recognizes that "an ICT ecosystem is…more than just a technological system; rather, it is a social system within which ICTs are embedded" (Smith and Elder 2010, 65). Moreover, contrary to popular belief, many or perhaps most (based on Google Scholar citations) recent uses of the term *open* do not depend on the existence of ICTs. Digitization is not a prerequisite for openness. Offline resources and processes can be open too. Of course, ICTs may be *a* factor facilitating social and economic change, but ICTs are neither sufficient nor necessary for a robust and holistic theory of open development. Smith and Seward (see chapter 2 of this volume) agree.

A technologically determined foundation for open development limits its theoretical potential. I suggest there is significant value in exploring openness outside of ICT-enabled contexts. Indeed, I believe this analytical shift is crucial to understand how openness affects development through innovation generally, beyond ICT4D. Doing so allows us to see that open models are everywhere, not just online. Without disconnecting openness from ICTs, it cannot be holistically conceived, implemented, tested, and improved as a model for development. A broader, crosscutting analysis also shows that the starting point for understanding openness is not the legal terms and conditions that govern access to software, but the social norms that inspired a community to seek out the appropriate legal tools to govern cocreated knowledge.

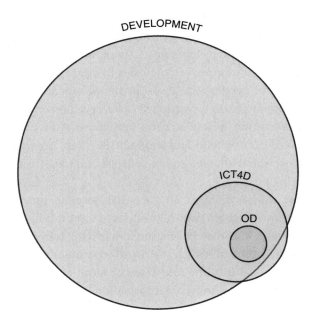

Figure 3.1
Open development (OD) conceived within the field of ICT4D.

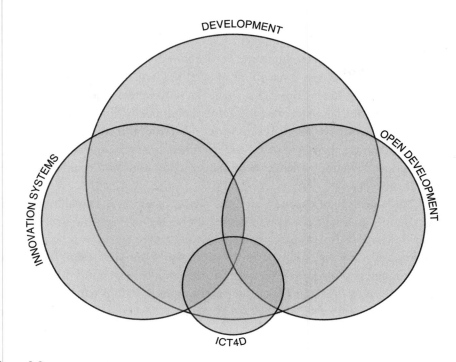

Figure 3.2
OD conceived as covering aspects of ICT4D and innovation systems.

Figures 3.1 and 3.2 demonstrate the expanded potential of reconceiving open development to cover aspects of ICTs and innovation systems, instead of a subfield or outgrowth of ICT4D research. Of course, open development might cover much more than innovation, just like innovation covers issues falling outside the concept of open development. However, enlarging the domain of open development beyond ICTs creates the possibilities of pushing the boundaries of development theory itself, as innovation systems thinking has done. Indeed, studying open development in connection with innovation systems, not just ICTs, has the added benefit of connecting the concept with a much richer body of knowledge on development generally (Lundvall 1992; Muchie, Lundvall, and Gammeltoft 2003; Kraemer-Mbula and Wamae 2010).

Furthermore, a key aspect of innovation strategy and policy that informs open development is knowledge governance. Indeed, the tension between control over and access to knowledge is a—perhaps *the*—unifying thread in open development (de Beer and Bannerman 2013). One of the most important legal tools for governing knowledge is intellectual property (IP). Laws, policies, and practices related to IP ownership can ultimately determine who benefits from open innovation. The potential of knowledge, in particular, to contribute to development has been well theorized and documented (Aghion, David, and Foray 2009; Juma and Yee-Cheong 2005).

There are challenges to past conceptions of openness, which both this chapter and chapter 2 confront in different ways. One challenge is that there is no common theory with which to learn and compare openness across a multiplicity of connotations, applications, and interpretations. This problem is not new. From the outset of its adoption in international development, *open* has been described as a fuzzy, trendy term susceptible to co-option: "a better marketing term than analytic concept" (Smith, Elder, and Emdon 2011, iii).

Davies (2012) sheds light on one reason the idea of openness is so malleable. As he explains: "There is an important distinction to observe between openness focussed on artifacts such as data, source code, or academic articles, and openness of processes, such as democracy and development." He further comments: "Formal definitions of the former may tend to be concerned more with the legal or technical status of the artifact, whereas definitions of the latter may focus on questions of who is participating, how they are allowed to participate" (Davies 2012). Davies is among numerous researchers who suggest that openness is often defined in oppositional terms. In the legal context, for example, *open* is the opposite of *proprietary* (Reilly and Smith 2013, 31). A question to answer using a more integrated theoretical framework, therefore, is: How might the relationship between open, proprietary, and blended models of innovation enlighten us on what open development is or is not?

Another challenge, also identified in chapter 2, is that openness is typically defined in universal legal and technical terms that are not sufficient for understanding the reality of openness in a development context. While the inclusion of some legal criteria is common across the openness discourse in various domains (Smith 2014, sec. 2.2), just saying that open resources are those that are *appropriately* licensed is too vague to be meaningful. Indeed, there are valid concerns about whether any kind of legal licensing requirement must be part of a definition of open. "[S]coping the concept of openness as legal permissions is an arbitrary boundary that doesn't reflect reality," explains Smith (2016, 6–7). That is because, as explained later in this chapter, legal rules may be less influential than social norms governing the appropriation of and access to knowledge in many developing countries. Smith's point about the arbitrariness of scoping openness through legal permissions, echoed in chapter 2, mirrors my previous point about the limitations of a technologically determined definition.

In the broader context of innovation systems, "the link between openness and innovation is not necessarily straightforward; openness may support some types of innovation, but there can be a dynamic and productive tension between open and enclosed systems. Closed technological innovations can often emerge from open systems, while open initiatives can take advantage of closed technologies or systems" (Reilly and Smith 2013, 35). Researchers have investigated whether open innovation might change innovation policymaking in catch-up economies (Karo and Kattel 2011), but they have not situated open innovation in the context of development policy more generally.

Significant uncertainty stems from the fact that many development scholars' understanding of openness is inconsistent with the literature on open innovation, especially with respect to knowledge governance systems. This discussion now turns to the open innovation literature.

Innovation through Openness

The open innovation literature is vast and well established. Numerous thorough reviews and syntheses of key sources among the thousands of works on this topic have already been published (e.g., Chesbrough and Bogers 2014; Dahlander and Gann 2010; Elmquist, Fredberg, and Ollila 2009; Fredberg et al. 2010; Huizingh 2011; Lichtenthaler 2011; Van de Vrande, Vanhaverbeke, and Gassmann 2010; West et al. 2014).

If another open *anything* movement is to move forward with credibility in the fields of innovation studies, management science, law, or economics, then a serious conceptual gap must be acknowledged and bridged. This is especially true with respect to open business models, where the focus is squarely on firm strategy, but the leading research is neglected (compare Mizukami and Lemos 2010 with Chesbrough 2006 and Teece 2010).

While there may be observable differences between developed and developing countries, such work should not continue in silos. It is impossible to be taken seriously by the business leaders or economic policymakers whom development researchers aim to influence without understanding the perceived connotation of terms like *openness* and *innovation*. The research gap is not just about North versus South or developed versus developing country; it is also cross-disciplinary and cross-sector. This subsection of the article summarizes the most relevant insights for open development.

"Open, user, collaborative, and related innovation concepts imply strategies and systems where ideas and knowledge flow across firm boundaries" (de Beer 2015, 11); that is the common thread in the literature on openness related to innovation. Beyond that point of convergence, however, a recent review by leading researchers identifies a "fault line" over the importance of appropriation (West et al. 2014, 808). The key divergence concerns how and why knowledge spillovers happen.

Research on user innovation, grounded in the work of Eric von Hippel, tends to view appropriation through IP rights as a drag on innovation, especially sequential or cumulative innovation, thus diminishing social welfare (von Hippel 2005). In this context, the word *open* is adopted as part of the phrase *open collaborative innovation* to mean "all information related to the innovation is a public good—non-rivalrous and non-excludable" (Baldwin and von Hippel 2011, 1400). The nonproprietary *innovation* is open.

Research on *open innovation*, a term associated with Henry Chesbrough's seminal book of that title, sees the appropriation enabled by IP as a tool facilitating inflows and outflows of knowledge between businesses (Chesbrough 2003). Recent work on open innovation by West et al. (2014, 806) has defined the phenomenon as "a distributed innovation process based on purposively managed knowledge flows across organizational boundaries, using pecuniary and non-pecuniary mechanisms." Chesbrough's first book has been cited almost 12,000 times, with subsequent related works being cited thousands more times.

It may surprise open development researchers to realize that within the most widely known and cited paradigm of open innovation, strong IP protection is a key facilitator of openness. That is because the openness that Chesbrough identifies is the firm's; in the process of innovation, the knowledge-exchanging firm, but not necessarily the knowledge, is open.

There is a parallel between the system's/firm's views of openness in innovation and the artifact/process distinctions of openness in development. Research following von Hippel's work on open and collaborative innovation centers on the open nature of the artifacts circulating within an innovation system. Research following Chesbrough's work on open innovation and open business models centers on the open nature of processes through which firms innovate.

From the firm-centric perspective, clearly delineated IP rights that can be purchased or sold by a business are among the important market institutions that explain the rise of open innovation during the second half of the twentieth century. The existing research on open innovation highlights several major trends driving the phenomenon: market institutions, labor mobility, product complexity, and technology platforms (de Beer 2015, 20).

Market institutions other than IP that promote open innovation include venture capital, securities exchanges, and other financing systems, as well as industry standards that require interoperability. Labor mobility is a crucial factor, as people no longer spend entire careers with one organization. As people move, so does knowledge. Increasing product complexity is also associated with open innovation because no single firm is able to produce all components working in isolation. Finally, technology platforms—ICTs in particular—make asynchronous collaboration across geographic boundaries possible. Technology is one (but not the only) factor responsible for open innovation, which is noteworthy for open development.

Much of open development research has seized upon only part of the literature on openness and innovation. Benkler's concept of *peer production*—decentralized, collaborative, nonproprietary production by widely distributed and loosely connected individuals (Benkler 2006)—has been the most influential (IDRC 2011; Reilly and Smith 2013; Smith and Elder 2010; Smith, Elder, and Emdon 2011). Regarding appropriation (or, rather, nonproprietary) approaches to knowledge management, Benkler's conceptual framework is more closely aligned with von Hippel's work on user innovation and open and collaborative innovation systems than with work on open innovation in the firm-centric paradigm (de Beer 2015, 28). A key question that this chapter raises is whether widely distributed and loosely connected peer production aptly characterizes much innovation that happens in the informal sector, which dominates economic activity throughout developing countries.

A "Source" of Openness to Interpretation

Other influential concepts imported into open development research include crowdsourcing and open sourcing, ideas that offer insights into the root causes of misunderstandings. Despite sharing the common word *source*, these terms cover very different ideas. Applying the various perspectives of open innovation/collaborative innovation/peer production to specific examples and applications, such as crowdsourcing and open-source software, illustrates the challenges and opportunities of integrating innovation into open development theory and practice.

Crowdsourcing is a term coined by Jeff Howe, first in an article for *Wired* magazine and then in a book by that title (Howe 2006; Howe 2008). A cross-disciplinary review of research later integrated forty original definitions, from over 200 sources, to propose this integrated definition: "Crowdsourcing is a type of participative online activity in which an individual, an institution, a non-profit organization, or company proposes to a group of individuals of varying knowledge, heterogeneity, and number, via a flexible open call, the voluntary undertaking of a task" (Estellés-Arolas and González-Ladrón-de-Guevara 2012, 197).

With their integrated definition, Estellés-Arolas and González-Ladrón-de-Guevara (2012, 197) offer eight criteria to determine whether an activity is crowdsourcing or not:

"(a) there is a clearly defined crowd;

(b) there exists a task with a clear goal;

(c) the recompense received by the crowd is clear;

(d) the crowdsourcer is clearly identified;

(e) the compensation to be received by the crowdsourcer is clearly defined;

(f) it is an online assigned process of participative type;

(g) it uses an open call of variable extent;

(h) it uses the Internet."

Two things are notable about the integrated definition of and criteria for crowd-sourcing. First, it is not always easy to delineate the boundaries between crowdsourcing as a form of firm-driven open innovation on one hand and open/collaborative/free peer production on the other. Take Wikipedia, for example, which in some ways seems like a form of crowdsourcing and in others seems like peer production. While there is a clear goal to create a free, publicly editable encyclopedia, via an online process involving an open (implicit and sometimes explicit) call to participate on an Internet platform owned and controlled by the nonprofit Wikimedia Foundation, there is no clearly defined recompense, at least not in the form of pecuniary compensation. Wikipedia meets more than half, but not all, of the eight characteristics of crowdsourcing. Open development researchers may conceive of Wikipedia not as crowdsourcing, but rather as a mode of peer production, in the sense imagined by Benkler. However, scholars in other fields may see it as a firm-centric open innovation strategy within Chesbrough's open innovation framework. Ambiguities about crowdsourcing demonstrate differences between certain conceptions of peer production and open innovation, and thus raise questions for open development researchers.

Second, several of the eight elements that describe crowdsourcing seem difficult to apply in the context of informal economic activities in the developing world. In particular, much open innovation in the informal economy happens offline in social, not technological networks (de Beer and Armstrong 2015; Kraemer-Mbula and Wunsch-Vincent 2016). Moreover, the firm-centric understanding of crowdsourcing presupposes a degree of order and organization that may not be easily observable in the informal sector. This contrasts with certain kinds of crowdsourcing, such as solutions-sourcing, in the formal sector of developed countries where topics like IP management are more easily studied (de Beer et al. 2017). Thus, is crowdsourcing a misnomer in open development, or is international development missing in the research on crowdsourcing?

Open source is often understood as the inspiration for open development through ICTs. Open-source software is a better example of peer production than crowdsourcing, although many firms practicing crowdsourcing may turn to open-source solutions. The original and still-leading research explains that *open source* refers to software licensed on particular terms. The license must meet the criteria for free redistribution, source code availability, and derivative works, among others (de Beer 2015; Perens 1999; Raymond 1999).

One key point is that, in the context of software, *open source* is defined primarily in reference to legal criteria. But another key point is that open-source software is *not*, legally speaking, nonproprietary. It is legally protected by copyright, patents, or both, but creatively licensed to require, instead of restrict, sharing (de Beer 2015, 32). A framework is also emerging to understand open-source hardware, in addition to software, based on similar legal principles and practices.

Chapter 2 classifies crowdsourcing as a contribution that the open innovation school of thought has contributed to an overarching framework for open development. It also positions open-source software as the school of thought that contributes ideas about peer production, open licensing, and user freedom. While crowdsourcing is one example of open innovation, and software is the most dominant model for understanding openness in ICT4D, this chapter argues that looking across other domains through the lens of innovation is appropriate to frame open development. The next section of this chapter, therefore, considers the relationships among innovation, appropriation, and development in the realm of open science, open access, and open data.

A Crosscutting Concept of Openness through Innovation in Practice

Both scholarly literature and practical experience belie the premise of classifying the study of innovation, business models, or both into a silo distinct from the domains of science, education, or data. Indeed, open innovation is inseparable from open science, open education, or open data. Through access to and exchanges of knowledge, innovation is intractably embedded in, and also transcends, each of these fields. The implementation and diffusion of new products, processes, and organizational and marketing methods (i.e., innovation as commonly understood) are the phenomena that make science, education, and data drive development in a knowledge society. Figure 3.3 depicts these relationships.

Therefore, this section of the chapter considers innovation-related aspects of knowledge governance across domains ranging from science to education to data. It takes up the challenge to move "beyond studying the qualities of openness within specific localized projects, and focus its energies on crosscutting studies that identify the factors driving quality openness" (Reilly and McMahon 2015, 48). It starts with an overview of open access, which straddles open innovation and each of the three focal areas

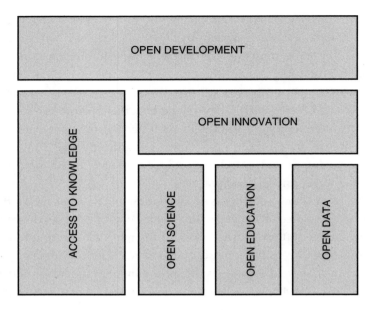

Figure 3.3
A framework for analyzing openness, situating knowledge and innovation (not ICTs) among science, education, data, and development outcomes.

of education, data, and science most closely connected with the concept of access to knowledge as a whole, which straddles open innovation and each of the three focal areas of science/education/data.

Open Access

Most definitions of openness include accessibility as a core feature. The term *open access* is related to, but not synonymous with, the concepts of open science, open data, and other applications of openness. It generally refers to published content that is digital, online, free of charge, and free of most copyright restrictions (Suber 2012). These freedoms address two separate barriers to accessibility. Making works available *gratis* removes financial barriers to access, while making works available *libre* removes permission barriers to access.

Both of these freedoms were emphasized in three formal declarations on open access publishing: the Budapest Open Access Initiative (Chan et al. 2002), the Bethesda Statement on Open Access Publishing (Stebbins 2003), and the Berlin Declaration on Open Access to Knowledge in the Sciences and Humanities (Max-Planek-Gesellschaft 2003).

A common theme is the understanding that: "[f]or a work to be OA [open access], the copyright holder must consent in advance to let users 'copy, use, distribute, transmit and display the work publicly and to make and distribute derivative works, in any digital medium for any responsible purpose, subject to proper attribution of authorship'" (Suber 2012, 8).

More so than open science, the term *open access* has long been associated with IP licensing, particularly copyrights. Imbued with this legal connotation, open access has since evolved in three related but distinct directions. First, the original issue of access to published scholarly literature continues to generate debate. Second, recent innovations have led to an increased use of open access to publish other types of content. Third, open access is moving to educational resources, both in artifacts and the process of learning.

In the first area, open access to scholarly literature, one of the strongest arguments for open access to literature is its potential to increase the impact of scholarly publications (Hess and Ostrom 2003). Early research suggested that journal articles received more citations when openly published (Antelman 2004; Eysenbach 2006). These findings generated significant interest within academia, leading to the "green and golden roads to open access" (Harnad et al. 2004, 310). By 2004, 90 percent of academic journals surveyed in one study were "green"—that is, they allowed authors to self-archive—while 5 percent of academic journals were "gold," which means publishing under open access licenses (Harnad et al. 2004, 313). More critical reviews call these impact effects into question, pointing to variability in findings and identifying various biases (Craig et al. 2007). However, a strong consensus remains that open access increases academic impact (Tennant et al. 2016).

The demand for open access to literature has never been higher. Elsevier's recent legal victory drew attention to the academic piracy site Sci-Hub, whose users downloaded 28 million papers between September 2015 and March 2016 (Bohannon 2016). However, limited research examines the economic impacts of open access to literature. A report to the United Kingdom's Open Access Implementation Group estimated that open access saves the public sector £26 million in access fees and £2.6 million in time (Look and Marsh 2012). Recognizing the economic and social value of open access literature, the Barack Obama administration announced in 2013 that federally funded research in the United States would be freely available within one year of publication (Stebbins 2013).

Second, as Internet bandwidth has increased, so have "remix culture" and the demand for freely available content (Lessig 2004, 965). The Creative Commons (CC) suite of copyright licenses has helped to meet this demand, allowing creators to publish their works gratis while selecting a range of libre-based requirements for attribution and use.[1] Over 1.4 billion works are openly accessible under CC licenses (Merkley

2018). Major Internet services offer options to publish under CC, including content on Wikipedia, video on YouTube, music on Soundcloud, and images on Flickr.

Open Education

Third, open access to educational resources has moved beyond textbooks and other content-based artifacts of education, to the process of learning. Educational resources are made open with the understanding that "access to the world's knowledge is a public good" (Smith and Casserly 2006, 10). Research in the field explores how open educational resources (OER) are produced, delivered (Wiley, Bliss, and McEwen 2014), and adopted, as well as their subsequent impacts (also see chapter 12 for more on OER). OER include open courses and learning materials, software for learning (e.g., learning management platforms), and repositories of learning materials (Downes 2007).

Downes (2007) highlights a number of business models being used to provide OER. Models include an endowment model, where funding comes from interest generated from large donations (e.g., Stanford's *Encyclopedia of Philosophy*); an institutional model, where funding is part of the organization's operational budget [e.g., the Open Courseware program at the Massachusetts Institute of Technology (MIT)]; and a conversion model, where for-profit organizations offer *freemium* options, with the goal of converting free consumers into paying customers (e.g., Coursera) (Downes 2007). Some governments have shifted spending from proprietary to open resources.

In terms of access to the *process* of education, massive open online courses (MOOCs) have emerged as particularly interesting (Haggard et al. 2013). These online courses are open for anyone to enroll in and access reading lists, lectures, and various learning experiences. Examples include edX, run by a consortium of universities including Harvard, the University of California, Berkeley, and the University of Adelaide; Coursera, run by Stanford, Princeton, and Arizona State University; and Udemy, a nonacademic skills training site that allows experts to create and administer courses.

As with OER, MOOCs have struggled to find sustainable business models (Wiley, Bliss, and McEwen 2014), although there are some emerging models such as charging for specializations, on-demand MOOCs, and verified certificates (Tirthali 2016). What is clear is that the development and maintenance of online learning materials are costly. For example, each course published on MIT's Open Courseware takes a minimum of 100 hours of effort to produce, at an annual cost of US$3.5 million.[2] The costs to produce and deliver MOOCs can also be quite high. A 2014 study found that the cost per course for MOOCs ranged between US$38,980 and US$325,330 (Hollands and Tirthali 2014), and a more recent paper noted that there are examples of high-end courses costing up to an estimated US$1 million (Tirthali 2016). These costs highlight the challenges that providers face in covering their costs while maintaining free access to course materials.

A number of other governance challenges exist for MOOCs. Although free, as in gratis, remains a common theme across MOOCs, now many courses are not offered free, as in libre. The debate about whether these courses are *massive, open,* and *online* or just *massive* and *online* demonstrates the ambiguity and controversy about what *open* really means. These developments have led some commentators to speculate whether massive online courses can remain free and sustainable (Tirthali 2016; Gee 2016).

Open access to both educational resources and processes is especially important for developing countries, as IDRC-supported research on open development clearly demonstrated (Armstrong et al. 2010). In the knowledge economy, access to information drives innovation and growth. Limited financial resources within developing countries constrain access to proprietary journals and other creative resources that are necessary for innovation. Education for innovation requires access to both materials and pedagogical tools for learning. As emerging concepts that require innovation in their implementation, open access and OER will also create opportunities for education in the process of innovation.

Moving forward, a leading thinker on OER forcefully argued that there is no longer any debate about the meaning of *open* in the context of OER: "As far as I can tell, the only people actively engaged in a debate about the meaning of the word 'open' in the educational context are (1) those who genuinely misunderstand it because they haven't become part of the community yet, and (2) those whose business models would collapse if the public had free access to and open licenses for their products" (Wiley 2016). The key phrase in Wiley's comment is "in the educational context."

Cutting across sectors—looking at innovation in education, science, data, and other areas—there is significant debate about what *open* really means. When organizations around the world say that they practice open innovation, it is not just naivete, or "openwashing" as Wiley suggests (Wiley 2016). These organizations may be adopting a bona fide understanding of openness based on renowned work by authors such as Henry Chesbrough. Work in the realm of open data helps to further highlight the conceptual challenges that still plague open development across domains.

Open Data

Data have become valuable with the rise of the digital era, informing and driving scientific discovery, underpinning business models, and supporting evidence-based policy. Developments in linked data provide incentives for firms to open their data for collaboration.

The *Open Data Handbook* (n.d.) defines "data" as data sets as opposed to a single data point, which it defines as "content". Data are considered to be "open" when they can be accessed, used, modified, or shared by anyone (*Open Data Handbook* n.d.). Within the open innovation literature, there is some consensus that open data require ICT—the data must be machine readable and accessible online (Chan 2013; Gurstein 2011). In contrast, open development scholars acknowledge that data take many qualitative forms, including maps, pictures, and paintings, and need not be machine readable or accessible online to be open (Hossain, Dwivedi, and Rana 2015; van Schalkwyk et al. 2014).

As an intangible resource, IP governs the ownership of data. By default, owners hold a proprietary right to their data. This is a result of a combination of legal mechanisms governing ownership of data, including copyright, sui generis database rights, technological protection measures (TPMs), trade secrets, and privacy (de Beer 2016). Copyright (the most commonly discussed mechanism) automatically protects original compilations of data in databases, but not fact-based content like statistics or formulas. More than one of these legal mechanisms may apply to a given data set, increasing the ambiguity of data ownership. Therefore, data are only considered "open" when they are published under an open license.

Proprietary ownership of data poses several challenges for open data artifacts. In practice, proprietary data hinder the growth of the linked data commons, making it impossible to apply open licenses to linked data sets containing proprietary data. The ambiguous nature of ownership rights in data means that licensing open data may not be as straightforward as other content. Conversely, clearer ownership rights could facilitate open data by enabling owners to apply open licenses to their data. Open data licenses transfer these rights, allowing anyone to access and use the data with attribution and other optional conditions (Open Data Commons n.d.; Creative Commons 2013).

Despite the challenges, firms are practicing open innovation by releasing their private data, recognizing the economic benefits and potential of open data systems (Dodds et al. 2014; Hammell et al. 2012; Open Data Institute 2016). Depending on the particular model adopted to share open data, these practices could reflect either the firm-centric version of open innovation, by using IP licenses to exchange data into and out of the organization, or a more systemic approach, in which data are put into the public domain without any IP protection at all. In either case, the economic impacts of open data are substantial.

It has been suggested that the market impact of public-sector information across the European Union (EU) in 2008 was €28 billion (Vickery 2011). An independent review in the United Kingdom estimated benefits of public-sector information at £6.8 billion in 2013 (Shakespeare 2013). Looking globally across public- and private-sector information, the McKinsey Institute estimates the widespread use of open data will globally unlock $3.2 trillion in economic value per year (Manyika et al. 2013). However, it is difficult to assess the reliability of these figures because little or no empirical work has been conducted on the macroeconomic impacts of open data.

Using business case studies, the Open Data Institute (2016) describes how three firms, Thomson Reuters, Arup, and Syngenta, have adopted an open data approach to gain an economic and competitive advantage. Thomson Reuters opened access to Permanent Identification (PermID), its key entities identifier system, to improve the richness and accuracy of their data (Dodds et al. 2014). They enjoy a reciprocal benefit when outside users link their open data to the PermID system, gaining access to outside data with little additional effort (Dodds et al. 2014). Arup, a design and engineering consulting firm, uses open data to enable nimble responses to new ideas inside and outside the organization. It allows Arup to "create IP without having to have complex legal agreements, lawyers, and background discussion that slows everything down" (Open Data Institute 2016). Syngenta, a global agricultural firm, has published six open data sets as part of their Good Growth Plan for sustainably growing their business by improving global food security (Open Data Institute 2016). Beginning as a strategy to engage stakeholders and build trust in their plan through transparency, Syngenta AG view open data as part of a shift toward a more collaborative business model.

There is considerable optimism surrounding open data among the development community. The World Bank sees their potential to help level the playing field for the communication of knowledge (Walji 2011). Such inclusivity is expected to generate more effective outcomes (Davies and Edwards 2012). For example, increased access to information allows policymakers and aid funding agencies to make evidence-based decisions (Linders 2013). But scholars warn that "openness must serve the interests of marginalised and poor people" (Davies and Edwards 2012), which in many cases is overlooked and has only a tangential bearing on the open data work being done.

Several challenges must be overcome before these opportunities are realized. Unequal access to ICT and open data creates a digital divide, excluding marginalized users from the benefits of open data while empowering users who already have expertise and access (Gurstein 2011). Developing countries and businesses often lack the capacity to digitize their data (Davies 2014).

When open data are available, they are often published in the aggregate (for a variety of reasons, including privacy). But the developing world needs disaggregated data to make evidence-based policy decisions (Addison et al. 2016; Chan 2013). Data intermediaries are recognized as part of the solution to these challenges (van Schalk-wyk et al. 2014), but more work is needed to increase ICT penetration and address the context of developing countries. (See chapters 10 and 11 in this volume for more on open government data.)

Open Science

Science is perhaps the broadest domain for open development research because it both produces and depends on scholarly literature and data. In a way, open science subsumes and transcends many aspects of open access publishing and open data (although, as chapter 13 in this volume suggests, open science may be interpreted differently in the context of development). It may be reasonable to treat certain open access issues, such as access to scholarly literature, primarily under the rubric of open science. The framework offered in this chapter, however, considers scholarly publishing alongside other forms of open access that share common roots (specifically, access to remixed cultural content and access to educational resources). Open science has different and earlier historical roots.

Dasgupta and David (1994, 487) explain the "new economics of science" as a synthesis of "the classic approach of Arrow and Nelson in examining the implications of the characteristics of information for allocative efficiency in research activities, on the one hand, with the functionalist analysis of institutional structures, reward systems, and behavioral norms of 'open science' communities—associated with the sociology of science in the tradition of Merton—on the other." The stylized term inspired by Merton (1973), *open science*, is now understood as being an institution with a self-reinforcing code of conduct. The scientific priority of original discovery is rewarded with monetary and social benefits, which create incentives for full disclosure and diffusion of scientific knowledge.

The open science model contrasts with one where exclusivity of property rights is the key incentive for investments in science. The tension over openness was described by Paul David and Bronwyn Hall (2006, 767) in this way, in the introduction to a special issue of *Research Policy* on IP issues affecting science: "[W]e have two distinctive regimes or environments for the conduct of research: the actors in the realm of 'open science research' expect reciprocal sharing of discoveries among themselves and the rest of the world, while those in the world of private profit-oriented and proprietary R&D expect to receive payment for the right to use their inventions (and to pay others for the use of theirs)." This and other seminal literature on open science define *openness* at least partly by reference to its opposite, *proprietary science* (see also David 2004). For more details, see chapter 13 in this volume.

The incentives produced by open and proprietary approaches have different impacts, depending on the system in which science operates. Indeed, it has been shown that open science contributes to scientific and economic inequalities in developed and developing countries (Carillo and Papagni 2014; also see chapter 13). That is because the larger the scientific system in terms of investments and involvement of the state in which one operates, the greater the social and professional rewards for openness tend to be. There are fewer rewards in smaller systems characterized by scant investments. Consequently, economic modeling shows a world with two stable equilibria, which "may explain the huge differences existing between scientific sectors of less developed and more developed countries" (Carillo and Papagni 2014, 52).

Distinctions between open and proprietary models of science had roughly tracked the divide between university- and industry-led processes. But this line is becoming increasingly blurry as universities face pressure to commercialize scientific research and industry experiments with new appropriation strategies that support more open models of innovation. IP rights play a central role here. One of the key conclusions flowing from leading research on academic science and entrepreneurship is that IP rights such as patents are "changing the 'rules of the game' for scientific exchange, scientific credit, and the commercialization opportunities arising from scientific discovery" (Jaffe et al. 2007, 575).

The most significant shift in academic entrepreneurship during the twentieth century occurred as a result of legislation in the United States, the Bayh-Dole Act, which permitted recipients of public funding to obtain private IP rights over research outputs. While the legislation, passed in 1980, may not have fundamentally changed processes at the few American universities that were already actively exploiting IP (Mowery et al. 2001), for most institutions the Bayh-Dole Act was "a major impetus towards increased university involvement in patenting and licensing" (Sampat 2006, 781; also see Berman 2008, 836–837). Indeed, Bayh-Dole is associated not just with increased IP awareness and acquisition, but with academic entrepreneurship more generally (Aldridge and Audretsch 2011; Grimaldi et al. 2011).

"[T]he intellectual foundations for this sea-change in federal patent policy were weak," explains Sampat (2006, 773), "based on a lack of understanding of the roles of universities in the innovation system." Nevertheless, in the early twenty-first century, the impacts of the Bayh-Dole Act, combined with the World Trade Organization's Agreement on Trade-Related Aspects of Intellectual Property Rights (TRIPS), have been rippling throughout the developing world. In a must-read review of economic evidence pertaining to IP's impact on science and technology in developing countries, Forero-Pineda (2006, 810) summarizes: "Scientific communities in developing countries are particularly vulnerable to limitations of cooperation and access to information, resulting from stronger intellectual property rights protection, as their efforts to obtain normal science results must be considerable."

There are basically two ways in which IP threatens open science: access costs and transaction costs (David 2004). Institutional innovations that privatize and commodify knowledge "have a potential to do serious damage in the field of scientific and technological research, with all the adverse implications that this may carry for the long-term course of innovation and economic welfare growth in the advanced, 'knowledge-driven' economies and the developing economies alike" (David 2004, 10). Empirical studies, using methods such as difference-in-differences estimators, show substantial benefits of academic openness for innovation (Murray et al. 2016). Economic modelling also shows that under the right conditions, open science is associated with higher social welfare than secrecy (Mukherjee and Stern 2009).

In developed countries, a possible "tragedy of the anti-commons" is among the biggest concerns around the push to propertize and commercialize scientific research (Heller and Eisenberg 1998). Empirical research is scarce, but some evidence shows that patents do have a "modest anti-commons effect" that hinders the free flow of scientific knowledge (Murray and Stern 2007, 649). A core challenge is developing an empirical methodological framework to test anti-commons and open science theories. This is very difficult in developed countries with data about patents and publications (Murray and Stern 2007, 656–661). It is even more difficult to conduct quantitative or statistical analysis in developing countries, where new concepts and metrics to measure informal innovation are just beginning to emerge (de Beer, Fu, and Wunsch-Vincent 2013).

Numerous researchers have called for reform of the Bayh-Dole system in the United States (Kenney and Patton 2009; Rai and Eisenberg 2003). There is also significant debate on whether the Bayh-Dole approach is appropriate for other developed countries. The most credible research suggests not: "efforts at 'emulation' of the Bayh-Dole policy elsewhere in the OECD are likely to have modest success at best without greater attention to the underlying structural differences among the higher education systems of these nations" (Mowery and Sampat 2005, 117). The problem is even worse when transplanting Bayh-Dole to developing countries (So et al. 2008, 262).

It is not surprising, therefore, that the emerging research on open science in development characterizes the issues very differently. Development-related research on open science frames the issues less in economic terms than as about "the ways in which colonial legacies, capitalist forces, and political repression continue to limit access to knowledge around the world" (Albornoz 2016, sec. 1).

While it is justifiably argued that "Open Science addresses development by expanding opportunities to create, share, and use knowledge" (Albornoz 2016), these are unfortunately not the terms on which policy debates are unfolding in real time in developing countries. New research by the Open African Innovation Research (Open AIR) network demonstrates that open science is under threat as a result of Bayh-Dole–like initiatives in numerous African countries. The conclusion from Open AIR's work in three countries thus far is as follows (de Beer et al. 2014, 391):

> It remains to be seen whether such an orientation, fashioned more than three decades ago in the world's strongest economy, will be helpful in contemporary or future African contexts. The evidence provided in this book suggests that the IP commercialisation orientation for public research outputs will have a relatively benign impact in South Africa; potentially damaging consequences in the context of Ethiopia (with its moribund university–industry linkages); and highly uncertain results in Botswana (where the policy-making is very recent and awareness among public researchers very low).

The main reason such a dramatic policy shift away from open science may not have serious unintended consequences in South Africa is that relatively sophisticated stakeholders are crafting workarounds to avoid the worst outcomes (Ncube, Abrahams, and Akinsanmi 2013). Not all researchers are optimistic that problems can be avoided, however (Barratt 2010). Regardless, the South African approach sets a dangerous precedent for the rest of the continent, as well as the developing world more generally. Concerns have been expressed about the threats from the propertization of science in research focusing on other developing countries and regions, including India (Sampat 2009) and Latin America (Forero-Pineda 2006). Future open development-related research on open science cannot ignore this crucial issue.

"The case for open scientific knowledge clearly needs to be reconstructed," argues at least one leading innovation economist, to acknowledge that "the scientific commons is in danger, the costs of having it erode further are likely to be high, and that we ought to move to protect it" (Nelson 2004, 456 and 470). Much work remains to be done to understand when and where an open or proprietary approach makes more sense, and time is of the essence.

Interestingly for the conceptual framing of this chapter, ICTs factor very little in the leading research on open science. There are two possible inferences to draw from its absence. Either there is a major gap in the research, with open science scholars failing to recognize the central role of ICTs and give them due analytical attention, or ICTs may not be the definitive driver of open science. If the latter explanation is true (or even possible), open development researchers would do well to study the broader social and economic forces at play when building grounded theories about openness in science, technology, and innovation policies for development.

Another interesting contrast exists between research on open science and open innovation regarding the direction of the shift toward openness. In the realm of science, openness is being supplanted by appropriation through IP rights as part of the push toward the commercialization of publicly funded research. As a result, science is under threat of becoming less open. In the realm of innovation more broadly, industry is becoming more open. Old models of closed innovation premised on isolation and secrecy are being replaced by more collaborative models based on the flow of knowledge across firm boundaries.

Is the trend similar with respect to other areas of open development, such as education and data? The following section of this chapter explores that question.

Summary and Next Steps

This chapter has highlighted theoretical gaps between the fields of open development and open innovation. It has suggested strategies to better integrate these two concepts, thus extending the potential of open development beyond its origins in ICT4D.

Significant discussion of the meaning of openness was contained in both major sections of the chapter. That discussion reveals that critics of openwashing may misunderstand the reason that companies call practices open, despite not meeting the criteria befitting one particular application of openness or another. The reason is that some practices may be labeled open according to the widely accepted meaning of *openness* in the management and innovation literature. This is not always a disingenuous or nefarious marketing ploy; it is an innovation strategy taught in introductory-level business school courses.

This chapter has also shown how the concepts of open innovation and access to knowledge provide crosscutting analysis of commonalities among applications including open science, open education, and open data. The practices that underpin open science are, in fact, modes of open innovation. Open education is itself an open innovation, and, whether they realize it or not, all (and maybe most) actors in the open education ecosystem are open innovators. Open data are among the key currencies exchanged via open innovation. Open innovation does not belong in a category with open science, open education, and open data; *it simultaneously subsumes, underpins, and permeates such things*. A new, theoretically integrated, and practically cross-cutting framework, as presented in figure 3.3, can facilitate more interdisciplinary and policy-relevant research.

As a final remark, there are two areas that stand out as priorities for future researchers who might use these insights to advance open development research. One relates to informality, the other to governance.

Regarding the informality of openness, it is critical to note the size and importance of the informal economy in many developing countries. The latest figures show that the informal economy contributes nearly two-thirds of gross domestic product (GDP) in the region of sub-Saharan Africa, and, in some Southeast Asian countries, such as India, informal economic contributions constitute half of GDP. Groundwork has recently been done to prove that (1) extensive innovation happens in the informal economy (de Beer, Fu, and Wunsch-Vincent 2016); and (2) informal-sector innovators openly collaborate or appropriate differently from their counterparts in the formal sector (de Beer and Wunsch-Vincent 2016). An agenda to better measure and value these contributions has been proposed, but the hardest work of developing and implementing new metrics remains to be done.

Despite the importance of the informal economy in developing countries, little or no research has been published that explores open science, open education, or open data in this specific context. An opportunity exists for researchers to take up this challenge by situating those topics in a framework integrating open innovation and development. Without more explicit and systematic coverage of the informal sector, open development cannot fulfill its explanatory potential or have the impact that it otherwise might.

On the issue of governance, further research is needed to understand the best approaches to mediate tensions among openness, access, and the appropriation of knowledge. Knowledge flows throughout innovation systems and influences the degree to which the benefits of science, education, and data lead to positive development outcomes for all of society. Access to knowledge was identified as a central concept animating the last decade of work on ICT4D (de Beer and Bannerman 2013). Now the time is ripe to take an analogous step in the emerging field of open development. It is heartening to see Smith and Seward accept that challenge, as they did in chapter 2.

One conceptual tool to better understand how knowledge governance affects innovation across science, education, data, and other domains is the *commons*. Numerous scholars have been inspired by the work of Nobel laureate Elinor Ostrom on governing the commons (Ostrom 1990). Her insights have been adapted to create a framework for research on governing the knowledge commons (Hess and Ostrom 2006; Frischmann, Madison, and Strandburg 2014). Interesting scholarship using this framework has been published on commons-driven initiatives in genomics, medical research, astronomy, aviation, journalism, military technology, and much more. Chapter 2, picking up on this idea, identifies the potential of a knowledge governance framework in open development. But the knowledge commons framework for governing open innovation in developing countries has not yet been well developed, nor well studied.

Informal innovation and knowledge governance are just two specific priorities that might be possible to explore once the concepts of open innovation and open development become better integrated. Moving open development out of the constraints of the ICT4D domain will help researchers address key questions around open science, open education, and open data. ICT4D researchers should be proud of the open development theory that they have spawned. The next step is to let it loose.

Notes

1. See the home page of Creative Commons (https://creativecommons.org/choose/).

2. See MIT Open Courseware (http://ocw.mit.edu/donate/why-donate/#how-much).

References

Addison, Chris, Isolina Boto, Ana Brandesescu, Hugo Besemer, Jerven Morten, Ben Schaap, and Isaura Lopes Ram. 2016. "CTA Discussion Paper: Data Revolution for Agriculture." Wageningen, Netherlands: Technical Centre for Agricultural and Rural Cooperation. https://brusselsbriefings.files.wordpress.com/2015/03/1937_pdf.pdf.

Aghion, Philippe, Paul A. David, and Dominique Foray. 2009. "Science, Technology, and Innovation for Economic Growth: Linking Policy Research and Practice in 'STIG Systems.'" *Research Policy* 38 (4): 681–693.

Albornoz, Denisse. 2016. "Understanding Openness: New Findings in Context-Sensitive Open Science." Open and Collaborative Science in Development Network (OCSDNet). http://ocsdnet.org/understanding-openness-new-findings-in-context-sensitive-open-science/.

Aldridge, T. T., and David Audretsch. 2011. "The Bayh-Dole Act and Scientist Entrepreneurship." *Research Policy* 40 (8): 1058–1067.

Altenburg, Tilman. 2009. "Building Inclusive Innovation Systems in Developing Countries: Challenges for IS Research." In *Handbook of Innovation Systems and Developing Countries: Building Domestic Capabilities in a Global Setting*, ed. Bengt-Åke Lundvall, K. J. Joseph, Christina Chaminade, and Jan Vang, chapter 2. Cheltenham, UK: Edward Elgar.

Antelman, Kristin. 2004. "Do Open-Access Articles Have a Greater Research Impact?" *College & Research Libraries* 65 (5): 372–382. doi:10.5860/crl.65.5.372.

Armstrong, Chris, Jeremy de Beer, Dick Kawooya, Achal Prabhala, and Tobias Schonwetter, eds., 2010. *Access to Knowledge in Africa: The Role of Copyright*. Ottawa: IDRC; Durbanville, South Africa: Shuttleworth Foundation; Johannesburg: LiNK Centre, Graduate School of Public and Development Management, University of the Witwatersrand; Cape Town, South Africa: Juta. https://idl-bnc-idrc.dspacedirect.org/bitstream/handle/10625/44667/IDL-44667.pdf?sequence=1&isAllowed=y.

Arrow, Kenneth. 1962. "Economic Welfare and the Allocation of Resources for Invention." In *The Rate and Direction of Inventive Activity: Economic and Social Factors*, ed. Universities-National

Bureau Committee for Economic Research, Committee on Economic Growth of the Social Science Research Council, 609–626. Princeton, NJ: Princeton University Press. http://www.nber.org /chapters/c2144.pdf.

Baldwin, Carliss, and Eric von Hippel. 2011. "Modeling a Paradigm Shift: From Producer Innovation to User and Open Collaborative Innovation." *Organization Science* 22 (6): 1399–1417.

Barratt, Amanda. 2010. "Lessons from Bayh-Dole: Reflections on the Intellectual Property Rights from Publicly Financed Research and Development Act (South Africa)." *Journal for Juridical Science* 35 (2): 30–69.

Benkler, Yochai. 2006. *The Wealth of Networks: How Social Production Transforms Markets and Freedom.* New Haven, CT: Yale University Press. http://www.benkler.org/Benkler_Wealth_Of_Networks.pdf.

Berman, Elizabeth P. 2008. "Why Did Universities Start Patenting? Institution-Building and the Road to the Bayh-Dole Act." *Social Studies of Science* 38 (6): 835–871. doi:10.1177/0306312708098605.

Bohannon, John. 2016. "Who's Downloading Pirated Papers? Everyone." *Science* April 28, 2016. http://www.sciencemag.org/news/2016/04/whos-downloading-pirated-papers-everyone.

Carillo, Maria R., and Erasmo Papagni. 2014. "'Little Science' and 'Big Science': The Institution of 'Open Science' as a Cause of Scientific and Economic Inequalities among Countries." *Economic Modelling* 43 (C): 42–56. doi:10.1016/j.econmod.2014.06.021.

Chan, Calvin M. L. 2013. "From Open Data to Open Innovation Strategies: Creating E-Services Using Open Government Data." *Proceedings of the 46th Hawaii International Conference on System Sciences*, 1890–1899. Wailea, HI, January. doi:10.1109/HICSS.2013.236.

Chan, Leslie, Darius Cuplinskas, Michael Eisen, Fred Friend, Yana Genova, Jean-Claude Guédon, Melissa Hagemann, et al. 2002. "Budapest Open Access Initiative." http://www .budapestopenaccessinitiative.org/read.

Chesbrough, Henry W. 2003. *Open Innovation: The New Imperative for Creating and Profiting from Technology.* Boston: Harvard Business School Press.

Chesbrough, Henry W. 2006. *Open Business Models: How to Thrive in the New Innovation Landscape.* Boston: Harvard Business School Press.

Chesbrough, Henry, and Marcel Bogers. 2014. "Explicating Open Innovation: Clarifying an Emerging Paradigm for Understanding Innovation." In *New Frontiers in Open Innovation*, ed. Henry W. Chesbrough, Wim Vanhaverbeke, and Joel West, 3–28. Oxford: Oxford University Press.

Craig, Iain D., Andrew M. Plume, Marie E. Mcveigh, James Pringle, and Mayur Amin. 2007. "Do Open Access Articles Have Greater Citation Impact?" *Journal of Informetrics* 1 (3): 239–248. doi:10 .1016/j.joi.2007.04.001.

Creative Commons. 2013. "Data." https://wiki.creativecommons.org/wiki/Data.

Dahlander, Linus, and David M. Gann. 2010. "How Open Is Innovation?" *Research Policy* 39 (6): 699–709.

Dasgupta, Partha, and Paul A. David. 1994. "Toward a New Economics of Science." *Research Policy* 23 (5): 487–521.

David, Paul A. 2004. "Can 'Open Science' Be Protected from the Evolving Regime of IPR Protections?" *Journal of Institutional and Theoretical Economics* 160 (0502010): 9–34.

David, Paul A., and Bronwyn H. Hall. 2006. "Property and the Pursuit of Knowledge: IPR Issues Affecting Scientific Research." *Research Policy* 35 (6): 767–771. doi:10.1016/j.respol.2006.04.002.

Davies, Tim. 2012. "What Is Open Development?" *Tim's Blog*, September 10. http://www.timdavies .org.uk/2012/09/10/what-is-open-development/.

Davies, Tim. 2014. *Open Data in Developing Countries: Emerging Insights from Phase I.* Berlin: World Wide Web Foundation. http://opendataresearch.org/content/2014/704/open-data-developing -countries-emerging-insights-phase-i.

Davies, Tim, and Duncan Edwards. 2012. "Emerging Implications of Open and Linked Data for Knowledge Sharing in Development." *Institute of Development Studies Bulletin* 43 (5): 117–127.

De Beer, Jeremy. 2015. "'Open' Innovation Policy Frameworks: Intellectual Property, Competition, Investment & Other Market Governance Issues." February 15. Ottawa: Industry Canada.

De Beer, Jeremy. 2016. "Ownership of Open Data: Governance Options for Agriculture and Nutrition." New York: GODAN. http://www.godan.info/sites/default/files/documents/Godan_Owner ship_of_Open_Data_Publication_lowres.pdf.

De Beer, Jeremy, and Chris Armstrong. 2015. "Open Innovation and Knowledge Appropriation in African Micro and Small Enterprises (MSEs)." *African Journal of Information and Communications* 16:60–71. http://wiredspace.wits.ac.za/bitstream/handle/10539/19315/AJIC-Issue-16-2015-De-Beer -Armstrong.pdf.

De Beer, Jeremy, Chris Armstrong, Chidi Oguamanam, and Tobias Schonwetter. 2014. "Current Realities of Collaborative Intellectual Property in Africa." In *Innovation and Intellectual Property: Collaborative Dynamics in Africa*, ed. Jeremy de Beer, Chris Armstrong, Chidi Oguamanam, and Tobias Schonwetter, 373–394. Cape Town, South Africa: University of Cape Town Press.

De Beer, Jeremy, and Sara Bannerman. 2013. "Access to Knowledge as a New Paradigm for Research on ICTs and Intellectual Property Rights." In *Connecting ICTs to Development: The IDRC Experience*, ed. Laurent Elder, Heloise Emdon, Richard Fuchs, and Ben Petrazzini, 75–90. London/Ottawa: Anthem Press/IDRC. https://www.idrc.ca/en/book/connecting-icts-development-idrc-experience.

De Beer, Jeremy, Kun Fu, and Sacha Wunsch-Vincent. 2013. "The Informal Economy, Innovation and Intellectual Property—Concepts, Metrics, and Policy Considerations." *World Intellectual Property Organization Economic Research Working Paper*. WIPO Economics & Statistics Series, Economics Working Paper no. 10. Geneva, Switzerland: Economics and Statistics Division, World Intellectual Property Organization. http://www.wipo.int/edocs/pubdocs/en/wipo_pub_econstat_wp_10.pdf.

De Beer, Jeremy, Kun Fu, and Sacha Wunsch-Vincent. 2016. "Innovation in the Informal Economy." In *The Informal Economy in Developing Nations: Hidden Engine for Innovation*, ed. Erika Kaemer-Mbula and Sacha Wunsch-Vincent, 53–99. Cambridge: Cambridge University Press.

De Beer, Jeremy, Ian P. McCarthy, Adam Soliman, and Emily Treen. 2017. "Click Here to Agree: Managing Intellectual Property When Crowdsourcing Solutions." *Business Horizons* 60 (2): 207–217.

De Beer, Jeremy, and Sacha Wunsch-Vincent. 2016. "Appropriation and Intellectual Property in the Informal Economy." In *The Informal Economy in Developing Nations: Hidden Engine of Innovation?* ed. Sacha Wunsch-Vincent and Erika Kaemer-Mbula, 232–295. Cambridge: Cambridge University Press.

Dodds, Leigh, Georgia Phillips, Tharindi Hapuarachchi, Bob Bailey, and Andrew Fletcher. 2014. *Creating Value with Identifiers in an Open Data World*, October. London/New York: Open Data Institute/Thomson Reuters. https://www.thomsonreuters.com/content/dam/openweb/documents /pdf/corporate/Reports/creating-value-with-identifiers-in-an-open-data-world-summary.pdf.

Downes, Stephen. 2007. "Models for Sustainable Open Educational Resources." *Interdisciplinary Journal of Knowledge and Learning Objects* 3:29–44. http://www.oecd.org/education/ceri/36781698.pdf.

Elmquist, Maria, Tobias Fredberg, and Susanne Ollila. 2009. "Exploring the Field of Open Innovation." *European Journal of Innovation Management* 12 (3): 326–345. doi:10.1108/14601060910974219.

Estellés-Arolas, Enrique, and Fernando González-Ladrón-de-Guevara. 2012. "Towards an Integrated Crowdsourcing Definition." *Journal of Information Science* 38 (2): 189–200. doi:10.1177 /0165551512437638.

Eysenbach, Gunther. 2006. "Citation Advantage of Open Access Articles." *PLoS Biology* 4 (5): e157. https://www.ncbi.nlm.nih.gov/pmc/articles/PMC1459247/.

Forero-Pineda, Clemente. 2006. "The Impact of Stronger Intellectual Property Rights on Science and Technology in Developing Countries." *Research Policy* 35 (6): 808–824. doi:10.1016/j.respol .2006.04.003.

Fredberg, Tobias, Eleni Giannopoulou, Anna Yström, Susanne Ollila, and Maria Elmquist. 2010. "Implications of Openness: A Study into (All) the Growing Literature on Open Innovation." *Journal of Technology Management & Innovation* 5 (3): 162–180. https://scielo.conicyt.cl/scielo.php ?script=sci_arttext&pid=S0718-27242010000300012.

Frischmann, Brett M., Michael J. Madison, and Katherine J. Strandburg. 2014. "Governing Knowledge Commons." In *Governing Knowledge Commons*, ed. Brett M. Frischmann, Michael J. Madison, and Katherine J. Strandburg, ix–xiv. Oxford: Oxford University Press. http://madisonian.net /downloads/papers/GKC.pdf.

Gee, Sue. 2016. "Coursera Commits Cultural Vandalism as Old Platform Shuts—UPDATE." *I Programmer.* http://www.i-programmer.info/news/150-training-a-education/9817-coursera-vandalism -as-old-platform-shuts.html.

Grimaldi, Rosa, Martin Kenney, Donald S. Siegel, and Mike Wright. 2011. "30 Years after Bayh-Dole: Reassessing Academic Entrepreneurship." *Research Policy* 40 (8): 1045–1057.

Gurstein, Michael S. 2011. "Open Data: Empowering the Empowered or Effective Data Use for Everyone?" *First Monday* 16 (2), February 7. http://firstmonday.org/article/view/3316/2764.

Haggard, Stephen, Tim Gore, Tom Inklaar, Stephen Brown, Roger Mills, Allan Tait, et al. 2013. *The Maturing of the MOOC: Literature Review of Massive Open Online Courses and Other Forms of Online Distance Learning*. BIS Research Paper no. 130. September. London: Department for Business, Innovation, and Skills. http://dera.ioe.ac.uk/18325/7/13-1173-maturing-of-the-mooc_Redacted .pdf.

Hammell, Richard, Carl Bates, Harvey Lewis, Costi Perricos, Louise Brett, and David Branch. 2012. "Open Data: Driving Growth, Ingenuity and Innovation." London: Deloitte. https://www2 .deloitte.com/content/dam/Deloitte/uk/Documents/deloitte-analytics/open-data-driving-growth -ingenuity-and-innovation.pdf.

Harnad, Stevan, Tim Brody, François Valliéres, Les Carr, Steve Hitchcock, Yves Gingras, et al. 2004. "The Access/Impact Problem and the Green and Gold Roads to Open Access." *Serials Review* 30 (4): 310–314. doi:10.1080/00987913.2004.10764930.

Heeks, Richard, Christopher Foster, and Yanuar Nugroho. 2014. "New Models of Inclusive Innovation for Development." *Innovation and Development* 4 (2): 175–185. doi:10.1080/21579 30X.2014.928982.

Heller, Michael A., and Rebecca S. Eisenberg. 1998. "Can Patents Deter Innovation? The Anticommons in Biomedical Research." *Science* 280 (5364): 698–701.

Hess, Charlotte, and Elinor Ostrom. 2003. "Ideas, Artifacts, and Facilities: Information as a Common-Pool Resource." *Law and Contemporary Problems* 66 (2): 111–146.

Hess, Charlotte, and Elinor Ostrom. 2006. "Introduction: An Overview of the Knowledge Commons." In *Understanding Knowledge as a Commons: From Theory to Practice*, ed. Charlotte Hess and Elinor Ostrom, 3–26. Cambridge, MA: MIT Press.

Hollands, Fiona M., and Devayani Tirthali. 2014. *MOOCs: Expectations and Reality*. New York: Center for Benefit-Cost Studies of Education, Teachers College, Columbia University. https://www .cbcse.org/publications/moocs-expectations-and-reality.

Hossain, Mohammad Alamgir, Yogesh K. Dwivedi, and Nripendra P. Rana. 2015. "State-of-the-Art in Open Data Research: Insights from Existing Literature and a Research Agenda." *Journal of Organizational Computing and Electronic Commerce* 26 (1–2): 14–40. https://www.tandfonline.com /doi/full/10.1080/10919392.2015.1124007.

Howe, Jeff. 2006. "The Rise of Crowdsourcing." *Wired*. 14 (6):1–4. https://www.wired.com/2006 /06/crowds/.

Howe, Jeff. 2008. *Crowdsourcing: Why the Power of the Crowd Is Driving the Future of Business*. New York: Crown Business.

Huizingh, Eelko K. R. E. 2011. "Open Innovation: State of the Art and Future Perspectives." *Technovation* 31 (1): 2–9. doi:10.1016/j.technovation.2010.10.002.

International Development Research Centre (IDRC). 2011. *Innovation for Inclusive Development: Program Prospectus for 2011–2016*. Ottawa: IDRC.

Jaffe, Adam B., Josh Lerner, Scott Stern, and Marie C. Thursby. 2007. "Academic Science and Entrepreneurship: Dual Engines of Growth?" *Journal of Economic Behavior & Organization* 63 (4): 573–576. doi:10.1016/j.jebo.2006.05.009.

Juma, Calestous, and Lee Yee-Cheong. 2005. *Innovation: Applying Knowledge in Development.* London: Earthscan.

Karo, Erkki, and Rainer Kattel. 2011. "Should 'Open Innovation' Change Innovation Policy Thinking in Catching-up Economies? Considerations for Policy Analyses." *Innovation: The European Journal of Social Science Research* 24 (1–2): 173–198. doi:10.1080/13511610.2011.586496.

Kenney, Martin, and Donald Patton. 2009. "Reconsidering the Bayh-Dole Act and the Current University Invention Ownership Model." *Research Policy* 38 (9): 1407–1422. doi:10.1016/j.respol.2009.07.007.

Kraemer-Mbula, Erika, and Watu Wamae, eds. 2010. *Innovation and the Development Agenda.* OECD Innovation Strategy. Paris/Ottawa: OECD/IDRC. https://www.idrc.ca/en/book/innovation-and-development-agenda.

Kraemer-Mbula, Erika, and Sasha Wunsch-Vincent, eds. 2016. *The Informal Economy in Developing Nations: Hidden Engine of Innovation?* Cambridge: Cambridge University Press.

Lessig, Lawrence. 2004. "Free(ing) Culture for Remix." *Utah Law Review* 2004: 961–971.

Lichtenthaler, Ulrich. 2011. "Open Innovation: Past Research, Current Debates, and Future Directions." *Academy of Management Perspectives* 25 (1): 75–93.

Linders, Dennis. 2013. "Towards Open Development: Leveraging Open Data to Improve the Planning and Coordination of International Aid." *Government Information Quarterly* 30 (4): 426–434. https://www.sciencedirect.com/science/article/pii/S0740624X13000737.

Look, Hugh, and Kevin Marsh. 2012. *Benefits of Open Access to Scholarly Research to the Public Sector: A Research Report to JISC from Rightscom Ltd and Matrix Evidence Ltd.* March. London: Rightscom and Matrix Evidence.

Lundvall, Bengt-Åke, ed. 1992. *National Systems of Innovation: Towards a Theory of Innovation and Interactive Learning. (Anthem Other Canon Series).* London: Pinter.

Manyika, James, Michael Chui, Peter Groves, Diana Farrell, Steve Van Kuiken, and Elizabeth A. Doshi. 2013. "Open Data: Unlocking Innovation and Performance with Liquid Information." London, San Francisco; Shanghai: McKinsey Global Institute: Washington, DC: McKinsey Center for Government; New Jersey: McKinsey Business Technology Office. https://www.mckinsey.com/~/media/McKinsey/Business%20Functions/McKinsey%20Digital/Our%20Insights/Open%20data%20Unlocking%20innovation%20and%20performance%20with%20liquid%20information/MGI_Open_data_FullReport_Oct2013.ashx.

Marshall, Alfred. 1920. *Principles of Economics.* London: Macmillan and Company.

Max-Planek-Gesellschaft. 2003. "Berlin Declaration on Open Access to Knowledge in the Sciences and Humanities." *Open Access: Max-Planck-Gesellschaft.* October 23. https://openaccess.mpg.de/Berlin-Declaration.

Merkley, Ryan. 2018. "A Transformative Year: State of the Commons 2018." *Creative Commons* (blog), May 8. Mountain View, CA. https://creativecommons.org/2018/05/08/state-of-the-commons -2017/.

Merton, Robert K. 1973. *The Sociology of Science: Theoretical and Empirical Investigations*. Chicago: University of Chicago Press.

Mizukami, Pedro N., and Ronaldo Lemos. 2010. "From Free Software to Free Culture Case Study: The Tecnobrega Scene of Belém Learning from the Social Commons Four Challenges Facing Open Business." In *Access to Knowledge in Brazil: New Research on Intellectual Property, Innovation, and Development*, ed. Lea Shaver, 13–35. London: Bloomsbury Publishing PLC.

Mowery, David C., Richard R. Nelson, Bhaven N. Sampat, and Arvids A. Ziedonis. 2001. "The Growth of Patenting and Licensing by U.S. Universities: An Assessment of the Effects of the Bayh–Dole Act of 1980." *Research Policy* 30 (1): 99–119. doi:10.1016/S0048–7333(99)00100–6.

Mowery, David C., and Bhaven N. Sampat. 2005. "The Bayh-Dole Act of 1980 and University-Industry Technology Transfer: A Model for Other OECD Governments?" *Journal of Technology Transfer* 30 (1/2): 115–127. https://deepblue.lib.umich.edu/bitstream/handle/2027.42/43108 /10961_2004_Article_5384361.pdf?sequence=1.

Muchie, Mammo, Bengt-Åke Lundvall, and Peter Gammeltoft, eds. 2003. *Putting Africa First: The Making of African Innovation Systems*. Vol. 125. Aalborg, Denmark: Aalborg University Press.

Mukherjee, Arijit, and Scott Stern. 2009. "Disclosure or Secrecy? The Dynamics of Open Science." *International Journal of Industrial Organization* 27 (3): 449–462. doi:10.1016/j.ijindorg.2008.11.005.

Murray, Fiona, Philippe Aghion, Mathias Dewatripont, Julian Kolev, and Scott Stern. 2016. "Of Mice and Academics: Examining the Effect of Openness on Innovation." *American Economic Journal: Economic Policy* 8 (1): 212–252. doi:10.3386/w14819.

Murray, Fiona, and Scott Stern. 2007. "Do Formal Intellectual Property Rights Hinder the Free Flow of Scientific Knowledge?" *Journal of Economic Behavior & Organization* 63 (4): 648–687. https://www.nber.org/papers/w11465.

Myers, Michael D., and Heinz K. Klein. 2011. "A Set of Principles for Conducting Critical Research in Information Systems." *MIS Quarterly* 35 (1): 17–36.

Ncube, Caroline, Lucienne Abrahams, and Titilayo Akinsanmi. 2013. "Effects of the South African IP Regime on Generating Value from Publicly Funded Research: An Exploratory Study of Two Universities." In *Innovation and Intellectual Property Collaborative Dynamics in Africa*, ed. Jeremy de Beer, Chris Armstrong, Chidi Oguamanam, and Tobias Schonwetter, 281–315. Cape Town, South Africa: University of Cape Town Press.

Nelson, Richard R. 2004. "The Market Economy, and the Scientific Commons." *Research Policy* 33 (3): 455–471. https://pdfs.semanticscholar.org/c943/a9ceb66f2740615c6ea38057cf1d876b3 d65.pdf.

Nussbaum, Martha C. 2011. *Creating Capabilities: The Human Development Approach*. Cambridge, MA: Belknap Press of Harvard University Press. https://www3.nd.edu/~ndlaw/prog-human-rights /london-symposium/CreatingCapabilities.pdf.

Open Data Commons. n.d. "Licenses." Open Data Commons. http://opendatacommons.org /licenses/.

Open Data Handbook. n.d. "What Is Open Data?" http://opendatahandbook.org/guide/en/what-is -open-data/.

Open Data Institute. 2016. *Open Enterprise: How Three Big Businesses Create Value with Open Innovation*. London: Author. https://theodi.org/article/open-enterprise-how-three-big-businesses-create -value-with-open-innovation/.

Organisation for Economic Co-operation and Development (OECD). 2005. *Oslo Manual: Guidelines for Collecting and Interpreting Innovation Data. Guidelines for Collecting and Interpreting Innovation Data*. 3rd ed. Paris: OECD.

Organisation for Economic Co-operation and Development (OECD). 2015. *Innovation Policies for Inclusive Growth*. Paris: OECD. http://dx.doi.org/10.1787/9789264229488-en.

Ostrom, Elinor. 1990. *Governing the Commons: The Evolution of Institutions for Collective Action*. Cambridge: Cambridge University Press.

Perens, Bruce. 1999. "The Open Source Definition." In *Open Sources: Voices from the Open Source Revolution*, ed. Chris DiBona, Sam Ockman, and Mark Stone. Sebastopol, CA: O'Reilly & Associates, Inc.

Pomerantz, Jeffrey, and Robin Peek. 2016. "Fifty Shades of Open." *First Monday* 21 (5), May 2. doi:10.5210/fm.v21i5.6360.

Rai, Arti K., and Rebecca S. Eisenberg. 2003. "Bayh-Dole Reform and the Progress of Biomedicine." *Law and Contemporary Problems* 66 (12): 289–314. https://scholarship.law.duke.edu/cgi /viewcontent.cgi?article=1282&context=lcp.

Raymond, Eric S. 1999. *The Cathedral and the Bazaar: Musings on Linux and Open Source by an Accidental Revolutionary*. Sebastopol, CA: O'Reilly Media, Inc.

Reilly, Katherine M. A., and Rob McMahon. 2015. "Quality of Openness: Evaluating the Contributions of IDRC's Information and Networks Program to Open Development." Ottawa: IDRC. https://assets.publishing.service.gov.uk/media/57a0897d40f0b652dd000248/61205_Openness_ Evaluation_Final_Report.pdf.

Reilly, Katherine M. A., and Matthew L. Smith. 2013. "The Emergence of Open Development in a Network Society." In *Open Development: Networked Innovations in International Development*, ed. Matthew L. Smith and Katherine M. A. Reilly, 15–50. Cambridge, MA/ Ottawa: MIT Press/IDRC. https://idl-bnc-idrc.dspacedirect.org/bitstream/handle/10625/52348/IDL-52348.pdf?sequence=1 &isAllowed=y.

Rostow, Walt W. 1960. *The Stages of Economic Growth: A Non-Communist Manifesto*. Cambridge: Cambridge University Press.

Sampat, Bhaven N. 2006. "Patenting and US Academic Research in the 20th Century: The World before and after Bayh-Dole." *Research Policy* 35 (6): 772–789. doi:10.1016/j.respol.2006.04.009.

Sampat, Bhaven N. 2009. "The Bayh-Dole Model in Developing Countries: Reflections on the Indian Bill on Publicly Funded Intellectual Property." UNCTAD-ICTSD Project on IPRs and Sustainable Development. Policy Brief no 5 (October): Geneva, Switzerland: ICTSD. https://www .ictsd.org/downloads/2011/12/the-bayh-dole-model-in-developing-countries-reflections-on-the -indian-bill-on-publicly-funded-intellectual-property.pdf.

Sen, Amartya. 1999. *Development as Freedom*. Oxford: Oxford University Press.

Shakespeare, Stephan. 2013. *Shakespeare Review: An Independent Review of Public Sector Information*. May. London. https://www.gov.uk/government/uploads/system/uploads/attachment_data /file/198752/13-744-shakespeare-review-of-public-sector-information.pdf.

Smith, Marshall S., and Catherine M. Casserly. 2006. "The Promise of Open Educational Resources." *Change: The Magazine of Higher Learning* 38 (5): 8–17. doi:10.3200/CHNG.38.5.8–17.

Smith, Matthew L. 2014. "Being Open in ICT4D." November 17. https://papers.ssrn.com/sol3 /papers.cfm?abstract_id=2526515.

Smith, Matthew. 2016. "Open Is as Open Does." *ROER4D Newsletter*. http://roer4d.org/wp -content/uploads/2014/01/ROER4D-Newsletter-February-March-2016.pdf.

Smith, Matthew L., and Laurent Elder. 2010. "Open ICT Ecosystems Transforming the Developing World." *Information Technologies & International Development* 6 (1): 65–71.

Smith, Matthew L., Laurent Elder, and Heloise Emdon. 2011. "Open Development: A New Theory for ICT4D." *Information Technnologies & Information Development* 7 (1): iii–ix.

Smith, Matthew L., and Katherine M. A. Reilly. 2013. "Introduction." In *Open Development: Networked Innovations in International Development*, ed. Matthew L. Smith and Katherine M. A. Reilly, 1–14. Cambridge, MA/Ottawa: MIT Press/IDRC. https://idl-bnc-idrc.dspacedirect.org/bitstream /handle/10625/52348/IDL-52348.pdf?sequence=1&isAllowed=y.

So, Anthony D., Bhaven N. Sampat, Arti K. Rai, Robert Cook-Deegan, Jerome H. Reichman, Robert Weissman, and Amy Kapczynski. 2008. "Is Bayh-Dole Good for Developing Countries? Lessons from the US Experience." *PLoS Biology* 6 (10): e262. http://journals.plos.org/plosbiology /article?id=10.1371/journal.pbio.0060262.

Stebbins, Michael. 2003. "Expanding Public Access to the Results of Federally Funded Research." Whitehouse.gov. https://www.whitehouse.gov/blog/2013/02/22/expanding-public-access-results -federally-funded-research.

Suber, Peter, ed. 2003. "*Bethesda Statement on Open Access Publishing*." June 20. http://legacy .earlham.edu/~peters/fos/bethesda.htm.

Suber, Peter. 2012. *Open Access*. Cambridge, MA: MIT Press. https://openaccesseks.mitpress.mit .edu/.

Teece, David J. 2010. "Business Models, Business Strategy, and Innovation." *Long Range Planning* 43 (2–3): 172–194. doi:10.1016/j.lrp.2009.07.003.

Tennant, Jonathan P., François Waldner, Damien C. Jacques, Paola Masuzzo, Lauren B. Collister, and Chris H. J. Hartgerink. 2016. "The Academic, Economic, and Societal Impacts of Open Access: An Evidence-Based Review." *F1000Research* 5(632).

Tirthali, Devayani. 2016. "Are MOOCs Sustainable?" In *From Books to MOOCs? Emerging Models of Learning and Teaching in Higher Education*, ed. Erik De Corte, Lars Engwall, and Ulrich Teichler, 115–123. London: Portland Press Publishing.

Van de Vrande, Vraska, Wim V. Vanhaverbeke, and Oliver Gassmann. 2010. "Broadening the Scope of Open Innovation: Past Research, Current State, and Future Directions." *International Journal of Technology Management* 52 (3/4): 221–235. http://citeseerx.ist.psu.edu/viewdoc/download ?doi=10.1.1.466.8313&rep=rep1&type=pdf.

van Schalkwyk, François, Michael Cañares, Sumandro Chattapadhyay, and Alexander Andrason. 2014. "Open Data Intermediaries in Developing Countries." *Journal of Community Informatics* 12 (2): 9–25.

Vickery, Graham. 2011. *Review of Recent Studies on PSI Re-use and Related Market Developments. Information Economics*. Paris: European Commission.

von Hippel, Eric. 2005. *Democratizing Innovation*. Cambridge, MA: MIT Press. https://mitpress.mit .edu/books/democratizing-innovation.

Walji, Aleem. 2011. "Let's Move Beyond Open Data to Open Development." *Let's Talk Development* (blog). July. http://blogs.worldbank.org/developmenttalk/are-we-the-world-bank-or-the -data-bank.

West, Joel, Ammon Salter, Wim Vanhaverbeke, and Henry Chesbrough. 2014. "Open Innovation: The Next Decade." *Research Policy* 43 (5): 805–811. doi:10.1016/j.respol.2014.03.001.

Wiley, David. 2016. "The Consensus Around 'Open.'" *Iterating toward Openness* (blog). January 29. http://opencontent.org/blog/archives/4397.

Wiley, David, T. J. Bliss, and Mary McEwen. 2014. "Open Educational Resources: A Review of the Literature." In *Handbook of Research on Educational Communications and Technology*, ed. J. Michael Spector, M. David Merrill, Jan Elen, and M. J. Bishop, 4th ed., 781–789. New York: Springer. doi:10.1007/978-1-4614-3185-5.

II Governing the Open Development Ecosystem

4   Gender and Equity in Openness: Forgotten Spaces

Sonal Zaveri

Introduction: Why Is Gender Equity Important?

Gender equity[1] is recognized by many to be critical to ensure an inclusive society that benefits all people. A gap in gender parity across the world has been well documented. The World Economic Forum's *The Global Gender Gap Report 2017* (Leopold, Ratcheva, and Zahidi 2017), which measures the gap between men and women in four key areas of health, education, economy, and politics, indicated that in 2017, an average gap of 32 percent remained to be closed between men and women. Some countries showed a reversal, and others some positive steps forward, indicating that context and sustained efforts are important while tracking gender measures. Yet these persistent gender gaps have focused global attention and stimulated a call for action to track progress and close these gaps (Leopold, Ratcheva, and Zahidi 2016).

Although the promise of open development is that it will be neutral, inclusive, and gender-fair, operationalizing openness to ensure that men and women benefit equally can be problematic. This is largely because gender asymmetries and the inherent social structures that fuel them are often not addressed adequately, even when technological and operational concerns are attended to. Addressing technological challenges faced by women is just that—a service delivery that reaches out to women. But participation is much more than numbers and attendance; it is about speaking up, sharing ideas, and being heard. Gender asymmetries in participation and voice have been attributed to a failure to address entrenched cultural and traditional biases and a lack of gender-sensitive policies (Neuman 2016). Participation is important for many open processes, but it does not happen on its own. Steps toward greater inclusion and participation involve gender-sensitive policymaking, strategies such as gender targeting (addressing the specific needs of women to ensure gender parity and representation), engagement with women's civil society organizations, information flows that include women, and greater decision-making by women.

This chapter takes a closer look at inclusiveness and nondiscrimination in the open processes where, collaboratively, knowledge is produced, shared, and consumed. The argument is that knowledge itself is not gender neutral because it depends on who, what, and how it is created and used. To unpack inclusiveness, this chapter nuances the processes of participation and engagement in relation to gender—how participative, equitable, and gender responsive are open production, distribution, and consumption processes, and are they truly nondiscriminatory? To do so, it uses a gender transformative viewpoint that places issues of power at the center of the discussion. The argument is that it is important to recognize that all openness processes are affected by structural inequities and imbalances of power that engender social norms and interactions. Therefore, to be gender equitable, gender fair, and nondiscriminatory, one must address the power and structure that underpin open social processes.

The chapter progresses as follows. In the first section, it looks at open development processes through a gendered lens, examining the differences in men's and women's[2] experiences of open processes *from the point of view of their socially constructed, ascriptive*[3] *roles*. This enables us to question the power relations between men and women which, in turn, intersects with power related to race, caste, class, abilities, and sexual orientation and keeps women in subordinate positions. Without using a gendered lens, one cannot address gender equity. In particular, it looks at the ways that open processes interact with and affect gender equity. Next, it describes gender concepts relevant to our discussion on open development and then explains how open processes (open production, open distribution, and open consumption of knowledge—see chapter 2 of this volume) can be engendered from or endowed with a gender perspective. The third section develops an analytical framework with guiding questions to determine the extent to which open processes are gender equitable, and then it illustrates the use of this framework with two case studies. The chapter concludes with recommendations for next steps.

Social Inclusion and Exclusion

Social inclusion is the removal of institutional barriers and the enhancement of incentives to increase the access of diverse individuals and groups to development opportunities (Dani 2003). Between the two extremes of inclusion and exclusion, there are shades and levels of both, which are largely dependent on institutional and social barriers. It is important to note that one may be included in one domain but excluded from another. In other words, social inclusion is a multidimensional, contextual and relational process capable of enhancing integration, cohesion, and solidarity (Silver 2015).

Thus, the process of inclusion *necessarily* means that someone or something is or can be excluded.[4]

Historically, exclusion has been linked to gender, class, caste, age, religion, ethnicity, disability, and geolocation. While discussing his research on the use of digital technologies by Filipinos to improve transparency and accountability, Roberts (2017) points to digital technology emerging as a factor of exclusion. He identifies five A's of digital access: *availability, affordability, awareness, ability,* and *accessibility* as a series of concentric circles that structurally exclude particular groups whenever digital technologies are deployed. Exclusion *from* and inclusion *in* social structures imply that someone has more power over others and that there is either an explicit or implicit power relationship influencing praxis (World Bank 2013).

The idea of inclusion is to some extent *sameness*—that is, everyone should be able to use the same facilities, take part in the same activities, and enjoy the same experiences, including people who have a disability or other disadvantage. The concept of sameness is recognized in formal gender equality, as it is premised on the principle of the sameness of women and men. It assumes that if women and men are given the same opportunity and women are treated similarly to men, equality will be achieved (Murthy and Kappen 2017). Thus, one way to ensure gendered inclusion (and nondiscrimination) is through this principle of *sameness*. Much of the research on differential access to the Internet or to open artefacts is related to this principle.

However, we could also consider a more *substantive* gender equality, which recognizes that men and women have to be treated differently to achieve equality because women's disadvantages need to be addressed first, such as less mobility, lower buying power, different workloads such as child care, lower education, and lack of skills (Facio and Morgan 2009; Kabeer 2001; Kapur and Cossman 1993). Sen (1989) argues that outcomes cannot be judged in terms of access to resources, but rather people's capabilities to engage in different functions (i.e., a disabled, or differently abled, person might require more support to engage in the same activity as an able-bodied person). But it is substantive gender equality that stresses that it is power and hierarchy (not just capabilities) that discriminate against women.

It is for these reasons that this chapter frames the discussion regarding inclusive open practices by addressing the socially and culturally constructed gender roles and relationships that often limit the capacity of women and men to participate on equal terms, even when open processes are available. We do this from a strong belief that open practices can be fundamental for societal transformation; but to better understand how this can happen, we need to understand the barriers to gender inclusiveness.

Gender Equity

Analytical frameworks related to gender have attempted to assess *to what extent* and *how* we address gender equity. Displaying change on a continuum, the Gender Results Effectiveness Scale (GRES) analyzes the extent and process of structural transformation resulting from a project/intervention (UNDP 2015, 46). The scale prioritizes *systemic* change and suggests that access to opportunities and resources, or changes in laws and policies, is not enough to make a difference.

These categories necessarily evolve over time and are contextual. Gender-targeted or gender-responsive results have the potential to become transformative because they

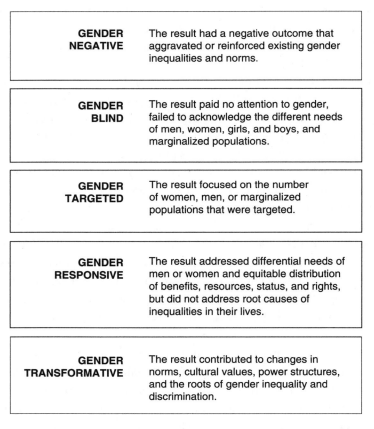

Figure 4.1
The Gender Results Effectiveness Scale.
Source: Based on table 3 from UNDP (2015).

describe the differential needs of men and women and the unequal distribution of resources and rights. However, they are on a continuum and indicate the importance of moving forward toward the gender transformative category, which explicitly addresses the power structures and the roots of gender inequality.

Often, gendered responses have taken on a technocratic, apolitical form in an effort that appears to steer away from the structural challenges inherent in achieving gender equality.

> Represented to technocrats and policymakers in the form of tools, frameworks, and mechanisms, "gender" appears as neutralised of political intent. Diluted, denatured, depoliticized, included everywhere as an afterthought, "gender" has become something everyone knows that they are supposed to do something about (Cornwall, Harrison, and Whitehead, 2004, 1).

Fundamental to any discussion on gender transformative change is the principle that patriarchal bias exists systemically and is manifest in structures (media, government, family, and other institutions), in interpersonal relationships, and daily lived experiences. In other words, gender permeates all that we do. As Hay (2012, 336) argues, "A gendered lens is recognition that the underlying structures and systems that create inequities cannot be programmed away within contexts that perpetrate and reinforce those systems."

Applying a gender transformative approach to open processes would mean addressing gendered perspectives along with *intersectionality*, which refers to the intersection of gender with race, class, sexuality, ability, and other identities that marginalize and subordinate in the context of power. Such intersectionalities indicate how complex it is to address gender inequities. However, by using the gender transformative approach, open processes can demonstrate how the theoretical underpinnings of inclusion and nondiscrimination can be translated to practice.

A first step toward addressing gender and equity issues in openness is to better understand how access, participation, inclusion, and nondiscrimination are gendered, and how this affects decision-making and valuing knowledge that is created, shared, and consumed.

Interface between Gender and Openness: Key Concepts

The Sustainable Development Goal (SDG) 5b on women's empowerment has as one of its targets to "enhance the use of enabling technology, in particular information and communications technology [ICTs], to promote the empowerment of women" (UNCTAD, n.d., n.p.). Women's empowerment is undoubtedly important for the attainment of this goal. Unlike the Millennium Development Goals (MDGs), which concluded in

2015, the SDGs are not just for the developing world; they are necessary for all nations, rich and poor, to address whatever inequities exist in *every* society. This means that we cannot talk about gender without talking about equity, and vice versa. Gender is only one axiom of inequity and cannot be abstracted from important identities, including race, ethnicity, class, culture, age, sexual identity, and physical ability. Gender (male, female, or other) injustice, a manifestation of exclusion and discrimination, is inextricably linked to these multiple identities. One may also argue whether it is possible to address equity without addressing gender, such as addressing poor people's access to the Internet or the needs of Indigenous communities, or making Internet accessibility affordable. Such approaches focus on efficiency and effectiveness but are gender blind and assume that there is no difference in the position of men and women. But we know that women's roles are gendered, ascribed by social roles, customs, and cultures that skew the power balance in favor of men. So, it is only when we *align* gender and equity that we are truly inclusive, we have ensured our commitment to having "no one left behind," and we have addressed the broader, intersectional concerns of inclusion.

Past experience in the field of information and communication technologies for development (ICT4D) indicated that although there was a vision of being inclusive and gender-fair, in reality, men and women did not equally participate and benefit.[5] At first, the slower inclusion of women was considered to be an artifact of digital access and paucity of skills. Then came the realization that the situation was more complex, and one needed to frame differences in terms of discrimination and barriers in participation that were structurally inherent in societies, often rooted in hierarchy and patriarchy. For example, Internet penetration rates among women from western Asia are lower than in any other place on the globe (Perryman and Arcos 2016). Citing research studies in Uganda and India, Perryman and Arcos (2016) show that women's digital exclusion in some developing countries is due to oppressive gender-based norms, as well as low mobile phone ownership (in India, for instance, only 30 percent of mobile phones are owned by women). They observed that many of the inequalities posing a barrier to ICT use in the developing world replicate broader social inequalities: lack of education, poor ICT infrastructure, self-efficacy to use ICT, and lack of gender-sensitive policies (165–166).

Recent data on access and participation indicate a complex web of gender differences in the way that women participate in different countries and contexts.[6] A recent set of household surveys found that, for the most part across the Global South, men have higher access to mobile phones than women, except in a few countries such as South Africa, Colombia, Paraguay, and Argentina. However, in all those countries except Argentina, men have a higher percentage of smartphones than women. Also interesting is that women in Ghana, Nigeria, South Africa, and Kenya use the Internet more for education than men do, and this effect is particularly strong for rural women in Nigeria. Similarly, in contrast to the rest of the countries surveyed, there are only two—Nigeria and Paraguay—where women use the Internet more than men for work-related activities (e.g., in Paraguay, 29 percent of women use the Internet for work, as opposed to only 16 percent of men). We need more data and analysis to understand why women do not possess high-value phones, and, when compared to men, why Internet and social media use is lower—what are the reasons for such differences, and how do they affect women?

Both men and women have reported online bullying and posting of inappropriate content, with more women reporting such complaints in Kenya and Tanzania and more men reporting them in Rwanda, Mozambique, Ghana, and South Africa.[7] We need more research to understand the nature of the bullying and why it is gender specific.

Open development, typically predicated on ICTs, is subject to many of the same issues that emerged in the ICT4D field. In the same way that the diffusion of ICTs and their inclusion in development projects did not guarantee equitable benefits regardless of gender, open processes take place in the larger context of systemic inequities and do not necessarily transcend them. However, openness brings a particular subset of issues into focus and the normative impetus is gender equitable.

Looking through a gendered lens raises many questions regarding open processes and their underlying assumptions. For instance, in what ways are open practices engendered, and do those practices address hierarchical structures controlling knowledge production and dissemination? How and in what contexts are open development processes inclusive, nondiscriminatory, and therefore truly transformative *in practice*? When and how do open practices need to address power relationships that exist in society? What are the barriers for equitable participation of men and women across the intersections of class, ethnicity, status, and geographical location, and how do different openness processes address or affect them? Whose responsibility is it to ensure open and inclusive processes?

Engendering Open Concepts

Open processes have distinguishing characteristics of being free, voluntary, and non-discriminatory (see chapter 2 for a more in-depth discussion of these characteristics). However, spotlighting these characteristics through a gender lens illuminates how open processes affect and are affected by the social differences between men and women and the power relations between them. Table 4.1 explains how engendering open processes can provide insights into the participation in and the development of knowledge artifacts.

Table 4.1
Engendering open concepts.

Open processes and principles	Open practices	Applying a gendered lens
Open production of content/knowledge	Creation of content and knowledge is participatory, anyone can contribute, and, in theory, no one is restricted from contributing. This means that whether peer produced or crowdsourced, all contributions to content/ knowledge are equally valued (i.e., are nondiscriminatory).	Knowledge and values are culturally, socially, and temporally contingent. Knowledge is filtered through the person who knows. Thus, knowledge is not value free. It is influenced by one's own experiences, realities, and identities. It is contextual, privileging the knowledge of some people over others. Knowledge's value depends on the power of the decision-maker. In other words, who creates knowledge, how it is created, with whom it is shared, and for what depends on who is doing the decision-making. Women are particularly affected in this scenario because they have less power.
Open distribution and consumption	Anyone, without restriction of proprietorship or cost, can access, modify, remix, share, use, and republish the content/ knowledge created.	Access is not just technological. Also, access does not necessarily mean use. There are gatekeepers for access and use—social, cultural, educational, financial, and geographical—representing privilege, power, opportunity, and agency. Those who have access to resources are able to control the process of modifying, sharing, and using. A resource may be free (no cost and in relation to participation), but social, cultural norms, and/or lack of agency (or skills) may restrict who can *actually* modify, share, and use. Women are especially affected, and open processes may not privilege women (or other marginalized groups). As a result, participation in the sharing and use of content/knowledge is not always equitable.
Principles of non-discrimination and freedom to participate	In theory, open processes are nondiscriminatory and provide a platform for anyone to participate.	In practice, inclusiveness and equality in participation both depend on various social cleavages such as gender, age, class, ethnicity, education, and geography. Inclusion and full and equal participation usually depend on existing socially structured power asymmetries. Even if there is no explicit exclusion, there may be implicit exclusion and discrimination.

Although open processes are based on technical principles of nondiscrimination, it is clear that they do not automatically mean that women will participate, or that women will participate in the same way as men (Buskens 2011). This is, of course, not surprising. What type of participation is valued (or not) is itself gendered—for example, *good* participation means that women participate with reference to their socially constructed, ascriptive roles or that they participate in ways that men do. But participation may not be *good* or valued if women participate, but do so differently from men.

Access and Participation

To address gender and open processes meaningfully, we need a nuanced understanding of both access and participation. Participation cannot be understood as a binary function—either participation or nonparticipation. Rather, it is a continuum of various types of engagement and activity (Cousins and Whitmore 1998; Ramirez 2008).

A clear finding in the research is that access does not necessarily lead to participation. Access suggests the ability to use the information and the resources provided. Also, one may have access to resources but have no control over them, which means that participation is limited, particularly in decision-making. Graham (2014) and Warschauer (2002) acknowledge that greater access and participation driven by technological and operational innovations have not necessarily affected gender asymmetries, and they argue that much more work is needed to overcome inequalities in visibility, voice, and power in the networked society. A detailed discussion by Graham and De Sabbata (see chapter 5 of this volume) outlines the geographic asymmetries in openness participation. Information societies around the world are not free from existing and gendered global frameworks of governance, ownership, and control over resource access.

The analyses by Cornwall (2002) and Gaventa (2002) of how people participate are valuable for understanding how to frame participation in the digital world and, by extension, the social processes that define openness. Spaces for participation are important so that people can be directly involved and be able to exercise autonomous action. However, such spaces are *produced* spaces, never neutral, and reflect the interplay of existing power and difference (Gaventa 2002). It is no surprise that these spaces need to be situated not only within that context and its practices, but also with the multiplicity of *other* spaces with which they are in turn connected. Online participatory processes may serve simply to reproduce "echoes of dominant knowledge rather than to amplify the alternative, 'bottom-up' perspectives that are claimed for them" (Cornwall 2002, 9). All spaces have boundaries within which processes operate, acknowledging that "power must be analyzed as something that circulates," meaning that we need to ask questions such as who is inviting participation and who is taking part, what they think participation is about, and how people in different spaces perceive it (Cornwall 2002; Foucault 1980, 102). A valuable framing of participation and power (Gaventa 2002) is expressed through the Power Cube and relates to how important it is to interrogate not only visible power (laws, rules) and hidden power (such as with exclusionary rules), but also invisible power (internalized self-limiting self-beliefs).[8] Women and marginalized groups may not see their participation as valuable because they are told that it is not valued as much as that of men.

The concept of spaces of participation (and spaces of power) has value in our discussion of openness because no matter how open social processes are, they are always imbued with underlying status, class, and social position issues, which are reproduced in the ways that people communicate with each other in any social space, even those that are meant to be free (Kohn 2008). These prescriptors defining participation resonate with Lane's discussion that educational divisions between people arise through a combination of factors—social, cultural, geographical, attitudinal, political, and economic (Lane 2009). These educational divisions can be easily extended to the digital world.

These issues are reflected in the data. For instance, a study of 3,705 responses of civic technology users who use mySociety's open-source software extensively found the participation of women in civic applications such as FixMyStreet to be low. The fairly high gender imbalance among users diminishes women's voices and marginalizes issues that are important to them – and consequently, the issues are less likely to be addressed (Rumbul 2015). Free and open-source software (FOSS) researchers Kuechler et al. (2012) make a comparison across a sample of open-source projects showing that although 25 percent of people employed in the information technology sector are women, only 7 percent of people who post online in open-source forums (i.e., post at least once) are women, and merely 2.5 percent of people who post regularly (i.e., ten or more contributions) were women. Women may have an online presence but do not contribute or speak out if they think differently from the online moderators, indicating a gendered pattern of participation that suggests women are "not supposed to" push back, assert themselves, or be otherwise expressive. A 2013 survey found that of more than 2,000 open-source developers who indicated their gender, only just over 10 percent were women (an increase from 2 to 5 percent in the early naughts) (Robles, Reina, Gonzalez-Barahona, and Dominguez, 2016). In this sense, the low and gendered participation is closely linked to autonomy and decision-making (World Wide Web Foundation 2015).

Studies have suggested that women tend to self-select what they do or do not do due to gender norms and social status rather than their technical skills and abilities.

Some of these considerations, such as time use of women at work and home, have been well documented. Lam et al. (2011) confirm the presence of a large gender gap among editors and a corresponding gender-oriented disparity in the content of Wikipedia's articles. They also hint at "a culture that may be resistant to female participation" (Lam et al. 2011). A Wikipedia Foundation survey found that only 13 percent of contributors were women and 9 percent of editors were women (Moeller 2009[9]; Wikipedia n.d.[10]). The reasons analyzed by Gardner (2011) elaborate on why women felt discouraged while contributing. Eight out of nine reasons cited by women had nothing to do with their skills but rather were related to women's gendered roles and male privilege and dominance. The major reasons were not having enough free time, aversion to conflict and lengthy edit wars, belief that their contributions would be reverted or deleted, a misogynistic culture, sexual overtones that distress women, lack of comfort with using the male grammatical gender as part of language, and lack of self-confidence. This was followed by another study, Bear and Collier (2016), which explores the issue by analyzing a subset of the original 2008 Wikipedia survey data (1,589 occasional American contributors, of whom 17.5 percent were female) and finding clear differences along gender lines. Women reported feeling less confident about their expertise, being less comfortable with editing others' work (a process that often involves conflict), and reacting more negatively to critical feedback than men (Bear and Collier 2016). There is already some research on the difference between men and women regarding confidence—but women do not actually score lower on ability and expertise (Torres 2016). Other studies have shown that while women are less confident than they should be, men are overconfident (Niederle and Vesterlund 2007).

Terrell et al. (2017) quote a study by Stack Overflow, a question-and-answer community for programmers, which found "a relatively 'unhealthy' community where women disengage sooner, although their activity levels are comparable to men's." A large-scale study of gender bias at GitHub shows that women's acceptance rates of contributions are higher only when they are not identifiable as women. Their study indicates how deeply gendered responses are: women demonstrate a self-selection bias in how long they survive on the platform, but what was surprising is that there are different expectations for women's and men's work—women's work is likely to be less valued or judged against higher standards than men's.

What these data points illustrate is that, in practice, if we want openness to enable people to engage equitably, open spaces will have to address the particular needs of excluded groups and provide mediation between the various actors in that particular context.

Inclusion and Nondiscrimination

Lessig (2003) questions whether the neutrality of the Internet is able to break boundaries influenced by power and ensure inclusion. But the reality is that knowledge institutions, producers, and distributors remain concentrated in a few locations, adding to inequity. The reasons Lessig identifies are the economic power of large knowledge institutions and the existing structure of intellectual property (IP) rights. Many organizations believed that correcting this imbalance was possible through a series of new-generation Internet tools that enabled global access to knowledge, as well as affording the opportunity to establish new institutions for sharing, peer production, and remixing of knowledge (Graham et al. 2011).

For instance, research on microwork has highlighted the complexity of addressing gender. Some argue that microwork and online jobs can benefit women because working online allows women to juggle family, work, and time use. A World Bank report (Rossotto, Kuek, and Paradi-Guilford, 2012) shows how microwork is successful in reshaping the global market, but it also points to a gender and age imbalance.[11] A recent study of a Latin American microwork platform by Galperin et al. (2015), however, shows how nuanced the gender dynamics can be. For example, overall, they found that, all else being equal, women were more likely to be hired over men (a small, but statistically significant effect). Yet women engage in microwork on the platform in smaller numbers than men *and* tend to submit lower bids for jobs than men do. However, when it is clear that women are doing the hiring, women will bid as much as men and will be chosen more often. There appears to be also a self-driven gendered perception which is nuanced across cultural perceptions of the value of men's and women's work.

Power is central to how gender affects open processes. Thus, it is crucial to address power and hierarchy if one expects everyone, including women, to participate in the open processes of production, consumption, and dissemination in an inclusive and nondiscriminatory way. If we address power differentials, which are often embedded in cultural norms and hierarchical values that impede women's full participation, we will necessarily have to frame progress on gender in transformative terms. We can do so by ensuring that we address both the practical and strategic needs of women such as connectivity access, skills acquisition, and understanding dynamics related to family responsibilities. Addressing the strategic needs of women targets equity issues, such as education, mobility, economic participation, empowerment, and norms, which have the potential to transform gender relations. In other words, questioning, researching, and analyzing gender disparities and gendered differences of openness have the potential to ensure true inclusion and prevent discrimination in open processes.

Situating Knowledge

Looking at how knowledge is produced, shared, and used, it is imperative to understand the knowledge economy (i.e., who produces and reproduces, who has access, and how people are represented and excluded). It is also about discussing inequalities in traditional knowledge and information geographies before moving on to examine the Internet's potential to have new and more inclusionary patterns. However, studies show the divisiveness that exists in the knowledge economy. Graham (2014), in a study on the knowledge economy and digital labor, concludes that rather than democratizing platforms of knowledge sharing, the Internet seems to be generating a gendered digital division of labor, in which the visibility, voice, and power of the Global North are reinforced rather than diminished. Which knowledge system we value is clearly gendered—the knowledge system with more power is privileged over another, less powerful one. This is similar to modern knowledge being valued more than traditional ways of knowing (see also chapter 13 in this volume), or productive work being valued more than reproductive or caring work. Ann Weiner (2016, 1) writes that code is not neutral, as it is a creation, and that "[s]oftware products would be more powerful, more accessible, and more democratic—Twitter, for example, would look a lot different today if it had been built by people for whom online harassment is a real-life concern." She claims that algorithms and code embody values and have been a concern for many years, quoting Ellen Ullman, one of the first women to enter the coding community in the 1970s, "[t]he engineer's assumptions and presumptions are in the code" (Weiner 2016). Recent research acknowledges that gender bias pervades the open-source community (Terrell 2017). In interviews with women working in open source, Nafus (2012, 669 and 672) revealed that "men monopolize code authorship and simultaneously de-legitimize the kinds of social ties necessary to build mechanisms for women's inclusion," meaning that values are gendered, politeness is favored less by men, and "sexist behavior is … as constant as it is extreme."

Rather than neutral and value-free, knowledge is deeply connected to a time, place, and social context. Feminist theorists talk about the *situatedness* of knowledge to a context and the effects of power on its production and validation (Brisolora, Seigart, and SenGupta 2014; Haraway 1988). This means that those who are marginalized have access to knowledge and viewpoints that are unique, not mainstream and dominant. Sandra Harding (1991, 185) asserts that such an approach is more objective and fair than traditional approaches to enquiry, which favor the dominant to shape knowledge, giving rise to a partial (and therefore distorted) view of reality. "Starting off research from women's lives will generate less partial and distorted accounts not only of women's lives but also of men's lives and of the whole social order" (Harding 1993, 56). For knowledge to be constructed fairly, one must be aware of the skewed sociopolitical power and, more important, recognize that there are voices that have been left out and need to be heard.

This concept is important for openness because the cocreation (and cosharing and coconsuming) of knowledge assume that everyone has partial and contingent knowledge, and by participating in the crowdsourcing and peer-production processes, one achieves a shared knowledge. Similarly, perspective and experience shared through blogs and communities of practice provide important spaces for sharing, all adding to knowledge building. Knowledge sharing has become democratic (i.e., experts are not the only source of knowledge), valuing one's experiences and thoughts, which can be created, accessed, and shared immediately. Here, one must recognize that it is filtered through the knower's own realities, identities, and experiences, which shape the construction of shared knowledge. So knowledge has a social milieu and culture in which it is created and shared.

Situating knowledge helps us to be vigilant about who is *not* contributing to knowledge development. Masculine hierarchy can block and disregard the knowledge held by women. It is likely that the ones who are silent and have the least privilege may actually have the insight and knowledge that are valuable. Such knowledge may be traditional and gendered, and therefore less valued. Traditional bearers of local and Indigenous knowledge, be they men or women, may find themselves cut off from the networked society, where information, communication, and knowledge are tradeable goods. This is similar to the way that IP rights have taken away Indigenous ownership over traditional foods, medicines, and overall biodiversity (Thas 2008, 12). It has become essential that legal instruments are framed to recognize and protect knowledge created, developed, and enhanced by communities of people. These instruments need to be developed with the full participation of all parties who hold such knowledge, including men and women, and should acknowledge that men and women have differential access to the structures that shape knowledge systems (Primo 2003, 52).

Which knowledge is relevant and how it is expressed, therefore, depend upon one's standpoint. The dominant paradigm is influenced by the politics of location combined with a specific scientific methodology (Baghramian and Carter 2017). Many researchers have commented that the dominant logic of the scientific knowledge paradigm (methods, writing style, and assumptions) is shaped by discourse that privileges dominant groups, such as the male European paradigm (Euro-androcentric), and shuts off alternative perspectives, typically held by less privileged groups. So, observations, expressions of lived realities, and the diversity of women's experiences are often dismissed as subjective and irrelevant, and this overlooks the fact that there are often differences in how men and women think, what they think about, and what they consider important (Brisolara et al. 2014, 7). A project in the Open and Collaborative Science in

Development Network (OCSDNet)[12] (called Understanding Open Hardware and Citizen Science) used language that was not part of mainstream science, such as the use of the word *design* rather than *engineering*. The project's advisors from mainstream academia faced the dilemma of whether to use words that are commonly seen as "objective" (such as those commonly used in mainstream science) or to privilege women's experiences (see Chapter 13 in this volume for more on OCSDNet).[13]

So how does one navigate gendered open processes to create opportunities for systemic inclusion of marginalized or minority groups? In the next section, a framework is introduced that helps to illuminate gendered differences, which become apparent when a research framework exposes gendered patterns and contributing factors for those dynamics.

Gender Analysis of Open Practices

A gender analysis of open practices describes a systematic approach to examining factors related to gender and identifying and understanding the various roles, relationships, situations, benefits, constraints, needs, and interests of men and women in a given sociocultural context. Further research and analysis can contribute to understanding the nature of structural inequities in specific contexts and how they affect open practices. It is important to question preexisting differences that skew the distribution of positive impacts to men more than women, as well as analyze if the impacts themselves reinforce gender differences.

A number of researchers have explored the framing of gender analysis in relation to power relationships among men and women. Ineke Buskens looks at researcher intent, which she categorizes into three types: conformist (aims to produce knowledge), reformist (to produce knowledge in order to understand how to reform existing unequal gender relationships), and transformist (to enable women to produce knowledge themselves) (Roberts 2015). The latter type enables a better understanding for women about existing unequal gender relations and the structural power interests that support them so that these can be transformed.

Using a Gender Analysis Framework for Openness

In this section, I develop the novel Gender Analysis Framework for Openness (GAFO), which incorporates key questions that can help to assess the extent of gender inclusion in open development projects.[14] The GAFO framework suggests that power is pervasive and can be described as power to, with, over, and within (Rowlands 1997), as well as power to empower (Chambers 2012). These categories can be described as follows:

- *Power to:* The increase in skills and capabilities so that one can contribute, decide, and take the lead. An example of how knowledge production can increase the power that comes from an OCSDNet project in Kyrgyzstan,[15] which notes an increased participation of girls in citizen science in testing their communities' water quality.

- *Power with:* Seeking collaborative and collective action for the collective good and to create an enabling environment. An OCSDNet project in Lebanon notes that the group of "community volunteers" testing well water were all women, and the team in Southeast Asia exploring open science through open hardware design workshops report that using the phrase "design and collaboration" drew more participation from women than did "tools and infrastructure" (see chapter 13 of this volume for more details).

- *Power within:* Leads to increase in motivation, confidence to contribute, sense of belief to bring change, excel, and lead change. Power within is usually expressed once power to, power over, and power with has been experienced. Both the previous examples, in Kyrgyzstan and Lebanon, indicate the power to confidently contribute.

- *Power over:* A person's ability to overcome resource and power constraints to reach one's potential and take control of one's own personal and professional decisions and, in doing so, enable the person to increasingly influence and have a voice. The notion of *cognitive justice* used by the OCSDNet team from Haiti and Francophone Africa is one such example, which talks about empowered and confident researchers using all kinds of epistemologies and methods, not only those from the North (see chapter 13).

- *Power to empower:* Inspiring others, working on, and influencing broader agendas to multiply opportunities (i.e., being a champion). Examples can be found in the attempts of various forums to increase women's representation and participation. The International Open Data Conference (IODC), a place for sharing experiences, networking, and discussing the most crucial issues of the movement toward open data, reported that only 34 percent of the speakers were women at its 2015 conference. This prompted an open letter to IODC 2016 from Mor Rubinstein, who called for gender-balanced panels for IODC 2018. "Let's aspire (and commit) to have 50 percent women speakers this round" (Rubinstein 2016). It is not only important to see the increase in numbers, but also to review how men and women participate and engage in the open spaces provided for producing, reviewing, and using knowledge. Power to empower is possible only when there is power within to contribute. For example, Open Heroines created an online blog, providing a visible platform and public voice for women to express their thoughts, ideas, and critiques. This space emerged mainly because, despite women contributing to the open spaces, many felt their voices remained unheard, and were frustrated by this "underrepresentation."[16]

Vignettes: GAFO Analysis

In this section, I test the usefulness of the GAFO by using vignettes from various research projects supported by the International Development and Research Centre (IDRC)[17] to understand how gender affects open processes. I chose relevant questions from the framework to describe gender dynamics, determine how gendered the open processes were, explain how power relationships were affected, analyze the various types of empowerment, and discuss the impact of doing so.

Case study: Teacher professional learning communities—A participatory open educational resource (OER) creation and adaptation approach in Karnataka state, India (a subproject of the ROER4D program)[18]

The Research on Open Educational Resources for Development (ROER4D)[19] network aims to provide evidence-based research from a number of countries in the Global South (see chapter 12 of this volume). One ROER4D project in Karnataka used a bottom-up approach for teacher professional development, where teachers collaboratively and actively cocreated educational resources to respond to local needs.

The project worked with sixty-seven mathematics, science, and social science high school teachers and teacher educators in Karnataka. This group was embedded within a larger professional learning community of around 15,000 teachers across Karnataka, developed through the Subject Teacher Forum, an in-service teacher education program in the public education system. The research approach included periodic workshops with the sixty-seven participants, where they attended collaborative OER adoption processes. Analyses of data regarding the outcomes of the project indicated that teachers found meaning in reuse, creation, revision, remixing, and redistribution of resources on the mailing lists and the OER portal they used; experienced professional development and agency in using the digital platform; and increased their skills.

Questions from the GAFO (table 4.2) provide insight into the interrelationship between gender and openness. The project had to make special efforts to ensure that 50 percent of the teachers participating were women. Although female teachers are 41.42 percent of the total teacher population in Karnataka, only 20.9 percent (or a little over one in five) of the participant teachers in the OER project were women.[20] The selection process of science and math teacher resource persons was open and not discriminatory, and yet women's participation was low. Here, it would be useful to enquire why many women lacked the *power to*. For example, the researchers might ask: What challenges do women face in order to participate and benefit from these open processes?

Table 4.2
The Gender Analysis Framework for Openness (GAFO).

Engendered processes	Open production: open to more people (e.g., crowdsourcing, peer production)
	Open distribution: sharing, republishing; nondiscriminatory access, use at no cost
	Open consumption: create, retain, reuse, revise, and remix for use
Power to do Choosing to do	What are the differences in who, what, and how knowledge is created? Is it inclusive or not, and, if so, for whom and how? To what extent is traditional knowledge expressed? How is it done, and who does so?
	How does such engendered knowledge creation (e.g., sex-disaggregated statistics) affect the quantity and quality of research that can help to fill the gaps in knowledge?
	To what extent do women have access to resources to produce, share, and use knowledge?
	What challenges do women have to face in order to participate and benefit from these open processes?
	What advantage do women have when involved in open processes, as opposed to a more conventional way to produce knowledge?
	To what extent do women have the freedom (and choices) to develop, publish, share, use, and be free to innovate?
	To what extent are women's voices heard so that they lead open practices?
Power with Do together	How did women's collaborative work, such as through peer-to-peer (P2P) and crowdsourcing, affect what knowledge was created, shared, and used?
	What barriers do women face in communication and engagement with others in open processes? In participating and/or leading collective or collaborative action?
	What opportunities were created for women to produce, share, and use collectively?
	Was there a change in the profile of users, types of usage, and new avenues opened up or avenues closed down?
Power within Agency	How confident did women feel about producing, sharing, and adapting open content? How confident are they to share the knowledge of their lived realities and traditional knowledge in the way they choose?
	Was there greater assertiveness in taking on new tasks?
	Did women understand their strengths and weaknesses, and how to manage them better to advance their work?
	How did women personally benefit? Did it change the way that women produced knowledge?
	Do women feel "safe" to share or participate?
Power over Control	What opportunities are (or should be) provided to overcome underlying resource and power constraints so that women can contribute, lead, and inspire?
	How do women's voices and achievements influence a larger audience in open processes?
	To what extent are women able to exert control over their personal and professional decisions, so that they can realize their full potential?
Power to empower Being a champion	What leadership contributions are women making to open processes? How did they change the nature of open processes?
	How are women and men inspiring other women and multiplying their opportunities?

This OER project team made attempts to encourage women teachers to join in (*power to empower*) and to address the challenges faced by women teachers, both online and offline. We find that the participating women teachers had limited *power with*. While some women did participate in communicating through emails and sharing information from home, they contributed only 7 percent of all the emails; 93 percent of the emails were from male teachers.

The project explored a key *power with* question: What barriers do women face in communication and engagement with others in open processes – and/or in participating and/or leading collective or collaborative action? Women participants cited their various household and childcare responsibilities and a lack of time, preventing them from using their computers at home. Interestingly, male teachers reported that using the computers at home was more acceptable, and they did not categorize doing so as *work*. Such barriers affect the creation, sharing, and use of knowledge; limit participation in social processes; and, by extension, make them exactly the opposite of what they were meant to be—discriminatory and not inclusive. Although women who participated did show increasing confidence to participate (*power within*), the observation and gendered perspective of the project lead revealed greater nuance: women did not like conflict during discussions, were worried about being wrong, and were willing to go along with their male colleagues. The analysis indicated how gendered women's (and men's) responses to participation are, and, to ensure that open processes are transformative, strategies for inclusion, participation, and power have to be formulated right from the beginning.

The offline situations for the same group of participating women teachers included logistical barriers, such as the residential nature of the training program (which led to difficulties with childcare, seeking permission to travel from in-laws, and other issues); poor arrangements at the training venue, like dysfunctional toilets, lack of drinking water, and nonavailability of food arrangements; and public transport facilities close to the training venue. Some of the district training centers were far from the city center and not easily accessible. Women also mentioned that they did not feel safe at these centers. Those who did come said, "We came in spite of the home, we braved it" (*power within* and *power over*), indicating an attempt to exert control over barriers.

If we review this OER project on the gender effectiveness scale (see figure 4.1), the project could be classified as gender targeting—trying to get more women involved in the project by specifically addressing their practical gender needs. To be gender transformative, the project would need to question and address the power relations between men and women teachers and the roles that they played in their daily lives, which in turn affected their contribution to the OER development, sharing, and use.

Case study: Indigenous Knowledge and Climate Change Adaptation (a subproject of OCSDNet)[21]

OCSDNet explores the role of openness and collaboration in science as a transformative tool for development thinking and practice with researcher-practitioners from the Global South. The Indigenous Knowledge and Climate Change Adaptation project used a political and ecological approach to understand the relationship between climate change, IP, and Indigenous peoples, focusing on these facets as they pertain to Khoe peoples, and the Griqua and Nama groupings in particular, in South Africa. The project used participatory action research design and methods to reduce the power relations within and between researchers and the researched and hierarchies of knowledge production by involving marginalized groups within the design, implementation, and outcomes of the research. By doing so, these community researchers would be able to influence and contribute to the coproduction of knowledge.

Analyzing the case using the questions provided in the *power to do* category in table 4.2 helps reveal the role of gender in knowledge sharing and use in this project. Because men were the herders, they were de facto *holders* (or owners) of the knowledge about changes in the environment, and, within this group, it was the older and more experienced ones who held the *power to do*. In other words, gender roles influenced who possessed the knowledge; women did not have the *power over* to overcome the access to this knowledge, and neither could they have the *power to* nor the *power within* to access knowledge. However, there were some caveats to this scenario. For instance, some women had taken over herding, as they were widows or because their husbands were migrating for work. In these cases, they *did* possess knowledge, and had the *power to* contribute. But researchers noted that women were not comfortable coming to meetings, and, even if they did come, the male elders preferred to talk to researchers and express their views to them. Women had little *power within* or *power over* to overcome the barriers. In fact, it was easier to have more interactive conversations separately with women.[22] Clearly, the filtration of Indigenous knowledge, despite its coproduction, is still gendered. Researchers involved in this project mentioned that to explore the role of gender deeply, it is important to have more time, resources, and expertise at their disposal.

If we review the project using the Gender Results Effectiveness Scale (see figure 4.1), it could be considered gender discriminatory because it did not question at all the place of women in sharing the knowledge. In fact, the researchers in the example noted that men were given precedence, even though there were circumstances where single women herders were the holders of knowledge. To be gender transformative, they had to challenge the male hierarchy so that women could participate in joint meetings, have their voices heard and valued, and reconstruct Indigenous knowledge through a gender lens. This is possible only if the research design and openness values of inclusiveness specifically articulate such questions.

Enabling Spaces for Gendered Participation

As can be seen from the examples given here, many criteria need to be considered in making openness inclusive and nondiscriminatory. Open spaces are not neutral, and definitely not gender neutral. In some cases, these spaces are pointedly gender discriminatory. The following sections attempt to address how open spaces can be gender-fair and safe.

Making Open Spaces Less Discriminatory

A few of the ROER4D projects have shown that women need much more than mere persuasion and open space to participate. For example, Maria Pilar Saenz Rodriguez from the Colombia OER project spoke during her interview about the need for a collaborative and supportive space, where women teachers can talk freely about their personal lives, as well as work professionally.[23]

Some other OER project leaders also noted a similar trend during interviews; Lauryn Oates and Mubarak from Afghanistan[24] mentioned that in their OER project, men and women had separate times to access a computer lab, which is itself telling. Men tended to dominate discussions, even though teachers were university educated and the training was located in capital cities, where a more equitable attitude was expected. There were more male teachers in Afghanistan, but the project had ensured a 50:50 representation. Similar to the Karnataka project, there was a difference in the online participation of men and women, with more men uploading the material and using the data. Men were more used to the technology and stayed longer to use the computers, unlike the women.

But gender can work the other way, too, as happened in an OER project in Sri Lanka, where female teachers in Colombo managed to attend more workshops while juggling childcare, whereas male teachers preferred to pursue other degrees where there was greater monetary gain.[25] This example indicates that participation is often nuanced and contextual, and the perception of benefit can differ between men and women.

Need for Safe Spaces to Contribute Productively

Generally, as power structures get disrupted due to increases in inclusion and participation of women in development, we are warned of the possibility of a backlash. This is equally true of digital spaces.

Susan Herring's research on gender dynamics in participation in online discussion lists provides plausible reasons for the gender gap reflected in the 2011 Wikipedia editor's survey; more women than men gave their main reason for not participating in online posting as that they felt unsettled by the "tone of the discussions" and "antagonistic exchanges" (Herring 2011).[26] Similarly, Reagle (2011) points to the presence of a "culture of hacker elitism," which can deter female contributors from utilizing free culture projects like Wikipedia and free and open-source software. Reagle (2011) suggests that the "ideology and rhetoric of freedom and openness can then be used (1) to suppress concerns about inappropriate or offensive speech as 'censorship' and (2) to rationalize low female participation as simply a matter of their personal preference and choice."[27]

Linked to safe participation is the need to promote digital rights, which is not a very commonly known set of human rights issues, especially in the South Asian context. At the *Hamara Internet—Ending Online Violence against Women* conference, held in Pakistan during November 2016, Shumaila Jaffrey of the British Broadcasting Corporation (BBC) referred to a recent report of the Federal Investigation Agency on cybercrimes, which suggested that 45 percent of the victims in the 3,000 cases of online harassment in Pakistan were females.[28] Thus, digital security and protection is critically important in our discussions of gendered inclusion in open processes. Buskens's (2011, 72–73) experience with the Gender Research in Africa and Arab Countries into ICTs for Empowerment (GRACE) project indicates that power dynamics in the environment have the potential to corrupt "the quality of openness," despite the intentions of stakeholders and role players.[29] She points out that "even within this network space, open sharing between the researchers had to be mediated by their need for safety. There was an awareness that.... GRACE researchers are also members of many social systems in their countries of origin, as well as regionally and internationally, which are very diverse, and not all share enlightened perspectives on women's empowerment and gender equality. The GRACE social platforms were therefore managed through a rhythm of openings and closures" (Buskens 2011, 74).

There is a need to address the context and the sociocultural milieu so that women are motivated to contribute to the cocreation of knowledge without being threatened. For example, on realizing the low number of female editors, Wikipedia initiated "edit-a-thons," with the idea of (1) increasing the coverage of topics related to women in Wikipedia; (2) encouraging more women to edit Wikipedia through projects like VisualEditor; and (3) providing a user-friendly environment for female newcomers through the Teahouse project. The Wikipedia initiatives show the possibility of having two strategies: (1) women need to be targeted separately from men, and (2) the setting should include both men and women and be sensitive to women's concerns. Both strategies have their advantages and disadvantages and can be used creatively by other organizations besides Wikipedia.[30]

These examples exemplify *power to empower* to provide safe online space to women contributors. Women's *power to* contribute, to be able to exercise *power over* online harassment, and the *power within* to challenge safety issues link to the work-in-progress GAFO framework.

Whether a radical idea such as the feminist Internet (Association of Progressive Communication n.d.)[31] is the answer, or if there must be rules that protect women in social praxis until cyberprotection is ensured, discussion of openness as being nondiscriminatory is limited.

Conclusion: What Have We Learned?

Roberts (2017)[32] discusses how, by focusing on the excluding mechanisms, designers of digital development projects can use different and imaginative ways to seek the participation of marginalized groups, including blending offline and online activities and using analog as well as digital technologies. He underscores that if there is an intent to include the most marginalized in digital development initiatives, then there is a "need to design for equity from the outset."

While openness implies a normative principle of inclusion, if we do not explicitly populate it with inclusion principles, it will only reflect the dominant paradigms existing in society. What is evident is that if gender is not addressed specifically, any discussion on openness is likely to bypass it—that is, "If you don't ask about gender, you don't learn about gender" (ROER4D 2016). Most likely, the knowledge created, accessed, and shared will reflect the dominant experience, which is likely to be male and white. To reach truly equitable representation, it is clear that one has to create conditions that address the barriers that prevent participation.

At the simplest, one must assess the differential use rates of men and women. It is important to then assess the direct impact on women (in terms of communication, decisions, and information); compare the impact among men and women, in terms of the relationships and the gendered actions, roles, and resources available; and finally examine the forces (sociocultural, institutional, and organizational) that influence gender (and gendered) norms, power, and practices (Heeks and Molla 2009).

Since openness, which is about production, sharing, and use, is ultimately a collaborative endeavor, it is often necessary to accommodate dynamic teams that are more geographically distributed. This is important, as it is one of the more positive and significant predictors of productivity (Terrell et al. 2017). Bias mitigation activities can be useful here, such as (1) "bias busting" workshops,[33] (2) open-source codes of conduct,[34] (3) blinded interviewing,[35] and (4) acknowledgments by the community that biases are widespread, so that it can make a practical impact on the practices of open development (Terrell et al. 2017).

The need to create and nurture a safe and nonbullying atmosphere for the Internet in general, and open processes specifically, as a global concern cannot be overstated.

It is imperative to tackle barriers to women's empowerment by enhancing their participation and representation in decision-making processes at all levels. Only this long-term process can have a sustained impact on developing a gendered Internet space and, therefore, on openness.

However, several steps and strategies may be initiated so that this extensive endeavor becomes manageable. The following actions are suggested for centering gender in openness. First, as one's gendered orientation will determine whether gender will be addressed in open development, it is important to build the capacities of all those involved in open production, cocreation, sharing, and usage to review processes using a gender lens. If you put on a different lens, you can ask: "How is this issue for women?" "How is it different for men and women?" "Why and how can we change it?" Second, having gender consultants involved in the open development process of a project could be a short-term way out, but the long-term approach of training all those involved and creating a gender equal work ethos would be more sustainable. It is essential to improve the capacity of program leaders and partners to develop and scale up gender-responsive programming to advance gender-related outcomes in program areas. Third, the inclusion of team members and consultants, trained for gender analysis, needs to be accompanied by the appropriate resources for developing a strategy for engendering openness—right from the start. Fourth, there is a need to address women's practical needs and expand safe spaces for voices, choices, and access; good practices like HarassMap and the Government of Canada's commitment to feminist strategies in international development need more visibility. Fifth, we must encourage good practices and critical feedback from reviewers and evaluators to remove the defensiveness within networked economies about gender-related concerns.

Gender equity in openness needs much more than just wishful thinking. It requires a head-on discussion regarding the power interplay, explicit and implicit, that colors gender in open development.

Notes

1. Gender is different from sex. *Sex* refers to biological differences, whereas *gender* refers to the socially constructed roles and relationships between men and women. Some theorists go beyond

the description of binaries of male and female and discuss sexual identities when referring to gender inequities. In this chapter, we use *gender* as a reference to women's lived realities. *Gender equity,* sometimes used interchangeably with *gender equality,* is different. Gender equality requires equal enjoyment by women and men of socially valued goods, opportunities, resources, and rewards. Where gender inequality exists, it is usually women who are disadvantaged. Gender equity, on the other hand, is the process of being fair to women and men, one that facilitates strategies and measures for compensating for women's historical and social disadvantages. Gender equity helps to level the unequal playing field and empower women and thus becomes essential to achieving true equality (according to the United Nations Populations Fund). (Also see http://www.unfpa.org/resources/frequently-asked-questions-about-gender-equality.)

2. We can extend this argument to include other population groups of diverse gender identities because sex and gender are not binaries.

3. By "ascriptive," we mean that the position describes the gender, such as a brother is a male and a sister is female. It also refers to describing, assuming, and accepting a gendering role (e.g., that a director is male and an assistant is female when there is no biological reason why this should be so).

4. There is a body of literature on inclusion and exclusion defined by various social science paradigms. This chapter does not critique them; rather, it uses these concepts to discuss how gender and the dynamics of inclusion affect participation in open development.

5. The Beijing Platform for Action, Section J, affirmed the importance of gender inclusion in ICT policy development at local, national, regional, and international levels. By 2000, policies to direct the ICT tools, so celebrated for their potential to effect change in developing nations, were implemented only sparsely toward programs for women's development (see Dumas 2006).

6. See IGF 2017 Panel. 2018. *After Access: Let the People Speak Using Evidence from the Global South to Reshape Our Future.* Geneva: Internet Governance Forum (IGF) Geneva. https://researchictafrica.net/wp/wp-content/uploads/2018/01/AfterAccess_IGF2017-1-2.pdf.

7. See Calandro and Mothobi (2017).

8. See http://www.powercube.net/analyse-power/forms-of-power/. To identify visible power, we ask "who decides"—they are seen as legitimate decision-makers since they 'represent us' (e.g., government, international bodies). To identify hidden power, we ask 'who influences'; they are less visible but are very influential (e.g., corporations, religious institutions, or others who exclude certain groups from decision-making or dismiss their concerns). To identify invisible power, we ask "what are the norms and who benefits" (e.g. women do not use public forums, being socialized that girls do not speak up, therefore benefiting men's voices).

9. See https://blog.wikimedia.org/2009/04/16/first-preliminary-results-from-unu-merit-survey-of-wikipedia-readers-and-contributors-available/.

10. See https://en.wikipedia.org/wiki/Gender_bias_on_Wikipedia#cite_note-Gardner110219-21.

11. See World Bank, ICT Note no. 3. June 2012. https://olc.worldbank.org/sites/default/files/New%20Frontiers_0.pdf.

12. See "Understanding Open Hardware and Citizen Science." https://ocsdnet.org/projects/hita -ordo-natural-fiber-honf-foundation/.

13. "Our applications and efforts at getting female participation in workshops backs up previous research that pits framing of workshops in 'design' rather than 'engineering' or other socially gendered terminology as more accessible for female participants," feedback from OCSDNet June monthly reports and communicated via email by Becky Hillard, August 30, 2016.

14. The chapter draws from Naila Kabeer's social transformation framework and adapts it to open processes. Kabeer's framework conceptualizes gender as central to development thinking. It helps to analyze existing gender inequalities in the distribution of resources, responsibilities, and power. For more detail, see http://www.ilo.org/public/english/region/asro/mdtmanila/training /unit1/socrelfw.htm.

15. For more detail, see Kyrgyz Mountains Environmental Education and Citizen Science, https:// ocsdnet.org/projects/kmeecs/.

16. See Open Heroines (2016).

17. Projects were selected for the vignettes using these criteria: (1) projects identified gender as an important issue and maintained relevant data or (2) were willing to reflect and respond to questions related to gender and had documented the data. Others may have addressed gender but had not maintained data on it; therefore, they were not selected for the vignettes.

18. For more detail, see "Teacher Professional Learning Communities: A Collaborative OER Adoption Approach in Karnataka, India." http://roer4d.org/collaborative-creation-of-oer.

19. For more detail, see "ROER4D Overview." http://roer4d.org.

20. Source: Interviews and emails with Anita Gurumurthy, October 3, 2016.

21. https://ocsdnet.org/projects/natural-justice-empowering-indigenous-peoples-and-knowledge -systems-related-to-climate/.

22. Interview with Dr. Laura Foster, October 13, 2016.

23. Interview with Maria Pilar Saenz Rodriguez, Project Leader of "ROER4D Subproject 6—Collaborative Co-creation of OER by Teacher Educators and Teachers in South Western Colombia: A Participatory Action Research Study."

24. Interviews with Lauryn Oates and Mubarak, Project Leaders of "ROER4D Subproject 10.4: Impact of the OER Darakht-E Danesh (Knowledge Tree) Library on Educators in Afghanistan," October 19, 2016 (Lauryn) and October 20, 2016 (Mubarak).

25. Interview with Shironica Karunanayaka, Project Leader of "ROER4D Subproject SP10.6: Impact of OER in Sri Lanka / Impact of Integrating OER in Teacher Education at The Open University of Sri Lanka," October 20, 2016.

26. See http://www.nytimes.com/roomfordebate/2011/02/02/where-are-the-women-in-wikipedia /communication-styles-make-a-difference.

27. See https://www.nytimes.com/roomfordebate/2011/02/02/where-are-the-women-in-wikipedia /open-doesnt-include-everyone.

28. See http://nation.com.pk/30-Nov-2016/hamara-internet-helpline-launched-to-tackle-online -harassment.

29. See https://www.apc.org/en/news/grace-project-state-research.

30. See https://en.wikipedia.org/wiki/Gender_bias_on_Wikipedia.

31. See https://feministinternet.org/.

32. Tony Roberts, "Digital Technologies Exclude." *Making Real Voices Count* (blog), May 2, 2017. http://www.makingallvoicescount.org/blog/digital-technologies-exclude/.cescount.-exclude/

33. See http://www.forbes.com/sites/ellenhuet/2015/11/02/rise-of-the-bias-busters-how-unconscious -bias-became-silicon-valleys-newest-target.

34. See http://contributor-covenant.org.

35. See https://interviewing.io.

References

Association of Progressive Communication. n.d. "Feminist Principles of the Internet—Version 2.0." https://www.apc.org/en/pubs/feminist-principles-internet-version-20.

Baghramian, Maria, and J. Adam Carter. 2017. "Relativism." In *The Stanford Encyclopedia of Philosophy*, ed. Edward N. Zalta. https://plato.stanford.edu/archives/sum2017/entries/relativism/.

Bear, Julia B., and Benjamin Collier. 2016. "Where Are the Women in Wikipedia? Understanding the Different Psychological Experiences of Men and Women in Wikipedia." *Sex Roles* 74:254–265. https://link.springer.com/article/10.1007%2Fs11199-015-0573-y#citeas.

Brisolara, Sharon, Denise Seigart, and Saumitra SenGupta, eds. 2014. *Feminist Evaluation and Research: Theory and Practice*. New York: Guilford Press.

Buskens, Ineke. 2011. "The Importance of Intent: Reflecting on Open Development for Women's Empowerment." *Information Technologies & International Development* 7 (1): 71–76. http:// itidjournal.org/itid/article/viewFile/698/296.

Calandro, Enrico, Chenai Chair, and Onkokame Mothobi. 2017. *Africa Digital Policy Project*. Geneva, Switzerland: IGF Geneva, United Nations. December 18. https://researchictafrica.net/wp/wp -content/uploads/2018/01/2017_What_Digital_Future__IGF_2017-1.pdf.

Chambers, Robert. 2012. "Robert Chambers on the Fifth Power (the power to empower)." *From Poverty to Power* (blog). November 29. https://oxfamblogs.org/fp2p/robert-chambers-on-the-fifth -power-the-power-to-empower/.

Cornwall, Andrea. 2002. "Making Spaces, Changing Places: Situating Participation in Development." IDS Working Paper no. 170, October. Brighton, UK: Institute of Development Studies.

http://www.ids.ac.uk/publication/making-spaces-changing-places-situating-participation-in-development.

Cornwall, Andrea, Elizabeth Harrison, and Ann Whitehead. 2004. "Introduction: Repositioning Feminism in Gender and Development." *Repositioning Feminisms in Development. IDS Bulletin* 35 (4): 1–10.

Cousins, J. Bradley, and Elizabeth Whitmore. 1998. "Framing Participatory Evaluation." *New Directions for Evaluation* 80:5–23.

Dani, Anis A. 2003. *Social Analysis Sourcebook: Incorporating Social Dimensions into Bank-Supported Projects*. Washington, DC: Social Development Department, World Bank.

Facio, Alda, and Martha I. Morgan. 2009. "Equity or Equality for Women: Understanding CEDAW's Equality Principles." IWRAW Asia Pacific Occasional Papers No. 14 (2009). Kuala Lampur.

Foucault, Michel. 1980. "Two Lectures." In *Power/Knowledge: Selected Interviews & Other Writings 1972–1977*, ed. Colin Gordon, 78–108. New York: Pantheon Books.

Galperin, Hernan, M. Fernanda Viecens, and Catrihel Greppi. 2015. In *Discrimination in Online Contracting: Evidence from Latin America*, ed. Judith Mariscal, 1–20. Lima: Diálogo Regional sobre Sociedad de la Información.

Gardner, Sue. 2011. "Nine Reasons Why Women Don't Edit Wikipedia." *Sue Gardner's Blog*. February 19. https://suegardner.org/2011/02/19/nine-reasons-why-women-dont-edit-wikipedia-in-their-own-words/.

Gaventa, John. 2003. "Towards Participatory Local Governance: Assessing the Transformative Possibilities." Prepared for the Conference on Participation: From Tyranny to Transformation. Manchester, UK, February 2003. https://dspace.library.uvic.ca/bitstream/handle/1828/6433/Gaventa_John_TowardsParticipatoryLocalGovernance_2003.pdf.

Graham, Mark. 2014. "The Knowledge-Based Economy and Digital Divisions of Labour." In *Companion to Development Studies*, 3rd ed., ed. Vandana Desai and Rob Potter, 189–195. London: Routledge.

Graham, Mark, Scott A. Hale, and Monica Stephens. 2011. *Geographies of the World's Knowledge*, ed. Corinne M. Flick. London: Convoco! Edition. https://www.oii.ox.ac.uk/archive/downloads/publications/convoco_geographies_en.pdf.

Gurumurthy, Anita. 2006. "Saying No to a Hand-Me-Down Information Society: The Digital Gap, Gender, and Development." Keynote address at the Know-How Conference. Mexico City, August 23–25.

Gurumurthy, Anita. 2009. "The Internet and Citizenship: Applying a Gender Lens." *Internet Governance Forum*. Sharm el Sheikh, Egypt. November. http://nuovo.netmundial.org/session/573 #sthash.S5YMRGFp.dpuf.

Haraway, Donna. 1988. "Situated Knowledges: The Science Question in Feminism and the Privilege of Partial Perspective." *Feminist Studies* 14 (3): 575–599.

Harding, Sandra. 1991. *Whose Science? Whose Knowledge?* Ithaca, NY: Cornell University Press.

Harding, Sandra. 1993. "Rethinking Standpoint Epistemology: What Is Strong Objectivity?" In *Feminist Epistemologies*, ed. L. Alcoff and E. Potter, 49–82. London: Routledge.

Hay, Katherine. 2012. "Engendering Policies and Programmes through Feminist Evaluation: Opportunities and Insights." *Indian Journal of Gender Studies* 19 (2): 321–340.

Heeks, Richard, and Alemayehu Molla. 2009. *Compendium of Impact Assessment of ICT-for-Development Projects*. Ottawa: IDRC. https://idl-bnc-idrc.dspacedirect.org/bitstream/handle/10625/45567/132030.pdf?sequence=1&isAllowed=y.

Herring, Susan C. 2011. "Communication Styles Make a Difference." *The New York Times*. February 4. http://www.nytimes.com/roomfordebate/2011/02/02/where-are-the-women-in-wikipedia/communication-styles-make-a-difference.

Kabeer, Naila. 2001. "Discussing Women's Empowerment—Theory and Practice." SIDA Studies no. 3. Stockholm: Swedish International Development Cooperation Agency (SIDA).

Kapur, Ratna, and Cossman, Brenda. 1993. "Communalising Gender/Engendering Community: Women, Legal Discourse, and the Saffron Agenda." *Economic and Political Weekly* WS35–WS44.

Kohn, Margaret. 2008. "Homo Spectator: Public Space in the Age of the Spectacle." *Philosophy & Social Criticism* 34 (5): 467–486.

Kuechler, Victor, Claire Gilbertson, and Carlos Jensen. 2012. "Gender Differences in Early Free and Open Source Software Joining Process." In *Open Source Systems: Long-Term Sustainability. OSS 2012. IFIP Advances in Information and Communication Technology*, vol. 378, ed. Imed Hammouda, Björn Lundell, Tommi Mikkonen, and Walt Scacchi, 78–93. Berlin and Heidelberg: Springer. https://doi.org/10.1007/978-3-642-33442-9_6.

Lam, Shyong T. K., Anuradha Uduwage, Zhenhua Dong, Shilad Sen, David R. Musicant, Loren Terveen, and John Riedl. 2011. "WP: Clubhouse? An Exploration of Wikipedia's Gender Imbalance." In *Proceedings of the 7th International Symposium on Wikis and Open Collaboration*, 1–10. https://doi.org/10.1145/2038558.2038560.

Lane, Andy. 2009. "The Impact of Openness on Bridging Educational Digital Divides." *International Review of Research in Open and Distance Learning* 10 (5): 1–12.

Leopold, Till Alexander, Vesselina Ratcheva, and Saadia Zahidi. 2016. *The Global Gender Gap Report 2016*. Geneva, Switzerland: World Economic Forum. http://reports.weforum.org/global-gender-gap-report-2016/.

Leopold, Till Alexander, Vesselina Ratcheva, and Saadia Zahidi. 2017. *The Global Gender Gap Report 2017*. Geneva, Switzerland: World Economic Forum. http://www3.weforum.org/docs/WEF_GGGR_2017.pdf.

Lessig, Lawrence. 2003. "An Information Society: Free or Feudal?" *World Summit on the Information Society*. http://www.itu.int/wsis/docs/pc2/visionaries/lessig.pdf.

Moeller, Erik. 2009. "First Preliminary Results from UNU-Merit Survey of Wikipedia Readers and Contributors." *Wikimedia Foundation*, April 16. https://blog.wikimedia.org/2009/04/16/first-preliminary-results-from-unu-merit-survey-of-wikipedia-readers-and-contributors-available/.

Murthy, Ranjani K., and Mercy Kappen. 2017. *Gender Equality and Sustainable Development Goals: A Trainer's Manual*. Bangalore, India: Visthar.

Nafus, Dawn. 2012. "'Patches Don't Have Gender': What Is Not Open in Open Source Software." *New Media & Society* 14 (4): 669–683. http://journals.sagepub.com/doi/abs/10.1177/1461444811422887.

Neuman, Laura. 2016. "Great Ideas for OGP Action Plans: Open Government for Whom? Committing to Women." *Open Government Partnership* (blog). March 8. https://www.opengovpartnership.org/stories/great-ideas-for-ogp-action-plans-open-government-for-whom-committing-to-women/.

Niederle, Muriel, and Lise Vesterlund. 2007. "Do Women Shy Away from Competition? Do Men Compete Too Much?" *Quarterly Journal of Economics* 122 (3): 1067–1101. https://doi.org/10.1162/qjec.122.3.1067.

Open Heroines. 2016. "Hello, We Are Open Heroines" *Open Heroines* (blog). May 19. https://medium.com/open-heroines/hello-we-are-open-heroines-8e7830e3b3a0.

Perryman, Leigh-Anne, and Beatriz de los Arcos. 2016. "Women's Empowerment through Openness: OER, OEP, and the Sustainable Development Goals." *Open Praxis* 8 (2): 163–180. http://oro.open.ac.uk/46371/1/OpenPraxis%20Gender.pdf.

Primo, Natasha. 2003. "Gender Issues in the Information Society." Paris: UNESCO. http://unesdoc.unesco.org/images/0013/001329/132967e.pdf.

Ramirez, Ricardo. 2008. "A 'Mediation' on Meaningful Participation." *Journal of Community Informatics* 4 (3). http://ci-journal.net/index.php/ciej/article/view/390/424.

Reagle, Joseph M. 2011. "'Open' Doesn't Include Everyone." *The New York Times*, February 4. http://www.nytimes.com/roomfordebate/2011/02/02/where-are-the-women-in-wikipedia/open-doesnt-include-everyone.

Roberts, Tony. 2015. "Is a Transformist ICT4D Possible?" *Appropriating Technology* (blog). May 18. http://appropriatingtechnology.org/?q=node/208.

Roberts. Tony. 2017. "Digital Technologies Exclude." *Making All Voices Count Blog* (blog). May 2. http://www.makingallvoicescount.org/blog/digital-technologies-exclude.

Robles, Gregorio, Laura Arjona Reina, Jesus M. Gonzalez-Barahoma, and Santiago Duenas Dominguez. 2016. "Women in Free/Libre/Open Source Software: The situation in the 2010s" In Open Source Systems: Integrating Communities, vol 472, ed. Crowston, K., Imed Hammouda, Björn Lundell, Gregorio Robles, J. Gamalielsson, J. Lindman, 163–173. Gothenburg, Sweden, May 30 June 2. Cham: Springer. https://hal.inria.fr/hal-01369061/document.

ROER4D. 2016. "October 2016 Newsletter." http://roer4d.org/wp-content/uploads/2016/10/ROER4D-Newsletter-OctoberNovember-2016.pdf.

Rossotto, Carlo M., Siou Chew Kuek, and Cecilia Paradi-Guilford. 2012. "New Frontiers and Opportunities in Work: ICT Is Dramatically Reshaping the Global Job Market." ICT Note no. 3. June. Washington, DC: World Bank. https://olc.worldbank.org/sites/default/files/New%20Frontiers_0.pdf.

Rowlands, Joanna. 1997. *Questioning Empowerment: Working with Women in Honduras*. Oxford, UK: Oxfam.

Rubinstein, Mor. 2016. An Open Letter to IODC. March 21. https://medium.com/@Morchickit/an-open-letter-to-iodc-2016-eb343389fe8a.

Rumbul, Rebecca. 2015. "Who Benefits from Civic Technology? Demographic and Public Attitudes and Public Attitudes Research into the Users of Civic Technology." London: mySociety.

Sen, Amartya. 1989. "Development as Capability Expansion." *Journal of Development Planning* 19:41–58.

Silver, Hilary. 2015. "The Contexts of Social Inclusion." UN DESA Working Paper no. 144. ST/ESA/2015/DWP/144. October. http://www.un.org/esa/desa/papers/2015/wp144_2015.pdf.

Terrell, Josh, Andrew Kofink, Justin Middleton, Clarissa Rainear, Emerson Murphy Hill, Chris Parnin, and Jon Stallings. 2017. "Gender Differences and Bias in Open Source: Pull Request Acceptance of Women versus Men." *PeerJ Computer Science,* May 1. https://peerj.com/articles/cs-111/.

Thas, Angela M. K. 2008. "An Empowerment Approach to Gender Equality in Information Society: Perspectives from East Asia." In *Empowerment Approach to Gender Equality in the Information Society,* ed. Anita Gurumurthy, Parminder Jeet Singh, and Anja Kovacs, 11–50. Bangalore, India: IT for Change. https://idl-bnc-idrc.dspacedirect.org/bitstream/handle/10625/41796/129459.pdf?sequence=1.

Torres, Nicole. 2016. "Why Do So Few Women Edit Wikipedia?" *Harvard Business Review*, June 2. https://hbr.org/2016/06/why-do-so-few-women-edit-wikipedia.

United Nations Conference on Trade and Development (UNCTAD). n.d. "Goal 5; Gender Equality: Target 5b: Women Empowerment through ICT." http://stats.unctad.org/Dgff2016/people/goal5/target_5_b.html.

United Nations Development Programme (UNDP). 2015. "Evaluation of UNDP Contribution to Gender Equality and Women's Empowerment." New York: Author. http://web.undp.org/evaluation/evaluations/thematic/gender.shtml.

UN Women. n.d. "Concepts and Definitions." http://www.un.org/womenwatch/osagi/conceptsandefinitions.htm.

UN Women. n.d. "SDG 5: Achieve Gender Equality and Empower All Women and Girls." http://www.unwomen.org/en/news/in-focus/women-and-the-sdgs/sdg-5-gender-equality.

UN Women. 2013. *How to Handle Gender-Responsive Evaluation: Evaluation Handbook*. New York: Author. http://genderevaluation.unwomen.org/en/evaluation-handbook.

Warschauer, Mark. 2002. "Reconceptualizing the Digital Divide." *First Monday* 7 (7), July 1. http://firstmonday.org/article/view/967/888.

Wiener, Anna. 2016. "Hacking Technology's Boys Club." *New Republic*. February 1. https://newrepublic.com/article/128795/hacking-technologys-boys-club.

Wikipedia. n.d. "Gender Bias on Wikipedia." https://en.wikipedia.org/wiki/Gender_bias_on_Wikipedia.

World Bank. 2013. *Inclusion Matters: The Foundation for Shared Prosperity*. Washington, DC: Author. http://siteresources.worldbank.org/EXTSOCIALDEVELOPMENT/Resources/244362-1265299949041/6766328-1329943729735/8460924-1381272444276/InclusionMatters_AdvanceEdition.pdf.

World Wide Web Foundation. 2015. *Women's Rights Online Translating Access into Empowerment*. http://webfoundation.org/docs/2015/10/womens-rights-online21102015.pdf.

5   The Geographic Contours of Openness

Mark Graham and Stefano De Sabbata

Introduction

Even though the Internet is theoretically open to anyone, it is characterized by deep geographic inequalities. Some people and places are far more likely to participate or be represented than others. This chapter explores the geography of participation and representation in open platforms across the globe. It begins by looking at the geography of Internet penetration as a prerequisite to participation, exploring which parts of the world are better connected than others. It then moves to an in-depth exploration of two types of participation in open platforms. First, it looks at the geographies of participation through Wikipedia (as a proxy for content generation) and GitHub (as a proxy for code development). Second, it looks at the geographies of representation (in other words, the parts of the world that have more or less data about them) through OpenStreetMap, the world's largest open map, and GeoNames, the world's most used open gazetteer. The discussion asks which Internet users are more likely to participate in the global web of knowledge than others. Once technological barriers to participation (i.e., Internet access) have been bridged, why do significant barriers remain for large parts of the planet?

Can We Map Openness?

Information has always had a geography. It is from somewhere, about somewhere; it evolves and is transformed somewhere; and it is mediated by networks, infrastructures, and technological tools, all of which exist in physical, material places. Information has also always been mobile. The most commonly used definition of *information*, as noted by the Oxford English Dictionary (2015), is "the imparting of knowledge." It emphasizes the transmission and movement of information in an ongoing and dynamic process. In short, information, ranging from standardized measurements to instruction manuals to stories and legends, emerges from and is adapted to a range of local contexts and geographies.

If information has a geography, then so does open information. In the context of this research, we define *open information* (or *open informational resources*) as information that is freely and publicly shared, typically (but not exclusively) over the Internet. Some individuals, groups, networks, and institutions are more likely to produce and share open information than others. Also, some parts of the world are more likely to have more open information about them than others.

In theory, open information is equally accessible and usable by all, and therefore portends more equality with respect to the meaningful use of this information. However, if information itself is characterized by large inequalities in terms of both who produces and what and where it is produced, then this will likely translate into large inequalities in terms of who can make meaningful use of open information. The idea that better access to technology and to informational resources and open information might be a force for inequality as well as equality is not new to the literature (e.g., Zook et al. 2010; Foster and Graham 2016). This chapter specifically focuses on the geographies of open information as a component or function of inclusion in and exclusion from the meaningful use of open information.

In focusing on the information geography of open information, this chapter specifically accesses patterns of mutability (i.e., the tendency for the information to be changed), mobility, and underlying power relations relative to historical arrangements in the production and use of information. It is precisely this mobility and mutability of information that provide the motivation to constrain the mutability of information through the creation of what Latour (1986) refers to as "immutable mobiles" (i.e., information that can be transported without significant change to its inherent characteristics or meaning). The printing press, for instance, made it relatively cheap to create and transport information within the container of printed paper, while simultaneously limiting how its form could change. As information technology–based nonproximate communication emerged and was adopted by governments and companies, the ability to create *immutable mobiles*, or shared understandings of information by people separated in both time and space, became vital. Information and power thus became intimately intertwined as people capitalized on the value associated with epistemic control: information represented *this* and not *that* (Schech 2002; Foucault 2000).

A key characteristic of immutable mobiles is their ability to crystalize informational layers of places in a moveable container in order to create particular geographies of information (Wilson 2015). A map, a tourist guide, and a postcard all annotate a bounded part of the world tied to a relatively immutable form that can be physically moved to different locations. Thus, immutable mobiles affect representations of places that are used both in the locales referenced and in other parts of the world (Kitchin and Dodge 2007; Kitchin, Dodge, and Perkins 2011). Information about any location can be abstracted from an immutable mobile and be placed in the relatively immutable form of printed paper, thus simultaneously fixing information to a physical object and untethering it to a locale, as the printed form can be easily moved through space. In the era of print, the geography of immutable mobiles such as maps or books largely defined the geography of codified and geographically referenced information. In other words, the scope for the spread of open information was always constrained by the geographies of immutable mobiles that transported and contained it.

Information communication technologies (ICTs) have also facilitated an evolution of information beyond immutable mobiles through the creation of *(im)mutable augmentations* characterized by the layering of dynamic information across and over geographic space. Thus, not only does information have particular geographies, but geography itself is layered, defined, and augmented by information that is more or less immutable (i.e., both mutable and immutable, or (im)mutable) depending upon the institutions and practices associated with it (Perkins 2014). The Taj Mahal, for instance, is not just a building made from marble and mortar, nor is it simply represented by guidebook entries, postcards, or other immutable mobiles that are trapped within their containers. It is also overlaid with digital images, videos, descriptions, reviews about tours and past performances, and innumerable stories told about experiences associated with it, which are stored in online maps, annotations, and websites.

All those things are informational, but they are also part of the place itself; they are part of how we enact and bring the place into being (Graham 2013; Graham, Zook, and Boulton 2013; Floridi 2011).[1] The advent of the (im)mutable augmentations and mobile tools that allow us to access this information while in situ (for shopping, wayfinding, driving, sightseeing, protesting, and many other geographic activities) places an ever-greater value in the epistemic control to fix informational layers of place (Shaw and Graham 2017). The fact that contemporary (im)mutable augmentations are digital means that they hold much potential with respect to open information. In theory, anyone with access to the right tools and modes of connectivity can produce, share, and access a world of information.

Geographies of the production of data matter because they can reinforce a world in which some people have a more substantial voice than others. In a world in which digital information is even more crucial to almost every facet of daily life, it is crucial to understand whether some groups of people have more of a say in how our digital world is constructed than others do. The question that could be asked is: What sort of global information society are we building if large groups of people rarely participate in it as producers? Furthermore, the (im)mutable augmentations of information about places matter because they shape how we are able to find and understand different parts of the world (Shelton et al. 2014). Places that are invisible or discounted in representations are equally invisible in practice to many people. A restaurant omitted from a map can cease to be a restaurant if no one finds it. Likewise, how places are presented within informational augmentations fundamentally affects how they are used or brought into being (Graham and Zook 2013). In other words, geographic augmentations are much more than just representations of places. They are part of the places themselves, and they shape it rather than simply reflect it; the map again becomes part of the territory (Floridi 2014; Pickles 2004). This fusing of the spatial and informational augmentations that are (im)mutable can result in high stakes as annotations of place emerge as sites of political contestation, with different groups of people trying to impose different narratives on informational augmentations (Zook and Graham 2007).

In short, the *geography of information*, which refers to the geographic distribution of information either as a phenomenon in its own right or as a representation of some other underlying process (Wilson 2015), has long been a key means of control and power formation. The rise of *information geographies* (i.e., informational augmentations to places) represents a key and emerging area of inquiry for scholars of information.

After giving a brief review of predigital geographies of information, this chapter explores how open information geographies have their own geographic distributions: first in terms of geographies of participation (contributing content to a digital platform), and second in terms of representation (what informational augmentations exist about a place). The chapter does this by examining platforms that play a particularly important role in the production and sharing of open information and information-embedded goods—and thus play a critical role in the ecosystem and political economy of information flows.

Predigital Geographies of Information

In the predigital age, the affordances of technologies and associated sociotechnical systems for collecting, storing, and disseminating information meant that information was both scarce and geographically embedded. For instance, at the dawn of the nineteenth century, the tools for collating encyclopedic information about places (e.g., compasses, paper, and sextants) were concentrated with just a few individuals in a few places, making the ability to engage in large-scale data collection relatively rare. This was even more the case because the required propinquity to the object of measurement inherent in collecting information about places entailed a scale of organization not widely available. Likewise, the state of the art for containing information—the book—required specific points of access to codified content for its production. Books were also constrained by a particular form—two-dimensional printed material of prespecified parameters, which is usually part of a linear reading trajectory from start to finish, and features a method of physical storage in particular places.

Other key bottlenecks in the processing of information included the availability of requisite skill sets to manage, validate, merge, modify, classify, sort, analyze, and manipulate information into particular forms and formats. The institutions that emerged to meet this challenge, such as universities, associations, and guilds, required resources. These in turn often needed to be *spatially fixed* as a result, and a formalized education in information-handling practices was necessarily place-bound and concentrated in specific locales. These geographic centers of calculation meant that the ability to access codified information, let alone contribute to it (i.e., the professionalization of knowledge work), was also highly constrained.

Although the affordances of predigital technologies (and their associated systems of governance, economization, and socialization) allowed the movement of codified information (shifted from its point of creation to other locations), it could never transcend the innate materiality of its medium or the world. In short, the frictions of mobility associated with transmitting and storing information, the place-bound rules and forms of governance, and the availability of requisite technologies have all shaped the geographies of information in this era. In practice, these constraints manifest into hegemonic representations and hegemonic modes of participation (cf. Gramsci 1971). As knowledge and codified information are always produced under conditions of power (Crampton 2008; Pickles 1994), control over hegemonic representations has been a way of exerting economic, social, and political power (Laclau and Mouffe 2001).

Books, newspapers, and patents, for instance, were all far more likely to be published from (and about) the Global North, with the Global South playing a relatively minor role in producing, using, and controlling codified information (Zhang et al. 2013; Graham et al. 2011; Thompson and Fox-Kean 2005).[2] This information power and power over information manifest in distinct spatial patterns and almost all traditional media of information are characterized by significant spatial inequalities, leading Castells (1999, 3) to conclude that "most of Africa is being left in a technological apartheid." The systemic and uneven relationships between information production/use and socioeconomic exclusion and marginalization are characterized as the "black holes of informational capitalism" (Castells 1997, 162).

Changing Geographies after the Information Revolution?

Against this backdrop, the past decades have seen a sea change in the availability of information. The terms *information revolution* (Floridi 2014) and *data revolution* (Kitchin 2014) signify the radical changes in the ways that information is produced and used, implying that we are now in an age of postinformation scarcity. In this age, information has moved from being proprietary and closed to becoming shared and shareable, and it no longer is confined to a narrow selection of containers and places. This transformation has been brought about by the proliferation of new sociotechnical systems of the so-called information age. These systems are underpinned by greater accessibility to computers that can readily receive and transmit information nonproximately, as well as by a host of associated social, economic, and political practices. As a result, many of the barriers to the production, processing, and proliferation of information in the predigital era have been drastically lowered.

Some have argued that this emerging digital age offers a potentially radically different political economy of information[3] (Benkler 2007; Bruns 2008; Jenkins 2006). Tapscott and Williams (2006) and Shirky (2011) highlight the ways that digitally mediated participation and representation are broad-based, circumventing traditional mediators of information that allow citizens to play a more significant role in shaping the content and augmentations that play key roles in their lives (also see, e.g., Sui and Goodchild 2011). Lawrence Lessig, a key scholar of the effects of information systems on property rights, has made some particularly hopeful observations on the democratic power of the Internet. At the 2003 World Summit on the Information Society, he remarked on the significant possibilities afforded by the web, noting that "[f]or the first time in a millennium, we have a technology to equalize the opportunity that people have to access and participate in the construction of knowledge and culture, regardless of their geographic placing" (Lessig 2003, 1).

Lessig's characterization is not unique; such sentiments also infuse the worlds of policy and business. In 2012, Hamadoun Touré, the secretary-general of the International Telecommunication Union (ITU), claimed that once Internet connectivity arrives, "all the world's citizens will have the potential to access unlimited knowledge, to express themselves freely, and to contribute to and enjoy the benefits of the knowledge society" (Touré 2012). Echoing similar lines of rhetoric, Wikipedia, according to its cofounder Jimmy Wales, seeks to "contain the sum of all human knowledge" (Miller 2004). And Google's stated core mission is to "organize the world's information and make it universally accessible and useful" (Google 2015).

Similar rhetoric has accompanied the emergence of openness whose influence has piggybacked on the growth and diffusion of ICTs. There were hopes that openness would make a difference to practices and processes of development at the world's economic margins (Bentley and Chib 2016; Graham and Haarstad 2011; Smith 2013). This is in part because the global or macro picture is one of extreme connectivity—currently, there are 3.5 billion people and 25 billion devices attached to the global network. Furthermore, the total amount of accessible information online, both open and closed, has dramatically increased (Hilbert 2012). But has this increase in access and availability of freely available open information had any effect on the political economy or geographies of information? Has it altered participation or representation? If people can, in theory, create and access open information about and from almost anywhere on Earth, are we seeing different geographies of participation and representation or new layers of digital augmentations [i.e., data shadows (Graham 2010)] associated with places?

To answer these questions, we engaged in a broad-scale survey of the contemporary geographies of key digital and Internet-mediated platforms for open information. Some of this information is produced through the open production practices of crowdsourcing or peer production. We produced a series of mappings based on the most definitive sources available. Some data is emerging from established informants such as the ITU, which provides relevant indicators of information use (and as a result, these data have been fairly widely disseminated). By contrast, much of the data used in this chapter were generated using bespoke data collection tools making for a unique analysis of rarely used data.

Geographies of Participation

To understand the geographies of participation, we explore GitHub (as a measure of contributions to the world's largest open software repository) and edits to Wikipedia (as a measure of contributions to the world's largest open encyclopedia). While both measures are shaped in part by local cultural practices, such as the awareness of and interest in contributing to GitHub or Wikipedia, they also represent global communities of practice that transcend the particularities of any one place.

Collaborative Coding

GitHub is the largest code-hosting service in the world, containing 17 million repositories. In 2015, it had 3.5 million registered users, as well as countless unregistered users. Programmers can use GitHub to publish their code for others to download and use, as well as to collaborate with others on shared projects, tracking changes and contributions. No other code-hosting service has anywhere near the same number of users, making GitHub a useful proxy for the extent to which Internet users create and share code.

Data for the map of GitHub users and commits (i.e., contributions of software or code for others to use) in figure 5.1 come from the GitHub archive (GitHub 2014) and include all freely shared contributions logged by the service. The 2013 data contain over

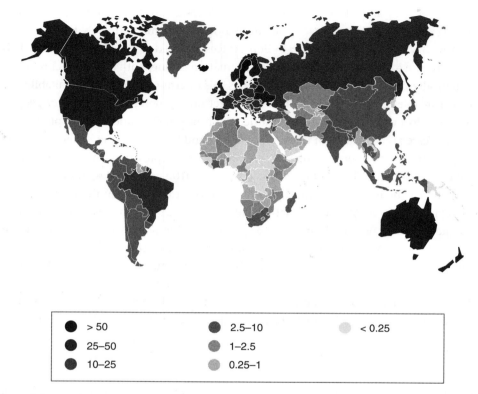

Figure 5.1
Number of GitHub users or commits per 100,000 users in every country in 2013.
Sources: Github.com; World Bank data.

65 million commits made by about 1.1 million users who were active that year. Users are able to specify their home locations as a string of text, and 26 percent of users' entries were geolocatable using the Edinburgh Geoparser (2015) web service at the University of Edinburgh. Another 2 percent of entries were given in nongeographic terms (e.g., "Internet," "127.0.0.1," "Planet Earth," or "everywhere"), with the remaining 72 percent of profile entries being empty. The 26 percent of locatable users account for over 44 percent of the commits. While this is a relatively small percentage of all users, we are not aware of any systemic bias that would significantly overcount or undercount contributions from particular countries.

Figure 5.1 shows the number of GitHub users and commits by these users relative to the number of Internet users. While Internet penetration explains about one-third of the variability in the number of GitHub users per country, large differences remain in the rate at which people from various parts of the world contribute. North America and Europe each account for over one-third of the total number of GitHub users, and the rate of participation—34 GitHub users and 21 GitHub users per 100,000 Internet users (hereafter referenced as G per 100 K), respectively—well exceeds the global average of 11.4 G per 100 K. The platform is particularly popular in northern Europe and eastern Europe; for instance, Iceland and Sweden have more than 50 G per 100 K apiece. It is also popular in New Zealand and Australia, with about 35 G per 100 K.

A majority of the remaining third of GitHub users (17 percent) are located in Asia, including Singapore, with 27 G per 100 K, and Taiwan, with 10 G per 100 K, which per capita represent the two largest. In absolute terms, China is home to 5.6 percent of GitHub users but has fewer than 3 Github users per 100 K. The Middle East, North Africa, and sub-Saharan Africa stand out with the lowest levels of participation, and, combined, the regions are home to less than 1 percent of GitHub users and commits, comparable to the level of activity in Switzerland.

In addition to being home to the majority of users, North America and Europe contribute at higher rates than the rest of the world. For example, the United States is home to 31 percent of users but contributes 35 percent of commits. The statistics for users and commits for other standout countries include the Netherlands (1.7/2.4) and Switzerland (0.9/1.4). The opposite pattern is evident in much the rest of the world, with India accounting for 3.6 percent of users but only 1.7 percent of commits; Brazil, with 3.7 percent of users and only 2.5 percent of commits; and South Africa, containing 0.46 percent of users but only 0.36 percent of all commits.

In summary, this analysis of GitHub shows that Europe and North America are significantly more involved in collaborative code development than other parts of the world. Africa and the Middle East contain considerably fewer people accessing or contributing software than would be expected, given the level of Internet access in those places. One potential inference from these data is that factors such as skills, education, and income play a more significant role than connectivity (Ojanperä et al. 2017).

Wikipedia Contributions

While code is central to the functioning of contemporary societies, its creation is a particularly specialized endeavor. In contrast, Wikipedia—a platform that allows all Internet users to write and edit its articles—offers an indicator of a more generalized level of content creation and contribution. Not only is Wikipedia by far the world's largest and most used encyclopedia (1,600 times larger than the *Encyclopedia Britannica*), it is also extremely popular. More than 15 percent of Internet users access it on any given day, and it is in the top twenty most accessed websites in 95 percent of the world's countries

(Graham et al. 2014). Part of its popularity can be tied to its articles being written in 282 languages, with 40 of those language versions containing more than 100,000 articles each. In other words, edits to Wikipedia have a tremendous power to shape the content accessed by the majority of Internet users around the world.

Wikipedia's approach to contributions, in theory, allows anyone with an Internet connection to contribute; the platform's strapline is "the free encyclopedia that anyone can edit." However, based on the number of edits to every language version of Wikipedia coming from all countries and territories in the last quarter of 2014 (the most recent data available),[4] figure 5.2 shows that the geography of participation on Wikipedia is highly uneven.

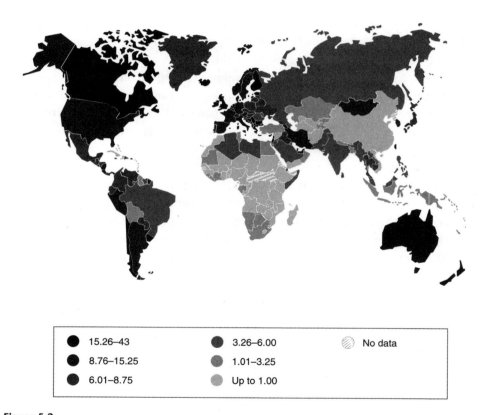

●	15.26–43	●	3.26–6.00	◌	No data
●	8.76–15.25	●	1.01–3.25		
●	6.01–8.75	●	Up to 1.00		

Figure 5.2
Wikipedia edits per capita (monthly average values) in 2014.
Source: Stats.wikimedia.org.

Stark inequalities are readily apparent, as Europe and North America contribute 35.2 percent and 23.6 percent of Wikipedia's edits, respectively, while Africa as a whole contributes only 1.3 percent of the world's total. In fact, contributions from Africa are so low that there are actually more edits that originate in the Netherlands than the whole continent. While some of these disparities can be explained by the total number of Internet users in a country, even normalizing by the percentage of the population online, far fewer edits are registered in Africa than would be expected (for a detailed statistical analysis on the topic, see Graham et al. 2014).

A key way that these geographies of participation matter is tied to how content and locales or places are created in different parts of the world. Figure 5.3 shows the percentage of local edits to articles that reference places within the users' own countries.[5]

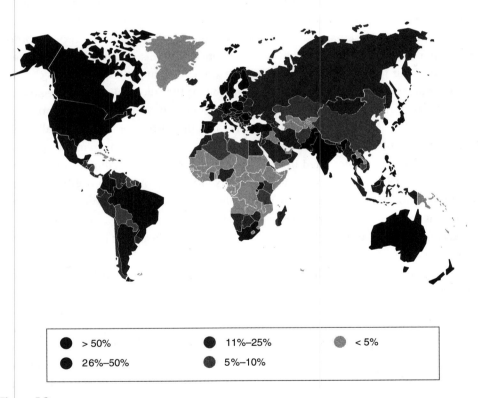

> 50%   11%–25%   < 5%

26%–50%   5%–10%

Figure 5.3
Percentage of edits to English-language Wikipedia articles from local people in specific countries in 2013.
Source: Oxford Internet Institute.

In other words, this map illustrates the percentage of edits about a country (i.e., articles that fall within the boundary of a country) that come from users within that country. In this specific instance, we were only able to use data about the English version of Wikipedia because the method of geolocating user profiles involved parsing unstructured English-language text. While many places have a high percentage of content created by local people (e.g., 85 percent and 78 percent of content about the United States and the United Kingdom, respectively, comes from users located there), the percentages in Africa are much lower. Only 16 percent of content about Nigeria and 9 percent of content about Kenya are created by locals, and, in much of the rest of the continent, less than 5 percent of content is generated locally.

We can also analyze the locality of voice and participation using figure 5.4 (originally published in Graham et al. 2016). It depicts seven world regions (Europe, Oceania, North America, Middle East and North Africa, Latin America and the Caribbean, sub-Saharan Africa, and Asia) as dots. The y-axis of the graph indicates the proportion of edits that a region receives internally (a high score would mean that the region largely is written about from within the region). The x-axis indicates the proportion of edits that a region commits internally (a high score means that most edits from a region are about that region). It is worth noting that even though a region like sub-Saharan Africa and a region like Europe commit roughly the same proportion of edits internally, sub-Saharan Africa has far fewer locally produced digital representations than Europe. This is, in part, because, as presented in figure 5.4, there are far more editors from Europe, and it only takes a few editors writing about sub-Saharan Africa to result in articles about the region being dominated by nonlocally produced content. Compounding this problem is the fact that editors in other parts of the world with very limited locally produced content (such as in the Middle East) end up exporting a lot of their editing power by writing about other parts of the world.

In summary, this section shows the spatial distribution of participation in two open production processes. While both data sources have their own idiosyncrasies and display different patterns (to be explored in future research), the general refrain remains consistent. Thus, the Global North is characterized by the greatest levels of participation and is creating the bulk of digital content, while the Global South contributes very little. The continent of Africa, in particular, is almost entirely omitted from these processes of digital generativity. Moreover, these distributions stand in marked contrast to the geographies of Internet users. While this is cause for concern in a number of arenas, we now turn to a direct impact of these differences—namely, the ways in which places are represented (or not) within information geographies.

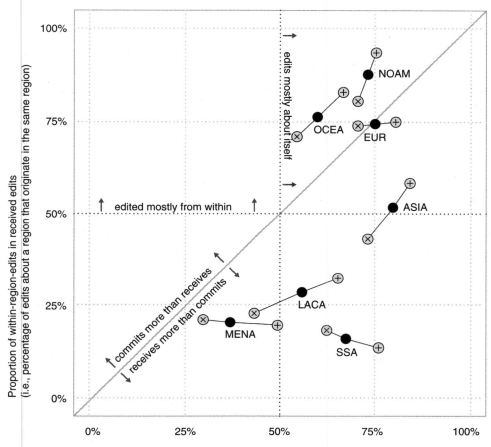

Figure 5.4

Proportion of within-region edits in total committed edits (*x*-axis) and total received edits (*y*-axis) to geocoded articles per each world region. Data shows anonymous edits only (+); registered edits only (×); and both edit types combined (•). The seven world regions are Europe (EUR), Oceana (OCEA), North America (NOAM), Middle East and North Africa (MENA), Latin America and the Caribbean (LACA), sub-Saharan Africa (SSA), and Asia.

Geographies of Representation

To better understand the contours of representation within the (im)mutable augmentations of the world, we present a series of visualizations (i.e., we ask what informational
augmentations exist about a place): OpenStreetMap (OSM) (the world's largest open
map) and the Semantic Web, as defined by GeoNames (one of the world's largest open
gazetteers), both of which are examples of the crowdsourcing of information. In both
of these cases, the popularity of these systems provides useful ways to gauge the spatial
differences in digital representation on these crowdsourcing platforms.

Mapping OpenStreetMap

As the world's largest road map, and because it is free and open source, OSM is used
as a base map for thousands of other digital platforms and services. Therefore, it is
important to understand how much content OSM contains about various parts of the
world.[6] Figure 5.5 is based on data downloaded from GeoFabrik.de in December 2013,
containing all 2 billion nodes (i.e., elements used to represent any point feature) in
OSM at that time. The number of nodes in each cell of the 0.1-degree grid were tal-
lied and mapped. The node density was then calculated for square area units with
side length of 10 kilometers and a neighborhood radius of 25 kilometers. The United
States accounts for the largest total amount of content, hosting 21 percent of all nodes
present in OSM, followed by France, Canada, Germany, and Russia, with each containing more than 100 million nodes. These five countries alone comprise 58 percent of
all the content in OSM, and the group of 36 high-income Organisation for Economic
Co-operation and Development countries contains almost 80 percent of the total
number of nodes.

The Netherlands has the highest density of content, with an average of over 1,000
nodes per square kilometer. Belgium follows with over 700 nodes per square kilometer.
Germany, the Czech Republic, Switzerland, and France all have about 400 nodes per
square kilometer. In contrast to the high density in Europe, the Southern Hemisphere is
far more sparsely covered. Africa and Latin America are each represented by less than 5
percent of the world's content in OSM. In contrast, California alone accounts for almost
as much content as the whole continent of Africa. Furthermore, Iceland has as much
content as Egypt, despite being a tenth of its size and having 0.4 percent of its population.

GeoNames and the Contours of the Semantic Web

The Semantic Web is a movement to make the web more efficient by creating common frameworks that allow data to be easily shared and reused across sites, services,

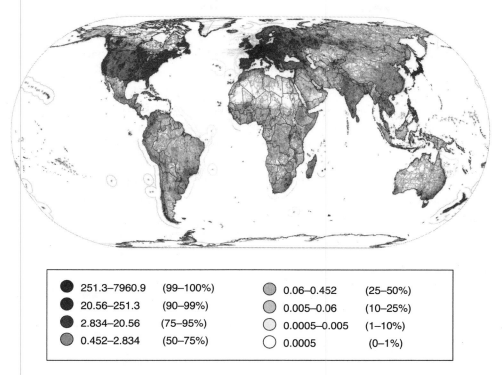

Figure 5.5
The number of nodes in OSM per square kilometer. Squared area units 10 km x 10 km, neighborhood radius 25 km. The value 0.0005 indicates one object per area unit.
Source: Openstreetmap.org, Geofabrik.de. Data comes from "*-latest.osm.bz2" files available per world region as of December 12, 2013.

and places. Google, for instance, has recently employed what it terms its *knowledge graph* as a way of reacting to user queries. Instead of displaying a simple list of links to websites in response to a search query, the search engine looks for implicit meaning embedded in a request (such as "What is the capital of France?") and then displays structured information about that query on the right side of the search page (e.g., the word *Paris,* the population of Paris). Because Google is the primary interface to the web for approximately 67.6 percent of Americans and over 90 percent of Europeans (European Commission 2013), information in its knowledge graph plays an important role in how hundreds of millions of people view and interpret the world.

Information contained in the Semantic Web (such as the answer that Paris is the capital of France) is derived from centralized databases that feed facts into Internet services like Google, Bing, Facebook, and many others. One of the most important back-end geographic databases for the Semantic Web is GeoNames, the world's largest and probably most used gazetteer or directory of place names. The service is a combination of freely available national gazetteers and data sets,[7] as well as volunteered geographic information that is constructed such that, in theory, anybody with an Internet connection can enter or edit data. We obtained data from the gazetteer's data dump,[8] and figures 5.6 and 5.7 illustrate the density of place names listed in the gazetteer. In this map, darker shades indicate higher numbers of place names per square kilometer.

The geography of GeoNames is not a simple reflection of the distribution of population. For instance, the United States accounts for 25 percent of the entire database (Graham and De Sabbata 2015), which means that there is more content about the United States than in all of Asia, which contains only 23 percent of place names, and Europe, with 19 percent of place names. India is the most underrepresented country in the world, with only 0.6 percent of the collection (figure 5.7 shows the relationship between population and geographic content in more detail).

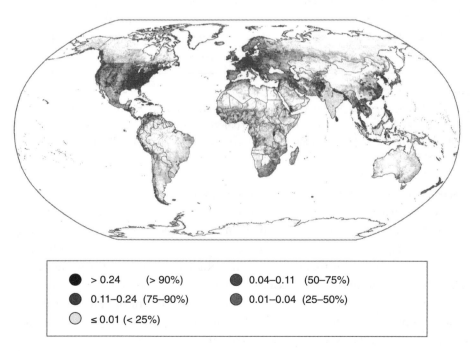

● > 0.24   (> 90%)   ● 0.04–0.11 (50–75%)

● 0.11–0.24 (75–90%)   ● 0.01–0.04 (25–50%)

○ ≤ 0.01 (< 25%)

Figure 5.6
Distribution of place names in GeoNames throughout the world.
Source: Oxford Internet Institute.

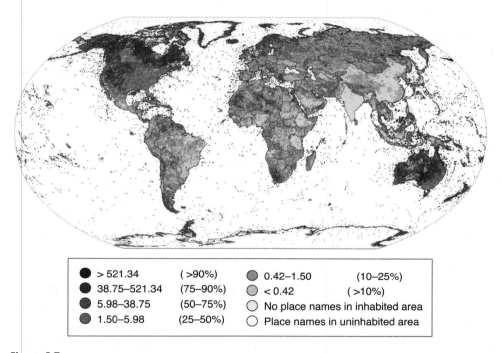

Figure 5.7
Distribution of place names per 1,000 inhabitants in GeoNames.
Sources: GeoNames.org; SEDAC.ciesin.columbia.edu.

Intriguingly, the standard patterns of concentration in the Global North and absence in the Global South are also accompanied by some less expected patterns. Nepal, for instance, has more content than all but ten other countries and contains more place names than India and the United Kingdom combined. We suspect that this is tied to the significant efforts of a 2001 project funded by the European Union (Budhathoki and Chhatkuli 2004) to create a geographical information infrastructure in Nepal. Also noteworthy is that Iran is augmented by almost as many place names as Germany, and North Korea and Sri Lanka are referenced in almost as much detail as Austria. It is likely that some of these patterns appear because many of the place names for locations outside North America and Europe are sourced from the National Geospatial-Intelligence Agency in the United States, and therefore reflect the interests of the US intelligence services. We also note that there are indications that a significant amount of content has been created by crisis mappers (Zook et al. 2010). Haiti, for instance, is annotated by more content than Denmark, which likely is a result of work done following the 2010 earthquake in the country (for more details about the efforts of crisis mappers in Haiti, see Meier 2015).

Because GeoNames is now an essential component of many contemporary digital services (e.g., the geocoding of social media), the presences and absences outlined here have the potential to have a significant impact on how we understand, interact with, and use other digital information. GeoNames may seem like a small corner of the web, but the imbalances noted here can have large reverberations throughout broader information ecosystems.

Similar to the section "Geographies of Participation," earlier in this chapter, this section has shown that there are broad patterns of unevenness throughout platforms that facilitate the representation of places. Although each platform is characterized by its own idiosyncrasies, some parts of the world are massively overrepresented (i.e., North America and Europe), while the rest of the world is severely underrepresented.

Conclusions

This chapter offers a review of key geographies of access, participation, and representation with respect to open information, using a combination of existing statistics and bespoke data. Through this effort, it demonstrates that in addition to uneven geographies of access to contemporary modes of communication, uneven geographies of participation and representation in open information are evident; and in some cases, they are being amplified rather than alleviated.

Too much should not be read into the specific differences between the geographies of participation and representation. However, apart from the Global South having low scores on every metric, it is noteworthy that rates of representation of Africa and South America are generally higher than rates of participation from Africa and South America. This is because, as noted in "Wikipedia Contributions," nonlocals can often choose to get involved in the representation of far-off places.

Moreover, there are few signs that global informational peripheries are achieving comparable levels of participation or representation with traditional information cores, despite the hopes of policymakers and the promises of openness. Open (i.e., freely shared information) information geographies seem to follow a pattern similar to other information geographies such as book publishing or academic journal article production; that is, the Global North produces, and is the subject of, exponentially more content than the Global South[9] (Chan and Gray 2014; cf Dicken 2010; Graham et al. 2011). Even the fast-paced spread of the Internet to 3.5 billion people worldwide has done little to change this basic pattern.

This matters, even though the platforms analyzed in this chapter are all open platforms in principle, because significant barriers remain for people and places in the

Global South. As this discussion has shown, these barriers cannot simply be explained by lack of connectivity. As such, any research on obstacles to a broad base of participation in the creation and meaningful use of open information must also seek to consider the impacts of postcolonial modes of informational governance; the culturally contingent ways through which participation and representation take place; shifts in the political economy of control of information (Leszczynski 2012; see also chapter 6); the affordances of platforms and infrastructures of connectivity (see chapter 8 for more on this topic); the constraints of explicit and implicit censorship; gendered or socioeconomic constraints to access or production (see chapters 4 and 9 for more information); and the availability or absence of a broader information ecosystem of local content.

This chapter is a first but important step in showing that global uneven geographies of open information are not simply an outcome of the idiosyncrasies in particular platforms. It also contributes to the literature illustrating how openness itself is always structured and socially embedded (Smith and Reilly 2013), and consequently, it could work to deepen existing exclusions rather than expanding inclusion (e.g., Graham et al. 2016). Openness, therefore, can mean very different things in different places, and it is important to look beyond the term to see what different platforms make visible, invisible, possible, and probable, not just in theory but in practice.

Despite this rather gloomy summation, we see this work as a beginning rather than an end, and also as part of an effort to confront these stubborn realities. This chapter offers an initial broad-scale survey of the contemporary geographies of the production and representation of open information. Future work needs to seek to better understand the contextual causes (using inferential statistics and in-depth qualitative research) and to better explicate some of the contextual nuances (i.e., why certain types of information on certain platforms are more or less likely to be produced in certain places) of these uneven geographies.

Acknowledgments

This work was made possible by research grants from the International Development Research Centre (Canada), the Philip Leverhulme Fund (PLP-2016–155), and the European Research Council under the European Union's Seventh Framework Programme for Research and Technological Development (FP/2007–2013)/ERC Grant Agreement no. 335716. The authors are also grateful for the help of numerous colleagues and collaborators. In particular, we would like to thank Matthew Zook, Bernie Hogan, Ralph Straumann, and Ahmed Medhat.

Notes

This chapter is an adapted version of Graham, De Sabbata, and Zook (2015).

1. This is not an attempt to argue that augmented geographies already exist. We instead follow the arguments of Kitchin and Dodge (2007, 2011) in viewing information geographies as ontogenetic (i.e., in a state of becoming that emerges through practices).

2. These patterns have even been described as "a new phase in a long history of the West's attempt to colonize not only the territory and the body but also the mind of the Third World 'other'" (see Sardar 1996, cited in Schech 2002, 18).

3. It should also be noted that hype around the transformational power of technology is not limited to the Internet. For a historical example, see Graham et al. (2015).

4. These data were obtained from http://stats.wikimedia.org/wikimedia/squids/SquidReportsCo untriesLanguagesVisitsEdits.htm. See Graham and Hogan (2014) for more detail on geolocation methods that can be employed to determine the origin of edits.

5. This method of understanding the locality of content about places is particularly methodologically challenging (for more on the method, see Graham et al. 2016). As such, we are relying on older, already published 2011 data to create this particular map.

6. For more detailed research on the quality of OSM's coverage in different parts of the world, see Haklay (2010), who compared OSM data to high-quality data from government agencies (which makes it difficult to focus on parts of the world, where high-quality official data are lacking).

7. See www.geonames.org/data-sources.html.

8. See download.geonames.org/export/dump/.

9. The *Scimago Journal and Country Rank* database of all journals in the Scopus database (https://www.scimagojr.com/), for instance, shows that the United States has the most published academic articles of any country, and moreover that there are more articles from the United States than the combined total of the bottom 225 countries on the list.

References

Benkler, Yochai. 2007. *The Wealth of Networks: How Social Production Transforms Markets and Freedom.* New Haven, CT: Yale University Press.

Bentley, Caitlin M., and Arul Chib. 2016. "The Impact of Open Development Initiatives in Lower- and Middle-Income Countries: A Review of the Literature." *Electronic Journal of Information Systems in Developing Countries* 74 (1): 1–20.

Bruns, Axel. 2008. *Blogs, Wikipedia, Second Life, and Beyond: From Production to Produsage.* New York: Peter Lang.

Budhathoki, Nama, and Raja Ram Chhatkuli. 2004. "Building Geographic Information Infrastructure at National Level: Nepalese Experience." Paper presented at the GSDI 7th Conference, Bangalore, India, GSDI 7, January 30–February 6.

Castells, Manuel. 1997. *The Power of Identity.* Vol. 2 of *The Information Age: Economy, Society, and Culture.* Oxford, UK: Blackwell.

Castells, Manuel. 1999. *Information Technology, Globalization and Social Development.* Geneva, Switzerland: United Nations Research Institute for Social Development.

Chan, Leslie, and Eve Gray. 2014. "Centering the Knowledge Peripheries through Open Access: Implications for Future Research and Discourse on Knowledge for Development." In *Open Development: Networked Innovations in International Development,* ed. Matthew L. Smith and Katherine M. A. Reilly, 197–222. Cambridge, MA/Ottawa: MIT Press/IDRC. https://idl-bnc-idrc.dspacedirect .org/bitstream/handle/10625/52348/IDL-52348.pdf?sequence=1&isAllowed=y.

Crampton, Jeremy W. 2008. "Will Peasants Map? Hyperlinks, Map Mashups, and the Future of Information." In *The Hyperlinked Society: Questioning Connections in a Digital Age,* ed. Joseph Turow and Lokman Tsui, 206–226. Ann Arbor: University of Michigan Press.

Dicken, Peter. 2010. *Global Shift.* 6th ed. London: SAGE Publications.

European Commission. 2013. "Antitrust: Commission Seeks Feedback on Commitments Offered by Google to Address Competition Concerns," news release, April 25. http://europa.eu/rapid /press-release_IP-13-371_en.htm.

Floridi, Luciano. 2011. *The Philosophy of Information.* Oxford: Oxford University Press.

Floridi, Luciano. 2014. *The Fourth Revolution: How the Infosphere Is Reshaping Human Reality.* Oxford: Oxford University Press.

Foster, Christopher, and Mark Graham. 2016. "Reconsidering the Role of the Digital in Global Production Networks." *Global Networks* 17 (1): 68–88.

Foucault, Michel. 2000. *Power (The Essential Works of Foucault 1954–1984. Vol. 3),* ed. James D. Faubion, trans. Robert Hurley. London: Allen Lane/Penguin.

GitHub. 2014. "GitHub Archive." https://www.githubarchive.org.

Google. 2015. "Company Overview." https://www.google.com/intl/en/about/our-company/.

Graham, Mark. 2010. "Neogeography and the Palimpsests of Place: Web 2.0 and the Construction of a Virtual Earth." *Tijdschrift voor economische en sociale geografie* 101 (4): 422–436.

Graham, Mark. 2013. "Geography/Internet: Ethereal Alternate Dimensions of Cyberspace or Grounded Augmented Realities?" *Geographical Journal* 179 (2): 177–182.

Graham, Mark, and Stefano De Sabbata. 2015. "Mapping Information Wealth and Poverty: The Geography of Gazetteer." *Environment and Planning A: Economy and Space* 47 (6): 1254–1264.

Graham, Mark, Stefano De Sabbata, and Matthew A. Zook. 2015. "Towards a Study of Information Geographies: (Im)mutable Augmentations and a Mapping of the Geographies of Information." *Geo: Geography and Environment* 2 (1): 88–105. https//:doi:10.1002/geo2.8.

Graham, Mark, and Håvard Haarstad. 2011. "Transparency and Development: Ethical Consumption through Web 2.0 and the Internet of Things." *Information Technologies & International Development* 7 (1): 1–18.

Graham, Mark, Scott A. Hale, and Monica Stephens. 2011. *Geographies of the World's Knowledge*, ed. Corinne M. Flick. London: Convoco! Edition. https://www.oii.ox.ac.uk/archive/downloads/publications/convoco_geographies_en.pdf.

Graham, Mark, and Bernie Hogan. 2014. *Uneven Openness: Barriers to MENA Representation on Wikipedia*. Oxford: Oxford Internet Institute.

Graham, Mark, Bernie Hogan, Ralph K. Straumann, and Ahmed Medhat. 2014. "Uneven Geographies of User-Generated Information: Patterns of Increasing Informational Poverty." *Annals of the Association of American Geographers* 104 (4): 746–764.

Graham, Mark, Ralph K. Straumann, and Bernie Hogan. 2016. "Digital Divisions of Labor and Informational Magnetism: Mapping Participation in Wikipedia." *Annals of the Association of American Geographers* 105 (6): 1158–1178. https//:doi:10.1080/00045608.2015.1072791.

Graham, Mark, and Matthew Zook. 2013. "Augmented Realities and Uneven Geographies: Exploring the Geo-linguistic Contours of the Web." *Environment and Planning A: Economy and Space* 45 (1): 77–99.

Graham, Mark, Matthew Zook, and Andrew Boulton. 2013. "Augmented Reality in the Urban Environment: Contested Content and the Duplicity of Code." *Transactions of the Institute of British Geographers* 38 (3): 464–479.

Gramsci, Antonio. 1971. *Selections from the Prison Notebooks of Antonio Gramsci*. Trans. Geoffrey N. Smith and Quinton Hoare. London: Lawrence & Wishart.

Haklay, Mordechai. 2010. "How Good Is Volunteered Geographical Information? A Comparative Study of OpenStreetMap and Ordnance Survey Datasets." *Environment and Planning B: Planning and Design* 37 (4): 682–703.

Hilbert, Martin. 2012. "How Much Information Is There in the 'Information Society'?" *Significance* 9 (4): 8–12.

Jenkins, Henry. 2006. *Convergence Culture: Where Old and New Media Collide*. New York: New York University Press.

Kitchin, Robert. 2014. *The Data Revolution: Big Data, Open Data, Data Infrastructures and Their Consequences*. London: SAGE Publications.

Kitchin, Robert, and Martin Dodge. 2007. "Rethinking Maps." *Progress in Human Geography* 31:331– 344.

Kitchin, Robert, Martin Dodge, and Christopher Perkins. 2011. "Power and Politics of Mapping." In *The Map Reader: Theories of Mapping Practice and Cartographic Representation*, ed. Martin Dodge, Robert Kitchin, and Christopher Perkins, 387–394. Chichester, UK: Wiley.

Laclau, Ernesto, and Chantal Mouffe. 2001. *Hegemony and Socialist Strategy: Towards a Radical Democratic Politics*, 2nd ed. London: Verso.

Latour, Bruno. 1986. "Visualization and Cognition: Thinking with Eyes and Hands." *Knowledge and Society: Studies in the Sociology of Culture Past and Present* 6:1–40.

Lessig, Lawrence. 2003. "An Information Society: Free or Feudal?" *World Summit on the Information Society*, Geneva, Switzerland, December 10–12. https://www.itu.int/net/wsis/docs/pc2/visionaries/lessig.pdf.

Leszczynski, Agnieszka. 2012. "Situating the Geoweb in Political Economy." *Progress in Human Geography* 36 (1): 72–89.

Miller, Robin. 2004. "Wikimedia Founder Jimmy Wales Responds." *SlashdotMedia*, July 28.

Ojanperä, Sanna, Mark Graham, Ralph Straumann, R., Stephano De Sabbata, and Matthew Zook. 2017. "Engagement in the Knowledge Economy: Regional Patterns of Content Creation with a Focus on Sub-Saharan Africa." *Information Technologies and International Development* 13:33–51.

Oxford English Dictionary. 2015. "Information." *OED Online*. Oxford: Oxford University Press. http://www.oed.com/viewdictionaryentry/Entry/95568.

Perkins, Chris. 2014. "Plotting Practices and Politics: (Im)mutable Narratives in OpenStreetMap." *Transactions of the Institute of British Geographers* 39 (2): 304–317.

Pickles, John. 1994. *Ground Truth: The Social Implications of Geographic Information Systems*. London: Guilford Press.

Pickles, John. 2004. *A History of Spaces: Cartographic Reason, Mapping, and the Geo-Coded World (Frontiers of Human Geography)*. London: Routledge.

Schech, Susanne. 2002. "Wired for Change: The Links between ICTs and Development Discourses." *Journal of International Development* 14(1): 13–23. https://onlinelibrary.wiley.com/doi/10.1002/jid.870.

Shaw, Joe, and Mark Graham. 2017. "An Informational Right to the City? Code, Content, Control, and the Urbanization of Information." *Antipode* 49 (4): 907–927.

Shelton, Taylor, Ate Poorthuis, Mark Graham, and Matthew Zook. 2014. "Mapping the Data Shadows of Hurricane Sandy: Uncovering the Sociospatial Dimensions of 'Big Data.'" *Geoforum* 52:167–179.

Shirky, Clay. 2011. *Cognitive Surplus: Creativity and Generosity in a Connected Age*. London: Penguin.

Smith, Matthew L., and Katherine M. A. Reilly, eds. 2013. *Open Development: Networked Innovations in International Development*. Cambridge, MA/Ottawa: MIT Press/IDRC. https://idl-bnc-idrc.dspacedirect.org/bitstream/handle/10625/52348/IDL-52348.pdf?sequence=1&isAllowed=y.

Sui, Daniel, and Michael Goodchild. 2011. "The Convergence of GIS and Social Media: Challenges for GIScience." *International Journal of Geographical Information Science* 25 (11): 1737–1748.

Tapscott, Don, and Anthony D. Williams. 2006. *Wikinomics: How Mass Collaboration Changes Everything*. New York: Penguin.

Thompson, Peter, and Melanie Fox-Kean. 2005. "Patent Citations and the Geography of Knowledge Spillovers: A Reassessment." *American Economic Review* 95 (1): 450–460.

Touré, Hamadoun I. 2012. "U.N.: We Seek to Bring Internet to All." *Wired*, November 7. http://www.wired.com/2012/11/head-of-itu-un-should-internet-regulation-effort/.

Wilson, Matthew W. 2015. "Morgan Freeman Is Dead and Other Big Data Stories." *Cultural Geographies* 22 (2): 335–349.

Zhang, Qian, Nicola Perra, Bruno Gonçalves, Fabio Ciulia, and Alessandro Vespignani. 2013. "Characterizing Scientific Production and Consumption in Physics." *Scientific Reports* 3 (1640).

Zook, Matthew A., and Mark Graham. 2007. "The Creative Reconstruction of the Internet: Google and the Privatization of Cyberspace and DigiPlace." *Geoforum* 38 (6): 1322–1343.

Zook, Matthew, Mark Graham, Taylor Shelton, and Sean Gorman. 2010. "Volunteered Geographic Information and Crowdsourcing Disaster Relief: A Case Study of the Haitian Earthquake." *World Health and Medical Policy* 2 (2): 7–33.

6 Ecologies of (Open) Access: Toward a Knowledge Society

Laura Czerniewicz

Introduction

New forms of networked participation and open access in education and scholarship offer great opportunities to expand learning and growth. At the same time, they must flourish and compete in a world of great inequality that is fraught with contradictions. Open access in itself cannot solve the issues of unequal representation in science and scholarship; nor can it solve the tensions between the market and the commons that are inherent in the fluid and unstable global knowledge ecosystem, both of which are compounded by divisions between the Global South and Global North. In fact, this chapter argues that some innovations in openness, such as open access to scholarly publishing, can actually exacerbate those very tensions and inequalities in the system.

The geopolitics of knowledge are characterized by deep fissures and inequalities between the Global South and Global North. These are caused partially by differential resources, but also by historical power relations and determinants of legitimacy. In the academic domain, knowledge patterns reflect physically based geopolitical realities where knowledge from the Global South is treated as peripheral while knowledge from the Global North maintains dominance in terms of all the conventional metrics (Beigel 2014; Czerniewicz, Goodier, and Morrell 2016; Canagarajah 2002; Florida 2005; King 2004). The patent and citation maps produced by Florida (2005) highlight this relationship, showing peaks of these measures of innovation and knowledge clustered almost exclusively in the Global North, with the vast majority clustered in the United States and Europe. The one significant shift since Florida's 2005 description has been the dramatic rise of China in the citation rankings (Jia 2017). Aside from China's rise, however, northern dominance remains. At the same time, these knowledge realities are vigorously contested, and also powerfully fueled in higher education today by networked technologies (e.g., Internet and mobiles) in research and education, as well as new forms of scholarship, with new ecologies of access coming into existence.

Widening income disparity around the world, according to the World Economic Forum (2013), is a top global trend and a growing concern. In higher education, inequality is exacerbated by reduced state spending on higher education. For example, between 2005 and 2011, two-thirds of countries who were member countries of the Organisation for Economic Co-operation and Development (OECD) decreased their proportion of public expenditure devoted to education (OECD 2014), and more than half of developing countries reduced their spending on education between 2008 and 2012 (Seery and Arendar 2014, 91). Research funding across developed and developing countries is also inequitable. The gross domestic spending on research and development for the United States in 2012, for example, was 2.76 percent of the gross domestic product (GDP), while for South Africa, it was only 0.73 percent of GDP.[1] Declining funding has led to what can only be understood as the ironically termed *cost sharing* (i.e., sharing the costs of higher education with students and parents, a much criticized phenomenon).

In this fragile terrain, openness (featuring open content and open scholarship in particular) is often promoted as one means to level these inequalities. Yet ironically, these fissures may actually be intensified by the ways that openness is structured and regulated in the knowledge domains. Of interest in this chapter are the consequences of inequality for educational and scholarly resources. The cost of books, for instance, has risen dramatically—starkly so in developing countries when considered as a proportion of income (Liang 2009).[2] A related concern is that educational resources are generally not easily accessible to those in the Global South (Trotter et al. 2014).

This crisis in scholarly resources is playing out in a broader context of an increasingly commercialized and financialized education. Of particular concern to the access ecosystem are the threats posed by increased intellectual property (IP) rights, privatization, commodification, corporatization, lack of governmental and corporate transparency, and loss of privacy and overall disempowerment (Hess 2013).

It is in this context that digital technologies and openness are often promoted as one means to decrease inequality. The networked age also promises global digital cultures with flattened power relations, given the affordances of information and communication technologies (ICTs) to collapse distance, enable easier cross-country collaborations, and create new opportunities for knowledge production and sharing (Castells 1996).

The possibilities of the digital world have fueled demands for openness, transparency, creative contribution, and more egalitarian knowledge production and dissemination policies and practices, coupled with a greater consciousness about how knowledge is produced, by whom, for whom, and for what purpose (Comaroff and Comaroff 2012). New formations that have come into existence make it possible for those previously marginalized by infrastructural and physical constraints to participate in global education and scholarship; indeed, networked environments provide potentially hospitable places for collaboration and communication (Trotter et al. 2014). The counternarrative lies in the affordances of the Internet to change the nature of networks by making them more inclusive and easy to participate in (Castells 1996).

This openness is expressed in changing roles and emergent new practices in higher education for all stakeholders forming part of the access ecosystem. For scholars and students, the confluence of the digital with the globalization of education and the mainstreaming of open access (at least in the Global North) has seen reshaped and digitally mediated scholarly practices emerging. At every stage and level of scholarship, new ways of doing research have merged, and boundaries between the old and the new have become increasingly blurred. Within this shifting terrain, openness has been a central characteristic and an emergent practice. Open practices feature increased visibility, more collaboration, and earlier access to research. Ideas and resources have become easily shareable and more granular. New modes, methods, and genres have come into existence, and audiences have become more diverse. Forms of engagement have become multifaceted, and participation more smoothly enabled.

Publishers are also reimagining their positions and contributions to the ecosystem. Until recently, publishers would have known that their core business was concerned with content and that their business model, entrenched for centuries, was lucrative, clear, and understood by all. Now they are moving into the larger field of learning delivery and support, becoming full-spectrum service providers for classroom learning and research; encroaching on tasks performed by libraries, bookstores, teachers and administrators, and technology providers; and incorporating a variety of other student support services. Increasingly, educational publishers understand their competition not as other publishing companies, but as telecommunications companies, software companies, and information-retrieval providers (Gray and Czerniewicz 2018).

What this means for open access in education and scholarship is that assumptions have been profoundly challenged regarding content, its production, and its role in the access ecosystem. The status quo sees traditional and emergent models coexisting and jostling for dominance and legitimacy. The evolving transition to new services and licensing models is not fully understood in terms of who benefits and whose interests are being served. Also, it is clear that the role of openness in this nascent terrain is not yet settled, given the unresolved tensions in the ecosystem of access.

In this chapter, three tensions within the open access ecosystem are identified and discussed: (1) the inclusive versus exclusive nature of openness, (2) digitally open versus free content, and (3) copyright versus open content. Following that, the argument is made that the IP system itself requires rethinking if openness is to be structured in a manner that produces more equitable outcomes.

Tensions of Openness in the Access Ecosystem

Tension 1: Open as Abundant and Exclusionary?

Openness is associated with availability, with access, and indeed with abundance. It is widely agreed that with networked technologies, digital affordances, and granular multilayered provision, there has been a shift from a *scarcity* model of education to an *abundance* model. This has led to what has become known as the "age of abundance" through digital distribution and an end to content scarcity (Colombani and Videlaine 2013); indeed, the total amount of data on the Internet is estimated to be in excess of 7,900 exabytes (Gantz and Reinsel 2011). As the marginal cost of digital products has decreased to essentially zero, perfect digital copies can be produced at no extra cost, making copying essentially free (as well as extremely easy), with profound implications—and opportunities therefrom. There has simultaneously been an explosion in user-generated content. For example, as of May 2019, there are roughly 500 hours of video uploaded to YouTube every minute (Clement 2019). It is the end of the age of scarcity and the models of scarcity on which traditional access systems are founded. Scarcity models are by definition exclusionary, while abundance models promise inclusion. The question is whether they deliver on that promise.

Networked technologies have made the costs of distribution negligible. The ubiquity of open content now offers much to universities, and this is especially compelling given universities' otherwise resource-constrained circumstances. At a time when a key question has been what can be handed over to technology to save costs, improve efficiency, create opportunities, and derive other benefits, open education and open content would seem to be promising viable solutions, bringing together a set of values and assumptions about shareable knowledge and enabling technology diffusion (see, e.g., Smith and Casserly 2006; Smith 2013). In addition to these efficiencies, the opportunities align with the missions of public universities to serve the public good and the needs of civil society. Thus, there is a clear alignment with the intentions of the famous Budapest Open Access Initiative (BOAI) and the Cape Town Open Education Declaration (CTOED), which both address the Internet's potential to be an "unprecedented public good" (BOAI 2002) and serve a "collaborative, interactive culture" (CTOED 2007).

However, abundance is not equally distributed and collaboration is unlikely to be equitably experienced. An overt example of these divisions is in the ways that openness does not necessarily serve scholars and students from the margins, such as from the

Global South (see Chan and Gray 2013; Rohs and Ganz 2015). There is nothing intrinsically open about the so-called digital sphere, and, therefore, it cannot be assumed that because it enables equitable openness and abundance, it determines or creates it. Rather, it often seems that because the digital educational ecosystem echoes and feeds into the power dynamics of those in the material sphere, it likely reflects those values and indeed may exacerbate or create new forms of exclusion.

An example helps to illustrate this point. The many open access research policy mandates across Europe and North America have led to increased access and availability for scholarship from the Global North, while actually decreasing the visibility of scholarship from the Global South. Without resources (in the form of infrastructure and expertise), scholars on the margins are not able to curate their scholarship in ways that make it openly visible and discoverable. Increasingly, if it cannot be found online, it does not exist. This invisibility and discrepancy are not trivial, given that what is found online feeds into the formation of knowledge production and therefore shapes what comes to be known everywhere (Czerniewicz and Goodier 2014). While access may appear to be more widespread and models seemingly provide abundance, representation and voice are unevenly constituted in new, digitally afforded ways.

Tension 2: Open as Digital, Free, and Legal?

In a climate of abundance, there is a widespread assumption that *digital* equals *open* and *open* equals *free*. However, it is important to note that digital can also afford closed systems and analog resources (i.e., paper) sometimes can offer affordances that can be more open than a particular piece of digital resource might be. The move to digital content is a move from tangible to intangible, and often from ownership to license and digital rights management (the practice of imposing technological restrictions that control what users can do with digital media). In other words, these new digital systems are not neutral. Whether or not they lead to open or closed content is a function of value-laden decisions made by people who impose specific legal and technological frameworks.

Within these new legal and technological frameworks, a complex ecosystem of access is emerging, which exists on continua from analog to digital and from legal to illegal. Legal and open licensed content is only one option in this new ecology. New cultural practices have arisen, including piracy cultures; for many, these are considered both open and free, despite the fact that they are not legally open. Castells and Cardoso (2013, 6) have noted that "All over the world, we are witnessing a growing number of people building media relationships outside [of] institutionalized sets of rules," and that "a very significant proportion of the population is building its mediation through alternative channels of obtaining content." They also observed that "piracy cultures have become part of our everyday life in the network society, sometimes even without us fully acknowledging them as such," and they go so far as to say that "the pirates are more often than not all of *us*" (Castells and Cardoso 2013, 6). The culture has also been described as an "affective economy," which introduces an emotional aspect: as has been observed, "filesharing has emerged as one of the most popular dimensions of the new affective economy, in which it simply feels good to share and then it feels even better to embellish, remix, and share again" (Fleming 2012, 685).

There has been what might be called a *quiet encroachment*. Informal practices are becoming mainstream and acceptable as the blurring of boundaries and the breaking of rules have become the norm. These informal access practices constitute a global phenomenon that are not only limited to the developing world,[3] where common misconceptions imagine them to be neatly aligned to deficits of availability. Thus, a narrow view of openness, limited to copyrighted or legally licensed, is not an accurate reflection of the practices and understandings, even by scholars and students (Smith and Seward 2017). This conflation of *digitally* and *freely available* with *legal* is a central tension in nascent ecologies.

Research undertaken under the auspices of research on open educational resources for development (ROER4D) illustrates this tension (see chapter 12 of this volume). It revealed that educators are often unaware of the difference between an openly licensed open educational resource (OER) that can be reused legally and copyrighted material that can be downloaded from the Internet. Educators often assume that online resources are legally available for their educational use (*fair use*, in legal terms). Less than a third of university lecturers surveyed across nine countries in the Global South said that they had shared their teaching materials with an open license.

Similarly, another study, of 1,000 university students in South Africa, showed a blurring in their understanding of legal and illegal practices and a view that copyright should serve educational imperatives rather than the other way round. Students distinguished between plagiarism, with the author's right to be attributed, and copyright, which they associated with monetary gains that might be made at the expense of their right to education. The students argued that access to education must be the primary right (Czerniewicz 2017).

Tension 3: Open as Bureaucracy?

In an era where *open* generally means removing barriers, the legal sphere is one of the few areas where barriers are being added and where the terrain is becoming more complex. Legally, *open* means specifying permissions, adding layers of bureaucracy, and ironically, perhaps engaging more closely with copyright, rather than less so. This is happening at a time when the general discourse around copyright is about serious criminal actions—piracy, illegal downloading, and file sharing. Copyright is fraught, disabling, enclosing, and bureaucratic. Making copyright better through permissions processes may inadvertently make it more opaque and inaccessible, adding layers of bureaucracy instead of easing access.

This increased bureaucracy is even more problematic given that copyright is now legally the default, as noted by Liang (2005, 105): "Initially, the practices of people operated on the presumption that everything was in the public domain, except where otherwise stated, and copyright did not play much of a role. The history of copyright has centred on a reversal of this presumption to the extent that everything is assumed to be protected unless specifically stated to be in the public domain."

Thus, openness as a legal solution to the current copyright regime works to legitimize this underlying assumption of automatic copyright—and also undermines the public domain. This adds layers of complexity to a system that previously was more straightforward and presumed openness unless otherwise stated.

Beyond the Tensions: Rethinking Copyright

Given the tensions noted here, it is useful to consider that copyright in its current form may be the problem and requires rethinking. In the digital world, copying is such an essential action, and so bound up with the way that computers work, that control of copying provides, in the view of some, unexpectedly broad powers—in fact, considerably beyond those intended by copyright law (National Research Board, Computer Science and Telecommunications Board, and Committee on Intellectual Property Rights in the Emerging Information Infrastructure 2000).

It is worth looking at the original intentions of copyright—namely, as a necessary evil for the greater good that should be kept to as short a time span as possible. Baron Thomas B. Macaulay noted in 1897, "Copyright is monopoly, and produces all the effects which the general voice of mankind attributes to monopoly....It is good that authors should be remunerated; and the least exceptionable way of remunerating them is by a monopoly. Yet monopoly is an evil. For the sake of the good we must submit to the evil; but the evil ought not to last a day longer than is necessary for the purpose of securing the good" (Young 1952).

The fostering of a rich and diverse public domain has always been one of the principal rationales for copyright—"the public domain is not an unintended byproduct, or 'graveyard' of copyrighted works, but its very goal" (Birnhack 2006, 60). The intention always was to keep works in copyright for as short a time as possible—which is notably of benefit to the producer, not the intermediary—and works always were assumed to be in the public domain unless they specifically were not. The battle for the public domain remains woefully current, as exemplified by a number of recent disputes over copyright that continue to make headlines—for instance, concerning the works of Sir Arthur Conan Doyle and the "Happy Birthday to You" song.

It is hardly a new argument that knowledge should be free—"as free and general as air or water," as argued by Lord Camden in 1774, during the court case *Donaldson v. Becket*—though it has become lost in the current era of commercialization. Goethe proclaimed 400 years ago that "everything that I have seen, heard, and observed I have collected and exploited. My works have been nourished by countless different individuals....My work is the work of a collective being that bears the name of Goethe" (Frosio 2017). It is a truism to say that knowledge is an accretion, enabled by openness; it was Sir Isaac Newton, in 1676, who famously repeated the maxim of "standing on the shoulders of Giants" [as cited in Turnbull (1959, 416)]. Indeed, scholars cannot produce knowledge without access to other knowledge.

There is presently a serious risk that knowledge, which we could argue based on historical precedent ought to be free and open, is in the "vice grip of commerce," as "we are in the midst of an enclosure movement in our information environment" (Benkler 1999). Accordingly, it "is caused by the conflicts and contradictions between IP laws and the expanded capacities of new technologies. It leads to speculation that the records of scholarly communication, the foundations of an informed, democratic society, may be at risk" (Hess and Ostrom 2003, 112).

There is a need to rethink the policy environment. The IP frameworks that shape higher education's engagement with knowledge are anachronistic and outdated, and they are out of sync with the urgent needs of a digitally mediated and extremely unequal world. As discussed previously, it is in part the current IP regime that is shaping the access ecosystem in a manner that tilts the benefits toward those who already hold positions of relative power and voice.

The situation is in danger of getting worse. Many multinational trade agreement negotiations have been vehemently criticized for lack of transparency and the overreaching provisions on IP. The final version of the IP chapter of the now-defunct Trans-Pacific Partnership (TPP), for example, presented these terms: life plus 70-year copyright term (up from 50); toughened rules against circumventing digital rights management (DRM); targeting whistleblowers and journalists with criminal penalties for accessing secrets online; greater liability on Internet intermediaries; and adopting heavier criminal sanctions. Although the TPP, absent the United States, has now become the Comprehensive and Progressive Trans-Pacific Partnership at the time of writing, these proposed rules show the trajectory of IP negotiations. All these proposals are of serious concern.

How can creativity, scholarship, and learning—elements that are protected in the foundational principles of copyright—flourish in an environment of increasing control? There is a growing need for sustainable IP balances, a landscape of privacy with lots of public spaces, and sustainable development for creativity and public access for everyone to use (Aoki, Boyle, and Jenkins 2006). What happens in the copyright IP arena matters profoundly to education, and new kinds of alliances between stakeholders (including educators and public interest lawyers) are essential. At the very least, institutional IP policies need updating to reflect the changing digital environment, and academics and educators should be taking their IP contracts seriously.

Moving from a Knowledge Economy to a Knowledge Society

The tensions regarding openness in shifting access ecosystems that are explored in this chapter are being played out and disputed through fundamental contestations in education and scholarship. At the heart of these dilemmas, and thus in the tensions regarding openness, lie disagreements about the purpose of knowledge itself and the interests it serves. The tensions point to the imperative to reclaim the commons and knowledge as a public good. Here, *the commons* refers to people working together in self-governing groups that govern themselves independent of the state in order to solve problems and share knowledge and resources. While the prevailing dominant imaginary in today's information societies is *market led*, the alternative imaginaries are best described as *open* or *commons-led* (Mansell 2013). Of course, the current dominance of the copyright regime in its current form is one manifestation of the market-led imaginary. Thus, one step to achieving an alternative imaginary is the rethinking of copyright as discussed earlier in this chapter. But there is more to do.

For those wishing to ensure that knowledge remains free, with education that is fully inclusive and scholarship for the purview of all, increased attention needs to be paid to the nature and governance of the commons (specifically the digital commons). The commons are *institutions* that fall between markets and states and are vulnerable to social dilemmas and threats of enclosure (Hess 2013). It is an often-used term, with the knowledge commons or cultural commons forming only one part. Originally, it was applied to the natural commons, and it is important not to conflate the two. In the natural commons, physical resources can be overused, and one encounters depletable and exhaustible participation, rivalry, and scarcity—the so-called tragedy of the commons, wherein individuals acting in their own self-interest deplete the shared commons (Hardin 1968, 1244). In this context, *open access* has very different and negative connotations.

The digital knowledge commons, by contrast, is physical but also intangible, generative and regenerative, wherein peer production is nonrivalrous and offers abundance.

Open access in this context is a very good thing, and, if anything, there is a threat of underuse (Hess 2013). The commons for education places knowledge producers in charge. Here, cocreation and ethical and social benefits become the norm, and the knowledge *economy* shifts to a knowledge *society*. This is not merely a semantic shift; it is actually a profound conceptual shift.

Academic scholarship is premised on collaboration and sharing, and it is an educator's prerogative to reclaim knowledge as a nonrivalrous and nonexclusive public good. Individuals, alone, are not enough to stake this territory. If support for OER does not come from public bodies, such as governments and universities, the OER movement could lead to control of the system residing within a technological elite, a narrow band of activist producers, and a corporate takeover of the business side (Jones 2015).

For equitable openness to be achieved, the state has an important role to play, although not in organizing and managing education in a homogenous way. The state needs to support the 2012 Paris OER Declaration of the United Nations Educational, Scientific, and Cultural Organization (UNESCO) and policy frameworks to enable open education, to invest in the knowledge commons, and to steer the market through light touch interventions and disincentives. Universities play an essential role in owning, controlling, and managing knowledge production and dissemination, and in a digital age, they should be asserting their rights to manage their own assets. They should assert the priority of academics and authors as the agents and owners of knowledge, protect the autonomy at the heart of commons-based structures for knowledge, and develop and support collaborative initiatives in knowledge dissemination. Overall, open education is a means to an end, and it is only one—albeit an important—strategy toward an equitable, democratic, and peaceful world.

Acknowledgments

Grateful thanks for the rich resources provided by Giancarlo Frosio LLM, whose presentation (Frosio 2017) provided links to valuable references used in this chapter.

Notes

1. See OECD, "Gross Domestic Spending on R&D," https://data.oecd.org/rd/gross-domestic -spending-on-r-d.htm.

2. Liang (2009) provides the example of a dictionary, the actual cost of which is $47 in South Africa, more than double the $21.50 cost in the United States; worse, the projected cost is actually $504.50 when calculated at South African proportions of income.

3. Examples of this in the Global North include the Netherlands, where in 2014, only 10 percent of all ebooks on devices were actually paid for and most digital books were pirated (Kozlowski 2014); the United Kingdom, where up to 76 percent of the fifty most popular textbooks used by students are available as pirated ebooks (Izundu 2013); and Russia, where 92 percent of ebook readers have been found to have obtained their books by illegally downloading them (Indvik 2013).

References

Aoki, Keith, James Boyle, and Jennifer Jenkins. 2006 *Bound by Law: Tales from the Public Domain*. Durham, NC: Duke Center for the Study of the Public Domain. https://law.duke.edu/cspd/comics/zoomcomic.html.

Beigel, Femanda. 2014. "Publishing from the Periphery: Structural Heterogeneity and Segmented Circuits. The Evaluation of Scientific Publications for Tenure in Argentina's CONICET." *Current Sociology* 62 (5): 1–23.

Benkler, Yochai. 1999. "Free as the Air to Common Use: First Amendment Constraints on the Enclosure of the Public Domain," *New York University Law Review* 74 (2): 414–426.

Birnhack, Michael D. 2006. "More or Better? Shaping the Public Domain." In *The Future of the Public Domain: Identifying the Commons in Information Law,* ed. Lucie Guibault and P. Bernt Hugenholtz, 59–86. Alphen aan den Rijn, Netherlands: Kluwer Law International.

Budapest Open Access Initiative (BOAI). 2002. February 14. http://www.budapestopenaccessinitiative.org/read.

Canagarajah, A. Suresh. 2002. *A Geopolitics of Academic Writing*. Pittsburgh: University of Pittsburgh Press.

Cape Town Open Education Declaration (CTOED). 2007. "Cape Town Open Education Declaration: Unlocking the Promise of Open Educational Resources." http://www.capetowndeclaration.org/read-the-declaration.

Castells, Manuel. 1996. *The Rise of the Network Society (Information Age) Vol 1*. Oxford, UK: Blackwell.

Castells, Manuel, and Gustavo Cardoso, eds. 2012. "Editorial Introduction." *International Journal of Communication* 6 (2012): 826–833.

Chan, L, and Eve Gray. 2013. "Centering the Knowledge Peripheries through Open Access: Implications for Future Research and Discourse on Knowledge for Development." In *Open Development: Networked Innovations in International Development*, ed. Matthew L. Smith and Katherine M. A. Reilly, 197–222. Cambridge, MA/Ottawa: MIT Press/IDRC. https://www.idrc.ca/en/book/open-development-networked-innovations-international-development.

Clement, J. 2019. "Hours of Video Uploaded to YouTube every minute 2007–2019." statista.com, August 9. https://www.statista.com/statistics/259477/hours-of-video-uploaded-to-youtube-every-minute/.

Colombani, Laurent, and François Videlaine. 2013. *The Age of Curation: From Abundance to Discovery.* Boston: Bain & Company. http://www.bain.com/publications/articles/the-age-of-curation-from-abundance-to-discovery.aspx.

Comaroff, Jean, and John L. Comaroff. 2012. "Theory from the South: Or, How Euro-America Is Evolving toward Africa." *Anthropological Forum* 22 (2): 113–131.

Czerniewicz, Laura. 2017. "Student Practices in Copyright Culture: Accessing Learning Resources." *Learning Media and Technology* 42 (2): 171–184.

Czerniewicz, Laura, and Sarah Goodier 2014. "Open Access in South Africa: A Case Study and Reflections." *South African Journal of Science* 110 (9): 1–9.

Czerniewicz, Laura, Sarah Goodier, and Robert Morrell. 2016. "Southern Knowledge Online? Climate Change Research Discoverability and Communication Practices." *Information, Communication & Society* 20 (3): 386–405. doi:10.1080/1369118X.2016.1168473.

Donaldson v. Becket, 17 Parl. Hist. Eng. 953, 970–71 (H.L. 1774); 4 Burr. 4th ed. 2408, 98 Eng. Rep. 251, 257 (H.L.1774).

Fleming, Dan. 2012. "Poisoning the Affective Economy of RW Culture: Re-mapping the Agents." *International Journal of Communication* 6:669–688.

Florida, Richard. 2005. "The World Is Spiky: Globalization Has Changed the Economic Playing Field, But Has Not Levelled It." *Atlantic Monthly* 296 (3): 48–51.

Frosio, Giancarlo. 2017. "Digital Copyright: Peer Production, User-Generated Content, Access, Enclosure and the Public Domain." April 21. *Slide presentation.* http://slideplayer.com/slide/6380572/.

Gantz, John, and David Reinsel. 2011. *The 2011 Digital Universe Study: Extracting Value from Chaos.* Framingham, MA: IDC. https://www.slideshare.net/llevine/idc-report-extractingvaluefromchaos.

Gray, Eve, and Laura Czerniewicz. 2018. "Access to Learning Resources in Post-Apartheid South Africa." In *Shadow Libraries: Access to Educational Materials in Global Higher Education*, ed. Joe Karaganis, 107–157. Cambridge, MA/Ottawa: MIT Press/IDRC. https://idl-bnc-idrc.dspacedirect.org/bitstream/handle/10625/56942/IDL-56942.pdf?sequence=2&isAllowed=y.

Hardin, Garrett. 1968. "The Tragedy of the Commons." *Science* 162 (3859): 1243–1248. https://www.sciencemag.org/site/feature/misc/webfeat/sotp/pdfs/162-3859-1243.pdf.

Hess, Charlotte. 2013. "Crafting New Commons: Designing for Robust Collaboration, Participation, and Sustainability." Keynote address at Infrastructuring the Commons Conference, Aalto University, School of Arts, Design, and Architecture, Helsinki, November 7.

Hess, Charlotte, and Elinor Ostrom. 2003. "Ideas, Artifacts, and Facilities: Information as a Common-Pool Resource." *Law and Contemporary Problems* 66 (1): 111–145. April. https://scholarship.law.duke.edu/cgi/viewcontent.cgi?article=1276&context=lcp.

Indvik, Lauren. 2013. "92% of E-book Downloads in Russia Are Pirated." *Mashable.com,* July 9. http://mashable.com/2013/07/09/russia-ebook-piracy/.

Izundu, Chi Chi. 2013. "Students 'Worst' at E-book Piracy, Says Data Monitor." BBC.com. October 17. http://www.bbc.co.uk/newsbeat/article/24540745/students-worst-at-e-book-piracy-says-data-monitor.

Jia, Hepeng. 2017. "China's Citations Catching Up." natureindex.com, November 30. https://www.natureindex.com/news-blog/chinas-citations-catching-up

Jones, C. 2015. "Openness, Technologies, Business Models, and Austerity." *Learning, Media, and Technology* 40 (3): 328–349. doi:10.1080/17439884.2015.1051307.

King, David A. 2004. "The Scientific Impact of Nations." *Nature* 430 (July): 311–316.

Kozlowski, Michael 2014. "eBook Piracy a Big Deal in the Netherlands." Goodereader.com. February 5. http://goodereader.com/blog/e-book-news/ebook-piracy-big-deal-netherlands.

Liang, Lawrence. 2005. "Copyright, Cultural Production, and Open-Content Licensing." *Indian Journal of Law and Technology* 1:96–157. http://ijlt.in/wordpress/wp-content/uploads/2015/08/Liang-Copyright-Cultural-Production-and-Open-Content-Licensing-1-Indian-J.-L.-Tech.-96.pdf.

Liang, Lawrence. 2009. "Piracy, Creativity, and Infrastructure: Rethinking Access to Culture." *Alternative Law Forum*, July 20. https://papers.ssrn.com/sol3/papers.cfm?abstract_id=1436229.

Mansell, Robin. 2013. "Imagining the Internet: Open, Closed, or in Between." In *Enabling Openness: The Future of the Information Society in Latin America and the Caribbean*, ed. Bruce Girard and Fernando Perini, 9–20. Montevideo, Uruguay/Ottawa: Fundación Comunica/IDRC. https://www.idrc.ca/en/book/enabling-openness-future-information-society-latin-america-and-caribbean.

National Research Board, Computer Science and Telecommunications Board, and Committee on Intellectual Property Rights in the Emerging Information Infrastructure. 2000. *The Digital Dilemma: Intellectual Property in the Information Age*. Washington, DC: National Academies Press.

Organisation for Economic Co-operation and Development (OECD). 2014. *Education at a Glance 2014: OECD Indicators*. Paris: OECD Publishing. doi: 10.1787/eag-2014-en.

Rohs, Matthias, and Mario Ganz. 2015. "MOOCs and the Claim of Education for All: A Disillusion by Empirical Data." *International Review of Research in Open and Distributed Learning* 16 (6): 1–18. http://www.irrodl.org/index.php/irrodl/article/view/2033.

Seery, Emma, and Ana Caistor Arendar. 2014. *Even It Up: Time to End Extreme Inequality*. Oxford, UK: Oxfam. http://www.oxfamamerica.org/static/media/files/even-it-up-inequality-oxfam.pdf.

Smith, Marshall S. 2013. "Open Educational Resources: Opportunities and Challenges for the Developing World." In *Open Development: Networked Innovations in International Development*, ed. Matthew L. Smith and Katherine M. A. Reilly, 129–170. Cambridge, MA/Ottawa: MIT Press/IDRC. https://www.idrc.ca/en/book/open-development-networked-innovations-international-development.

Smith, Marshall S., and Catherine M. Casserly. 2006. "The Promise of Open Educational Resources." *Change: The Magazine of Higher Learning* 38 (5): 8–17. https://doi.org/10.3200/CHNG.38.5.8-17.

Smith, Matthew L., and Ruhiya Seward. 2017. "Openness as Social Praxis." *First Monday* 22 (4), April 3. http://firstmonday.org/ojs/index.php/fm/article/view/7073.

Trotter, Henry, Catherine Kell, Michelle Willmers, Eve Gray, and Thomas King. 2014. *Seeking Impact and Visibility: Scholarly Communication in Southern Africa.* Cape Town, South Africa: African Minds.

Turnbull, H. W., ed. 1959. "Letter to Robert Hooke Dated February 5, 1676." In *The Correspondence of Isaac Newton: 1661–1675*, Vol. 1, 416. London: Cambridge University Press.

World Economic Forum Team. 2013. *Outlook on the Global Agenda 2014.* New York: Author. http://reports.weforum.org/outlook-14/.

Young, G. M., compiler. 1952. "Speech Delivered in the House of Commons on 5th February 1841, Opposing Proposed Life+60 Years Copyright Term." In *Macaulay Prose and Poetry*, 731–743, London: Rupert Hart Davis.

7 Open Provision: Changing Economic and Human Development Perspectives

William Randall Spence and Matthew L. Smith

Introduction

This chapter starts with the premise that the impacts of open activities on economic and human development are large and increasing. These impacts come through a variety of mechanisms and are affecting all sectors. Governments are starting to recognize the opportunities presented thereby and are enacting related policies. As of early 2020, seventy-eight countries have made commitments to "make their governments more open and accountable"[1] (see chapters 10 and 11 for more on open government activities). Many countries are enacting policies in support of open educational resources (OER), with the hope of improving quality while reducing costs for education (see chapter 12 for more on OER). Nongovernmental organizations (NGOs) and community organizations are taking advantage of free software tools, content, and the ease of connecting with others. To wit, around the world, there have been over 90,000 deployments of Ushahidi, an open-source crowdsourcing platform, to address local issues.[2] Private-sector companies are similarly extracting economic value through new open business models. Studies by the Computer and Communications Industry Association have estimated the share of open activities in economic production in the United States to be about one-sixth of gross domestic product (GDP) in 2010 (Benkler 2011, 314–315), and it is growing fast.[3]

In this chapter, we focus specifically on how these changes, brought about through various open practices, might necessitate new economic understandings and explanations, specifically concerning the role of economic policy and theory in international development. The perspective is primarily micro, with some more macro dimensions of open provision explored later.

The starting point for this exploration is *open provision;* that is, the provision of the innumerable goods, services, and benefits that the private, public, and nonprofit sectors make available to consumers and recipients free of direct charge or price. The viability of open provision is based on leveraging open informational resources and voluntary human resources at little or no direct cost, together with—in the private sector in particular—revenue streams from many kinds of marketing, as well as selling consumer and/or market data to suppliers. Its expansion has been very innovative with respect to inventing and applying new provision processes and institutions. As we will see in this chapter, open provision is happening in the context of the rapidly expanding number and form of open practices throughout economic, political, social, and cultural endeavors.

This chapter begins by further defining and providing examples of open provision, and then briefly sketches two main frameworks to examine the economic dimensions of open activities: normative welfare economics, which focus on the provision of goods and services (henceforth referred to as *goods*); and the human development and capability approach (HDCA), which focuses on the expansion of human capabilities and freedoms (economic, political, social, cultural, and ethical). Following this is a policy-oriented exploration of the relationships among private, public, and open goods. This exploration reveals, in particular, that open provision extends (or, with negative goods, diminishes) both public and private goods and freedoms, thus changing the role of markets, nonprofits, and governments in providing them. Finally, the chapter provides a number of perspectives on policy and practice, with the objective of expanding the roles of open activities in the provision of goods and the advancement of human well-being.

Openness and Open Provision

Openness has many uses and meanings (Lundgren and Westlund 2016; Pomerantz and Peek 2016). Here, we draw on Smith and Seward (2017), who argue that openness is better understood in terms of processes and practices (e.g., sharing), rather than artifacts (e.g., open goods or services). They identify three main types of open processes: *open production, open distribution,* and *open consumption*. Each process consists of a series of open practices that drive the process. A quick overview of open processes and practices, with examples from the private, nonprofit, and public sectors, is provided in table 7.1.

Open Provision Definitions and Dimensions

If the provision of goods amounts to their production, distribution, and consumption, we define *open provision* to be the provision of goods and freedoms that include open practices in one or more of the provision components (production, distribution,

Table 7.1
Open practice examples in the nonprofit, public, and private sectors.

Open practice	Nonprofit sector	Public sector	Private sector
Peer production	Open-source software production; Wikipedia; open (collaborative) science (e.g., consulting blogs to solve math proofs)	Open legislation	iFixIt (a collaboratively produced repair knowledge base)
Crowdsourcing	Ushahidi applications (e.g., HarassMap) Citizen-science crowdsourcing (e.g., crowdsourcing research questions) Kiva (online development lending organization)	ICT-enabled citizen-voice (e.g., Maji Voice, Por Mi Barrio) Citizen-sourcing (e.g., e-consultation, online referendum, editing and commenting on city design plans)	TripAdvisor, Yelp Outsourcing tasks (e.g., Mechanical Turk) Crowdsourced innovation (e.g., collecting ideas from customers) Crowdfunding (e.g., Kickstarter.com)
Share, republish	Open data; OER; open access repositories; MOOCs	Open government data	OER such as MIT's OCW; Java programming language; MOOCs
Retain, reuse, revise, remix	Teachers, students reusing OER; NGOs reusing government data; researchers replicating research or working with open data	Public data interpretation	Global positioning system (GPS) data applications (companies using open government data)

or consumption). The examples provided in this chapter indicate that few (if any) goods and freedoms are completely open; at a minimum, most have important information and communication elements that use information and communication technology (ICT) infrastructure and services provided by nonopen proprietary market practices.

In terms of artifacts, open goods and open freedoms have open practices *prominently* in their provision components. But as noted, we prefer a process view of provision due to its accuracy and clarity. In this view, open provision is the provision of goods and freedoms that include open practices in one or more of its components. The provision components—production, distribution, and consumption—are further disaggregated in the following examples. The principal open practices are *peer production*, *crowdsourcing*, *sharing/republishing*, and *retaining/reusing/revising/remixing* (the 4 Rs). In addition, *nonproprietary* is a characteristic common to open practices, and *free to consumers* is typical of goods with open practices prominent in their provision.

Open Provision Cases

In this section, we present a few types of open provision that incorporate the three open practices of sharing, peer production, and crowdsourcing. All of the examples presented here are important in both less and more developed economies and societies, with some having particular importance within developing countries. It is important to note the following:

- These examples cover the full provision process (input provision, production, distribution, and consumption) of the good or freedom.

- These are stylized provision business models that do not include any focus on revenue and viability issues.

- These are types rather than specific cases (e.g., open-source software versus Mozilla Firefox or Open Office).

- These tables leave out intermediate inputs and focus on the provision of value-added and end-use consumption. Intermediate inputs typically include open activities in their provision; as a result, there are few (if any) goods and freedoms that are completely nonopen.

While we provide five case types in the following discussion, we have outlined provision models for many other specific cases. The striking feature of these instances is not that they fit easily into specific typologies, but in fact that they are dramatically diverse. The extent of innovation and adaptation of open practices in provision of goods and freedoms is truly remarkable.

Open Peer Production Provision

Examples of open peer production provision (e.g., open-source software) abound and include the popular web browser Mozilla Firefox and the Apache web server that, as of April 2017, was estimated to serve about half of all the existing websites.[4] The Open Medical Records System (OpenMRS) is a collaboratively developed, open-source electronic medical record system platform that was developed to work in resource-constrained environments.

When open-source code is developed and maintained collaboratively, open-source software provision entails open practices throughout the provision process, with market components mainly being in the ICT platforms used. However, like many other open informational resources, there are also private-sector companies that make their code open source for a variety of reasons.

This commons-based peer production model is also applied in areas outside software development, typically with the same set of open practices throughout the provision

Table 7.2
Commons-based peer production provision and the role of open and nonopen practices throughout the provision cycle.

Provision cycle	Open practices	Nonopen practices
Input provision		
Finance	Little	Market
Knowledge	Voluntary contributions	Market
Labor, skills	Volunteer	Market
Physical capital	Little	Market
Connectivity/ICT		Market/public
Management	Peer production	Market
Production/assembly	Peer production	Market
Marketing and delivery	Sharing (often via a searchable repository)	
Consumption or use	Retain, reuse, revise, remix	

cycle. For example, India's Open Source Drug Discovery project hosts an open and collaborative research platform "to accelerate drug development for neglected diseases" (Masum et al. 2013, 113). Wikipedia, one of the most highly accessed and used websites in the world, is also a variant of the peer production model. Similarly, iFixIt is a wiki-based, privately run website with collaboratively produced do-it-yourself (DIY) repair manuals for devices. Their business model includes selling the parts and tools required.

A critical element of peer production is that the open practices it entails can spawn cycles of knowledge growth, reuse, and sharing, which lead to increasing returns and knowledge spillovers (Garzarelli et al. 2008).

Crowdsourced Provision Models

Ushahidi is an open-source crowdsourcing platform developed in Kenya (and is now also offered as a software service by a private software company).[5] It has been locally implemented tens of thousands of times in both developed- and developing-country contexts for a variety of purposes, such as security, transparency, and crisis survival and management. One Ushahidi implementation, HarassMap,[6] is an Egyptian crowdmapping site for reports and testimonials of sexual harassment. The NGO that implemented HarassMap goes beyond the collection of knowledge voluntarily from participants (crowdsourcing) and leverages the open sharing of data as part of a larger process of social mobilization and sensitization, as well as change.

The public sector can also engage in *citizensourcing*, the crowdsourcing of data by soliciting information from citizens. Citizensourcing is one of a larger set of open

Table 7.3
NGO-implemented, crowdsourcing-based provision and the role of open and nonopen practices throughout the provision cycle.

Provision cycle	Open practices	Nonopen practices
Input provision		
Finance	Little	External donor funding
Knowledge	Voluntary contributions	
Labor, skills	Sharing (volunteer)	
Physical capital	Little	
Connectivity/ICT		Market
Management	NGO-led	
Production/assembly	Crowdsourcing	
Marketing and delivery	Sharing	
Consumption or use	Retain, reuse, revise, remix by NGOs	

government practices that taps into the collective knowledge of the public to produce public value creation (Hilgers and Ihl 2010).

Similar examples, but with different social and economic implications, are private sector–based crowdsourcing initiatives that then share the gathered information as part of a service. For example, TripAdvisor is a travel information service that can be accessed via either a website or a mobile app.[7] The principal data for this service come by crowdsourcing the knowledge of travelers in their reviews of places, hotels, restaurants, and other travel businesses, freely provided and shared with everyone. The rest of the provision activities are market provided (see table 7.4). Revenue to the site appears to come primarily from advertising and the selling of user data to travel and other service providers. Many similar private services, such as Yelp, also hinge on views, reviews, and evaluations by consumers and users.[8]

These services are expanding in every subsector of the economy. In finance and investment, for example, direct trading platforms provide free market data and research to investors, deriving revenue from large volumes of trades and sale of market activity and user data. In real estate, sites increasingly provide free data (e.g., assessments) and links to service providers (e.g., financial, legal, or staging).

Sharing and Republishing

In this section, we will examine two examples: OER and open government data. OER are defined as "teaching, learning, and research resources that reside in the public domain or have been released under an intellectual property (IP) license that permits

Table 7.4
Private sector–based crowdsourcing provisions (e.g., TripAdvisor) and the role of open and nonopen practices throughout the provision cycle.

Provision cycle	Open practices	Nonopen practices
Input provision		
Finance		Market
Knowledge	Voluntary contributions	
Labor, skills	Sharing (volunteer)	Market
Physical capital	Little	
Connectivity/ICT		Market
Management	Firm-led crowdsourcing	
Production/assembly	Crowdsourcing	
Marketing and delivery		Market
Consumption or use		

free use and re-purposing by others" (Smith and Casserly 2006, 9). The first prominent example of OER came in the form of the Open CourseWare (OCW) offered by the Massachusetts Institute of Technology (MIT), where MIT made the content of their courses openly available on their website in 2002.[9] Since then, OER have taken thousands of forms, from open textbooks to online course modules to massive open online courses (MOOCs), with important implications for the societies and governments of countries in the Global South (Smith 2013).

There are a huge variety of OER available and a very diverse set of production models for their creation. For example, Siyavula Education, an education technology company in South Africa, emerged out of a group that facilitated a collaborative authoring process of openly licensed textbooks. Open textbooks are freely available to teachers and students across the country to download and use as desired. Another model of open production was tried in the state of Utah, when the government decided to support open textbooks in key curriculum areas in 2012. A pilot study found that this model of producing open textbooks can reduce costs by 50 percent or more (Wiley et al. 2012).

OER have many users, and educational initiatives can leverage the existence of a wide variety of high-quality OER. For example, the Darakht-e Danesh project, run by the nonprofit group Canadian Women for Women in Afghanistan, created a web portal for open educational content from around the world, and curated and translated to fit the Afghanistan curriculum (Oates and Hashimi 2016). Afghanistan's teachers can and do contribute content to the web portal as well. Another example is the Rumie

Table 7.5
Typical OER provision model showing the role of open practices throughout the provision process.

Provision cycle	Open practices	Nonopen practices
Input provision		
Finance		Market
Knowledge	Sharing, 5 Rs	
Labor, skills		Market
Physical capital		(Little)
Connectivity/ICT		Market
Management		NGOs
Production/assembly	Crowdsourcing	
Marketing and delivery	Sharing	
Consumption or use	Retain, reuse, revise, remix	

Initiative, run by a nonprofit organization based in Canada. Experts and communities choose top-quality open educational materials, put them on tablets, and provide them to underresourced schools in developing countries and to First Nations communities in Canada. The principal inputs for the Rumie Initiative are OER, ICT connectivity, very low-cost tablets produced by a supplier in China, financing (partly crowdsourced online), and management (a virtual network of individuals and organizations).

Open government data are publicly shared governmental informational resources. Governments typically disclose their data for a variety of reasons that "run on a spectrum between *service delivery* and *public accountability*" (Yu and Robinson 2012, 182) ideally resulting in a wide range of potential economic, social, and political benefits (Verhulst and Young 2016). One example of a public accountability application of open data in Uruguay is A Tu Servicio, an app that provides an easy-to-use interface to open government health data, allowing citizens to compare local healthcare providers based on a variety of key indicators (A Tu Servicio is discussed in more detail in chapter 11). The traditional provision cycle of open government data contains only a few open practices at the delivery and consumption end (see table 7.6).

There are several other models of open government data provision beyond governments making existing data available. Governments and NGOs, for example, run crowdsourcing processes to generate relevant data. Assessments of when such ICT-enabled citizen voices lead to government responsiveness is provided by Peixoto and Fox (2016). It is also common for intermediaries such as NGOs to work with open government data, often repackaging and republishing the information for a particular purpose and audience (van Schalkwyk et al. 2014). In other instances, NGOs might

Table 7.6
Typical open government data provision model showing the role of open practices throughout the provision process.

Provision cycle	Open practices	Nonopen practices
Input provision		
Finance		
Knowledge		Public
Labor, skills		Public
Physical cap.ital		Little
Connectivity/ICT		Market
Management		Public (bureaucracy)
Production/assembly	Crowdsourcing	Public (bureaucracy)
Marketing and delivery	Sharing	
Consumption or use	Retain, reuse, revise, remix	

gather government-held data through a variety of means (such as freedom of information requests), compile and curate them, and then share them publicly as open government data. For example, in Mexico, the Mejora Tu Escuela (Improve Your School) project works to encourage parents' engagement in the education of their children and to combat corruption in the education sector (Verhuslt and Young 2016). It does so through a portal that presents (mostly previously inaccessible) data from Mexico's Ministry of Education, including information on school infrastructure, locations, standardized test results, and teacher assessments. The portal also includes some national census data, which were not originally released by the government but were leaked to NGOs (Verhulst and Young 2016).

Open Provision Platforms

Key parts of the open provision ecosystem are the platforms that enable open practices and the provision of goods and freedoms, which themselves have varying provision models. The platforms can be either technological infrastructure (such as the Internet) or the application layer (typically websites or apps). The Internet is mainly privately provided and not free to users. The major access and social platforms, including those of Google and Apple as well as Facebook and Twitter, are generally free to users. Their services do come at some cost to the user in terms of privacy and loss of control over the data that they generate from using the platforms; indeed, the huge number of users makes the platforms highly valuable for advertising, as well as consumer and market data acquisition.

Emergence and Economics of Open Provision

Sharing digital informational resources at scale, typically over the Internet, has emerged as a central practice since the middle of the 1990s. The rise of the prevalence of open processes is directly linked to the increasing spread of low-cost connectivity and information capabilities of the digital revolution, in the form of increasingly accessible and less costly Internet and information technology platforms and means.

This rise of open processes and provision in all institutional economic sectors— public, private, nonprofit, and personal (individual and household)—has meant that the economic impacts of open provision have grown considerably in the last two decades (Benkler 2013). This economic activity emerges not just from new models of peer-to-peer production that fall outside of the public and private sectors, as Benkler describes, but also from state (e.g., open government data) and private actors.

The reason that open practices are gaining in significance is because they can add value and reduce cost (i.e., increase efficiency in the provision of goods and freedoms) or provide novel and more effective means to accomplish specific goals or fill particular demands (see table 7.7 for a brief overview of the benefits and costs of engaging in the various open practices). Of course, there is no such thing as a free lunch—content might be free (in terms of price), but there are always some associated costs, be they connecting to the Internet or other resource costs or abdicating control over personal data and privacy. These costs need to be covered in some manner in order for provision to be viable. Open practices in provision also often help to reduce information asymmetries between providers and users, thus helping with another aspect of inefficiency in market provision.

Many of the kinds of benefits and costs in table 7.7 are very difficult, if not impossible, to measure. This is because open activities typically are free to users, and their inputs are often voluntary—that is, there is no wage or price attached to them or they are difficult or impossible to value for other reasons. Consequently, their value does not receive proper consideration or weight in national accounts and productivity estimates.

Economic Frameworks and Open Provision

Normative Welfare Economics

Economic analysis of open provision needs a particular economic framework. Here, we draw on what we consider to be the two most relevant frameworks: normative welfare economics (market economics plus public finance) and the human development and capability approach (HCDA). The former, which focuses on the provision of goods and services, has been at the heart of the postwar Western economies and globalization.

Table 7.7
Benefits and costs of engaging in open practices.

Open practice	Benefits	Costs
Sharing	Democratization of knowledge (increasing access to knowledge) Improved quality of content through self-monitoring (knowing that content will be seen by many) and building reputation	Hosting costs Time to produce and share content Reinforcing/exacerbating existing inequalities The risk that sharing poor-quality content hurts reputation
Transparency	Build legitimacy, trust Greater efficiency and effectiveness of services through reduced corruption	Cynicism (negative information decreases trust and legitimacy) Resistance and undermining of transparency measures
Reuse	Time and cost savings Innovation around shared content (e.g., apps based on open data)	Time to find content Filtering poor content Cost of support, maintenance, support
Revise	Locally appropriate content Economic/cultural innovation	Time, cost of customization Training staff
Remix	Creation of novel content Economic/cultural innovation	Time
Crowdsourcing	New, low-cost source of ideas, data, content, funds, and human resources	Costs (e.g., running a crowdsourcing platform) Verification and validation of data sources
Peer production	Improved quality of content through peer feedback High-quality content New communities	Costs of hosting and governance of the peer-production process Lack of support for produced content

Source: Adapted from Smith (2014).

The latter is, in fact, much broader than an economic framework per se, as it focuses on the provision of capabilities and freedoms—economic, political, social, cultural, and ethical.

Normative welfare economics, as described by Smith et al. (2011, 83n13), are observed to be a "body of economic theory that addresses maximizing the material welfare of a society and its individuals—welfare derived from consumption of goods and services— and public finance for public goods and services.... Normative welfare economics includes equity as well as efficiency considerations, and provides analysis of equity characteristics of market functioning and of public economic activity—expenditures, taxes, policies, and regulations."

Normative welfare economics recognize that governments play a key role in the provision of public goods such as national defense, health, education, law/justice, environmental protection, and social services. These goods are either not typically organized by market mechanisms (defense and justice) or privately provided in suboptimal amounts (health and education). Public goods comprise about a quarter of the GDP of most economies, and, next, we explore their characteristics in detail in comparison with those of open goods.

The Human Development and Capability Approach

Our second economic framework is the HDCA. A detailed introduction of this concept is beyond the scope of this chapter, but its central ideas include human functionings, capabilities, freedoms, and agency.

The definitions of the key terms of the HDCA are as follows:

- *Functionings*, as noted by Sen (1999a, 75), are defined as "the various things a person may value doing or being." In other words, functionings are valuable activities and states that make up people's well-being, such as being healthy and well nourished, being safe, being educated, having a good job, and being able to visit loved ones. They are also related to goods and income, but they describe what a person is able to do or be with these. For example, when people's basic need for food (a commodity) is met, they enjoy the functioning of being well nourished.

- *Capability* refers to the freedom to enjoy various functionings. In particular, the term is defined, by Sen (1992, 40), as "the various combinations of functionings (beings and doings) that the person can achieve…reflecting the person's freedom to lead one type of life or another." In other words, capabilities are "the substantive freedoms [that a person] enjoys to lead the kind of life he or she has reason to value" (Sen 1999a, 87).

- *Agency*, in turn, is defined as the ability to pursue goals that one values and has reason to value. An agent, therefore, is "someone who acts and brings about change" (Sen 1999a, 19).

Perhaps the key area of difference between normative welfare economics and the HDCA framework is that the latter focuses on more dimensions of human prosperity or flourishing—specifically, social, political, cultural, and ethical dimensions—than just material (i.e., economic) ones (Sen 1999a). Table 7.8 provides an overview of the differences between normative welfare economics and the HDCA.

Table 7.8
Comparing normative welfare economics with the HDCA.

	Normative welfare economics	HDCA
Principal goal	Economic growth; the expansion of material production/consumption on average	Human flourishing as the expansion of freedoms (with agency) for everyone
Equity	Disputed	Built-in
Dimensions of prosperity	Material (economic)	Economic, social, political, cultural, and ethical

Welfare economics draws a blank on what specific public goods should be produced and consumed because consumers' preferences do not translate directly into production decisions, as with markets and private goods. One central pursuit of the HDCA, therefore, has been to develop workable theories and processes of social choice and justice (Sen 1999b). In this respect as well, work that has extended the original HDCA conceptualization recognizes and emphasizes the central role of power—and the interests of the powerful—in governance and policymaking (Spence and Deneulin 2010). This is a dimension often absent in the analytic focus of normative welfare economics on efficiency and equity.

Open informational resources, practices, and provisions appear to have strong implications, in terms of both potential and challenges, for equity, informed public discourse, social and public choice, and the provision of all varieties of freedoms.

Open, Public, and Private Goods and Freedoms

Many meanings of the term *public goods* are in current use, based on attributed characteristics of the goods (artifacts). We review these perspectives here before suggesting better process (provision) views or definitions of public goods.

As previously mentioned, normative welfare economics considers public goods as those that the market or the nonprofit sector would not provide in the right amounts (or forms), and thus their provision is organized and also might be carried out by government. In this conception, public goods, in fact, are mostly services. Government provides physical goods, such as roads and military equipment, but most government economic involvement is by providing services, including organizing the provision of services, financing them, and actually producing and delivering them. Government organizes and finances defense, for example, and military forces (which are essentially governmental) deliver the service, while private industry provides military hardware and much of the technology. In many countries, sectors such as education and health are both publicly and privately provided. Government is also involved in regulation in all sectors, and regulatory services are particularly prominent in some.

Public goods have also been characterized in terms of two main aspects—excludability (whether individuals can be excluded from use of the good) and rivalry (whether one individual's use of a good reduces its availability to others). These concepts have been key to arguments about why their provision is not done at all, or not done well, by markets. A well-known matrix that characterizes (material) goods and services is shown in table 7.9.

Public Goods in the Digital World

We suggest that this characterization of public and private goods requires some updating. The world has changed considerably since this original formulation, in particular with the advent of increasingly abundant free and open informational resources and the emergence of open practices and provision. Hence, it would be informative to bring this table up to date and include newer examples of goods and services that contain open processes. These examples challenge the idea that goods are rivalrous or excludable by nature, regardless of how the component activities of their provision are organized. They also help to explain the underlying reasons for rivalry and exclusion, which look particularly important in the current world of digital content. In this section, we offer an alternative to the rivalrous or excludable matrix to understand public and private goods in relation to open goods.

The notion behind excludable goods, which include doughnuts and journal subscriptions, is that it is possible to restrict who can consume them. Because each individual receives all the benefit, sellers can appropriate the revenue, and these goods are

Table 7.9
Private and public goods.

		Excludability	
		Easy (exclusive)	Difficult (nonexclusive)
Subtractibility (Rivalrousness)	High	Private goods Personal computers, doughnuts, food, cars, and personal electronics	Common-pool resources Libraries, irrigation systems, fish stocks, timber, and coal
	Low	Toll or club goods Journal subscriptions, day-care centers, private parks, cable and satellite television, Netflix	Public goods Useful knowledge, sunsets, free-to-air television, national defense

Source: Adapted from Hess and Ostrom (2007).

generally provided and sold by private market organizations. Nonexclusive goods, such as libraries and free-to-air television, are typically provided by public and nonprofit organizations (although sometimes by the private sector as well) free of direct charge (i.e., price) to consumers.

However, the distinction between exclusive and nonexclusive goods, as originally made, does not hold as accurately now, particularly with the advent of the Internet and digital goods. In practice, it is perhaps more accurate to assess exclusion versus inclusion on the basis of how the good is provided (process), rather than its inferred nature (artifact). Movies and television programs, for example, are nonexclusively provided on free-to-air television via antennae (of which there are few left), exclusively on cable or paid Internet services (such as Netflix or Hulu), and inclusively on free-to-user Internet services (such as YouTube).

The notion of rivalry is also not as clear cut in a digital world. The basic notion is that consumption or use by one person either prevents or detracts from use by, and benefit to, others. On the side of exclusive goods, this separates out *club goods*, which are physically consumed jointly by users (cinemas, private parks, or airplane, train, and bus rides) but still are paid separately by each consumer. Some club goods (movies) can be rivalrous or not in different provision models (cinemas, Netflix). Club goods comprise a relatively small subset of exclusive goods—those physically consumed collectively.

On the side of nonexclusive goods, rivalry is said to separate out *common goods*, such as timber and fish stocks, because their supply is so large relative to demand that they are considered to be effectively free. However, are there many common goods left? Real wilderness areas (not public parks that people pay fees to visit), for example, remain a dwindling luxury in most developed countries, and increasingly so in developing ones. Even clean water and air are increasingly scarce in many cities around the world. Unlike the diminishing physical commons, the knowledge commons is growing rapidly, with growing populations and communications adding to stocks rather than diminishing them. Nonrivalry—one user not diminishing availability to others—is in fact a powerful basis of much of the explosion of the open provision of goods and freedoms.

Given the revisions just indicated, we propose a revised matrix of exclusiveness and openness in goods provision, shown in table 7.10.

In this schema, open goods are found in five categories: open publicly (state) provided goods and services, open private services that are free to users, common goods, knowledge commons, and other largely open goods, including open-source software and OER provided often by the nonprofit or voluntary sector.[10]

Many publicly provided services are starting to incorporate open practices in their provision. Indeed, this even means that sometimes the benefits of some government

Table 7.10

Exclusively and nonexclusively provided goods: Proposed revised list.

	More exclusively provided goods (individual/household benefit)	More inclusively provided goods (collective benefit)

Nonopen goods	Privately (market) provided goods and services
	    Food and medicines (private, perishable goods)
	    Clothing and electronics (private, semidurable goods)
	    Cars and housing (private, durable goods)
	    Insurance, travel, and entertainment (private, business services)
	    Education and health (private, social services)	

	Publicly (state) provided exclusive goods and services
	    Fish, timber, minerals, oil, and gas (public, licensed resources)
	    Toll roads, electricity, and water (public utilities)
		Publicly (state) provided nonexclusive goods and services (public goods)
		    Education, health, and social security (public social services)
		    Defense, police, and justice (public security services)
		    Telecom and finance regulation (public regulatory services)
		    Public roads and airports (public, infrastructure)

	Privately provided club goods (cinemas, private parks, and airline/bus trips, Netflix, e-books, software such as Microsoft Word)	

Openly provided (shared) goods		Open public-sector goods
		    Open government data, accountability, and consultation/referenda services
		Open private services
		    TripAdvisor reviews, iFixIt repair manuals, Google search results
		Common goods (goods from common-pool resources)
		    Clean water and air, inhabitable climate
		Knowledge commons goods
		    In public domain or released under an IP license that permits free use and repurposing by others (e.g., OER, open-source software, Wikipedia, open access to scholarly publishing)

activities, such as funding open textbooks as part of their education provision, can spread beyond the borders of that government's particular jurisdiction. Further, within the public sector, there are highly open goods and freedoms based on the provision of open informational resources (e.g., open data initiatives and referendums).

How much insight does one gain by categorizing goods in these ways? In normative welfare economics, the defining of *public goods* was intended to specify which goods are not provided (either efficiently or at all) by markets, yet are demanded by people, so their provision needs to be organized by government. The emergence of open goods adds complications and a more nuanced view of government roles.

More specifically, open provision models arguably offer alternatives where both markets and the public sector fall short of supplying goods and freedoms that are in demand. To market provision, they add new goods (such as free applications and content) and services (such as user reviews) that help to reduce information asymmetries between sellers and buyers. To public provision, they add new ways (such as referendums) to identify demand for public goods and freedoms, greater reach and quality of public services (e.g., through OER or by offering open government data to make public expenditures and activities more transparent), and new goods and freedoms (such as crowdmapping and crisis management) that need voluntary input to succeed.

Although public policy has many purposes in addressing public goods, key questions in both normative welfare economics and the HDCA frameworks is about what public goods to provide and how to organize the provision. With the explosion of new open goods and freedoms now occurring, reformulating the theory of public goods is needed to guide public provision decisions and policy and improve informed public discourse, social choice, and social justice.

In this context, an important feature of open provision in the personal and non-profit sectors is simply the possibility that people can organize the provision of collective benefit goods and freedoms without the process requirements and constraints of public organization, consensus requirements, and funding. On the whole, this should add greatly to the overall efficiency of providing valued goods and freedoms and, hence, to the flourishing of humanity. However, as chapters 1 and 6 illustrate, open provision can lead to the increased efficiency of provision of social *bads* as well as goods. This concept will be discussed briefly in the following section.

Policy and Research Implications

Phenomena as large as open provision might be expected to have a wide range of major implications for public policy and action. Here, we have picked out some main areas from the analysis—namely, public provision of digital goods and freedoms, IP, employment and social protections, privacy and security, and a cluster that includes agency, social choice, and political freedoms.

Public Provision

To what extent should governments be active in the provision of open goods and freedoms? While the particulars of each national government will be highly influential, we provide next just a quick review of a few areas where governments are engaged or could benefit from engaging in open provision. This brief discussion is indicative rather than comprehensive, focusing on goods provision; public curtailment of the provision of bads is addressed separately in the "Privacy and Security" section later in this chapter.

Education   Given the public goods nature of an educated population, it is not surprising that most governments attempt to provide public education for all. However, there is variation in the abilities and commitments of governments to cover the cost of educational resources. Some governments are adopting open practices in the provision of educational resources, such as making all educational resources that are funded by the government openly licensed, and thus reusable for free by students. There are some emerging models that seem to be working. For example, in British Columbia, Canada, the Ministry of Advanced Education launched the BC Open Textbooks project to provide open textbooks in the subject areas with the highest enrollment levels. With this model, the government pays comparatively less than the original outlay to have the books updated annually. This means that not only are the books free to teachers and students, but they are also more up to date than previously published alternatives. Such an approach may be doubly beneficial for developing countries if there is a focus on working with in-country authors, considering that foreign publishers are often highly active in developing-country markets (Toledo et al. 2014).

Governance   As discussed previously, open data initiatives by governments have expanded rapidly, with the potential to improve governance across a wide range of areas. The availability of open government data is also argued to enable much value creation by the private sector—estimated by some to be in the trillions worldwide (Manyika et al. 2013). Furthermore, there are also many examples of government use of crowdsourcing to improve service delivery in education, health, water, waste management, and other areas, as well as a means to foster broader public participation (Bott and Young 2012; Gigler and Bailur 2014; Peixoto and Fox 2016). In many countries, both less and more developed, improving the public, private (e.g., social media), and nonprofit mechanisms furthering political engagement and consensus building is a key public policy challenge.

Intellectual Property Protection   While IP has a long history, its relative significance for economic and human development is arguably only increasing given our shift toward increasingly knowledge-based societies. IP protection has been supported mainly on the ideas of fairness to inventors and incentive for research and development, and, on the other hand, it has been challenged throughout its history on the grounds that it stifles innovation. The current copyright regime hampers one of the core affordances of the Internet (easily sharing digital goods) and thus limits the sharing of ideas, knowledge, and resources that are fundamental to key social functions such as education (Wiley 2017). The emergence of open provision provides a fundamental challenge to the current dominant IP regime and competition policy. Drawing on examples of the major innovations in the Internet, Yochai Benkler (2011, 318–320) argues that the freedoms extended by more flexible IP policy ("freedom to operate") are more important than strong IP protection in driving this innovation.

There is also an emerging body of knowledge on practical ways in which knowledge is appropriated and used for innovation in informal sectors of developing countries. In a synthesis of five case studies of informal sector innovation in sub-Saharan Africa, de Beer and Armstrong (2015) found that informal sector innovators adopted open practices (particularly sharing), although they were not necessarily digital. The key point is that the protection of IP rights did *not* play a significant role in spurring innovation.

Similarly, Mizukami and Lemos (2008) describe a business model for local Technobrega musicians in Brazil that is also predicated on giving away their music to street vendors, who then sell it. The goal for the musicians is to share their music broadly to gain popularity. Then they host street concerts for which they can charge admission. It mirrors online freemium models, which give away some basic services or content, but then charge for extras. These perspectives are particularly significant, given that in many developing countries, the informal economy constitutes the majority of the economic activity.

Much more could be said about IP policy and the law. Open innovation analysis, for example, describes the relationship between open innovation and IP and recommends appropriate IP and other marketplace framework policy measures (de Beer 2016). For example, there is an argument for policy neutrality between the proprietary firm-based system developed throughout the Industrial Revolution and the rapidly emerging open and collaborative needs of open innovation and provision.

Nonneutrality of infrastructure poses another large set of diverse interests facing IP and competition policy (Fuster Morell 2014). Monopolization occurs in many ways through a demand-side discoverability dynamic where, for example, despite the wide diversity of a particular type of content, those elements that are easily found on Google will dominate greatly, while the rest exist in the long shadow of dwindling use (see also chapter 6).

Employment and Social Protection   It is difficult to measure the current extent of open provision and how far and fast it will expand. Available studies suggest that open provision—in the sense of industries that depend on and benefit from limitations to copyright, rather than its extension—comprise about one-sixth of the US GDP (Benkler 2011). In the case of open provision, trends or limits might be easier to approach than current levels. One interesting perspective on the potential is the aggregate amount of time that individuals spend on the consumption of open-activity goods and freedoms. According to Shirky (2010, 10), "Americans watch roughly two hundred billion hours of TV every year.... Even tiny subsets of this time are enormous: we spend roughly a hundred million hours every weekend just watching commercials."

Open provision looks likely to expand greatly on the basis of so-called big data and data exhaust, as well as sheer innovation, rather than the amounts of human and capital resources used in provision. The impact of artificial intelligence (AI), for example, is already substantial and growing fast. One large area includes the studying of user and market behavior and the tailoring of provision and marketing to individual preferences. Where AI may lead is hard to guess. Its possible applications were suggested by Sebastian Thrun, founder of Google X (Thrun 2017):

> My students and I recently did work on artificial intelligence for detecting skin cancer, and we found that if we train an artificial intelligence with about 130,000 images, we can find skin cancer basically using an iPhone as accurately as the best board-certified dermatologist.... Every time I talk through my phone—and it's probably about an hour a day—it could analyze my speech and thereby find things like Alzheimer's much, much, much earlier than we find it today.

Open provision in many cases displaces jobs and employment (e.g., appliance repair people and real estate agents). AI and robotization extend this potential in both lower- and higher-skilled employment. This is one part of a picture of uncertain employment prospects associated with technology, automation, digitalization, and globalization, among other areas. Employment and social security implications require public policy responses.

It is noted that open provision models, including intelligent job search and matching, counter the "fatalism that we are powerless to harness what we create to improve our lives—and indeed our jobs" (Spence and Manyika 2015, 1). Nevertheless, open provision contributes to the possibility of widespread prosperity without widespread employment and the need for political action and social protection (e.g., guaranteed income) to resolve who gets what. In many developing countries, where social and economic security mechanisms are not very developed and where full-time employment is rarer and temporary or freelance work more common, current and coming challenges are substantial.

Privacy and Security   It is clear that open provision can provide bads and restraints, as well as goods and freedoms. One example is the use of online platforms where the ease of sharing can support the recruitment and radicalization of individuals, who in turn may participate in terrorist activities. Similarly, one can use these platforms for bullying, hate campaigns, and political manipulation where provision reduces rather than expands freedoms. Another set of privacy and security concerns surrounds major open platforms and the theft and misuse of personal data from user repositories (cybercrime). These and other concerns (e.g., cyberwarfare) apply to proprietary (corporate, military) provision processes, as well as open ones and, while important, are well beyond the scope of this chapter. One thing that seems clear is that the Internet and the high-volume provision that it enables—both open and proprietary—are facing much higher security and privacy costs than in the past, as both security and privacy are essential to sustain openness and broad public participation. They are also facing major substantive challenges for public policy and participation, reflecting greater difficulty than expected in identifying and managing or countering highly negative behavior.

Agency, Social Choice, and Political Freedoms   Open provision can promote agency, social choice, and political freedoms, which are three major concerns of the HDCA. The idea that open provision activities tend to promote agency does not seem far-fetched when one looks at people's personal contributions in terms of commitment, time, effort, skills, knowledge, experience, management, and finance. In many cases, connectivity and platforms allow people to be engaged in the provision of goods and freedoms that they value and have reason to value. Open activities certainly can serve the provision of informed public discourse, social choice, social justice, and political freedoms, which are not small matters. For instance, public consultation processes are examples from the public sector, and many of the Ushahidi-based initiatives are examples on the nonprofit side.

On the other hand, open activities can also pollute public discourse and thus effectively reduce political freedoms and social choice. One prominent example is the emergence of deliberate misinformation as legitimate news stories (i.e., what has become known as *fake news*) as a genuine threat to democratic governance. The prevalence of misinformation has become significant enough that some social media platforms, such as Twitter, have proposed measures to counter its spread. Security dimensions of fake news have also been highlighted by Russia's activities before and after the 2016 election in the United States. Given the effectiveness of these techniques, such interference in political processes is increasing—with organized disinformation campaigns found in 48 countries in 2018 (Bradshaw and Howard 2018.)

Furthermore, the tailoring of free content based on an individual's past actions by social media platforms serves only to further fragment society, creating separate realities and alternative facts, dramatically undermining the possibility for meaningful dialogue. Indeed, it is an open question as to whether democracies will survive in such a context.[11]

Afterword

The reality and rapid expansion of open provision necessitate a change in the nature of economic theory and analysis. A simple example from this chapter is that it is no longer adequate to address economic efficiency, equity, and stability in terms of private and public goods. Rather, one must include open provision across the public, private, nonprofit, and personal sectors. Digital provision—both open and proprietary—is transforming economies in terms of goods and freedoms provided, work, IP, competition, and security. Because proprietary provision has been the dominant mode of market economies, the large open portion of digital provision is, in our view, the most transformative part. Like the future of open provision, its ultimate impact on economic thinking is in the early stages and very hard to predict. Nevertheless, the discussion should prove both valuable and interesting.

Notes

1. See Open Government Partnership (n.d.).

2. See Ushahidi (n.d.).

3. As freely shared goods have no price and often have voluntary labor and inputs, data on their extent come only from infrequent studies.

4. See W3Techs (n.d.).

5. See Ushahidi (n.d.). Its Twitter account is at https://twitter.com/ushahidi.

6. See HarassMap (n.d.).

7. See TripAdvisor (2018).

8. Benkler's (2015) view of TripAdvisor and Yelp as examples of firm-based peer production is also a reasonable way of viewing their provision models.

9. See MIT (2018). Over 200 other universities around the world have subsequently made courseware openly available online. For more information, consult http://www.oeconsortium.org/members/.

10. Some of these services aim to make governments more open or responsive, but these are organized outside government and so are distinguished from open public activities, where governments themselves are the providers.

11. See Helbing et al. (2017).

References

Benkler, Yochai. 2011. "Growth-Oriented Law for the Networked Information Economy: Emphasizing Freedom to Operate over Power to Appropriate." In *Rules for Growth: Promoting Innovation and Growth through Legal Reform: The Kauffman Task Force on Law, Innovation, and Growth*, ed. The Kauffman Taskforce on Law, 313–342. Kansas City, MO: Ewing Marion Kauffman Foundation. http://www.kauffman.org/~/media/kauffman_org/research%20reports%20and%20covers/2011/02/rulesforgrowth.pdf.

Benkler, Yochai. 2013. "Foreword." In *Open Development: Networked Innovations in International Development*, ed. Matthew L. Smith and Katherine M. A. Reilly, vii–ix. Cambridge, MA/Ottawa: MIT Press/IDRC. https://www.idrc.ca/en/book/open-development-networked-innovations-international-development.

Bott, Maja, and Gregor Young. 2012. "The Role of Crowdsourcing for Better Governance in International Development." *Praxis the Fletcher Journal of Human Security XXVII*, 47–70.

Bradshaw, Samantha, and Philip N. Howard. 2018. "Challenging Truth and Trust: A Global Inventory of Organized Social Media Manipulation," Oxford Internet Institute's Computational Propaganda Research Project. July. http://comprop.oii.ox.ac.uk/wp-content/uploads/sites/93/2018/07/ct2018.pdf.

De Beer, Jeremy. 2016. "Evidence-Based Intellectual Property Policymaking: An Integrated Review of Methods and Conclusions: Evidence-based Intellectual Property Policymaking." *Journal of World Intellectual Property* 19 (5–6): 150–177. https://doi.org/10.1111/jwip.12069.

De Beer, Jeremy, and Chris Armstrong. 2015. "Open Innovation and Knowledge Appropriation in African Micro and Small Enterprises (MSEs)." *African Journal of Information and Communication (AJIC)* Iss. 16. http://wiredspace.wits.ac.za/bitstream/handle/10539/19315/AJIC-Issue-16-2015-De-Beer-Armstrong.pdf.

Fuster Morell, Mayo. 2014. "Governance of Online Creation Communities for the Building of Digital Commons: Viewed through the Framework of the Institutional Analysis and Development." In *Governing Knowledge Commons*, ed. Brett M. Frischmann, Michael J. Madison, and Katherine J. Strandburg, Chapter 8. Oxford: Oxford University Press. https://papers.ssrn.com/sol3/papers.cfm?abstract_id=2842586.

Garzarelli, Giampaolo, Yamina R. Limam, and Bjørn Thomassen. 2008. "Open Source Software and Economic Growth: A Classical Division of Labor Perspective." *Information Technology for Development* 14 (2): 116–135.

Gigler, Björn-Sören, and Bailur, Savita, eds. 2014. *Closing the Feedback Loop: Can Technology Bridge the Accountability Gap?* Washington, DC: World Bank. http://elibrary.worldbank.org/doi/book/10.1596/978-1-4648-0191-4.

HarassMap.org. n.d. "HarassMap." http://harassmap.org/en/.

Helbing, Dirk, Bruno S. Frey, Gerd Gigerenzer, Ernst Hafen, Michael Hagner, Yvonne Hofstetter, Jeroen van den Hoven, Roberto V. Zicari, and Andrej Zwitter. 2017. "Will Democracy Survive Big Data and Artificial Intelligence?" *Scientific American*, February 25. https://www.scientificamerican.com/article/will-democracy-survive-big-data-and-artificial-intelligence/.

Hess, Charlotte, and Elinor Ostrom. 2007. "Introduction: An Overview of the Knowledge Commons." In *Understanding Knowledge as a Commons: From Theory to Practice*, ed. Charlotte Hess and Elinor Ostrom, 3–26. Cambridge, MA: MIT Press.

Hilgers, Dennis, and Christoph Ihl. 2010. "Citizensourcing: Applying the Concept of Open Innovation to the Public Sector." *International Journal of Public Participation* 4 (1): 67–88.

Lundgren, Anna, and Hans Westlund. 2016. "The Openness Buzz in the Knowledge Economy: Towards Taxonomy." *Environment and Planning C: Government and Policy* 35 (6): 975–989.

Manyika, James, Michael Chui, Diana Farrell, Steve Van Kuiken, Peter Groves, and Elizabeth Almasi Doshi. 2013. *Open Data: Unlocking Innovation and Performance with Liquid Information.* London; San Francisco; Shanghai; Washington, DC; New Jersey: McKinsey Global Institute, McKinsey Center for Government, McKinsey Business Technology Office. https://www.mckinsey.com/business-functions/digital-mckinsey/our-insights/open-data-unlocking-innovation-and-performance-with-liquid-information.

Massachusetts Institute of Technology (MIT). 2018. "About OCW." http://ocw.mit.edu/about/.

Masum, Hassan, Karl Shroeder, Myra Khan, and Abdallah S. Daar. 2013. "Open Source Biotechnology Platforms for Global Health and Development: Two Case Studies." In *Open Development: Networked Innovations in International Development*, ed. Matthew L. Smith and Katherine M. A. Reilly, 129–170. Cambridge, MA/Ottawa: MIT Press/IDRC. https://www.idrc.ca/en/book/open-development-networked-innovations-international-development.

Mizukami, Pedro N., and Renaldo Lemos. 2008. "From Free Software to Free Culture: The Emergence of Open Business." In *Access to Knowledge in Brazil: New Research on Intellectual Property, Innovation, and Development*, ed. Lea Shaver, 25–66. New Haven, CT: Information Society Project.

Oates, Lauryn, and Jamshid Hashimi. 2016. "Localizing OER in Afghanistan: Developing a Multilingual Digital Library for Afghan Teachers." *Open Praxis* 8 (2): 151–161.

Open Government Partnership. n.d. "About OGP." https://www.opengovpartnership.org/about/.

Peixoto, Tiago, and Jonathan Fox. 2016. *When Does ICT-Enabled Citizen Voice Lead to Government Responsiveness?* 2016 World Development Report Background Paper. Washington, DC: World Bank. https://openknowledge.worldbank.org/bitstream/handle/10986/23650/WDR16-BP-When-Does-ICT-Enabled-Citizen-Voice-Peixoto-Fox.pdf.

Pomerantz, Jeffrey, and Robin Peek. 2016. "Fifty Shades of Open." *First Monday* 21 (5) May. https://firstmonday.org/article/view/6360/5460.

Sen, Amartya. 1992. *Inequality Re-examined*. Oxford, UK: Clarendon Press.

Sen, Amartya. 1999a. *Development as Freedom*. New York: Knopf.

Sen, Amartya. 1999b. "The Possibility of Social Choice." *American Economic Review* 89 (3): 349–378.

Shirky, Clay. 2010. *Cognitive Surplus: How Technology Makes Consumers into Collaborators*. New York: Penguin Press.

Smith, Marshall S. 2013. "Open Educational Resources: Opportunities and Challenges for the Developing World." In *Open Development: Networked Innovations in International Development*, ed. Matthew L. Smith and Katherine M. A. Reilly, 129–170. Cambridge, MA/Ottawa: MIT Press/IDRC. https://www.idrc.ca/en/book/open-development-networked-innovations-international-development.

Smith, Marshall S. and Catherine M. Casserly. 2006. "The Promise of Open Educational Resources." *Change: The Magazine of Higher Learning 38* (5): 8–17.

Smith, Matthew L. 2014. "Being Open in ICT4D." *SSRN*, November 17. http://ssrn.com/abstract=2526515.

Smith, Matthew L., and Ruhiya Seward. 2017. "Openness as Social Praxis." *First Monday 22* (4) April. http://dx.doi.org/10.5210/fm.v22i4.7073.

Smith, Matthew L., Randy Spence, and Ahmed T. Rashid. 2011. "Mobile Phones and Expanding Human Capabilities." *Information Technologies and International Development* 7 (3): 77–88, 83n13.

Spence, Michael, and James Manyika. 2015. "Job-Saving Technologies." *Project Syndicate*. October 15. http://www.project-syndicate.org/commentary/online-talent-platforms-strengthen-employment-by-michael-spence-and-james-manyika-2015-10.

Spence, Randy, and Séverine Deneulin. 2010. "Human Development Policy Analysis." In *An Introduction to the Human Development and Capability Approach: Freedom and Agency*, ed. Séverine Deneulin and Lila Shahani, 275–299. London/Ottawa: Earthscan/IDRC. https://www.idrc.ca/en/book/introduction-human-development-and-capability-approach-freedom-and-agency.

Thrun, Sebastian. 2017. "Will Artificial Intelligence Help Us Solve Every Problem?" *PBS Newshour*, May 25. http://www.pbs.org/newshour/bb/will-artificial-intelligence-help-us-solve-every-problem/.

Toledo Hernández, Amalia, Carolina Botero, and Luisa Guzmán. 2014. "Public Expenditure in Education in Latin America. Recommendations to Serve the Purposes of the Paris Open Educational Resources Declaration." *Open Praxis* 6 (2). https://doi.org/10.5944/openpraxis.6.2.119.

TripAdvisor. 2018. "TripAdvisor Canada." https://www.tripadvisor.ca/.

Ushahidi. n.d. "About Ushahidi." https://www.ushahidi.com/about.

van Schalkwyk, François, Michael Cañares, Sumandro Chattapadhyay, and Alexander Andrason. 2014. *Open Data Intermediaries in Developing Countries*. Session at ICEGOV, Guimaraes, Portugal,

October 27–30. http://webfoundation.org/docs/2015/08/ODDC_2_Open_Data_Intermediaries_15 _June_2015_FINAL.pdf.

Verhulst, Stefaan, and Andrew Young. 2016. *Open Data Impact: When Demand and Supply Meet.* March 24. http://thegovlab.org/open-data-impact-when-demand-and-supply-meet/.

W^3Techs. n.d. "Usage Statistics and Market Share of Apache for Websites." https://w3techs.com /technologies/details/ws-apache/all/all.

Wiley, David, John Hilton III, Shelley Ellington, and Tiffany Hall. 2012. "A Preliminary Examination of the Cost Savings and Learning Impacts of Using Open Textbooks in Middle and High School Science Classes." *International Review of Research in Open and Distributed Learning* 13 (3): 262–276. http://www.irrodl.org/index.php/irrodl/article/view/1153/2256.

Yu, Harlan, and David G. Robinson. 2012. "The New Ambiguity of 'Open Government'." *UCLA Law Review Discourse* 59 (178). http://www.uclalawreview.org/pdf/discourse/59-11.pdf.

8 Openness in Telecommunications Reform and Practice: The Case of Open Access Broadband Networks, Public Wi-Fi, and Zero-Rating

Alison Gillwald

Introduction

Open access has had a positive effect on all things digital, including broadband. However, there is limited empirical research on its application as policy in developing countries or its impact or effectiveness in such contexts. Many of the assumptions underlying the theories and practices of *open* reflect conditions of abundance and freedom that are characteristic of mature, competitive economies and democracies of the Global North (see, e.g., Benkler 2013, vii–ix). As such, open access strategies cannot be applied uncritically to developing countries where the local context may not be conducive for success. There is also limited research on the potential of leveraging private and public resources through open systems to deliver public goods such as broadband, where states may not have the capacity to do so on their own.

This chapter seeks to contribute to a better understanding of open access regulation as a policy instrument in the context of developing countries. Building on the notion of private provisioning of social and public goods (Hirschman 1958), the argument presented in this chapter is that where there are no resources or institutional endowments for the state to provide social and public goods, the only way of doing so (in this case ensuring digital inclusion) may be accomplished by leveraging private resources. Drawing on Frischmann (2005, 2012), this chapter also makes the case for recognizing the often-ignored demand-side value of infrastructure, especially in the case of redressing digital inequality and citizens being unable to pay for services essential to their economic and social participation in modern society (see also Gillwald 2016).

The theories discussed in this chapter are used to create a framework to conceptualize and examine various types of open access in developing countries: (1) the mandatory open access regulatory regimes that emerged with the liberalization of markets and the regulation of former monopolies, in the interests of enabling the interoperability of networks and access to wholesale networks and facilities by service providers; (2) the mandatory and voluntary competitive models that have evolved with new broadband networks required to meet the demand for data with the popularization of the Internet; and (3) the resource management form of open access found in the theory and practice of the commons. In some cases, the latter is a subset of the governance framework described in the first point. This is true, for example, in the unlicensed spectrum set aside for public use that is examined here in the case of free public Wi-Fi as a state intervention to meet the communications needs of its citizens. What can be seen as a commercial variant of this service is also examined here: private operators zero-rate products or services by allocating bandwidth for open use in order to attract customers by providing free access to a product or service.

The chapter proceeds as follows. First, it discusses the evolution of open access regulation. It then extends this conceptualization by discussing the three approaches outlined previously: mandatory open access, voluntary open access, and commons-based approaches. It then assesses the outcomes and policy implications of these approaches. Finally, the chapter concludes by highlighting the need for context-specific considerations of open access applications, particularly when the use of these strategies in the Global South could disrupt existing systems without offering better access conditions or enhancing developmental outcomes.

Evolution of Open Access Regulation in Telecommunications

Despite its common usage in infrastructure regulation, there is no single, formal definition of *open access* in telecommunications policy and regulation. However, there is some consensus around open access principles in policy and regulation.[1] Common tenets include nondiscrimination and price transparency, wherein nondiscrimination is defined as equal access to networks and wholesale services;[2] and price transparency, meaning that prices are displayed to the public and customers understand how prices, based on actual costs, have been set.

The rationale for adopting open access regulation in telecommunications is to enhance overall consumer welfare, through both access and price, by improving both market competition and the efficiency of the telecommunications network. In the policy context of universal service, open access theoretically overcomes the problems associated with the high sunk costs required in infrastructure industries that make the duplication of certain network elements uneconomical.

Open access has long been a favored instrument of regulators to guarantee seamless access for consumers to competing networks and services, which nowadays include the Internet. The core principle of open access regulation is nondiscriminatory access to communication-enabling efficiencies, which would create surpluses for investment in network extension. Krämer and Schnurr (2014, 5), on the basis of this broad consensus, define open access in relation to infrastructure as follows:

> Open Access regulation refers to the mandated or voluntary provision of access to an upstream resource which must be based on the principle of non-discrimination. The concept may apply to publicly or privately owned access providers that are vertically separated, integrated, or represent a cooperative of multiple entities. Open Access regulation usually refers to the network layer, but may also be applied to other layers of the telecommunications value chain.

A growing body of evidence from more mature regulated markets indicates that the adoption of mandatory open access network strategies may come at the expense of investment and innovation (e.g., Bauer and Bohlin 2008). These trade-offs need to be assessed not only by means of the kind of static efficiency and instrumental competition models that are typically used to regulate the telecommunications sector, but also through dynamic efficiency models more suited to the rapidly changing and fluid Internet environment.

Open access regimes exist, then, to address the interrelated problems of (1) inflated prices, (2) reduced consumption of services as a result, and (3) insufficient investment and innovation. The first two contexts can best be understood in terms of static economic effects (i.e., at a given point in time). The dynamic economic effects associated with the third, innovation and investment, are the most difficult to solve with an open access regime (Gillwald, Odufuwa, Rademan, and Esselaar 2016b).[3]

As we have moved from a regulated telecommunications environment to that of the unregulated Internet, notions of *open* as regulated and unregulated access have collided. This is illustrated by the contested terrain of net neutrality, which has evolved with changes in technology and markets, as well as the propensity to regulate them over time. *Net neutrality* means many things to many people, but, at its core, it is about open access and control. An unwavering principle for proponents of *the free and open Internet* type of net neutrality is demonstrably a fluid concept in regulation, depending on definitions of the Internet as content or carrier.[4] The net neutrality debate has its roots in telecommunications regulation, particularly in the context of the US common carrier rules and in liberalizing markets to ensure interconnection with incumbent or dominant players. It also emerged with the popularization of the Internet and the shift in focus to informational resources.

In the net neutrality discourse, the argument has been around retaining the end-to-end architecture that has characterized the free and open Internet and is regarded as neutral; this arguably places limitations on the quality of services and product innovation. The argument put forward by operators and service providers, on the other hand, is for a shift to intelligent network design capable of allocating access to the infrastructure based on the identity of users. The former favors realizing the social value of the Internet, while the latter privileges private value (Goldsmith and Wu 2006).

Most recently, net neutrality has found expression in the zero-rating debate, and the calls by advocacy groups for zero-rating to be banned for fostering discrimination among providers of online content and content applications in ways that may skew incentives for subscribers (i.e., users may choose to access the free services of identified partners instead of the services of competitors). As discussed further later in this chapter, the issue of net neutrality has arisen starkly in the Global South over the zero-rating of Internet services, particularly the offer of free access to social networking platforms (e.g., Facebook's Free Basics, formerly Internet.org). Net neutrality proponents argue that such zero-rated services create *walled gardens* that limit access to and use of the free and open Internet. Many advocates have called for Free Basics to be regulated, and even banned. Some have been successful, the highest profile case being that of India.

Yet, from a pricing point of view, the concept of zero-rating has underpinned the expansion of the free and open Internet; in regulation, it has referred to the relationship between the network providers or Internet service providers (ISPs), depending on who is providing the service to the customers (and in mobile broadband markets, such roles are increasingly conflated), and content providers, who are prevented from charging fees for access to their customer base. As pointed out by Lee and Wu (2009, 63), since its inception in academia in the 1980s to its mass popularity in the 1990s and beyond, the Internet has maintained a pricing structure that is unique among information networks: "users and content providers typically pay ISPs access fees—fixed fees to get on the Internet at all—and usage fees—variable fees paid based on time or bandwidth usage; however, there have not generally been any additional charges for one user of the network to reach another user or content provider, reflected in the concept of the peering (free exchange) rather than paid interconnection, associated with traffic exchange in telecommunications networks."

As the balance of profitability shifted from the network providers and ISPs to the platforms and over-the-top[5] (OTT) applications (e.g., Skype and WhatsApp), especially ones that replaced high-cost local and international voice calls, telecommunications operators began calling for regulatory intervention that would enable them to charge certain users of the Internet, such as, notably, large application or content providers, additional fees to reach their subscribers, and enable forms of revenue sharing. Research by the European Telecommunications Network Operators' Association (ETNO 2012), for example, discusses ETNO's efforts to have regulations on revenue-sharing with OTT services adopted at the World Conference on International Telecommunications.

As Brett Frischmann (2005) recognizes, however, things are not as straightforward as they might appear. Prevention of quality of service discriminates in favor of various applications in the end-to-end architecture debate on net neutrality grounds. Additionally, by extension, it safeguards the commons, which favors data applications, at the expense of time-sensitive applications such as voice and video. The latter are being pushed generally by private and, particularly, giant companies requiring intelligent networks to manage network profitably and are viewed as being not net neutral in these generally polarized debates. But such arguments treat the generation of private value and social value as mutually exclusive. This chapter demonstrates the importance of creating incentives for private investments to deliver social value in countries where public resources do not exist.

Frischmann (2005) further argues that shifting to a quality of service regime where use is determined solely by private property owners that are able to offer such services (including arguably significant social value in the ability to offer greater cybersecurity) also is clearly not net neutral. He highlights the prioritization of innovation in the arguments that are made for optimal Internet design. Private property owners, on the one hand, argue strongly for incentives for innovation in private allocative models that are responsive to market demands. The counterarguments to this are made by those who advocate for the extension of the commons precisely to enable innovation (Lessig 2001). Frischmann (2005, 1008–1016) points out that innovation and competition in upstream and downstream markets, where the debate invariably lands in liberalized markets, is an important part of the policy debate. He notes, however, that "the Internet supports a substantially wider range of socially valuable downstream activities that are neither innovative nor commercial," have public or nonmarket value, and require equal policy consideration. He concludes, after a lengthy analysis of the arguments of Wu (the main proponent of net neutrality to safeguard a free and open Internet) and Lessig (the main proponent of the innovation commons), that while a theoretically neutral system has significant benefits, true neutrality is not attainable.

Besides the questionable attainability of net neutrality, the debate around neutrality and zero-rating is generally based on assumptions of universal access, or at least widespread access and quality of service thresholds that do not even pertain to the developing countries where such regulatory principles are now being instrumentally adopted.

The zero-rated approach to access contrasts with the typical private provision of the Internet at regulated or unregulated data tariffs. However, free services are not new. The major social platforms, including Facebook and Twitter, are free to users, with a business model based on two-sided markets where marketers and advertisers pay high prices to exploit user data (Bauer 2014; Economides and Tåg 2012). There are few, if any, open goods that are free of cost or nonproprietary in all stages of provision. Thus, as Spence and Smith point out (see chapter 7 of this volume), while free services offered by private companies may be surprising, private companies have long developed innovative ways to use open practices to generate revenue streams and to capture value in other areas of the business, or, in the sum of it, by deploying such strategies.

Conceptualizing Open Access

While the rationale for the monopoly provisioning of communications infrastructure in the form of public utilities was based on demand-side value associated with public goods, as markets became liberalized and the delivery of public services shifted to the private sector, the focus of regulation shifted to the supply-side value associated with private goods, and the extraction of rents. Yet, these were not ordinary private goods; they were public goods delivered by the private sector, and thus they required regulation to ensure that they were delivered affordably (Hirshmann 1958). In both the analysis of these problems and the proposed solutions, "complex motivational structures and…diverse private-for-profit, governmental, and community institutional arrangements that operate at multiple scales to generate productive and innovative, as well as destructive and perverse outcomes (North 1990 and 2005)" (Ostrom 2009, 408), need to be taken into account.

Historically, debates about resource management have been polarized into market versus state control of resources. Markets are narrowly seen as closed or proprietorial, while state ownership is potentially more public and open, although if monopolies are the providers, this is not necessarily the case. Advocates of open access frequently call for the creation or protection of the commons as an alternative to state control. This is, generally, a rejection of the management of resources, even if regulated, through market relations that are associated with private control. However, as pointed out by Frischmann (2005, 1), this "prescriptive call" arising from the revisiting of the commons is underdeveloped both from an economic perspective and in terms of the level required for policy implementation; meanwhile, on the private control side, there is a robust economic theory supporting the market mechanism with minimal government regulation that informs the approach to best practice infrastructure reform, and there is little theoretical support for the implementation of infrastructure commons (Frischmann 2005, 2–5).

Drawing on Ostrom's theory of common pool resources (Ostrom 2009), Frischmann (2005, 2012) presents an economics-based case for why some classes of key resources need to be managed in an accessible manner. Conventional economic analyses of infrastructure focus primarily on the supply-side value of infrastructure and the profit imperative in network investment and regulation, but Frischmann (2012) explores demand-side considerations to analyze how infrastructure resources generate value for consumers.

Three key insights emerge from this demand-side, value creation–focused analysis. The first, as also found in other infrastructure theories, is that infrastructure resources are fundamental and generate value when used as inputs into a wide range of productive processes. The second highlights that the outputs of infrastructure industries are generally public and nonmarket goods that create positive multipliers in both the economy and society. The third is that "managing infrastructure resources in an openly accessible manner may be socially desirable when it facilitates these downstream activities" (Frischmann 2005, 918).

Frischmann (2005), building on traditional economic concepts used in welfare analyses of infrastructure resources and the societal demand for such resources, puts forward a new theory of infrastructure. He notes that despite the extensive role of private and commercial delivery of information infrastructure, with the increased positive externalities derived from information infrastructure, the role of the state as coordinator and regulator in ensuring its provision and management is still required to ensure widespread access by citizens and the overall distribution of social gains (Frischmann 2005, 919–921).

The following section provides an empirical examination of different open access models, including mandatory-, voluntary-, and commons-based approaches to access regulation of competitive networks, open access broadband networks, free public Wi-Fi, and zero-rated services. The types of open access presented here, and shown in figure 8.1, are all intended to enable or enhance Internet access in developing-country contexts. The analysis of the cases and the conclusions presented thereafter highlight both the need to find new ways of addressing digital inequality and the dangers of static and instrumental regulation.

Cases: Mandatory Open Access, Voluntary Open Access, and Variations on the Commons

Mandatory Open Access Regimes

The first case looks at the application of open access to the mandatory regulation of more traditional telecommunications networks within the context of supply-side valuation associated with economic and competition regulation. Because markets were liberalized and competitors to public monopolies entered the market, open access regulation was mandatorily applied to ensure access to the remaining natural monopoly

SUPPLY VALUE

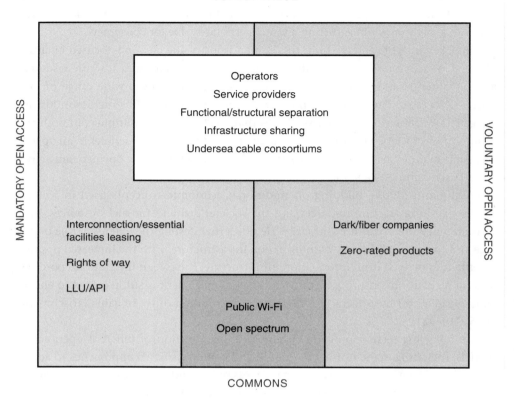

Figure 8.1
Depiction of various mandatory and voluntary open access forms.
Source: Author.

elements of backbone networks and fixed access network infrastructure. Open access regulation helps to ensure the seamless connection of customers on different networks by mandating the nondiscriminatory interconnection of networks. Facilities are thus available to connect other network operators, especially those that might otherwise have formed bottlenecks, including the wholesale segments of the market (backhaul[6] and the access network) where few suppliers exist and markets naturally tend toward oligopoly or monopoly.[7] This has led to the creation of open access regimes that compel dominant operators to provide access to rival operators to enhance competition.

Europe's open access regulation introduced competition into various monopoly elements of the market by mandating access at multiple layers of the network. This can be implemented through the separation and opening up of network elements, particularly the *last mile* or *access networks*, which have been the most uneconomical to duplicate from a fixed-line perspective. Unbundling of the local loop[8] has been a requirement of European and American regulators to enable competitive access to the last mile. At the backbone level, fair access to networks built with public investments as public utilities prior to any privatization has been accomplished through the structural separation of the network and the services, which are then offered independently to customers.

Local Loop Unbundling   One way of implementing open access on traditional copper access networks has been through local loop unbundling (LLU). The rationale here is to foster competition and reduce telecommunications costs by eliminating the duplication of large investments required for last-mile infrastructure. South Africa, as one of the only markets in sub-Saharan Africa with any significant copper networks, has long had LLU on the reform agenda. This is in line with claims made by dominant epistemic communities within the Organisation for Economic Co-operation and Development (OECD), International Telecommunications Union (ITU), and World Bank a decade ago to the effect that LLU was a best practice scenario. The stated argument was that it would enable telecommunications providers to innovate and differentiate their product offerings, promote competition in the provision of broadband services, offer opportunities for innovation to drive product and price differentiation, speed up national economic growth, and even increase competitiveness in the global market and create employment opportunities. With the identification of a second network operator by the South African government after none had met the public policy–determined criteria to be licensed by the regulator, an environment more conducive to new entrants had to be established.[9] Prevarication on the issue continued for years as a result of the conflict of interest of the government in South Africa. This conflict resulted because the government was responsible for market reform of a sector in which the state held a significant share of the incumbent operator, Telkom (Gillwald 2005), thereby preventing the second network operator from benefiting from market reform of the previous monopoly market.

The public process proceeded at a snail's pace. This was because the regulator, the Independent Communications Authority of South Africa (ICASA), was facing its own internal leadership crisis. It was also pursuing other urgent activities with more powerful interests (e.g., spectrum) than the second network operator. Despite the publication by the regulator of a findings document identifying four options for unbundling, including an easily implementable bitstream option, ICASA never published any regulations from that round of hearings. This was widely perceived as being a result of the obstructionism by the incumbent, Telkom (Ellipsis 2011).

As all elements of mobile networks are considered replicable (other than termination, which is inherently monopolistic), open access to mobile networks through an enabling application programming interface (API) or API access has not yet been considered mandatory. However, given the dominance of mobile operators in developing-country markets, this is being reviewed in the context of mandatory infrastructure sharing.[10]

Functional and Structural Separation Market restructuring through functional and even structural separation is a more drastic form of intervention to deal with incumbency or dominance in the market. Essentially, this restructures the market by separating out vertically integrated operations and compelling them to treat their downstream operations in the same way that they treat their competitors. With the network and services separated structurally, the network is often transformed into an open access, carrier of carriers network that can offer services only under the separated sister company. In South Africa, Telkom, which had been partially privatized in 1996, was required by the Competition Commission to functionally separate its activities as part of the remedies imposed after it was found guilty of anticompetitive practices in 2013. This separation did not restructure the market, but it did give effect to the policy and regulatory framework that required the incumbent to operate its wholesale and retail activities independently enough from each other to allow operators and service providers to compete fairly. Following several proposed turnaround strategies, including complete privatization and renationalization, and in the face of growing competition and price undercutting from new fiber companies, Telkom voluntarily undertook to separate structurally under the mantle of the national broadband champion (Padayachee interview, 2016). Given the voluntary nature of this restructuring exercise, the effects on the market may not be as dramatic as mandatory separation; but the effect on bandwidth prices in the market has been positive, and Telkom's own balance sheet has improved consistently throughout the early days of this transition despite the harsh economic climate in South Africa (Telkom 2016, 2017).

Outcomes of various forms of mandatory open access regulation are mixed and are context specific, and comparative data is limited. However, there is evidence that while such initiatives might have resulted in short-term positive consumer gains, they can negatively affect investment and innovation (Bauer and Bohlin 2008). In most African jurisdictions with barely any fixed local loops to unbundle, the focus has been instead on extending wireless networks. Since it is more economically feasible to invest in competitive wireless access networks, there has been little effort to require dominant players to provide access to competitors, despite the fact that outside the main urban centers, there is often only one operator network, or possibly two, available to consumers, with very little choice. As yet, very limited attention has been paid to mandating API access to mobile networks, which would have a similar effect to unbundling the fixed local loop. Rather, the focus of policymakers and regulators has been on mandating national roaming by new entrants on incumbent mobile networks. Without very extensive fiber networks in most African countries, open access, state-owned broadband networks have been set up in several countries (e.g., Botswana, South Africa, Tanzania, and Uganda).

National Open Access Broadband Networks (Carriers of Carriers)   Competition at the infrastructure level is not viable in many developing economies (indeed, it is not in many developed ones as well). Also, given the high cost of rolling out broadband, states have instead opted to deploy a single national fiber backbone open to all service providers on a nondiscriminatory price basis as a way of enhancing network expansion and access. Australia is one country that has led the way in this regard. Consolidating use on a single backbone enables economies of scale and cost reductions that translate into lower access prices for service providers. Competition then takes place at the service rather than at the network level. This could still foster the efficiencies usually associated with competition and contribute to consumer welfare through bypassing the high input costs for service providers arising from the duplication of facilities or networks.[11] State-owned broadband companies have had anticompetitive effects by either squeezing out private-sector investment (e.g., in Tanzania), or by governments requiring the public sector (often the single biggest collective user in many countries) to exclusively use the state-owned broadband services (e.g., in Uganda) (Lumu 2015).

Mandatory open access broadband networks, especially in developing countries where there is already significant private-sector investment, have not been successful. The high sunk cost associated with the rollout of fixed networks is difficult to replicate profitably. Without conscientious efforts to enable competition, the ability to challenge the market dominance of incumbents is limited. The case of South Africa illustrates these challenges.

The fiber-optic networks of the public rail network (Transnet) and the power utility (Eskom) were set aside for the creation of a second network operator at the end of Telkom's exclusivity in 2003. However, as the second operator was about to be licensed to Neotel in 2006, and broadband was starting to take off, the Department of Public Enterprises withdrew the mandatory setting-aside of holdings so that the transport communication network could create a new, state-owned, open access broadband company, Broadband Infraco (BBI). Since this decision happened without public consultation and cut across the emerging competitive convergence policy, the process was delayed.

Licensed for the provision of wholesale services, BBI became operational in 2009 (see Gillwald 2007 for a detailed case) following additional delays related to the determination of the type of services that the entity would be entitled to offer. BBI has since invested in national and international backbone communications networks and is one of the main investors in the West Africa Cable System (WACS).[12] However, state coordination has been weak and arguably lacking sufficient investment in BBI to deploy even the roughly 12,000 kilometers of backbone planned (not a great distance for a national backbone for a country the size of South Africa). The decision to create an open access network failed to consider the market dominance of the incumbent, which now has over 50,000 kilometers of unduplicated fiber and over 75,000 kilometers in all. Furthermore, international bandwidth capacity in the country had already increased significantly in terms of quality and pricing by then (Gillwald 2007; Nkhereanye interview, 2016).

Initially, there was some concern that BBI would squeeze out private-sector investment. However, having fallen victim to the lack of coordination between the Department of Public Enterprises and the Department of Communications, which was responsible for allocating BBI's license, BBI could no longer represent the interest of its target clients, the network operators, that in 2009 went on to cobuild an alternative national infrastructure network, while in the process undermining the viability of the BBI business model.[13]

Nigeria announced a similar open access model in 2012, but the process has been delayed. So far, there has not been an intervention in wholesale markets, and market regulation based on a comprehensive study is long overdue (see the Nigeria case in Gillwald et al. 2016a).

National Open Access Wireless Networks   Within infrastructure industry policy and regulation, the creation or enforcement of open access wireless networks has been identified as a mechanism to reduce infrastructure that is not economical to duplicate, and also as a remedy for monopoly. Open access networks have been tried in Kenya and Mexico to counter the extreme dominance of incumbents (above 80 percent of market share), and where such primary markets for achieving universal service were deemed uncompetitive. In these cases, the implementation of open access often takes the form of a consortium-owned mobile network. Here, spectrum is to be shared by any operator or service provider who wishes to offer wireless services on the designated spectrum. In Kenya, the dominant network operator Safaricom backed out of the deal before the proposed network became operational resulting in the collapse of the consortium. In the case of Mexico (discussed next), only the digital dividend spectrum has been set aside for this experiment (Gillwald et al. 2016a).

In Mexico, which is the only remaining country pursuing open access wireless, there is considerable concern about the risks emerging from the constitutional obligations to continue with the process in the face of growing evidence that it might not ultimately fulfill its mandate. A state company, Red Compartida, has been established to hold the spectrum licenses in an attempt to mitigate the risk of failure (Borjón Figueroa interview, 2016). In the meantime, other regulatory reforms in Mexico, which enabled the introduction of classical asymmetrical remedies for the market in which operators were exercising significant market power and distorting market outcomes, were implemented during the six years that it took to finally set up the open access wireless consortium (Labardini interview, 2016), reducing the dominance of the dominant operators to around 60 percent (from 80 percent).

South Africa's Integrated ICT White Paper (RSA 2016) proposes the introduction of an exclusive wireless network, not limited to the digital dividend spectrum, as proposed by Mexico and Kenya, but rather extending across the entire high-demand spectrum that is currently unassigned (2.6 GHz and the 700 MHz digital dividend spectrum). It also proposes the incorporation of other mobile spectrums when the operators' 15-year licenses expire so that the full spectrum is held in the open access wireless network (RSA 2016). As discussed previously, the extreme complexities of such proposals require a sophisticated understanding of the mobile market.

Although the white paper provides no insight into the business plan or ownership structure of the wireless open access network (WOAN), a consortium of the kind embarked on for the successful, voluntary, and partially open access undersea cable company consortia (WACS, Seacom, and Eassy) has been suggested as a model. The business model for the construction and maintenance of a single end-to-end cable with a 25-year life span, however, cannot be readily applied to a common carrier model in the dynamic and fast-changing mobile wireless market, where operators' control of the spectrum determines the competitive advantage.

International expert inputs into the consultative process for SA Connect, the national broadband plan, which was unpublished but publicly available at the time, contended that at least one of the bigger mobile operators needs to be inside the network for it to enjoy economies of scale and scope. Consultants appointed by the National Treasury of the Republic of South Africa to establish the viability of the WOAN also cautioned against its establishment (Bedi and Schumann 2013). To work, the model requires incentives to make the investment in the open access network more attractive to the mobile operators than investing and controlling their own networks. In another scenario, if operators are unable to access any of the additional long-term evolution (LTE) spectrum necessary for the cost-effective development of their businesses (as has been the case in South Africa), then there is no need for them to invest in their own networks. Instead, they can simply access wholesale networks at regulated open access prices.

There are at least two problems: first, capital for the open access network has to come from somewhere, fast; and second, the history of the public open access broadband company does not bode well. With some pressure from government, but also given the promise of low-cost access to BBI (the new state-owned company), the dominant mobile operators, MTN Group Limited (MTN) and Vodacom, opted not to build out fiber networks once the incumbent's exclusivity period expired, and they were permitted to do so. However, the delays to the licensing process, and subsequently the operationalization of the license and the clear undercapitalization of it for national champion purposes, drove MTN, Vodacom, and the second network operator, Neotel, to build their own intercity transmission network. Because the government again is trying to cut across the policy framework (flawed as it may be, it nevertheless is the result of a consultative process to force an exclusive wireless network), it appears that no lessons have been learned from its own recent history.

The proposed open access wholesale wireless network in South Africa could result in negative unintended consequences, particularly the inhibition of the current extremely high level of private investment in mobile network extension and upgrades. The opportunity costs of this to the country, already lagging on 4G[14] deployment, are potentially enormous and include negative impacts on economic growth and employment, which would take years to correct.

State efforts to intervene in the successful mobile market with mandatory open access wireless networks for the high-demand spectrum in South Africa may be counterproductive if the goal is to meet development objectives. Furthermore, there is anxiety about whether there is the institutional capacity and sophistication to oversee the complexity of creating a viable, single, open access network. After all, the absence of state coordination in relation to the spectrum has plagued far simpler processes. The WOAN may well fail for the same reasons that complex auctions, as an alternative to open access and other models, may also fail. The lack of success of any auction in Africa is cited by open access advocates (Song interview, 2017; Rey-Moreno interview, 2017) to argue against the multilateral best practice orthodoxy on spectrum assignment of auctions.

There are a couple of rejoinders to this position. There are few ways, other than auctions, of valuing and assigning spectrum set aside for commercial use competitively and in ways that will ensure optimal efficiency in the use of the spectrum (including regulated spectrum trading to enable the correction of any auction outcome errors). For example, the South African Treasury is regarded as a highly effective government department, and the high standing of the financial sector in South Africa and the long view taken on the economy is attributed to them. The Treasury already provides technical assistance to most departments through its Government Technical Assistance

Committee (GTAC). Within policy and regulatory confines that would contain fiscal interests in maximizing the pricing of the spectrum, the department could assist the regulator with the technical dimensions of the auction and the management of any external consultants who are brought in. This could be implemented far more quickly than an exclusive open access network, which is bound to face multiple rounds of legal review before the network could even be established and become operational. The release of the high-demand spectrum has already been delayed by six years.

The best case scenario if legal hoops were navigated, using the Mexican model as some measure, even with some lessons learned, is probably a minimum of five years. That would already place South Africa ten years behind early adopters of LTE in the allocated and cost-effective bands (although operators have refarmed alternative, less-cost-effective spectrum that they hold currently to make it available for LTE). All operators are offering such services in the major centers. With the urgent release of high-demand spectrum, and with all the previously mentioned caveats for making available unlicensed and open access spectrum, regulators should be focusing on creating incentives for infrastructure sharing, channeling complementary investments, and moving to an industry-coordinating role by enabling voluntary models that allow the participants to assume the risk associated with high sunk-cost infrastructure investments.

Voluntary Open Access Networks

Voluntary Open Access International Backbone Networks (Commercial Models) An example of successful voluntary open access in Africa is the provisioning of undersea international bandwidth by Seacom (and arguably WACS as well). Seacom broke the monopoly that SAT-3 (South Atlantic 3 submarine cable) had on Africa operating as a closed club consortium consisting of incumbents. The commercial logic of Seacom, and to some degree the shared infrastructure consortium that operates WACS, is similar to that of the commercial, open access, dark fiber national transmission networks (described next), and some have argued that that should be the form of the wireless open access network in South Africa.

Voluntary Open Access Fiber Networks (Commercial) With the opening of backbone competition, commercially operated, voluntary, open access networks operate in the South African market in complementary ways with existing broadband network investments and OTT platforms and applications. Commercial companies that operate voluntary open access models have managed to optimize their traffic flows and maximize their return on investments in as short a period as possible, allowing them to refinance the next phase of network rollout and contribute to the cost of network extension.

Open access companies such as Dark Fibre Africa (DFA) and FibreCo created competitive alternatives to Telkom on main intercity routes (MyBroadband 2014). This competitive pressure in the national data transmission market compelled Telkom to review its strategy in the market and adopt an open access model, undergoing a voluntary structural separation of its wholesale and retail divisions, as already mentioned. This has largely been welcomed, although it has not entirely eradicated the lingering skepticism of the incumbent's competitors and clients represented by the industry association that brought the initial anticompetitive case against Telkom. A voluntary regime could be reversed at any time, and there is still a view among some stakeholders that, given that Telkom is the dominant backhaul provider, oversight of the open access regime by the regulator is still necessary (Cull interview, 2016; Cohen interview, 2016; Nkereanye interview, 2016).

This open competitive environment results in the duplication of networks, certainly in the metro areas where competition can be easily sustained. However, there is also extensive evidence of complementary investments by different tiers and types of operators, and procurement or sharing of infrastructure for primary and redundancy use for national coverage (Hussein interview, 2016).

As the acting director general of the then-Department of Telecommunications and Postal Services (DTPS) in South Africa[15] indicated, commercial fiber "has been one of the most phenomenal developments in the sector, a game changer that demonstrated that open access networks are viable, unlike what the traditional operators have argued" (Mjwara interview, 2016).

The success of voluntary, open access, commercial fiber networks demonstrates that delivery of social goods through supply-side value can be enabled through demand-side valuation of those services and the creation of incentives for operators, such as the government anchor tenancy identified in the South African national broadband policy, SA Connect. It was the success of this voluntary open access model that led SA Connect to propose that instead of building another state-owned network for the public sector, as was being suggested in government circles but for which there was no state funding, that the extensive private networks be provided with the incentives to extend their nearby networks to underserved areas. The proposal was to aggregate public-sector demand and smart procure services from existing providers at cost-effective prices. In this way, incentives such as government anchor tenancies through demand aggregation in underserved areas could foster broadband investment in areas that would otherwise be uneconomical to service.

Despite this potential of leveraging private investment to furnish public-sector broadband services as proposed in SA Connect, little to no progress has been made since 2013 in this regard. The lack of capacity within the ministry to coordinate the plan across government departments is the main stumbling block.

Variants of the Commons

Free Public Wi-Fi—Bring Your Own Device   The use of universal service funds to reach underserved communities and to provide access to the Internet was locked into fixed-lined models for a long time, and today it remains largely focused on subsidizing network extension and the aggregation of demand through computer-based telecenters. However, with the advent of mobile broadband and smart devices, the price and skill barriers that the computer-based Internet access created were essentially removed. This undermined the logic of access aggregation of this kind. Mobile devices can now offer adequate user experiences, with web browsing, email access, messaging, and an increasing variety of applications for using the Internet without having to travel to single points of presence.

While increased Internet penetration (with its widening coverage), mobile technology upgrades to 3G (and now LTE), and the relative affordability of smart devices have combined to increase mobile data uptake, the majority of people in the Global South still lack access (see www.afteraccess.net). Limited coverage and slow data speeds outside the major centers, together with the relatively high cost of services, exclude the poor and inhibit the optimal use of mobile data by most users (Rey-Moreno 2013; Stork, Calandro, and Gillwald 2013). Yet in only a few countries have universal service funds or agencies made this transition to supporting user access.

Nevertheless, in some countries, such as Rwanda and South Africa, metropolitan governments are offering free public Wi-Fi (FPW) as part of their strategy to provide citizens with connectivity to access government services and the Internet more widely. Given the widespread use of Internet-enabled phones with sufficient computer power and adequate screen sizes for meaningful use (even among lower-income groups), FPW is a promising solution. FPW sponsored by a local authority is popular in many major Asian and North American cities; and the South African broadband plan, SA Connect, requires that all public buildings be connected to broadband and that, whenever these connections occur, they include a FPW hot spot. But provinces and cities in South Africa are moving even more swiftly by actively investing in both central business districts and underserviced areas, rolling out FPW. The traction with citizens has been overwhelming.

There are various models of public Wi-Fi in South Africa, but the two largest initiatives, in Gauteng and the Western Cape provinces, respectively, implemented assessable initiatives by 2016. These are the wealthiest provinces in the country and are highly urbanized (Gauteng almost entirely). There are projects in the four largest metropolitan areas: Tshwane (formerly Pretoria); Johannesburg and Ekurhuleni (in Gauteng); and Cape Town (in the Western Cape).

FPW projects typically emanate from authorities that already have broadband development strategies and plans in place, as is the case in both Gauteng and the Western Cape. Most FPW plans are linked to initiatives to interconnect government buildings via fiber networks. FPW projects tend either to piggyback on these fiber deployments (Western Cape, Ekurhuleni, Johannesburg, and, to some extent, eThekwini in KwaZulu-Natal province), or to benefit from existing municipal fiber (Tshwane and Cape Town) (Geerdts et al. 2016).

Of all the projects, the state-funded Tshwane Free Wi-Fi, Project Isizwe, is the most advanced in terms of scale and impact. The project began in 2013 and is based on two investment justifications: first, broadband, as a basic right for every citizen, should be offered across the country, fully funded by government; and, second, increased broadband penetration will drive economic growth, increase commercial and financial activity that will expand the tax base, and altogether will exceed the city's initial investment. On this basis, public Wi-Fi should be furnished for free (Geerdts and Gillwald 2017).

The results, in terms of network deployment, have been impressive. The content portal and program launched to generate local video illustrate the potential for Wi-Fi and broadband to enhance employment opportunities, improve health and education, and connect government to citizens. In line with the national broadband plan, SA Connect, the focus has been on connecting educational institutions.

In the longer term, Project Isizwe expects that input pricing will reduce to the point where free Wi-Fi is no longer considered a significant expense. Until then, the model is entirely dependent on substantial public funding, which has been large for a relatively small-scale, low-cost, public Wi-Fi network, at around $75,000 a month (Geerdts and Gillwald 2017).

The model for the Western Cape is more complex. The province and city take a holistic view of promoting broadband on multiple fronts. One of the foundations of this model is to stimulate private-sector investment in broadband by improving market information (RIA 2016) to help investors understand the costs, by creating demand (with government as an anchor tenant), and by reducing the capital outlay requirements (by paying for part of the infrastructure). At the provincial level, the government is implementing a fiber/Wi-Fi contract to connect government buildings and selected Wi-Fi sites. What was intended to be a public-private open access network was scuttled by the national State IT Agency (SITA), which asserted its prerogative to undertake a regular competitive tender under its auspices. As a result, a privately operated, closed network was created, with premiums significantly above those offered by the public open access network initially proposed.[16] The winning proposal allowed the second

Table 8.1

Comparison of Tshwane Free Wi-Fi and Western Cape Broadband Initiative (WCBBI).

	Tshwane Free Wi-Fi	Western Cape Broadband Initiative (WCBBI)/CoCT	Development outcomes
Production	Closed	Public-private community interplays: multiple players, but not open	Tshwane sustainability dependent on state-funded project; single service provider; closed system
Distribution	Closed	Multiple players/models	Tshwane fastest deployment
Consumption	Open/free	Open/free Paid (premium services)	Tshwane: free, more users, consistent quality and capacity WCBBI: mixed free/pay models, building sustainability with public backbone/private Wi-Fi model

Source: Alison Gillwald, using Smith and Seward's (2017) open access conceptual framework.

network operator, Neotel, to deliver services to government, as the anchor tenant, via both fiber and Wi-Fi, but also to exploit the private-sector market (Geerdts et al. 2016).

On the other hand, the City of Cape Town (CoCT) is encouraging private investment by reducing the upfront capital outlay required. The CoCT provides connectivity from a central point to remote locations while also supporting access points (APs). The ISP only has to offer data connectivity. This model is more expensive to implement than the Tshwane model, but includes the private sector and fosters innovation and competition. See comparisons in table 8.1.

What this natural experiment demonstrates is that various models of public Wi-Fi can be justified on the basis of the demand-side value of the network, as the Tshwane municipality has done to justify the substantial subsidy that it provides to offer limited free access to the Internet. Although the supply-side value of public Wi-Fi has been more difficult to institute across the world, the Western Cape government has attempted to support the private provisioning of public goods by enabling access to low-cost bandwidth and providing start-up subsidies, but, ultimately, it intends them to become self-sustaining and economically viable. See comparisons in table 8.1.

Free, Limited Access and Use: Zero-Rating Services   *Zero-rating* has been defined as tariff plans that enable mobile (wireless) customers to download and upload online content without incurring data usage charges or having their usage counted against data usage limits (Eisenach 2015). In developing countries, zero-rating allows mobile subscribers to access certain or preselected online content for free (i.e., without having the associated data usage counted against their usage allowances under wireless service plans). Zero-rating practices, therefore, are considered a violation of the net neutrality principle by some regulators. In India, this led to the mobilization of civil society to produce a million-signature campaign, which subsequently led to the banning of Free Basics and other zero-rated products by the Indian regulator, Telecom Regulatory Authority of India (TRAI). Most African countries, which tend to follow European Union (EU) regulatory trends rather than those in the United States, have been slow to develop positions on net neutrality, with the EU itself only adopting net neutrality rules late in 2015. The EU rules enshrine the principle of net neutrality in law: no blocking or throttling of online content, applications, and services. Under these rules, efforts to prohibit ISPs from blocking, throttling, and discrimination with regard to Internet traffic are largely focused on the quality of the service and treatment of traffic.

Services that are typically zero-rated by providers in developing countries include the world's biggest web properties, such as Google, Facebook, and Twitter, as well as messaging services such as WhatsApp, KakaoTalk, and WeChat that can reduce the high cost of communicating through phone calls and short message service (SMS)/text messages. See the comparisons in table 8.2.

Table 8.2
Zero-rating models for different platforms.

Platform/offering	Who subsidizes consumer?	Content
Free Basics	Does not pay carriers to zero-rate access and does not receive payments from carriers	Facebook Zero + mix of public-interest websites, including government, nongovernmental organizations (NGOs), and businesses (e.g., Smartbusiness, Girl Effects, and BBC News)
Wikipedia Zero	Does not pay carriers to zero-rate access to the Wikimedia sites and does not receive payments from carriers	Access to the regular mobile version of Wikipedia and other Wikimedia sites, in all languages
Mozilla Equal Rating	Low cost + unlimited talk + text + 500 MB of data for six months/watch ads to access other sites	All content equally available

Source: Gillwald et al. (2016a).

Assessment of Outcomes and Policy Implications

Mandatory Open Access Regulation and Broadband Networks

The empirical assessment of the cases demonstrates how the long history of mandatory open access regulation, derived from both regulation in the EU and multilateral agency reform programs as a way to enable market entry and manage market dominance and anticompetitive practices, has not transformed easily into fixed broadband network extension in South Africa and Nigeria, an open access wireless network extension in Kenya, or, as yet, South Africa (e.g., Gillwald et al. 2017).

All the national open access broadband cases highlight the institutional constraints on implementation, with the failure to implement since 2012, the planned wholesale open access national broadband network as cornerstones of national public policy. Inadequate funding and insufficient institutional and regulatory capacity to create a level playing field for the new entrants and investors, especially in upstream segments, explain this failure. See the comparisons in table 8.3.

State-Owned Open Access Wholesale Broadband Companies The introduction of open access wholesale networks in countries with very low per-capita incomes or small population sizes, such as Tanzania and Botswana, in countries where the duplication of competitive networks may not be feasible, and in countries unable to attract competitive private investments may have resulted in the extension of broadband networks across the country. As shown, however, this does not necessarily mean that such networks meet national objectives of digital inclusion, either because of the unavailability of access networks or consumers' inability to afford the Internet-enabled devices needed to access them.

The cases of state-initiated, open access, wholesale networks examined here demonstrate that the more sophisticated mandatory open access arrangements requiring institutional expertise to control or manage resources are limited or entirely absent in many developing countries. Even in more dynamic markets, such as Kenya, Nigeria, and South Africa, where state-owned entities needed to compete with or attract private operators, they have largely failed. In South Africa, the national broadband company never really thrived due to undercapitalization and inability to compete in the dynamic and fast-growing voluntary open access market. In Kenya and Nigeria, state-owned wireless and regional wholesale broadband networks proposed in those countries' national development plans were never even implemented.

Early efforts to intervene in the successful mobile market with early mandatory open access wireless networks for high demand spectrum in Kenya and South Africa have faced similar institutional constraints, perhaps even more so than in the case

Table 8.3

Comparison of mandatory and voluntary open access.

Purpose	Open access	Outcomes (combined private and social value)
Dominant/public operators required to provide interconnection with other operators or provide facilities to downstream competitors or be the "common carrier" to all service providers in order to reduce wholesale prices for facilities and services.	MANDATORY: Open access regulation, including termination (monopoly) rate regulation, to ensure interoperability of networks, and seamless interconnection of customers, serving to drive down prices for users. Wholesale regulation of dominant markets. Essential facilities regulation to ensure access to network elements, enhance competition, and level the playing field so that service providers can compete in vertically integrated operations.	Resource-intensive access regulation, but if effectively done, enables competition, enhances efficiency of resource allocation, reduces wholesale prices, and enhances consumer welfare. Reduces access price/data prices for users to access services/internet. The basis of intervention is supply-side value (cost-based/profitability studies), but social benefits ensue.
	VOLUNTARY open access fiber network investment has complemented incumbent high-speed backbone networks, stimulating competition in the market and driving down wholesale prices. With the correct incentives, such as aggregating demand and offering government anchor tenancies, providers could be induced to go to underserved areas.	No regulatory transaction costs; avoid unnecessary duplication of services; commercial imperative likely to produce the most efficient outcomes, with associated cost saving and price reductions (reduce regulatory scrutiny). Private-value driven, but public and social value is derived.
Ensure a fair and competitive environment and access for downstream competitors to vertically integrated incumbent networks.	MANDATORY unbundling/structural and functional separation of networks from services or LLU of incumbent access networks in an open access wholesale network and separate services company (functional separation as behavioral remedy to anticompetitive practices (e.g., South Africa: Competition Commission, Telkom).	Creates a fair, regulated environment for downstream competitors, access to facilities and competition in fixed access network. Public good imperatives, but private value considerations.
Seeks to create trusted environment for downstream competitors (clients) by removing anticompetitive incentives in incumbent.	VOLUNTARY functional or structural separation (South Africa: Telkom) of services from open access wholesale networks.	Introduces more competitive pricing to attract clients (who are also service competitors), more profitable, more investment in network extension. Services with a similar cost base compete on quality-enhancing consumer choice.
Common carrier network/fiber extension to reduce duplication of investments in infrastructure to enable affordable access.	MANDATORY: National open access wholesale broadband company (not competing with downstream players' services). Aggregated demand into a low-cost national provider, usually state owned, and sometimes a monopoly provider.	State-owned open access carrier network in South Africa failed to extend access or reduce prices; Nigeria appears not to have the institutional capacity to get proposed regional infrastructure companies under way.

Table 8.3 (continued)

Purpose	Open access	Outcomes (combined private and social value)
	VOLUNTARY: Commercial open access models providing complementary investment have resulted in considerable network extension and driven down wholesale prices.	Potential to leverage private investments (supply-side value) for public goods (demand-side value), such as anchor tenancies offered by the state to connect remote public buildings such as schools, clinics, and police stations.
Intended to deal with extreme dominance in mobile markets, by either excluding dominant players from the low-cost open access network (Mexico) or compelling them in through exclusive spectrum holding by the network to lower barriers to entry for new entrants by providing low-cost, high-demand spectrum.	MANDATORY: Open access wireless network to operate as a wireless common carrier network, offering smaller players access to the spectrum.	No successful examples yet to draw from, and it is not clear how the proposed model in South Africa will overcome the problems faced in Kenya and Mexico around risk management, investment incentives, and institutional capacity to implement and oversee. Mobile markets with high levels of concentration or dominance. Effectively asymmetrical access regulation can reduce prices and spur take-up more rapidly and with less risk than the exclusive open access networks being proposed.
	VOLUNTARY: Mobile virtual network operators generally gain access to the market through late entrant network (API) wishing to complement revenues through roaming agreements.	Increasing competition in the market and driving down prices.
To enable or enhance broadband access to public services or to complement commercial access for price sensitive users.	Public Wi-Fi exploits spectrum commons for unlicensed low-power use. FPW provided by government recognizes demand-side value of broadband connectivity for citizens by enabling free access, either through government subsidies or public–private interplays. Various free commercial offerings tied to commercial dimensions of either telecom or other businesses attracting clientele or collecting information on their behavior.	In most African contexts, where even cost-based broadband is not affordable to many, this enables social and economic inclusion (though not necessarily equality).
Zero-rating, intended to attract new and price-sensitive users onto mobile networks by offering limited access to social networking products for free.	Zero-rated bandwidth provides open access to limited content of popular social networking platforms.	Private value for mobile operators who attract customers to their networks, who go on to become paying customers for full services or other products. Demand-side value in the provisioning of primary or complementary access and use to users.

of fixed broadband, where there was not much competition at the time of the initial interventions. Open access initiatives in the extremely successful mobile sector, where billions of dollars are being invested in broadband network extension while access prices are coming down, may turn out to be counterproductive in terms of meeting development objectives.

The voluntary open access undersea cable company consortia (WACS, Seacom, and Eassy) successfully broke the dominance of the club consortia of incumbent operators that monopolized the provisioning of international bandwidth, the high cost of which has prevented Internet proliferation in Africa for decades. A similar consortium model applied in the dynamic mobile market will require clear incentives to make the investment in open access networks more attractive than operators investing in and controlling their own networks. In all the countries assessed in the case studies, the dominant mobile operators are also the largest investors in broadband rollout. If they are permitted to access the high demand spectrum while continuing to operate their own networks, then any competitive open access network will most likely be marginalized. On the other hand, if mobile operators are not permitted to access the desired spectrum in an attempt to compel them to use the WOANs, then there is no need for them to invest in the latter, as they can simply access wholesale networks at regulated open access prices instead of investing in a shared pool. This is the impasse faced in South Africa.

Additionally, anxiety persists about the existence of the institutional capacity and sophistication necessary to oversee the complexity of creating a viable single, open access network. The absence of state coordination in relation to broadband, first with the state-owned company, BBI, and then in relation to spectrum, is evidence of the institutional risks associated with the management of complex processes. The decade-long digital television migration debacle in South Africa, which has now been overtaken by global events, together with the six-year ministerial delay in issuing a policy directive on the release of high-demand spectrum, which has now resulted in a legal standoff between the Ministry of Telecommunications and Postal Services and the regulator, provide evidence of both the complexity and risk of this undertaking. The traditional asymmetries of information between operators, regulators, and the ministry that have plagued far simpler processes, such as licensing hearings or the successful completion of market reviews, are unlikely to be overcome in the short run.

In the context of limited capacity and resources, alternative approaches that leverage private capital and skills, lower regulatory risk, and use the large public-sector demand for broadband as an incentive for investment by the private sector are required. The unintended consequences and potential policy and regulatory failure in Mexico,

Kenya, and Rwanda, all with far less competitive and far more concentrated markets than South Africa, should be taken as a caution to policymakers. Without the institutional capacity and sophistication to oversee the complexity of creating a viable, single, open access network, more stringent enforcement of competition in the market to deal with dominance through well-established practices of asymmetrical economic regulation may be more feasible, as the case of Mexico demonstrates.

Finally, the high levels of risk associated with the likely protracted legal battles that would ensue from an exclusive open access network, as proposed in South Africa, would delay the release of high-demand spectrum, at considerable cost to the economy.

Voluntary Open Access Fiber Networks The commercial companies in South Africa that operate voluntary open access models to optimize their traffic flows and maximize their short-term return on investments so that they can refinance the next phase of network rollout are contributing to network extension in a cost-effective manner. Although this results in the duplication of networks, this is certainly the case in metropolitan areas, where competition can be easily sustained, and there is also ample evidence of complementary geographic investments by different tiers and types of operators. Moreover, procurement or sharing of infrastructure for primary and redundant use for national coverage is taking place.

New Ways of Extending the Commons

Accepting that large numbers of Africans will not be able to afford to be optimally online, even if markets were effectively regulated and prices were cost based, deploying spectrum to create and extend the commons (i.e., the unlicensed spectrum) would be a key enabler. Extending commercially available public Wi-Fi from elite urban areas, possibly through deploying poorly utilized universal service funds or other public resources to all public spaces, offers a viable way of increasing the intensity of use in urban areas and enhancing network effects that would contribute to more inclusive digital development.

This chapter argues for an innovative policymaking approach that understands the need for a new interplay between state and market. It looks at novel models of access, service delivery, investment, and risk that leverage private and community knowhow, low-cost technology innovations, and complementary access solutions such as FPW.

There is a need for even greater regulatory agility and insight to manage tensions between the various policy objectives of competitive efficiency, innovation, and consumer welfare, as well as the safeguarding of the public and social value of the Internet through the extension of spectrum commons (i.e., an unlicensed and social use spectrum). In developed and developing countries alike, most of the spectrum is largely unused outside main metropolitan areas. In the sharing economy of the Internet era, we are already seeing voluntary infrastructure sharing by operators. These types of approaches need to be embraced by governments from a critical resources management perspective. Enabling secondary spectrum use would enable new dynamic spectrum sharing, which operates at a fraction of the cost of the Global System for Mobile Communications (GSM) network (originally known as Groupe Spécial Mobile) to be deployed on new business models in the largely unused spectrum in rural areas. Such an approach could instantly provide low-cost, high-quality bandwidth.

With the long-term evolution of fifth generation (5G) under way, African governments need to ensure that the potential of this technology, which operates within a spectrum-sharing environment with data offloads to proprietorial and open public Wi-Fi, is harnessed for public purposes, not just for niche commercial applications.

Similarly, one of the main arguments in favor of zero-rating is that it brings down the cost of access to and use of information in developing countries. A user of Wikipedia Zero, for example, has unlimited, no-cost access to everything in the online encyclopedia. Furthermore, providing free access to popular content and services is preferable, from an access to information perspective, to restricted access or no access at all. Such free access may drive the demand for general-purpose, mobile Internet access that can stimulate demand and fund investment in infrastructure. If the unverified data provided by Facebook can be used as an indication, it may be that zero-rated services provide, to some extent, a gateway to the Internet. Facebook claims that 50 percent of Internet.org/Free Basics users move on to use some paid data service within a month of using the free service for the first time (Internet.org 2015[17] quoted in Futter and Gillwald 2015).

Traditionally, the net neutrality argument has been applied to ensuring equivalent quality of service to everyone who accesses the Internet by preventing positive pricing discrimination. The main problem with the net neutrality argument for banning zero-rated products, however, is that it prioritizes the principle of net neutrality over other public interest principles of universality and equality (of access, not quality) (Gillwald et al. 2016a). Applying net neutrality to zero-rating through negative pricing discrimination affects not the technical quality of the Internet, but the entry to and use of it. In African countries, where affordable access is the main factor inhibiting Internet take-up, and where even cost based prices may be unaffordable to many, zero-rated services may provide access to the Internet that otherwise would not be at all possible.

The critique of zero-rating on the grounds of breaching net neutrality in the mobile prepaid environment also tends to conflate different competitive outcomes for different players and elements, which, if found to have anticompetitive outcomes, may require different policy and regulatory remedies to address them at the level at which they occur, rather than through blanket bans or restrictions.

RIA's detailed pricing of products across the African markets also confirms that zero-rating is one of multiple short term market strategies to grow market share by late market entrants. If most users do not buy data at some point, it will not make sense as a business strategy for mobile network operators to continue to discount their data use of this platform (Gillwald et al. 2016a).

With regard to the mobile market, which is the market providing access to the majority of Internet users in Africa, zero-rating of products by late entrant operators in fact may be competition enhancing; and regulators should refrain from regulating it, so long as it does not establish or entrench anticompetitive practices or long-term dominance in a market. While it can be argued that zero-rating enhances the dominance of the platform that is being supported (e.g., Free Basics) and channels users to it, it should be noted that social networking in general, and Facebook in particular (whether it is zero-rated or not), is driving Internet take-up.

Conclusions

The cases of open access discussed in this chapter highlight the need for a case-by-case, context-specific consideration of open access applications. In highly resource-constrained environments, those resources that are available must be optimized to deliver on the social good promised by broadband and digital economy policies.

While open access policies and strategies have again become part of the best practice telecommunications reform templates to deal with absence or bottlenecks in broadband networks,[18] and the principle of openness underpins the public Internet, the uncritical use of open access strategies in developing countries operating under conditions of scarcity and constraint can end up disrupting existing systems without offering more favorable access conditions or enhancing planned developmental outcomes. Network competition is still seen as producing the best outcomes regarding public policy objectives in more developed economies; but the duplication of infrastructure and the fragmentation of demand typical in such cases are not feasible in most developing markets, or even in some more mature ones (Gillwald et al. 2016b). Where states are weak and lack the institutional capacity to enable or enforce open access, the instrumental application of open access solutions may have unintended consequences or promote elite outcomes that can end up exacerbating current bottlenecks or digital exclusion.

In much of the literature on open access and in the advocacy that accompanies its implementation, the value attached to the infrastructure tends to be siloed according to the delivery mechanism. Yet the information infrastructure underpinning our modern economy and society is now a mixed commercial, public, and social infrastructure. In practice, communications resource management has become far more complex than ever, with value being delivered through various hybrid regulated and unregulated models. Communications infrastructure is no longer simply a national communications system, manageable through national policy or regulation. Policy, regulation, and practice develop in response to technology developments in global markets, and increasingly through global governance, although they play out at the national and local levels. We see public and private networks delivering market goods with social value (productive use in downstream activities) and using nonmarket and public goods to transact and produce private goods, as people move from simply being users or producers to being both within the new forms of content development and provision in the platform economy. While the current practices largely undervalue public and social value, as this is classically understood in public goods or the commons, considerable social and public value is offered by private infrastructure investments driven by profit imperatives. This is particularly so in places where, without private provisioning, there was not, or would not be, much delivery of communications infrastructure at all.

Policymakers and regulators need to gear themselves up to the complex adaptive systems that have developed globally; regulators should be focusing on enabling and creating incentives to ensure that the underlying network necessary to support the high-value informational infrastructure is affordably available. This will require reducing cost drivers in developing markets through the regulation of infrastructure sharing through incentives and enabling rights of way regimes, as well as enforcing limitations on fruitless duplications in trenching and masts. Instead of adopting instrumental static regulation of competition derived from telecommunications regulation, regulators need to see how they can be channeling complementary investments and moving toward an industry-coordinating role by enabling voluntary models that allow the participants to assume the risk associated with high-sunk-cost infrastructure investments and open innovation.

Acknowledgments

The case studies used in this chapter draw on research undertaken for (1) Research ICT Africa policy papers on open access networks, by Alison Gillwald and with Fola Odufuwa, Broc Rademan, and Steve Esselaar; (2) on public Wi-Fi deployment in South Africa, by Alison Gillwald with Christopher Geerdts, Chenai Chair, Enrico Calandro, Mpho Moyo, and Broc Rademan; and (3) on zero-rating, by the author with Chenai

Chair, Ariel Futter, Fola Odufuwa, Kweku Korateng, and John Walabengu. For more information, see http://www.researrchictafrica.net.

The author thanks the editors and reviewers of this chapter for their invaluable comments, and especially Raul Zambrano, who contributed extensively to the chapter's structure. Any errors or omissions are those of the author.

Notes

1. OECD (2013), the ITU (2011), the New Partnership for Africa's Development (NEPAD 2010), the Body of European Regulators of Electronic Communications (BEREC 2011), and the European Commission (2011) have generally accepted a set of open access principles, but no common definition.

2. Nondiscrimination does not exclude volume discounts or other market segmentation tools, so long as they are available to all customers (i.e., customers would qualify, provided that they meet transparent volume requirements) (Gillwald et al. 2016b).

3. Within this regulatory framework, *openness* is not equated with *free*. Concepts of free (as in no cost to users) emerged in regulatory theory more with regard to regulation to deal with market failure and the need for subsidized access to services found in universal service regulation. In practical terms, free or subsidized services were realized through obligations on operators to contribute to universal service funds or to cover certain percentages of the population, or the provisioning of telecenters and, more recently, the provisioning of free public Wi-Fi.

4. The shifting and contentious position of the US Federal Communications Commission (FCC) in its latest regulations, called "Restoring Internet Freedom Order," which took effect on June 11, 2018, has outraged net neutrality proponents. It claims to provide "a framework for protecting an open Internet while paving the way for better, faster, and cheaper Internet access for consumers." It overturns former "unnecessary, heavy-handed regulations that were developed way back in 1934 with strong consumer protections, increased transparency, and common-sense rules that will promote investment and broadband deployment" (FCC n.d.).

5. OTT services and platforms are those that are delivered over the Internet, typically by broadband.

6. According to the Wikipedia "Backhaul (Telecommunications)" entry, "[T]he backhaul portion of the network comprises the intermediate links between the core network, or backbone network, and the small subnetworks at the 'edge' of the entire hierarchical network.... Visualizing the entire hierarchical network as a human skeleton, the core network would represent the spine, the backhaul links would be the limbs, the edge networks would be the hands and feet, and the individual links within those edge networks would be the fingers and toes" (Wikipedia 2018a).

7. The initial telecommunications reforms in the mid-1990s, which helped establish an independent regulatory authority and the liberalization of markets, introduced the first transparent access regime through interconnection and facilities leasing guidelines in compliance with General Agreement on Trade in Services (GATS) agreement on basic telecommunications.

8. According to the Wikipedia "Local-Loop Unbundling" entry, "Local loop unbundling...is the regulatory process of allowing multiple *telecommunications* operators to use connections from the telephone exchange to the *customer*'s premises" (Wikipedia 2018b).

9. In 2007, the Honorable Minister Ivy Matsepe-Casaburri, the minister of communications, appointed an LLU Committee, which in May of that year issued a report called *Local Loop Unbundling: A Way Forward for South Africa*.

10. Passive sharing is most common and occurring voluntarily as operators manage their costs with the transition to data. However, mandatory requirements on mobile operators to offer virtual private networks or access point name access to ISPs, in a way similar to bitstream on fixed lines, is emerging in some African countries.

11. See Williams (2010) for an example of the World Bank's philosophy of competition, where network competition is not feasible.

12. The West Africa Cable System (WACS) is a high-capacity, fiber-optic, underwater cable that links South Africa and western Africa to Europe via the United Kingdom.

13. It was clear by the time of the diagnostic report undertaken in 2011 for the National Development Plan that BBI was perceived as having failed. The company was undercapitalized and unable to compete with the low-cost, commercial open access companies that had emerged to fill the vacuum left by the incumbent Telkom's failure to embrace emerging broadband technologies. BBI had a single client, Neotel, and was unable to service its own network; in addition, Neotel had not built out its own intercity transmission network with the mobile operators Vodacom and MTN (Cohen, then the chief corporate services officer of Neotel, interview 2016).

14. *4G* refers to the fourth generation of the GSM technology standards developed by the European Telecommunications Standards Institute (ETSI) to describe the protocols for the second-generation (2G) digital cellular networks used by mobile phones, first deployed in Finland in July 1991, to the 5G currently being deployed in mature markets. As of 2014, it has become the default global standard for mobile communications, with over 90 percent market share, operating in over 219 countries and territories. For more information, see https://www.gsma.com/futurenetworks/faq/gsm/.

15. The DTPS was merged into the Department: Communications and Digital Technologies (DCDT) in June 2019.

16. The author served on the Western Cape Broadband Initiative advisory group between 2012 and 2014 to review the public-private delivery plan.

17. See https://info.internet.org/en/blog/2015/11/19/internet-org-myths-and-facts/.

18. Although initially there was resistance by African governments, largely as a result of pressure from their telecommunications incumbents, at the policy level, open access found currency through its extensive promotion by infoDev, a World Bank organization, a decade ago. This had a significant impact on telecom reform policy and practice. Open access regulation in areas such as interconnection (and, later, local loop unbundling) was emulated from the European

Commission by many African regulators. Also, infoDev described open access as being "about creating competition in all layers of the IP network, allowing a wide variety of physical networks and applications to interact in an open architecture" (Spintrack 2005, 8).

References

Bauer, Johannes M. 2014. "Platforms, Systems Competition, and Innovation: Reassessing the Foundations of Communications Policy." *Telecommunications Policy* 38 (8–9): 662–673. https://doi.org/10.1016/j.telpol.2014.04.008.

Bauer, Johannes M., and Erik Bohlin. 2008. "From Static to Dynamic Regulation: Recent Developments in U.S. Telecommunications Policy." *Intereconomics: Review of European Economic Policy* 43 (1): 38–50.

Bedi, I., and R. Schumann. 2013. "Market Structure and Open Access for South Africa Broadband: A Discussion Paper for the DTPS and GTAC." London: Analysys Mason Ltd. (unpublished).

Benkler, Yochai. 2013. In *Open Development: Networked Innovations in International Development*, eds. Matthew L. Smith and Katherine M. A. Reilly, vii–ix. Cambridge, MA/Ottawa: MIT Press/IDRC. https://www.idrc.ca/en/book/open-development-networked-innovations-international-development.

Body of European Regulators for Electronic Communications. 2011. *BEREC Report on "Open Access,"* BOR (11) 05. Riga, Latvia: BEREC. http://www.berec.europa.eu/eng/document_register/subject_matter/berec/reports/?doc=212.

Economides, Nicholas, and Joacim Tåg. 2012. "Network Neutrality on the Internet: A Two-Sided Market Analysis." *Information Economics and Policy* 24:91–104.

Eisenach, Jeffrey A. 2015. *The Economics of Zero Rating.* NERA Economic Consulting. www.nera.com/content/dam/nera/publications/2015/EconomicsofZeroRating.pdf.

Ellipsis. 2011. "ICASA Releases Findings on Local Loop Unbundling Framework." *Ellipsis*, November 30. https://www.ellipsis.co.za/icasa-releases-findings-on-local-loop-unbundling/.

European Commission. 2011. "The Open Internet and Net Neutrality in Europe." P7_TA(2011) 0511 European Parliament Resolution on the Open Internet and Net Neutrality in Europe 2013/C 153 E/15. https://eur-lex.europa.eu/legal-content/EN/TXT/?uri=CELEX%3A52011IP0511#ntr1-CE2013153EN.01012801-E0001.

European Telecommunications Network Operators' Association (ETNO). 2012. *ETNO Contribution. ITR's Proposal to Address New Internet Ecosystem.* https://etno.eu/datas/itu-matters/etno-ip-interconnection.pdf.

Federal Communications Commission (FCC). n.d. "Restoring Internet Freedom." Washington, DC: Federal Communications Commission. https://www.fcc.gov/restoring-internet-freedom.

Frischmann, B. M. 2005. "An Economic Theory of Infrastructure and Commons Management." *Minnesota Law Review* 89:917–1030.

Frischmann, B. M. 2012. *Infrastructure: The Social Value of Shared Resources*. New York: Oxford University Press.

Futter, Ariel, and Alison Gillwald. 2015. *Zero-Rated Internet Services: What Is to Be Done?* Policy Paper 1: Broadband for Africa. September. https://www.researchictafrica.net/docs/Facebook%20 zerorating%20Final_Web.pdf.

Geerdts, Christopher, and Alison Gillwald. 2017. "Developing Smart Free Public Wi-Fi in South Africa: Can Public Wi-Fi Help Redress Digital Inequality, and If So, How? Emerging Lessons from South Africa's Diverse Implementations." *SSRN*. https://papers.ssrn.com/sol3/papers.cfm ?abstract_id=3043690.

Geerdts, Christopher, Alison Gillwald, Enrico Calandro, Chenai Chair, Mpho Moyo, and Broc Rade- man. 2016. *Developing Smart Wi-Fi in South Africa*. Cape Town, South Africa: Research ICT Africa. https://www.researchictafrica.net/publications/Other_publications/2016_Public_Wi-Fi_Policy _Paper_-_Developing_Smart_Public_Wi-Fi_in_South_Africa.pdf.

Gillwald, Alison. 2005. "Good Intentions, Poor Outcomes: Telecommunications Reform in South Africa." *Telecommunications Policy* 29 (7): 469–491.

Gillwald, Alison. 2007. "Between Two Stools: Broadband Developments in South Africa." *Southern African Journal of Information and Communication*. Johannesburg: LINK Centre, Witwatersrand Uni- versity. http://wiredspace.wits.ac.za/bitstream/handle/10539/19787/SAJIC-Issue-8-2007-Gillwald .pdf?sequence=1&isAllowed=y.

Gillwald, Alison. 2016. *Beyond Access: Addressing Digital Inequality in Africa*. Paper Series no. 48. Waterloo, Canada/London: Centre for International Governance Innovation (CIGI)/Royal Insti- tute of International Affairs.

Gillwald, Alison, Chenai Chair, Ariel Futter, Kweku Koranteng, Fola Odufuwa, and John Walubengo. 2016a. *Much Ado about Nothing: Zero Rating in the African Context*. Policy Paper 1. vol. 4. Cape Town, South Africa: Research ICT Africa.

Gillwald, Alison, Fola Odufuwa, Broc Rademan, and Steve Esselaar. 2016b. *An Evaluation of Open Access in Africa: The Cases of Nigeria and South Africa*. Policy Paper no. 2, vol. 4. Cape Town, South Africa: Research ICT Africa. https://researchictafrica.net/publications/Other_publications/2016 _Integrated_Policy_Paper_-_Open_Access_Broadband_Networks_in_Africa.pdf.

Goldsmith, Jack L., and Tim Wu. 2006. *Who Controls the Internet? Illusions of a Borderless World*. Oxford: Oxford University Press.

Hirschman, Albert O. 1958. *The Strategy of Economic Development*. New Haven, CT: Yale University Press.

International Telecommunications Union (ITU). 2011. "Open Access Regulation in the Digital Economy." GSR 2011 Discussion Paper. www.itu.int/ITU-D/treg/Events/Seminars/GSR/GSR11 /documents/02-Open%20Access-E.pdf.

Internet.org. 2015. "Free Basics: Myths and Facts," *Internet.org by Facebook*, November 19. https:// internet.org/press/internet-dot-org-myths-and-facts.

Krämer, Jan, and Daniel Schnurr. 2014. "A Unified Framework for Open Access Regulation of Telecommunications Infrastructure: Review of the Economic Literature and Policy Guidelines." *Telecommunications Policy* 38 (11): 1160–1179.

Lee, Robin, and Tim Wu. 2009. "Subsidizing Creativity through Network Design: Zero-Pricing and Net Neutrality." *Journal of Economic Perspectives* 23 (3): 61–76.

Lessig, Lawrence. 2001. *The Future of Ideas: The Fate of the Commons in a Connected World.* New York: Vintage Books.

Lumu, D. 2015. "Museveni Directs Gov't Agencies to Use UTL." *New Vision*, January 29 (1, 5).

Ministry of Communications, Department of Communications, Independent Communications Authority of South Africa. 2007. *Local Loop Unbundling: A Way Forward for South Africa.* Pretoria, South Africa: Ministry of Communications. https://www.ellipsis.co.za/wp-content/uploads/2014/03/local_loop_unbundling.pdf.

MyBroadband. 2014. "XDSL Signs Agreement with Dark Fibre Africa and Conduct for More Fibre, Faster." *MyBroadband.* April 14. http://companies.mybroadband.co.za/blog/2014/04/14/xdsl-signs-agreement-with-dark-fibre-africa-and-conduct-for-more-fibre-faster/.

New Partnership for Africa's Development (NEPAD). 2010. "Protocol on Policy and Regulatory Framework for NEPAD ICT Broadband Infrastructure Network for Africa." https://www.nepad.org/fr/fr-nepad/publication/protocol-policy-and-regulatory-framework-nepad-ict-broadband-infrastructure.

North, Douglass C. 1990. *Institutions, Institutional Change, and Economic Performance.* New York: Cambridge University Press.

North, Douglass C. 2005. *Understanding the Process of Institutional Change.* Princeton, NJ: Princeton University Press.

Organisation for Economic Co-operation and Development (OECD). 2013. *Broadband Networks and Open Access.* OECD Digital Economy Papers, no. 218. Paris: OECD Publishing. http://dx.doi.org/10.1787/5k49qgz7crmr-en.

Ostrom, Elinor. 2009. "Beyond Markets and States: Polycentric Governance of Complex Economic Systems." Prize Lecture, Workshop in Political Theory and Policy Analysis, Indiana University Bloomington. https://www.nobelprize.org/prizes/economic-sciences/2009/ostrom/lecture/.

Republic of South Africa (RSA). 2016. *National Integrated ICT White Paper.* Pretoria, South Africa: Department of Telecommunications and Postal Services. https://www.ellipsis.co.za/wp-content/uploads/2016/10/National-Integrated-ICT-Policy-White-Paper.pdf.

Research ICT Africa (RIA). 2016. *Western Cape Digital Readiness Assessment.* Cape Town, South Africa: Research ICT Africa; University of Cape Town; University of the Western Cape.

Rey-Moreno, Carlos. 2013. *Alternatives for Affordable Communications in Rural South Africa: Innovative Regulatory Responses to Increase Affordable Rural Access.* Submission to the Parliament of South Africa. http://www.r2k.org.za/wp-content/uploads/Policy-brief-Cost-to-Communicate_13092016_FOR-SUBMISSION.pdf.

Spintrack, A. B. 2005. *Open Access Models: Options for Improving Backbone Access in Developing Countries (with a Focus on Sub-Saharan Africa)*. Washington, DC: infoDev/World Bank. http://www .infodev.org/en/Publication.10.html.

Stork, Christoph, Calandro Enrico, and Gillwald Alison. 2013. *Understanding Internet Going Mobile. Internet Access and Use in Eleven African Countries*. Policy Paper 14. Cape Town, South Africa: Research ICT Africa.

Telkom. 2016. Group Annual Results for the Year Ended 31 March 2016. http://www.telkom.co .za/ir/apps_static/ir/pdf/financial/pdf/Telkom_Annual_Results_Booklet_WP_2016_Final.pdf.

Telkom. 2017. Group Annual Provisional Results for the Year Ended 31 March 2017. http://www .telkom.co.za/ir/apps_static/ir/pdf/financial/pdf/Telkom_Annual_Results_Booklet_WP_2017_Final .pdf.

Wikipedia. 2018a. "Backhaul (Telecommunications)." https://en.wikipedia.org/wiki/Backhaul.

Wikipedia. 2018b. "Local-Loop Unbundling." https://en.wikipedia.org/wiki/Local-loop_unbundling.

Williams, Mark D. J. 2010. *Broadband for Africa: Developing Backbone Communications Networks*. Washington, DC: World Bank. License: CC BY 3.0 IGO. https://openknowledge.worldbank.org /handle/10986/2422.

Interviews

Brooks, Ant, former coordinator, October 2017.

Clatterbuck, Byron, chief executive officer, Seacom, March 2016.

Cohen, Dr. Tracy, chief services officer, Neotel, 2016.

Cull, Dominic, regulatory advisor, Internet Service Providers' Association (ISPA), 2016.

Edmunson, Kerron, advisor; Graham Mackinnon, legal regulatory executive; and Herman Pretorius, strategy executive, Cell C, May 2016.

Fernando Borjón Figueroa, Luis, secretary (DG), Communication and Transport Department, Mexico, 2016.

Hawthorne, Ryan, economist, Acacia Economics, May 2018.

Hussein, Arif, chief executive officer, FibreCo, 2016.

Johnson, Jo-Ann, deputy director-general, Department of Economic Development and Tourism, Western Cape Government, May 2016.

Labardini, Adriana, Comisionada del Instituto Federal de Telecomunicaciones (Regulator Mexico), discussion at net neutrality seminar, CIDE, 2016.

Mjwara, Joe, acting director general, Department of Telecommunications and Postal Services (DTPS), 2016.

Nkhereanye, Phatang, regulatory affairs and government relations manager, Broadband Infraco (BBI), 2016.

Nyoka, Nkateko, chief officer of legal, regulatory, and risk, Vodacom SA, March 2016.

Padayachee, Prenesh, chief of sales and marketing, Openserve, 2016.

Rey-Moreno, Carlos, postdoctoral fellow, University of the Western Cape, 2017.

Roux, Kobus, manager, strategic initiatives, Meraka Institute, CSIR, March 2016.

Smit, Gustav, chief executive officer, Dark Fibre Africa (DFA), 2015.

Song, Steve, founder, Village Telco project, 2017.

9 Who Benefits from Open Models? The Role of ICT Access in the Consumption of Open Activities

Roxana Barrantes and Paulo Matos

Introduction

The Internet and other information and communication technologies (ICTs) are transforming the ways in which people communicate and interact. People are now actively participating and interacting online in ways that are unthinkable in the physical world and were unimaginable just a decade ago.

In this context, the concept of *open practices* has arisen in the literature (see chapter 2 of this volume and Smith and Seward 2017). Open practices are a specific set of ways that people engage and participate online that involve collaborative production processes, as well as the distribution and use of free content. As articulated throughout this volume, under the right conditions, these practices have the potential to help achieve human development targets.

Yet, despite the promised benefits that these practices bring, and the great optimism with which they are sometimes treated in the literature, the reality is that society as a whole is far from benefiting equally from open activities because a large sector of the population is excluded from said benefits (Kularski and Moller 2012; Fairlie 2017; see also chapters 1 and 5 of this volume). As discussed in chapter 2, key features of what is called *open* are that in theory, there is no direct cost for participating in a certain platform, and anybody can do it. In practice, however, there are barriers such as hidden costs and skills that are needed in order to participate. Participation typically assumes access to the Internet, or at least a mobile network connection, and that users have reached a level of education that allows them to engage in a meaningful manner. In some cases, it is even necessary to belong to a certain social circle to even hear of the possibility of participation. The upshot of these factors is that the benefits of open practices do not accrue equitably.

In this chapter, we explore the relationship of personal factors surrounding the use of ICTs and the extent to which and how someone benefits from open activities or, conversely, remains excluded. The data used in this chapter come from the After Access Survey–2017 carried out by the DIRSI[1] network. The survey collected information about access to and use of the Internet for five Latin American countries, each with a different per-capita income level: Argentina (high-income), Colombia and Peru (upper-middle-income), Paraguay (lower-middle-income), and Guatemala (low-income).

The data and analysis show that the socioeconomic context in which people are embedded, which affects a broad range of issues, from where people live, to education status, to how they access the Internet, to work opportunities, matters a great deal. In particular, we explore how the devices that people use and the places where people access the Internet, coupled with personal characteristics, affect their engagement and potential benefit from open activities.

Two main findings stand out. First, the more people in these countries engage in more open activities, the more familiar they are with the Internet, as reflected by the number of years they have used the Internet, or the more devices they can use. The second result is that socioeconomic context still matters: people with higher levels of education, who have a higher socioeconomic status, or who live in richer countries will engage more in open activities. The first finding gives us room to recommend sector-specific policies. The second finding leaves us recommending sound macroeconomic policies.

The chapter unfolds as follows. The next section presents the theoretical framework in which we discuss the meaning of the term *open* and outlines the contextual elements that we have identified. The three subsequent sections provide an analysis of the data on the open use practices in the five countries. The first of these defines user profiles based on socioeconomic information and how they access the Internet. The second presents a descriptive analysis of the effect of the diverse Internet access forms on the number of open practices that the agents engage in, associated with educational purposes, government relations, job search, entertainment, and current events. Finally, the third presents our detailed analysis, using a multivariate econometric model, which outlines the impact of context (personal characteristics and type of access) on the probability that individuals engage in open practices, specifically focusing on education, government, and job search. The final section offers our concluding thoughts.

The Analytical Framework: What We Mean by *Open* and *Context*

In this section, we define what we mean by *open*, drawing on the analytical framework proposed in chapter 2. This is a necessary first step in trying to understand how the *context* (in this case, one's personal characteristics and type of access) shapes the ways in which one benefits from open practices (or not). After the clarification of the term *open*, we then explain the way in which the context creates barriers or enables our use of digital platforms, the Internet, and open practices. This gives content to the context, and therefore to the mechanisms that condition the use of technology and the practice of open activities.

Defining *Open* and Different Online Uses as a Proxy of Benefits

This chapter focuses on the open practice of open consumption, understood as the liberty to use content and platforms created and distributed by other people or organizations. By focusing on use, we do not consider how people contribute to the creation or expansion of the platform, but we do emphasize the benefits they receive (and perceive) from open activities. According to Smith and Seward (2017), "Consumption of content is ultimately what allows people to benefit (or not) from open processes, and through those benefits, realize other impacts, such as saving money or achieving better grades." In this way, the consumption of open activities not only determines who benefits, at least directly, from the open process, but it also shapes other relevant social impacts. Critically, open consumption is highly influenced by the individual's context, which we define as the means of access and some individual personal characteristics, as shown in figure 9.1.

Before developing a more accurate definition of context, it is necessary to explain what we mean by "benefits of open consumption." As mentioned, the term *open consumption* refers to people's usage of free online platforms or freely distributed resources. Therefore, the actual use of a platform or online resource in a specific area, such as education, job searching, work, or entertainment, implies a benefit. In this chapter, the number of open tasks that a person engages in serves as a proxy of the benefits that one obtains from open consumption. For example, if person A enrolls in a free online course, checks free digital libraries, and accesses a free database, while person B reads literature online, we could argue that person A is receiving more benefits from open education consumption than person B. Of course, the proxy is not perfect; for example, person's B usage could be more complex and in-depth, while person A's usage quite superficial.

The Content of the Context: From ICT Access to the Use and Appropriation of Digital Benefits

In this section, we develop two analytical models that complement the concepts proposed previously. These models explain the role that personal characteristics and the form of access play in the appropriation of the benefits obtained through open activities.

The first analytical model is the one elaborated by Selwyn (2010 and 2015), in which the connection between the use of technologies and the acquisition of relevant

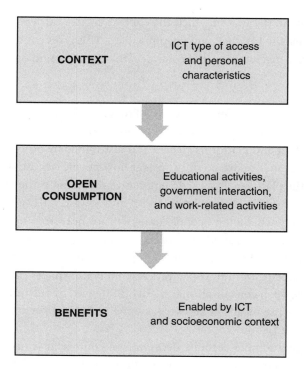

Figure 9.1
Context as a benefit facilitator in open activities.

variables influences the welfare of people. According to the model, simply having access to a set of technologies does not guarantee the appropriation of the benefits that these technologies can bring. Access is only the first step in the acquisition process.

Dodel (2015) proposed two additional levels—usage and appropriation—that are required before achieving the positive results of technology-based activities. Usage of ICTs concerns the frequency, the familiarity, and the diversity of digital uses that an individual can have. *Appropriation* means that the individual not only uses the technology, but also understands how the digital system with which he or she interacts works, what benefits can be gained, what damage it can cause them, and what their role is in that interaction structure. The addition of these levels helps illustrate why the consumption of content and use of digital platforms do not have a homogeneous impact on all individuals. The benefits depend on the familiarity they have with the platform, their level of education, their socioeconomic characteristics, and other factors. See figure 9.2 for a summary of this process.

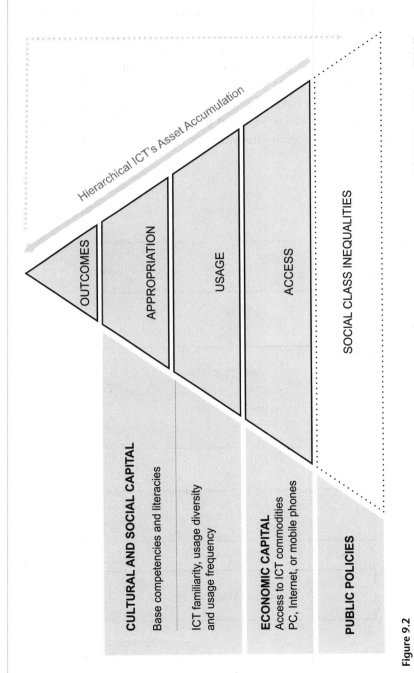

Figure 9.2
The ICT Appropriation Model and the relevant dependent variables for development, according to Dodel (2015) and Selwyn (2010).

Based on the conditions necessary for the digital benefits appropriation process, Van Dijk and Van Deursen (2014) propose something similar to Dodel (2015) and Selwyn (2010) (see figure 9.3). Van Dijk and Van Deursen suggest that four dimensions are required before achieving the expected benefits: motivation, material access, abilities, and time. The first dimension is the individual's motivation to use the technologies. For example, some people may have negative perceptions about the use of ICTs or of a particular service, and so they can be reluctant to utilize them. The second dimension is the physical access to the necessary infrastructure, which is still a relevant issue for

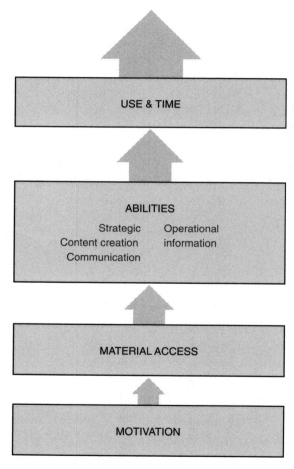

Figure 9.3
Digital benefits appropriation process determinants, adapted from Van Dijk and Van Deursen (2014).

developing countries. For instance, in the countries analyzed in this chapter, despite the fact that their teledensities exceed 100, there are still gaps in smartphone, tablet, and laptop access, which leaves a significant group of the population at a disadvantage.

The third element refers to the abilities that people have to utilize the devices. The authors mention five groups of relevant activities: strategic (knowing which platform to use for which end), creation of content, communication, operational, and news gathering. People who lack these abilities will not be able to obtain the benefits that the digital platforms can provide. The final dimension refers to the time available for the individuals to use the technologies. Van Dijk and Van Deursen (2014, 2) label this latter process as "the new digital divide," as opposed to the digital divide, which takes into account only access to ICT devices.

These models assume a neutral access dimension. In other words, they do not differentiate in terms of the kinds of access (a computer versus a feature phone, or at home as opposed to at a cybercafé). However, the way in which users access the digital infrastructure is not homogeneous; rather, it is differentiated by geographic location and/or the different devices users possess or use, as shown in figure 9.4. For example, for one individual to access the Internet from her or his home is not the same as the same individual accessing it from a workplace or school. In the latter, individuals may interact

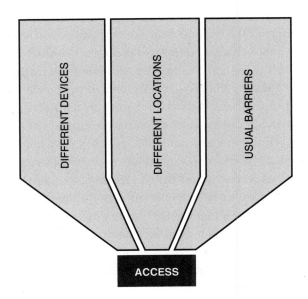

Figure 9.4
Elaborating on factors that affect the nature of access to open practices.

with others and learn about the Internet in ways not available when accessing it alone at home, as explained by Mazimpaka, Mugiraneza and Thioune (2015) and Rabab'ah et al. (2015). This way, certain locations will allow the development of a particular set of skills, while other locations might not. This differentiated access could have a similar effect when considering types of devices: mobile phones may represent a higher level of use of types of certain platforms (mobile applications), while laptops or desktops provide the ability to interact in different ways. As Donner (2015, 78) explains, there is a trend to design websites to be displayed in a different way on different devices, but not all "services residing on Internet servers are being configured to support user interactions across multiple devices." For this research, we combine these various models to develop a framework for understanding the key factors that determine the nature of use of open practices that we use in this study.

Creating User Profiles by Different Types of Internet Access

The first step in our analysis is to create user profiles. These profiles are the most commonly occurring groups of characteristics in terms of each of the following: access location, access devices, and socioeconomic category.

Access from Different Locations

The After Access Survey–2017 includes four possible places where people access the Internet: at home, a public space, a workplace, and a place of study (e.g., school, technical college, or university setting). We grouped those surveyed by the places of access. The first step toward creating the profiles is finding all the possible combinations of places from which people access the web, as shown in table 9.1. The most relevant combinations of the sample are in bold: all places mentioned (30 percent); all places except study (17 percent); home and public (14 percent); only home (13 percent); all places except workplace (10 percent), and home and work (7 percent). Each of the remaining combinations represents less than 5 percent of the sample.

The next step is distinguishing the relevant access combinations by sociodemographic information, which includes gender,[2] position in the household (head, spouse, or child), age group, education level, main occupation, and socioeconomic level. Table 9.2 shows the percentages of access within a certain group (sociodemographic) for each proposed category (access combination). For example, the percentage shown for women indicates the extent of access from a particular combination of locations within the women's sample (i.e., 32 percent of women access the Internet from all the places

Table 9.1
Internet access location combinations.

Home	Public	Work	Study	Observations	%
No	No	No	No	146	2.8
No	No	No	Yes	10	0.2
No	No	Yes	No	16	0.3
No	No	Yes	Yes	3	0.1
No	Yes	No	No	88	1.7
No	Yes	No	Yes	38	0.7
No	Yes	Yes	No	20	0.4
No	Yes	Yes	Yes	25	0.5
Yes	**No**	**No**	**No**	**651**	**12.6**
Yes	No	No	Yes	80	1.5
Yes	**No**	**Yes**	**No**	**369**	**7.1**
Yes	No	Yes	Yes	73	1.4
Yes	**Yes**	**No**	**No**	**728**	**14.1**
Yes	**Yes**	**No**	**Yes**	**500**	**9.7**
Yes	**Yes**	**Yes**	**No**	**889**	**17.2**
Yes	**Yes**	**Yes**	**Yes**	**1,546**	**29.8**

Note: The most relevant combinations are in bold.
Source: After Access Survey–2017.

identified while 28 percent of men do so). This is telling us that women tend to specialize less than men do when choosing where to access the Internet. The categories that stand out from each group appear in bold in table 9.2, taking into account two criteria: the score for that category should be the highest in the category, at least by one percentage point, and should represent more than 10 percent of the whole sample that accesses the Internet. Sticking to the previous example, we highlighted the female gender because it is more than 1 percent higher than the male percentage and it represents more than 10 percent of the total sample. The same analysis is carried out for the rest of the categories. In the case that one group meets just one of the criteria, we also highlight a second group that meets both. That is why the under-age is highlighted in the age category as they compose less than 10 percent of the sample that uses the Internet.

Table 9.3 shows the main access location categories for various socioeconomic profiles.

Table 9.2

Relevant access locations and socioeconomic characteristics, and the percentage of the total of each category in each access combination.

		All places (30%)	All places except study (17%)	Home and public (14%)	Only home (13%)	All places except work (10%)	Home and Work (7%)	All the rest of the categories (9%)	Total
Gender	Female	**32.3**	**18.9**	9.8	**13.3**	9.5	7.2	8.9	100.0
	Male	27.9	15.7	**17.4**	12.0	9.8	7.0	**10.2**	100.0
Relationship with head of household (HH)	Head of HH	25.9	**23.9**	11.5	14.6	3.8	**11.3**	9.1	100.0
	Spouse	26.1	12.8	**23.2**	**18.0**	4.4	6.2	9.2	100.0
	Son/Daughter	**38.2**	11.1	10.5	6.6	**20.5**	2.4	**10.7**	100.0
	Other	31.5	14.5	15.4	7.1	18.5	3.7	9.3	100.0
Age group	Under age	30.0	4.7	12.0	5.5	**32.3**	0.4	**15.2**	100.0
	Young	**38.8**	11.6	12.9	8.4	16.0	2.7	9.8	100.0
	Adult	27.2	**22.1**	14.5	13.9	3.9	**10.3**	8.2	100.0
	Elderly	13.5	13.8	**19.1**	**31.6**	0.7	6.4	**14.9**	100.0
Education level	Incomplete secondary	16.6	12.2	15.1	**23.0**	9.8	**10.9**	**12.9**	100.0
	Complete secondary	24.1	18.6	**18.1**	12.8	9.9	7.0	9.6	100.0
	> Secondary	**39.1**	**18.0**	10.7	8.4	9.4	6.2	8.3	100.0
Main occupation	Unemployed	29.9	7.3	**31.2**	15.4	6.4	2.1	7.7	100.0
	Student	**36.1**	3.7	6.7	3.4	**37.4**	0.4	**12.3**	100.0
	Employee	**36.3**	**27.5**	7.1	7.5	2.1	10.8	8.6	100.0
	Employer	**37.1**	**27.0**	3.4	9.6	2.2	**14.6**	6.2	100.0
	Independent	25.9	**28.2**	9.2	12.4	3.0	**13.0**	8.3	100.0
	Nonactive*	20.4	4.7	**30.7**	**25.4**	6.0	2.0	11.0	100.0

*The Nonactive category includes people who are currently not working, not looking for work, and are not studying. Standout categories are in bold.

Source: After Access Survey–2017.

Table 9.3
Socioeconomic profiles and access groups, and locations.

	All places	All places except study	Home and public	Only home	All places except work	Home and work (7%)
Gender	Female	Female	Male	Female	Either	Either
Relationship with HH*	Son/ daughter	HH*	Spouse	Spouse	Son/ daughter	HH*
Age group	Young	Adult	Elderly	Elderly	Young or under age	Adult
Education level	> Secondary	Complete secondary or more	Complete secondary	Incomplete secondary	Either	Incomplete secondary
Main occupation	Student, employee, or employer	Employee, employer, or independent	Unem- ployed or nonactive	Nonactive	Student	Employer or independent

* HH means head of household.
Source: After Access Survey–2017.

Access from Different Devices

In this second subsection, we apply the same procedure to identify combinations of devices: smartphone, tablet, and PC. Four relevant combinations were obtained, which in total represent more than 95 percent of the total sample, and these appear in bold in table 9.4. These combinations are access to all devices except tablet (48 percent), mobile phone only (34 percent), PC or laptop only (8 percent), and access to all devices (6 percent).

Within each access device combination, the percentages and the socioeconomic profiles are shown in tables 9.5 and 9.6, respectively. For the first relevant access combination, "All devices except tablet," there are no significant differences between the female and male groups. Nevertheless, with regard to the rest of the categories, the following groups are highlighted: "Son/daughter," "Young," "Under-aged," "Higher than secondary [education]," and "Student." As expected, people under 25 tend to be mostly students. As millennials, this population has grown up with the Internet and is typically familiar with these access devices.

The increasing affordability of the smartphone is allowing more people than ever to access the Internet, to enter the digital economy, and to benefit from life-enhancing opportunities. In Latin America, there has been a tremendous increase in the consumption of mobile Internet data: it grew from 5 million gigabytes in 2010 to 956 million

Table 9.4

Possible Internet access device combinations.

Mobile Phone	Tablet	PC or Laptop	Observations	%
No	No	No	117	2.3
No	No	Yes	**400**	7.7
No	Yes	No	10	0.2
No	Yes	Yes	27	0.5
Yes	No	No	**1,788**	34.5
Yes	No	Yes	**2,472**	47.7
Yes	Yes	No	42	0.8
Yes	Yes	Yes	**326**	6.3

Note: The more relevant combinations in the sample are in bold.
Source: After Access Survey–2017.

in 2017 (Ericsson 2017)—an exponential increase over the seven-year period. Perhaps unsurprisingly, then, individuals who responded "Mobile phone only" in the After Access Survey were users with the fewest years of Internet experience, these are further highlighted in our sociodemographic categories as "Female," "Spouse," "Elderly," "High school dropout," and "Nonactive." From an inclusion perspective, it is important to understand what activities these users can realistically perform on a mobile phone alone.

Finally, the group that has access to all devices is characterized as being young or adult, and having education higher than the secondary level. Unsurprisingly, those with the most online skills and formal education are those who also have the greatest diversity of access.

The next section analyzes the effect of the type of access, both physical and digital, on the number of open activities carried out by an individual.

The Effect of Forms of Access in the Different Uses of Open Activities

The second part of the analysis presented here focuses on the correlation between the profiles of access defined previously and the use of Internet, as defined by a set of activities related to education, work (job search or job-related activities), and engaging with government for services. Table 9.7 shows the types of activities, which we use as a proxy for open consumption practices.

In particular, we divide the practices into *open* and *mostly open*. In the case of *open*, we refer to tasks that do not imply any kind of cost (free). *Mostly open* activities are

Table 9.5

Main Internet access device combinations, percentage of the total of each category in each access combination.

		All devices except tablet (48%)	Only mobile phone (34%)	Only PC (8%)	All devices (6%)	All the rest of the categories	Total
Gender	Female	47.9	**35.9**	6.9	5.9	3.5	100.0
	Male	47.6	33.4	**8.4**	6.6	4.0	100.0
Relationship with head of household	Head of household	42.0	39.2	8.4	6.2	**4.2**	100.0
	Spouse	38.7	**40.7**	9.3	6.9	**4.4**	100.0
	Son/daughter	61.7	23.5	6.1	6.0	2.7	100.0
	Other	53.7	31.5	4.9	6.2	3.7	100.0
Age group	Under age	**63.9**	21.5	7.5	4.1	3.0	100.0
	Young	**56.3**	29.3	4.8	**6.7**	2.9	100.0
	Adult	42.8	38.5	8.4	6.6	3.7	100.0
	Elderly	29.8	**40.4**	**15.6**	4.3	**9.9**	100.0
Education level	Incomplete secondary	31.2	**55.1**	7.8	2.0	**4.1**	100.0
	Complete secondary	43.8	40.3	7.5	4.1	**4.5**	100.0
	Higher than secondary	**56.9**	22.4	7.8	**9.5**	3.3	100.0
Main occupation	Unemployed	47.0	31.6	9.8	7.7	3.8	100.0
	Student	**67.1**	18.8	5.4	6.9	1.9	100.0
	Employee	49.4	33.7	6.5	**6.8**	3.6	100.0
	Employer	48.9	29.8	7.3	**10.1**	3.9	100.0
	Independent	44.5	37.9	8.0	5.6	4.1	100.0
	Nonactive*	34.3	**45.2**	**10.3**	5.2	**5.1**	100.0

*The Nonactive category includes people who are currently not working, not looking for work, and are not studying. Standout categories are in bold.

Source: After Access Survey–2017.

Table 9.6
Socioeconomic profile and access groups, and devices.

	All devices except tablet	Mobile phone only	Only PC	All devices
Gender	Either	Female	Male	Either
Relationship with head of household	Son/daughter	Spouse	Head of household or spouse	Any
Age group	Young or under age	Elderly	Elderly	Adult or young
Education level	> Secondary	Incomplete secondary	Either one	> Secondary
Main occupation	Student	Nonactive	Nonactive	Any except independent or nonactive

Source: After Access Survey–2017.

those that might have a minimal cost. For example, for education, the search and download of literature may involve a download cost, but the survey did not ask about these potential costs.

In total, we identified twenty-five tasks (outlined in table 9.7): nine in education, seven in terms of job searching or work, and nine for government services.

Figure 9.5 displays the number of activities that each individual carries out within each task group, related with the access location. The number of realized tasks by the agents is very low on average (in the sample, only three of the twenty-five tasks were used), but the standard deviation is relatively high (over 4). Moreover, the median value is zero, which means that more than 50 percent of Internet users in the sample did not engage in open activities. To facilitate the statistical treatment, the analysis is carried out in relative terms (i.e., the variable is normalized).[3]

For education-related activities, people who access from all the places mentioned or all places except work demonstrate a higher level of activity than the other groups. In contrast, people who access only from home or home and a public place tend to engage in the lowest amount of education-related activity.

Regarding job search or work activities, logically, people who work access from their workplace, and people who study access more from where they study. However, what is interesting here is that workers usually do some online education activities, while students do not tend to engage in work- or job search–related activities online. Moreover, on average, people engage in more educational than job search–related activities.

Open government activities are the least performed, with only two of nine activities reported on average (compared with two of seven for job search or work activities, and

Table 9.7
The most important variable to use in the study and the classification of open tasks.

Variable	Description	
Purposes of Internet use	Education Job search or work Government interaction	
Educational-related activities	Open: To take free online courses To search and use open access databases To take part in Facebook groups related to studying, training, or learning To follow educational institutions and courses on Twitter To take part in WhatsApp groups related to studying	Mostly open: To check digital libraries To search, download, or read literature online To read study-related news To check study-related web pages
Work- or job search–related activities	Open: To have a professional profile in some web page or social network, such as LinkedIn To take part in Facebook groups related to their jobs or to job searching To follow their possible employers on Twitter	Mostly open: To check job offers from different organizations To put a résumé online To check the "Jobs" section in online newspapers To use WhatsApp, Facebook, or another platform to contact clients or sell something
Internet government-related activities	Open: To get informed about government activities or a government-related organization To check Facebook page of government and/or governmental organization To report a complaint To follow politicians on Twitter or Facebook To follow government organization on Twitter, YouTube, or another social network To make queries in general To book an appointment To take part in social network groups related to politics	Mostly open: To fill out applications or follow procedures (i.e., obtaining a national identification card or applying for a passport)

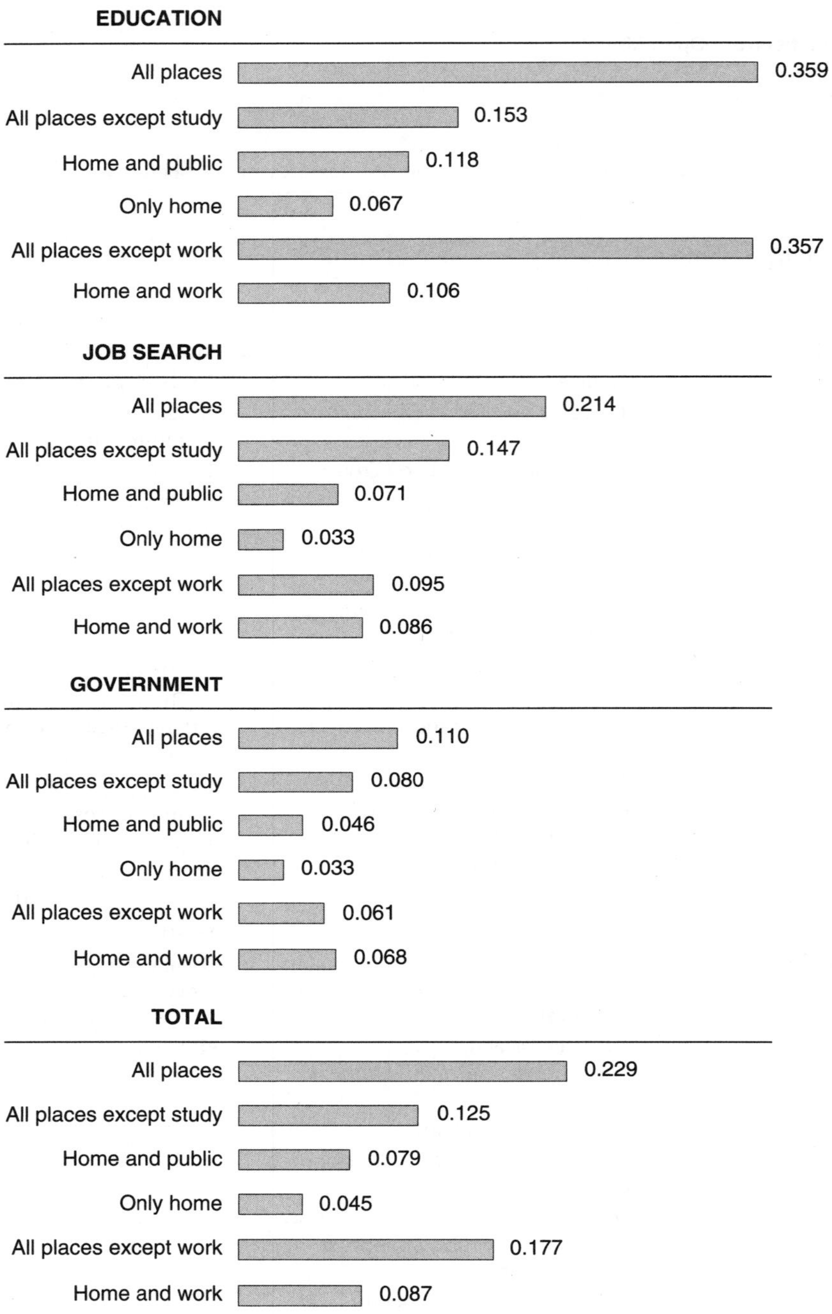

EDUCATION

All places	0.359
All places except study	0.153
Home and public	0.118
Only home	0.067
All places except work	0.357
Home and work	0.106

JOB SEARCH

All places	0.214
All places except study	0.147
Home and public	0.071
Only home	0.033
All places except work	0.095
Home and work	0.086

GOVERNMENT

All places	0.110
All places except study	0.080
Home and public	0.046
Only home	0.033
All places except work	0.061
Home and work	0.068

TOTAL

All places	0.229
All places except study	0.125
Home and public	0.079
Only home	0.045
All places except work	0.177
Home and work	0.087

Figure 9.5

Access location and types of ICT use and average of number of tasks for each access location. Normalized variables: Education (nine tasks), Job Search (seven tasks) and Government (nine tasks). The numbers shown are the mean of the normalized numbers of tasks, which follow this formula:

$task_{normalized} = \dfrac{\#tasks - \#tasks_{min}}{\#tasks_{max} - \#tasks_{min}}$. It is worth mentioning that a normalized variable only takes

values from zero to 1 and reflects the relative variation between the sample.

Source: After Access Survey–2017.

three of nine for education activities). Then, with regard to the differences in access places, the same pattern, as open job-search and work activities, remains. Additionally, the grouping for the total of tasks shows that those who access from all places do the most open activities online, whereas those who access only from home do the least.

Figure 9.6 shows the same analysis implemented in figure 9.5, but with differentiation by device.

There are observable differences in the number of tasks carried out by each group. For all cases, not surprisingly, the people who access from all the devices, as well as from mobile phone and PC, maintain a higher number of tasks. People who access the Internet only through a mobile phone perform the fewest tasks.

Multivariate Analysis: Determining the Probability of Carrying out Open Activities

In the previous section, we performed a bivariate analysis of access location and type of device on the number of activities performed on the Internet, either relating to education, job search and work, or government. It is clear from this analysis that the access locations or devices used affect the types and number of open tasks in which users engage.

The results obtained in the previous section do not control for other relevant factors, such as general traits of the individual, her or his home, and other digital characteristics. This section, on the other hand, executes a multivariate analysis using probability and regression models, which allows us to observe the effect of the type of access (location and devices) while controlling for other personal characteristics. It is important to note that the regression includes country per-capita income, thereby controlling for the differences in wealth in each country.

Table 9.8 shows the first set of results: the impact of a series of variables on both the probability of using the Internet for the three tasks in question (columns 1 through 3), and the number of tasks realized (columns 4 through 6). Given the different nature of the dependent variables, we ran two regressions. In the first, we use a dichotomous variable that takes the value of 1 if any kind of open activity is performed, and 0 if not.[4] The marginal effects results are shown in columns 1 through 3. For the second regression, the dependent variable is continuous and corresponds to a normalized tasks index.[5] This set of results is shown in columns 4 through 6.

Next, we describe the results, starting with the effect of the general characteristics of the individual and her or his home: gender, age category, education level, type of occupation, socioeconomic level, rural area population, and local native language spoken.

With regard to gender, being female positively affects the probability of using the Internet to get an education, but negatively affects the number of and the probability

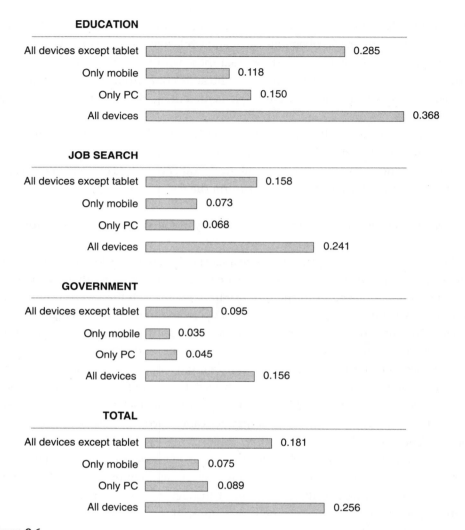

Figure 9.6
Access devices, types of ICT use, and average of number of tasks for each access device.

Table 9.8

Probability of using devices for different purposes and number of digital tasks (discrete marginal effects and regression coefficients).

	(1)	(2)	(3)	(4)	(5)	(6)
	Probablity			Number of tasks		
Variable	EDU	JOB SEARCH	GOV	EDU	JOB SEARCH	GOV
Women	0.03**	−0.04***	−0.02**	0.01	−0.03***	−0.02***
	(0.01)	(0.01)	(0.01)	(0.01)	(0.01)	(0.01)
Young	0.01	0.17***	0.09***	0.05***	0.08***	0.04***
	(0.03)	(0.02)	(0.01)	(0.02)	(0.01)	(0.01)
Adult	0.04	0.17***	0.13***	0.07***	0.09***	0.07***
	(0.03)	(0.02)	(0.02)	(0.02)	(0.02)	(0.01)
Elderly	0.01	0.06**	0.10***	0.05*	0.03	0.05***
	(0.04)	(0.03)	(0.03)	(0.02)	(0.02)	(0.02)
Education (years)	0.02***	0.01***	0.01***	0.01***	0.01***	0.00***
	(0.00)	(0.00)	(0.00)	(0.00)	(0.00)	(0.00)
Student	0.19***	−0.15***	0.03	0.20***	−0.09***	0.01
	(0.04)	(0.03)	(0.03)	(0.02)	(0.02)	(0.01)
Employee	−0.01	−0.09***	−0.00	0.01	−0.07***	−0.00
	(0.03)	(0.03)	(0.03)	(0.02)	(0.02)	(0.01)
Employer	0.02	0.03	0.02	0.03	0.01	−0.01
	(0.05)	(0.04)	(0.04)	(0.03)	(0.02)	(0.02)
Independent	−0.04	−0.09***	−0.02	−0.01	−0.08***	−0.01
	(0.03)	(0.03)	(0.03)	(0.02)	(0.02)	(0.01)
Nonactive	−0.04	−0.16***	−0.04	−0.03	−0.10***	−0.02
	(0.03)	(0.03)	(0.03)	(0.02)	(0.02)	(0.01)
NSE	0.17***	0.15***	0.15***	0.11***	0.06***	0.07***
	(0.04)	(0.04)	(0.03)	(0.02)	(0.02)	(0.02)
Rural	0.01	−0.03**	−0.01	−0.01	−0.02***	0.00
	(0.02)	(0.01)	(0.01)	(0.01)	(0.01)	(0.01)
GDP	0.00**	0.00**	0.00***	0.00**	0.00**	0.00***
	(0.00)	(0.00)	(0.00)	(0.00)	(0.00)	(0.00)
Native language	−0.01	0.04	0.04*	0.02	0.02	0.01
	(0.03)	(0.03)	(0.02)	(0.02)	(0.01)	(0.01)
Social ICT	0.01**	0.02***	0.01	0.01***	0.01***	0.00
	(0.01)	(0.01)	(0.00)	(0.00)	(0.00)	(0.00)

(*continued*)

Table 9.8 (continued)

	(1)	(2)	(3)	(4)	(5)	(6)
	Probablity			Number of tasks		
Experience ICT	0.01***	0.01***	0.01***	0.01***	0.01***	0.01***
	(0.00)	(0.00)	(0.00)	(0.00)	(0.00)	(0.00)
All devices except tablet	0.18***	0.06*	0.06**	0.10***	0.03*	0.03*
	(0.03)	(0.03)	(0.03)	(0.02)	(0.02)	(0.01)
Only mobile phone	0.11***	0.02	0.01	0.04*	0.00	–0.00
	(0.03)	(0.03)	(0.03)	(0.02)	(0.02)	(0.01)
Only PC	0.20***	0.09**	0.03	0.08***	0.02	–0.00
	(0.04)	(0.04)	(0.03)	(0.02)	(0.02)	(0.02)
All devices	0.19***	0.10***	0.10***	0.14***	0.07***	0.06***
	(0.04)	(0.04)	(0.03)	(0.03)	(0.02)	(0.02)
All places	0.18***	0.14***	0.05**	0.15***	0.11***	0.03***
	(0.03)	(0.02)	(0.02)	(0.02)	(0.01)	(0.01)
All places except study	–0.02	0.07***	0.01	–0.03	0.03**	–0.01
	(0.03)	(0.02)	(0.02)	(0.02)	(0.01)	(0.01)
Home and public	–0.01	0.01	0.02	–0.01	0.01	–0.01
	(0.03)	(0.02)	(0.02)	(0.02)	(0.02)	(0.01)
Only home	–0.06**	–0.04*	–0.01	–0.03*	–0.01	–0.01
	(0.03)	(0.02)	(0.02)	(0.02)	(0.01)	(0.01)
All places except work	0.12***	0.05*	–0.00	0.09***	0.03*	–0.00
	(0.03)	(0.03)	(0.02)	(0.02)	(0.02)	(0.01)
Home and work	–0.04	0.02	0.01	–0.04**	–0.01	–0.00
	(0.03)	(0.03)	(0.03)	(0.02)	(0.02)	(0.01)
Constant				–0.34***	–0.16***	–0.19***
				(0.04)	(0.03)	(0.03)
Observations	5,182	5,182	5,182	5,182	5,182	5,182
R-squared				0.26	0.17	0.12

Note: Standard errors in parentheses. Significance level: *** $p<0.01$, ** $p<0.05$, * $p<0.1$.
NSE stands for nivel socioeconómico, or socioeconomic grouping. This is constituted by five socioeconomic groupings in Peru: A, B, C, D and E, with "A" being the richest and "E" the poorest. Variables used for the grouping include: education, household expenditure, income, quality of the house (house made out of bricks, for instance), and connection to water and sewage.
Source: After Access Survey–2017.

of performing job searches and government-related tasks. With regard to the number of education-related tasks carried out, there is no significant effect, meaning that women do just as many educational activities as men.

Concerning age group, we include three categories in the regression analysis (young, adult, and elderly), and the coefficients and marginal effects must be interpreted as increase/decrease with respect to being under age (which is the omitted category). In almost all cases, except in educational activities, there is a significant advantage for all the age groups with respect to the omitted category in the regression. This makes sense because it is the adults who have more job search needs and interactions with government. Nevertheless, it is important to be cautious with this result because in general, the literature observes a negative impact of age on the acquisition of digital skills, with the elderly holding the most vulnerable position in that sense (Barrantes and Cozzubo 2015).

Education level shows a statistically significant effect on all the inspected variables, which brings out the importance of this variable in explaining digital skill appropriation and the realization of open activities. This is not a surprising result, as it extends the findings of other research that shows the importance of level of education for engaging online to include open activities.

When analyzing occupation, we include five categories (student, employed, employer, independent, and nonactive),[6] and the coefficients and marginal effects must be interpreted as increasing/decreasing with respect to being unemployed (similar to the age group analysis). First, as expected, being a student has a positive impact on engaging in education-related tasks, both in the probability to engage in open education activities and in the number of tasks associated with education. Also, as expected, this same category has a negative impact on the realization of job search–related Internet activities, again both in probability and in number of tasks. This result confirms what our intuition suggests: students' work- and job search–related needs are usually lower in relation to the rest of the sample; thereby, this group performs fewer job search–related activities on the Internet. With relation to government activities, students do not show a statistically significant difference from the omitted category (the unemployed).

On the other hand, the Employees, Independent, and Nonactive categories follow a similar pattern in terms of open job search–related activities. In particular, they show a statistically negative relationship with respect to the unemployed (the omitted category) in both the probability and the number of tasks. This is an expected result, however, because the unemployed have significantly greater needs to look for a job. Both employees and independent workers, by definition, have a current job, so they have less of a need to actively look for one.

When looking at educational and government-related activities, neither shows a significant level of correlation with any occupational category. This could be due to the general nature of the occupational categories. For example, the Employer category could be referring to jobs in very different economic sectors, thereby generating an average of zero.

To finish with the general characteristics of the individuals and household members, the socioeconomic level shows a positive, statistically significant impact in all cases, although it is of low magnitude. This finding is unsurprising, as it supports the literature that has reported an important effect that this variable has on the use of digital devices: usually, the poorest members of society are excluded from different Internet activities (Mendonça, Crespo, and Simões 2015; Galperin, Mariscal, and Barrantes 2014). Along the same line, a country's gross domestic product (GDP) also plays a positive role in explaining the probability of engaging in open activities, although it is limited compared to the other explanatory variables considered.

Additionally, we included as independent variables rural location and local (Indigenous) languages spoken. For rural location, there is a significant negative impact in the case of job search–related activities for both the probability and number of tasks, and it is not significant in the rest of cases. For local (Indigenous) language speakers, there is no significant impact on any of the open activities shown in table 9.8. This could be due mainly to the heterogeneity of the surveyed population in the five countries analyzed. For example, in Paraguay, which contributes about 70 percent of the local language speakers in the sample, the Guarani language is not necessarily a reason for discrimination and exclusion, as it is in Peru, Guatemala, or Colombia.[7]

The rest of this chapter seeks to explain the effect of the ICT characteristics, locations, and types of access on the probability of engaging in different open activities. One finding is that the number of years of experience using the Internet is positively correlated with the probability and number of open tasks performed. However, this relationship changes with the age group. As Barrantes and Vargas (2017) found, Internet users at some point in time tend to converge with respect to the number of online engagement activities, but this convergence is conditional on their age group. In other words, no matter how much Internet experience mature adults have, they will always engage in fewer Internet activities on average than younger people. So, for certain populations, no matter how much Internet experience they have, they will not be able to increase their skills and use the web without some kind of intervention.

On the other hand, ICT social capital (e.g., the number of friends on Facebook or WhatsApp) is significantly and positively correlated to educational and job search–related open activities, in terms of both the probability to engage and the number of tasks performed. The previous relationship highlights the relevance of the informant's social circle to engaging and appropriating online activities (Nam 2014; Norris 2003; Smoreda and Thomas 2001). However, in the case of open government activities, the previous relationship is not statistically significant. This could possibly be explained by the fact that is not enough to have friends who use a particular ICT device or a social media platform to engage in open government activities; supply being a key factor, or when government platforms are available, trust may be a key variable in using them. The survey did not allow us to capture the effect shown by Nam (2014), who finds that in engaging with government through open platforms, friends using this kind of service are key.

For the case of access devices and locations, the most important results are portrayed in table 9.8. For example, using all devices has the largest magnitude of significant impact in most cases. Regarding location, there is a similar trend—the informants who have access from all places tend to engage in more online activities than the rest, as shown in table 9.8 (recall that these users tend to be young and possess more than a secondary education). Additionally, some other regularities can be identified. Obviously, when study place is included within the set of access locations, a higher level of educational activities is observed, both in probability and in number of tasks, as was the case for the bivariate analysis. The opposite happens when we analyze Internet access from the workplace, where a positive effect of using the Internet for a job search is observed, both in probability and in number of tasks. Likewise, the locations associated with lower levels of both the probability of engaging in open activities and the number of activities are the home and public spaces. For a more detailed analysis, figures 9.7, 9.8, and 9.9 show a graphic analysis of the effects of the type of access on the probability of realizing different Internet activities.

In figures 9.7, 9.8, and 9.9, the average marginal effects of the type of access on the probability of carrying out an Internet activity are shown. It is necessary to note that the interpretation of these marginal effects is different from the interpretation of the discrete marginal effects, presented previously. The discrete effect shows how a dependent variable changes when a unit of the independent variable moves. On the other hand, the average marginal effect, presented in the figures, represents the probability that the dependent variable takes the value of 1, given a certain average level of the categorical variable. What the estimation shows, then, is the probability of realizing open activities on the Internet for different types of access. The calculation of these effects is done using the Probit model, presented in table 9.8.

Figure 9.7 shows how the various types of access affect the probability of using the Internet for educational purposes. The effects of using different devices are shown in the upper section, and the effects of locations are shown in the lower section. Regarding the different devices, all the relevant combinations that included PC/laptop showed higher probability to engage in open educational activities, except for "Only PC." This could possibly highlight the mobile phone's inability to adapt to the educational user's needs. Educational platforms sometimes require advanced features like more advanced multimedia capabilities and more flexible software tools. While the mobile phone can be a more efficient and appropriate tool than a PC for some types of educational activities (Lee 2015), it is not yet the predominant mode for accessing educational opportunities online.

Concerning the location of access, the set of locations where a higher probability of carrying out educational activities is "All Places Combinations," 0.5, followed by "Home, Study Place, and Public," with 0.45. After that, the next combinations show similar probabilities.

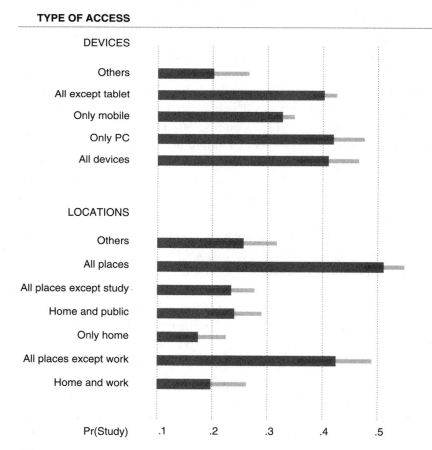

Figure 9.7
The marginal average effects of access locations and devices for Internet activities associated with education.

Figure 9.8 shows the average marginal effects for the probability of carrying out open activities related to a job search. Similar to the education case, the combinations of devices that show the highest probability are "All Devices" and "Only PC," highlighting again the necessity of a PC or laptop to engage in these kinds of activities. On the other hand, only mobile phone and other combinations (e.g., mobile phone and PC) present the lowest probability of carrying out open activities related to a job search among the device categories.

Considering different locations, similar to the education case, the "All Places" access alternative presents the highest probability to engage in job search online activities, while "Only Home" and "Home and Public" provide the lowest. Coupled with the

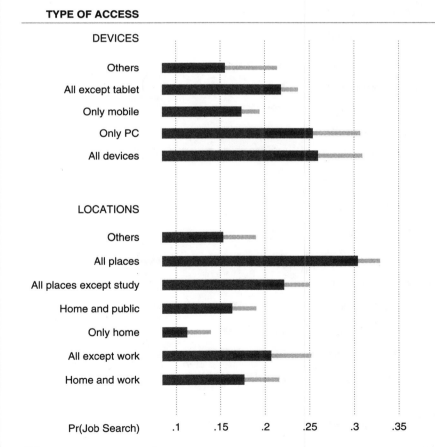

Figure 9.8
The marginal average effects of access locations and devices for Internet activities associated with job search.

results from education, this highlights the necessity of multiple location alternatives for users to engage in an open activity related to education or job search, which could also suggest that it is continuity in access that is important to users. It seems that the availability of accessing the Internet from multiple locations matters more for job search than other considerations.

Finally, figure 9.9 shows the results for open activities associated with government. Regarding devices, the person who uses "All Devices" has a slightly higher level of average probability of interacting with government than the other categories. The other levels are statistically the same. In the case of access locations, something similar happens because there is a high uncertainty in the effect of different kinds of access. In

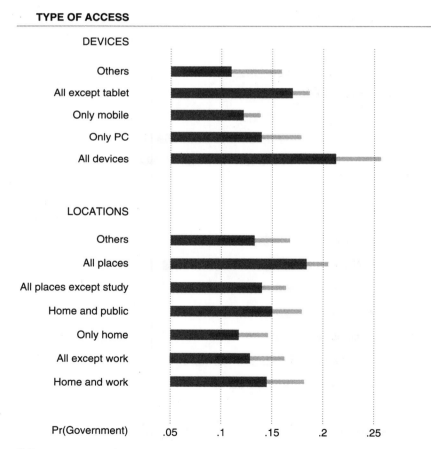

Figure 9.9
The marginal average effects of access locations and devices for Internet activities associated with government.

particular, the only significant effect is "All Places," which could be explained by the reduced number of people who engage in open government activities (only around 12 percent of the sample).

Conclusion

In this chapter, we have tried to show how context, understood as the individual's characteristics and her or his ways of accessing the Internet, affects the possibility of benefiting from the consumption of open activities, as proxied by use.

The analysis shows that both the location of the access (home, work, study place, or public space) and the access device (PC, mobile phone, laptop, and other) affect the probability and extent of engagement in various types of open activities. As one might expect, access from more locations or with more devices positively affects the number of open activities performed. This gives rise to two possible lines of explanation. The first relates to familiarity with the Internet, as proxied by diversification of devices and places of access, which matters more than device or place in explaining open consumption. The other is continuity of access, with people connecting wherever possible and preferring to change devices in order to remain connected, as mobile Internet access is not yet affordable in these Latin American countries (Agüero 2015; Viecens and Callorda 2016).

The econometric analysis confirmed this bivariate analysis, showing that the forms of access (from home or work, or using a PC or a smartphone) are correlated to the probability and extent of open activities. The data also showed that other characteristics, such as gender, age, education level, and socioeconomic status, significantly affect the number and type of open activities. For example, access from fewer devices, only from home, or characteristics associated with unemployment or nonactivity generate a lower number of open activities being realized. Furthermore, the locations and devices used can affect the number and type of online open tasks performed by the individual, as well as her or his capability to benefit from open activities. One interesting finding is that, while smartphones are touted as the solution to Internet access issues, a large part of the population does not take advantage of this access to engage in the open activities asked about in After Access 2017 survey.

The results emphasize the need for complementary policies addressed at including a larger portion of the population in the benefits that come from open activities. To exploit the benefits of open activities that Internet access can provide, affordable tariffs and devices are as important as the expansion of the infrastructure that is associated with high teledensity levels. Policies to improve home Internet access, which could begin with programs to encourage government employees to buy PCs or upgrade their mobile phones, could contribute to more people engaging in open consumption activities.

Likewise, the results suggest which locations (home, school, public spaces, or workplaces) should be prioritized in ICT policies for each kind of digital activity. For example, if the government sets a goal to carry out a digital literacy policy for the use of open data, it would make more sense that the core of the policy focuses on workplaces rather than on homes, given the results of this study. Given the low levels of benefit obtained from people who access the Internet only from public places, another example of relevant policy could be to encourage a set of ICT activities related to job searching or even work, education, or government in public spaces. This way, the public spaces could be rediscovered and upgraded, and the appropriation of the ICT benefits of the most excluded groups could be improved.

Regardless of the ubiquity of Internet access, or teledensities well over 100 percent per country, data from these five Latin American countries show that the locations and forms of access, combined with people's characteristics, matter. Reducing the consumption gaps of open activities is a pending task. By providing evidence on the factors associated with these gaps, this research hopes to have contributed to the design of sound policies to address them.

Notes

1. DIRSI stands for the *Dialogo Regional sobre Sociedad de la Información*.

2. The survey only asked about male or female.

3. When normalizing a variable, all possible real values are converted into a range between zero and 1, following the formula: $task_{normalized} = \frac{\#tasks - \#tasks_{min}}{\#tasks_{max} - \#tasks_{min}}$. By taking this limited range, the normalized variable reflects the relative variation within the sample.

4. This allows the use of a Probit model, a nonlinear probability model.

5. Here, we use ordinary least squares.

6. The characteristics of nonactive people are as follows: on average, they are forty-eight years old; 68 percent are women; about 31 percent access the Internet from home and public spaces; and 45 percent of them access from only a mobile phone.

7. In these three countries, speaking a local language is highly correlated with living in a rural area. Thus, in the regression analysis, the effect of language may be captured in the coefficient for rural.

References

Agüero, Aileen. (2015). *Banda Ancha en América Latina: Precios y tendencias del mercado* [Broadband in Latin America: Prices and market trends]. Diálogo Regional sobre Sociedad de la Información.

Lima: DIRSI. http://dirsi.net/web/web/es/publicaciones/detalle/banda-ancha-en-america-latina--precios-y-tendencias-del-mercado.

Barrantes, Roxana, and Angelo Cozzubo. 2015. "Edad Para Aprender, Edad Para Enseñar: El Rol Del Aprendizaje Intergeneracional Intrahogar En El Uso de Internet Por Parte de Los Adultos Mayores En Latinoamérica" [Age to Learn, Age to Teach: The Role of Intergenerational Learning in Internet Use by Older Adults in Latin America]. *Departamento de Economía PUCP* Documento (411): 78. http://files.pucp.edu.pe/departamento/economia/DDD411.pdf.

Barrantes, Roxana, and Eduardo Vargas. 2017. "¿Caminos Distintos Y Destinos Iguales? Análisis de La Convergencia En Patrones de Uso de Internet Entre Diferentes Grupos Etarios" [Different Paths and Equal Destinations: Analysis of Convergence in Patterns of Internet Use Among Different Age Groups]. Documento de Trabajo 438. Departamento de Economía, Pontificia Universidad Católica del Perú (PUCP), Lima.

Dodel, Matias. 2013. "Las Tecnologías de La Información Y Comunicación Como Determinantes Del Bienestar: El Papel de Las Habilidades Digitales en la Transición Al Empleo en la Cohorte PISA 2003" [Information and Communication Technologies as Determinants of Well-Being: The Role of Digital Skills in the Transition to Employment in the PISA Cohort 2003]. Universidad de la Republica, Montevideo.

Dodel, Matias. 2015. "E-skill's Effect on Occupational Attainment: A PISA-Based Panel Study." *The Electronic Journal of Information Systems in Developing Countries* 69 (3): 1–22. https://doi.org/10.1002/j.1681-4835.2015.tb00497.x.

Donner, Jonathan. 2015. *After Access: Inclusion, Development, and a More Mobile Internet*. Cambridge, MA: MIT Press.

Ericsson. 2017. "The Ericsson Mobility Report." Stockholm. https://www.ericsson.com/assets/local/mobility-report/documents/2017/ericsson-mobility-report-november-2017.pdf.

Fairlie, Robert W. 2017. "Have We Finally Bridged the Digital Divide? Smart Phone and Internet Use Patterns by Race and Ethnicity." *First Monday* 22 (9). http://firstmonday.org/ojs/index.php/fm/article/view/7919.

Galperin, Hernan, Judith Mariscal, and Roxana Barrantes. 2014. "The Internet and Poverty: Opening the Black Box," Lima: DIRSI. http://dirsi.net/web/files/files/Opening_the_Black_Box.pdf.

Kularski, Curtis M., and Stephanie Moller. 2012. "The Digital Divide as a Continuation of Traditional Systems of Inequality." *Sociology* 5151 (December): 1–23.

Lee, Myung Kyung. 2015. "Effects of Mobile Phone-Based App Learning Compared to Computer-Based Web Learning on Nursing Students: Pilot Randomized Controlled Trial." *Healthcare Informatics Research* 21 (2): 125–33. doi:10.4258/hir.2015.21.2.125.

Mazimpaka, Jean Damascène, Théodomir Mugiraneza, and Ramata Molo Thioune. 2015. "Impact of Public Access to ICT Skills on Job Prospects in Rwanda." In *Public Access ICT across Cultures: Diversifying Participation in the Network Society*, ed. Francisco J. Proenza, 35–58. Cambridge, MA/Ottawa: MIT Press/IDRC. https://idl-bnc-idrc.dspacedirect.org/bitstream/handle/10625/54174/IDL-54174.pdf?sequence=1&isAllowed=y.

Mendonça, Sandro, Nuno Crespo, and Nadia Simões. 2015. "Inequality in the Network Society: An Integrated Approach to ICT Access, Basic Skills, and Complex Capabilities." *Telecommunications Policy* 39 (3–4): 192–207. doi:10.1016/j.telpol.2014.12.010.

Nam, Taewoo. 2014. "Determining the Type of E-Government Use." *Government Information Quarterly* 31 (2): 211–220. doi:10.1016/j.giq.2013.09.006.

Norris, Pippa. 2003. "Social Capital and ICTs: Widening or Reinforcing Social Networks?" *International Forum on Social Capital for Economic Revival*. http://www.esri.go.jp/en/workshop/030325/030325paper6-e.pdf.

Rabab'ah, Ghaleb, Ali Farhan AbuSeileek, Francisco J. Proenza, Omar Fraihat, and Saif Addeen Alrababah. 2015. "User Perceptions of Impact of Internet Cafés in Amman, Jordan." In *Public Access ICT across Cultures: Diversifying Participation in the Network Society*, ed. Francisco J. Proenza, 11–34. Cambridge, MA/Ottawa: MIT Press/IDRC.

Selwyn, Neil. 2010. "Degrees of Digital Division: Reconsidering Digital Inequalities and Contemporary Higher Education." *RUSC. Revista de Universidad Y Sociedad Del…* 7(1): 33–42. http://rusc.uoc.edu/rusc/ca/index.php/rusc/article/download/v7n1_selwyn/660-454-1-PB.pdf.

Smith, Matthew L., and Ruhiya Seward. 2017. "Openness as Social Praxis." *First Monday* 22 (4). http://dx.doi.org/10.5210/fm.v22i4.7073.

Smoreda, Zbigniew, and Frank Thomas. 2001. "Social Networks and Residential ICT Adoption and Use." *France Telecom R&D* December: 1–11. http://citeseerx.ist.psu.edu/viewdoc/download;jsessionid=0338D0C93486A6E85DE91D045825AEBB?doi=10.1.1.203.5162&rep=rep1&type=pdf.

Van Dijk, Jan A. G. M., and Alexander Van Deursen. 2014. *Digital Skills: Unlocking the Information Society*. New York: Palgrave Macmillan.

Viences, Maria F. and Fernando Callorda. (2016). *The Digital Divide in Latin America: Broadband Price, Quality and Affordability in the Region. Lima: Regional Dialogue on the Information Society*. Lima: DIRSI. http://dirsi.net/web/web/es/publicaciones/detalle/the-digital-divide-in-latin-america--broadband-price--quality-and-affordability-in-the-region.

III Governing Open Development Applications

10   Open Government Data for Inclusive Development

François van Schalkwyk and Michael Cañares

Introduction

This chapter examines the relationship between open government data and social inclusion. Twenty-eight open data initiatives from the Global South are analyzed to find out how and in what contexts the publication of open government data tends to result in the inclusion of habitually marginalized communities in governance processes, such that they may lead better lives.

The relationship between open government data and social inclusion is examined by presenting an analysis of the outcomes of open data projects. This analysis is based on a constellation of factors that were identified as having a bearing on open data initiatives with respect to inclusion.

The findings indicate that open data can contribute to an increase in access and participation—both components of inclusion. In these cases, this particular finding indicates that a more open, participatory approach to governance practice is taking root. However, the findings also show that in the cases studied here, access and participation approaches to open government data have not successfully disrupted the concentration of power in political and other networks, and this has placed limits on open data's contribution to a more inclusive society.

The chapter begins by presenting a theoretical framework for the analysis of the relationship between open data and inclusion. The framework sets out the complex relationship between social actors, information, and power in the network society. This is critical, we suggest, to developing a realistic analysis of the contexts in which open data activates their potential for transformation. The chapter then articulates the research question and presents the methodology used to operationalize those questions. The findings and discussion section that follows examines the factors affecting the relationship between open data and inclusion and how these factors are observed to play out across several open data initiatives in different contexts. The chapter ends with concluding remarks and an attempt to synthesize the insights that emerged in the preceding sections.

Structural Inequality and Development in the Information Society

It is a truism to describe digital technology in general, and the Internet in particular, as having a pervasive and profound impact on the development of humankind. So much so that Castells and Himanen (2014) propose a new mode of development—*informational development*—that drives material wealth creation in the twenty-first century. While the creation of material wealth does not necessarily result in the betterment of the lives of all (Ravallion 2016), Castells and Himanen suggest that a synergistic relationship between informational and human development has the potential to underpin sustainable and egalitarian social progress. This comes with the recognition that development is not only about capital accumulation or social and economic progress, but about the widening of people's choices (Haq 1998), the removal of *unfreedoms* (Sen 1999), as well as improvements in living conditions and the provision of basic needs (Nayyar 2003).

The relationship between informational and human development is dependent, however, on "social interests and power relationships" (Castells and Himanen 2014, 17). For example, if informational development drives material wealth creation, unequal access to information may create further imbalances and inequalities in people's material conditions. As growth tends to favor higher-income groups to the detriment of those at the lower end of the income scale (Chen and Ravallion 2007; Ravallion 2016), the availability of information may empower the empowered without proper safeguards in place. Therefore, the role of government is critical, as it is government that determines the corrective and redistributive policies required to create the conditions for balanced, inclusive development (Castells and Himanen 2014; Kohli 2004; Chang 2003).

At the same time, however, governments are not immune to the politics of accumulation and distribution. Governments have used the mechanisms of the welfare state for political patronage and clientelism, often resulting in the double-edged sword of a disempowered citizenry on one side (through increased dependency on the state) and a government tightly coupled to the financial sector, to the exclusion of a significant portion of its population, on the other (Castells and Himanen 2014). This latter condition is made possible by the fact that knowledge-intensive, globally connected, and technologically advanced sectors of national economies operate in the ahistorical, placeless space of flows that characterize the new social order of the network society

(Castells 2007, 2009). Castells and Himanen (2014, 14) comment, "This is, in fact, the structural basis for the growing inequality, polarization, and marginalization that characterize the situation in most countries in the world, despite high rates of growth in many areas of the planet." Therefore, development strategies must contest and contend with the new structuration of society if it is to deliver equitable progress toward better lives for all.

Open Data and Inclusion as Political Participation

Data are a valuable resource in informational development, prized and exploited by those small and highly advanced sectors of globally networked economies. Open government data [i.e., data free to be reused without any restriction (GovLab and Laurence 2014)] are also of value to these exclusive sectors, and bold claims have been made that open data are worth, in financial terms, $3 trillion per annum to the global economy (Manyika 2013). Yet it remains an open question who will benefit from this purported boost to the global economy.

Open government data, as a public rather than a private resource, are embedded in principles of universal access, participation, and transparency, and, according to advocates,[1] promise to restore trust between citizens and government by making the latter more accountable and inclusive (Horrigan and Rainie 2015; O'Hara 2012). Ideally, increasing transparency should empower citizens to participate in and hold public institutions to account for the distribution of benefits that support human development. Accountable governments, in turn, are more likely to put in place the kinds of policies required to restore a developmental balance in the form of a socially productive synergy between informational and human development.

Open data can play a role in restoring such a balance between informational and human development that proprietary data are precluded from playing. Common to all definitions of open data is the condition of universal access. Access is critical when there is an expectation for open data to lead to data use and impact of a more inclusive kind. If one dispenses with unfettered access to the data, one foregoes transparency and accountability (in governance); replicability, verifiability, and efficiency (in science); and, particularly in the case of open government data, equal opportunity and socioeconomic development. A core value held by many proponents of open data is that it is inherently inclusive as such, and (theoretically at least) it democratizes access to informational resources (Kitchin 2014).

But some have highlighted several issues about the theorized benefits of open data. As far back as 2010, Gurstein expressed concern about the false hope of open data automatically resulting in greater social inclusion. He took his cue from early evidence emerging from real-world outcomes: "By raising fundamental issues in understanding the societal aspects of e-governance, it highlights the need to replace politically neutered concepts like 'transparency', 'efficiency', 'governance', and 'best practice' with conceptually more rigorous terms that reflect the uneven terrain of power and control that governance embodies" (Gurstein 2010). Peixoto (2013) contends that open data as a form of transparency do not necessarily lead to accountability if political agency is absent. A survey of the contribution of open development by Bentley and Chib (2016) finds that the research literature does not support claims that open development projects nor open data initiatives typically result in the inclusion of poor and marginalized communities. One reason is that the benefits of openness are largely dependent on the capacities of users to exploit it as a resource for public benefit (Gurstein 2011; Davies and Bawa 2012; Canares and Shekhar 2016). How openness is structured and the contexts in which it is embedded are at least two further determinants of who benefits (Gurstein 2011; Johnson 2014). Research on open data, while cognizant of the lack of deep knowledge on the topic (Davies and Bawa 2012), has not explicitly been directed toward this fundamental concern raised from the outset.

One of the central challenges of open data, then, is to actualize the core value of inclusion. To do so requires an understanding of how and in what contexts open initiatives are inclusive, which open initiatives have been successful and which have been unsuccessful, who is included and who is excluded from the outcomes of these initiatives, and whether the inclusion made possible by open data has empowered those included to reprogram the network so that the benefits of development are more equitably distributed throughout society. To explore the relationship between open data and inclusion, this chapter deals with the following questions: Do open data contribute to inclusive development? More specifically, how, for whom, and in what contexts do open data contribute to inclusive development?

Networks, Data, Power, and Inclusion

The literature on inclusion differs across disciplines. Inclusion, in economic development, occurs when growth is accompanied with falling inequality and decreasing levels of poverty (Piketty 2014; Ravallion 2016). In sociology, inclusion is an amalgamation of processes intersecting at both the individual and societal spheres that result either in the welcoming, acceptance, and provision for, or the ostracism, rejection, and nonacknowledgment of a person or a group of people (Allman 2013). In development studies, inclusion takes place when all people contribute to creating opportunities, participate in decision-making, and share in the social and economic benefits of development processes (Hickey, Sen, and Bukenya 2015). Castells, possibly attempting a supradisciplinary definition of *inclusion,* defines the concept as the systematic ability of individuals or groups to access the means for meaningful survival (Stalder 1998).

In this chapter, we anchor our view of inclusion in *political participation*—that is, whether individuals or groups of people enjoy equitable opportunities in shaping how they are governed and achieve and benefit from desired governance outcomes (Habermas 1996; Yuval-Davis 2011). Our approach to inclusion is political because it is inseparable from power, as highlighted by Gurstein (2010, 2011) and others [see, e.g., Arnstein's citizen control (1969), Pretty's self-mobilization (1995), and Hurlbert and Gupta's adaptive governance (2015)]. Access and broad forms of participation are important stepping stones to inclusiveness but do not necessarily confer agency on or empower those being included; access and participation may simply result in a "voice without agency … [and] presence without politics" (Singh and Gurumurthy 2013, 186) for previously excluded communities.

Inclusion is meaningful if material wealth and nonmaterial benefits (such as dignity and health) accrue to those habitually excluded. For those benefits to accrue, though, access to information networks and participation in the decisions taken by powerful nodes[2] in those networks are necessary conditions, as networked information flows have become the primary setting for human agency (Castells 1996; Stalder 2005). As Castells (2017, 72) states,

> There has been no economy and no society in the world in which wealth and power do not depend on information and knowledge. It has always been the absolutely critical matter for wealth generation and power generation. What has changed is … the information and communication technology revolution … with all its consequences: the ability to create organizational forms; the infrastructure and the rapidity of processing information, transforming it into knowledge; and using these transformations into knowledge to make actual changes in the production system.

Reilly and Smith (2013) argue that openness signifies more than access to technology; it entails changes to the patterns of development and the distribution of information, cultural production, and knowledge in the direction of what Walton et al. (2016, 4) refer to as "networked social morphologies." According to the rules for such openness, traditional hierarchically controlled modes need to make way for spaces that support networked social arrangements. While open data promise universal access and democratized participation, any developmental strategy focused on "spaces for achieving openness" needs to be mindful of the space of information flows and the new networked social arrangements that this space introduces, including the unavoidable binary condition of inclusion in and exclusion from global networks of wealth and power (Castells 1996, 2009; Stalder 1998).

The social dynamics of networks draw attention to a critical missing element in the assumed revolutionary potential of open data. If access and participation are to have meaningful outcomes, the habitually and systematically excluded must be able to access and participate in networks with something of value to offer the powerful established nodes in networks where decision-making is concentrated and the program for the network is determined. Once included, the opportunity arises to attempt the reprogramming of the dominant logic of the network to redirect the distribution of benefits in a more equitable fashion (Castells 2009). This shaping is unavoidably a struggle for power (Gurumurthy and Singh 2016).

Castells (2007, 29; 2009, 42–47) identifies four types of power in the network society. *Networking power* is the power of social actors in global networks over those who are not included in these global networks. It operates along the binary conditions of exclusion and inclusion. *Network power* is the power exercised by those in networks (typically those at the source of the network's formation) who prescribe the standards or protocols that determine the rules of acceptance. In this sense, those who execute network power coordinate social interaction in the networks according to rules for inclusion. *Networked power* is the relative power of social actors over other social actors in the same network; and the forms and processes of networked power are specific to each network. *Network-making power* is the power to program specific networks according to the interests and values of the programmers, and the ability to connect and ensure the cooperation of different networks, while defending the network from competition from other networks.

Programmers hold the power to program and reprogram networks; switchers hold the power to control the connecting points between networks. Crucially, within this formulation, people, collectives, and organizations are understood to be social actors who have the ability to disrupt the dominant power switches, and/or to push for change through what Castells calls "counterpower" (Castells 2007, 2009). Counterpower in the network society is exerted when social actors attempt to change the programs of specific networks or disrupt the switches that represent the dominant programmatic logic of the network.

In defining inclusion in this way, we acknowledge that we are setting the bar high by insisting that, in line with human potential paradigms, inclusiveness requires empowerment in the forms just described. Without inclusion culminating in those habitually excluded being in a position to negotiate different (and, hopefully, more equitable) decision-making outcomes by disrupting existing network power arrangements, we see little by way of meaningful returns from access and participation for those typically excluded from governance processes. At the same time, we acknowledge that a fully inclusive society is a utopian ideal. As Castells (1999) contends, exclusion is a structural condition of the network society and openness can be limited to certain constituencies. Nevertheless, open data make new power arrangements possible by disrupting previously closed information flows and by democratizing the monitoring of powerful actors to enforce the maintenance of a balance between informational and human development. This discussion will consider whether and how open data disrupt the existing distribution of power, and whether they activate different forms of counterpower in networks to yield a more inclusive, synergistic development.

Methodology

The Open Data for Development (OD4D)[3] initiative consists of a network of partners with the ambition of "empowering women and men around the world to achieve their own development goals and actively participate in decisions affecting their lives" (OD4D 2016, 44). OD4D has supported several initiatives to explore the connections between open data and development, with a particular focus on developing countries where the gaps between rich and poor, formal and informal economies, and skilled and unskilled are at their most acute.

A first round of analysis comprised an examination of OD4D projects that had formulated their own theory of change with regard to the inclusion of marginalized publics in decision-making as an outcome of the project.[4] Projects were selected for analysis on the basis of the following criteria: (1) open data must have been published by the project or the project resulted in the use of existing open data; and (2) there were tangible, recorded outcomes that are attributable to the release or use of open government data. A total of fifteen projects were included in the analysis (see table 10.1).

Following the analysis of the OD4D projects, it was clear that many of the OD4D projects did not provide sufficient evidence to explore how, for whom, and in what contexts open data contribute to inclusive development. It was decided, therefore, to broaden the scope of the analysis by purposively selecting from the literature additional open data projects that would be informative in terms of an analysis of the relationship between open data and inclusion. A total of fourteen projects were selected based on the existence of reported outcomes and impacts, and the bearing of these on inclusion (see table 10.2).[5]

Table 10.1

OD4D projects included in the first round of analysis.

Name of project	Short description
A Tu Servicio (At Your Service)	A Tu Servicio is a web-based app that uses data from the Ministry of Health to compare health service providers by providing Uruguayan citizens with information on which to base their annual selection of a health service provider.
Respiraciudad.org	The project engaged three cities in Latin America (Buenos Aires, Mexico City, Montevideo) in the collection, curation, and publication of air quality data. It allowed the cities to understand the challenges of producing updated data in order to report on air quality in three urban centers.
Cuidando do meu bairro 2.0	Cuidando do meu bairro 2.0, whose name means "Caring for my neighborhood" in Portuguese, created tools so that communities could better understand the public budget and exercise the control and inspection of public expenditures in the city to promote action in city neighborhoods.
OD4Environment Gjakovo	Citizens of Gjakovo, Albania, reported that illegal dumps have a negative effect on health and tourism. A partnership among local youth, the Municipality of Gjakova, Open Data Kosovo, and UNDP's Support to Anti-Corruption Efforts in Kosovo project led to the creation of the first heat map showing where 687 illegal dumps were located in the city. Local communities volunteered as data collectors.
Open budgets in Ukraine	Lviv, Ukraine, with a population of 730,000, publishes its annual $178 million municipal-level budget and expenditure data using the Open Budget tool. The data allows citizens to monitor the income and expenditure of the city.
Budi Odgovoran Montenegro	Budi Odgovoran, which means "be responsible" in Croatian, is a mobile app that allows the citizens of Montenegro to report local problems such as illegal waste dumps, misuse of official vehicles and irregular parking, failure to comply with tax regulations, and failure to issue fiscal receipts.
RISE Moldova	RISE Moldova, a Chisinau-based nongovernmental organization, brought together journalists, programmers, and activists from Moldova and Romania. RISE promotes and uses investigative journalism to uncover corruption, the misuse of office, and conflicts of interest. Using government data, RISE has published several stories on corruption in Moldova. The app also supports other investigative journalists: In 2015, it organized a "hackathon" and various workshops on data journalism, as well as training on data security.
Open procurement Kosovo	UNDP and Open Data Kosovo initiated a partnership that led to the opening of procurement databases in five municipalities in Kosovo. The databases covered three to five years, providing insights into local government spending

Table 10.1 (continued)

Name of project	Short description
	and access to over 10,000 public tenders. The cleaning and visualization of data were done in each municipality, with engagement of the local developer communities that underwent digital capacity-building. In addition to visualizations and mapping, the tech activists developed algorithms that automatically detect suspicious tenders.
Using open data to create transparent value chains in Rwanda	African Minds brought together stakeholders in a coffee value chain to discuss what data they own, what data they would like to have, and what data they are prepared to make open. The project is interested in finding out whether open data can create a more transparent value chain that is beneficial to all stakeholders in the chain.
Unlocking the value of open data through problem-focused subnational networks	Palmer Development Group working with Open Data Durban, engaged the city of Durban, South Africa, and convened a range of stakeholders to resolve how open data might be used in managing the city's water resources. The project was interested in discovering how a net-worked, problem-focused approach could unlock the value of open data at the local level.
Disrupting illicit financial flows in the extractives industry	African Network of Centre for Investigative Reporting sup-ported journalists across Africa to investigate corruption in their respective countries. The project was interested in finding out how open data contribute to the work of investigative journalists as they compile the evidence that supports their stories.
Linking follow the money initiatives for better transparency	The Center for Local and Regional Governance explored how open data can link follow-the-money communities together, particularly at the local level. This entailed mapping fiscal data requirements and producing an open data model for fiscal transparency and accountability. This was done by doc-umenting four cases of CSOs that audit or participate actively in budgeting and auditing processes at the local level.
Exploring political interest and asset ownership	Using international data standards, the Sinar Project built a sophisticated public visualization tool to explore politi-cal networks, conflicts of interest, and voting behavior of public servants in Malaysia.
Making smart city initiatives open and inclusive	The Center for Innovation Policy and Governance ana-lyzed and assessed smart city initiatives in Jakarta, Indone-sia, to see how these involve and benefit citizens.
Open data and interactive commu-nity mapping: Empowering local community tourism in Jamaica	This initiative employed partnerships with community organizations, government agencies, local businesses, and academia for the development of an interactive community-mapping ecosystem that provided the basis for community tourism activities. Interactive community mapping was employed for the creation of a community map as open geodata using the OpenStreetMap platform.

Table 10.2

Open data projects and outcomes analyzed.

Name of project	Short description
Esoko—Ghana	Smallholder farmers generate much of Ghana's agricultural production. However, they have only limited access to important information that underlies increasingly complex global food chains, and this prevents them from fully maximizing the value of their crops. Esoko, a company operating in Ghana, sought to address this problem by using multiple data sources, including open government data, to permit farmers to secure better prices for their produce and level the playing field in price negotiations between farmers and buyers.
Medicine Price Registry (MPR)—South Africa	In 2014, Code for South Africa took a little-known open data set from the national Department of Health website and created the Medicine Price Registry (MPR) app, an online tool that allows patients to compare medicine prices. The app allows patients to compare the costs of doctor-prescribed medicines with those of other medicines (e.g., generics) containing the same ingredients. It also helps patients verify that they are not being overcharged by their pharmacies and ensures cost savings for both patients and society without compromising on efficacy.
Open Education Dashboards—Tanzania	The Tanzanian public's knowledge of public school performance was limited by a lack of information about the country's primary and secondary education sectors. Two portals tried to remedy that situation, providing the public with more data on examination pass rates and other information related to school quality: • The Education Open Data Dashboard: A project established by the Tanzania Open Data Initiative, a government program supported by the World Bank and the UK's Department for International Development to support open data publication, accessibility, and use. • Shule: Developed by Arnold Minde, a programmer, entrepreneur, and open data enthusiast.
GotToVote—Kenya	In the lead-up to Kenya's 2013 general election, the country's Independent Electoral and Boundaries Commission (IEBC) released information about polling center locations on its website. The information, however, was difficult to access. Code for Kenya, a governance innovation initiative, scraped[6] the IEBC data and built a simple website where information could be more easily accessed. The result was the initial version of GotToVote, a website that provided citizens with voter registration center information and helped them navigate the complex registration procedures.
Predicting dengue fever outbreaks in Paraguay	Dengue fever has been endemic in Paraguay since 2009. Recognizing that the problem was being compounded by the lack of a strong system for communicating dengue-related dangers to the public, the National Health Surveillance Department published open data on dengue morbidity.

Table 10.2 (continued)

Name of project	Short description
	Leveraging this data, researchers created an early warning system that can detect outbreaks of dengue fever a week in advance. The data-driven model can predict dengue outbreaks, so long as data on morbidity, climate, and water are available.
A Tu Servicio—Uruguay	A Tu Servicio, a web-based app, uses data from the Ministry of Health in Uruguay to compare—and improve—care standards offered by health service providers. Uruguayans select a new service provide at the beginning of every year.
Bhoomi Program—Bangalore, India	The Bhoomi Program (promoted by the government of the Indian state of Karnataka) digitized and made public 20 million land records in Bangalore (India). The initiative was considered a best practice model of e-governance, to be replicated in other parts of India and elsewhere in poor countries.
Burkina Faso elections	In 2015, Burkina Faso held its first truly free, open, and transparent democratic presidential election. Planning and delivering a democratic election in Burkina Faso raised numerous challenges for the Commission Électorale Nationale Indépendante (CENI). The main challenges were to build trust in the election and to prevent a prolonged period of uncertainty about the results. In overcoming these challenges, CENI worked to secure political buy-in for the rapid processing and publication of verified election results. They committed to a turnaround time that would be unprecedented in Burkina Faso: just one day. Through a results transmission system and web app, along with media sources that had been briefed in advance, results information was made accessible to citizens and interested parties. The winner of the election was announced a little over twenty-four hours after the polls closed, and the result was accepted by the losing candidates.
Open Development Cambodia	Cambodia has shown impressive improvements in political, economic, and social conditions over the last ten years. The country has managed to end civil war, grow the economy, and improve health and education outcomes. Despite this, there are underlying weaknesses in Cambodia's political institutions that constrain its development. These include a growing opacity in decision-making and a lack of information regarding development efforts sweeping across the country. Open Development Cambodia (ODC) was born out of a desire to address these issues. Its goal is to provide access to current and historical information about Cambodia's development via an open data platform compiling data from a wide range of public sources. Launched in 2011, ODC's online portal provides information to government, civil society, media, and the public sector.

(continued)

Table 10.2 (continued)

Name of project	Short description
Electricity Supply Monitoring Initiative (ESMI)—India	Across the developing world, roughly 1.2 billion people do not have access to electricity. Of this number, at least 30 percent live in India. In addition, at least 247 million people experience irregular access to electricity, with many receiving only around four hours a day. While the Ministry of Power and the Central Electricity Authority have released several data sets on electricity service provision on the national open data portal, these relate to power generation, supply and demand, and tariffs—all useful information, but not about power quality. In 2007, the Prayas Energy Group (PEG), an Indian NGO, launched the Electricity Supply Monitoring Initiative (ESMI) to collect real-time power quality information by installing Electricity Supply Monitors (ESMs) in various locations. With a Google grant, it expanded to 200 locations in eighteen Indian states across the country. The initiative was able to make power supply–monitoring data available for different users across the country, to make people aware of the state of electricity supply, advocate for better service provision, and influence policy at both the state and country levels.
iParticipate—Uganda	In 2011, the Collaboration on International ICT Policy for East and Southern Africa (CIPESA) began promoting the use of ICT in monitoring good governance and service delivery in Uganda funded by the Swedish Program for ICT in Developing Regions (SPIDER). Building on the experience and networks developed by CIPESA through this project, iParticipate, a project funded by SPIDER in 2013, was designed to leverage open government data as an enabler of citizen participation and accountable governance. CIPESA used open data available from government portals and from other sources to analyze health service delivery and public investments in health. Mapped data of health providers was compared against the budgetary allocations to the subcounties for the health sector. The maps illustrated that areas with large populations had limited facilities for public health, while some areas received limited funding aimed at improving public health facilities.
Mining governance in Indonesia	Gerak Aceh, an anticorruption advocacy group in Banda Aceh, Indonesia, used open data to influence provincial mining policy. Gerak Aceh worked with the provincial information officers of Aceh province to convince the provincial government agencies to disclose mining-related information. Because of several challenges in working with provincial mining officials, the group took on the task of proactively disclosing mining data through its own portal. It then trained CSOs to use the open data and came up with analysis and visualizations of tax payments; outstanding payments of mining companies to governments; and permit issuance, among other functions. The outputs of the training were used to educate other organizations on the need for a moratorium on the issue of mining permits to be extended to allow reforms in mining governance. It also organized rallies to put pressure on the

Table 10.2 (continued)

Name of project	Short description
	provincial government to extend the moratorium. Gerak Aceh, in collaboration with other actors, was able to convince the provincial government to extend the moratorium. Data-based advocacy was the main factor in this victory, as Gerak Aceh and its partners were able to show through the data they gathered and analyzed that the provincial government still needs to do more through reforms before considering issuing more permits.
Public sanitation in Chennai, India	Transparent Chennai is an action-research group that uses data to improve urban governance in Chennai. In the course of their research, they observed several problems with the way government data is stored and shared with citizens. Transparent Chennai obtained data that do not have geospatial information, timelines, and administrative and sectoral boundaries, all of which have proved to be barriers to their use. Consequently, Transparent Chennai collected data sets with each of these aspects and processed them to improve their quality. For instance, they obtained lists of public toilets and mapped their physical locations. Its researchers also collected data on whether these toilets were functional according to some simple parameters: whether there was water, lights, and doors, and if they were clean. It then made interactive maps that overlay administrative boundaries with a layer of the location of public toilets and information on whether they are usable.
Disaster relief in Nepal (Kathmandu Living Labs' Quakemap and other initiatives)	After two devastating earthquakes in 2015, Nepal faced a lengthy and costly relief effort and recovery. Nepali open data activists sought ways to crowdsource and deploy open data to identify the most urgent needs of citizens, target relief efforts most effectively, and ensure that aid money reached those in need. A number of initiatives created postquake maps that were used by relief agencies, alerted rescuers to Nepalis in need of urgent assistance, provided opportunities for citizens to share feedback on the recovery with government, and ensured fiscal accountability for aid. One of the initiatives implemented was that of Kathmandu Living Labs, which mapped the areas affected by the earthquake and was used by search and rescue teams, via a website called Quakemap, where users could articulate their needs to responders, and coordinate relief and emergency response efforts.

Our approach in analyzing the fourteen projects was to develop an analytical framework. This framework was based on the proposition that for open data's contribution to inclusion to be meaningful in the sense that it supports equitable development, it should (1) take into account both the processes and outcomes of the supply and use of open data, (2) incorporate an appreciation of the networked nature of society, and (3) be placed within the context-specific distribution of power in the network society. To analyze these projects in a methodical and systematic manner according to these propositions, the following questions were developed to guide the analysis of each project:

- To what extent is social inclusion a stated objective of the project?
- How is access to data or information changed because of the publication of open data?
- What evidence exists regarding the result of open data on the type and level of participation of communities in a decision-making process?
- To what extent was the outcome of access and participation beneficial to habitually excluded groups?
- What were the contextual factors that resulted in an increase in the inclusion or exclusion of marginalized individuals or groups?

From the data collected on the processes, outcomes, and contextual factors of the projects, a set of conditioning factors was developed to capture what emerged from the projects as possible determinants of the observed outcomes in relation to open data and inclusion. The factors were developed by analyzing a random selection of eight projects before being stress tested and refined by an analysis of the remaining six projects in the sample.

Findings and Discussion

Open Data Project Outcomes and Inclusion

In most of the fifteen OD4D cases examined, we found that there is insufficient data on the outcomes and impacts of the projects to make conclusive statements about open data's role in including marginalized groups. In some instances, the interventions designed by projects were no longer active or in use at the time the research was being conducted (e.g., open procurement in Kosovo; reporting illegal dumping in Gjakovo, Albania; and air quality data in three Latin American cities), suggesting that these projects could not have had any sustained impact in terms of inclusion.

In other cases, we found evidence of an increase in the number of users of the information made available. For example, in the case of A Tu Servicio, an app that provides information on healthcare service providers in Uruguay, there was an increase in users from 30,000 (1% of the population) to 60,000 in its second year of operation. In the case of open budgeting information published by the city of Lviv in the Ukraine, there is evidence of 116,273 data downloads. But the number of hits, downloads, or users recorded reveals little about the demographics of those users—whether their composition reflects existing socioeconomic stratification in a particular country or region, or whether the composition of users is more diverse, providing previously excluded communities access to information that may yield new benefits for them through more informed decision-making. Neither do these kinds of data reveal any insights on how the lives of those users were changed.

This finding draws attention to a fundamental challenge for open data: how to measure and track the use of open data in such a way so as to be able to make robust claims about both their use and usefulness as a driver of change. As Janssen et al. (2012, 258) point out, "A conceptually simplistic view is often adopted with regard to open data, one which automatically correlates the publicizing of data with use and benefits." This is borne out in some of the cases analyzed where measurement terminates at data provision, regardless of whether the data were used. In the open procurement initiative in Kosovo, for example, success measurement stops at the number of data sets made publicly available. In the case of A Tu Servicio in Uruguay, the number of users of the app is used as a metric, while Budi Odgovoran in Montenegro uses the number of reports filed and the use of that data to issue fines.

If inclusion is a valued indicator of success, then funders of open data initiatives and designers of open data projects should take seriously the development of metrics that provide insights into the outcomes of data use, including the extent to which marginalized communities were among those who benefited from the intervention.

If we use, as an analytical lens, participation of marginalized groups in open data initiatives implemented by OD4D partners, then we find that the roles of marginalized groups in most of the projects are confined to informants, trainees, and beneficiaries—who are only consulted in some of the cases. As such, they may benefit from an intervention but are not necessarily involved in shaping them. This lack of attention to how marginalized groups participate in the design, implementation, or monitoring of these initiatives is viewed as an outcome rather than as a process. Had inclusion been incorporated as a process in the OD4D framework, reporting may have been more explicit in clarifying the roles of the marginalized in the life cycle of OD4D projects.

A project that was purposeful in its design in terms of the inclusion of marginalized people was the open data project in São Paulo, Brazil, called *Cuidando do meu bairro* (Caring for My Neighborhood). It sought to make online tools available so that citizens in marginalized city districts could better understand the public budget and exercise control and inspection of public expenditure in the city to promote action in their neighborhoods. The project came to the realization, however, that despite high levels of interest in using open budget data to monitor the city government, the enthusiasm of the diverse group of citizens who gathered in poor and often excluded parts of the city was thwarted by a lack of internet connectivity.

The São Paulo example illustrates that access to data, as well as the technical and cognitive skills combined with the domain expertise needed to interpret data to create meaning (Zuiderwijk et al. 2012), will often limit the possibility of the most vulnerable and marginalized to participate in or influence decisions that affect them. This is a major challenge for open data. Johnson (2014) points out that the open data community fails to understand the constructed nature of data, leading to three problems, one of which is the differential capabilities of data users. Others point to the contributions of intermediaries in bridging capability gaps to catalyze the flow and use of open data (Schrock and Shaffer 2017; van Schalkwyk et al. 2015).

A way in which OD4D projects were found to be more inclusive is through their convening effect. In other words, while the OD4D projects were not inclusive in their design, they do appear in their execution to convene a diverse and more inclusive range of stakeholders. An open mapping project in Kingston, Jamaica, brought together a range of stakeholders that, importantly, included representatives from a marginalized community in the city. Similarly, the Using Open Data to Create Transparent Value Chains in the Rwanda project convened multiple stakeholders (coffee producers, importers, roasters and retailers, as well as specialists in technology, agronomy, and research) who are not in the habit of interacting or sharing information to explore more transparent value chains in the coffee sector. The Health and Open Data project in Uruguay and the Unlocking the Value of Open Data through Problem-focused Sub-national Networks project in South Africa may not have been as inclusive in their convening of only civil society organizations (CSOs) and governments, but they nevertheless brought together stakeholders who had traditionally been in an adversarial rather than a cooperative relationship.

In many cases, a clear problem focus was evident. These projects positioned themselves less as open data projects and more as problem-specific projects interested in how open data could be deployed to solve the problem. A project in Kosovo focused on environmental health brought together local youth, community volunteers, the municipality, an open data CSO, and a United Nations Development Programme (UNDP) initiative to create a heat map of 687 illegal dumps in the city. In Malaysia, a project focused on corruption in the public sector created detailed profiles of elected officials using open data and resulted in the bringing together of various partners in

Malaysia (academia, CSOs, hackers, and even government officials) and, unexpectedly, partners from the technology community in Myanmar. While these projects did not result in the publication or use of open data, they did introduce a greater diversity of stakeholders into discussions of how open data can be used to solve social problems.

Whether more inclusive design or the convening of a more diverse group of stakeholders results in greater benefits for the habitually excluded remains unclear. Bringing the programmers and switchers of different networks together or creating spaces for locally excluded communities to connect to global networks may be a step forward, but it also may nevertheless reinforce exclusion or the entrenchment of existing power structures, as would be apparent from the outcomes and impacts of open data initiatives. It is to these outcomes and impacts that we now turn our attention.

Factors Affecting the Relationship between Open Data and Inclusion From a synthesis of the outcomes across the fourteen open data initiatives, a set of factors that condition the relationship between open data and inclusion was identified. These factors include the disruption of existing data flows, opportune niches and the interventions of intermediaries, and value creation and transfer. Each of these conditioning factors is explained and discussed in the sections that follow, with reference to the relevant cases.

It should be noted that the order in which the conditioning factors are presented should not be interpreted as indicating a linear or cumulative progression of factors. Neither are they a sequence of temporally dependent steps. For some of the factors, progression is implicit. For example, an opportune niche must be present before it can be occupied, and value transfer can take place only once value exists. However, it is also possible for value transfer to take place following disruption if the data already hold sufficient value for specific networks. We see the conditioning factors as a set of interlinked factors or conditions determined by the networked nature of society; some factors may occur in series, while others occur in parallel.

Disruption of Data Flows In all cases, we found open data to be a disruptor in the flow of data in one way or another, to varying degrees, and in both positive and negative ways. By implication, therefore, open data have the potential to change the distribution of power within information networks by making new flows of data in and between networks possible. If we use as a starting point the assumption that power is concentrated in certain nodes in networks and that data are a fundamental resource for social actors in establishing and protecting central nodes in the global network society, then the disruption of information flows is triggered by the release of open data that have currency in a particular network and are accessible and reusable by all actors in the network. This is not to say that all open data will disrupt existing flows in networks—but rather that their disruptive property is a factor of their openness and their currency.

It is important to be specific about the type of value that confers currency to data. For open data to be disruptive, they need to be of value to those social actors that occupy the central nodes of power in networks. If this is the case, noncentral nodes, and potentially those outside a network, will be in a position to use data to challenge the program of the network.

Several cases illustrate this point. The Department of Health in South Africa publishes data on medicine prices—data that are highly valuable to pharmaceutical companies in protecting their positions of power in a network programmed according to a capitalist market logic. An entrepreneur and a government agency in Tanzania with the support of a supranational institution make data on secondary-school pass rates available. These data are valuable to the ruling political elite in protecting their central position in a network programed to ensure its continued rule by meeting the expectations and needs of the majority of the electorate. Kathmandu Living Labs collects and publishes geolocation data that becomes valuable to a network of disaster relief agencies in postquake Nepal programmed according to logics of transparency and effectiveness. In Paraguay, the release of disease outbreak and morbidity data by the Direccion General de Vigilancia de la Salud (National Health Surveillance Department of Paraguay) is valuable to the political networks of the country, as well as to the network of supranational health agencies, each with a different programmatic logic (i.e., retaining political power versus equitable access to healthcare). In all cases, the data are disruptive because of their value to the network and they are made publicly available for other global networks and local communities to use.

The relevance of the value of open data in relation to specific programs of networks is perhaps most telling in the case of the Bhoomi Program in India (Benjamin et al. 2007). The government of the Indian state of Karnataka digitized and made public 20 million land records in Bangalore. In this case, the intended outcome was for the data to be of value to rural farmers who require title-deed data to apply for financial loans. However, as it turned out, the data were of value to surplus-seeking actors in the global financial network that were able to use the data to acquire land by various methods, and, in so doing, expel farmers from the local agricultural network and further entrench their own positions of power in financial networks.

The Bhoomi Program also illustrates that disruption is triggered in the first instance by data, not by nondigitized information. With the digitization of those records, lawyers, brokers, and financial experts who had previously relied on paper records gained immediate access to the raw land records data and could, by virtue of their expert knowledge, extract value from the information. Farmers, in contrast, were dependent on intermediaries to translate the raw data into usable information, and on information kiosks to access that information. Globally networked actors with the requisite skill sets and knowledge could act more rapidly, and thus exclude the intended beneficiaries. It is only when other factors activate opportune niches—the creation of value for marginalized communities by intermediaries and the transfer of value back into global networks as discussed later in this chapter—that information, as "data that have been organized and communicated" (Porat 1977, 2), also assumes its disruptive potential.

Who the publishers or communicators of open data are, and what type of data is published, were also observed to be relevant to the disruptive potential of open data. In nongovernmental institutional settings, such as private research labs and universities, funding agencies are disrupting the flow of scientific data by requiring grantees to make the research data publicly available. In five of the cases examined in this study, open data were published by nongovernment actors. In the cases of GotToVote in Kenya and the elections in Burkina Faso, it was the independent election oversight body that published the relevant open data. In both Nepal and Cambodia, it was a civil society–based organization that collected and published open map data, while in Banda Aceh, Indonesia, it was a CSO that published open government data, even though the data were collected by government. In only three cases were the open data published comprised exclusively of open government data.

In most of the cases, open government data was combined with other data, which included open and closed data, sometimes crowdsourced and sometimes from nongovernmental sources, to disrupt the flow of data in a network. For example, in India, open government data on electricity supply was supplemented by crowdsourced data on the quality of the supply for it to be disruptive. In Indonesia, provincial information officers of Aceh province and a CSO (Gerak Aceh) worked together, along with the national government, to make mining data available to the CSO so it could publish the data on its portal. In these cases, government acted cooperatively with nongovernmental actors.

There were instances in which government agencies attempted to prevent disruptive open data flows, possibly indicating attempts by network programmers or switchers to protect existing flows from being disrupted. In the case of Cambodia, certain government agencies failed to publish open data such as environmental impact assessment data, despite legal requirements for them do so. Open Data Cambodia resorted to scraping and publishing the data as open data on its own portal. In Tanzania, a project that relied on data scraped from Portable Document Format (PDF) files on a government agency's website, received no support when requests were made to government for the data to be published in open formats, which ultimately scuppered the publication of open examination results data.

These cases illustrate that open data have the potential to disrupt network information flows because it is universally accessible, but that disruption takes place in those networks only where the data have currency. Disruption is limited in some instances by the fact that while access is universal, usability is not. Open data may have to be converted to information or delivered by supplementary channels for the data to be of use to the intended beneficiaries, including to those who are habitually excluded. Moreover, further limits may be brought into play if there is an absence of suitably connected and able actors who can achieve the conversion from data to information. The lag from open data that are of value to selected globally connected networks to information that is of value to those typically outside of networks may further exclude, as network programmers or switchers use open data to protect their positions. Nevertheless, once open data have been translated into usable information, they may still be deployed to challenge the programs of dominant networks. How this process plays out is explored in more detail in the following sections on opportune niches, intermediaries, and value creation and transfer.

Opportune Niches and Intermediaries   The disruption of flows does not take place in a vacuum, but rather in a particular social and environmental context, each with a unique configuration of networked capabilities, resources, and power. Disruption of data flows in networks as described in the previous section may take place in contexts that create spaces, or *opportune niches*, that attract new social actors to networks. In a study of opportune niches in an open data ecosystem, Andrason and van Schalkwyk (2017, 11) suggest that a "niche emerges at the point where the data users, the data source, and resource owners intersect."[7] While an intersection is located within ecosystems in the Andrason and van Schalkwyk study, intersections also form part of networks, with dense convergences creating network nodes.

Not all opportune niches present equal opportunities. While open data imply universal access, access to opportune niches is not universal and depends in part on the configurations of material and nonmaterial capitals of social actors (van Schalkwyk et al. 2016). The advantage for some actors over others to enter a niche will depend both on their capitals and on the nature of the niche itself. In sum, the ability of actors to enter into or reposition themselves close to emerging niches in networks will depend on their constellations of capital, the situated material and nonmaterial advantages that they bring to the network or to those who occupy central nodes (Andrason and van Schalkwyk 2017; Castells 2009, 2017).

The importance of specific properties required by social actors to exploit opportune niches, and their effects once they establish themselves, point to the difference between those who are able to exploit opportune niches and those who cannot. Here, social actors located between those who occupy positions of power and those who are excluded from networks come into focus: namely, open data intermediaries (van Schalkwyk et al. 2015, 2016).

An *open data intermediary* is any social actor positioned at some point in a data supply chain that incorporates an open data set, positioned between two actors in the supply chain, and facilitates the use of open data that otherwise may not have been the case (van Schalkwyk et al. 2016). What is relevant in the definition to this analysis is the propensity of intermediaries to make possible new connections. Andrason and van Schalkwyk (2017, 17), in the following comment, discuss these possibilities:

> Each intermediary deploys the forms of the capital differently to connect…successfully. No intermediary necessarily has all the types of capital at their highest possible (notional) extents. Rather, intermediaries excel in some forms of capital (or even it sub-types of such forms) while the extent of other forms may be deficient… [T]hey are not only conditioned by their environment's structure and properties…but also actively modify the hosting milieu, as far as its configuration and characteristics are concerned. Overall, the intermediaries improve connectivity between the various agents in the ecosystem.

Intermediaries, due to their different constellations of capitals compared to that of excluded communities, are either established in networks or are able to access the opportune niches that emerge due to changes in the network's environment.

Opportune niches were noted in many of the cases (see table 10.3). In each of these cases, the niche in a particular network presented itself as a social problem and was exploitable by social actors because of (1) a simultaneous opportunity or enabling conditions that created a demand for data, (2) the availability of relevant open data, and (3) their particular constellation of capitals, the value and relevance of which are determined by the network in which the problem presents itself.

Social actors may predict the emergence of opportune niches. In the case of Gerak Aceh in Indonesia, the imminent expiry of a moratorium on the issuing of mining licenses was used to create an opportune niche. An Indonesian CSO negotiated with the government of Aceh to release data on mining in the province, which they used to mobilize other social actors effectively, drawing them into the network to apply collective pressure on the provincial government to extend the moratorium.

Opportune niches may emerge spontaneously, and they can disappear just as rapidly. Kathmandu Living Labs had been collecting and publishing open data for some time before the earthquake, but they remained largely unused. However, when the earthquake struck and information was needed to assist in the management of disaster relief efforts, the publicly available data were used by those coordinating the relief efforts. In other words, the earthquake created an unpredicted, spontaneous opportune

Table 10.3

Opportune niches in networks.

Actor	Product	Problem	Enabling conditions/demand for data	Open data	Capitals	Connections
Esoko	Information service	Illiterate farmers. Smallholder farmers unable to benefit from globalizing food chains.	Affordable and widespread mobile network. Inefficiencies of agricultural extension officers. Development funding.	Ministry of Agriculture, Government of Ghana US third-party provider	Economic ✓ Social ✓ Cultural ✓ Technical ✓ Symbolic ✓	Farming community Funding agencies National government
Code for South Africa	MPR	Lack of transparency and consistency in medicine pricing.	Increasing cost of healthcare. Expensive medicines. Computerization of surgeries. Attentive health ministry.	MPR, Ministry of Health	Cultural Technical ✓ Symbolic ✓	None
Tanzania Open Data Initiative	Open Education Dashboard	Lack of accountability for school performance. Lack of informed choices possible on the part of parents.	Poor examination results due to changes in the Tanzanian education system. Exposure of problem in the media. Mounting political pressure. Increase in interest in Tanzania by donors.	Examination pass rates, National Examination Council of Tanzania (NECTA) National Bureau of Statistics	Economic ✓ Cultural Technical ✓	Government Supranational funding agencies
Arnold Minde	Shule	Same as for Tanzania Open Data Initiative	Same as for Tanzania Open Data Initiative	Same as for Tanzania Open Data Initiative	Cultural Technical ✓	CSO
Code for Kenya	GotToVote	Limited access to information by the voting public.	Prior election chaos. New electoral process and constitution. Affordable and widespread mobile network.	Independent Electoral Commission, Kenya	Social ✓ Cultural ✓ Technical ✓	Oversight agency

					Value	Stakeholders
Latin American Open Data Initiative (ILDA)	Predicting dengue fever outbreaks in Paraguay	Dengue fever endemic in Paraguay since 2009. Problem compounded by the lack of a system for communicating dengue-related dangers to the public.	173,000 probable cases of dengue in the year 2016, with 48 cases of severe dengue and 16 deaths. Increased concern about other mosquito-borne diseases such as malaria, chikungunya, and Zika.	Dengue morbidity data, National Health Surveillance Department of Paraguay. Meteorological data, third party.	Cultural Technical ✓ Symbolic	Supranational funding agency
DATA Uruguay and Ministry of Health	A Tu Servicio	Lack of transparency and accountability of health service providers. Healthcare data not available in a format that allows citizens to make informed decisions. Additionally, the pressures from competing health providers led citizens to rely on marketing and advertising campaigns based on opinion rather than actual data.	Near-universal coverage of publicly funded healthcare provisions. February in Uruguay: public debate over the factors that influence citizens to choose (or leave) a health service provider; marked by heavy advertising on the part of providers, many of whom encourage citizens to join them and leave others and may even pay users to switch providers. Attentive health ministry.	Health service provider data, Ministry of Health.	Economic ✓ Social ✓ Cultural ✓ Technical ✓	Government Civil society
State of Karnataka, India	Bhoomi Program	Lack of access to land record data needed by farmers to secure loans.	Digitization of land records. Escalating land prices in Bangalore. Low levels of efficiency and high levels of corruption.	Land records data, State of Karnataka.	Economic ✓ Social ✓ Cultural ✓ Technical ✓	None

(continued)

Table 10.3 (continued)

Actor	Product	Problem	Enabling conditions/ demand for data	Open data	Capitals	Connections
Burkina Faso Open Data Initiative (BODI)	Burkina Faso election results	Low levels of trust in the electoral process, and trust needed to ensure postelection political stability.	Unstable and dictatorial past political means increased attention and interest in the elections. Interest from international open data community.	Election results data, CENI.	Economic ✓ Cultural ✓ Technical ✓	Government Oversight agency Supranational agencies International open data experts
Open Development Cambodia	Open data portal	Lack of access to natural resource data, including information related to agriculture which is one of Cambodia's key industries.	The failure of the Cambodian government to provide information on important country assets provided a role for ODC to fill. ODC had numerous requests in the past to get data on soil type published on its portal and was able to do so. This data were used by the Cambodian Rice Federation to determine potential growth areas in crop production.	Multiple sources, including scraped from government websites.	Social ✓ Cultural ✓ Technical ✓	Media Private sector
Prayas Energy Group	ESMI	Poor quality of electricity supply and lack of data on the quality of electricity supply.	The unequal access to quality electricity in India, where, for example, rural areas experience 500% more interruptions than district and urban centers. Interest from media and the funder (Google).	ESMs in various locations. Government data (Ministry of Power and the Central Electricity Authority).	Social ✓ Cultural ✓ Technical ✓	Government Regulators Media Civil society Private firms

CIPESA	iParticipate	Unclear; need for reforms in the healthcare sector?	Unclear: Funder-driven? Poor governance of health sector?	Open data on government portal.	Social ✓ Cultural ✓ Technical ✓	NGOs Media Donor funders
Gerak Aceh	Open data portal	Unaccountable mining companies, corruption, and adverse effects on local communities and their environment.	Lack of transparency and corruption in the mining sector in a province of Indonesia. A moratorium on the issuing of mining licenses expired in September 2016. This was seized on as an important moment for advocacy by the organization.	Provincial Mining and Energy Department and the local transportation, information, and communications agency.	Economic ✓ Social ✓ Cultural ✓ Technical ✓ Symbolic ✓	NGOs Local communities
Transparent Chennai	Enriched data on public facilities in Chennai	Health issues in Chennai's slums as a result of poor sanitation facilities.	Chennai's poor reputation as a city. Poor state of the public facilities as a result of the lack of consultation and grounding of public spending priorities. Government willingness to listen and accommodate the suggestions on data collection and quality.	Various municipal government sources. Data collected by Transparent Chennai to supplement government data.	Social ✓ Cultural ✓ Technical ✓	Local government
Kathmandu Living Labs	Quakemap	Lack of reliable data with which to plan and coordinate disaster relief and rescue efforts. Lack of accountability around the distribution of aid.	Earthquakes in Nepal. Attentive media and disaster relief network.	Crowdsourced data. Official statistical data.	Social ✓ Cultural ✓ Technical ✓	Disaster relief community Local communities

niche in the network of globally connected aid agencies that allowed Kathmandu Living Labs to enter the network of global relief agencies.

In some of these cases, opportune niches appear to be connected to powerful network nodes, while in others, this was not so. To illustrate, in the cases of Esoko, A Tu Servicio, Burkina Faso, Kenya, Bangalore, Gerak Aceh, Chennai, and electricity quality in India, social actors were connected to nodes of power (e.g., a government department or an independent oversight agency). On the other hand, in the cases of MPR, Dengue, iParticipate, Shule, and Open Development Cambodia, connections to power nodes were absent. While the absence of a connection between a powerful node and other social actors occupying an opportune niche does not prevent the addition of value to open data (as discussed next), the lack of a connection to a powerful node may account for why the latter group is more likely to fall short when it comes to transferring the value of the information across networks and, ultimately, to lower success rates in terms of inclusion. Similarly, those social actors without economic capital (e.g., Shule and Transparent Chennai) have not been able to maintain their position in the niche, and consequently are also unable to make a sustainable transformative contribution (see chapter 11 in this volume for more on the importance of government involvement in local, bottom-up open data initiatives).

What this section highlights is that opportune niches may be created by the simultaneous occurrence of opportunities in the environment and by the publication of open data. Opportune niches open up spaces in networks for intermediaries to occupy. Open data intermediaries are able to occupy and settle into niches if they possess the appropriate mix of capital that enables them to connect to existing actors in the network. Furthermore, once established, open data intermediaries make possible new connections between actors and resources within and between networks. Unresolved, however, is the question of whose interests open data intermediaries represent. Open data may have contributed to creating an opportune niche, but it is not yet apparent how open data contribute to a reprogramming of dominant networks in the interest of those excluded from networks.

Value Creation and Transfer   According to Castells (2009, 27), "value is what the dominant institutions of society decide it to be." In the network society, what constitutes value depends on the network and its program (or dominant logic) that is specific to each network (Castells 1996, 2009). In this sense, value is an expression of power, as those that have the power to program (or reprogram) the goals of the network determine what is of value to a specific network.

Janssen et al. (2012) say, "The main challenge is that open data has no value in itself; it only becomes valuable when used." In this sense, the use of open data is a proxy for their value in a network.

Converting data into usable information is the primary task of a particular type of intermediary: the infomediary (Fung et al. 2010; Pollock 2011; Chan et al. 2016). *Infomediaries* typically add value to open data by reinterpreting, mixing, or repackaging them. By doing so, they render the data more comprehensible, usable, and attractive, and this is in both senses of the word, to other actors in a network who typically share common programmatic objectives.

The case of Shule, one of the Open Education Dashboard projects in Tanzania, reveals evidence of a mismatch between the value created by open data and the needs of the intended users. The project scraped school examinations results data and made it available on a website, along with visualization and comparison tools. It also partnered with a CSO that is active in education to promote the use of the data by the parents of secondary school children. However, the project eventually came to an end when it became clear that the data were not being used. An interview with the project lead revealed that his initial intention was to supplement the exam pass data with more basic data on Tanzanian schools such as their addresses, contact numbers, facilities, admission policies, and the like. He felt that parents would find the basic information more useful, and his hope was that the basic information would attract users to the platform, creating an opportunity to expose them to the school performance data. However, he lacked the resources to collect and maintain the basic data on Tanzanian schools, and the data on school performance remained unused by parents.

Interestingly, the only real uptake was over a short period by the international media, which reported on the successful use of open data in Tanzania. The portal was of greater value to the global media network than it was to the local community of parents. In other words, open data did not create any value for the intended users who did not use them, but they did create unintended value for the global media.

Altering the value of data by converting them into usable information was found in most of these cases, where the intention was to create value for a group or groups of users identified by those who designed the project or intervention. In the case of Esoko, value was added to market price data by making it available in simple formats in multiple local languages via cell phones, and also by providing local-language call center support to smallholder farmers in Ghana. In South Africa, Code for South Africa added value to government data on the breakdown of medicine prices by publishing information via an online app in the form of comparable, single exit prices for patients. A Tu Servicio in Uruguay developed simple indicators from government health data, making it possible for citizens to compare health service providers. The project to prevent dengue fever in Paraguay combined government and other open data, such as meteorological data, to create a tool to predict outbreaks of dengue fever. In all these cases, there is evidence of use by the intended users.

The key question in terms inclusion and of value creation is for whom the value is being created. Adding value to data by converting them into usable information has the potential to attract new users to the network, such that they participate in the politics of decision-making, or to activate existing network actors to challenge the dominant logic of the network. If the locus of decision-making (i.e., central nodes of power) is located in a different network from the one in which the value was created, then the value created in one network, by intermediaries or other actors, for a specific group of users must be transferrable to the network in which power is vested in order for it to have an impact that challenges existing power relations. Yet the network in which decision-making is located likely may not share the same programmatic logic as the network in which the value was created. Recalling the definition of *value*, which is what the network determines it to be (Castells 2009), it is only when value is shared that transfer can occur.

If there is shared value, that value must be transferred by someone or something from one network to another. Switchers connect networks and allow value transfer. Switchers are powerful actors in networks because they have the "ability to connect and ensure the cooperation of different networks by sharing common goals and combining resources" (Castells 2009, 45). If a value is shared or if there are no switchers in place, then networks remain disconnected. We found the inability of the open data initiatives in the sample to connect the value of open data between or across networks to be the most significant reason hampering the potential contribution of open data to greater social inclusion. In particular, switching between development aid networks, the open data movement, and government networks where decisions on the distribution of public resources are concentrated was lacking.

The cases from Indonesia, Paraguay, and Uruguay best illustrate value transfer as a factor in the relationship between open data and inclusion. In the case of Gerak Aceh in Indonesia, new social actors were drawn into an opportune niche where various actors formed a collective advocating for reform in the governance of mining in the province. The inclusion of new social actors increased Gerak Aceh's ability to switch between networks (i.e., between a civil society network and a political one). This happened because Gerak Aceh was able to take advantage of networks and relationships within the provincial government, and, by mobilizing sufficient numbers of activist groups and citizens, political value was created. In other words, the collective nature of the action increased its constituent representivity and triggered the exploration of compatible goals.

Switchers are unlikely to be a single individual, but rather a group of actors. This not only negates the risks inherent in self-serving individual actors as switchers, but it also makes a bringing together of interests and influence that will connect networks more likely: "more subtle, complex, and negotiated systems of power enforcement must be established," and "the programmes of the dominant networks of society need to set compatible goals between these networks" (Castells 2009, 47).

In the case of the predicting dengue fever project, value was created in the scientific network (by an academic at a university in Paraguay). The new knowledge that it created using open data as a predictive tool is of value to the scientific network that seeks to establish verifiable truths about the world. But it is the government agency that must use the model created and its predictive capabilities to better manage the scourge of dengue fever for the benefit of marginalized rural and Indigenous publics. However, the value of new knowledge is not necessarily a value shared by the government agency; this is because it operates in a network with a different political programmatic logic that seeks to protect its position of political power. It is not that knowledge has no value in political networks, but rather that it is only when that knowledge serves the purpose of protecting the network that it takes on value.

New knowledge that allows a government to predict outbreaks in rural Paraguay may hold little value for government. Moreover, government operates at the national level, whereas the developers of the predictive model, when they are seeking validation for their truth claims, are operating at a different level in the global scientific network. The global health community also operates at the global level, according to a network logic more closely aligned with that of the global science network—and both are more communal. This allowed the project to switch effectively between the scientific and global health networks, but it has been less successful at switching between the scientific and political networks (for the time being, at least).

In the A Tu Servicio project, a notable shift took place when the civic tech company and the government department in the Ministry of Health were negotiating their cooperation agreement on creating an app that would use open government data to provide information on health service providers in Uruguay. The civic tech company's main purpose for repackaging open data on health service providers was to give the public a wider choice and to allow citizens to move from one service provider to another based on the information provided by A Tu Servicio. However, the government was not in favor of an annual mass migration of citizens between service providers; it was far more interested in the value of the information to make service providers more transparent and accountable to Uruguayans. The government also argued that promoting choice over accountability could destabilize the system, whereas the civic tech organization's starting position was in fact to disrupt the current system. In other words, the two parties saw different values in the data. Notably, the civic tech organization changed its position to align with that of the government department, thereby harmonizing the value proposition of the information and the intended outcomes of its use. The net result is a more transparent system in which health service providers are more accountable to government and citizens, there is more informed decision-making on the part of citizens, and there is a manageable number of transfers of less than 5 percent per annum to new health service providers.

Open government data is a "networked movement of technologists, activists, the private sector, and civil society actors" (Davies and Bawa 2012). Power in networks is corralled by the first-movers (knowledge workers and the technology savvy) and consolidated by those with historically endowed power. This networked nature of the global open data movement is highly relevant in relation to social inclusion. When switchers connect social actors in local networks to global networks, they must abide by and accede to the rules, protocols, and standards of global networks; these rules, protocols, and standards are determined by those who program global networks. The programmers of global networks provide the basis for inclusion. In other words, if a move from the local to the global does not conform to the network power in a global network, the switch will fail. The network power of global movements, including the open data movement, will, as a structural feature of networks, exclude by determining the rules of inclusion.

Network Inclusion versus Social Inclusion *Inclusion* was initially defined in network terms as meaningful participation in information networks by those habitually excluded. But the term could also be defined as the improvement of the position of those already in existing information networks in relation to central nodes where decision-making is concentrated. An improvement in a networked position, or being closer to more central nodes in networks, means having more information to contest the decision-making in central nodes that follow the logic of the network. This broader understanding of inclusion resonates with Castells's definition of one of the four forms of power in networks: *networked power* is "the power of social actors over other social actors in the network" (Castells 2007, 28). In other words, not all social actors share power equally in networks, leaving some social actors excluded from centralized power nodes. Bringing those actors within the same network closer to central nodes is also a form of inclusion.

In the case of Esoko, smallholder farmers were already participating in the agricultural network, but their relative position in the network was improved by information on the market prices—farmers were able to negotiate better prices with wholesalers. In the case of A Tu Servicio, almost all Uruguayan citizens have access to healthcare, and, as such, the provision of comparative information on healthcare service providers could not have resulted in more inclusive healthcare. But the availability of the information did empower some in the healthcare network to make more informed decisions about which healthcare service provider to select. In the case of the availability of comparable medicine price information in South Africa, the likelihood of the information leading to greater inclusion was stunted by the fact that patients in the public healthcare system pay a flat price for medicines dispensed by state-owned pharmacies. However, not all private healthcare patients are of equal means, and the information has empowered some private patients to make beneficial decisions in terms of the cost of their medicines. Moreover, the use of information by intermediaries, such as doctors in private practice, provided poorer private patients with access to cheaper medicines.

This type of inclusion may not sit well with those who are completely excluded from information networks, as they may see network inclusion as the social progression of those already privileged toward the network elites. For them, it is networking power and network-making that must be disrupted in order for true social inclusion to take place. However, it is possible that some social actors, particularly intermediaries, that are included in information networks may represent the interests of those who are excluded. By improving their position in networks, and in so doing improving their ability to challenge the programmatic logic of the network, these actors could disrupt power in the network, thereby creating new network nodes that allow the excluded to participate in a reprogrammed network. Such a route to inclusion, however, does depend on the propensity of those already in the network to act on behalf of those excluded from the network.

Most projects included for analysis show a redistribution of networked power but little disruption to networking power. In other words, improvements in the position of some social actors already within networks can be attributed to open data, but *open data did not redistribute networking power*. And in one case, as illustrated in the following section, open data strengthened existing nodes where power is concentrated, resulting in an increase in the exclusion of a marginal community from a financial network.

Exclusion While it has been shown thus far in this chapter that intermediaries play important roles in terms of adding value to open data and creating connections within and between networks, intermediaries should not be seen as a panacea in ensuring open data's positive impact on social inclusion. Intermediaries have their own vested interests and are not ideologically neutral (Schrock and Shaffer 2017). Furthermore, it cannot be assumed that the usual suspects (i.e., the most visible or vocal of the CSOs) represent those constituencies (including the marginalized) that they claim to represent (Enaholo 2017; Neubert 2011). While we had limited data at our disposal to explore the dark side of intermediaries, the possible negative effects that may accrue if, for example, Esoko were to marketize the personal data that it collects from farmers should not be glossed over; they require further investigation. In the case of the Bhoomi Program, the activities of legal professionals as intermediaries in conferring commercial value to land data have been shown to result in the exclusion of the very farmers who were meant to benefit from the public availability of the data (Benjamin et al. 2007).

Counterpower   Counterpower in the network society is exerted when social actors attempt to change the programs of specific networks, disrupt the switches that represent the dominant programmatic logic of the network, or both. We have shown that a disruption in data flows across networks may occur when data previously shared exclusively within one network or between selected nodes in a network are made openly accessible. We also showed that it may require the repackaging of data into usable information in order to challenge existing configurations of network power.

However, the analysis of the fourteen open data projects in table 10.3 shows that there were no instances where the dominant programs of existing global networks or the switches that connect across these networks were reprogrammed or disrupted—either by making data open or by making them both open and usable. In fact, in one case, the public availability of data had the opposite effect: it allowed an existing global network to consolidate its position at the expense of local communities. In other words, a disruption in the flow of data or its conversion into usable information does not necessarily equate to a disruption in the distribution of power.

At the same time, evidence was found of open data's propensity to create convening spaces (see the previous analysis of the fifteen OD4D projects in table 10.2), and it is conceivable that such spaces could open opportunities for counterpower to be exercised if programmers and switches are brought together. Similarly, opportune niches may create nonphysical networked spaces or moments in which existing power arrangements and distribution may be countered.

Conclusion

Castells's elaboration of the network society is not a theory per se (Stalder 1998); rather, it presents a way of thinking about and understanding society. Our approach has been the same. We have neither used nor offered a rigorous theory on the relationship between open data and social exclusion. Ours is a modest attempt to provide a grounded and empirically informed approach to understanding the relationship—one that will hopefully ignite robust debate and challenges to our framework and findings.

We acknowledge that what we have proposed as being influential factors in the relationship between open data and social inclusion is limited by our reliance on existing primary and secondary sources that describe and report on open data initiatives that were not expressly designed with social inclusion in mind. We take some refuge in the fact that, while they may not always be explicitly framed with social inclusion in mind, projects were nevertheless designed within an overarching framework that assumes social inclusion is a desired outcome of open data initiatives. We further acknowledge that our research would have benefited from in-depth interviews not only with those who designed and implemented the open data initiatives included in our analysis, but also with the intended beneficiaries of those initiatives. It was simply beyond the scope of this research to do so for the close to thirty open data initiatives implemented across the globe.

These limitations notwithstanding, we believe that we have offered an important first attempt to answer the ambitious question posed by this chapter: How, for whom, and in what contexts do open data contribute to inclusive development?

With the data at our disposal we were unable to show with any degree of confidence that the OD4D open data initiatives have resulted in greater inclusion, especially if inclusion is deemed to be meaningful only if it empowers those who are habitually excluded. On the other hand, one feature that was consistent across the open data projects analyzed is the catalytic and convening properties of open data. In a range of contexts, open data were found to bring together diverse stakeholders who shared a common interest in resolving a mutual problem using a free public resource.

The question arises as to whether there is something inherently special about open data—its perceived neutrality or the fact that access is nondiscriminatory—that complements the known preconditions required for collaboration to occur (Wood and Gray 1991). And further questions would need to be asked as to whether the potency of open data's convening power is dependent on the political sensitivity of the problem, particularly if, as Castells and Himanen (2014) suggest, government needs to participate as the central stakeholder in formulating and contributing to solutions that drive inclusive development. More politically sensitive problems may well exclude government but galvanize nonstate actors more effectively, leaving them at loggerheads in their perceptions on the use-value of open data as an instrument for inclusive human development. Recent shifts away from globalization and toward nationalism may not bode well as governments recede from public participation and attentive citizens become more demanding.

The analysis of the outcomes of fourteen open data projects in this chapter uncovered evidence of access and participation as components of inclusion. This could indicate that while there is insufficient evidence to support claims of open data's impact on social inclusion, there is nevertheless evidence of a more open and potentially participatory approach to governance practice.

It may be tempting to infer that the materialization of open data's causal relationship with more inclusive governance is simply a matter of time. That is, as open practices diffuse through and across public institutions, inclusiveness will tend to follow. However, a more holistic reading of the state of open data at a national level, and one that includes open data readiness and implementation indicators of open data practice, shows that governments are in fact regressing. In other words, open data practice as a contributor to more equitable governance is losing the foothold that it has established over the past three years (Brandusescu et al. 2017).

From our findings, we would offer that this regression occurs because open data practices centered around access and participation have not successfully disrupted the concentration of power in political and other networks. And where disruption of some kind is taking place, when opportune niches open up to attract new social actors (including intermediaries) into networks, and when these new actors add value to the open data, there remains a critical breakdown in the transfer of value between networks. Without transfer between networks (particularly, but not exclusively, to global political networks), the propensity for the uptake and use of information derived from open data by central nodes of power where decision-making is concentrated remains limited.[8] Where such value transfer takes place, the cases reveal instances of network inclusion.

In other words, open data improve the position of social actors already included in networks in relation to central nodes of power in those networks. Peripheral elites can either use open data to accumulate power and gravitate further toward the central elites or they can use open data to challenge the central elites and seek to redistribute power across new nodes by challenging the dominant program of the network. Such challenges may result in a more equitable distribution of resources, or else it may simply create revised network programs that fail to transform the rules of distribution.

While network inclusion makes this indirect form of social inclusion possible (though as risky as it is promising), our findings indicate that, at least in our sample, open data are thus far making at most a limited contribution to inclusion. While open data may well be delivering other benefits in terms of the accountability of public institutions and increased efficiency, those habitually excluded remain outside networks where those benefits accumulate, and open data are doing little to change the status quo in terms or resource distribution.

To return to Castells and Himanen's (2014) proposed conception of development in network societies, we found no evidence of open data leading to a more synergistic relationship between informational and human development, where the former is propelled by networked power according to a logic of informationalism and the latter is propelled by networking power according to a logic of welfarism. This leads us to suggest that open data are not contributing materially to the realization of the corrective and redistributive policies needed for a synergistic relationship to manifest. Nevertheless, it is hoped that this first foray into the relationship between open data and social inclusion—one that has attempted to uncover the dynamics of power accumulation, distribution, and disruption in network societies—will provide useful insights for the open data movement, as it mobilizes future resources and will open a promising line of inquiry for open data researchers who are eager to distill the true value and impact of open data for development.

Notes

1. See, for example, GovLab (n.d.), Open Knowledge International (n.d.), and Open Data Charter (2015).

2. Stalder (2005, 62) states, "At the interconnections of such flows, nodes arise. Nodes are structures built by the recurrent intersection of different flows which they, at the same time, process and direct. Nodes can have the form of large institutions, such as banks or government agencies that depend on the constant input of information which they process and feed back into the flow as new information."

3. For more information, see OD4D (http://www.od4d.net). For a detailed account of the evolution of the broader OD4D initiative's theory of change, see Davies and Perini (2016). For an evaluation of the OD4D initiative, see Acevedo-Ruiz and Pena-Lopez (2017).

4. An examination of the theories of change of the open data programs undertaken by the OD4D partners was done to assess how they describe the process by which open data leads to more inclusive development outcomes. While one may posit that theories of change are merely static, abstract ideations on how development projects are meant to take shape, theories of change nevertheless articulate the underlying rationale of why development interventions are executed, and, of relevance to this research undertaking, how they *presume* to improve the lives of certain communities. Theories of change of a total of nine OD4D partner programs were analyzed to determine whether and how they articulated a pathway from open data to inclusion. OD4D projects were selected from these programs.

5. The project A Tu Servicio was included in both the change theory and the outcomes analyses. It was the only project from the fifteen theories-of-change projects for which there was sufficient documented evidence for the outcomes analysis.

6. For more about data scraping, see https://en.wikipedia.org/wiki/Data_scraping.

7. See Andrason and van Schalkwyk (2016) for three examples of intermediaries taking advantage of opportune niches in the agriculture ecosystem in Ghana.

8. See Peixoto and Fox (2016), who reach a similar conclusion that the most successful cases are where civil society and government cooperate.

References

Acevedo-Ruiz, Manuel, and Ismael Peña-López. 2017. *Evaluation of the Open Data for Development Program: Final Report v 2.0.* Ottawa: OD4D. http://od4d.net/wp-content/uploads/2017/05/OD4D -Final-evaluation-report-v2_31-May.pdf.

Allman, Dan. 2013. "The Sociology of Social Inclusion." *Sage Open* January–March: 1–16. http:// journals.sagepub.com/doi/pdf/10.1177/2158244012471957.

Andrason, Alexander, and François van Schalkwyk. 2016. *Open Data Intermediaries in the Agricultural Sector in Ghana.* Washington, DC: World Wide Web Foundation.

Andrason, Alexander, and François van Schalkwyk. 2017. "Opportune Niches in Data Ecosystems: Open Data Intermediaries in the Agriculture Sector in Ghana." *SSRN* https://papers.ssrn .com/sol3/papers.cfm?abstract_id=2949722.

Arnstein, Sherry R. 1969. "A Ladder of Citizen Participation." *Journal of the American Institute of Planners* 35 (4): 216–224. https://lithgow-schmidt.dk/sherry-arnstein/ladder-of-citizen -participation.html.

Benjamin, Soloman, R. Bhuvaneswari, and P. R. Manjunatha. 2007. *Bhoomi: 'E-Governance', or, An Anti-Politics Machine Necessary to Globalize Bangalore?* A CASUM-m Working Paper. January. https://casumm.files.wordpress.com/2008/09/bhoomi-e-governance.pdf.

Bentley, Caitlin M., and Arul Chib. 2016. "The Impact of Open Development Initiatives in Lower- and Middle-Income Countries: A Review of the Literature." *Electronic Journal of Information Systems in Developing Countries* 74 (1): 1–20.

Brandusescu, Ana, Carlos Iglesias, and Kristen Robinson, lead authors; Jose M. Alonso, Craig Fagan, Anne Jellema, and Dillon Man, contributing authors. 2017. *Open Data Barometer: Global Report.* 4th ed. Washington, DC: World Wide Web Foundation. http://opendatabarometer.org /doc/4thEdition/ODB-4thEdition-GlobalReport.pdf.

Castells, Manuel. 1996. *The Rise of the Network Society. The Information Age: Economy, Society, and Culture.* Vol. 1. Oxford, UK: Blackwell.

Castells, Manuel. 2007. "Communication, Power, and Counter-power in the Network Society." *International Journal of Communication* 1 (1): 238–266.

Castells, Manuel. 2009. *Communication Power.* Oxford: Oxford University Press. http://socium.ge /downloads/komunikaciisteoria/eng/comunication%20power%20castells.pdf.

Castells, Manuel. 2017. "Rethinking Development in the Global Information Age." In *Castells in Africa: Universities and Development*, ed. Johan Muller, Nico Cloete, and Francois van Schalkwyk, 76–92. Cape Town, South Africa: African Minds. http://muse.jhu.edu/book/57259.

Castells, Manuel, and Pekka Himanen. 2014. "Models of Development in Global Information Age: Constructing an Analytical Framework." In *Reconceptualising Development in the Global Information Age*, ed. Manuel Castells and Pekka Himanen, 7–25. Oxford: Oxford University Press.

Chan, Mavis, Peter A. Johnson, and Malcolm Shookner. 2016. "Assessing the Use of Government Open Data and the Role of Data Infomediaries: The Case of Nova Scotia's Community Counts Program." *eJournal of eDemocracy & Open Government* 8 (1): 1–27.

Chang, Ha Joon. 2003. *Kicking Away the Ladder: Development Strategy in Historical Perspective*. London: Anthem.

Chen, Shoahua, and Martin Ravallion. 2007. "Absolute Poverty Measures for the Developing World, 1981–2004." *Policy Research Working Paper Series*. 4211. Washington, DC: World Bank. http://www.pnas.org/content/104/43/16757.

Davies, Tim, and Zainab A. Bawa. 2012. "The Promises and Perils of Open Government Data (OGD)." *Journal of Community Informatics* 8 (2). http://ci-journal.net/index.php/ciej/article/view/929/955.

Davies, Tim, and Fernando Perini. 2016. "Researching the Emerging Impacts of Open Data: Revisiting the ODDC Conceptual Framework." *Journal of Community Informatics* 12 (2).

Enaholo, Patrick. 2017. "Beyond Mere Advocacy: CSOs and the Role of Intermediaries in Nigeria's Open Data Ecosystem." In *Social Dynamics of Open Data*, ed. Francois van Schalkwyk, Stefaan Verhulst, Gustavo Magalhaes, Juan Pane, and Johanna Walker, 89–108. Cape Town, South Africa: African Minds. https://zenodo.org/record/1117797#.WoIwcedG2F4.

Fung, Archon, Hollie R. Gilman, and Jennifer Shkabatur. 2010. *Impact Case Studies from Middle Income and Developing Countries: New Technologies*. London: Transparency and Accountability Initiative. http://www.transparency-initiative.org/archive/wp-content/uploads/2011/05/impact_case_studies_final1.pdf.

GovLab. n.d. "Open Data's Impact: Open Data Is Changing the World in Four Ways." http://odimpact.org/.

GovLab, and Christian Laurence. 2014. "Open Data: What's in a Name?" *GovLab Blog* (blog), January 16. http://thegovlab.org/open-data-whats-in-a-name/.

Gurstein, Michael. 2010. "Open Data: Empowering the Empowered or Effective Data Use for Everyone?" *Gurstein's Community Informatics* (blog), September 2. https://gurstein.wordpress.com/2010/09/02/open-data-empowering-the-empowered-or-effective-data-use-for-everyone/.

Gurstein, Michael. 2011. "Open Data: Empowering the Empowered or Effective Data Use for Everyone?" *First Monday* 16 (2). http://journals.uic.edu/ojs/index.php/fm/article/view/3316/2764.

Gurumurthy, Anita, and Parminder J. Singh. 2016. "Open Development—a Focus on Organizational Norms and Power Redistribution." White Paper Series, Paper no. 5. Singapore: Singapore Internet Research Centre.

Habermas, Jürgen. 1996. *The Inclusion of the Other: Studies in Political Theory*, ed. Ciaran P. Cronin and Pablo De Greiff. Frankfurt: Suhrkamp.

Haq, Mahbub-ul. 1998. *Human Development in South Asia*. Karachi, Pakistan: Oxford University Press.

Hickey, Sam, Kunai Sen, and Badru Bukenya 2015. "Exploring the Politics of Inclusive Development: Towards a New Conceptual Approach." In *The Politics of Inclusive Development: Interrogating the Evidence*, ed. Sam Hickey, Kunai Sen, and Badru Bukenya, 3–32. Oxford: Oxford University Press.

Horrigan, John B., and Lee Rainie. 2015. "Americans' Views on Open Government Data." April 21. Washington, DC: Pew Research Center. http://www.pewinternet.org/2015/04/21/open -government-data/.

Hurlbert, Margot, and Joyeeta Gupta. 2015. "The Split Ladder of Participation: A Diagnostic, Strategic, and Evaluation Tool to Assess When Participation Is Necessary." *Environmental Science & Policy* 50 (June): 100–113.

Janssen, Marijn, Yannis Charalabidis, and Anneke Zuiderwijk. 2012. "Benefits, Adoption Barriers, and Myths of Open Data and Open Government." *Information Systems Management (ISM)* 29 (4): 258–268.

Johnson, Jeffrey A. 2014. "From Open Data to Information Justice." *Ethics and Information Technology* 16 (4): 263–274.

Kitchin, Rob. 2014. *The Data Revolution: Big Data, Open Data, Data Infrastructures, and Their Consequences*. Los Angeles: SAGE Publications.

Kohli, Atul. 2004. *State-Directed Development: Political Power and Industrialization in the Global Periphery*. Cambridge: Cambridge University Press.

Manyika, James, Michael Chui, Diana Farrell, Steve Van Kuiken, Peter Groves, and Elizabeth A. Doshi 2013. *Open Data: Unlocking Innovation and Performance with Liquid Information*. London: McKinsey Global Institute; McKinsey Center for Government; McKinsey Business Technology Office.

Nayyar, Deepak. 2003. "Globalization and Development." In *Rethinking Development Economics*, Book 1, ed. Ha-Joon Chang, 61–82. London: Anthem.

Neubert, Dieter. 2011. "'Civil Society' in Africa? Forms of Social Self-Organization between the Poles of Globalization and Local Socio-political Order." Bayreuth African Studies Working Paper No. 12: Civil Society in Africa? Bayreuth, Germany: Institute of African Studies, Universität Bayreuth. https://epub.uni-bayreuth.de/1697/1/BayWorkingpaper%20CSNeubertEnd_2.pdf.

O'Hara, Kieron. 2012. "Transparency, Open Data, and Trust in Government: Shaping the Infosphere." In *WebSci '12: Proceedings of the 4th Annual ACM Web Science Conference*, New York, June 22–24, 223–232. Evanston, IL: ACM Digital Library.

Open Data Charter. 2015. "Open Data Charter: Principles." September 25. https://opendatacharter .net/principles/.

Open Knowledge International. n.d. "Why Open Data?" http://opendatahandbook.org/guide/en/why-open-data/.

Peixoto, Tiago. 2013. "The Uncertain Relationship between Open Data and Accountability: A Response to Yu and Robinson's 'The New Ambiguity of Open Government'." *60 UCLA Law Review Discourse* 200 (2013). *SSRN.* https://ssrn.com/abstract=2264369.

Peixoto, Tiago, and Johnathan Fox. 2016. *When Does ICT-Enabled Citizen Voice Lead to Government Responsiveness?* World Development Report 2016 Digital Dividends. Washington, DC: World Bank. https://openknowledge.worldbank.org/bitstream/handle/10986/23650/WDR16-BP-When-Does-ICT-Enabled-Citizen-Voice-Peixoto-Fox.pdf.

Piketty, Thomas. 2014. *Capital in the Twenty-First Century.* Cambridge: Harvard University Press.

Pollock, Rufus. 2011. "Building the (Open) Data Ecosystem." *Open Knowledge Foundation Blog* (blog), March 31. https://blog.okfn.org/2011/03/31/building-the-open-data-ecosystem/.

Porat, Marc U. 1977. *The Information Economy: Definition and Measurement.* Washington, DC: Office of Telecommunications, US Department of Commerce.

Pretty, Jules N., 1995. "Participatory Learning for Sustainable Agriculture." *World Development* 23 (8): 1247–1263.

Ravallion, Martin. 2016. "Are the World's Poorest Being Left Behind? Reconciling Conflicting Views on Poverty and Growth." *Journal of Economic Growth* 21 (2): 139–164. http://www.ilo.org/wcmsp5/groups/public/---ed_emp/documents/publication/wcms_355712.pdf.

Reilly, Katherine M. A., and Matthew L. Smith. 2013. "The Emergence of Open Development in a Network Society." In *Open Development: Networked Innovations in International Development*, ed. Matthew L. Smith and Katherine M. A. Reilly, 15–50. Cambridge, MA/Ottawa: MIT Press/IDRC. https://idl-bnc-idrc.dspacedirect.org/bitstream/handle/10625/52348/IDL-52348.pdf?sequence=1&isAllowed=y.

Schrock, Andrew, and Gwen Shaffer. 2017. "Data Ideologies of an Interested Public: A Study of Grassroots Open Data Intermediaries." *Big Data & Society* (January–June): 1–10. http://journals.sagepub.com/doi/pdf/10.1177/2053951717690750.

Sen, Amartya. 1999. *Development as Freedom.* Oxford: Oxford University Press.

Singh, Parminder J., and A. Gurumurthy. 2013. "Establishing Public-ness in the Network: New Moorings for Development—A Critique of the Concepts of Openness and Open Development." In *Open Development: Networked Innovations in International Development*, ed. Matthew L. Smith and Katherine M. A. Reilly, 173–196. Cambridge, MA/Ottawa: MIT Press/IRDC. https://idl-bnc-idrc.dspacedirect.org/bitstream/handle/10625/52348/IDL-52348.pdf?sequence=1&isAllowed=y

Stalder, Felix. 1998. "The Network Paradigm: Social Formations in the Age of Information." *The Information Society* 14 (4): 301–308.

Stalder, Felix. 2005. "Information Ecology." In *Open Cultures and the Nature of Networks*, ed. New Media Center. Novi Sad, Serbia: Futura.

van Schalkwyk, François, Michael Cañares, Sumandro Chattanpadhyay, and Alexander Andrason. 2016. "Open Data Intermediaries in Developing Countries." *Journal of Community Informatics* 12 (2): 9–25.

van Schalkwyk, François, Michelle Willmers, and Maurice McNaughton. 2015. "Viscous Open Data: The Roles of Intermediaries in an Open Data Ecosystem." *Information Technology for Development* 22 (sup1): 68–83. http://dx.doi.org/10.1080/02681102.2015.1081868.

Walton, Marion, Andy Dearden, and Melissa Densmore. 2016. "Resources, Learning, and Inclusion in Open Development." Strengthening Information Society Research Capacity Alliance. SIRCA White Paper Series. Paper no. 2. Singapore: Singapore Internet Research Center.

Wood, Donna J., and Barbara Gray. 1991. "Toward a Comprehensive Theory of Collaboration." *Journal of Applied Behavioral Science* 27 (2): 139–162.

Yuval-Davis, Nira. 2011. *The Politics of Belonging: Intersectional Contestations*. London: SAGE Publications.

Zuiderwijk, Anneke, Marijn Janssen, Sunil Choenni, Ronald Meijer, and Roexsana S. Alibaks. 2012. "Socio-technical Impediments of Open Data." *Electronic Journal of e-Government* 10 (2): 156–172.

11   Governing Open Health Data in Latin America

Carla Bonina and Fabrizio Scrollini

Introduction

Civil society and governments around the world have recognized the potential developmental benefits that data released in open format could bring to the Global South. This *open data*, released in digital format, publicly available for anyone to use—promise to contribute to global development goals, such as economic growth, job creation, social and economic inclusion, and access to public services such as healthcare. Although emergent, there is growing evidence that in the right circumstances, open data could contribute to these goals (see Verhulst and Young 2016, as well as chapter 10 in this volume).

Despite the potential, there is also a body of literature suggesting that most open data initiatives are not having the desired impact, particularly in the Global South, for a variety of reasons. These include poor-quality or incomplete data, data in hard-to-use formats, and a mismatch between the data that are published and the data that are actually needed (World Wide Web Foundation 2017). Thus, it is becoming paramount to understand how to improve the connection between making the data available, sharing it, and fostering the actual uptake of open data to solve developmental problems. Recent evidence has shown that the governance relationship is an important factor in this equation. For example, in a review of twenty-three digital monitoring platforms of public services, Peixoto and Fox (2016) show that the existence of institutional arrangements increases the use and responsiveness of these initiatives. While valuable, these studies show broad patterns of the overall picture. In this chapter, we aim to delve into these patterns in detail.

This discussion explores the role of governance arrangements in fostering civic engagement and open data-use outcomes in the Global South by looking at three case studies. The cases all originate in Latin America: Mexico's La Rebelión de los Enfermos,[1] Uruguay's A Tu Servicio, and Peru's Cuidados Intensivos. All three share the use of digital technologies and open data and have the aim of improving health outcomes by producing and distributing information on health services. These cases also represent particular types of open data initiatives, where the resources are made open through the leading efforts of local activists and nongovernmental organizations (NGOs) instead of governments.

We apply the knowledge commons research framework developed by Madison, Frischmann, and Strandburg (2010; also see Frischmann, Madison, and Strandburg 2014c), which builds on the work of Elinor Ostrom and colleagues (Hess and Ostrom 2006; Ostrom 1990; Ostrom and Hess 2006). The framework provides a lens through which to understand the governance of open data and, in these cases, how bottom-up processes that build open data commons are related to stakeholder engagement and use of open data. For each case, we show in detail the different paths that bottom-up processes follow, how the community gets organized to build and sustain the commons, and the importance that governance arrangements can have to take the projects to the next level. The cases reveal that *collaboration among stakeholders promises better chances to scale and improve how open data can be used to solve social and developmental problems.* They also suggest that *the existence of rules to govern the process of sharing and producing resources in the data commons is important to increase the levels of engagement and use within the community.*

The chapter proceeds as follows. In the first section, we briefly introduce the linkages between open data and their potential to contribute to better health outcomes in international development. We then introduce the knowledge commons framework, link it to the field that we study, and expand on the relevant dimensions to analyze our empirical cases. An overview of our research methods, data collection, and analysis follows, and we then present the narrative of the three cases. Next, we discuss our findings, reflecting on three important dimensions: what problem is being solved, what institutional forms are chosen, and how these forms lead to modes of engagement. In the conclusion, we reflect on the main lessons and the value of the framework for this and similar studies.

Open Data Ecosystems in Public Health Services

As with the case of open government, open data can be conceived of in several ways, and often in ambiguous terms (Yu and Robinson 2012). The origins of open data can be traced to the open-source software community, although the connections between both communities of research have not materialized to a great extent yet (Lindman,

Rossi, and Tuunainen 2013; Willinsky 2005). In practice, within the open data community, open data are generally understood as *objects*—that is, a piece of data is open if it is accessible, with no limitations on the user's identity or intent; provided in digital, machine-readable format capable of being linked with other data; and provided free of restriction on use, reuse, or redistribution according to its actual licensing conditions. Nevertheless, as Scrollini (2018) notes, there are other ways of conceiving and using the term *open data*, such as a policy, a community of practice, or a problem-solving approach. More recently, some literature refers to open data as an entire ecosystem (e.g., Dawes, Vidiasova, and Parkhimovich 2016) composed of data objects, data infrastructure, and a set of actors that release, reuse, or consume open data.

Among the many potential benefits of open government are in how it contributes to improving healthcare systems. According to a recent mandate from the Sustainable Development Goals of the United Nations (UN)—specifically Goal 3—countries should aim to provide universal health coverage and access to quality essential healthcare services to their population by 2030. Further, corruption and inefficiency affect developing countries, leading to estimated losses of $1.26 trillion (UN 2015). As observed by Scrollini (2018), the promise is that open data approaches will contribute to these goals by delivering transparency and accountability to the health sector. The rationale is that open data can be particularly beneficial for increasing transparency, fighting corruption, and encouraging democratic values, which are all drivers for many open government data initiatives in Latin America (World Wide Web Foundation 2017). Through transparency and appropriate contextual information, open government data can contribute to holding health providers accountable.

The pathway from open data to transparency and accountability, however, is seldom straightforward. Open data portals prove themselves good repositories, but the demand for data sets is still low. There were (and are) several constraints about the provision of data, such as availability, quality, timeliness of the provision, and the will to open data in the first place (Attard et al. 2015; Charalabidis et al. 2016; Zuiderwijk et al. 2012). Furthermore, not all countries have the legal framework and the capacity to release open data in ways that are meaningful, particularly in the Global South (Davies and Perini 2016).

In sum, despite the potential benefits, the evidence is incomplete and inconclusive on how, to what extent, and in what contexts open data initiatives contribute to improved healthcare systems. As the cases presented in this chapter show, the way that open data ecosystems are mobilized and governed are critical factors that affect their influence on healthcare systems.

The Knowledge Commons Framework for Studying Open Data in Latin America

This chapter applies the knowledge commons framework that Frischmann and colleagues have proposed in recent years (Frischmann, Madison, and Strandburg 2014b). The framework builds on the Institutional Analysis and Development (IAD) framework that Elinor Ostrom developed to study community management arrangements for shared resources in natural environments (Ostrom 1990). Ostrom's IAD approach provided a seminal contribution to addressing collective action problems in settings of shareable but depletable natural resources such as water, trees, and fish. But governing shared knowledge and information resources, such as many of the examples covered in this volume, requires accounting for mechanisms or characteristics that are no longer constrained by geographic or physical boundaries. This new type of commons—knowledge and cultural commons— attracted the attention of scholars, including Ostrom herself (Hess and Ostrom 2006). The knowledge commons is thus "shorthand for the institutionalized community governance of the sharing and, in some cases, creation, of information, science, knowledge, data, and other types of intellectual and cultural resources" (Frischmann et al. 2014b, 3).

The knowledge commons framework is therefore proposed as a way to systematically investigate governance regimes in broader cultural environments, which, as opposed to natural environments, require dealing with producing or sharing information, innovation, or creative works.[2] The cases presented in this chapter represent interesting cases of the knowledge commons because of two characteristics. First, all three cases deal with knowledge and information resources that are largely nondepletable. This is mainly because the resources are either produced or reproduced digitally, in machine-readable, open formats—in other words, the health resources are made into, or sourced from, open data. Second, as happens with other digitally enabled commons (i.e., online creation communities like Wikipedia), the knowledge resources did not exist as *open* but had to be created in all three cases. Therefore, we can study and learn from the various arrangements put in place to produce and preserve these resources.[3]

Dimensions of the Knowledge Commons Framework for Open Data Cases

In their conceptualization, Frischmann et al. (2014b) suggest conducting comparative institutional analysis with a proposed series of commons-related questions, some of which are adapted from Ostrom's IAD framework and others are developed specifically to study knowledge commons. Table 11.1 summarizes the full list, which are grouped in four areas: background environment, attributes, governance, and patterns and outcomes. We then present an overview of an abbreviated set of relevant questions that guide our empirical analysis, together with an introduction of the categories in relation to our cases.

Table 11.1

Representative research questions of the knowledge commons framework.

Framework element		Research questions
Background environment		What is the background context (legal, cultural, etc.) of this particular commons?
		What is the default status of knowledge resources in this context (patented, copyrighted, open, etc.)?
		What is the culture of openness in this policy, and the social and cultural context?
Attributes:	Resources	What resources are pooled, and how are they created or obtained?
		What are the characteristics of the resources? Are they rival or nonrival, tangible or intangible? Is there shared infrastructure?
		What technologies and skills are needed to create, obtain, maintain, and use the resources at stake?
	Community members	What members of the community are managing commons resources, and what are their roles?
		Are there any community members that benefit from openness (women, disabled, etc.)?
		How does a culture of openness affect your project's engagement with the general public?
	Goals and objectives	What are the goals and objectives of the commons and its members, including obstacles or dilemmas to be overcome?
Governance		What are the relevant action arenas, and how do they relate to the goals and objective of the commons and the relationships among various types of participants and with the general public?
		What are the governance mechanisms (e.g., membership rules, resource contribution or extraction standards and requirements, conflict resolution mechanisms, and sanctions for rule violations)?
		Who are the decision-makers, and how are they selected?
		What are the institutions and technological infrastructures that structure and govern decision-making?
		What informal norms govern the commons?
Patterns and outcomes		What benefits (e.g., innovations and creative output, production, sharing and dissemination of knowledge, and social interactions) are delivered to members of the community?
		What costs and risks are associated with collaboration, including negative externalities?

Source: Adapted from Frischmann et al. (2014b, 20–21).

Background Environment   The initial dimension aims to set the background context and the default status of the resources involved. This includes the characterization of the environment in which the case takes place, such as prevalent social norms, laws, or traditions, as well as the differentiation of whether the resources available are patented, open, or something in between. In the empirical analysis in the section "Three Cases of Opening up Health Data in Latin America," we review the current healthcare system context, as well as the histories and motivations to build open, sharable resources as the characterization of the background environment of each case.

Basic Attributes: Resources, Community Members, and Goals and Objectives   The second cluster of questions focuses on identifying and describing the basic attributes of the commons—that is, the type and characteristics of the resources and skills needed to produce, maintain, or use them; who the community members are and what their roles are; and what goals and objectives are pursued. The framework allows for flexibility; some cases may have precise and fixed definitions of both resources and community membership, while others may be more fluid, with less clear boundaries or rules (Frischmann et al. 2014b).

In contrast to what happens with natural commons resources that are already there to be preserved, the pooled resources in the cases that we analyze in this chapter need to be built and then preserved. In general, it can be argued that the three cases consist of pooling dispersed data about health services—whether public or proprietary—and bringing together technical and cognitive capabilities to make data available as open knowledge resources. The resource characteristics entail a combination of nonrival, intangible resources (i.e., open and/or accessible data sets), with information available only in paper format, or closed data sets, to be shared over a digital infrastructure that has to be created and maintained.

As for their community members, the three cases entail small communities with similar attributes—their members are identified clearly and relatively simply. The communities mostly consist of civil society organizations (CSOs) seeking to open up information; government bodies with different levels of involvement; and technology experts who develop tools to contribute to the expansion of the knowledge resources. Because of the nature of the knowledge commons in these three cases, people from the general public are the default users, who in some instances may contribute to the commons with feedback and use cases.

The last set of questions in this cluster refers to understanding the goals and objectives of a knowledge commons—that is, what problems and social dilemmas are being solved. As the framework suggests, often, knowledge commons are purpose-built. Examples of problems that knowledge commons have tried to solve include the production of shareable resources for further creativity and the production of intellectual products to be shared (Frischmann et al. 2014b, 25). In the cases analyzed here, the goals are actually what trigger the commons to emerge: they all aim to produce and sustain open information and knowledge resources that may be beneficial for users of health services in their contexts.

Governance This set of questions is used to investigate the dynamics of knowledge commons governance—what Ostrom refers to as the *rules-in-use* of commons, or the interactions of knowledge commons participants and resources. Frischmann et al. (2014b) suggest three angles that are separated for analytical purposes, as some elements overlap: (1) the commons approach to openness, both with respect to resources and community; (2) the commons general governance structures, such as formal or informal entitlements and decision-making structures, legal structures, and institutional settings; and (3) those rules and norms that apply to particular action arenas.

In the analysis that follows, we focus on the relevant action arenas—that is, the spaces where goals, resources, and community members interact, constituting action situations. Ostrom (2008, 52) defines action situations as being "composed of participants in positions choosing among actions at a particular stage of a decision process in light of their control over a choice node, the information they have, the outcomes that are likely, and the benefits and costs they perceive for these outcomes." Action arenas result in patterns of interaction, and ultimately, those patterns may result in particular outcomes.

Patterns and Outcomes The framework suggests identifying and assessing the benefits that are delivered to members and nonmembers that emerge from the knowledge commons. For example, this may include innovations and creative outputs, production and dissemination of knowledge resources to a broader audience, and new social interactions that emerge from the commons. In the cases that we analyze, outcomes include the production, management, and maintenance of information resources in open digital format.

Research Methods and Significance of the Empirical Setting

Our analysis[4] applies a comparative, multiple-case-study method and reports findings from three cases in Latin America: specifically, in Mexico, Peru, and Uruguay (see table 11.2). The Mexican La Rebelion de los Enfermos and the Uruguayan A Tu Servicio cases were part of the Open Data for Development (OD4D) research program supported by IDRC, and the Peruvian case was originally supported by the International Center for Journalists (ICFJ). These cases represent different modes of engagement, in which citizen groups could foster transparency and accountability to improve service delivery (Scrollini 2018).

Table 11.2
General description of the cases.

Case	Description
La Rebelión de los Enfermos (Mexico)	An online-offline platform to express citizens' grievances with Mexico's healthcare system
Cuidados Intensivos (Peru)	A website on health service delivery capable to expose potential corruption issues through the dissemination of public information
A Tu Servicio (Uruguay)	A digital platform to help citizens choose their health service provider

Data Collection and Analysis

These three cases were researched under the umbrella of the Iniciativa Latinoamericana por los Datos Abiertos (ILDA, or the Latin American Open Data Initiative) and were previously documented in a paper published by the U4 Anti-Corruption Resource Centre (Scrollini 2018). The research design included a participatory action research approach, in which authors worked alongside their counterparts in the initiatives to generate evidence and develop practical solutions to identified issues (Herr and Anderson 2005). The research also included interviews with government champions and leaders of the initiatives, as well as extensive revision of resources available online, including blogs and news articles, narratives available on the cases' websites, and social media. We studied the cases retrospectively, covering a two-year period from 2014 to 2016.

To analyze the cases, this investigation used the set of relevant questions from the knowledge commons framework, which proceeded in an iterative manner. We first examined the narrative of the cases to understand the context and the basic features of their environment, the attributes of the resources, and their goals and governance. We paid particular attention to goals and objectives, following our understanding of the framework. Because the knowledge resources have to be built rather than governed in a particular community or geographical setting, starting with an understanding of the goals and objectives was useful to identify the narratives and action arenas, as well as the participants and the rules in place. We then reflected on the relevant questions and dimensions of the knowledge commons framework to elucidate findings based on a comparative analysis. In the analysis, we stress three points: What problem is being solved? What institutional forms did the cases choose to follow? What were the ways that those choices led to modes of engagement and problem-solving?

Three Cases of Opening up Health Data in Latin America

Latin American countries offer an interesting setting for studying open data and civic technology, given its rapid growth and importance in a variety of policy arenas (World Wide Web Foundation 2017). Countries like Mexico, Uruguay, and Brazil, for example, are top performers among countries in the Global South. They are among the top fourteen best-performing countries in the global Open Data Barometer of 2017—a global ranking that ranks countries according to the publication, readiness, and impact of open government data sets (World Wide Web Foundation 2018). In addition, Latin America now has five countries among the top twenty of the Open Data Index 2017, a survey coordinated by the Open Knowledge Foundation that measures the state of open government data around the world.[5] Moreover, the health service delivery sector has been considered strategic in consecutive open data conferences held in the region (known as Abrelatam/Condatos). In this section, we explore cases from Mexico (La Rebelion de los Enfermos), Peru (Cuidados Intensivos), and Uruguay (A Tu Servicio).

La Rebelión de los Enfermos: Engaging Mexico's Healthcare System

Background Environment   Mexico's healthcare system is complex and fragmented. While it is meant to cover the entire Mexican population, the system underserves or does not cover a significant portion of the population due to differences in who has access and how they seek care. A recent Organization for Economic Co-operation and Development (OECD) report notes: "Mexico's massive public investment in its health system … has failed to translate into better health and health system performance to the extent wished and a program of continued, extensive reform is needed" (OECD 2016, 13). There are six institutions that deliver health services in Mexico, and each has its own independent network of doctors, clinics, hospitals, and pharmacies (ManattJones 2015). As a result, this creates a large structure with several implementation problems.

At the same time, when it comes to open data, Mexico was ranked the sixth best performer by the Open Data Barometer (World Wide Web Foundation 2018), and the country leads the region. But the implementation of the open data policy faces several challenges (OECD 2016).

Goals and Objectives, Resources, and Community Members   Sonora Ciudadana—an NGO based in the state of Sonora in the north of Mexico working on transparency and human rights in Mexico—developed the initiative La Rebelión de los Enfermos with the objective of raising awareness about the difficult conditions that Mexican hospitals face, as well as providing a channel for grievances with health services. The motivation goes back to 2008, when Sonora Ciudadana received a complaint from an individual who was denied access to medicine and other services at ISSSTESON (one of the six Mexican institutions), on the basis of his previous health condition. Sonora Ciudadana filed litigation, taking the case to Mexico's Supreme Court of Justice (this was a rather common practice in the sector), and decided to push more cases before the Court as well.

The central resources of this commons—data or information on health services—are very limited, nonexistent, or very difficult to access, given the system's related high transactional costs. They consist of pooling dispersed data in the Mexican healthcare system, together with technical and cognitive capabilities to make it available for a wider audience. The activities and skills needed to do so typically entailed digitizing paper-based data, using tools to clean up data, and using digital tools and infrastructure to publish the information in a meaningful way.

The community member in this case is Sonora Ciudadana, which is a traditional human rights organization working on human rights and transparency issues, but not necessarily linked to the open data community (or the technology community overall). The NGO took on the role of translating or pooling the information resources, based on its own organizational identity.

Governance and Action Arena   To expand on the case of 2008, Sonora Ciudadana launched a set of access to information requests to obtain data about ISSSTESON's performance. The organization monitored a set of indicators about health performance through these requests. Interestingly, ISSSTESON did not deny the information that Sonora Ciudadana obtained, but the fact that requests were filed on paper made the process difficult for all parties involved. Because it was not a particularly tech-savvy organization, a common obstacle that it faced was to systematize the information and make it accessible in formats that could reach and benefit a wide range of people in the Mexican population.

With significant evidence collected, Sonora Ciudadana launched a campaign under the banner "La Rebelion de los Enfermos," which aimed to showcase the difficulties that users had when trying to get access to the healthcare system, as well as to document new cases of potential injustice in the sector. As the campaign advanced, they set up a website where users could document their complaints, which in turn became a useful endeavor in itself. The website used part of the information that Sonora Ciudadana obtained through freedom of information (FOI) requests, combined with available data sets from the federal government. The effort allowed people to map and understand the way that clinics and hospitals work across Mexico, as well as to put forward user complaints. The NGO decided to build a tool that would provide information and also allow people to denounce situations, which made sense in the context of the organization's longer-term litigation strategy. Further, Sonora Ciudadana decided that the new tool would cover all healthcare systems, not only ISSSTESON.

Most of the information came from FOI requests that were mostly paper based. As a result, Sonora Ciudadana had to invest in digitalizing this information, at significant cost. To explore how this data could be structured and eventually used, Sonora Ciudadana collaborated with ILDA and Codeando Mexico, a civic technology organization, to explore if and how Sonora Ciudadana could access better data from the public sector.

This process helped to identify significant problems in the government data available through FOI requests: there is no data structure, the formats are inconsistent or incompatible, and there are missing sources that otherwise would allow data reliability tracking. In short, while data were available, there was a significant cost to process that data, as well as to develop a tool that would enable comparisons across the systems. Codeando Mexico conducted an extensive review of the data infrastructure of ISSSTESON and other Mexican authorities, developing a standard to publish data about medical institutions, basic infrastructure, service metrics, human resources metrics, and cost metrics (Codeando Mexico 2015). The standard was designed to structure information in ways that could foster comparison and be realistically adopted by health institutions. While the standard is available (and open for all interested parties), the lack of resources to fully implement it and the difficulties in collecting the data prevented the project from scaling up.

Outcomes   An important outcome of this initiative has been the joint work of Codeando Mexico and Sonora Ciudadana to create an open data standard for health service delivery. The standard provided a template on how to scale and develop basic data infrastructure. The process of standardization proved to be complex due to the difficulties of structuring the data and getting accurate data to work with. But the work served as the basis to guide other iterations of related projects, such as A Tu Servicio, currently deployed in Colombia and Uruguay. In addition, the significant work put toward the creation of the standard, and the fact that it is freely shared online, are contributions that enhance the work in the long run.

La Rebelion de los Enfermos offers an example of how traditional campaigning is needed to deliver results for citizens' rights in a context of open data. The decision to embark on a digital journey also represents a change in strategy for a rather traditional, accountability-oriented organization. Nevertheless, better data alone would not help Sonora Ciudadana to follow and improve the monitoring and transparency of the sector. The initiative relies on the collaboration of users, who need to provide more data to enrich the system.

Cuidados Intensivos: Checking on the Peruvian Healthcare System

Background Environment Peru is one of the fastest-growing economies in Latin America, with an average of 5.3 percent growth in gross domestic product (GDP) and a rapidly expanding middle class (OECD 2016). Such growth is putting pressure on the public sector to deliver better social outcomes. Further, while open government efforts have been part of Peru's agenda for at least twenty years, there are several challenges in terms of integrity, corruption in public procurement, and access to information (OECD 2016). Peru is a member of the Open Government Partnership and has committed to the Open Government Principles, but, in practice, the lack of a unified open government policy (Casas 2012) has led to a fragmentation and poor implementation of open government initiatives. The result is that there is limited (or nonexistent) room for dialogue between government and civil society around the open government process. When it comes to open data, Peru has a medium score—forty-eighth globally and seventh in the region (World Wide Web Foundation 2017).

Like Mexico, the healthcare system in Peru is also fragmented. There are five entities coordinating health service delivery, including the Ministry of Health, EsSalud (the National Health Insurance system), the armed forces, the police, and the private sector. EsSalud and the private sector combined cover around 40 percent of the population. EsSalud contracts out part of its services and provides its own clinic services. In recent years, private providers have become critical for the provision of health services (Torres López and Huacles 2015).

Goals and Objectives, Resources, and Community Members OjoPúblico is an independent digital media outlet carrying out investigative journalism in Peru. Founded in 2014 by a group of journalists and programmers and evolving into an online journalism venture, it delivers traditional investigative reporting but also uses new digital tools and data journalism practices in the Peruvian context.

OjoPúblico decided to research the lack of transparency in the health sector and the powerful corporate interests operating in the private sector. Similar to the previous case, the information resources had to be pooled from different sources. Through the process, OjoPúblico encountered many problems with the official data. Most of the data were outdated, the formats in which they were provided were not open, and the team had to correct mistakes by hand and scrape Portable Document Format (PDF) files.[6] The Peruvian state organizations had problems handling the data due to its own lack of information technology (IT) systems and the legacy systems in place. Thus, the issue was not only about the will to be more open, but also about the capacity to engage.

Action Arena   OjoPúblico engaged in an investigative reporting strategy that included traditional journalism and the use of FOI laws and data journalism practices to explore the complex subject of health service provision. Cuidados Intensivos was part of this strategy, as OjoPúblico identified an opportunity to obtain and use data about health providers in order to provide more transparency, as well as to promote better choices. The project was supported by the ICFJ, the Knight Foundation, Hacklabs, and Friends of OjoPúblico.

OjoPúblico's strategy was to expose the complex situation of the healthcare system in Peru. Their investigative reporting uncovered three key issues: lack of regulation in the private sector to prevent potential abusive practices, lack of transparency and enforcement of fines for breaching terms of service, and lack of an effective redress mechanism for grievances. OjoPúblico's research also identified a private-sector concentration process, whereby eight economic groups developed systems wherein they provide the insurance, the clinic service, and the pharmaceuticals, effectively creating a vertical integration with little control by public authorities (López and Huacles 2015). OjoPúblico also identified the clinics with the most fines and established a ranking. Finally, their research established that none of these clinics paid their fines—they owed the Peruvian state around 10 million soles (approximately $3 million).

The website was designed to take advantage of the information released to raise awareness among the issues covered in the investigative reporting pieces. In other words, the website was supposed to be the *actionable* item of OjoPúblico's strategy. The website would allow people to understand who had permission to practice and the fines that they had accumulated over the years. The Peruvian open data portal had no information about these topics, nor was there an attempt to engage with the initiative from the Peruvian office of e-Government in order to obtain the data. The leaders of the project attributed the latter to the fact that the e-Government office has little political influence, as well as to the fact that sensitive health data could not be obtained via the mobilization of an open data agenda in that way. This seems plausible in light of a recent OECD review that noted the limited capacity of the e-Government agency to influence digital policies in Peru (OECD 2016).

OjoPúblico decided to follow an eclectic strategy to get the data. First, they filed fifty-two FOI requests, directed to several institutions including the National Competition Authority, the Copyright Authority, and agencies that were part of the National Authority on Health (SuSalud, EsSalud, the Ministry of Health, and the police). Furthermore, the news organization collected available reports that these sources published online. As in the Mexican case, most of the replies to the FOI requests were on paper. Once OjoPúblico got the data into whatever format was available, they compiled a database and started to systematize the information. Furthermore, hard-copy data (on paper) were crucial to obtain more reliable data, as the authorities were not processing the files. OjoPúblico had also to deal with the complex jargon, which had consequences for the way that data was presented. For instance, the concept of *operational risk* was a relevant one. As Hidalgo and Torres (2016, 83) observe:

> In the official jargon, this [operational risk] concept refers to the result of the evolution of private services and measures their degree of compliance with the standards of patient care (conditions and equipping of emergency services, intensive care units, pharmacies). *Susalud* inspectors registered a percentage for each service provider and this actually corresponded to the percentage of compliance. So, when reports said that a clinic had "operational risk level: 6%", what it actually meant was that the establishment did not meet 94% of the care standards. The impact of the data collected changed the knowledge radically.

The databases were later combined with relevant databases from the private and public sectors such as the National Health Institute, the Peruvian Stock Exchange, the tax authority, the judiciary, and the media. In some cases, OjoPúblico had to pay for the data. The key elements used to build Ciudados Intensivos were data on private clinics, data on insurance companies, and data on public health investments (Hidalgo and Torres 2016). OjoPúblico built its own open data commons collecting, treating, establishing categories, and eventually using the data.

Outcomes   OjoPúblico managed to gather information about 61,372 doctors, 9,920 clinics, and twenty-one insurance companies. They created an open data commons by merging available disparate databases or those obtained through different legal or social processes. In doing so, OjoPúblico collected better data than the government had, and the initiative allowed access to an unprecedented amount of information about the private healthcare sector in Peru. The launch of the story put OjoPúblico on the journalism map, as the healthcare system is one of the country's key controversies. Cuidados Intensivos also gave OjoPúblico more visibility nationally, establishing its reputation as a young and professional news outlet. Furthermore, it helped the group reach out to users' rights organizations working in the health field. OjoPúblico collected stories from these organizations and gave voice to issues surrounding malpractice and abuse in the healthcare system. As a result of this engagement, OjoPúblico also improved the capabilities of its own organization, equipped journalists with new skills, and managed to develop other projects.

Overall, the project improved the accountability of the Peruvian healthcare system by exposing several conflicts of interest and forcing authorities to correct data and to improve the control of the system. With more information available, more people were able to check the status of clinics in Peru and find out which were the best and worst performing. Surprisingly, the general public's use of the tools was relatively low, considering its potential. The main obstacle was reaching a general audience and sustaining efforts to release data on a relatively small budget. Nevertheless this was the first time that information was systematized in a way that could be used for accountability. As in the Mexican case, the lack of formal (or even informal) governance arrangements to secure and use the data conditioned the way that the project could have progressed.

Atuservicio.uy: Coproducing a Health Application

Background Environment   Every February, Uruguayans get to choose whether to change their health service provider. This opportunity is the result of a series of major reforms in the Uruguayan national healthcare system that lead to almost full coverage of the country's population. As a result, significant amounts of public funding go into the system, which offers a mix of public, semipublic, and private providers. The more customers a health provider gets, the more funding the provider obtains from the government. As a result, health providers compete relentlessly for every person. Health providers develop aggressive marketing campaigns through the media, and in some cases offer cash rewards to people if they switch services—the latter is illegal under Uruguayan regulations.

Concerned about these practices, the Ministry of Public Health, in 2008, started publishing information about various performance indicators for the system. The ministry published this data on its website using Microsoft Excel tables. This is not surprising—Uruguay has been among the top performers in open data, both in the region and globally. The press used these tables to produce news pieces about the system, but users seldom retrieved the tables. The language was difficult to understand, in part because the information was not displayed in a manner that was friendly to nonexperts and because it was difficult to make comparisons among providers. Moreover, the government assumed that users would have access to some kind of proprietary software in order to make sense of the information published.

Goals and Objectives, Resources, and Community Members   In 2013, a CSO called DATA Uruguay identified an opportunity to work with available data from the Ministry of Health. The organization partnered with a local online media outlet, 180 Ciencia, and developed a tool to visualize and rank providers according to user preferences. The project was aptly named Temporada de Pases (Transfer season), in reference to the short time frame that Uruguayans had to choose their health providers. DATA Uruguay extracted the data sets from the ministry's websites, cleaned them, and designed an interphase in which users were able to understand the data easily. The online media outlet helped to spread the word, and the website got around 6,000 visits in February 2014. The project was built using open-source software, with the rationale that the data could be audited by anyone in the community. The overall goal in the Uruguayan case, therefore, could be summarized as an effort to provide an online tool to inform health users about their choices at a critical time.

Temporada de Pases did not involve the Ministry of Public Health, but, because of the presence in the media and the reaction from early users, the government eventually began to work with them. Thus, the community included DATA Uruguay and collaborators, but also the government. A notable absentee from this commons, however, were users. Initially, DATA and the Ministry of Public Health aimed to include them, but due to the time and resource constraints to develop the app, they were not considered as relevant actors in the design phase. Yet users later become crucial in reporting missing data, as well as demanding that new data be incorporated.

Action Arena   The initiative Temporada de Pases created a baseline to which members of DATA and collaborators could scale the newly created open resources. DATA and the Ministry of Public Health explored making an alliance in 2015. The ministry had the intention to create a similar website to the one that DATA had created, but it was not possible to find a suitable provider. DATA had the expertise to carry forward this mission, but it had only a basic understanding of the technical and policy nuances of health data. Eventually, the Ministry of Public Health and DATA set up a formal partnership to cocreate and coproduce the web application. The partnership featured the ministry's commitment in terms of human and financial resources to assist DATA on the one hand, and the commitment of DATA to assist the ministry on the other. In turn, DATA pushed for developing this work on open-source software to allow the eventual replication and transparency of the process.

The initiative was an emergent and bottom-up process. DATA engaged with a group of midlevel managers who had the political support to proceed. DATA and the ministry's team held meetings defining the scope of the information to include. DATA would normally push for more information to be published, while the Ministry of Public Health would be more cautious about what to publish. The ministry had initially classified part of the information that they released as "reserved," following the provisions of the access to information law in the country. To solve this problem, DATA and the Ministry of Public Health constructively bargained for what information to include on the website.[7]

DATA had an initial bias toward user choice. In DATA's view, the more people exercising the right to switch providers, the better. On the other hand, the Ministry of Public Health argued that switching providers should not be the ultimate policy goal, as it could jeopardize the stability and sustainability of the healthcare system. Instead, the ultimate goal for the ministry was to encourage users to express their concerns to the health authority in order to improve the way that health services are offered.[8] DATA agreed to work within the framework of the ministry's policy objectives to move forward.

This discussion was important, as it affected several decisions about how information was represented, as well as about what health information users could eventually compare on the website. Once there was an agreement on what information to include, the ministry's team went to look for the sources of information. The government team found that most of the data was compartmentalized across the Ministry of Public Health, and it was not available in open format. Furthermore, collection processes were often manual. Through the identification and collection process, the ministry discovered that some of the data sources had quality problems or raised conflicts among different sources. The process of collecting data helped the ministry to understand its own sources of information and put them in order. On DATA's side, the team initially developed the back end of the app to import and process the data. Initial tests were run with data sets from the Ministry of Public Health to ensure compatibility. This process was lengthy and technically challenging for both parties. Problems with data standardization haunted the project until its first launch.

As the project evolved, DATA developed the first mock-ups (drafts) of the website and began the validation process with the ministry's team. Middle managers working on this project were usually on board with the design choices. The process also involved other managers and political appointees who were data providers. Most of them wanted to ensure that the data that they collected or created would not be misrepresented on the website. The discussion showed the asymmetry of technical knowledge between managers and technologists. Members of DATA would act as translators to ensure that all parties were on the same page.

DATA and the ministry made a set of basic decisions on which data to showcase and how to do it. Users would get to see data about wait times, prices, users' rights, the location of services, and performance targets on the home screen. Users then would be able to compare up to three providers from their administrative jurisdiction, allowing them to delve extensively into the data. The standardization of the data set on the government's side and technical capacity on both sides were considerable obstacles to the project.

The final stage was a sprint to get the site published before February 1, when Uruguayans would have an opportunity to choose between providers. At the end, with these challenges overcome, all the standardized data were added to the Uruguayan national open data portal, which received around 2,000 downloads in the rest of 2016.

Outcomes   As a result of the initiative, in the first year, around 35,000 Uruguayans got access to the data published via the A Tu Servicio portal. In the second year, the number of A Tu Servicio users increased to 60,000. In addition, the website was used to inform public debate and taken up by several media outlets with an interest in the subject (Sangakoya et al. 2016). Both government and the opposition used A Tu Servicio to argue about health policy in the Uruguayan parliament. The project also survived a change of government. In 2016, the ministry's team was able to increase its audience and impact. Table 11.3 provides the set of impacts on various intended beneficiaries of the project according to Sangakoya et al. (2016) and Scrollini (2016).

Governing Open Data Health Commons

Using the knowledge commons framework, we will now analyze these cases from a comparative perspective (see table 11.4). Following Madison (2014), we stress three points in the analysis: the problem that is being solved, the choice of institutional forms (including views on infrastructure), and the ways that those choices led to modes of engagement.

As we hinted at the beginning, all these cases try to solve a rather typical knowledge commons dilemma: the projects exist to manage existing resources and to sustain the production and contribution to a shared resource of open data pools in health services.

Arguably, the strategies on cooperation and confrontation contributed to the differences in outcome. For example, despite the initial interest from the government, the Peruvian case was never able to collaborate with the Ministry of Public Health. Likewise, the Mexican case was unsuccessful in getting the government on board to engage and respond to the initiative. Closer collaboration with government authorities and the provision of better data could have improved the process that Sonora Ciudadana developed. On the other hand, the Uruguay case showed that the initial willingness and open data capacities of the government contributed to building the initiative as a coproduction process.

Overall, the cases show different ways of engaging in the production of the commons. In these three cases, the more collaborative approach between leading actors in a given action area led to better use of the data to address the issue at hand. Nevertheless, confrontational approaches—that is, those in which civil society uses tools to hold the government to account—also offer value, as the commons are still available as a result of FOI requests or data scraping, as the Peruvian case demonstrates. In general, a mix of both approaches could be considered when starting a process in a given action arena.

The cases analyzed here also show that without a cooperation arrangement—whether formal or informal—to sustain the data commons, most of the applications

Table 11.3 Summary of A Tu Servicio's main outcomes.

Intended beneficiaries	Results	Indicators
Average citizens	Enabling the people of Uruguay to make better-informed health decisions as a result of actionable information	Previous to the existence of this initiative there was no way to compare providers in a systematic way
	Equipping citizens with data-driven evidence and tools to make better decisions on health-care choice	80,000 users in the last edition of A Tu Servicio in 2016
	Catalyzing citizens to act as agents of monitoring and evaluation around the health services they receive	Six reports on service delivery issues and requests of more information through social media
Health providers	Improving the quality and responsiveness of service based on data-driven demands from citizens	Providers adjusted at least five prices as a result of data publication
Media	Encouraging better data journalism efforts and data-driven arguments for public debate on healthcare	180 media reports using Atuservicio.uy data or quoting it
Civil Society, unions and politicians	Enabling better-informed argumentation and advocacy round the status of the healthcare system	At least six documented uses by MPs, Senators, union leaders, providers and citizens about Atuservicio.uy in public debates and discussions
Ministry of Health	Enhancement of the Ministry's regulatory role	Data from health providers for the second edition arrived on time to the Ministry
	Improvement of Ministry's own data sources and processes	The Ministry formalized data collection procedures
Open Data policy	Contribution to the Uruguayan open data portal in terms of data	During February 2015, it was the most demanded data set of the Uruguayan national open data portal Atuservicio.uy is used by the e-Government agency as an exemplar for other agencies
	Case study to showcase to other state institutions to promote the use of the portal	

Source: Based on Scrollini (2016) and Sangakoya et al. (2016).

Table 11.4
Summary of case analysis.

	Mexico La Rebelion de los Enfermos	Peru Cuidados Intensivos	Uruguay A Tu Servicio
Problem to be solved	Lack of public data to check health service delivery in Peru and expose potential corruption issues	Lack of an accountability channel to monitor exclusion and discrimination in Mexico's healthcare system	Lack of reliable, public, and accurate data to make decisions on Uruguay's health service providers
Background environment and existing resources	Country signed on to the Open Government Partnership, but lack of a unified open government policy Low levels of transparency in the health sector Low-to-nonexistent open data or shared knowledge resources Data obtained through several methods, including scraping	Country leading in open data policies in the developing world Complex, nontransparent, and corrupt healthcare system Some public data exist, but not structured in ways that can be used by the public Some data under protected licenses (proprietary systems), and some accessed through FOI requests	Existing capacities to produce open data in government Open data sets exist, but are poorly structured or incomplete
Choice of institutional form and rules	Largely local arrangements; network of activists contributing to maintaining the commons (OjoPúblico) No shared objectives with government and no institutional or legal arrangements in place to scale the project outside the organization	Largely informal network of users governed by Sonora Ciudadana; collaborative partnership with technical capabilities provided by an external community member (Codeando). No shared objective with government and no defined legal mechanisms to scale the project outside the initiative	Shared policy objectives and collaborative arrangement set between a leading NGO and government, governed by the existence of informal and formal rules Shared technical infrastructure of open characteristics
Results in engagement	Low Emerging engagement in the form of citizen control. Emerging engagement with interested but not digitally savvy communities in the space Some reactions from government but cocreation nonexistent	Low Limited engagement in the form of raised awareness of health injustices in Mexico, with changes in the provision of health service delivery in Sonora No engagement from government	Medium to high Notable engagement from government; limited engagement from users, who are able to use the data but not to contribute to the commons

are likely to disappear. For this reason, as Peixoto and Fox (2016) note, the involvement of the government in some form is crucial.

The cases also illustrate the different ways that institutional choices are made, particularly in regard to building a community. While the Peruvian and Uruguayan cases are confined to a small community of members (mainly NGOs governing the processes), the Mexican case required a broader community to engage with criticisms and the provision of data. Uruguay's A Tu Servicio and Peru's Cuidados Intensivos may be seen comparatively to be more successful in the ways that they achieve new forms of engagement because, in order to build and preserve the common resource, they have controlled and small communities with clear roles, with the potential to reach out to the wider community through media and civil society channels. This does not mean that to be successful, open data initiatives need small communities controlling the resources, but it reflects the well-known challenges of keeping a community engaged and motivated when there are no labor contracts or financial incentives in place (e.g., Benkler and Nissenbaum 2006; Madison 2014). When a voluntary or collaborative relationship is a precondition for producing the open resources, the chance to get it done will depend on the rules and arrangements put in place to manage the community.

Knowledge commons also often depend on shared infrastructure (Frischmann, Madison, and Strandburg 2014a). In some cases, technical infrastructure may be a substitute for formal rule-based governance (Fuster Morell 2014) and may be critical for the development of new uses (Scrollini 2018; Moncecchi 2012). The three cases in this chapter all included the development of open data sets held on different types of shared infrastructure that could (or should) be improved by actors in the ecosystem. However, in the absence of collaborative relationships and institutional mechanisms, the reutilization of the shared knowledge resources may not scale. For example, the way La Rebelion is organized suggests that users can contribute only in certain ways (i.e., what is defined in the technical standard). The community of users does not have control over the design of the platform of participation, and it may not define rules or licenses. In the Uruguayan case, on the other hand, the choice of developing the web application in open-source software, as well as sharing the new open resource on the national open data portal, meant that the initiative contributed to less dependency and more openness in terms of decision-making processes. In the Peruvian case, the data are open, but the tool is not. Thus, although the open-source nature of a commons project may enable better outcomes in terms of engagement and sustainability, it does not guarantee the sustainability or the replicability of the initiative.

Finally, the cases show the importance of politics—an evident factor, given the highly political character of healthcare systems anywhere. Although this is hardly novel, what the framework helps to stress is that in order to build open data commons, a shared vision of the value of openness and the mechanism to dispute the absence of or lack of quality of public data matter. The Mexican case serves to exemplify this point. The process of scraping all the data and setting up the portal, La Rebelion de los Enfermos, was almost heroic, taking into account how the data were initially structured. A governance setting that ensures access to basic data and incentives to the public sector to use that data could have changed the way that the project evolved, generating traction. Having said this, the dynamics to build trust and exchanges between parties remain elusive.

Conclusions

It is not a surprise that open data and open knowledge, and their potential impact for development and inclusion, have captured the interest of governments, civil society, and communities. The considerable enthusiasm created by open data in the Global South, however, has yet to translate into more systematized results and lessons to be shared and embraced. As in the case of other information and communication technologies for development initiatives, open data projects do not exist independent of ideas, techniques, technologies, systems, people, and contexts (Kitchin 2014). Understanding what goals and objectives drive open data initiatives, what arrangements they have in place, and what they can deliver in their context is critical to design effective governance arrangements and effective open data policies.

The three cases discussed in this chapter, while differing in scope and results, offer valuable lessons. The cases are useful to highlight that, as opposed to the prevalent government-centric, top-down view of knowledge production and distribution, innovation and problem-solving with open data can happen in distributed ways, with practices that could be best described as bottom-up and emerging from the activists in a local community. In addition, and in light of the available evidence, our empirical work shows that *collaboration among stakeholders promises better chances to scale and improve how open data can be used to solve social and developmental problems*. This echoes findings from related work on digital platforms for civic engagement suggesting that involving the government and achieving institutional responsiveness may be an enabling condition for success (Peixoto and Fox 2016).

At this point, we want to make a final comment on the knowledge commons framework that we applied. Despite its suitability for analyzing and understanding open data initiatives, it remains largely under the radar of open data students. We believe that through a knowledge commons lens, researchers and analysts could help to uncover important openness characteristics and governance traits that may increase the value of opening up welfare-enhancing resources such as healthcare services. We also recognize that there is no single way to apply a framework, and that poses challenges on researchers, as Frischmann et al. (2014a) appreciate. For example, the interconnected and evolving character of key variables such as resources, community members, and goals and objectives makes the operationalization of the framework rather difficult. Despite the complexities of the framework, we encourage scholars to perform more work on the subject by adding new comparative cases in other regions or by extending similar analysis to other sectors.

Given the centrality to the success of open data commons, future work should focus on understanding the role that shared infrastructure may have on open development initiatives, either as a substitute or complement for formal and rule-based governance and decision-making processes (Fuster Morell 2014). Although we have tried to offer some glimpses of the infrastructural resources created or used in the cases (i.e., the open-source software deployed), future studies could concentrate on identifying governance constraints or specific arrangements in this space. Future work could also explore questions related to the sustainability of open resource initiatives. The knowledge commons framework can offer a valuable lens to understand what emerging sustainable models underlie similar initiatives, by looking at the linkages between governance arrangements, commons resources, and outcomes. We believe that this could be a plausible alternative to the current debate around business models of open data and open resource projects. Overall, we hope that this work can inspire the building of more systematic explorations of the relationship between open data initiatives and developmental outcomes in the Global South.

Acknowledgments

We gratefully acknowledge the financial support received from the IDRC Open Data for Development program and Fundación Avina to conduct part of this research. This chapter builds on Scrollini (2018).

Notes

1. A loose English translation of this phrase is "the rebellion of the sick."

2. The knowledge commons framework generally assumes that intangible information and knowledge resources are nonrival and nonexcludable public goods, and therefore nondepletable in character. See Madison (2014) for more information.

3. Note that the cases we studied involve small communities—small organizations or groups of people that open up health data to distribute it or to give control back to their users to improve their knowledge on health services, to raise awareness, and contribute to accountability or transparency. These open data initiatives are different in scale from the usual examples in the knowledge commons literature, such as Wikipedia, the Human Genome Project, and ZooGalaxy.

However, they all have in common practices to produce, distribute, or consume open knowledge resources to achieve a social or public interest good.

4. This section is an adapted version of sections 3, 4, and 5 of Scrollini (2017). Here, we use the empirical material with a different framework to explain other dynamics of open data production and collaboration. We gratefully thank the U4 Anti-Corruption Resource Centre for its permission to reproduce parts of that work in this chapter.

5. See https://index.okfn.org/.

6. In a nutshell, parsing and scraping are methods for extracting data from the Internet.

7. One particular piece of information that was heavily debated was the number of affiliates at each institution.

8. The initial project contemplated feedback monitoring, which has not been possible to implement to date.

References

Attard, Judie, Fabrizio Orlandi, Simon Scerri, and Sören Auer. 2015. "A Systematic Review of Open Government Data Initiatives." *Government Information Quarterly* 32 (4): 399–418.

Benkler, Yochai, and Helen Nissenbaum. 2006. "Commons-Based Peer Production and Virtue." *Journal of Political Philosophy* 14 (4): 394–419.

Casas, Javier. 2012. "Mecanismo de revisión independiente: El Perú. Informe de avance 2012–13" [Independent Review Mechanisms: Peru. Progress Report 2012–13]. Independent Reporting Mechanism, Open Government Partnership, Washington, DC. http://sgp.pcm.gob.pe/wp-content/uploads/2017/11/Informe-de-Avance-Plan-AGA-2012-2013-del-MRI.pdf.

Charalabidis, Yannis, Charalampos Alexopoulos, and Euripidos Loukis. 2016. "A Taxonomy of Open Government Data Research Areas and Topics." *Journal of Organizational Computing and Electronic Commerce* 26 (1–2): 41–63.

Codeando Mexico. 2016. "Infrastructure, Budgets, and Health." Working Paper, Iniciativa Latinoamericana de Datos Abiertos (ILDA).

Davies, Tim, and Fernando Perini. 2016. "Researching the Emerging Impacts of Open Data: Revisiting the ODDC Conceptual Framework." *Journal of Community Informatics* 12(2). http://ci-journal.net/index.php/ciej/article/view/1281.

Dawes, Sharon S., Lyudmila Vidiasova, and Olga Parkhimovich. 2016. "Planning and Designing Open Government Data Programs: An Ecosystem Approach." *Government Information Quarterly* 33 (1): 15–27.

Frischmann, Brett M., Michael J. Madison, and Katherine J. Strandburg. 2014a. "Conclusion." In *Governing Knowledge Commons*, ed. Brett M. Frischmann, Michael J. Madison, and Katherine J. Strandburg, 469–484. Oxford: Oxford University Press.

Frischmann, Brett M., Michael J. Madison, and Katherine J. Strandburg. 2014b. "Governing Knowledge Commons." In *Governing Knowledge Commons*, ed. Brett M. Frischmann, Michael J. Madison, and Katherine J. Strandburg, 1–43. Oxford: Oxford University Press.

Frischmann, Brett M., Michael J. Madison, and Katherine J. Strandburg, ed. 2014c. *Governing Knowledge Commons*. Oxford: Oxford University Press. https://doi.org/10.1093/acprof:oso/9780199972036 .001.0001.

Fuster Morell, Mayo. 2014. "Governance of Online Creation Communities for the Building of Digital Commons: Viewed through the Framework of Institutional Analysis and Development." In *Governing Knowledge Commons*, ed. Brett M. Frischmann, Michael J. Madison, and Katherine J. Strandburg, 281–312. Oxford: Oxford University Press.

Herr, Katherine, and Gary L. Anderson. 2005. *The Action Research Dissertation: A Guide for Students and Faculty*. New York: SAGE Publications.

Hess, Charlotte, and Elinor Ostrom, eds. 2006. *Understanding Knowledge as a Commons: From Theory to Practice*. Cambridge, MA: MIT Press.

Hidalgo, David, and Fabiola L. Torres. 2016. *La Navaja Suiza del Reportero* [The Swiss Army Knife of the Reporter]. Lima: Consejo de la Prensa Peruana. https://navaja-suiza.ojo-publico.com/static /Manual_OjoPublico.pdf.

Kitchin, R. 2014. *The Data Revolution: Big Data, Open Data, Data Infrastructures, and Their Consequences*. Thousand Oaks, CA: SAGE Publications.

Lindman, Juho, Matti Rossi, and Virpi K. Tuunainen. 2013. "Open Data Services: Research Agenda." Presented at the 46th Hawaii International Conference on System Sciences (HICSS), Maui, Hawaii, January. In *46th Annual Hawaii International Conference on System Sciences*, ed. Ralph H. Sprague Jr., 1239–1246. Los Alamitos, CA: IEEE Computer Society.

Madison, Michael J. 2014. "Commons at the Intersection of Peer Production, Citizen Science, and Big Data: Galaxy Zoo." In *Governing Knowledge Commons*, ed. Brett M. Frischmann, Michael J. Madison, and Katherine J. Strandburg, 209–254. Oxford: Oxford University Press.

Madison, Michael J., Brett M. Frischmann, and Katherine J. Strandburg. 2010. "Constructing Commons in the Cultural Environment." *Cornell Law Review* 95 (2010): 657–709.

ManattJones. 2015. "Mexican Healthcare System Challenges and Opportunities." January. Washington, DC: ManattJones Global Strategies, LLC. https://www.wilsoncenter.org/sites/default/files /mexican_healthcare_system_challenges_and_opportunities.pdf.

Moncecchi, Guillermo. 2012. "Towards a Public Digital infrastructure. Why Do Governments Have a Responsibility to Go Open?" *Open Knowledge Foundation Blog* (blog), November 1. http:// blog.okfn.org/2012/11/01/towards-a-public-digital-infrastructure-why-do-governments-have-a -responsibility-to-go-open/.

Ostrom, Elinor. 1990. *Governing the Commons: The Evolution of Institutions for Collective Action*. Cambridge: Cambridge University Press.

Ostrom, Elinor. 2008. "Developing a Method for Analyzing Institutional Change." In *Alternative Economic Structures: Evolution and Impact*, ed. Sandra S. Batie and Nicholas Mercuro, 48–76. London: Routledge.

Ostrom, Elinor, and Charlotte Hess. 2006. "A Framework for Analyzing the Knowledge Commons." In *Understanding Knowledge as a Commons: From Theory to Practice*, ed. Charlotte Hess and Elinor Ostrom, 41–82. Cambridge, MA: MIT Press.

Organisation for Economic Co-operation and Development (OECD). 2016. *OECD Reviews of Health Systems: Mexico 2016*. Paris: OECD Publishing.

Peixoto, Tiago, and Johnathan Fox. 2016. "When Does ICT-Enabled Citizen Voice Lead to Government Responsiveness?" No. WDR 2016 Background Paper. Washington, DC: World Bank. https://openknowledge.worldbank.org/handle/10986/23650.

Sangokoya, Dave, Ali Clare, Stefaan Verhulst, and Andrew Young. 2016. "Uruguay's A Tu Servicio." New York: GovLab. http://odimpact.org/case-uruguays-a-tu-servicio.html.

Scrollini, Fabrizio. 2016. "Open Your Data and…Will 'They' Build It? A Case of Open Data Coproduction in Health Service Delivery." In *The Social Dynamics of Open Data*, ed. François van Schalkwyk, Stefaan G. Verhulst, Gustavo Magalhaes, Juan Pane, and Johanna Walker, 139–152. Cape Town, South Africa: African Minds. http://www.africanminds.co.za/wp-content/uploads/2017/06/9781928331568_txt.pdf.

Scrollini, Fabrizio. 2018. "Keeping Health on Check: Can Open Data Initiatives Improve Health Service Delivery?" Working Paper, U4 Anti-Corruption Resource Centre, Bergen, Norway.

Torres López, Fabiola, and José L. Huacles. 2015. *Los dueños de la salud privada en Perú* [The owners of private health care in Peru]. http://ojo-publico.com/93/los-duenos-de-la-salud-privada-en-el-peru.

United Nations (UN). 2015. *Sustainable Development Goals Fact Sheet*. New York: United Nations.

Verhulst, S., and Andrew Young. 2016. *Open Data Impact: When Demand and Supply Meet*. New York: GovLab.

Willinsky, John. 2005. "The Unacknowledged Convergence of Open Source, Open Access, and Open Science." *First Monday* 10 (8), August 1. http://firstmonday.org/article/view/1265/1185.

World Wide Web Foundation. 2017. *Open Data Barometer*, 4th ed. Washington, DC: World Wide Web Foundation. https://opendatabarometer.org/4thedition/report/.

World Wide Web Foundation. 2018. *Open Data Barometer*. Washington, DC: World Wide Web Foundation. https://opendatabarometer.org/doc/leadersEdition/ODB-leadersEdition-Report.pdf.

Yu, Harlan, and David G. Robinson. 2012. "The New Ambiguity of 'Open Government.'" http://papers.ssrn.com/sol3/papers.cfm?abstract_id=2012489.

Zuiderwijk, Anneke, Marijn Janssen, Sunil Choenni, Ronald Meijer, and Roexsana S. Alibaks. 2012. "Socio-technical Impediments of Open Data." *Electronic Journal of E-Government* 10 (2): 156–172.

12 Open Educational Resources and Practices in the Global South: Degrees of Social Inclusion

Henry Trotter and Cheryl Hodgkinson-Williams

Introduction

Across the Global South, educational institutions are under pressure to provide students with equitable access to affordable and good-quality education in economically constrained environments. The demand for equity of access to affordable and appropriate educational materials is felt in these countries that face growing student numbers, decreasing government funding, increasing textbook costs, and lack of locally relevant educational resources.

The rapid growth and broad deployment of digital technologies have provided educators and students with platforms for locating, creating, sharing, and using educational materials at an unprecedented scale. This is a development that many (e.g., Daniel, Kanwar, and Uvalić-Trumbić 2009; Smith and Casserly 2006) have hoped would expand equity of access for those from resource-constrained environments. However, not all the educational materials located on the Internet are legally adaptable or shareable. Moreover, even if learners and educators have access to materials on the Internet, whether openly licensed or not, the content may not be suitable for their needs or it may lack relevance because it is based on worldviews or contexts that do not speak meaningfully to their own.

Engaging with open educational resources (OER) and open educational practices (OEP), which entails creating materials, sharing them on public platforms, reusing the original materials verbatim, customizing them, combining them with other materials, and sharing these publicly, has been advocated as a way of reaching groups that are socioeconomically, geographically, linguistically, and epistemically marginalized. In many parts of the world, educators in schools, higher-education institutions, and non-governmental organizations (NGOs) are starting to collaboratively create educational materials with the intention of sharing these freely with other educators and students. These OEP include activities such as collaboration among educators, cocreation among learners and educators, the use of open technologies, and open peer review. If the materials created are given an open license (e.g., Creative Commons)[1] that specifies the reuse permissions, these materials can then be shared as OER. Due to the legal permissions granted by the creators of OER, other educators and learners can legally copy, adapt, keep, and reshare versions of resources in ways that best suit their contextual needs and foreground local knowledge.

This chapter explores the phenomena of OER and OEP and their relationship to social inclusion in developing countries. It asks the question: Whether, why, and how do OER and OEP contribute to the social inclusion of underserved communities in the Global South by widening access to education, encouraging educational participation, and fostering empowerment of educators and learners? To answer this question, we analyze findings from the Research on Open Educational Resources for Development (ROER4D) project,[2] which focuses on OER and OEP activities in three regions: South America, sub-Saharan Africa, and South and Southeast Asia. ROER4D consists of eighteen subprojects with more than 100 participating researchers and research associates in Afghanistan, Brazil, Chile, Colombia, Ghana, India, Indonesia, Kenya, Malaysia, Mauritius, Mongolia, Pakistan, the Philippines, Somalia, South Africa, Sri Lanka, Tanzania, Uganda, Uruguay, Zambia, and Zimbabwe.

This chapter starts by presenting a conceptual framing of the concepts of OER, OEP, and social inclusion. Next, it provides perspectives on how OER and OEP relate to social inclusion, as gleaned from the academic literature. Then it describes the meta-analytical methodology employed here. Finally, it goes through the findings as they pertain to the relationship between ROER4D's subprojects' data and OER and OEP, as well as summarizing the key points of this chapter.

Conceptual Framing of OER, OEP, and Social Inclusion

In this section, we provide a conceptual and theoretical framework for understanding OER, OEP, and social inclusion. This framework underpins the discussion of the findings that follow.

Open Educational Resources and Practices

In this chapter, we adopt the Hewlett Foundation's definition of OER, which conceives of them as "teaching, learning, and research resources that reside in the public domain or have been released under an intellectual property (IP) license that permits their free use and re-purposing by others."[3] Wiley, Green, and Soares (2012) expand on the terms *free use* and *repurposing*, coining the term *4 Rs* (which stands for *revise, reuse, remix, and redistribute*) to describe the rights associated with OER, and later extend this to the *5 Rs* framework (by adding *retaining* to the list) (Wiley 2014).

An early definition considered OEP as "the practice of creating the educational environment in which OER are created or used" (Conole and Ehlers 2010, 2). Subsequent practitioners and researchers have extended these practices more deliberately to include collaboration (Karunanayaka et al. 2015), "developing and applying open/public pedagogies in teaching practice" (Beetham et al. 2012, 1), crowdsourcing (Weller 2013), open peer review (Hegarty 2015), and "using open technologies" (Beetham et al. 2012, 2). More recently, Cronin (2017, 18) expanded the concept of OEP to include "collaborative practices that include the creation, use, and reuse of OER, as well as pedagogical practices employing participatory technologies and social networks for interaction, peer-learning, knowledge creation, and empowerment of learners."

In the ROER4D project, OEP are construed as individual and/or collaborative practices between educators and/or cocreation with students to create, use, and adapt OER through crowdsourcing of ideas and/or materials, open peer review of materials, participatory teaching practices, and open technologies to optimize sharing and reuse.

In 2014, Hodgkinson-Williams proposed an elaboration of the practices associated with OER (Okada et al. 2012; White and Manton 2011; Wiley 2014), framing them within a more comprehensive set of OEP encompassing ten distinct activities of an open education cycle (originally called the *10 Cs*—*conceptualize, create, curate, circulate, certify, critique, loCate, customize, combine, and copy*) posited to optimize the key value propositions of OER (namely, access to affordable, high-quality education). This model has evolved over the period of ROER4D research (Walji and Hodgkinson-Williams 2017) and been refined into an open education cycle, which is based on a common conceptualization activity, followed by three distinct phases: a creation phase, a use phase, and an adaptation phase (see figure 12.1).

For OER to exist, there must be prior OEP, such as individual or collaborative creation, curation (retention), and circulation (distribution) processes, in order for others to locate, copy (reuse in its unaltered form), or adapt (customize/revise or combine/remix) so as to recurate and recirculate (Hodgkinson-Williams 2014). Therefore, if OER are to contribute to more equitable, high-quality, and sustainable education, OEP must be taken up by educators and learners.

As explained by Hodgkinson-Williams et al. (2017, 32–33):[4]

The **conceptualisation** activity includes planning what OER and which pedagogical strategies might be most suitable in a specific context; it is implicit in the OER creation, use or adaptation phases. The **creation** phase refers to the development of original materials and/or tuition by the author or institution, either as a "self-use" of existing materials or as "born open" OER

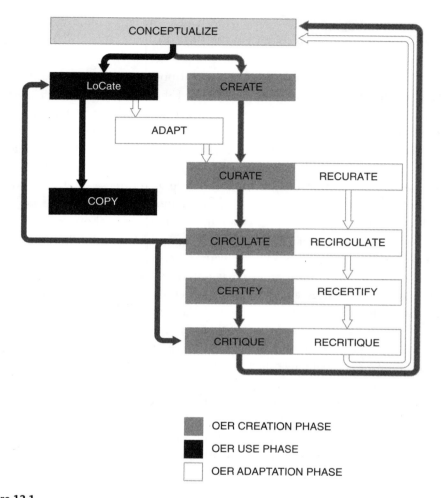

Figure 12.1
Proposed optimal Open Education cycle.
Source: Adapted from Hodgkinson-Williams (2014, 32); Walji and Hodgkinson-Williams (2017).

(i.e. developed with the view of being shared freely and openly). In order for these materials to be made publicly available, they need to be **curated**; that is, they need to be hosted on a publicly accessible platform with sufficient descriptive information (i.e. metadata) and appropriate open licensing (e.g. Creative Commons [CC]) for them to be easily found through Internet search tools and legally reusable. Further **circulation** amongst potential users of the OER is required to raise awareness of the existence of the OER (e.g. via social media, OER portals), which are then ideally **certified** through some type of quality assurance mechanism, either by the OER creator, their peers, an educational body or the hosting organisation. Best practice also requires that the OER can be **critiqued** to ensure that user feedback informs subsequent phases of conceptualisation regarding the OER. The **use** phase refers to finding OER (artificially referred to as "**loCate**" in this phase) so that it can be used in its original form (i.e. **copied**) in other contexts. This use phase, where OER are used "as is", implies a finite path as no subsequent OER are created from this activity. The **adaptation** phase refers to OER being customised (e.g. revised, modified) or combined (e.g. remixed with more than one set of OER) in order for these derivative OER to be re-curated, re-circulated, re-certified and re-critiqued.

Social Inclusion

For the analysis of ROER4D findings, we use the concept of social inclusion, which the World Bank (2013, 3) defines as "the process of improving the terms for individuals and groups to take part in society," to which Bonami and Tubio (2015, 100) further add: "It ensures that people have a voice in decisions which affect their lives and that they enjoy equal access to markets, services and political, social, and physical spaces."

This process counters an opposing reality of exclusion that faces a great many people, especially in the Global South. The World Health Organization defines *exclusion* as consisting of: "dynamic, multi-dimensional processes driven by unequal power relationships interacting across four main dimensions—economic, political, social, and cultural—and at different levels including individual, household, group, community, country, and global levels."[5]

According to Peters and Besley (2014), the concept of social inclusion first emerged as a guiding political priority in France during the 1970s, followed by Britain's New Labour government in the 1990s, with its Third Way approach to neoliberal governance. It has since then become more broadly accepted as a norm to strive for across all spheres of social activity, having become a dominant policy concept that is "seen as self-evident and part of the common-sense acceptance of the human rights framework" (Peters and Besley 2014, 108).

According to Gidley et al. (2010, 1), the following elements may, depending on the particular context, influence social inclusion, "socio-economic status, culture (including Indigenous cultures), linguistic group, religion, geography (rural and remote/isolated), gender, sexual orientation, age (including youth and old age), physical and mental health/ability, and status with regard to unemployment, homelessness and incarceration."

Aside from factors that influence social inclusion, Gidley et al. (2010, 2) suggest that there are "degrees" of social inclusion characterized by notions of access, participation, and empowerment. This means that inclusion should not be understood as a simple, binary, yes/no outcome. As they argue, "Social inclusion can be understood as pertaining to a nested schema regarding degrees of inclusion. The narrowest interpretation pertains to the neoliberal notion of social inclusion as *access*; a broader interpretation regards the social justice idea of social inclusion as *participation*; whilst the broadest interpretation involves the human potential lens of social inclusion as *empowerment*" (Gidley et al. 2010, 2).

Access   The most basic form of social inclusion revolves around the principle of *access,* one of the major preoccupations of the open movement. Gidley et al. claim that this is often tied up with neoliberal ideology, which sees access as being about "investing in human capital and improving the skills shortages for the primary purpose of economic growth as part of a nationalist agenda to build the nation's economy in order to better perform in a competitive global market" (2010, 2). This is an instrumentalist approach, seeing people as having certain deficits in skills, knowledge, and so forth, which should be overcome with greater access, leading to increased social capital, and, therefore, opportunities for the individuals concerned, as well as expanded economic growth for their societies.

Participation   A broader sense of social inclusion includes notions of participation, which are tied to questions of social justice. This goes beyond the more economically instrumental view of neoliberal access and addresses the frequently more challenging issues of "human rights, egalitarianism of opportunity, human dignity, and fairness for all" (Gidley et al. 2010, 4). Such social inclusion at the higher education level is exemplified through social responsibility activities such as those involved in university-community partnerships. The relationship between the university and civil society is what Cooper (2009, 153) calls the "fourth helix," which goes beyond the more traditional triple-helix relationship between University-Industry-Government. The theories associated with this aspect of inclusion include critical pedagogy, partnership theory, and feminist theories.

Empowerment   At the broadest level, social inclusion also includes a focus on personal empowerment, in that education should seek to "maximise the potential of each human being" (Gidley et al. 2010, 4). This is based on the recognition that each person is complex and multidimensional and that difference and diversity are strengths to be leveraged and enhanced rather than ignored or suppressed. "Through this, education can be understood as transformative" (Gidley et al. 2010, 5), fostering one's dignity and generativity. The theories associated with this element include adult developmental psychology theories, pedagogies of hope, and postcolonial development theories.

Perspectives on How OER and OEP Relate to Social Inclusion

With this understanding of social inclusion in mind, we can see how other scholars have tried to relate OER and OEP to these three elements of the concept (as shown in figure 12.2). Concerning the first element, *access*, from the very beginning of the open movement (Smith 2014), OER have been touted as having the power to overcome various forms of educational exclusion, especially for informal learners (McGreal et al. 2014) and those in marginalized contexts (Dutta 2016). Open advocates and scholars have argued that "at the heart of the movement toward OER is the simple and powerful idea that the world's knowledge is a public good and that technology in general and the World Wide Web in particular provide an opportunity for everyone to share, use, and reuse it" (Smith and Casserly 2006, 2). Many early studies focused on access as the foundational challenge to inclusion (OECD 2007), and the Millennium Development Goals (MDGs) prioritized universal access to primary education.[6] Access remains a challenge for many people today, as Willems and Bossu (2012, 185) contend: "[W]hile equity reasons often underpin the provision of OER, challenges continue to be experienced by some in accessing open digital materials for learning." Indeed, despite OER being "high on the agenda of social and inclusion policies and supported by many stakeholders, their use in higher education and adult education has not yet reached the critical threshold" (Ehlers 2011, 1). Thus, access is still at the core of social inclusion discussions in many contexts, especially the Global South.

However, as access has grown, OER proponents have broadened their understanding of social inclusion to incorporate notions of participation (Lane 2012), especially as it relates to social and educational justice (Richter and McPherson 2012). Richter and McPherson (2012, 202) elaborate on this perspective with this observation:

> Just providing those resources as a contextualized "give-away" cannot lead to reach the aim of educational justice throughout the world, but worse, without further action, the gap between the industrialized countries and the developing world may even be risen. Our research (Richter 2010) has shown that when implementing learning in foreign contexts, not taking the cultural context of the targeted learners into consideration can lead to their frustration and finally to a general denial of participation.

This has already permeated the approaches of many educational organizations, including the European Association of Distance Teaching Universities (EADTU) that views participation as being "limited for many learners by availability, affordability, accessibility and acceptability of opportunities to participate in education" (Lane 2012, 138). Richter and McPherson (2012) also note how the historical effects of colonialism, language, contextual gaps, and a lack of cultural diversity influence the production of educational materials globally, which affects participation.

Additionally, as remarked upon by Perryman and Coughlan (2013, 1),

> this vision of openness and of the connection between OER and social justice…is limited by the fact that OER-provision is typically top-down, driven by higher education suppliers with the needs of higher education (HE) in mind. As a consequence, the OER that are released can be hard to find for potential users outside HE and often fail to meet those potential users' needs in respect of the content, size, format and level of the OER.

To overcome this deficiency, Perryman and Coughlan (2013, 1) call for academics to become "public-facing open scholars" who work with "online communities outside HE to source OER to meet the specific needs of those communities." Thus, social inclusion at this level means allowing learners to identify the type of educational needs that they have, and educators to apply their expertise to meet those needs in an open fashion.

Moving beyond access and participation, scholars have also started to highlight the importance of empowerment for social inclusion. As Knox states in his critique of the OER movement: "Proponents of OER have focused disproportionately on the removal of barriers to accessing educational content, and studies into the activities and competences of self-direction are needed" (2013, 830). This type of empowered, self-directed activity forms part of a broader movement encouraging those who have been socially excluded in the past—such as scholars in the Global South vis-à-vis those in the Global North—to contribute their knowledge to the world in their own unique voices and through their own "theory from the south" (Comaroff and Comaroff, 2012). In this way, they may transcend the demeaning and exclusionary situation where "data gathering and application happen in the colony, while theorizing happens in the metropole" (Connell 2007, ix). Empowerment through OER can occur at multiple levels, such as between students and educators. Hodgkinson-Williams and Paskevicius (2012) have studied how postgraduate students at a South African university experienced a growing sense of personal agency from their efforts to help rework academics' teaching materials as OER. Thus, empowerment can occur not only in OER creation, but also in all forms of OER use (revising, remixing, redistributing, etc.).

These OER and OEP can be visually conceptualized as a nested development from access to participation through to empowerment (see figure 12.2).

Methodological Approach: Metasynthesis

To provide insights into the relationship between OER, OEP, and social inclusion, the findings across seventeen ROER4D empirical studies on OER adoption and impact in the Global South have been examined using a metasynthesis approach. Scruggs, Mastropieri, and McDuffie (2007, 395), based on their research, explain that the purpose of

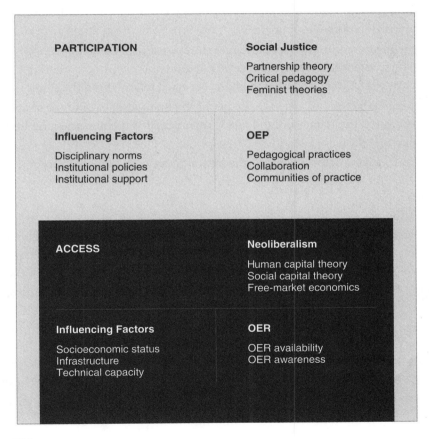

EMPOWERMENT

Human Potential

Postcolonial theories
Pedagogies of hope

Influencing Factors

Reputation enhancement
Personal fulfilment
Research-led teaching practice
Epistemological stance

OEP

OER creation
Cocreation with students

PARTICIPATION

Social Justice

Partnership theory
Critical pedagogy
Feminist theories

Influencing Factors

Disciplinary norms
Institutional policies
Institutional support

OEP

Pedagogical practices
Collaboration
Communities of practice

ACCESS

Neoliberalism

Human capital theory
Social capital theory
Free-market economics

Influencing Factors

Socioeconomic status
Infrastructure
Technical capacity

OER

OER availability
OER awareness

Figure 12.2
Degrees of social inclusion with regard to OER and OEP.
Source: Adapted from Gidley et al. (2010, 3), figure 1.

metasynthesis is "to integrate themes and insights gained from individual qualitative research into a higher order synthesis that promotes broad understandings of the entire body of research, while still respecting the integrity of the individual reports."

The draft research reports or chapters of the ROER4D volume, edited by Hodgkinson-Williams and Arinto (2017), serve as the data objects for this metasynthesis, which involves a number of stages, as follows:

1. Reading draft and final versions of the research reports or chapters (including, in some cases, primary microdata) and noting key similarities and/or differences according to key themes in the research question

2. Engaging directly with the researchers to clarify concepts, data, and/or findings to aid comparison of the findings

3. Using a literature-informed set of themes (access, participation, and empowerment) in the first instance to create a metalevel conceptual framework to identify the possible themes and indicators that might be expected to arise from the studies

4. Using this framework to code the themes in the findings of each of the studies and then adjusting the framework to include unanticipated themes emerging from the findings

5. Distilling insights according to the theoretical framework proposed here

Findings

In this section, we examine how the findings from the ROER4D studies relate to the social inclusion themes of access, participation, and empowerment. We aim to provide details from as many of the studies as possible to allow an understanding of the rich diversity of the research sites involved and to reveal the complexities, nuances, and differences that characterize the Global South's context.

Access

In this section, we assess educators' and learners' degrees of access to OER in the Global South. We do so through examining how the studies speak to several factors that shape the nature and extent of access: socioeconomic status, infrastructural access, technical capacity, OER availability, and OER awareness.

Socioeconomic Status

Whether OER use is positively related to higher levels of economic development was examined in a ROER4D study by de Oliveira Neto et al. (2017). Higher levels of development typically provide higher-education learners and educators with opportunities for accessing and engaging online learning platforms and online collaborative spaces. The question that must be asked, however, is whether that access translates into higher OER use rates. To find out, the researchers first looked at the OER use rates across the Global South and then compared them to the gross domestic product (GDP) per capita statistics for each country as a proxy for level of development. They did this for both higher-education lecturers and learners.

Based on data from de Oliveira Neto et al.'s cross regional, nine-country study, 51 percent of the 295 randomly selected educators surveyed reported having used OER at least once (2017, 81) (see table 12.1). Those from the South and Southeast Asia regions had the highest comparative use rates, with 56 percent claiming that they had used OER, while 49 percent of educators in South America and 46 percent in sub-Saharan Africa asserted that they had done the same.

A wide range of OER usage responses were found across the nine countries. Educators in Brazil (71 percent), India (70 percent), and Indonesia (70 percent) reported the highest levels of OER use; Malaysia (39 percent), South Africa (35 percent), and Colombia (22 percent) educators revealed the lowest OER use; and Ghana (53 percent), Kenya (49 percent), and Chile (45 percent) educators indicated intermediate use of OER. In another ROER4D study (Zagdragchaa and Trotter 2017), 48 percent of forty-two

Table 12.1

ROER4D cross-regional study—Educators' response as to whether they have used OER.

Region	Country	Yes (%)	Not Sure (%)	No (%)
South America	Brazil (*n* = 17)	71	24	6
	Chile (*n* = 33)	45	36	18
	Colombia (*n* = 9)	22	56	22
Regional total	*n* = 59	49	36	15
Sub-Saharan Africa	Ghana (*n* = 38)	53	32	16
	Kenya (*n* = 43)	49	30	21
	South Africa (*n* = 34)	35	32	32
Regional total	*n* = 115	46	31	23
South and Southeast Asia	India (*n* = 23)	70	22	9
	Indonesia (*n* = 44)	70	7	23
	Malaysia (*n* = 54)	39	15	46
Regional total	*n* = 121	56	13	31
Total	*n* = 295	51	25	24

Source: de Oliveira Neto et al. (2017, 81), chapter 3, table 3.

university lecturers surveyed in Mongolia reported having used OER for teaching and learning purposes. A qualitative study of teacher educators in education institutions in Tanzania, Uganda, and Mauritius revealed that the use of OER was highly fragmented and had yet to have any impact at the institutional or department level (Wolfenden et al. 2017). Furthermore, almost half of the forty-eight secondary school teachers in a study conducted in Afghanistan by Oates et al. (2017) indicated that they had used OER prior to the study.

Based on a similar survey given to students at the same twenty-eight universities as the educators (de Oliveira Neto and Cartmill 2017), table 12.2 shows that 39 percent of students said that they had used OER before, while 35 percent were unsure if they had and 26 percent stated that they had not. South and Southeast Asian students claimed the highest OER use rate, 51 percent, substantially higher than the 37 percent of South Americans, and 29 percent of sub-Saharan African students.

On the highest end of the use scale were students from India (85 percent), followed by Malaysia (47 percent), Colombia (41 percent), and Kenya (40 percent), then Brazil (38 percent), Chile (35 percent), Indonesia (33 percent) and Ghana (47 percent), and followed by the students of Kenya (41 percent) and Brazil (40 percent), then Chile (35 percent) and Indonesia (33 percent), and finally South Africa (25 percent) and Ghana (22 percent).

Table 12.2

ROER4D cross-regional study—Learners' response to whether they have used OER.

Region	Country	Yes (%)	Not sure (%)	No (%)
South America	Brazil (*n*=286)	38	33	29
	Chile (*n*=293)	35	34	31
	Colombia (*n*=170)	41	45	14
Regional total	*n*=749	37	36	27
Sub-Saharan Africa	Ghana (*n*=817)	22	45	33
	Kenya (*n*=798)	40	38	22
	South Africa (*n*=622)	25	41	34
Regional total	*n*=2,237	29	41	29
South and Southeast Asia	India (*n*=437)	85	5	9
	Indonesia (*n*=645)	33	42	24
	Malaysia (*n*=716)	47	25	28
Regional total	*n*=1,798	51	27	22
Total	*n*=4,784	39	35	26

Source: de Oliveira Neto and Cartmill (2017), appendix C.

However, when these figures are compared to GDP per capita data, figure 12.3 suggests that, at least for educators, the assumption about a positive relation between OER use and level of socioeconomic development does not stand. In two of the three regions—sub-Saharan Africa and South and Southeast Asia—the educators from the relatively less economically developed countries were most likely to use OER. In South America, this trend is only modified due to the very low OER use levels in Colombia (a country from which only nine educators responded to the survey, far below the thirty respondents that were aimed for in each survey, and that might explain this aberration).

As de Oliveira Neto et al. (2017, 84) state, "This perhaps suggests that instructors from these countries or regions have had to be more resourceful than their colleagues in more developed countries and regions in seeking out non-traditional educational materials that suit their needs from a cost and accessibility perspective." These authors also argue that it is likely that because all of the educators surveyed work in higher-education contexts, they appear to have access to the minimum level of technological infrastructure necessary for using OER without too much hindrance.

The student responses support this portrayal to some extent. In all three regions, the students from the lowest GDP per capita countries were more likely to have used OER than those from most developed countries within their own regions: Colombia more than Chile; Kenya more than South Africa; and India more than Malaysia (de Oliveira Neto and Cartmill 2017). Because of the mild variability within this pattern, it is worth remaining cautious about the link between GDP per capita and OER use. As suggested by de Oliveira Neto et al. (2017, 110), "OER use requires a certain minimum threshold of access to information and communication technology (ICT) infrastructure, which the HEIs [higher-education institutes] we surveyed provide," and it is likely that other factors are more influential than access with regard to negatively influencing OER use, at least for educators. Further research is required to ascertain this, however.

Infrastructure

Infrastructural conditions need to be favorable for learners and/or educators to gain access to digital OER and to be able to participate in online open education activities. While some OER are available in print, such as open textbooks (Goodier 2017), the majority are available via online platforms. These include those of the Khan Academy, used in a study in Chile (Westermann Juárez and Venegas Muggli 2017); Coursera and FutureLearn, used in a study in South Africa (Czerniewicz et al. 2017); and institutional- or government-supported repositories, such as Karnataka Open Educational Resources (KOER), used and extended in a study by Kasinathan and Ranganathan (2017). In addition, collaborative creation of OER with colleagues or cocreation with students usually

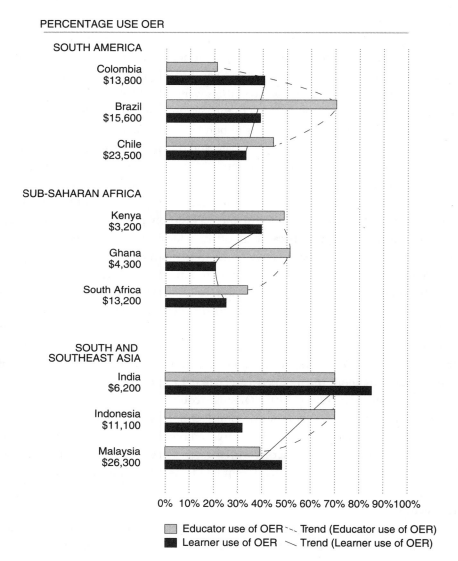

Figure 12.3
GDP per country* and educators' and learners' use of OER.
Source: *CIA (2016).
Adapted from de Oliveira Neto and Cartmill (2017).

requires the use of an online platform, such as Wikibooks, used in the Chilean study (Westermann Juárez and Venegas Muggli 2017). Necessary infrastructure, therefore, includes access to a stable power supply, appropriate hardware, and Internet connectivity. In many parts of the Global South, as ROER4D found, these foundational infrastructural requirements for OER use and creation cannot be taken for granted for either educators or learners.

Electricity

In most of the contexts where ROER4D research was engaged, local participants, especially educators, enjoyed some level of access to electricity, though this was sometimes compromised through random or scheduled power outages. Such outages severely hampered their general access to and use of desktop computers and other computing devices. For instance, teachers in the Karnataka state of India reported that power outages were quite common in many areas (Kasinathan and Ranganathan 2017), as did teacher educators in Tanzania, Uganda, and Mauritius (Wolfenden et al. 2017). In South Africa, one study found that university lecturers faced similar power disruptions (called *load shedding*), but at varying levels of inconvenience, with the urban universities enjoying longer, more stable periods of power than rural universities (Cox and Trotter 2017). This is a challenge over which educators and students have little control, but it creates additional pressure on educators and learners when they are able to use computers, forcing them to focus on essential activities while there is access to electricity. OEP may sometimes be a casualty of that pressure and constraint.

Hardware

Access to computers is also essential for OER activity. In the higher-education sector in which ROER4D subprojects were engaged, educators appeared to have good enough access to computing hardware to conduct their normal teaching work, and, by extension, to engage with OER. However, *good enough* does not necessarily mean *optimal*; it means that the computers likely belong to the institution and are as up to date and powerful as the institutions' or governments' budgets allow. This will shape the users' experiences with the machine, but for the most part it does not make OER adoption impossible.

However, such experiences can influence users' priorities around what to allocate time to while on the computer. For instance, nearly 25 percent of Indian higher-education educators surveyed by Mishra and Singh (2017) stated that poor technical infrastructure was a barrier to OER adoption. A dire challenge was noted by Indian schoolteachers, many of whom said that they did not always have sufficient access to functional computers, which inhibited their OER creation and use (Kasinathan and Ranganathan 2017).

Connectivity

The availability and quality of Internet connectivity are also major access issues in OEP. For most of the educators participating in ROER4D studies, connectivity was possible, allowing OER adoption activities, though that connectivity was characterized by varying levels of stability, speed, and cost. These variables did not necessarily prohibit OEP in any absolute sense, but it constrained it for some. For instance, secondary school teachers in Afghanistan said that because of Internet connectivity challenges, they required extra computer terminals to be located at their school so that they could access a particular digital library offline that was populated with OER (Oates et al. 2017). Teacher educators from Tanzania, Uganda, and Mauritius also reported an absence of fast, consistent Internet connectivity (Wolfenden et al. 2017). The same was true for some South African lecturers at a rural university, where it was more convenient for them to use private data dongles rather than the institutional network. The university recognized this problem, providing data dongles to many of its staff (Cox and Trotter 2017).

The urban/rural divide was often the key factor in whether connectivity was suitable for OEP. For many Indian schoolteachers interviewed in Karnataka, the "patchy" connectivity in certain rural areas limited their access to the collaborative development platforms and digital repositories necessary for OEP (Kasinathan and Ranganathan 2017, 527). In another study, South African lecturers at a distance education university worried about the lack of connectivity for their rural students, so they limited the amount of digital materials that they encouraged their students to use. This concern for their students' lack of connectivity in poorer, rural areas influenced their pedagogical strategies regarding OER (Cox and Trotter 2017).

Technical Capacity

The infrastructural aspects of OEP also rely on users having the requisite level of technical capacity to adopt such materials. As ROER4D's cross-regional survey established, this did not require an advanced level of digital expertise, but somewhere between a basic and intermediate level (de Oliveira Neto et al. 2017). With only the basic level of digital skills, OER use is a challenge. According to Cox and Trotter (2017, 296–297), OER technical capacity goes beyond a general sort of computer literacy because it requires OER agents to "possess an understanding of what differentiates OER from other educational materials as well as the technical skills to adapt (revise or remix), curate (include metadata to aid findability) and share these materials on a public platform. They [teachers] must, therefore, comprehend the role of open licensing and how this impacts Internet searching (to find OER) as well as materials development (for open sharing of educational resources)."

This is in line with the sentiments expressed by the Indian higher-education educators in one study, whose general interest in increasing their ICT skills opens a door to potential OEP as they gain exposure to the more specialized aspects of this activity (Mishra and Singh 2017). Similarly, course developers in Malaysia revealed in a focus group discussion that they would have reduced their time in searching for relevant resources if they had better technical skills (Menon et al. 2017). Teachers in the Indian study found the editing of content on a shared wiki platform difficult and intimidating, opting instead to share materials via a mailing list (Kasinathan and Ranganathan 2017). However, as was revealed at one South African university, the relevant technical capacity need not reside in all educators if they are able to call on institutional support, such as from staff members or student assistants, to help with their OER-related needs (Czerniewicz et al. 2017).

OER Availability

Another essential structural requirement for access is the availability of global, national, regional, and/or institutional platforms, repositories, aggregators, initiatives, and/or projects used to create and host OER—including open textbooks and massive open online courses (MOOCs)—and/or facilitate OEP. This is largely beyond the control of individual educators, as such availability relies on the collective efforts of educators to make their teaching materials available, and of relevant institutions to establish the digital platforms for the sharing of those materials. However, while there is a large number of OER available on the Internet for free use, this is not quite what we mean by *availability*, which requires that those materials are contextually suitable for educators and have the requisite quality. Thus, for our purposes, availability is less about the sheer volume of materials online and more about the relevance of those materials for a particular educator or learner who desires materials for a specific anticipated use (Cox and Trotter 2017).

Several ROER4D studies show that where such appropriate materials are made available to them, educators use the resources to enhance teaching of their subject matter. In Chile, educators reported using materials from the Spanish Khan Academy site for first- and second-year university students and the Wikibooks platform for a teacher-generated open textbook (Westermann Juárez and Venegas Muggli 2017). Indian teachers stated that they were pleased to use materials from the KOER platform (Kasinathan and Ranganathan 2017). In Afghanistan, teachers said that they used materials from the purpose-built online Darakht-e Danesh Library (DDL)[7] (Oates et al. 2017). In Africa, teachers from a number of countries revealed that they had used resources from the Teacher Education in Sub-Saharan Africa (TESSA)[8] platform (Wolfenden et al. 2017). With the assistance of an institutional MOOC development team, lecturers at one university in South Africa have so far contributed to four MOOCs on platforms such as FutureLearn and Coursera (Czerniewicz et al. 2017). In Sri Lanka, an OER-integrated Teaching and Learning (OERTL) learning management system played a key role in facilitating teachers' access to OER related to their subject areas and their integration of those resources into their teaching and learning practices (Karunanayaka and Naidu 2017). OERTL was organized to motivate and support teachers not only to search, identify, and integrate OER, but also to share OER with peers, upload OER-integrated lessons, upload concept maps, and reflect on experiences. In South Africa, the Department of Basic Education has engaged in at least two national OER initiatives: printing and distributing openly licensed textbooks produced by an independent OER publisher, Siyavula,[9] and producing, printing, and distributing the "Mind-the-Gap"[10] OER self-study guides to public schools (Goodier 2017).

However, many educators said that they also felt constrained by the current OER available. Some felt they were not of the best format for their teaching needs (e.g., they were text based rather than multimedia based), or there was not enough diversity of platforms catering to their specific regional context, or the materials were in languages that were difficult for them or their students to engage with. For example, educators in Sri Lanka have some familiarity with English, but a majority teach in Sinhala or Tamil (Karunanayaka and Naidu 2017). Teachers in Pakistan and Afghanistan also bemoaned the fact that OER available in their national languages is limited (Oates et al. 2017; Waqar et al. 2017).

One university in South Africa has taken a small step in ameliorating this type of deficit by establishing an open research, teaching, and learning repository where lecturers can share their teaching materials openly (Cox and Trotter 2017). Another South African university also plans to make a large proportion of its staff's teaching materials openly available, a project similar to the OpenCourseWare (OCW) initative at the Massachusetts Institute of Technology (MIT) (Cox and Trotter 2017). Such developments are crucial if educators and learners from poorer, marginalized regions and countries are to see OER as increasing their level of social inclusion.

OER Awareness

In order for open education to fulfill its potential, students, educators, learning designers, librarians, educational managers, and policymakers need to be aware of the concept of *openness*, OER, open textbooks, and MOOCs, as well as their associated open practices. Most important, they need to be aware of how these resources are different from any other content on the Internet and other online courses that do not allow legal retention, reuse, revision, remixing, and redistribution.

In the cross-regional survey, 75 percent of the educators reported that they were aware of OER to some extent, in that they were able to say definitively whether they had used OER or not, compared to 25 percent who said that they were unsure if they had ever used OER (de Oliveira Neto et al. 2017). This does not provide much detail as to the extent of that awareness, but it suggests that OER as a concept have some degree of familiarity in this particular education community.

Research at South African universities showed, however, great variation between levels of awareness at different institutions. At one urban residential university, which has a pro-OER policy and institutional support for OER activity (in the form of OER grants, workshops, and other offerings), awareness was relatively high (Cox and Trotter 2017). At a large distance education university that has an OER strategy (but not yet a policy), where OER workshops are featured every few months on campus, OER awareness was growing from a relatively low base (Cox and Trotter 2017). But at a rural residential university that had been historically disadvantaged during apartheid, OER awareness was decidedly low (Cox and Trotter 2017). This intracountry differentiation was common in many research contexts, including in India (Mishra and Singh 2017) and Mongolia (Zagdragchaa and Trotter 2017).

The picture becomes more challenging in the schooling context. For instance, prior to an OER workshop intervention in Sri Lanka, only 10 percent of teachers said that they had heard of the term *OER* before (Karunanayaka and Naidu 2017). This is partially due to a simple lack of exposure to the concept. However, it also appears due in part to the fact that there are already certain understandings of what can be used freely in teaching based on fair use guidelines and common pedagogical tradition. Thus, although the majority of teacher educators in institutions in Tanzania, Uganda, and Mauritius regularly drew on multiple online resources, many were uncertain as to which of these resources were *open* (Wolfenden et al. 2017). They used them regardless, as the relevance of the resources was more important than their licensing conditions (Wolfenden et al. 2017). Similarly, secondary school teachers in Afghanistan demonstrated little familiarity with the concept of OER, revealing some confusion as to what constituted the *open* in *OER:* "Most teachers had some idea that OER generally had to do with information that was online and many respondents assumed that OER had to do with the Internet, with libraries, books, or information" (Oates et al. 2017, 565).

This perception that essentially all Internet resources are available for educational use cuts across multiple educational levels. Among the Mongolian university educators as well, many felt largely free to download and use any type of educational material online (whether openly licensed or not), which means that the typical value proposition made by OER advocates—that OER are free—may not mean much when educators are already obtaining and using desired materials for free (Zagdragchaa and Trotter 2017). These findings are consistent with prior studies on students' download and use behaviors in the Global South (Czerniewicz 2016).

This variable and often laissez-faire understanding of what OER consist of as opposed to any other type of online materials was mirrored in educators' general lack of knowledge about open licensing. Among those who had used OER, most were at least marginally aware of the rights that a Creative Commons (CC) license might grant them, but they were rarely confident enough in their knowledge of such licenses to know how they would then apply a CC license to their own work to make it publicly open. The nuances involved in the legal rights expressed in the various licenses felt like specialized knowledge to most. Educators at one South African university were confronted with the challenges of copyright and open licensing when needing to make decisions around access to the resources of their MOOCs (including their own articles over which they did not have copyright) (Czerniewicz et al. 2017). Special permissions for reusing their articles in fully copyrighted journals or books were sought, and, if not granted, educators were not at liberty to use their published research in the MOOC.

Participation

If access is satisfactorily achieved, educators and learners can move on to the more profound social inclusion component of participation, which is linked to social and educational justice. We will focus here on the factors that are critical in determining educators' and learners' degrees of participation (in the Global South): disciplinary norms, institutional policies, institutional support mechanisms, pedagogical practices, and collaboration (including communities of practice).

Disciplinary Norms   One of the primary social cues that educators assess when making pedagogical decisions is what is conventional practice within their discipline. If OEP are common in their field, then they have to decide for themselves whether to participate in such practices. If it is not common, then it may not even require a conscious decision, either because they remain unaware of OER and OEP or because they see OEP as a niche or optional activity.

At South African universities, qualitative interviews revealed that educators were sensitive to the norms not only of their disciplines, but also those of their colleagues in their departments. While the disciplinary norms influenced them from within and beyond the university, their departmental settings provided personal peer pressure regarding their teaching choices, sometimes leading to OER use (Cox and Trotter 2017).

In the study of Mongolian universities, "Of the 76 percent of survey respondents who said that they had never created and shared OER, the highest percentage of them (25 percent) said that they had not done so because 'such sharing is not common in my discipline'" (Zagdragchaa and Trotter 2017, 408).

Institutional Policies   While disciplinary (and departmental) norms seem to shape the expectations of educators regarding their pedagogical options, institutional policies can play an even more determining role regarding whether they will be able to use or create OER. The institution's policies, some of which are based on national law (particularly regarding copyright), may ultimately decide at what level educators can enjoy or promote social inclusion, participation, and social justice.

In many countries, such as South Africa (as well as Canada and the United States), national copyright laws automatically grant employers copyright over any works created by employees in the course of their duties. This typically includes teaching materials created by educators for use with their students. Most South African universities explicitly note this in their IP policies (Trotter 2016), but some also state that they grant copyright over those teaching materials to the creators, thus allowing the latter to relicense those works and share them openly as OER if they so desire. Without that formal permission from the institution, educators are technically not allowed to share their teaching materials openly because they lack the right to relicense the materials (they legally belong to the institution).

For most educators, this does not influence whether they can download and use OER in their teaching, but it does affect whether they can create or redistribute OER (Trotter 2016). For instance, while one South African university in the ROER4D study had developed a pro-OER policy that formally encouraged educators to share their teaching materials openly on a purpose-built open platform hosted by the university, another university had created a mechanism whereby educators could petition their relevant tuition committees to gain permission to share their teaching materials as OER. Though not well known to the study's participants, this mechanism provides at least a technically viable avenue for some level of OER creation activity (Cox and Trotter 2017).

Other universities, such as the University of the Republic of Uruguay, which accounts for 90 percent of the country's total enrollment, has begun promoting OER as one of the open initiatives in an institutional policy that includes OEP, use of open-source software, and open access (Toledo 2017). Wawasan Open University in Malaysia has adopted a specific OER policy on new course development that requires that educators use existing OER wherever possible to avoid the use of copyrighted textbooks (Menon et al. 2017).

While institutional IP policies and broader OER-related policies offer general guidelines on how educators might participate in OEP (if at all), educators themselves often say that they are more responsive to the personally impactful policies regarding rewards and incentives. For instance, educators at four Indian higher education institutions identified the lack of recognition and reward systems as a major obstacle for developing OER (Mishra and Singh 2017). Half of forty-two Mongolian university educators surveyed felt that the lack of a reward system for OER creation was an important factor in their decision-making on this issue (Zagdragchaa and Trotter 2017). In addition, teachers in Tanzania, Uganda, and Mauritius highlighted an absence of institutional recognition for OER creation, noting that even in institutions where senior leaders expressed support for OER, there was little evidence of institutionwide implementation (Wolfenden et al. 2017).

Cox and Trotter (2016) suggest that an institution's dominant culture (collegial, managerial, bureaucratic, etc.) should be taken into account when determining which type of policy arrangement would work best in promoting OEP. However, as research participants from across numerous field studies reported, having any sort of policy clarity regarding OER would be a useful first step in many environments where there is no such clarity or awareness regarding policy's relationship to OER.

Institutional Support   While it is possible to use and create OER on one's own, it is useful to be surrounded by colleagues who also do so and be backed by policies that provide clarity on one's actions. Beyond this, educators appreciate any institutional support that they can get for adopting OER. For instance, this support that can come in many forms, such as OER creation grants, legal support personnel (for copyright management and licensing), an institutional OER platform, and an on-campus unit with OER specialists who are available to help staff, has been instrumental in the engagement with OER for a number of educators at one South African university (Cox and Trotter 2017; Czerniewicz et al. 2017). Because of the robustness of this support, the educators were able to go far beyond simply using OER as is, reworking their own materials as OER, contributing to larger projects, such as MOOCs, and making all their work open.

Institutional support does not have to be as extensive as this to be valuable. In one ROER4D study, Malaysian librarians and technical support staff assisted course developers in locating suitable OER for creating a research methodology course primarily from existing OER (Menon et al. 2017). This is a low-budget form of support, as it taps into intellectual capital rather than financial capital. It also builds networks and capacities for future OER-related activities.

In Africa, at three teacher education institutions in Tanzania, Uganda, and Mauritius, extended individual engagement with OER was found to have been stimulated by support from library staff, or staff leading internal staff development sessions, such as instructional design specialists who acted as a resource for practice (Wolfenden et al. 2017). However, in several institutions, the locus of OER expertise was seen to be located in the e-learning, distance learning, or ICT unit or department, resulting in a gap between the technical issues of OER and the social practice of their use in teaching (Wolfenden et al. 2017).

In general, the instances of institutional support that we identified in our research across the Global South were few. Most educators said that they worked in environments where they either did not know where to go institutionally for OER support, or they already knew that there was nowhere to go for such support. While they could often get ICT support from the ICT staff, they did not look to them for the more specialized knowledge required for OER activity. The same was true for the library staff, some of whom were familiar with open access issues that pertain to research publications rather than teaching and learning materials but not OER. For many of the educators, knowing of even one person on campus, such as an institutional champion of OER who tried to raise awareness among colleagues, was important.

Because of this, most institutional work regimes do not actively support OEP, thus making it an optional activity outside the scope of normal work. For instance, teachers in Colombia complained to the researchers that their institutions did not provide time for the creation of educational resources and that school principals, in particular, were unsupportive (Sáenz, Hernandez, and Hernández 2017). Without formal, or even tacit, institutional support, OEP will likely remain an individualized and niche activity that will never gain critical mass. This is a challenge for a social inclusion ethic surrounding participation that benefits from broad engagement.

Pedagogical Practices   There is a spectrum of OEP in which educators can engage to adopt OER. On the one hand, for some who are the lone OER users or creators in their departments or institutions, the work can be quite solitary. They and their students may benefit from this OEP, but it would not necessarily result in a broader change in practices. On the other hand, especially where there is some institutional support for open activities or where an institution has been the target of sustained OER interventions from outside groups, there exists the possibility that conventional pedagogical practices can be reexamined and altered to fit a new, more open paradigm.

Where educators' practices reside on this spectrum may be initially influenced by the level of informal sharing that occurs prior to a formal open intervention. For instance, 92 percent of teachers in the Sri Lankan study revealed that they informally shared materials that they were developing with each other or other interested parties (Karunanayaka and Naidu 2017). However, they rarely took the next step to make them formally open (licensed) or publicly available to anyone who may request them. This was a common approach among disciplinary and departmental colleagues in the many contexts we investigated. A culture of mild informal sharing among peers was common, and in some cases that could be used as the basis for encouraging educators to take the next step and enlarge the circle of people that they share with beyond their known associates (Kasinathan and Ranganathan 2017).

However, regardless of the predominant approach to informal sharing, pedagogical practices were observed to change in situations where educators were exposed to OER and OEP and given the necessary support to experiment with them. For instance, based on the long-term interventions promoted by one open educational initiative in three African countries, a number of OER champions at these teacher-educator institutions stated that they had observed a shift in educator thinking and practices. One educator, who was reporting on his colleagues' practices, suggested, "Exploring other OER gave them a quality benchmark, which sometimes caused them to feel they were doing a 'substandard' job compared to their international peers and that they were using 'old' methods" (Wolfenden et al. 2017, 271–272). Indeed, in the course of the intervention, participants' pedagogical thinking became more critical, creative, and collaborative, due to the integration processes involved in OEP (Wolfenden et al. 2017, 271–272). The educators themselves identified various factors that they believed were helpful for sustaining a shift to OEP, including extended study at another institution (usually abroad), improved technology or connectivity (such as personal acquisition of a laptop), and personal interaction with an external visitor who advocates and illustrates the use of OER (Wolfenden et al. 2017, 271–272). By the end of the intervention, the majority of the participants who remained were actively engaged not only in reusing OER, but also in repurposing them by translating them into local languages, adapting them to suit their contexts, and even creating OER on their own (Wolfenden et al. 2017, 271–272).

However, in some cases, the predominant culture among colleagues is hostile to the type of openness (i.e., sharing and collaboration) that can be built in for OER purposes. At one South African university, there was very little informal sharing, as educators felt possessive over their teaching materials and had a "conservative academic culture" (Cox and Trotter 2017, 322). This stance made the case for OER that much more difficult to sustain, as it relies on educators having a certain level of emotional and philosophical openness that can be leveraged and expanded.

Some teachers, such as more than half of those featured in the Afghanistan study, revealed that when they prepared lesson plans, they did not use any OER and relied solely on a textbook (Oates et al. 2017). This is a common approach in areas where teachers may not feel capacitated to construct their own learning materials from a broad array of resources, or where the textbook takes pride of place as the curricular guide.

A work environment need not be hostile to openness for the idea of OER and OEP to struggle there. In many cases, such as with teachers in India, educators do not have the necessary autonomy in their work or control over their responsibilities to introduce OER or OEP (Kasinathan and Ranganathan 2017). For these teachers, their role is to simply transmit the prescribed textbook-based information to their students, not to develop teaching materials themselves (Kasinathan and Ranganathan 2017). Thus, while they are open to the idea of OER and OEP, their own conventional teaching roles do not allow them to engage with teaching materials in the same way as, perhaps, at other institutions where teachers develop much of their own teaching materials. Thus, for these teachers, to enjoy the type of participation and social inclusion promised by open practices, they would need not only to engage with OER and OEP, but also to be given the right and time to do so from their institutions and/or provincial education departments.

Collaboration and Communities of Practice   If we extend this discussion on the idea of a spectrum of open practices from individual based to group based, then we can focus on the maximal form of OEP as advanced by the open community, that of sustained collaboration, or the development of communities of practice where creating, sharing, and peer reviewing of OER is a focal practice. For OER advocates, this represents the fulfillment at a developmental and practice level of the open ethic, in which educators collaborate with each other as a norm, building identities or communities around those collaborations. As this marks a high point of OEP, it is also relatively rare, at least when it is connected to OER outputs. Of course, in many disciplines such as the sciences, collaboration is already common, but the resulting outputs are often closed, copyright-protected materials. The kind of collaboration being addressed here is the kind that leads to and facilitates further open collaboration between educators and with students.

This type of sustained, open collaboration was glimpsed mostly in experimental contexts, as with the MOOC team at one South African university (Czerniewicz et al. 2017). Because the unit in which the MOOC was based happened to have a strong open ethos, the members of that unit were able to push for the MOOCs produced—and all future MOOCs to come out of its collaborations with other university staff members—to be based upon open, collaborative practices (Czerniewicz et al. 2017).

In Afghanistan, most secondary school teachers (76 percent) featured in the study said that they were willing to share resources found in the DDL, while 78 percent indicated that the OER in DDL helped them initiate collaboration among students (Oates et al. 2017). In addition, two-thirds also said that the OER would help them work collaboratively with other teachers. This was a relatively new idea among teachers in Afghanistan, but it was an educational context that was wide open to new ideas, as the educators recognized that their challenging environment called for imaginative strategies to overcome limitations while delivering relevant, high-quality education to their students (Oates et al. 2017).

Empowerment

If access and participation can be achieved, educators and learners can move on to the final social inclusion component of empowerment, which relates to capacitating individuals to live up to their full potential, whether as educators or learners. We focus here on the factors that relate to OER creation, reputation enhancement, personal fulfillment, research-led teaching praxis, cocreation with students, and epistemic stance, by which we can deduce educators' and learners' degrees of empowerment in the Global South.

OER Creation   OER creation represents the fulfillment of a relatively high level of social inclusion. It goes beyond mere OER use, especially if the OER is used as is because that type of OER engagement is only minimally transformative (at least for the educator, though inclusion of OER could enhance the learning experience appreciably for students). But when educators create and share their own teaching materials openly, they make a contribution to the broader world (beyond the classroom), asserting their unique voice along with that of the many others who share their materials. This is potentially transformative not only for the recipients, but also for the educators themselves. It reveals (and hopefully develops) a level of confidence that is especially necessary for educators in the Global South, whose knowledge production has been marginalized compared to their counterparts in the Global North.

According to the multiregion survey, 23 percent of the 295 educators stated that they had openly licensed (i.e., shared) their teaching materials in some fashion (de Oliveira Neto et al. 2017). This is just less than half the percentage who stated that they had used OER before. That there are fewer OER creators than users can be expected, given that there are lower barriers to OER use than to OER creation. But there is also a discernible relationship between users and creators, in that virtually all creators have used OER at some point as well (de Oliveira Neto et al. 2017). Their familiarity with

OER through use may have helped make OER creation an imaginable activity for themselves. Thus, the power of an OER use experience cannot be discounted for inspiring educators to contribute their own work as well.

At one South African university, OER creation activities appeared to result from both personal desire and from peer pressure (Cox and Trotter 2017). A number of individual lecturers profiled by one study saw the virtue of sharing their locally relevant materials so that they could fill a gap in the broader collection of OER available (Cox and Trotter 2017). However, others who joined in a collaborative MOOC creation process found themselves under pressure to release their particular contributions to the overall course openly along with everyone else (Czerniewicz et al. 2017). Although they had not anticipated that they would have to do so, a number of the educators involved were persuaded to make their content open so that the entire MOOC could be considered open, as preferred by the core team running the MOOC-making initiative (Czerniewicz et al. 2017). Through this process, the initially hesitant educators became converts to the cause, appreciating the value of making their own work open.

In India, a group of teachers created (from scratch) twenty-five Kannada-language video resources for the demonstration of various science concepts (Kasinathan and Ranganathan 2017), which eventually formed the core resource material for a statewide training program. This contribution has emboldened many of these Indian teachers to try to find further open opportunities, as they can see its value not only for them, but also for other educators in their region.

Reputation Enhancement   As can be imagined, one of the outcomes of educators sharing their materials—especially if they are high quality and suited to many potential users—is the enhancement of their reputation, both locally and globally. In some cases, such as at one South African university, educators may receive official recognition for their OER contributions (in this case, an award given at a public ceremony), although in most other instances, that recognition comes from feedback from users of the content, who share words of praise and gratitude and then share the resource further with their colleagues (Cox and Trotter 2017; Czerniewicz et al. 2017).

According to most Indian university lecturers in one study, sharing educational resources was perceived as improving their professional standing, enhancing their personal reputations, and boosting their institutional reputations (Mishra and Singh 2017). It also increased educators' networks and their sphere of influence, providing recognition at a global level. Additionally, in Mongolia, 60 percent of university educators in the study stated that they would be motivated to create OER, as it enhances their reputation among their peers (even though they had not yet contributed OER) (Zagdragchaa and Trotter 2017).

It is hard to overstate the importance of this form of empowerment for the sustainability of the open movement. While openness is based primarily on an altruistic ethical foundation, it leverages more self-centered personal ambitions for educators as well (Cox 2016). The combination of these desires—to enhance one's reputation while also making a contribution to society—allows a type of empowerment at multiple levels.

Personal Fulfillment   Beyond the competitive gains that educators can make through open practices, such as enhancing their reputations, they can also enjoy one of the more enduring forms of empowerment, which is simply personal fulfillment. Many educators from across the studies revealed that they got a great deal of satisfaction from sharing their materials openly. It addressed a deeply held desire concerning what type of educator they wanted to be, how they wanted to operate in the world, and how they imagined themselves to be at their most effective.

Among Indian university lecturers, the highest score that they collectively attributed to various attitudinal survey prompts (4.65 on a scale of 1–5) related to the pleasure they felt when adopting or adapting their educational resources (Mishra and Singh 2017). It also enhanced their sense of confidence, as it made them feel like they were an important part of a larger community [mean (M) = 4.46]. In addition, they felt that sharing OER was a useful way to disseminate their ideas (M = 4.29) and to obtain feedback (M = 4.58) (Mishra and Singh 2017).

In many ways, this is quite personal, as ROER4D researchers also met many educators who said that currently they would not get the same sense of fulfillment out of openly sharing their materials because they were concerned about their quality and the potentially critical assessment that they might receive from colleagues (Cox and Trotter 2017). It would expose them. For those able to get their materials into a state that they believed not only reflected well upon them as educators but also was of real value to others, the act of sharing their materials openly was a gratifying one (Czerniewicz et al. 2017).

Research-Led Teaching Praxis   Many educators engaged in the Global South would not have participated in OER creation activities without the intervention of an outside organization that had the capacity to help them develop materials and demonstrate what OEP looks like (Kasinathan and Ranganathan 2017; Sáenz, Hernandez, and Hernández 2017). This points to the continued relevance of the donor-funding community in creating opportunities for educators, especially teachers, to embark on an OER creation exercise within the safety of a larger group of collaborators, with quality assured by the rigor of the process.

In rural Colombia, one of the studies was a participatory action research (PAR) project conducted with forty-eight teachers and eleven teacher educators at eleven schools across four states (Sáenz, Hernandez, and Hernández 2017). Through that engagement, which was something new for the teachers, six schools and twenty-two teachers created sixteen OER.[11] Six OER were created by several authors to be used across their respective school areas, and ten were created by individual authors. This research-led interaction with the teachers took them from a point of relative disempowerment with regard to their feelings about their teaching materials to one where they were collaboratively creating a broad array of OER to be shared openly.

This kind of outcome can often only come through specialized OER-related interventions, driven by external funders (as in the Colombia example given in this chapter) or governments that have taken up an active role, as they have in three states in India (Kasinathan 2016). Such interventions represent not a norm for the future of all OER expansion, but one of a number of activities that helps educators experiment with OER and gradually build up their capacities and confidence.

Cocreation with Students

Beyond educator to educator collaborative practices, OER advocates have embraced the socially inclusive vision of learner-centered pedagogical practices to the point of encouraging students to become cocreators of OER. This represents a particularly deep and powerful form of empowerment for all concerned, disrupting the power dynamics traditionally associated with the teacher-student relationship.

In ROER4D's multiple studies, this was a very nascent phenomenon. In most cases, educators were not at a stage of pedagogical thinking that enabled them to embark on an experiment like this, as it combines two relatively radical approaches to teaching and learning—cocreation and openness.

In Pakistan, 31 percent of the teachers surveyed indicated that they shared OER with their students using Google Drive, while 22 percent shared resources through a personal website or blog (Waqar et al. 2017). They did this for the sake of their students, not so much to reach an online public. Thus, these teachers made OER central to their approach with their own students, who were also free to share these materials with others. Again, this represents only a gesture toward the broader empowerment goal discussed here. For the most part, such open cocreation is not happening, constrained as educators are by conventional teaching approaches, culturally informed notions of the teacher-student relationship, and a modest familiarity with OEP in general. However, whether or not educators and students interact at this level, from a social inclusion perspective, both are able to still seek the broader goal of empowerment that lies at the heart of the OER and OEP approach.

Epistemic Stance   Finally, perhaps the ultimate form of empowerment and social inclusion is being able to assert and define one's own understanding of what constitutes valuable knowledge. Due to a long history of imperialism and postindependence neocolonialism, the Global South has been dominated by Northern epistemic norms and understandings, making it difficult for Southern educators to insist on their own forms of knowledge. This is an intellectually debilitating situation to be in, and it is at the heart of educators' sense of global educational inequality (Mkandawire 2011). However, the affordances of the Internet create new opportunities for Southern educators to share their own knowledge (despite the various digital divides that also shape the ICT space), especially as OER. As our research shows, some educators were using this affordance as an opportunity to make epistemic assertions that not only challenged the hegemonic status of Northern knowledge systems, but also provided more locally relevant materials for other educators in the Global South. Thus, a South-to-South conversation was already in motion, if only tentatively, regarding the sharing of teaching materials.

For instance, at the South African university running a series of MOOCs, each MOOC had its own strategic goals, which, to varying degrees, included the provision of open educational opportunities to engage global participants with locally generated knowledge (Czerniewicz et al. 2017). Despite the fact that MOOC learners might be from anywhere in the world, they engaged with materials that were unashamedly Southern (in general), and South African (in particular).

The African teacher educators in Tanzania, Uganda, and Mauritius began altering their epistemic and pedagogical positions through their use of OER by (1) exhibiting greater confidence and competence in drawing on multiple forms of knowledge from OER and problematizing what was considered valued knowledge; (2) challenging traditional hierarchical teacher-learner relationships and instead beginning to position their students as autonomous agents in their learning; and (3) developing a learning culture embracing both formal and informal learning, in which learning is jointly constructed and distributed (Wolfenden et al. 2017).

These efforts were all congruent with a movement toward a more participatory pedagogy, but the evidence was still highly emergent and fragile. For almost all the educators for whom OER have become part of their lived practice, this is the result of personal choice rather than institutional policy or collaborative endeavour (Cox and Trotter 2017).

In addition, while a number of educators felt emboldened to challenge the epistemic status quo by asserting and sharing their own locally imbued materials openly, many others had yet to develop the confidence to do so. Thus, it is still early days in this regard, certainly in the educational resources domain, but it offers the greatest scope for transformative impact if more educators continue to develop their own Southern voices and share their resources with others. They will then be able to educate a generation of learners for whom epistemic inequality will not be as great as it has been up to now.

Conclusion

In this concluding section, we summarize the key findings and arguments made in this chapter.

First, engagement with OER and OEP contribute to social inclusion through three nested components of this broader concept: access, participation, and empowerment. The first tier, access, is underpinned by a relatively narrow neoliberal understanding of the term, focused on how educational access can provide marginalized people with more economically useful skills for contributing to their national economies. The open activity most associated with this basic form of social inclusion is the use of OER as is. With the creation of OER platforms around the world, but primarily in the Global North, any educator or learner with an Internet connection can download OER and use them for teaching or learning purposes. As our research shows, this the primary form of engagement that people in the Global South have with OER, as it has the lowest barrier to engagement compared to other forms of OER adoption. There are few policies or regulations against OER use in the education sector, and the ability of educators to use those materials in an unmodified form requires little specialized skill. At its most elementary level, this form of OER use can indeed foster social inclusion through access, broadening the scope of available materials with which educators and learners can engage.

Nevertheless, educators and students exhibit variable OER awareness based on a widespread confusion about which materials are free or open to use on the Internet. This confusion is due, in part, to fair use legal provisions and common educational practices, but it is also exacerbated by the ease with which online materials may be downloaded free of charge, regardless of license. Our research indicates that educators and students use online materials based on their perceived relevance rather than on their open licensing conditions.

In the Global South, there seems to be greater uptake of OER from higher-education institutions than schools. This may be partially because universities, which are mostly urban based, typically enjoy greater infrastructural capacity than many schools which are spread across both urban and rural (often poorer) areas. As we have seen in this chapter, university students have had better access to a sufficient number of functional computers, uninterrupted power supply, and fast, stable, and affordable connectivity.

While most educators and learners had the necessary computer literacy to find and download some OER, they did not necessarily have the specialized knowledge needed for doing anything more than using OER as is.

The second tier of social inclusion is participation, which derives from a number of social justice ideologies. With regard to OER and OEP, this factor is evident in the incipient shifts of teachers' and lecturers' pedagogical practices toward greater collaboration, sharing, and OER engagement. Although ROER4D studies did not find that the creation and sharing of teaching materials were the usual practices for the schoolteachers researched, there was some evidence that, with the necessary support and time to engage in collaborative materials-development activities, they were eager to adapt or create and share materials with each other having content appropriate for their contexts and in languages most readily understood. While the use of the textbook as the core source of information was still the norm within the schooling sector, many teachers seemed to be eager to use OER as a supplement in a localized or summarized form. Despite infrastructural challenges, they appeared willing to share their materials, if in a more informal manner (such as emailing each other) than by uploading their materials to a public repository.

Because current OER repositories host mostly English-language materials, lack of OER in languages relevant in the Global South remains a challenge. It forms a barrier to full access and participation. However, as we have seen, some educators from India, Sri Lanka, and Afghanistan have started contributing materials in local languages to various local platforms with the help of government or foreign donor funding. The ongoing support for these existing and new communities of collaborative OER developers may be a strategy for surmounting the need for linguistically appropriate materials.

Participation in collaborative creation of OER takes a slightly different form in higher education where lecturers are more likely to collaborate with librarians, learning designers, course developers, content production teams, platform hosts, and some of their disciplinary and departmental colleagues. However, this traditional form of collaboration—and informal sharing of resources between colleagues—has not yet been infused with the open ethic. But because this type of sociability already exists in many higher-education contexts, it represents a foundation on which more collaborative activities can develop, shifting to a more participatory space for everyone involved.

Although relatively few examples of cocreation with students were reported in ROER4D studies, this nascent student participation is indicative of a more learner-centered approach and a challenge to the traditional teacher-learner hierarchies. The pedagogical shifts to more learner-centered approaches become more pronounced with the development of MOOCs, where lecturers must not only consider the needs of a wider audience than their immediate student cohort, but also think of ways of conveying their course content in multimedia formats, preparing assessments that are suitable for large numbers of students, and engaging in online support activities with large groups of students. One of the key challenges here is ensuring that the materials referred to in the MOOCs have open licenses that can be easily accessed, as MOOC participants do not enjoy the same access to university libraries as fee-paying students. For this reason, it is useful to distinguish between OER-based MOOCs and so-called xMOOCs (eXtended Massive Open Online Courses), which do not openly license their materials for future reuse.

Finally, the third tier of the social inclusion concept concerns empowerment, a notion that is ideologically informed by human potential theories. This high-level form of social inclusion through OEP was embryonic within ROER4D studies. It was emerging in the contribution of original OER to public repositories by educators and the offering of MOOCs by university lecturers in association with their own institutions and hosting platforms. For schoolteachers, this represented the development of a new level of agency in privileging their own perspectives on what constitutes valuable knowledge, thereby increasing their accountability and influencing their reputation beyond their usual sphere of influence. Likewise, for university lecturers, the offering of MOOCs provided an opportunity to assert alternative epistemic perspectives on a global scale involving both personal and institutional reputational risks. By contributing original OER and/or offering MOOCs, teachers and lecturers were offering knowledge to the world in their own unique voices and through their own "theory from the South," engaging in a dynamic conversation with hegemonic epistemic perspectives while strengthening their sense of self-identity.

In sum, it appears that the use, adaptation, and creation of OER (including OER-based MOOCs), as well as collaboration and cocreation practices, foster social inclusion along a continuum from enabling access, to encouraging participation, to gradually cultivating empowerment more markedly with educators (especially in higher education) than with learners in the Global South. At least, that is the picture currently. What is clear is that these social inclusion processes take time to develop and unfold and need ongoing nurturing.

Acknowledgments

This work was carried out with the aid of a grant from Canada's International Development Research Centre. The authors wish to thank the ROER4D researchers, whose original research contributed to this analysis. We also thank the ROER4D network hub for generous assistance (namely, Michelle Willmers for her editorial support). Also, we thank Sarah Goodier for visuals, Tess Cartmill for quantitative data analysis, and Thomas King for data curation. We extend our gratitude to the ROER4D team at Wawasan Open University and the ROER4D researchers who helped with the review process, specifically Patricia Arinto, Shironica Karunanayaka, Sanjaya Mishra, Maria Lee Hoon Ng, and Freda Wolfenden. Additionally, we give special thanks to Marshall Smith and the other volume contributors who provided excellent feedback during the chapter's development, to J. Lynn Fraser for her attentive copyediting, and to the volume editors, Ruhiya Kristine Seward and Matthew Smith, for their careful and insightful comments.

Notes

1. See Creative Commons (n.d.).

2. See ROER4D (2018).

3. See William and Flora Hewlett Foundation (2018).

4. Emphasis in bold, as in the original.

5. See World Health Organization (2018).

6. See United Nations (n.d.).

7. See Darakht-e Danesh Library (n.d.).

8. See TESSA (n.d.).

9. See Siyavula (n.d.).

10. See "Mind the Gap Study Guide" (http://www.education.gov.za/Curriculum/LearningandTea chingSupportMaterials(LTSM)/MindtheGapStudyGuides.aspx).

11. See Proyecto de Co-Creación Colaborativa de Recursos Educativos Abiertos (REA). n.d.

References

Beetham, Helen I., Isobel Falconer, Lou McGill, and Allison Littlejohn. 2012. "Open Practices: Briefing Paper." Jisc, 2012. https://oersynth.pbworks.com/w/page/51668352/OpenPracticesBriefing.

Bonami, Beatrice, and Maria L. Tubio. 2015. "Digital Inclusion, Crowdfunding, and Crowdsourcing in Brazil: A Brief Review." In *Handbook to Comparative Approaches in the Digital Age Revolution in Europe and the Americas* (A volume in the Advances in Electronic Government, Digital Divide, and Regional Development ((AEGDDRD) Book Series), ed. Brasilina Passarelli, Joseph Straubhaar, and Aurora Cuevas-Cerveró, 77–100. Hershey, PA: Information Science Reference (IGI Global). https://www.igi-global.com/chapter/digital-inclusion-crowdfunding-and-crowdsourcing-in-brazil /138027.

Central Intelligence Agency (CIA). 2016. *CIA World Factbook*. https://www.cia.gov/library/publications/the-world-factbook/rankorder/2004rank.html.

Comaroff, Jean, and John L. Comaroff, 2012. "Theory from the South: Or, How Euro-America is Evolving toward Africa." *Anthropological Forum* 22 (2): 113–131.

Connell, Raewyn W. 2007. *Southern Theory: The Global Dynamics of Knowledge in Social Science*. Cambridge, UK: Polity.

Conole, Grainne C., and Ulf-Daniels Ehlers. 2010. "Open Educational Practices: Unleashing the Power of OER." Paper presented to UNESCO Workshop on OER in Namibia 2010. Windhoek, Namibia. https://oerknowledgecloud.org/sites/oerknowledgecloud.org/files/OEP_Unleashing-the-power-of-OER.pdf.

Cooper, David. 2009. "University-Civil Society (U-CS) Research Relationships: The Importance of a 'Fourth Helix' Alongside the 'Triple Helix' of University-Industry-Government (U-I-G) Relations." *South African Review of Sociology* 40 (2): 153–180.

Cox, Glenda. 2016. "Explaining the Relations between Culture, Structure and Agency in Lecturers' Contribution and Non-contribution to Open Educational Resources in a Higher Education Institution." PhD thesis, University of Cape Town, South Africa. http://open.uct.ac.za/handle/11427/20300.

Cox, Glenda, and Henry Trotter. 2016. "Institutional Culture and OER Policy: How Structure, Culture, and Agency Mediate OER Policy Potential in South African Universities." *International Review of Research in Open and Distributed Learning* 17 (5). https://doi.org/10.19173/irrodl.v17i5.2523.

Cox, Glenda, and Henry Trotter. 2017. "Factors Shaping Lecturers' Adoption of OER at Three South African Universities." In *Adoption and Impact of OER in the Global South*, ed. Cheryl Hodgkinson-Williams and Patricia B. Arinto, 287–347. Cape Town, South Africa/Ottawa: African Minds/IDRC; Cape Town, South Africa: Research on Open Educational Resources for Development. https://www.idrc.ca/en/book/adoption-and-impact-oer-global-south.

Creative Commons. n.d. "Creative Commons." https://creativecommons.org/.

Cronin, Catherine. 2017. "Openness and Praxis: Exploring the Use of Open Educational Practices in Higher Education." *International Review of Research in Open and Distributed Learning* 18 (5): 15–34. http://www.irrodl.org/index.php/irrodl/article/view/3096.

Czerniewicz, Laura. 2016. "Student Practices in Copyright Culture: Accessing Learning Resources." *Learning, Media, and Technology* 42 (4): 1–84. http://www.tandfonline.com/doi/full/10.1080/17439884.2016.1160928.

Czerniewicz, Laura, Andrew Deacon, Sukaina Walji, and Michael Glover. 2017. "OER in and as MOOCs." In *Adoption and Impact of OER in the Global South*, ed. Cheryl Hodgkinson-Williams and Patricia B. Arinto, 349–386. Cape Town, South Africa/Ottawa: African Minds/IDRC; Cape Town, South Africa: Research on Open Educational Resources for Development. https://www.idrc.ca/en/book/adoption-and-impact-oer-global-south.

Daniel, John, Asha Kanwar, and Stamenka Uvalić-Trumbić. 2009. "Breaking Higher Education's Iron Triangle: Access, Cost, and Quality." *Change: The Magazine of Higher Learning* 41 (2): 30–35.

Darakht-e Danesh Library. n.d. "Home Page." http://www.darakhtdanesh.org/.

de Oliveira Neto, José D., and Tess Cartmill. 2017. "OER Adoption by Higher Education Instructors and Students in the Global South." *ROER4D* (blog), November 16. http://roer4d.org/3305.

de Oliveira Neto, José D., Judith Pete, Daryono, and Tess Cartmill. 2017. "OER Use in the Global South: A Baseline Survey of Higher Education Instructors." In *Adoption and Impact of OER in the Global South*, ed. Cheryl Hodgkinson-Williams and Patricia B. Arinto, 69–118. Cape Town, South Africa/Ottawa: African Minds/IDRC; Cape Town, South Africa: Research on Open Educational Resources for Development. https://www.idrc.ca/en/book/adoption-and-impact-oer -global-south.

Dutta, Indrajeet. 2016. "Open Educational Resources (OER): Opportunities and Challenges for Indian Higher Education." *Turkish Online Journal of Distance Education* 17 (2): 110–121.

Ehlers, Ulf-Daniel. 2011. "From Open Educational Resources to Open Educational Practices." *E-learning Papers* 23: 1–8. https://www.researchgate.net/publication/260423349_Extending_the _territory_From_open_educational_resources_to_open_educational_practices.

Gidley, Jennifer, Gary Hampson, Leone Wheeler, and Elleni Bereded-Samuel. 2010. "Social Inclusion: Context, Theory, and Practice." *Australasian Journal of University-Community Engagement* 5 (1): 6–36. https://researchbank.rmit.edu.au/view/rmit:4909.

Goodier, Sarah. 2017. "Tracking the Money for Open Educational Resources in South African Basic Education: What We Don't Know." *International Review of Research in Open and Distributed Learning* 18 (4): 16–34. http://dx.doi.org/10.19173/irrodl.v18i4.2990.

Hegarty, Bronwyn. 2015. "Attributes of Open Pedagogy: A Model for Using Open Educational Resources." *Educational Technology* (July–August): 3–13. https://upload.wikimedia.org/wikipedia /commons/c/ca/Ed_Tech_Hegarty_2015_article_attributes_of_open_pedagogy.pdf.

Hodgkinson-Williams, Cheryl. 2014. "Degrees of Ease: Adoption of OER, Open Textbooks, and MOOCs in the Global South." Keynote address at the OER Asia Symposium 2014, Penang, Malaysia, June. https://www.slideshare.net/ROER4D/hodgkinson-williams-2014-oer-asia.

Hodgkinson-Williams, Cheryl, and Patricia B. Arinto, eds. 2017. *Adoption and Impact of OER in the Global South*. Cape Town, South Africa/Ottawa: African Minds/IDRC; Cape Town, South Africa: Research on Open Educational Resources for Development. https://idl-bnc-idrc.dspacedirect.org /bitstream/handle/10625/56823/IDL-56823.pdf?sequence=2&isAllowed=y.

Hodgkinson-Williams, Cheryl, Patricia B. Arinto, Tess Cartmill, and Thomas King. 2017. "Factors Influencing Open Educational Practices and OER in the Global South: Meta-synthesis of the ROER4D Project." In *Adoption and Impact of OER in the Global South*, ed. Cheryl Hodgkinson-Williams and Patricia B. Arinto, 27–67. Cape Town, South Africa/Ottawa: African Minds/IDRC; Cape Town, South Africa: Research on Open Educational Resources for Development. https:// www.idrc.ca/en/book/adoption-and-impact-oer-global-south.

Hodgkinson-Williams, Cheryl, and Michael Paskevicius, 2012. "The Role of Post-graduate Students in Co-authoring Open Educational Resources to Promote Social Inclusion: A Case Study at the University of Cape Town." *Distance Education* 33 (2): 253–269. http://dx.doi.org/10.1080 /01587919.2012.692052.

Karunanayaka, Shironica P., and Som Naidu. 2017. "Impact of Integrating OER in Teacher Education at the Open University of Sri Lanka." In *Adoption and Impact of OER in the Global South*, ed. Cheryl Hodgkinson-Williams and Patricia B. Arinto, 459–498. Cape Town, South Africa/Ottawa: African Minds/IDRC; Cape Town, South Africa: Research on Open Educational Resources for Development. https://www.idrc.ca/en/book/adoption-and-impact-oer-global-south.

Karunanayaka, Shironica P., Som Naidu, Joseph C. N. Rajendra, and Hemali U. Ratnayake. 2015. "From OER to OEP: Shifting Practitioner Perspectives and Practices with Innovative Learning Experience Design." *Open Praxis* 7 (4): 339–350.

Kasinathan, Gurumurthy. 2016. "Scaling Open Education Resource-Based Teacher Professional Development in India." Unpublished technical report. Cape Town, South Africa: Research on Open Educational Resources for Development (ROER4D) project, August 5.

Kasinathan, Gurumurthy, and Sriranjani Ranganathan. 2017. "Teacher Professional Learning Communities: A Collaborative OER Adoption Approach in Karnataka, India." In *Adoption and Impact of OER in the Global South*, ed. Cheryl Hodgkinson-Williams and Patricia B. Arinto, 499–548. Cape Town, South Africa/Ottawa: African Minds/IDRC; Cape Town, South Africa: Research on Open Educational Resources for Development. https://www.idrc.ca/en/book/adoption-and -impact-oer-global-south.

Knox, Jeremy. 2013. "Five Critiques of the Open Educational Resources Movement." *Teaching in Higher Education* 18 (8): 821–32.

Lane, Andy. 2012. "A Review of the Role of National Policy and Institutional Mission in European Distance Teaching Universities with Respect to Widening Participation in Higher Education Study through Open Educational Resources." *Distance Education* 33 (2): 135–150.

McGreal, Rory, Dianne Conrad, Angela Murphy, Gabi Witthaus, and Wayne Mackintosh. 2014. "Formalising Informal Learning: Assessment and Accreditation Challenges within Disaggregated Systems." *Open Praxis* 6 (2): 125–133. https://openpraxis.org/index.php/OpenPraxis/article/download /114/88.

Menon, Mohandas B., Bhandigadi Phalachandra, Jasmine S. Emmanuel, and Ch'ng Lay Kee. 2017. "A Study on the Processes of OER Integration for Course Development." Unpublished final research report. Cape Town, South Africa: Research on Open Educational Resources for Development (ROER4D) project, November 7.

Mishra, Sanjaya. 2017. *Promoting Use and Contribution of Open Educational Resources*. New Delhi: Commonwealth Educational Media Centre for Asia (CEMCA). http://oasis.col.org/handle/11599/2659.

Mishra, Sanjaya, and Alka Singh. 2017. "Higher Education Faculty Attitude, Motivation and Perception of Quality and Barriers towards OER in India." In *Adoption and Impact of OER in the Global South*, ed. Cheryl Hodgkinson-Williams and Patricia B. Arinto, 425–458. Cape Town, South Africa/

Ottawa: African Minds/IDRC; Cape Town, South Africa: Research on Open Educational Resources for Development. https://www.idrc.ca/en/book/adoption-and-impact-oer-global-south.

Mkandawire, Thandika. 2011. "Running While Others Walk: Knowledge and the Challenge of Africa's Development." *African Development* 36 (2): 1–36.

Oates, Lauryn, Letha K. Goger, Jamshid Hashimi, and Mubaraka Farahmand. 2017. "An Early Stage Impact Study of Localised OER in Afghanistan." In *Adoption and Impact of OER in the Global South*, ed. Cheryl Hodgkinson-Williams and Patricia B. Arinto, 549–73. Cape Town, South Africa/ Ottawa: African Minds/IDRC; Cape Town, South Africa: Research on Open Educational Resources for Development. https://www.idrc.ca/en/book/adoption-and-impact-oer-global-south.

Okada, Alexandra, Alexander Mikroyannidis, Izabel Meister, and Suzanne Little. 2012. "'Colearning'— Collaborative Networks for Creating, Sharing and Reusing OER through Social Media." In *Cambridge 2012: Innovation and Impact—Openly Collaborating to Enhance Education*, April 16–18, Cambridge, UK: The Open University. http://oro.open.ac.uk/33750/2/59B2E252.pdf.

Organisation for Economic Co-operation and Development (OECD). 2007. *Giving Knowledge for Free: The Emergence of Open Educational Resources*. Paris: Centre for Educational Research and Innovation; Organisation for Economic Co-operation and Development. http://www.oecd.org/edu /ceri/38654317.pdf.

Perryman, Leigh-Anne, and Tony Coughlan. 2013. "The Realities of 'Reaching Out': Enacting the Public-Facing Open Scholar Role with Existing Online Communities." *Journal of Interactive Media in Education*.3.

Peters, Michael A., and Tina A. C. Besley. 2014. "Social Exclusion/Inclusion: Foucault's Analytics of Exclusion, the Political Ecology of Social Inclusion, and the Legitimation of Inclusive Education." *Open Review of Educational Research* 1 (1): 95–115. http://www.tandfonline.com/doi/full/10 .1080/23265507.2014.972439.

Proyecto de Co-Creación Colaborativa de Recursos Educativos Abiertos (REA). n.d. "Banco de REA." https://karisma.org.co/cokrea/?page_id=1079.

Research on Open Educational Resources for Development (ROER4D). 2018. "ROER4D Overview." ROER4D.org.

Richter, Thomas. 2010. "Open Educational Resources im kulturellen Kontext von e-Learning. Zeitschrift für E-Learning" (ZeL), Freie elektronische Bildungsressourcen." *Journal for e-Learning, Open Educational Resources* (Special Issue) 3 (September): 30–42.

Richter, Thomas, and Maggie A. McPherson. 2012. "Open Educational Resources: Education for the World?" *Distance Education* 33 (2): 201–219.

Sáenz, Maria P., Ulises Hernandez, and Yoli M. Hernández. 2017. "Co-creation of OER by Teachers and Teacher Educators in Colombia." In *Adoption and Impact of OER in the Global South*, ed. Cheryl Hodgkinson-Williams and Patricia B. Arinto, 143–185. Cape Town, South Africa/Ottawa: African Minds/IDRC; Cape Town, South Africa: Research on Open Educational Resources for Development. https://www.idrc.ca/en/book/adoption-and-impact-oer-global-south.

Scruggs, Thomas E., Margo A. Mastropieri, and Kimberley A. McDuffie. 2007. "Co-teaching in Inclusive Classrooms: A Metasynthesis of Qualitative Research." *Exceptional Children* 73 (4): 392–416. http://www.schoolturnaroundsupport.org/sites/default/files/resources/Scrugg_2007.pdf.

Siyavula, n.d. Siyavula: Technology Powered Learning. https://www.siyavula.com/.

Smith, Marshall S. 2014. "Open Educational Resources: Opportunities and Challenges for the Developing World." In *Open Development: Networked Innovations in International Development*, ed. Matthew L. Smith and Katherine M. A. Reilly, 129–179. Cambridge, MA/Ottawa: MIT Press/IDRC. https://www.idrc.ca/sites/default/files/openebooks/541-1/index.html#ch06.

Smith, Marshall S., and Catherine M. Casserly. 2006. "The Promise of Open Educational Resources." *Change: The Magazine of Higher Learning* 38 (5): 8–17. https://www.hewlett.org/wp-content/uploads/2016/08/ChangeArticle.pdf.

Teacher Education in Sub-Saharan Africa (TESSA). n.d. http://www.tessafrica.net/.

Toledo, Amalia. 2017. "Open Access and OER in Latin America: A Survey of the Policy Landscape in Chile, Colombia, and Uruguay." In *Adoption and Impact of OER in the Global South*, ed. Cheryl A. Hodgkinson-Williams and Patricia B. Arinto, 121–141. Cape Town, South Africa/Ottawa: African Minds/IDRC; Cape Town, South Africa: Research on Open Educational Resources for Development. https://idl-bnc-idrc.dspacedirect.org/bitstream/handle/10625/56823/IDL-56823.pdf?sequence=2&isAllowed=y.

Trotter, Henry. 2016. "How Intellectual Property (IP) Policies Affect OER Creation at South African Universities." *ROER4D* (blog), June 1. http://roer4d.org/2298.

United Nations. n.d. "Goal 2: Achieve Universal Primary Education." (website). "We Can End Poverty. Millennium Development Goals and Beyond 2015." http://www.un.org/millenniumgoals/education.shtml.

Walji, Sukaina, and Cheryl A. Hodgkinson-Williams. 2017. "Factors Enabling and Constraining OER Adoption and Open Education Practices: Lessons from the ROER4D Project." Slide presentation at World Conference for Online Learning, Toronto, October 15–19. https://www.slideshare.net/ROER4D/factors-enabling-and-constraining-oer-adoption-and-open-education-practices-lessons-from-the-roer4d-project.

Waqar, Yasira, Sana Shams, Naveed Malik, Muhammad Ahsan ul Haq, and Syed M. M. Raza. 2017. "An Exploratory Case Study: Enabling and Inhibiting Factors and Extent of Use of Open Educational Resources (OER) in Pakistan." Unpublished final research report. Penang, Malaysia: Research on Open Educational Resources for Development (ROER4D) Project, February 7.

Weller, Martin. 2013. "The Battle for Open–A Perspective." *Journal of Interactive Media in Education* (3). https://www-jime.open.ac.uk/articles/10.5334/2013-15/.

Westermann Juárez, Werner, and Juan Ignacio Venegas Muggli. 2017. "Effectiveness of OER Use in First Year Higher Education Students' Mathematical Course Performance: A Case Study." In *Adoption and Impact of OER in the Global South*, ed. Cheryl Hodgkinson-Williams and Patricia B. Arinto, 187–229. Cape Town, South Africa/Ottawa: African Minds/IDRC; Cape Town, South

Africa: Research on Open Educational Resources for Development. https://www.idrc.ca/en/book/adoption-and-impact-oer-global-south.

White, David, and Marion Manton. 2011. *Open Educational Resources: The Value of Reuse in Higher Education.* Oxford: University of Oxford. http://www.jisc.ac.uk/media/documents/programmes/elearning/oer/OERTheValueOfReuseInHigherEducation.pdf.

Wiley, David. 2014. "Clarifying the 5th R." *Iterating Toward Openness* (blog), March 15. https://opencontent.org/blog/archives/3251.

Wiley, David, Cable Green, and Louis Soares. 2012. "Dramatically Bringing Down the Cost of Education with OER: How Open Education Resources Unlock the Door to Free Learning." Colorado: Educause Center for American Progress. https://library.educause.edu/resources/2012/2/dramatically-bringing-down-the-cost-of-education-with-oer-how-open-education-resources-unlock-the-door-to-free-learning.

Willems, Julie A., and Carina Bossu. 2012. "Equity Considerations for Open Educational Resources in the Glocalization of Education." *Distance Education* 33 (2): 185–199.

William and Flora Hewlett Foundation. 2018. "Open Educational Resources: Overview." http://www.hewlett.org/strategy/open-educational-resources/.

Wolfenden, Freda, Pritee Auckloo, Allison Buckler, and Jane Cullen. 2017. "Teacher Educators and OER in East Africa: Interrogating Pedagogic Change." In *Adoption and Impact of OER in the Global South*, ed. Cheryl Hodgkinson-Williams and Patricia B. Arinto, 251–286. Cape Town, South Africa/Ottawa: African Minds/IDRC; Cape Town, South Africa: Research on Open Educational Resources for Development. https://www.idrc.ca/en/book/adoption-and-impact-oer-global-south.

World Bank. 2013. *Inclusion Matters: The Foundation for Shared Prosperity.* New Frontiers of Social Policy 81478. Washington, DC: World Bank. http://documents.worldbank.org/curated/en/114561468154469371/pdf/814780PUB0Incl00Box379838B00PUBLIC0.pdf.

World Health Organization. 2018. "Social Determinants of Health: Social Inclusion." Geneva, Switzerland: World Health Organization (WHO). http://www.who.int/social_determinants/themes/socialexclusion/en/.

Zagdragchaa, Batbold, and Henry Trotter. 2017. "Cultural-Historical Factors Influencing OER Adoption in Mongolia's Higher Education Sector." In *Adoption and Impact of OER in the Global South*, ed. Cheryl Hodgkinson-Williams and Patricia B. Arinto, 389–424. Cape Town, South Africa/Ottawa: African Minds/IDRC; Cape Town, South Africa: Research on Open Educational Resources for Development. https://www.idrc.ca/en/book/adoption-and-impact-oer-global-south.

13   Toward an Inclusive, Open, and Collaborative Science: Lessons from OCSDNet

Rebecca Hillyer, Denisse Albornoz, Alejandro Posada, Angela Okune, and Leslie Chan

Introduction

The idea of *open science* has gained momentum over the past few years, emerging along-side other open initiatives—including open access, open government, open source, open data, and others (Bartling and Friesike 2014). A common conception of open science is the opening of the entire research cycle, from designing the question and methods, to collecting and analyzing data, through to the communication and dissemination of the findings (Fecher and Friesike 2014; Nielsen 2013). In principle, these practices allow increased transparency of scientific processes, as well as the expansion of participation in and opportunities for diverse forms of knowledge production. As such, open science provides a key opportunity to critically reflect on who is involved in knowledge-making processes, what tools are used, and what forms of knowledge are being produced and legitimized. Ultimately, open science provides a unique lens for understanding how science could be made fairer to and more inclusive of groups and worldviews that have been previously marginalized from scientific discourses.

Despite this potential, the majority of action and discussion on open science has been dominated by actors and institutions in the Global North, with a tendency to concentrate on the tools, infrastructure, and cost models of producing knowledge openly (OECD 2015; Orth, Pontika, and Ball 2016; Schmidt et al. 2016), with less focus on the underlying power structures that tend to determine who can or cannot participate in knowledge-production processes, and for what aims (Chan et al. 2015; Czerniewicz 2015; Graham, Sabbata, and Zook 2015; Moletsane 2015; Okune et al. 2016; see also chapter 5 in this volume). In such a framing, openness has become a universal set of technical requirements and standards to be met,[1] rather than a dynamic process of negotiation between knowledge producers within particular social, historical, and institutional contexts.

The Open and Collaborative Science in Development Network (OCSDNet) is an international research network launched in 2015 to address the fundamental question of whether and how open science has the potential to contribute to the achievement of development goals and opportunities (Chan et al. 2015; Chan et al. 2019). Funded by Canada's International Development Research Centre (IDRC) and the UK's Department for International Development (DFID), with coordination support from iHub[2] (based in Kenya) and the University of Toronto, OCSDNet is composed of twelve international research teams[3] throughout Latin America, Africa, the Middle East, and Asia. The teams are composed of individuals with highly diverse academic and practical backgrounds, including in law, art, education, climate change, the maker movement, intellectual property rights, biodiversity, health, and environmental conservation. Over the course of two years, and using an array of diverse research methods, each team explored the challenges and opportunities for imagining science as open and collaborative, as well as the potential of open science to contribute toward inclusive and sustainable development in their local contexts.

OCSDNet recognizes that in recent history, the processes of knowledge production and dissemination have been shaped and solidified by a privileged and exclusive set of actors who have influenced how the world understands valid and legitimate scientific knowledge and research. This limited representation of knowledge has led to an incomplete and distorted understanding of the world and the issues affecting local populations (Moletsane 2015; Sillitoe 2007). Unchallenged, this system will continue to entrench knowledge and research inequalities and will have serious consequences for sustainable and equitable development (Hall and Tandon 2017a).

This chapter synthesizes the lessons from the twelve projects within the network, which have shaped how the OCSDNet members have reimagined the potential of open science to transform knowledge production and contribute to sustainable development. It is important to note the diversity of projects across the network. Some projects have contributed to the practice of open science at the grassroots level by implementing small-scale citizen science projects at the community level. Other projects have contributed to reimagining the field through case-study analysis of existing, longer-term open science initiatives by unpacking the challenges and social tensions that can arise as openness scales up within or between institutions and their networks. Finally, other research teams have applied network-defined open science principles within their unique contexts to develop new tools and frameworks for understanding how open science contributes to complex development and societal challenges.

The chapter begins with a discussion of the network's background, including the methodologies that have guided the research conducted between 2015 and 2017. This is followed by an overview of how individual projects have contributed to coconstructing a new and more nuanced understanding of open science. Through the application of a contextualized or situated approach to defining and practicing open science, the chapter concludes with key lessons for making the theory and practice of open science more amenable to a diverse set of actors and epistemic traditions in the achievement of development objectives.

Conceptual Framework and Methodologies of OCSDNet

The initial research questions for the network were based on the Institutional Analysis and Development (IAD) framework developed by Elinor Ostrom and her colleagues, which is grounded in the assumption that knowledge is a common community resource.[4] Ostrom's work challenged conventional wisdom around the need for government regulation of public resources (such as forests and fisheries) in order to attain sustainability and benefit sharing, highlighting that communities often formulate their own rules and procedures for governing shared resources without top-down intervention (Ostrom 1991, 2005).

More recently, the IDA framework has been applied to knowledge as a commons that cuts across national and disciplinary boundaries (Hess 2012; Hess and Ostrom 2005), which makes it distinct from natural resources. Frischmann, Madison, and Strandburg (2014) developed a "knowledge commons framework" to aid researchers with empirical research on different forms of commons. The concept of the commons also includes open-source commons (Schweik and English 2012), art commons (Guayasamín and José 2014), and medical knowledge commons (Strandburg et al. 2017). The revised framework provides guiding research questions around the types of communities, the resources in use, the existing institutional arrangements, and the interactions that take place within the community. These questions were used and adapted by OCSDNet projects to structure data collection activities, and also provided valuable information about how different groups, institutions, and cultures might implement principles of openness differently.[5]

The bulk of the data collected from OCSDNet projects came from monthly and annual reports, project publications, interviews with team members, and group discussions throughout the funding cycle of the network. However, less structured observations around team and network working dynamics were drawn from exchanges within a closed Google Group[6] established for network communication, as well as from discussions on social media (e.g., Facebook groups and Twitter), while also including participation in various public speaking forums, including academic conferences. Project teams were encouraged to share events, resources, and best practices as part of the field and network-building exercises.[7]

OCSDNet also explored the potential of participatory, consensus-building exercises through the design of an *OCSDNet Manifesto*, which consolidates the shared values and understanding of the importance of open and collaborative science to scientific research and development.[8] These discussions and the subsequent seven open science principles that were developed have influenced the way that projects assess their findings and ways of working.

OCSDNet's diverse geographies, skill sets, and epistemologies required a different kind of rigour (Chambers 2017, 91) beyond a Newtonian cause-and-effect epistemology that anticipates predictable, linear change. "Inclusive rigour" (Chambers 2017, 94) acknowledges the complexity of research for development and focuses on "critical observation and analysis of the processes of knowledge formation, including distortions resulting from power relations...positionality, relationships, and interactions" (Chambers 2017, 98). The core concepts of this approach include eclectic methodological pluralism, diversity and balance, improvisation and innovation, adaptive iteration, triangulation, and inclusive participation for plural perspectives. OCSDNet employed this approach in its analysis to uncover themes and ideas and to allow a broader comparison among diverse and complex projects. As a result, the cases reveal innovative ways that open science principles can be applied to complex development questions and scenarios, and also include the sociocultural contexts that enable (or curtail) open science as an effective approach for achieving sustainable development objectives.

Furthermore, OCSDNet members broadly agreed on a notion of development that builds on Appadurai's (2006) "Right to Research," which acknowledges that all humans have the capacity to imagine their own knowledge and future. This echoes Amartya Sen's Capabilities Approach, which suggests that human development is the process of enlarging a person's "functionings and capabilities to function, the range of things that a person could do and be in her life," expressed in terms of one's agency to exercise "choice" (Sen 1989, 48). A primary goal of development is thus to improve human lives by expanding the range of things that a person can be and do, such as to be well nourished and healthy, to be knowledgeable by taking part in *making* knowledge, and to participate actively in community life. In this regard, the Latin American and Indigenous tradition of *buen vivir*[9] (meaning "good living" in Spanish) and the African concept of Ubuntu (which celebrates the strength of humans working and living in community with one another) both informed the network's conceptual framework (Dolamo 2013).

OCSDNet also recognized that inclusivity and cognitive justice are both key for open science and to achieve development objectives that are fair and meaningful for a broad array of groups, particularly those who have been historically marginalized in knowledge-creation processes. Inclusivity is actualized through questioning and reflection, and cognitive justice "demands recognition of knowledges, not only as methods but as ways of life" (De Sousa Santos 2014; Visvanathan 2009), to ensure that all people have the right to access and create locally relevant knowledge with epistemologies, tools, and modes of collaboration of their choice.

Taken together, these ideas comprise a framework of inclusive development that positions human beings as agents working toward common goals, using tools and forms of knowledge that are most relevant to their unique sociocultural contexts.[10] It is in this context that we assess whether the practice of open and collaborative science has the potential to achieve positive development outcomes.

The next section will discuss key findings from the twelve individual research projects. The intention is to frame open science beyond the tools and cost models commonly associated with working openly.

Findings from OCSDNet Projects

The diversity of the network afforded a unique opportunity to interrogate the manifestation of open science practices ranging from the grassroots community level to the institutional, national, and regional levels. While some teams sought to implement practical, hands-on open science projects with tangible development outcomes for local communities, others analyzed and documented the challenges and implications of existing, longer-term open science initiatives, or developed new tools, modes of collaboration, and theoretical frameworks that explore open science as an inclusive approach to development. As such, the projects have been divided into three categories, with the intention of viewing open science from the perspective of (1) the local grassroots level, using an insider approach (four projects); (2) the metalevel outsider view to understand the challenges of scaling and sustaining larger open science projects (two projects); and (3) by exploring the potential of open science principles in the creation of new tools and frameworks for addressing local development issues (six projects).

Practicing Open Science at the Grassroots Level

Grassroots development refers to development activities driven by local communities. It facilitates a bottom-up approach to development, which allows ordinary people to be directly involved in activities meant to improve their lives (Escobar 1992). OCSDNet borrows from grassroots development because it is similar to the localized and small-scale citizen science initiatives that exist in four of the projects, which allowed people to initiate, manage, and assess community-based open science initiatives with minimal funding and in a relatively short time frame. They permit a unique, insider perspective regarding the day-to-day negotiations and complexities associated with the practice of open science, as well as a chance to compare dilemmas and opportunities across contexts. Most important, they provide the opportunity to assess whether the small-scale, open science project approach could have positive implications for sustainable community development.

All four projects in table 13.1 position citizen science as central to their respective methodologies and conceptual frameworks. In general, *citizen science* refers to "the involvement of the public in scientific research—whether community-driven research or global investigations" (Citizen Science Association 2017).[11] Although numerous forms of citizen science may have important outcomes for knowledge production and development, they do not always acknowledge members of the public as local experts or co-researchers who could provide valuable insight during all stages of the research cycle.

All four projects use participatory action research (PAR) methodologies in their research design and data collection.[12] PAR methodologies tend to position citizens as local experts who are likely to be involved in all (or many) stages of the research cycle that include the identification of local challenges, research design, data collection, analysis, implementation, and communication of results. Within OCSDNet, there is a

Table 13.1
Practicing open science at the grassroots level.

OCSDNet project name	Keywords
Water quality and social transformation in rural Kyrgyzstan	citizen science, environmental conservation, Kyrgyzstan, open science motivation, participatory action research, rural communities, water quality, students, teachers
Community-driven environmental conservation in Costa Rica and Colombia	adaptive capacity, biodiversity, citizen science, Colombia, Costa Rica, human capabilities, Model Forests, participatory action research, sustainable development
Water quality and community development in Lebanon	bottom-up policymaking, citizen science, community-based environmental management, empowering conservation, Lebanon, participatory action research, water quality
Open science hardware for development in Southeast Asia	citizen science, do-it-yourself, Indonesia, little science, Nepal, open science hardware, participation, right to science, Southeast Asia, Thailand, tinkering, tools, transnational networks

strong overlap between the use of PAR methodologies and the intentional practice of citizen science and, as a result, citizen scientists involved in network projects were often engaged in various capacities throughout stages of the research cycle. For instance, in Kyrgyzstan, the OCSDNet research team worked with rural schoolteachers and students to design an experiment for testing local water quality after communities acknowledged that water pollution was a significant issue in the area. This was not a simple act of designing and rolling out an experiment, but instead involved complex discussions with teachers, students, and research organizations that focused on who should be able to participate in scientific knowledge production, and for what purposes. Throughout the project, teachers and students began to redefine their ideas of who a scientist is and what scientific research could entail.

This was similar to the research team in Lebanon, which recruited a group of local volunteers (all of whom were women) to conduct water-quality testing in fifty rural villages. After intensive training to equip them to use specialized tools, the women located problematic wells and conducted water-quality analysis. Through these activities, not only did these citizen scientists feel more informed about water issues in their respective areas, they felt empowered to begin making demands on the government to pay attention to water-quality issues.

In the case of the projects based in Costa Rica and Colombia, citizen science was negotiated differently. Here, the team sought to bring together local community members and academic researchers to discuss and negotiate how the Model Forest[13] approach to sustainable development could be adapted in the context of open science. Input from both parties was used to construct opportunities for collaboration and knowledge-sharing to achieve local development goals. In the end, seven new, community-based open science initiatives were devised around the theme of local adaptation to climate change, including a farming agroecology network, a rainwater harvesting program, a tree nursery, and ecotourism awareness.

For the fourth project based in Southeast Asia, a more subtle version of citizen science was enacted in order to facilitate and assess project activities, through what the team refers to as *small science*. This team built on the practice and philosophy of the increasingly popular global maker movement and hacker communities, which position the creative building and codesign of tangible tools and processes for innovative problem-solving. Using these concepts as a starting point, the team hosted four multiday workshops that brought together a diverse group of participants (including artists, designers, students, and teachers) to test opportunities for facilitating creative spaces, which would allow participants to identify and discuss issues of importance to the local communities, as well as the potential to develop strategic tools for addressing these challenges.

As a result of these exchanges, the team suggests that, within their context, open science could be imagined as a process of creative engagement among diverse participants, often without a tangible social or development objective in mind. One interesting cross-project outcome from these exchanges was the design and construction of a cost-effective microscope, which was taken up by the OCSDNet team in Kyrgyzstan for use in rural schools with underresourced science labs.

The first two projects in Kyrgyzstan and Lebanon highlight instances where, given the opportunity to participate in processes of creating and analyzing locally relevant knowledge, otherwise-marginalized communities used their knowledge to address a pertinent local challenge and altered the way that they feel about themselves as active and informed citizens within their communities. Additionally, given the notable voluntary participation from women (in Lebanon) and female schoolchildren (in Kyrgyzstan), the research suggests that a local, exploratory approach to open science could be a means for increasing the representation of women and girls in scientific initiatives.

Overall, the four projects highlight the nuances of positioning citizen science in the context of open science in development, the specifics of which vary depending on the theory of change used by the individual project. In all instances, the framing of who are citizen scientists and what role they play within a given project has important implications for assessing who has power within the scope of the research cycle, and hence who has the power to create relevant, local knowledge. To varying degrees, all four projects were designed to increase opportunities for regular citizens to participate in processes of knowledge creation and discussions that could have implications for influencing their lives. Importantly, each project sought to challenge the traditional idea of who constitutes a scientist and to reimagine the tools and processes required for legitimate scientific discovery and local innovation. Finally, all four projects position citizens as agents of change with important, preexisting expertise, rather than as mere volunteers involved in data collection for a preestablished project agenda.

These factors all demonstrate the ability to engage in inclusive open science. These projects worked with diverse actors who otherwise would tend not to be involved in the creation of scientific knowledge and/or would be unlikely, as defined experts, to be involved in knowledge creation with local communities. They were able to do so through collaboration and learning across disciplinary silos, and they do not follow the technocratic, instrumentalist, top-down route of previous development initiatives.

Analyzing Existing Open Science Projects

Two projects within OCSDNet sought to examine the challenges and opportunities for larger, complex, ongoing open science initiatives that extend beyond two to three years of funding. These projects provide insight into the complexities and longer-term

Table 13.2
Analyzing existing open science projects.

OCSDNet project name	Keywords
Evaluating open science e-infrastructure in Brazil	botany, Brazil, e-database, interdisciplinary collaboration, open science infrastructure, virtual herbarium
Negotiating open science in Argentina	Argentina, boundary objects, negotiating openness, opening process, open science

challenges of existing open science projects in the Global South, both for individuals and institutions, as well as the practical implications that these challenges could have for achieving sustainable development through the practice of open science.

In the Brazilian case study, shown in table 13.2, the research team sought to understand how and for what purpose diverse users were accessing a Brazilian-based, open access e-database, and documented any benefits to data providers. Known as a virtual herbarium, the open access database consists of pooled botany and fungi records from a large network of Brazilian research institutions. The initial idea behind the virtual herbarium was to create a centralized hub of information that could be easily accessed by any individual interested in research on Brazil's rich and diverse plant and fungi kingdoms. The herbarium was initiated in 2008 and is currently composed of 106 associated national herbaria, 25 herbaria from abroad, and 20 other herbaria that are not directly associated with the project but contribute their data through a shared provider. As a whole, the e-infrastructure combines over 5.5 million data records from 191 data sets and more than 1.4 million images (Canhos et al. 2015).

The OCSDNet research team recorded impressive results around the use of herbarium records, documenting not only the surprising frequency with which data is accessed and used (1.7 billion records were accessed between 2012 and 2017), but also the diversity of the users ranging from PhD, master's, and secondary school students, to government representatives, local research organizations, nongovernment organization (NGO) workers, and the private sector. Importantly, 94 percent of users were residents of Brazil, highlighting the immense importance of providing access to local knowledge through accessible, online tools in local languages.

Most surprising to the team were the complex negotiations and cultural shifts that occurred over the years that supported the project's success. For instance, the preliminary requirement for data providers was the complete openness of all data—but through a series of negotiations, this requirement changed to allow data providers flexibility in deciding which records would be made openly available and how. This was largely in response to one of the larger data providers, who felt that full data availability through the virtual herbarium reduced visitor traffic to its own site, hence diminishing its own reputation. At the same time, all decisions regarding the technological aspects of the network's architecture and e-infrastructure were left to those equipped with the relevant technical skills. It seems that it was important for key actors to have some degree of power over their contributions to maintaining the herbarium, while also having appropriately defined roles that allowed efficient, longer-term planning and governance of the infrastructure. Communication, transparency, and participation, according to the team, were indispensable for building trust, understanding, and ownership among all actors.

In the Argentinian study, the team assessed four locally initiated open science case studies encompassing a broad range of disciplines—namely, the New Argentinian Virtual Observatory (NOVA) (astronomy), Argentinian Project of Monitoring and Prospecting the Aquatic Environment (PAMPA2) (limnology), e-Bird Argentina (ornithology), and the Integrated Land Management Project (geography, chemistry, and environmental science). The team sought to understand what is being opened within the specific cases, how it is being opened, and who is participating in the opening process. They were particularly interested in understanding the consequences of scaling up open initiatives and how the transition from the laboratory to the institutional level occurs in practice, particularly because institutional models of open science do exist, but there is usually less emphasis on the initiation of openness at the laboratory level.

The team noted in its analysis that while the four Argentinian case studies employed different methodologies and actors for the collection of data, all strove to make collected data more accessible to the general public. Furthermore, their findings suggest that as each of the four open science case studies moved to a new phase of the research cycle (from project planning to data collection to analysis to dissemination), there was a need to reflect on and reconsider the tools, resources, and infrastructure required for each new phase. At these junctures, open scientists are forced to create and confront boundary objects (i.e., tools and/or forms of communication that allow for the translation of complex ideas across diverse communities). From a sociocultural perspective, this process puts new strains on open science practitioners, as each phase may entail new contradictions of (and hence negotiations with) traditional institutional norms and structures.[14]

Looking at both the Brazilian and Argentinian case studies, several key observations can be made regarding the complexities of sustainable, longer-term open science initiatives. First and foremost, effective open science is more than the design of new tools that allow easier collaboration among individuals. Instead, it demands complex negotiations around roles and responsibilities, principles and priorities, and timelines and resources. Second, open science practices require new and innovative thinking at each stage of the research cycle and reflection on how such practices may coincide with existing cultural and institutional norms. Third, from a practical perspective, large-scale initiatives also require a comprehensive consideration of long-term funding, particularly when multiple institutions are involved. Indeed, despite the success of the Brazilian virtual herbarium and its deployment since 2008, the infrastructure is still described as a project because the sustainability of funding is by no means a guarantee (Canhos et al. 2015).

Exploring the Potential of Open and Collaborative Science through New Tools and Frameworks

Other OCSDNet teams imagined the potential of open science through a variety of new tools and frameworks. Two teams drew on network principles of open science to create new, practical, and usable tools to negotiate complex development issues within their specific contexts, while four other teams used these principles to develop new ways of framing possibilities around open science to address particular local challenges (see table 13.3).

In the case of new, practical, and usable tools, the OCSDNet team in South Africa employed open science ideologies to negotiate a community-researcher contract to

Table 13.3
Exploring the potential of open science through new tools and frameworks.

OCSDNet project name	Keywords
Researcher contracts for Indigenous knowledge in South Africa	climate change, decolonizing research methodologies, Indigenous knowledge, intellectual property rights, research contract, South Africa, terra nullius
Disaster management tools for small island-states	design science, disaster recovery plans, knowledge broker artifact, regional collaboration, Small Island Developing States,
Commercialization and open science in Kenya	collaboration, commercialization, Kenya, IP laws, open science, private sector, research partnerships, universities
Sustainable development and the potential for open citizen science in Brazil	diverse actors, open science, participatory action research, social change, sustainable development, Ubatuba
Social problems and the potential of open science in Latin America	cognitive exploitation, collaborative science, Latin America, nonhegemonic countries, openness, social problems
Building open science social networks in West Africa and Haiti	cognitive justice, Haiti, open repository, open research, open science networks, participatory action research, science shops, West Africa

safeguard Indigenous communities' knowledge around climate change and adaptation. Originally, the team planned to investigate what climate knowledge exists within Indigenous communities (and hence what knowledge might be openly shared) to promote learning around adaptation to climate change. However, after becoming aware of the historical and present-day exploitation that tends to occur during research with Indigenous communities, the team shifted their focus to be more reflective of the community's needs. It developed an innovative research contract in close consultation with community members and legal professionals that could be used as a tool for negotiating community rights in all future knowledge collaborations (Traynor 2017).

Similarly, to address the challenges of limited resources for climate change adaptation and disaster response, the Caribbean-based OCSDNet project developed a *knowledge broker artifact* to facilitate and mainstream a common vocabulary across Small Island Developing States to improve collaboration during disaster-management responses. Using a design science[15] approach, the team engaged with diverse stakeholders to negotiate the creation of an *artifact* that could be used to plan and streamline a coordinated disaster response efficiently. Similar to other case studies, the team suggested that beyond the complex debates associated with developing shared terminologies, a more important challenge was in negotiating the diverse institutional and social arrangements among collaborating stakeholders.

Beyond tools, four other projects used case studies to examine the application of an open science research framework to various development challenges. In Kenya, the team sought to understand how open science may be harmonized with commercialization practices that tend to prioritize personal and intellectual property. The Brazilian team applied an open science lens to a complex social situation in Ubatuba to examine whether open science can facilitate the achievement of sustainable development outcomes across a range of actors and activities. The Kenyan example revealed the complexities of sustaining and scaling up open science initiatives in academic and policy environments that have ongoing relationships with the private sector, as these partnerships tend to value the protection of data and forms of collaboration that offer value for money. In particular in many southern global contexts, financially constrained research institutions face enormous pressure to procure research funding, often through systems of intellectual property (IP) protection, including copyright and patenting, and must actively pursue partnerships with the private sector. At the same time, the team found that most Kenyan institutions also use (where possible) open access tools such as repositories. These issues highlight the fact that institutional environments must be willing to embrace both open and closed systems of knowledge production.

In the Ubatuba case in Brazil, the team raised the fundamental question of development—*for whom?*—when determining to what extent open science can support sustainable development. The team looked at environmental conservation issues in Ubatuba by engaging stakeholders from diverse sectors, including policymakers, members of the private sector, community groups, and academics. The authors suggest that while open and collaborative science does create new spaces and methods for traditionally marginalized groups to engage in scientific discussions and local problem-solving, these spaces may be limited by top-down management cultures, particularly within policymaking contexts. Participatory management is key to allowing the communication of complex scientific ideas and for diverse audiences to engage in the creation of new, socially relevant scientific data.

The OCSDNet team based at the National Scientific and Technical Research Council (Spanish: *Consejo Nacional de Investigaciones Científicas y Técnicas*, CONICET) in Argentina selected four case studies in Latin America to explore the degree and varying outcomes of collaborative knowledge creation and knowledge use. In particular, the team sought to inquire whether the practice and intention of open science could be used to achieve social needs, particularly in the case of neglected socioscientific topics that are important to local communities but may not be viewed as worthy of investigation by mainstream knowledge makers (e.g., pharmaceutical companies) due to their low profit potential. Through their analysis, the team identified that drivers (i.e., the individuals or groups initially engaged in mobilizing scientific knowledge for particular outcomes) are the key to gauging the anticipated degree of openness within processes of knowledge production. For instance, in a case study examining research on Chagas disease (an understudied tropical disease that affects poor communities), the team identified traditional scientists as the primary drivers of knowledge creation. In turn, a case study on the Jáchal-Veladero mining controversy revealed citizen activists and community groups as the main producers and distributors of knowledge.

In the first instance, the degree of openness (in the sense of equitable distribution of, access to, and creation of relevant knowledge) was primarily limited to scientific experts in molecular biology. Even when the scientific publications and the genetic information about Chagas were made open, a high degree of technical competency was required in order to access the information and translate it into usable knowledge. In the case of the Jáchal-Veladero dispute, a more horizontal flow of knowledge and communication around the environmental pollution problem was possible because the primary driver of knowledge use was a coalition of local miners and community organizations who wanted the mine to be closed to stop cyanide leaching. In this case, they actively worked with experts who translated the technical reports into accessible knowledge so that citizens could use them for advocacy purposes.

Two other case studies were conducted by this Argentinian team. One involved conservation of the endangered jaguar in Argentina, and the other involved studies of migrant population in Mexico. In the conservation case, citizens were easily attracted to support such studies as data collectors as biodiversity efforts are relatively free from social conflict. In this case, both the citizen scientists and researchers see the jaguar as the benefactor of the knowledge being produced to address a local problem. Thus, there was no dispute over which knowledge mattered more. Further, in the case of the study of migrant issues in Mexico, the social scientists have to balance a number of delicate social political issues, as well as how migrants see their own positions and what they identified as challenges. As a result, the researchers were more reluctant to make their knowledge open.

These four case studies illustrate that the degree of openness of knowledge produced from research depends on the kinds of research being performed, who drives the research agenda, and, importantly, for whom the research is being performed. Thus, openness is situated and highly conditioned by the conditions of knowledge production.

Finally, using a network-building and advocacy approach with the assistance of social media tools, surveys, and workshops, another OCSDNet research team (Project SOHA) sought to define and promote open science and open access across a number of universities in French-speaking West Africa and Haiti. Considering the lack of access to academic journals experienced by many institutions within these regions, the team engaged university students and staff in discussions about access to research and the lack of representation of southern global (particularly French-speaking African and Haitian) researchers in the production of scientific knowledge. This group in particular engaged the idea of cognitive justice within the network—to challenge the colonial and neocolonial practices of erasure of local knowledge, and to advocate for the right of local citizens to participate in the creation of knowledge that is relevant to their own lives, experiences, and worldviews.

As a result of the extensive social network created across West Africa and Haiti, we have witnessed the emergence of several dynamic early-career researchers who have become local advocates of change within their respective countries and institutions. They have leveraged the importance of cognitive justice for Southern researchers and for *fair* open science within many international speaking forums. The project team also emphasized the importance of self-autonomy through do-it-yourself publishing and employing the methodologies of the open science hardware movement as a means for creating sustainable local development. Unlike other projects within the network, this action-oriented initiative is continually building its foundation and methodologies. What the project demonstrated is that shared values, through a commitment to claiming cognitive justice, is a precondition to local knowledge-making.

In this sense, the SOHA project is consistent with the first examples on the development of tools in South Africa and the Small Island Developing States, as they demonstrate that open science can be imagined as a loose ideology or mindset rather than a fixed set of practices or one-size-fits-all protocol. Imagining open science in this way allows flexibility in solving complex development challenges and issues. At the same time, this process of negotiation can be deeply complex and time consuming, particularly when working across heterogeneous communities with different sociocultural and institutional arrangements. By comparison, the Kenyan, Brazilian, and Argentinian case studies demonstrate the tensions that can emerge among various communities of knowledge actors, particularly those in pursuit of financial goals versus those concerned with social objectives. They highlight the importance of building partnerships across diverse sectors, with different actors involving complex negotiations that establish trust and defined roles for resource sharing to maximize the potential of open science in development.

Together, these six cases illustrate the power and complexity of multiactor collaborations, particularly in southern global contexts where independent institutions often lack sustained funding and resources but can nevertheless harness diverse skill sets to innovate. These projects provide grounded examples of how open science can be adapted and applied to promote new forms of collaboration, knowledge sharing, and innovation to be used to tackle a wide range of issues.

Cross-Cutting Lessons and Conclusions

Despite the diversity of these projects, an overlapping set of themes and conditions emerged across all or many of the projects. These themes highlight some important aspects to consider when implementing an inclusive open science agenda that aims to meet development goals.

First and foremost is the importance of *building a common language* among open science practitioners. As we have seen with the disaster management artifact in the Caribbean, the harmonization of open science and commercialization in Kenya, the virtual herbarium in Brazil, and the community conservation project in Colombia and Costa Rica, the engagement of diverse stakeholders in collaborative processes requires a deliberate and reflective process around shared principles and goals, to ensure that everyone is striving toward a common objective. Within the network, we found the creation of the *OCSDNet Manifesto*[16] was indispensable in this regard. The intense process of debate and cocreation has led to a shared set of values, the establishment of trust among members, and a common vocabulary through which to pursue and discuss network goals and objectives.

The second point is that *a contextual or situational framing of open science* is key to encouraging local buy-in and ownership of a project. As we have seen through the diversity of projects in the network, there is no one-size-fits-all approach to open science. It is, instead, a flexible concept that should be adapted to reflect local norms and realities. In this way, a contextual approach to open science is one that encourages the inclusion of diverse actors and ways of knowing and helps in the actualization of cognitive justice. For instance, the approach to openness in post-Soviet Kyrgyzstan (where democracy and collaboration are often viewed with suspicion) is quite different from the one employed in Brazil, where participatory spaces are built into the constitutional fabric of the country.

Third is the need to *be critical of the processes and the information to be shared* within the design and negotiation of open science architectures. Complete openness is not always feasible, nor is it desirable in all situations for historical or sociopolitical reasons or due to differing work priorities of diverse collaborators. Evidence of this was clearly demonstrated in the South African case, in which the team worked to safeguard the traditional knowledge of Indigenous communities; and in the Brazilian virtual herbarium project, which recognized that data providers should have a say in deciding which data are made openly accessible to the public. When contributors have no say in whether their data is made open or not, the result could be disempowering rather than empowering. This finding reinforces similar lessons drawn from openness activities in other domains (Smith and Reilly 2013).

Fourth is the *potential importance of an active civil society and pursuing open science goals that are relevant to larger populations.* For instance, the Ubatuba-Brazil team recognized the importance of community groups in terms of their intentional engagement with policymakers and the private sector to collaborate on development issues within the region, while the Argentinian team acknowledged the role of community activists as key drivers in the success of an antimining campaign in the region. While the involvement of civil society may not be a precursor for all open science objectives, it nonetheless has a key role to play in leveraging community issues and demanding knowledge resources and accountability from those in traditional positions of power.

The fifth point is that *understanding the feasibility of funding and timelines of that funding is critical to the success of larger, long-term open science projects.* Ambitious open science projects in southern global institutions have a vital role to play in providing the general public with knowledge and information that are useful for determining development priorities and local decision-making, but realistically, they are also constrained by lack of access to viable, long-term funding and resources. The project-based timelines of most funders make it difficult to plan and implement long-term, larger-scale open science initiatives that demand flexibility, reflection, and adaptation at all stages of the research cycle to tackle complex development challenges. Funding institutions interested in seeing a real impact around open science in development should take these considerations into account when defining their priorities and criteria for funding allotment.

The sixth point is that evidence from the network demonstrates the *value of collaboration across disciplines* for solving complex development challenges and practicing more inclusive forms of science. Our study suggests that the notion of open science has been underconceptualized and underproblematized. Hence, advocates and practitioners of open science must strive to work beyond their respective silos and explore relevant work that has been done in other domains. A considerable body of literature has been written since the 1970s about development, with lessons and best practices for facilitating inclusive and participatory processes of community engagement.[17] Likewise, gender and critical race theorists have produced highly relevant critiques of Western positivist science that must be taken into consideration for the development of a situated and inclusive open science (Haraway 2008; Harding 2006, 2015).

Seventh, and in a similar vein, there is a need for *increased interdisciplinary and cross-sector collaborative research, particularly between actors in the Global South*. As described throughout this chapter, collaboration, in a multitude of forms, is essential when combining open science and social needs. Whether this is at the local level, between teachers and students (as seen in Kyrgyzstan), among communities, government, and the private sector (as seen in Ubatuba, Brazil, and Kenya), or among different students from different institutions and regions (as seen in West Africa), collaboration allows the sharing of skills, ideas, and resources for tackling complex development issues over the long term. It can also generate the momentum and ownership needed to disrupt the institutional norms that limit the potential of open partnerships.

In summary, the OCSDNet teams recognize that open science has the potential to transform the foundational structures of knowledge creation in new and important ways. It offers spaces, tools, opportunities, and principles that facilitate opportunities for historically marginalized groups to participate in knowledge production. It also validates new and existing forms of local knowledge. For instance, the high participation rate of female schoolchildren and women in citizen science projects in Kyrgyzstan and Lebanon, and the strong engagement of Indigenous leaders in the South African climate change project both illustrated this potential. At the same time, powerful actors such as the oligarchic multinational science publishers (Larivière et al. 2015) continue to resist the idea of knowledge as a public good and to maintain the status quo of keeping knowledge as a commodity for consumption by elites (Fyfe et al. 2017). The anthropologist Paul Sillitoe (2007, 16) observed, "The idea is not that the small local knowledge stone should knock Goliath science over.... It is that we should create space for others' ideas. This is necessary not only because it should continue to add to global science's awesome fund of knowledge, but also because it might help us to manage this knowledge more effectively for the planet and humankind."

Positioning this conclusion more broadly, the United Nations (UN) Sustainable Development Goal number nine recognizes the need to "build resilient infrastructure, promote inclusive and sustainable industrialization, and foster innovation" (UN 2016, 11). In this regard, effective, inclusive open science has a key role to play in ensuring that infrastructure and innovation are locally appropriate, inclusive, and hence sustainable in the longer term. This calls for local participation and dialogue at all levels, including resources and policies from the top that must be grounded in and designed with knowledge from local communities. It is only through the inclusion and consideration of diverse human actors and experiences that open science might offer the opportunity for transformational human development.

Notes

1. See, for example, this widely accessed website: European Union (n.d.).

2. See https://ihub.co.ke/.

3. Visit www.ocsdnet.org for full project descriptions.

4. This framework was developed over several decades of work on natural resource commons and their governance.

5. We did this by including the questions in monthly and annual report templates, semistructured interview questions, and general group discussions throughout the funding duration of the network.

6. A Google Group is a closed, online forum that allows written discussion on a variety of topics.

7. The OCSDNet Research Coordination team, consisting of five members in five countries around the world, also participated in similar processes of reflection and discussion around their own observations of and contributions to power dynamics within the network.

8. See Albornoz et al. (2017) for ELPUB and for more information about the manifesto creation process.

9. For a description of *buen vivir*, see Monni and Pallottino (2015).

10. For more information, see the annotated bibliography and reading list that we consulted (https://docs.google.com/document/d/10g0U2_aNsOWCSNulfsw3Ea0TEhbx18JoCL8I7a8QLZ8 /edit).

11. The most common conception of a citizen scientist is as an individual who voluntarily spends time contributing to the crowdsourcing of data (often using online tools and infrastructure) as part of a larger research investigation with predefined questions and objectives. See chapter 14 of this volume for more on crowdsourcing in development. For instance, Silvertown (2009, 467) refers to a citizen scientist as "a volunteer who collects and/or processes data as part of a scientific enquiry," while Cohn (2008, 193) defines them as "volunteers who participate as field assistants in scientific studies."

12. PAR methodologies were originally conceived by development practitioners in the 1970s. These methods have been touted for their ability to uncover highly nuanced and locally relevant data, as well as their potential to achieve more sustainable outcomes, as they tend to focus on social transformation or citizen empowerment as concurrent research objectives (Chambers 1994; Hall 1992).

13. *Model Forests* are "social, inclusive, and participatory processes that seek the sustainable development of a territory and thus contribute to global targets related to poverty, climate change, desertification and sustainable development." See http://www.bosquesmodelo.net/en/bosques -modelo/ for more information.

14. Similar findings have been presented by the Research on Open Educational Resources for Development (ROER4D) Network, under a discussion of the tensions around operational openness within research processes; for further information, see King et al. (2016).

15. In the field of information systems, design science is a research paradigm that seeks to "extend the boundaries of human and organizational capabilities by creating new and innovative artifacts" (Hevner et al. 2004, 75).

16. The *OCSDNet Manifesto* is available in English, Spanish, French, and Afrikaans and can be accessed at https://ocsdnet.org/manifesto/open-science-manifesto/. See also Albornoz et al. (2017).

17. For example, see Chambers (1994) and Hall and Tandon (2017b).

References

Albornoz, Denisse, Alejandro Posada, Angela Okune, Rebecca Hillyer, and Leslie Chan, 2017. "Co-constructing an Open and Collaborative Manifesto to Reclaim the Open Science Narrative." In *Expanding Perspectives on Open Science: Communities, Cultures, and Diversity in Concepts and Practices, Proceedings of the 21st ELPUB Conference*, ed. Leslie Chan and Fernando Loizides. Amsterdam: IOS Press. http://ebooks.iospress.nl/book/expanding-perspectives-on-open-science-communities -cultures-and-diversity-in-concepts-and-practices-proceedings-of-the-21st-international -conference-on-electron.

Appadurai, Arjun. 2006. "The Right to Research." *Globalisation, Societies, and Education* 4 (2): 167–177.

Bartling, Sönke, and Sashca Friesike, eds. 2014. *Opening Science: The Evolving Guide on How the Internet Is Changing Research, Collaboration and Scholarly Publishing.* Berlin: SpringerOpen. http://www.openingscience.org/get-the-book/.

Canhos, Dora A. L., Marian S. Sousa-Baena, Sidnei de Souza, Leonor C. Maia, João R. Stehmann, Vanderlei P. Canhos, Renato De Giovanni, Maria B. M. Bonacelli, A. Wouter Los, and A. Townsend Peterson. 2015. "The Importance of Biodiversity E-infrastructures for Megadiverse Countries." *PLOS Biology* 13 (7): e1002204. https://doi.org/10.1371/journal.pbio.1002204.

Chambers, Robert. 1994. "The Origins and Practice of Participatory Rural Appraisal." *World Development* 22 (7): 953–969.

Chambers, Robert. 2017. *Can We Know Better? Reflections for Development.* Rugby, UK: Practical Action Publishing Ltd.

Chan, Leslie, Angela Okune, Rebecca Hillyer, Denisse Albornoz, and Alejandro Posada. 2019. *Contextualizing Openness: Situating Open Science.* Ottawa: University of Ottawa Press/IDRC. https://www.idrc.ca/en/book/contextualizing-openness-situating-open-science.

Chan, Leslie, Angela Okune, and Nanjira Sambuli. 2015. "What Is Open and Collaborative Science and What Roles Could It Play in Development?" In *Open Science, Open Issues,* ed. Sarita Albagli, Maria Lucia Maciel, and Alexandre Hannud Abdo, 87–112. Brasília: Instituto Brasileiro de Informação em Ciência e Tecnologia (IBICT). http://livroaberto.ibict.br/bitstream/1/1061/1/Open%20Science%20open%20issues_Digital.pdf.

Citizen Science Association. 2017. "The Power of Citizen Science." http://citizenscience.org/.

Cohn, Jeffrey P. 2008. "Citizen Science: Can Volunteers Do Real Research?" *BioScience* 58 (3): 192–197. http://dx.doi.org/10.1641/B580303.

Czerniewicz, Laura. 2015. "Confronting Inequitable Power Dynamics of Global Knowledge Production and Exchange." *Water Wheel* 14 (5): 26–28. http://journals.co.za/content/waterb/14/5/EJC176212.

De Sousa Santos, Boaventura. 2014. *Epistemologies of the South: Justice against Epistemicide.* New York: Routledge.

Dolamo, Ramathate. 2013. "Botho/Ubuntu: The Heart of African Ethics." *Scriptura* 112:1–10. https://journals.co.za/content/script/112/1/EJC148117.

Escobar, A. 1992. "Reflections on 'Development': Grassroots Approaches and Alternative Politics in the Third World." *Futures* 24 (5): 411–436. https://doi.org/10.1016/0016-3287(92)90014-7.

European Union. n.d. "Open Science Guidelines." https://www.fosteropenscience.eu/taxonomy/term/101.

Fecher, Benedickt, and Sascha Friesike. 2014. "Open Science: One Term, Five Schools of Thought." In *Opening Science: The Evolving Guide on How the Internet is Changing Research, Collaboration and*

Scholarly Publishing, ed. Sönke Bartling and Sascha Friesike, 17–47. Cham, Switzerland: Springer International. http://dx.doi.org/10.1007/978-3-319-00026-8_2.

Frischmann, Brett M., Michael J. Madison, and Katherine J. Strandburg, eds. 2014. *Governing Knowledge Commons*. Oxford: Oxford University Press.

Fyfe, Aileen, Kelly Coate, Stephen Curry, Stuart Lawson, Noah Moxham, and Camilla M. Røstvik. 2017. *Untangling Academic Publishing: A History of the Relationship between Commercial Interests, Academic Prestige and the Circulation of Research*. May 25. https://zenodo.org/record/546100#.WpdoZvTtSQM.

Graham, Mark, Stefano De Sabbata, and Matthew A. Zook. 2015. "Towards a Study of Information Geographies: (Im)mutable Augmentations and a Mapping of the Geographies of Information." *Geo: Geography and Environment* 2 (1): 88–105. http://dx.doi.org/10.1002/geo2.8.

Guayasamín, Cagigal, and Pedro José. 2014. *Art Commons in a Social Knowledge Economy. Cultura Digital*. London: King's College London. http://repositorio.educacionsuperior.gob.ec//handle/28000/1674.

Hall, Budd. 1992. "From Margins to Center? The Development and Purpose of Participatory Research." *American Sociologist* 23 (4): 15–28. https://doi.org/10.1007/BF02691928.

Hall, Budd L., and Rajesh Tandon. 2017a. "Decolonization of Knowledge, Epistemicide, Participatory Research, and Higher Education." *Research for All* 1 (1): 6–19. https://doi.org/10.18546/RFA.01.1.02.

Hall, Budd L., and Rajesh Tandon. 2017b. "Participatory Research: Where Have We Been, Where Are We Going?—A Dialogue." *Research for All* 1 (2): 365–374. https://dspace.library.uvic.ca/handle/1828/8562.

Haraway, Donna. 2008. "Situated Knowledges: The Science Question in Feminism and the Privilege of Partial Perspective." *Feminist Studies* 14 (3): 575–599.

Harding, Sandra. 2006. *Science and Social Inequality: Feminist and Postcolonial Issues*. Urbana: University of Illinois Press.

Harding, Sandra. 2015. *Objectivity and Diversity: Another Logic of Scientific Research*. Chicago: University of Chicago Press.

Hess, Charlotte. 2012. "The Unfolding of the Knowledge Commons." *St Antony's International Review* 8 (1): 13–24.

Hess, Charlotte, and Elinor Ostrom. 2005. "A Framework for Analyzing the Knowledge Commons." In *Understanding Knowledge as a Commons: From Theory to Practice*, ed. Charlotte Hess and Elinor Ostrom, 41–82. Cambridge, MA: MIT Press.

Hevner, Alan R., Salvatore T. March, Jinsoo Park, and Sudha Ram. 2004. "Design Science in Information Systems Research." *MIS Quarterly* 28 (1): 75–105.

King, Thomas W., Cheryl-Ann Hodgkinson-Williams, Michelle Willmers, and Sukaina Walji. 2016. "Dimensions of Open Research: Critical Reflections on Openness in the ROER4D Project." *Open Praxis* 8 (2): 81–91.

Larivière, Vincent, Stafanie Haustein, and Philippe Mongeon. 2015. "The Oligopoly of Academic Publishers in the Digital Era." *PLOS ONE* 10 (6): e0127502. https://doi.org/10.1371/journal.pone.0127502.

Moletsane, Renebohile. 2015. "Whose Knowledge Is It? Towards Reordering Knowledge Production and Dissemination in the Global South." *Educational Research for Social Change* 4 (2): 35–47. http://ersc.nmmu.ac.za/articles/Vol_4_No_2_Moletsane_pp_35-48_October_2015.pdf.

Monni, Salvatore, and Massimo Pallottino. 2015. "A New Agenda for International Development Cooperation: Lessons Learnt from the Buen Vivir Experience." *Development* 58 (1): 49–57.

Nielsen, Michael. 2013. *Reinventing Discovery: The New Era of Networked Science*. Reprint ed. Princeton, NJ: Princeton University Press.

Okune, Angela, Becky Hillyer, Denisse Albornoz, Nanjira Sambuli, and Leslie Chan. 2016. "Tackling Inequities in Global Scientific Power Structures." *The African Technopolitan*. 4 (1). https://tspace.library.utoronto.ca/handle/1807/71107.

Organisation for Economic Co-operation and Development (OECD). n.d. *Open Science*. Paris: OECD. https://www.oecd.org/science/inno/open-science.htm.

Orth, Astrid, Nancy Pontika, and David Ball. 2016. FOSTER's Open Science Training Tools and Best Practices. In *Positioning and Power in Academic Publishing: Players, Agents and Agendas: Proceedings of the 20th International Conference on Electronic Publishing* (135). Amsterdam: IOS Press. http://ebooks.iospress.nl/publication/42908.

Ostrom, Elinor. 1991. *Governing the Commons: The Evolution of Institutions for Collective Action*. New York: Cambridge University Press.

Ostrom, Elinor. 2005. *Understanding Institutional Diversity*. Princeton, NJ: Princeton University Press.

Schmidt, Birgit, Astrid Orth, Gwen Franck, Iryna Kuchma, Petr Knoth, and José Carvalho. 2016. "Stepping up Open Science Training for European Research." *Publications* 4 (2): 16. http://www.mdpi.com/2304-6775/4/2/16/htm.

Schweik, Charles M., and Robert C. English. 2012. *Internet Success: A Study of Open-Source Software Commons*. Cambridge, MA: MIT Press.

Sen, Amartya K. 1989. "Development as Capability Expansion." *Journal of Development Planning* 19:41–58.

Sillitoe, Paul. 2007. "Local Science vs. Global Science: An Overview." In *Local Science vs. Global Science: Approaches to Indigenous Knowledge in International Development*, ed. Paul Sillitoe, 1–22. Oxford, UK: Bergahn Books.

Silvertown, Jonathan. 2009. "A New Dawn for Citizen Science." *Trends in Ecology and Evolution* 24 (9): 467–471.

Smith, Matthew L., and Katherine M. A. Reilly. 2013. "Introduction." In *Open Development: Networked Innovations in International Development*, ed. Matthew L. Smith and Katherine M. A. Reilly,

1–13. Cambridge, MA/Ottawa: MIT Press/IDRC. https://idl-bnc-idrc.dspacedirect.org/bitstream/handle/10625/52348/IDL-52348.pdf?sequence=1&isAllowed=y.

Strandburg, Katherine J., Brett M. Frischmann, and Madison J. Madison, eds. 2017. *Governing Medical Knowledge Commons*. New York: Cambridge University Press.

Traynor, Cath. 2017. "Contracting Justice Workshop—Exploring Socially Just Research Processes." Open and Collaborative Science in Development Network (OCSDNet), March 30. https://ocsdnet.org/contracting-justice-workshop-exploring-socially-just-research-processes/.

United Nations (UN). Economic and Social Council. 2016. *Progress toward the Sustainable Development Goals: Report of the Secretary-General,* E/2017/66, 11–12. Reissue June 2017. http://www.un.org/ga/search/view_doc.asp?symbol=E/2017/66&Lang=E.

Visvanathan, Shiv. 2009. "The Search for Cognitive Justice." In *Knowledge in Question: A Symposium on Interrogating Knowledge and Questioning Science* 597, May. http://www.india-seminar.com/2009/597.htm.

14   The Inclusivity of Crowdsourcing and Implications for Development

Savita Bailur and Raed Sharif

Introduction

"When one starts to look at the power of crowdsourcing in developing regions, there is optimism in a nascent paradigm shift of the realities of a poverty-stricken community" (Fisher 2012). As this quote suggests, there is hope that crowdsourcing can be an effective approach to tackling some development problems in an inclusive manner. In this chapter, we take crowdsourcing to be "the act of taking the job traditionally performed by [a] designated agent (usually an employee) and outsourcing it to an undefined, generally large group of people in the form of an open call" (Howe 2006, 99). Reflecting its origins as an innovation strategy in the private sector, crowdsourcing is seen as a means to improve efficiency, reduce costs, and enhance creativity. While these potential benefits are relevant to international development, there is an added normative rationale—that gathering information (which may lead toward making a decision), should be as inclusive as possible. As Fisher (2012) states, this may even include "poverty-stricken communit[ies]" and helping their voices be heard.

It is unclear, however, what inclusivity looks like in crowdsourcing for development. A number of questions remain: How is it defined? How, to what extent, and in what contexts can it occur? Who is included? This chapter seeks to improve our understanding of inclusivity in crowdsourcing activities for international development. This includes deepening our knowledge of the enabling conditions that make a certain activity more inclusive than another, as well as the challenges faced.

To explore these questions, this chapter examines the premise of inclusivity of crowdsourcing initiatives through an analysis of seven projects that either researched or operationalized crowdsourcing (HarassMap;[1] Peaceful Truth and Una Hakika, both run by the Sentinel Project;[2] Cuidando do Meu Bairro (CMB), two microwork projects with DIRSI[3] and LIRNEAsia, and one with iHub on the analysis of Twitter in Kenya). Three highlights emerge in this chapter regarding inclusivity in crowdsourcing in the Global South:

- Inclusivity in crowdsourcing is relative—it is defined in different ways by different project owners and as a result, operationalized in different ways at different stages.
- Inclusivity in crowdsourcing is influenced by a number of factors, the key being the vision and strategy around the initiative.
- Inclusivity can happen indirectly and tangentially—for example, through intermediaries.

The chapter begins with an overview of the key terms used throughout: namely, *crowdsourcing* and *inclusivity*. Next, it introduces Sharma's (2010) framework for crowdsourcing success, which we then apply to analyze the seven initiatives. Finally, we conclude with the problematization of inclusivity that we encountered in the crowdsourcing projects.

Crowdsourcing and Inclusivity

As discussed in other chapters in this volume, a core promise of openness is inclusivity. In open data, *inclusivity* is meant to democratize access to informational resources (see chapter 10). In open education, Trotter and Hodgkinson-Williams (see chapter 12) cite Smith and Casserly: "at the heart of the movement towards OER [open educational resources] is the simple and powerful idea that the world's knowledge is a public good and that technology in general and the World Wide Web in particular provide an opportunity for everyone to share, use and reuse it" (Smith and Casserly 2006, 2). In chapter 13, Hillyer et al. state that open science is the "opening of the entire research cycle" … [to] "allow increased transparency of scientific processes, as well as the expansion of participation in and opportunities for diverse forms of knowledge production." Likewise, crowdsourcing has the potential to be inclusive, as the process itself is designed to not discriminate and therefore to theoretically facilitate participation (see chapter 2).

Before we examine the concept of inclusion within crowdsourcing, we first define crowdsourcing itself. Estellés-Arolas and González-Ladrón-de-Guevara (2012) undertook a comprehensive review of six academic databases between January and August 2011 to source forty varied definitions of crowdsourcing. They found eight characteristics that defined crowdsourcing:

1. There is a clearly defined crowd.
2. There is a task with a clear goal.
3. The recompense received by the crowd (not always financial) is clear.
4. The crowdsourcer is clearly identified.
5. The compensation to be received by the crowdsourcer is clearly defined.

6. It has an online assigned participative process.

7. It uses an open call of variable extent.

8. It uses the Internet.

We should also recognize here the different types of crowdsourcing (expanding on point 7). Crowdsourcing usually refers to an *open and ongoing/active call*—anyone with the skills and interest can participate. However, other initiatives (such as Una Hakika and Peaceful Truth) employ *crowdseeding*—selecting members of the crowd to give them a more focused role. *Microwork*, on the other hand, is work comprising small tasks (such as photo tagging), which is crowdsourced. What Sambuli et al. (2013, 8) call *passive crowdsourcing* is more of a research method in terms of analyzing types of tweets on Twitter.

From its commercial origins, cost reduction, more real-time data, and diversity of inputs are often cited as the key outcomes of crowdsourcing (Kleemann, Voß, and Rieder 2008; Parameswaran and Whinston 2007; Surowiecki, 2004). Howe's (2006) perspective of "taking a function once performed by employees and outsourcing it to an undefined, generally large group of people in the form of an open call," emerged from within a business context.

While these benefits also apply in international development, especially gathering data from remote areas and in the crisis and emergency response fields, and reducing costs for already cash-strapped nongovernmental organizations (NGOs), more as well as diverse voices in the production of data are not just valued as innovative or cost-effective but, in addition, it is normatively valued as the right thing to do. In development, crowdsourcing has evolved to apply to activities aligned with more normative values, such as participatory theory (Chambers 2006, 2014; Cooke and Kothari 2001), or the open-source software principles of information systems (Mansell 2013), with the idea that inclusion provides voice and ownership. For example, Mansell (2013, 267) argues that Ushahidi "provided a way of breaking [the] monopoly on crisis data previously held by organizations such as the Red Cross and the United Nations, yielding data which enhanced situation awareness for small NGOs without the resources to collect or manage data independently."

Table 14.1 contains some examples of well-known crowdsourcing platforms in development. These platforms were intended to "democratize" data, as crowdsourcing "data now stands to be the great leveler and democratizer" (Fisher 2012). According to Fisher (2012), the process of crowdsourcing itself is inclusive for development because "by supplying someone in a developing region with the physical means to access data, one not only automatically brings them into the loop of communication, but also introduces them into a whole new business infrastructure powered by crowdsourcing methodologies."

Table 14.1

Examples of crowdsourcing platforms in development.

Name	Summary
Ushahidi https://www.ushahidi.com/	Perhaps the best-known of the crowdsourcing platforms borne out of the postelection riots in Kenya. Aims to gather and verify local informal reports crowdsourced through email, SMS, or social platforms to ensure that people have access to the information they need. This can range from the location of the nearest medical supplies to which areas of town to avoid due to severe outbreaks of violence.
Medic Mobile https://medicmobile.org/	A mobile app that allows community health workers in twenty-three countries to register pregnancies, track disease outbreaks, communicate about emergencies, and keep inventory of critical medicines.
Plantwise initiative https://www.plantwise.org/	Launched by the Center for Agricultural Bio-Science International (CABI), Plantwise collects information on soil health and other risk factors from thousands of farmers in twenty-four countries. In exchange for providing data, farmers receive technical assistance via SMS and/or voice messages on how to remove or avoid pests and, as a result, reduce crop loss.
iCow http://www.icow.co.ke	Dairy farmers in Kenya, Tanzania, and Ethiopia can track livestock through aggregating and mapping their crowdsourced data, but they also use this app to increase their bargaining power by facilitating collective buying of input and enabling larger sales volumes.
Ipaidabribe http://www.ipaidabribe.com/	An anticorruption platform that emerged in India to report corrupt and praise honest public-sector officials. Now also used in Kenya, Ghana, and Sri Lanka, among other countries.

Yet Fisher's perspective makes many assumptions—crowdsourcing does not necessarily guarantee access to the crowdsourced data—and, even if access is granted, not everyone will have the infrastructure, skills, or motivation to use them. In both Mansell and Fisher's points, it is unclear exactly how inclusion occurs and at what stage; is it in producing the data, distributing them, or consuming them? And how does this "[automatic bringing] into the loop of communication" occur? Furthermore, inclusion is separate from participation—inclusion is likely to be the effort of the provider/platform owner, while participation is largely on the part of the platform user—and people may opt out for many reasons. Even if the skills, infrastructure, and other tangible aspects exist, participation will not be possible if there is no alignment with the aims of the platform provider.

Finally, Silversmith and Tulchin (2013) add that in a development context, both the users' access devices and motivations are important to consider when it comes to inclusion. In the Global South, the main device for access is a mobile phone rather than a desktop, laptop, or tablet. In addition, as they argue, participation in agriculture-related crowdsourcing activities has generally been motivated by cash, or cash-alike payments such as airtime or important information that can be linked to ways to improve or secure income. Understanding the tools that people use and what incentivizes them to participate in crowdsourcing activities in development is critical in successfully designing and implementing an inclusive crowdsourcing initiative in a development context.

So, what do we understand *inclusivity* in crowdsourcing to mean? Fisher's (2012) definition of inclusivity is an "intention or policy of including people who might otherwise be excluded or marginalized," and therefore the leveling of access to data. However, first, there are different understandings of types of inclusion, as discussed by other authors in this volume. There is a difference between inclusion in terms of quantity or numbers of people, and inclusivity in terms of *representativity*—types of people, specifically those who might normally be marginalized. For example, van Schalkwyk and Cañares (see chapter 10) discuss the difference between numbers (more people are included) and representativity (minorities are included). They also provide an additional definition of *inclusion* in terms of whether "more people participated in governance after an open data initiative" (i.e., contributing to the outcome of inclusivity).

Similarly, Trotter and Hodgkinson-Williams (see chapter 12) use the World Bank's definition of social inclusion: "the process of improving the terms for individuals and groups to take part in society.... It ensures that people have a voice in decisions which affect their lives and that they enjoy equal access to markets, services and political, social and physical spaces" (see World Bank 2013 and Bonami and Tubio 2015, cited in chapter 12), which correlates to inclusion as an outcome or a consequence rather than a process.

Thus, there are different categories or types of inclusion that different people and institutions adopt. Many microwork platforms,[4] for example, are considered inclusive (in terms of numbers and improving citizens' access to work), even though they have severe imbalances in gender, age, and other characteristics among participants. Civic reporting sites also show similar imbalances. For example, Swan (2016) found that in the mobile-based civic reporting tool U-Report, two-thirds of U-Reporters are male, 90 percent are under thirty-five years of age, and urban residents are likely to be overrepresented. Similarly, in analyzing eleven citizen-reporting platforms across the world, Rumbul (2015) found a tendency for the participants to be male, older (although the opposite was found in Kenya and South Africa), part of a majority ethnic group, and educated and employed.[5] Therefore, such platforms may be inclusive in terms of including more people, but not necessarily in terms of including minorities (not as a concerted effort anyway).

As Trotter and Hodgkinson-Williams (see chapter 12) state, the hierarchy of access, participation, and empowerment often reveals that the first (access) and the second (participation) occur in the case of open educational resources (OER), but the third is hard to achieve. This could be a fundamental weakness of the theory of change of inclusion, as illustrated in Fisher (2012) and Mansell (2013); both see inclusion mainly in terms of access to data, which then can be consumed freely. However, Smith and Seward (see chapter 2) make the distinction between production, distribution (sharing), and consumption (use) of data in open processes, including crowdsourcing, with the idea that inclusion (as in Gidley et al.'s 2010 nested stages of access, participation, and empowerment) can occur at any of these points (Smith and Seward 2017; Gidley et al. 2010). Yet, as Graham and De Sabbata (see chapter 5) and Zaveri (see chapter 4) note, geography and gender are just two of the factors that make inclusion at any of these stages problematic. We discuss further factors for inclusion in crowdsourcing next.

A Framework for Inclusion in Crowdsourcing

Sharma (2010) suggests that there are six factors that contribute to successful crowdsourcing. *Successful* here refers to a quantitative rather than a representative notion of inclusion, where inclusion is concerned with whether "there are sufficient members of the crowd participating in it" (Sharma 2010, 8), rather than deliberately including the otherwise excluded or marginalized. We return to this distinction in our analysis.

Sharma (2010) lays out the key factors for including as many members of the crowd as possible: human capital, infrastructure, linkages and trust, external environment, vision and strategy, and motive alignment of the crowd (see figure 14.1 for an illustration). We use this framework for the analysis of our International Development Research Centre (IDRC) case studies, while also problematizing it.

As a prerequisite, *human capital* involves ensuring that individuals have the literacy, digital literacy, language skills, and other necessary characteristics to participate online. A critical mass of skills is needed to ensure inclusive and usable platforms (Alonso et al. 2008). A second important prerequisite is that of a dependable, affordable *infrastructure*, particularly of mobile and mobile Internet, as that is increasingly the mode of access (Silversmith and Tulchin 2013). A more complex factor is that of *linkages and trust*, where those who are using the crowdsourcing platform trust that their input is being taken into consideration, with appropriate checks and balances, especially in relation to privacy and security. De Beer et al. (2017) also point out that there may be a concern

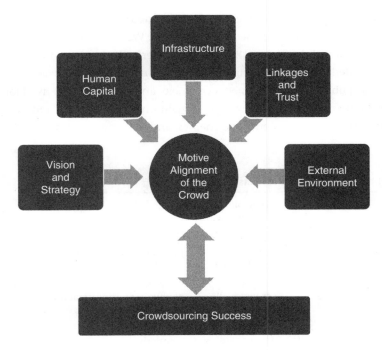

Figure 14.1
Crowdsourcing success factors.
Source: Sharma (2010).

about intellectual capital on the part of users—what will happen to the data they input, and who owns them? The *external environment*, another critical success factor, affects this, in terms of the amount of support and freedom given to the platform (a problematic issue arising for a number of platforms that we discuss in the following sections). Finally, the two critical factors that we will examine in terms of inclusion are the *vision and strategy* of the platform and the *motive alignment* of the crowd (i.e., the extent to which the crowd aligns with the platform intentions). We use this framework for the analysis of our IDRC case studies in this chapter, while also problematizing it.

Methodology

The research was designed as a multicase, comparative case study. We conducted in-depth, semistructured interviews with seven project managers who have either used or researched crowdsourcing in their projects. Table 14.2 contains more details on the projects, summarizing the objectives and background of the projects. The appendix at the end of this chapter presents the interview guide. We conducted interviews between December 2017 and February 2018 via Skype. Interviews were each about one hour long and recorded with the participants' permission. We also reviewed project documents such as published reports, media coverage, and other publicly available materials. Data were then analyzed following the qualitative data analysis tradition: making sense of the data, finding patterns and themes, and drawing conclusions.

Table 14.2
Objectives and background of the projects.

Project name	Type of crowdsourcing	Problem	Geographic location
HarassMap http://harassmap.org/en/	Active and open (all can participate)	Addressing sexual harassment, particularly in public spaces	Egypt
Una Hakika https://www.unahakika.org/	Targeted crowdseeding	Addressing and countering misinformation and interethnic violence	Tana Delta, Kenya
Peaceful Truth https://www.peacefultruth.org/	Targeted crowdseeding	Addressing and countering misinformation	Myanmar
Nubelo (now Freelancer.com)[a] https://www.freelancer.es/nubelo	Microwork	Addressing unemployment by matching employers who post contracts for short-term jobs with workers who bid for these jobs	Based in Spain, with suppliers largely in Spanish-speaking countries
Online freelancing and microwork in Sri Lanka[b]	Microwork	Like Nubelo, connecting employers with contract workers for specific tasks	Sri Lanka
Cuidando do Meu Bairro[c]	Open and active	An open data civic platform mapping public spending in São Paulo	Brazil
Kenyan elections monitoring[d]	Passive crowdsourcing	An analysis of participation on Twitter after the 2007 Kenyan elections	Kenya

[a]Galperin and Greppi's (2017) paper is found here: https://papers.ssrn.com/sol3/papers.cfm?abstract_id=2922874.
[b]See http://lirneasia.net/projects/inclusion-in-business-process-outsourcing/.
[c]See https://colab.each.usp.br/blog/tag/cuidando-do-meu-bairro/.
[d]See https://ihub.co.ke/ihubresearch/jb_VsReportpdf2013-8-29-07-38-56.pdf.

Understanding Inclusivity through Sharma's Framework

Infrastructure

Drawing lessons from inclusive crowdsourcing activities in development, Silversmith and Tulchin (2013, 3) argue that "tools should be structured based on the needs and behaviors of the users, not on the technology or developmental goals." Another important factor is that the user interface should be simple to ensure easy and quick signup and usability. All the project managers recognized that appropriate infrastructure is critical for inclusion. Una Hakika and Peaceful Truth both conducted baseline surveys to understand what technologies would be most used by targeted populations. In the Tana Delta in Kenya, where Una Hakika started, a baseline survey found that WhatsApp and Viber were more widely used than short message services (SMS); in Myanmar, where Peaceful Truth is based, 92.1 percent of respondents said that they use the Internet, while 97.3 percent of respondents owned a mobile phone (Boyd 2016). Una Hakika also uses radio extensively to raise awareness (Tuckwood 2017). In the case of HarassMap, Rebecca Chiao stated that being SMS and online based improved the system's ability to reach women and empower them to report sexual harassment incidents more frequently and on time. Yet, she was aware that it was harder to reach women who did not have access to technical infrastructure. While HarassMap ran committed awareness campaigns, it also relied on some intermediaries who did have access to infrastructure and could report harassment.

The mode of access also affects inclusion. In *After Access: Inclusion, Development, and a More Mobile Internet* (2015), Jonathan Donner makes the point that while most Internet access, particularly in developing countries, is achieved through mobile phones, this presents a restricted production scenario, with a limit to mobile capacity in terms of interface, methods of input, and screen size. So while this may work for HarassMap or Una Hakika, access via mobile phone limits the types of microwork activities that users can engage in. LIRNEAsia, for its part, found a significant discrepancy in terms of inclusion. While buying and selling between supplier and vendor happened through mobile phones, the "heavy parts of the work, design or translation comes from desktops" (Sriganesh Lokanathan, LIRNEAsia, interview, January 27, 2017). They conclude that "inclusion is not binary—it also means what kind of devices people have" (Lokanathan, interview, January 27, 2017). Other aspects of infrastructure in microwork related to what affordances vendors have for payment (as PayPal does not currently operate in Sri Lanka), or the 15 percent to 20 percent fees that platforms ask for as a membership fee. This returns to the implications of inclusion for development—those who can afford desktop computers will theoretically have greater access opportunities to be included as distributors and producers of data rather than consumers.

The challenge is that if you do not have access to infrastructure, you cannot participate online, and thus you cannot be represented. Lokanathan gives an example of an app that tracks bumps (e.g., Street Bump, for the city of Boston) and uses this crowdsourced data to keep the city council informed of where road repairs are needed. In Sri Lanka, Lokanathan points out, this would reflect only the richer areas—where users with smartphones would crowdsource the data while poorer areas would simply be "blackspots" (as it happens, this also tends to be the case with Street Bump). As he says, the question of infrastructure means that "you need to think about that lack of representation in terms of inclusion" (Lokanathan, interview, January 27, 2017). Similar sentiments were raised for CMB (Craveiro and Martano 2015), Kenyan election monitoring (only those who are on Twitter can be captured for that analysis of representation), and for Nubelo, in terms of what kind of jobs that suppliers can access, and on what devices.

Human Capital

Who is included and how are partly dependent on infrastructure, but also on skills. It seems obvious to state it, but only those who have access to infrastructure and are skilled enough—in terms of digital literacy, social media use, and other technological abilities—can actually use Twitter (Kenyan election monitoring), Nubelo, or the microwork platforms analyzed by LIRNEAsia in Sri Lanka.

In the context of microwork where participation is competitive, winning a bid may include not just the requisite skills, but also effective strategies. For example, on the Nubelo platform, women consistently bid lower than men for the same jobs. This is potentially a strategy for getting one's foot in the door (it is important to have done work on the platform in order to get new work) but also as a way to counter potential bias against female workers and high competition against men. As a result, while there appears to be comparatively low participation of women in crowdsourcing platforms compared to men (Raja et al. 2013; Rossotto, Kuek, and Paradi-Guilford 2012), on the Nubelo platform, women are more likely to win bids than men (Galperin et al. 2017).

Finally, human capital is not just in terms of users, but also staff, volunteers, and intermediaries to run platforms. As part of a community engagement effort, establishing a local presence and training local volunteers (or partners) to provide technical assistance are critical to encouraging adoption and long-term participation in the crowdsourcing activity. In the HarassMap case, the organization relies on volunteers, especially in university settings, and the idea of *safe areas*, with local store owners or neighbors acting as volunteers; inclusion here is also of the HarassMap staff, to inculcate the idea of public spaces as inclusive to all (Fahmy et al., 2014; Farid 2015). In São Paulo, CMB relied on staff and students for mapping public expenditure data. The Sentinel Project partners with a local organization and trains the local staff to be the project representatives on the ground. For example, the team hired local staff in Kenya and positioned them in the local community. In Myanmar, the team partnered with the Smile for Education and Development Foundation. They wanted to partner with this organization because simply, in the Myanmar context, they were trusted—leading us to the theme of linkages and trust, discussed next.

Linkages and Trust

The two factors of linkages (i.e., what the platform is being associated with) and trust are critical to shaping the contours of inclusion in crowdsourcing processes. In Nubelo, Galperin and Greppi (2017) find that foreign job-seekers (i.e., not Spanish) are 42 percent less likely than job-seekers from Spain to win contracts from Spanish employers, who represent two-thirds of all employers on the platform. Because the client-supplier relationship appears stronger if both are Spanish, Spanish suppliers are able to charge 16 percent more than similarly qualified foreign suppliers. This emerges partly because of an implicit trust by employers that there will be lower communication costs and higher worker quality if the vendor is local. Galperin states that employers "resort to stereotypes about what is a good or a bad worker, what is the quality of the work and inevitably they have a bias towards their own country of origin because they understand better about the quality of distribution in their own countries. So they're always a bit more reluctant to hire somebody from a different country, just because of a lack of information or information surety about whether that worker is of good quality" (Galperin, interview, January 30, 2017). Therefore, in some cases, even where the infrastructure and skills might be equal or close to equal (Spanish and non-Spanish), employers still place more trust in Spanish workers, thereby excluding non-Spanish workers. Of course, microwork platforms may have no social imperative to actively include marginalized members of the community. As Galperin states: "they're interested in more matches, … they make revenues and they grow as more matches are made" (interview, January 27, 2017).

For crowdsourcing for international development initiatives, building trust is essential for success. As Drew Boyd says of Peaceful Truth, the greatest lesson was the importance of constantly reassuring users, particularly in Myanmar, who had privacy concerns and suspicions of what would happen with the data collected. In Una Hakika too, Boyd et al. (2015) spoke of deliberately conducting *barazas* (village meetings), especially with village heads, to raise awareness of Una Hakika, and that it was aiming to alleviate misinformation, not increase it by setting up yet another media platform.

External Environment

As Graham and De Sabbata (see chapter 5) state, geographies of participation matter to the production of open content. That is, one's geographic location, and all that it entails, has a high level of influence on participation patterns. Besides infrastructure and skills, one's geography includes factors such as the current political climate, culture, and economic context.

For example, in the case of the microwork platforms in Sri Lanka, LIRNEAsia found that many of those applying for jobs online are from smaller cities in Sri Lanka, rather than Colombo—perhaps because residents of smaller cities find it hard to find physical job positions and easier to find opportunities online, whereas in Colombo, it might be easier for applicants to find opportunities in person.

Crowdsourcing initiatives that seek to be disruptive of the current status quo can bring challenges. While authors like Swan (2016) call for more crowdsourcing platforms to challenge public institutions (e.g., reporting corruption), such a system is never deployed in a vacuum. For HarassMap, Chiao raised the delicate balance in working with government: "there were times when the issue of harassment became very politicized, the government accused the Muslim Brotherhood of being responsible for harassment, and the Brotherhood said that it was the government and security forces who were responsible. HarassMap does not engage in politics and is politically neutral, but there are broader political issues around the issue of harassment" (Chiao, interview, January 30, 2017).

Another concern was that the Egyptian government did not want any organization or activity to "paint Egypt in a negative light" (Chiao, interview, January 30, 2017). This may have led to concerns around using the platform, or that no change was happening as a result of the initiative because the government was not taking it seriously (Abdelmonem and Galán 2017). Similarly, Una Hakika and Peaceful Truth are affected by the broader political situations in Kenya and Myanmar, as well as by whether citizens feel they can participate safely.

Vision and Strategy: What Types of Inclusion, and at What Stage

Vision and strategy emerged from the interviews as the most critical factor shaping inclusion. What are the vision and strategy behind the crowdsourcing initiative?

Sharma states as an essential prerequisite of success that all crowdsourcing initiatives have a set of ideals, goals, and objectives that are well defined and clear to the participating crowd (Brabham 2009). While incentivization of the crowd is important (Kittur, Chi, and Soh 2008; Sharma 2010), this does not necessarily need to be financial. Incentives could be social or political as well.

In the IDRC studies on microwork (Nubelo and LIRNEAsia's research), the platform owners and employers understandably make no attempt at *representative* inclusion, as that is not the focus of the platforms. Lokanathan and Perampalam find that in Sri Lankan microwork platforms, "the majority of people are engaged in some kind of employment, but they want to increase their income by earning a little extra" (Lokanathan and Perampalam, interview, January 27, 2017). It is, therefore, not the unemployed who find their way to the microwork platforms, but already-employed individuals who want to enhance their income. Galperin and Greppi (2017, 27) unequivocally state that "there is no such thing as a flat world in digital labor," and echoing Pallais's (2014) findings, that stereotypes are strengthened online, where there is little opportunity for redress (e.g., in the offline world, by meeting in person). As Galperin states in an interview (January 30, 2017), in the online world, "there is no job interview and there are no recommendations. It is just four or five pieces of information that you have against 30–50 other people who have similar information."

Both the LIRNEAsia and Nubelo microwork-related projects conclude that there are negative implications for representative inclusion on these platforms. If these platforms continue the way they are now, only a small elite will commandeer the online labor market—or, as Galperin finds, build their own pyramids, such as the "superstars" (Galperin, interview, January 30, 2017), who win contracts but then outsource the work to others and take a commission. However, Lokanathan (interview, January 27, 2017) argues that this is not the aim of the platforms, so the issues are larger and implicate broader stakeholders: "[Y]our answers lie elsewhere in terms of education [e.g., have the skills to be on an online job platform], which will be what will facilitate greater inclusivity."

Galperin and Greppi (2017) provide a number of policy suggestions to make microwork platforms more inclusive. They suggest first, that operators could "discourage the display of information unrelated to productivity on workers' profiles" (e.g., nationality, location, gender, and other characteristics); second, implement mechanisms to validate skills and previous work experience (e.g., use algorithms that locate job-seekers without previous contracts higher in the results and provide online third-party certification); and third, provide more networking opportunities for women, because, as the LIRNEAsia research finds, men network more than women do on online labor platforms.

In contrast, the other IDRC projects had a deliberate aim of inclusion, although it is accomplished through different means. For instance, HarassMap is open to all—anyone with access can report her own or other individuals' experience of sexual harassment, while for CMB, though the vision was inclusion of all in terms of who can use the data, the production of the data was limited to staff, students, and volunteers. Craveiro (interview, January 31 2017) also speaks of a different civic action crowdsourcing tool, Promise Tracker,[6] a mobile phone–based tracker of public-sector promises and performance that identified senior citizens as those who would be more engaged; senior citizens were then targeted to receive training on smartphone usage.

Similarly, Una Hakika, instead of crowdsourcing with an open call, where anyone can participate, employed targeted crowdsourcing or crowdseeding that gathered data from trained, trusted informants. This approach results in smaller amounts of data being gathered, but that data, theoretically, would be of better/more trustworthy quality (see also a similar initiative in South Kivu, referenced by Tuckwood 2014). Therefore, while representativity is important, for Una Hakika, it is purposefully selected: "[I]nclusivity is a really high priority for us because we are dealing with information and misinformation and rumors of the type we are normally seeing circulate from person to person and word of mouth, so the more people from different demographics and diversity from the community, the more effective we will be in achieving our goals. Inclusivity is really important…in terms of reaching different demographics, be they ethnic, gender-based, age-based or religious or anything else" (Tuckwood, interview, February 2, 2017).

The Una Hakika team emphasizes the importance of having committed subscribers, or as it calls them, a "captive subscriber base," as the focus of their crowdsourcing activities. Tuckwood explains that "though it is possible for people to make one-time submission of information, what we really prefer is having people really engage, subscribers who sign up to the service" (interview, February 2, 2017). Thus, at this level, the aim is not to be as inclusive of the entire population as possible, but already restrict inclusion to a more strategic selection (Tuckwood, interview, February 2, 2017):

> Crowdsourcing, at least in our interpretation, is about putting this information out there and asking anybody and everybody to submit this information. Useful in some applications, but what we found more interesting is to strategically place people within the community, that is civil society, average residents, members of religious communities, even members of security and government apparatus who can act as a collection point as well as a loudspeaker, a much more targeted approach, rather than saying anybody and everybody inputs information and then you might have to sift through a lot more information which might not have any inherent value. So with crowdseeding, the public is always welcome to submit and we always broadcast that, but we strategically place people, only make connections with that community, so it's a much more targeted approach.

If inclusion depends in part on the platform owner's motivation, this then emerges in design and deployment. As Nanjira Sambuli comments: "a lot of the challenges that we are discussing, even in terms of inclusion at the design level, we need to think about who is designing the platform—as well as the research and analysis of the data produced." HarassMap aims to be as inclusive as possible, running public awareness campaigns and partnering with local NGOs, community leaders, and even store owners. At the Sentinel Project, Tuckwood and Boyd also iterate the necessary pursuit of community engagement in Una Hakika. This is important, of course, but it also comes with a high cost, as they explain: "[it] has been very time-consuming. You might spend a few hours driving to a village and you might get around twenty people to sign up to the service" (Tuckwood, interview).

If we think about inclusion at the stages of production, distribution, or consumption in a crowdsourcing process, there are several strategies that depend upon the nature and purpose of the platform. Microwork platforms do not have an explicit inclusion strategy, although it is certainly possible that they could. All other projects discussed in this chapter invite inclusion at the stage of producing data. However, how they go about facilitating inclusion differs. For example, Una Hakika and Peaceful Truth employ crowdseeding rather than the open-call crowdsourcing approach of HarassMap. Another interesting note regarding the Una Hakika and Peaceful Truth approach is that while the initial input is inclusive, the remaining stages are not broadly inclusive in order to contain the spread of misinformation—while rumors are input through voice, SMS, email, and the web (desktop or mobile) by the 200 or so community members, they are parsed by moderators, who also aggregate, analyze, and can provide counter-messaging (so as to ensure facts, not misinformation, are available).

Thus, in some crowdsourcing platforms, inclusion can be indirect, where a population is included via the activities of intermediaries. The role that these intermediaries play is key to the vision and strategy of the crowdsourcing initiative. In Una Hakika, Peaceful Truth, and HarassMap, we can see that these were critical.

Motive Alignment of the Crowd

Linkages, trust, and the external environment all contribute to whether the motivations of the crowd align with the platform's vision and strategy. In Una Hakika, Tuckwood and Boyd (interview, February 2, 2017) from the Sentinel Project reflect on the challenge of "the famous quote [that] … 'we can't eat information.' People liked the idea, but didn't feel that it would really benefit them. So we tried to share this idea that they would go hand-in-hand, so you might build a school, but if it gets burned down, then what was the point?" Equally, in HarassMap, Chiao speaks of the frustration (and therefore the disincentive) that many faced in reporting harassment—the feeling that the situation might not change. In addition, only major instances may be reported, rather than catcalls for example, which may skew reporting data. In CMB, Craveiro (interview, January 31 2017) spoke of the frustration that most government officials (some of the intended consumers, if not producers) "did not work with the mapped public budget data anyway." The idea that the situation may not change reflects Sharma's motive alignment, a major failure factor in other crowdsourcing initiatives such as Maji Matone (Raising the Water Pressure) in Tanzania, where citizens were meant to report malfunctioning water sources, but the initiative failed to gain critical mass (see Gigler and Bailur 2014).

Similarly, in their Twitter analysis, Sambuli et al. (2013) argue that we should analyze why some people are opting out too. In her interview, Sambuli points out the need to understand black holes: "we really need to understand not only who is included, but who is opting out. So what if someone decides they just don't want to be connected—people switching off after the [2016] US election for example—how do we make sure their views are represented? Women particularly may decide to opt out because politics is designed to be harsh towards women. What do we do then?" (Sambuli, interview, February 3, 2017). This reflects Masika and Bailur's (2015) argument on the adaptive preference of women, who may act sometimes to preserve the status quo simply because challenging it is too problematic. Similarly, Chiao acknowledges that people are opting out of HarassMap due to "participation fatigue"—wondering if it is worth contributing anything: "at the time you might be furious, and want to report something, but when it happens again and again, maybe you don't want to. The fact that it's happened so much—that's what happened to me, that you're fed up and you think, really, is this going to help?" (Chiao, interview). The incentives and patterns for participation, then, may differ between crowdsourcing information in slow-burn situations (e.g., a culture of harassment) and highly acute situations (election monitoring or disaster response), and each may need different strategies to encourage inclusion.

Table 14.3 summarizes our analysis of inclusion practiced by the IDRC projects we researched.

Conclusion

"Inclusivity, that's a tricky one. Even the way it is defined implicates the person who is defining it. Who decides what is inclusive or not?" (Sambuli, interview). Sambuli's words get to the heart of this discussion about inclusion in crowdsourcing models. It

Table 14.3
Inclusion in practice.

Project name	Type of crowdsourcing	Inclusion in practice
HarassMap	Active and open	Inclusion happens at the initial (production) stage, but not so much at the consumption and distribution stages by users (distribution and analysis occur by HarassMap). Access and participation are actively encouraged.
Cuidando do Meu Bairro (CMB)	Active and open	Production is not inclusive, but distribution and consumption are, and it is unclear whether there is a concerted strategy in terms of access, participation, and empowerment. The premise is that open data will be a gateway to further participation (which is contested by the open data critics). See chapter 10.
Una Hakika and Peaceful Truth	Crowdseeding	Selective inclusion occurs at the initial (production) stage, but not so much at the consumption and distribution stages by users (distribution and analysis occur by Una Hakika). Access and moderated participation is encouraged.
Nubelo (now Freelancer.com) and online freelancing and microwork in Sri Lanka[7]	Microwork	No deliberate strategy for inclusion by platform implementers, whether production, distribution, or consumption. Those who access and participate are more likely to be empowered financially.
Kenyan election monitoring	Passive crowdsourcing	No deliberate strategy for inclusion by Twitter, whether production, distribution, or consumption. Questionable whether those who access and participate are more likely to be *empowered*.

appears that unless an active inclusion process is pursued by a crowdsourcing initiative, it is likely that crowdsourcing platforms will be characterized by elite capture (Rumbul 2015 and Swan 2016) (i.e., addressing only concerns by those populations who participate because they have the technical skills and access to do so). Even when it takes place in an open information environment, some suggest that crowdsourcing is fostering a new elite, which may reproduce power dynamics simply because they have the resources to participate (Wexler 2011). In sum, we found the following:

- Inclusivity in these crowdsourcing initiatives is relative—it is defined in different ways by different project owners, and as a result, is operationalized in different ways at different stages (production, distribution, and consumption).

- Inclusivity in crowdsourcing is influenced by a number of factors, the key one being the vision and strategy around the initiative that influences the operationalization of inclusivity. This makes sense given the centralized nature of a crowdsourcing process.

- Inclusivity can happen indirectly and tangentially, such as through intermediaries, but this may introduce other power dynamics (e.g., superstar online workers who outsource to lower tiers).

- There is a difference between microwork and passive crowdsourcing and other types of crowdsourcing in terms of inclusion—microwork in general does not have inclusion as an explicit goal in a normative sense.

Perhaps the most important takeaway from this chapter is that crowdsourcing, of all types, *can* be representatively inclusive—but the inclusion needs to be clearly defined and designed from the start of a project. Inclusion needs to permeate through the vision and strategy of the implementers. Depending on the strategy, this inclusion within crowdsourcing can occur at various stages of production, distribution, and consumption of data in crowdsourcing (where distribution and consumption are not always a given).

There are a few recommendations emerging from the case studies for those who are seeking to expand representative inclusion of their crowdsourcing activities. Implementers need to think about target populations—what it might take to engage them and how to build trust. Active and open crowdsourcing needs to deal with the problem of trust and user fatigue. Crowdseeding needs to strike a careful balance between relying on a few trustworthy seeders and ensuring that they do not dominate, therefore remaining inclusive in a broader sense. Microwork platforms can intentionally try to be more inclusive, particularly in terms of algorithms and rules for employers.

Crowdsourcing in development typically includes a normative value to expand representative inclusion. This type of inclusion in crowdsourcing initiatives requires concerted efforts, particularly by the crowdsourcing implementer, to reach out and engage target populations. Without this engagement, representative inclusion most likely will not occur. Of course, despite the best intentions to expand representative inclusion, success is not assured. Users may choose not to participate for a variety of reasons, such as being suspicious of the initiative or because they do not see the value of participating. This chapter offers some early insights into how crowdsourcing implementers hopefully can increase their chances of success by expanding the diversity of their platforms' participants.

Appendix

Semistructured Question Guide

Have you used crowdsourcing/researched crowdsourcing (tied to what is your definition of crowdsourcing?) in your project?

Why did you use/focus on crowdsourcing? What was the aim of the project?

Who were the intended users and beneficiaries?

What is your overall sense of satisfaction (positive impacts?)

How inclusive do you think the process of crowdsourcing has been? How do you assess the level of inclusivity?

How do you assess this impact?

What are the gender implications of crowdsourcing in your project?

How do you address any questions of ethics in your project?

Using a specific example, what do you think were the challenges of crowdsourcing in your project?

Using a specific example, what were the dangers or unintended consequences of crowdsourcing in your project?

If you had one comment/piece of feedback for IDRC with regard to your example of crowdsourcing, what might that be?

Is there anything else you would like to add/ask?

Notes

1. Project objective: To test strategies and tools for scaling HarassMap to other geographical locations and for other social issues, with the ultimate goal of reduced harassment and corruption.

2. Project objective: To enable a greater understanding of how and whether networked technologies can both influence the process and be deployed to counter misinformation in Kenya and Burma (Myanmar) with the broader aim of reducing conflicts in these regions.

3. Project objective: To improve our understanding of the dynamics and distributional effects of digital labor by exploring potential discrimination against women and workers from less developed countries in an online labor platform serving Latin America.

4. Microwork (such as on platforms like Amazon Turk, Premise, or Upwork), could be a type of crowdsourcing in which a number of prospective employees bid on a task, but there may also be contracts that do not include crowdsourcing (i.e., with already established suppliers).

5. The platforms include FixMyStreet (UK); TheyWorkForYou (UK); GovTrack (US); SeeClickFix (US); AskTheEU (EU-wide); Atlatszo (Hungary); OpenPolis (Italy); Aduanku (Malaysia); Mzalendo (Kenya); People's Assembly (South Africa); OpenAustralia (Australia).

6. See http://promisetracker.org/.

7. See http://lirneasia.net/projects/inclusion-in-business-process-outsourcing/.

References

Abdelmonem, Angie, and Susana Galán. 2017. "Action-Oriented Responses to Sexual Harassment in Egypt: The Cases of HarassMap and WenDo." *Journal of Middle East Women's Studies* 13 (1): 154–167.

Alonso, Omar, Daniel E. Rose, and Benjamin Stewart. 2008. "Crowdsourcing for Relevance Evaluation." *ACM SIGIR Forum* 42 (2): 9–15.

Boyd, Drew. 2016. "Myanmar's State of (Mis)information." *The Sentinel Project*, November 17. https://thesentinelproject.org/2016/11/17/myanmars-state-of-misinformation/.

Boyd, Drew, John Green, Christine Mutisya, and Christopher Tuckwood. 2015. *Una Hakika: Mapping and Countering the Flow of Misinformation in Kenya's Tana Delta*. Final Report. December. Nairobi, Kenya, and Ottawa: IHub/The Sentinel Project and IDRC. https://thesentinelproject.org/wp-content/uploads/2015/12/UHPublicReport_Final.pdf.

Brabham, Daren C. 2009. "Crowdsourcing the Public Participation Process for Planning Projects." *Planning Theory* 8 (3): 242–262.

Chambers, Robert. 2006. "Participatory Mapping and Geographic Information Systems: Whose Map? Who Is Empowered and Who Disempowered? Who Gains and Who Loses?" *Electronic Journal of Information Systems in Developing Countries* 25 (2): 1–11.

Cooke, Bill, and Uma Kothari, eds. 2001. *Participation: The New Tyranny?* London: Zed Books.

Craveiro, Gisele S., and Andrés M. R. Martano. 2015. "Caring for My Neighborhood: A Platform for Public Oversight." *Agent Technology for Intelligent Mobile Services and Smart Societies*, ed. Fernando Koch, Felipe Meneguzzi, and Kiran Lakkaraju, 498:117–126. Heidelberg/Berlin: Springer.

De Beer, Jeremy, Ian P. McCarthy, Adam Soliman, and Emily Treen. 2017. "Click Here to Agree: Managing Intellectual Property When Crowdsourcing Solutions." *Business Horizons* 60 (2): 207–217.

Donner, Jonathan. 2015. *After Access: Inclusion, Development, and a More Mobile Internet*. Cambridge, MA: MIT Press.

Estellés-Arolas, Enrique, and Fernando González-Ladrón-de-Guevara. 2012. "Towards an Integrated Crowdsourcing Definition." *Journal of Information Science* 38 (2): 189–200.

Fahmy, Amel, Angie Abdelmonem, Enas Hamdy, Ahmed Badr, and Rasha Hassan. 2014. "Towards a Safer City: Sexual Harassment in Greater Cairo: Effectiveness of Crowdsourced Data." https://harass map.org/storage/app/media/uploaded-files/Towards-A-Safer-City_executive-summary_EN.pdf.

Farid, Farid Y. 2015. "Keep Off: The App That Wants to Make Egypt's Streets Safer for Women." https://qz.com/434606/the-app-that-wants-to-make-egypts-streets-safer-for-women/.

Fisher, Lauren. 2012. "How Crowdsourcing Is Tackling Poverty in the Developing World?" *Forbes*, March 21. https://www.forbes.com/sites/benkerschberg/2012/03/21/how-crowdsourcing-is-tackling -poverty-in-the-developing-world/.

Galperin, Hernan, Guillermo Cruces, and Catrihel Greppi. 2017. "Gender Interactions in Wage Bargaining: Evidence from an Online Field Experiment." *SSRN*. https://papers.ssrn.com/sol3 /papers.cfm?abstract_id=3056508.

Galperin, Hernan, and Catrihel Greppi. 2017. Geographical Discrimination in the Gig Economy. *SSRN*. https://ssrn.com/abstract=2922874.

Gidley, Jennifer, Gary Hampson, Leone Wheeler, and Elleni Bereded-Samuel. 2010. "Social Inclusion: Context, Theory, and Practice." *Australasian Journal of University-Community Engagement* 5 (1): 6–36. https://researchbank.rmit.edu.au/view/rmit:4909.

Gigler, Björn-Sören, and Savita Bailur. 2014. *Closing the Feedback Loop: Can Technology Bridge the Accountability Gap?* Washington, DC: World Bank. https://openknowledge.worldbank.org/handle /10986/18408.

Howe, Jeff. 2006. "The Rise of Crowdsourcing." *Wired* 14 (6): 1–4.

Kittur, Aniket, Ed H. Chi, and Bongwon Soh. 2008. "Crowdsourcing for Usability: Using Micro-Task Markets for Rapid, Remote, and Low-Cost User Measurements." *CHI Conference on Human Factors in Computing Systems*, 453–456. Florence, Italy, April. http://citeseerx.ist.psu.edu/viewdoc /summary?doi=10.1.1.532.2255.

Kleemann, Frank, G. Günter Voß, and Kerstin Rieder. 2008. "Un(der)paid Innovators: The Commercial Utilization of Consumer Work through Crowdsourcing." *Science, Technology and Innovation Studies* 4 (1): 5–26.

Mansell, Robin. 2013. "Employing Digital Crowdsourced Information Resources: Managing the Emerging Information Commons." *International Journal of the Commons* 7 (2): 255–277.

Masika, Rachel, and Savita Bailur. 2015. "Negotiating Women's Agency through ICTs: A Comparative Study of Uganda and India." *Gender, Technology, and Development* 19 (1): 43–69.

Pallais, Amanda. 2014. "Inefficient Hiring in Entry-Level Labor Markets." *American Economic Review* 104 (11): 3565–3599.

Parameswaran, Manoj, and Andrew B. Whinston. 2007. "Social Computing: An Overview." *Communications of the Association for Information Systems* 19 (37): 762–80. http://aisel.aisnet.org/cgi /viewcontent.cgi?article=2680&context=cais.

Raja, Siddhartha, Saori Imaizumi, Tim Kelly, and Cecilia Paradi-Guilford. 2013. *Connecting to Work. How Information and Communication Technologies Could Help Expand Employment Opportunities*. Washington, DC: World Bank.

Rossotto, Carlo M., Siou C. Kuek, and Cecilia Paradi-Guilford. 2012. *New Frontiers and Opportunities in Work: ICT is Dramatically Reshaping the Global Job Market*. Brief 78266, Vol. 1. Washington, DC: World Bank.

Rumbul, Rebecca. 2015. *Who Benefits from Civic Technology? Demographic and Public Attitudes Research into the Users of Civic Technology*. London: mySociety, October. https://www.mysociety .org/files/2015/10/demographics-report.pdf.

Sambuli, Nanjira, Angela Crandall, Patrick Costello, and Christopher Orwa. 2013. *Viability, Verification, Validity: 3Vs of Crowdsourcing. Tested in Election-based Crowdsourcing*. Nairobi, Kenya: iHub Research. https://ihub.co.ke/ihubresearch/jb_VsReportpdf2013-8-29-07-38-56.pdf.

Sharma, Ankit. 2010. "Crowdsourcing Critical Success Factor Model: Strategies to Harness the Collective Intelligence of the Crowd." Working Paper 1. London: London School of Economics.

Silversmith, A., and D. Tulchin. 2013. "Crowdsourcing Applications for Agricultural Development in Africa." Briefing Paper. Washington, DC: USAID. http://pdf.usaid.gov/pdf_docs/PA00J7P7.pdf.

Smith, Marshall S., and Catherine M. Casserly. 2006. "The Promise of Open Educational Resources." *Change* 38 (5): 8–17.

Smith, Matthew L., and Ruhiya Seward. 2017. "Openness as Social Praxis." *First Monday* 22 (4), April 3. http://dx.doi.org/10.5210/fm.v22i4.7073.

Surowiecki, James. 2004. *The Wisdom of Crowds*. New York: Doubleday.

Swan, Anthony. 2016. "Bridging Data Gaps for Policy Making: Crowdsourcing and Big Data for Development." *DevPolicyBlog,* July 8. http://devpolicy.org/bridging-data-gaps-policymaking -crowdsourcing-big-data-development-20160708/.

Tuckwood, Christopher. 2014. "The State of the Field: Technology for Atrocity Response." *Genocide Studies and Prevention: An International Journal* Article 9, 8 (3): 80–86. http://scholarcommons .usf.edu/cgi/viewcontent.cgi?article=1275&context=gsp.

Tuckwood, Christopher. 2017. "Tune into Tana: On the Air with Amani FM." *The Sentinel Project*, September 4. https://thesentinelproject.org/2017/09/04/tune-into-tana-on-the-air-with-amani-fm/.

Wexler, Mark N. 2011. "Reconfiguring the Sociology of the Crowd: Exploring Crowdsourcing." *International Journal of Sociology and Social Policy* 31 (1/2): 6–20.

World Bank. 2013. *Brief: Social Inclusion*. August 15. http://www.worldbank.org/en/topic /socialdevelopment/brief/social-inclusion.

15   Open Innovation in Africa: Current Realities, Future Scenarios, and Scalable Solutions

Jeremy de Beer, Chris Armstrong, Shirin Elahi, Dick Kawooya, Erika Kramer-Mbula, Caroline Ncube, Chidi Oguamanam, Nagla Rizk, Isaac Rutenberg, and Tobias Schonwetter

Introduction

When many people think of Africa, *innovation* is not a word that springs to mind. It should be. The continent of Africa is among the most dynamic, innovative places on Earth. The issue is that too few people have been looking for the ways and the places in which African innovation is happening.

A goal of the Open African Innovation Research[1] (Open AIR) network has been to help the world recognize Africa's role in the global knowledge economy. One of the ways that Open AIR does this is through empirical research. The network's research proves that innovation is flourishing, and will continue to, in various forms across the African continent. Open AIR's research has also shown that, in many ways, innovation systems in Africa are more inclusive than elsewhere.

Stereotypes may suggest that to be valuable, innovation ought to involve radical breakthroughs driven by large-scale investments of financial capital and human resources into a linear process of formal research and development. From that point of view, innovation is driven primarily by individual entrepreneurs or single firms, incentivized by the ability to appropriate returns on investment via intellectual property rights (IPRs) and related mechanisms. Many people in society are excluded from participating in, or sharing the benefits of, such forms of innovation.

Another perspective is that innovation is an incremental process involving experimentation, adaptation, improvisation, and collaboration. In this paradigm, the openness of innovation ecosystems encourages local, sustainable problem-solving. Formal appropriation mechanisms like IPRs are irrelevant (or even impediments) to the exchanges of knowledge that facilitate open and collaborative innovation. Often, although not always, such innovation systems are more inclusive than exclusive.

Which perspective, or combination of perspectives, best reflects innovation in Africa at the current time? Which is most appropriate to inform policy and practice going forward?

In answer to such questions, this chapter summarizes findings from two interrelated research initiatives carried out by the Open AIR network between 2010 and 2014: a series of case studies exploring open and collaborative innovation and a strategic fore-sight exercise exploring the future of knowledge governance.[2] Chapter 3 of this volume explores in detail the concept of open innovation and its links to development, which this chapter does not repeat. Rather, this chapter connects Open AIR's findings about current realities and future scenarios with the network's ongoing efforts to deepen understanding of how openness may affect the scalability of African innovation.

Current Realities: The Collaborative Dynamics of African Innovation

Africa is an enormous and diverse continent, with many countries, cultures, and con-texts. Open AIR's exploration of the role of IPRs in systems of innovation and creativity in African settings seeks to avoid the perpetuation of stereotypes of African homo-geneity. This perspective emerges from an awareness that in the context of human-ity's striving for innovation and creativity, Africa's contributions have tended to be, in our experience, confined to the prehistoric era, sometimes via dubiously benevolent attempts to acknowledge the continent's role as the starting place (the *cradle,* no less) of humankind. Africa has also tended to be depicted as a dark continent—that is, as a disease- and affliction-ridden hot spot dominated by poverty, violence, and corruption. Juxtaposing the concept of *innovation* with the word *African* has, for much of the past century, been depicted as a contradiction in terms.

Various intellectual property (IP)–related reasons might explain the power of nar-ratives suggesting that creativity and innovation in most parts of Africa appear to fall short of innovative and creative activity in other regions, particularly developed world regions. Research by Open AIR investigates two possible reasons in particular. First, African creativity and innovation are not properly valued by prevalent IP systems and assumptions. Second, African creativity and innovation are being constrained by sub-optimal IP-related policies and practices. To explore those issues, in 2011, the Open AIR network released an open call for research that would help answer the following question: How can existing or potential IP systems be harnessed to appropriately value and facilitate innovation and creativity for open development in Africa?

This framing provoked a range of connected questions. Practically, how do African innovators or creators exploit, adapt to, or work around, IP environments? Conceptu-ally, are exclusive IP rights compatible with collaborative, openness-oriented innova-tion and creativity in Africa, and with inclusive development more generally? What are the on-the-ground interplays between openness and protection in relation to IP in

African innovative and creative settings? At a more systemic level, to what extent, and how, have policymakers in Africa attempted to calibrate IP frameworks in such a way that they can maximize innovative and creative potential?

The research examines such questions clustered around the following topics: (1) informal appropriation, (2) trademarks and geographical indications, (3) traditional knowledge, (4) copyrights, (5) patents, and (6) publicly funded research. Collectively, these six interconnecting research foci offer insights into the extent to which IP systems are being, or could be, harnessed in African contexts to enable successful collaborative peer production and distribution of knowledge-related goods and services.

Open AIR researchers were mindful of overlaps among these topics. Any innovator, creator, entrepreneur, or supporting policymaker can attest to the fact that the key, overarching, real-world issue is how valuable intangible resources of any sort are protected, managed, and mobilized. Whether the legal regime of patents or trademarks or copyrights is the particular tool being utilized in an effort to perform the desired management or mobilization is of secondary importance to ultimate objectives. Many of the stakeholders affected by IPRs in any particular setting are unaware of the technical distinctions among branches of IP. A holistic approach is, therefore, appropriate.

Based on comparisons and contrasts of specific research findings, Open AIR research draws conclusions regarding three key topics: (1) collaborative innovation and creativity, (2) openness, and (3) IPRs. The research reveals the need for restraint in drawing generalized impressions of the modes of innovation and creativity on the African continent. There are inherent and profound divergences among African countries' sociocultural compositions and among their environments. At the same time, it cannot be denied that there is evidence of similarities at play across the African innovation landscapes. Such similarities point to systemic, albeit emergent or open-ended, insights into innovation and creativity as the continent responds to the transformational pressures of market liberalization and global IP norms.

The results from our case studies make it apparent that in Africa, innovation and creativity are not endeavors that inevitably take place in the context of market economic surveillance. Deliberate reification of commercial or organizational strategies for business and entrepreneurial advancement may be aspirational constructs, but they are not necessarily the mainstream of African orientation toward innovation. Indeed, at present the African context seems predisposed toward innovations and creations of necessity. Outside conventional straitjacketing, innovations and creations in African settings often consist of endeavors that create value and add value to societies, through pragmatic means. Innovations occur in multiple contexts, including through transformations, reorientations, and renegotiations of Indigenous knowledge systems.

The innovation creation dynamics reflected in most of the case studies unavoidably generate doubt over the veracity, in African contexts, of the firm or the organization as the default unit for knowledge transfer. In the African settings examined, the configurations of cultural strands, nodes, and clusters interact in formal and informal ways to generate knowledge outside presumed organizational paradigms. Knowledge transmission is mediated by a myriad of factors, including necessities generated by present dynamics, intergenerational obligations, and cultural sensitivities to experiences and knowledge from the (deep and/or recent) past.

Tabulations of the quantity of science and engineering publications, yearly patent totals, and other forms of research and development statistics reified by orthodox audits of innovation are extremely blunt instruments for anyone seeking to distill the essences of the innovations and creations present in the African settings analyzed in Open AIR's research. Given the predilection of such research and development benchmarks for the detection of so-called frontier technologies, it should not come as a great surprise that the often-incremental, informal, traditional, and/or accidental innovations and creations highlighted are not readily captured by such benchmarks.

Current interest shown by some governments in Africa in calibrating university/ industry liaisons through patenting and commercialization of publicly funded research outputs symbolizes a response to the globalizing world's innovation measurement imperative. Such attempted calibrations reflect exploration of the expansion of formal institutional channels for knowledge transformation in which the firm and other forms of local organizational structures were conduits for knowledge transfer. The expansion of such formal institutional collaborations for innovation would likely result in increased relevance of orthodox benchmarking of innovation. But such changes might come at the expense of more context appropriate approaches that better reflect realities in African settings. Quite unlike the orthodox, firm-centric organizational structure featured in conventional innovation discourse, actors in the African settings probed by Open AIR are situated within heterogeneous sociocultural ecosystems characterized by ongoing hybridizations among the modern and the traditional, the developed, and the developing, the Western, and the African.

The Open AIR case studies also display pluralities of social units, associational frameworks, and contexts for innovative and creative endeavors. Africa's diversity of social constructs cannot readily be compacted into a simplistic binary between so-called individualistic and collectivist societies. However, it is true that many of Africa's innovation contexts (including several of the contexts examined in Open AIR's book) do not affirm the privileging of individualist cultures over collectivist ones. The research findings suggest that the individual, the family, the community, and various other social units and contingent entrepreneurial clusters, are all implicated in knowledge generation, innovation, and creativity in the settings studied.

In contemporary African settings, innovative/creative modalities tend toward optimized hybrids: nonabsolutist, adaptable mixes of sharing and preserving, of informal and formal, of new and old, of open-source and IP-protected. Such hybrids, arrived at via selective pragmatism, have the potential to accentuate the diversity of African innovation/creation practices and allow individuals, communities, regions, and nations on the continent, and diasporic Africans, to more optimally participate in global IP structures. IP lawmaking and policymaking in service to optimized hybrids is and will be complex, particularly given the fluidity of these hybrids.

Across Open AIR's studies, we see examples of what seem to be potential middle-ground models of IP policies and practices based on underlying principles of *inclusion* and *collaboration*. This middle ground emerges when one is willing to accept that absolute openness is not required to facilitate knowledge sharing; and, at the same time, nor does IP protection inevitably preclude access to everyone but the individual proprietor. Situated in this middle ground are various forms of IP that can be used as tools to facilitate collaboration within or across communities of many kinds.

For example, research by Ncube, Abrahams, and Akinsanmi (2014), Belete (2014), and Ama (2014) suggests that appropriate IP management policies and practices can contribute to the ability of publicly funded researchers to put open science models into practice (i.e., to engage in wide online sharing of research data in order to spur collaborations and dissemination). The research shows that patents are rarely the best way to develop, commercialize, and disseminate innovation from publicly funded research in African countries.

South Africa is leading Africa's policy emphasis on institutional patenting of publicly funded research outputs, via its Intellectual Property Rights from Publicly Financed Research and Development (IPR-PFRD) Act of 2008 and associated regulations of 2010. The IPR-PFRD Act encourages publicly funded research institutions to prioritize protection and patenting of their findings. The Open AIR South African researchers, Caroline Ncube, Luci Abrahams, and Titi Akinsanmi, conducted a case study of research management practices at two universities, the University of Cape Town and the University of the Witwatersrand, and found that the IPR-PFRD Act's patent focus was suboptimal, "It calls itself an IPR Act, but it's a patent act," says Abrahams, who is director of the Wits LINK Centre, "[a]nd it neglects issues of how to transfer knowledge, and socialize knowledge, in line with development of a knowledge-intensive economy" (Open AIR 2014, 1). According to Ncube, who now holds the South African Research Chair in Innovation (SARChI), Intellectual Property, and Development, the IPR-PFRD Act is to some extent misdirecting university resources: "The danger is encouraging mindless filing of patent applications. Because of the legislation, there is a tendency to disclose any and everything, and the technology transfer office staff at [the University of Cape Town] now spend a lot of time trolling through reams of paper" (Open AIR 2014, 1). Ncube, Abrahams, and Akinsanmi found that many researchers at the University of Cape Town and the University of the Witwatersrand are adopting workaround solutions to ensure that, as well as complying with the IPR-PFRD Act, they can disseminate their innovative research findings quickly and widely, on an online open science basis, via self-archiving and open access journals.

The findings in South Africa are reinforced by Open AIR research on Ethiopia's Science, Technology and Innovation (STI) Policy of 2012. Among other things, the policy calls for increased innovation transfers between the country's public universities and industry players, and for universities to pursue patents on inventions generated by their publicly funded research. But according to Open AIR Ethiopian researcher Wondwossen Belete, "the STI Policy puts the cart before the horse" because "in the Ethiopian context, the major problem is the weak research capacity of the universities, not research outputs which are piling up in university laboratories because of some sort of lack of incentive to be transferred to industry" (Open AIR 2014, 1). Belete, an IP expert with the Society for Technology Studies (STS) in Addis Ababa, found a dearth of research at Ethiopia's universities and scant private-sector capacity to absorb and commercialize innovations. Thus, Belete concluded, the Ethiopian government needs to focus policy not on downstream IP rights, but rather on building the upstream capacities of university research departments. Belete argues that a key element of this support should be ensuring Ethiopian researcher participation in international online sharing of research data on an open science basis.

A related Open AIR study in Botswana, conducted by Njoku Ola Ama, found that patents are largely irrelevant to the priorities of the country's researchers (Ama 2014; Open AIR 2014, 1). The survey of dozens of African national patent offices conducted by Ikechi Mgbeoji (2014) shows that even if researchers wanted to prioritize patenting, most patent authorities on the continent lack the institutional capacity to optimally regulate the granting and enforcement of such rights. Given these realities, it is open and collaborative innovation approaches that are often the most practical business models in African settings.

Both the Ethiopian and South African policy approaches mirror elements of the Bayh-Dole Act of 1980 in the US, also known as the Patent and Trademark Law Amendments Act (Pub. L. 96–517, December 12, 1980). This act encouraged American public research bodies to pursue IP protection of their research outputs. According to the findings of Belete (2014) in Ethiopia, and Ncube, Abrahams, and Akinsanmi (2014) in South Africa, Bayh-Dole-style policies do not appear to be directly transferable to current African national research contexts.

Moreover, open innovation strategies are not mere charity, but rather are cutting-edge commercialization techniques that build platforms for spin-off business opportunities, good jobs, economic growth, and social benefits. Collaborative models help to build the trust essential for productive partnerships. Open AIR research findings suggest that policies blindly encouraging more patenting of African publicly funded research outputs are largely misguided.

Open AIR researchers also shed light on previously understudied modes of appropriation in the informal economy. What the researchers describe in relation to the informal economy would be commonly understood, in high-income countries, as trade secrecy. Trade secrets, confidential information, and sharing or nondisclosure agreements are all well-accepted forms of IP management and play important roles in innovation systems. Yet because secrecy does not produce a quantifiable output (e.g., a patent), its use and value in Africa's informal sectors are too-often ignored.

For example, Kawooya (2014) shows that automotive mechanics and university researchers can and do share trade secrets among themselves, often pursuant to informal agreements enforced by social rather than legal norms. Informal-sector artisans in Kampala with no formal education or training made parts for a widely celebrated Kiira EV, the electric vehicle prototype produced at Makerere University, Uganda. IPRs were not central but were important to the collaboration. Kawooya's interviews revealed that the artisans are not interested or even aware of formal IPRs. What is captivating to the artisans is the idea that university professors with formal training and PhDs in engineering are coming to them to translate their ideas into a product. At the same time, however, IP is involved because the university (due to pressure to protect the patentability of inventions from their publicly and donor funded research) requires artists to sign nondisclosure agreements regarding confidential information.

The studies by Oguamanam and Dagne (2014) and by Adewopo, Chuma-Okoro, and Oyewunmi (2014) found that groups of agricultural or industrial producers and retailers invoke place-based protections. Meanwhile, as evidenced by the Ouma (2014) study and the research of Cocchiaro et al. (2014), Indigenous peoples manage cultural heritage or medicinal knowledge through a mix of customary laws and cultural norms, and/or through more formal mechanisms such a biocultural community protocol (BCP). Rizk (2014) found that musicians choose to confront the realities of copyright unenforceability through alternative business models, and Sihanya (2014) looked at how scholars and publishers can use copyright creatively to openly license learning materials. Dos Santos and Pelembe (2014) and Awad and Abou Zeid (2014) found evidence to suggest that the patent system could play a role in the sharing of technological knowledge between rights holders and communities of potential users or collaborators, thus furthering particular industrial policy objectives, with respect to clean energy technologies.

In none of these observed cases would IP owners be likely to see an advantage in exercising the power to fully exclude others from the protected knowledge. Doing so would be counterproductive to underlying social, cultural, and economic objectives present in the settings in which the knowledge is being deployed.

When Open AIR began this phase of research, potential confusion around the concept of openness stemmed from the elusiveness of agreement about what it is. Whether a system can be considered open depends on a variety of factors, including, significantly, the degree to which people are free, or even empowered, to universally access a system and to participate, collaborate, and share within that system (Smith et al. 2011). Open AIR's early brainstorming around the idea of openness for development centered around principles of collaboration, participation, and inclusiveness in the political, legal, economic, social, cultural, technological, and other institutions (broadly conceived) that shape people's lives.[3] Examples in practice might include open government, open communications networks, open access to content, open-sourced research, open product development, and commons-based peer production (Benkler 2006; Wunsch-Vincent and Vickery 2007). Similar principles can be found in discussions using the label "inclusive development," both generally (IDRC 2011) and in the specific context of innovation (OECD 2013).

Proponents of the value of open or inclusive development paradigms tended to gravitate toward calls for increasing democratic engagement, and they tend to emphasize the distributive implications of the benefits that accrue from such modes of development to the most marginalized segments of society. It can even be argued that openness breeds more openness, so that it is a game-changing force for unlocking innovation and creativity. That said, the potential downsides of openness should not be overlooked, including in the realm of IP protection, the risk of misappropriation and, perhaps, the challenges faced in seeking to find financial incentives for innovative and creative activity. The potential advantages and disadvantages make it necessary to consider appropriate degrees of openness that balance benefits with costs. Such balancing tends to be a constantly dynamic process, which further complicates a possible definition of openness in the context of developmental processes.

Another challenge in arriving at a clear understanding of open development and related openness-focused concepts is the paradox that one person's freedom often requires another's constraint. Despite these conceptual and definitional challenges, and also to a great extent *because* of them, Open AIR sought to help build a better understanding of what the concept of open development might look like in one particular set of contexts: African contexts involving elements of IP, innovation, and creativity.

In some of Open AIR's case studies, we see what appears to be a strong emphasis on openness, with an almost-complete absence of restrictions or closures, in relation to certain innovative collaborative outputs. For instance, Ugandan mechanics do not, as is the nature of the very open paradigm in which they innovate and develop their livelihoods, seek proprietary control over access to their innovative ideas and solutions. But in other contexts, we see that collaboration does not mean absolute openness. In one Indigenous community in South Africa, healers are committed to openness among the participants in their *traditional knowledge commons*, but their cultural protocol controls access to this commons by both participants and nonmembers. Likewise, leather and textile makers in Nigeria seek to share within their unions and associations, but at the same time, they seek to prevent their designs from being used by nonunion/association members. And while Kenyan scholarly authors are enthusiastic about the potential of open access publishing, they also want protection of their economic rights as creators.

To the extent that Open AIR's studies suggest that collaboration is a primary engine of innovation and development in many African settings, then the conceptual emphasis of open development's proponents, with the focus on networked collaboration, seems to fit. But it must also be kept in mind that the builders of the open development framework acknowledge that absolute openness will often not be beneficial or possible in developmental settings; there will usually need to be some parameters and restrictions (Smith et al. 2011). The findings generated by the studies in this book support the contention that open development cannot be conceived as a binary proposition, either open or closed. Nor would a metaphor of a spectrum, from more open to more closed, necessarily be apt. Socioeconomic development, especially when conceived as open development, is a far more complex process.

Overall, the IP approaches identified as suitable by the research done by Open AIR (i.e., approaches identified as being compatible with innovation and creativity in the African settings studied) tended to be characterized by a strong degree of openness and a balance between knowledge protection and collaboration.

Open AIR's key recommendations are, therefore, to (1) patiently avoid importing and entrenching foreign IP approaches that may not suit local conditions, (2) broaden conceptions of relevant IP rights beyond merely formal mechanisms in order to create collaborative knowledge governance systems, and (3) focus on the future rather than the past or present when implementing IP policies.

Through on the ground qualitative and quantitative data gathering, Open AIR researchers have demonstrated the rapidly evolving dynamics of IP, innovation, creativity, and development in African settings. This evidence provides a sense of the current realities in a wide variety of contexts. But simply observing the past and present cannot adequately prepare policymakers and stakeholders for the future. Many African states appear to be at a crossroads in their paths toward negotiating their places in an increasingly globalized IP order. A narrative of Africa as *emerging* has gained currency in recent years. This more positive view of the continent's prospects is potentially a welcome boost for African nations seeking to attract investment and partners. But this narrative, whereby Africa is emergent, also brings with it the danger of intensified pressure on African states to fine-tune national and regional laws and reorient knowledge production traditions into a globalized paradigm predicated on the market economy in which orthodox approaches to IP rights have typically been positioned as sacrosanct.

The findings about current realities from the Open AIR network suggest that going forward, African policymakers, as with the innovators and creators whom they are supposed to serve, must seek to harness IP rights on their own terms. To prepare for multiple plausible futures, Open AIR conducted a massive strategic foresight exercise (Elahi et al. 2013), described in the next section of this chapter.

Future Scenarios: Knowledge Governance Models for Multiple Futures

In an uncertain world, there is little point in trying to predict the future. Yet Nelson Mandela observed, "One cannot be prepared for something while secretly believing it will not happen" (1995, 374). An alternative approach is to find a framework, or a map, for thinking about possible futures and their implications. Scenarios are maps of the future and, like any map, they link the world and our existing knowledge to new terrain such as new experiences, ideas, and thought processes. With these maps, policymakers, communities, researchers, and anyone else with an interest in how the future might unfold can take steps to rehearse the future and explore how these three diverse worlds might affect their actions or policies.

Scenarios also enable dialogue. Talking and exploring differences allow stakeholders with diverse perspectives and interests to find common ground. The aim is not to find a single answer, but to have strategic conversations that open possibilities and enable participants to acknowledge different worldviews and perspectives. The process increases fairness, if not in the outcomes, then at least in the procedure, as all are given a voice. Using scenarios also allows strategists and policymakers to anticipate events and prevent mistakes.

The Open AIR network spent several years constructing scenarios through literature reviews, key informant interviews, and workshops. The following section of the chapter describes three scenarios developed by the Open AIR network, as well as their implications for future research, policy, and practice around knowledge and innovation in Africa.

Forces Driving Change

As a first step, Open AIR's research identified five major forces simultaneously driving countries around the continent of Africa in multiple, uncertain directions. Driving forces affect the perception of progress, the shape of innovation systems, and the governance of knowledge. How these forces converge or diverge will determine which scenario will dominate the future in specific places at specific times. The five driving forces identified are as follows:

- *Global relationships:* The countless interconnections and interdependencies that span the globe to unite its people or distance them. Will these relationships be collaborative, competitive, or coercive? Who benefits?
- *Statehood and governance:* The role of the state in relation to citizens, balancing the innate tension between individual rights and freedoms and state power. Will African governance be cohesive, challenging, or communal? Whose interests are being served?
- *Identities and differences:* The values that evolve in the face of social, political, and economic changes taking place at the global, local, and personal levels. Will multiplicity, fluidity, or stability hold sway as African identities and values evolve?
- *Infrastructure and technology:* Disruptive enablers to leapfrog conventional structures, and methods to create new economic, social, and political development and disrupt the status quo. Will infrastructure and technology investment be inclusive, strained, or reconceived?
- *Employment and livelihoods:* The ability to create opportunities for a growing workforce, so providing the means to reduce poverty and to create economic growth, social empowerment, or even social cohesion. Will African economies diversify, render informal, or reconfigure to meet the needs of the increasingly youthful population?

In addition to these driving forces, there are several possible wild cards or shocks that could catapult the continent of Africa into a different future at present entirely unforeseen. These include violence, military action, and terrorism; major clashes of civilizations or religions; epic natural disasters or climate changes beyond predicted extremes; or human, animal, or agricultural pandemics.

Considering the many combinations of ways that these drivers of change may intersect with one another, Open AIR developed a set of three scenarios that reflect different, plausible scenarios: futures for knowledge and innovation in Africa dominated by:
(1) high-tech hubs, (2) informal innovation, and/or (3) Indigenous entrepreneurship.

Box 15.1

High-tech hubs

In this scenario, which Open AIR titled "Wireless Engagement," countries in Africa have
strong international roles, and African enterprise is interconnected with the global service-
oriented economy. Savvy, young, educated, and mobile business leaders are forming a new
and vocal middle class. Engaged citizens are able to participate both politically and economically, thereby holding their governments accountable. Uneducated or underresourced
individuals are excluded by their inability to conform to homogenous technical, legal, and
socioeconomic standards.

Box 15.2

Informal innovation

In a scenario of "Informal, the New Normal," dynamic informalities cross every aspect of
African societies economically, politically, and socially. Increasingly diverse regions of the
continent are constantly changing, affecting and affected by the endless ways in which
people pursue their livelihoods. Ideas constantly recombine within communities built
upon interpersonal trust, triggering innovations adapted to this relentless change. Who
you know matters more than what you know. Those people unable to establish local grassroots relationships will fail to build thriving businesses or social influence.

Box 15.3

Indigenous entrepreneurship

Open AIR's third scenario was titled "Sincerely, Africa," a future in which global instabili-
ties and external pressures allow Africans to focus inward, building strength by exploiting
for themselves valuable endowments including a youthful population and natural resource
riches. With scarcity threatening the rest of the world, African societies ensure sustainability by reengaging and reinterpreting their traditional knowledge systems and sociocultural
institutions. Who you are matters most. Outsiders lacking community roots lose the ability
to participate socially, politically, and economically.

Every scenario is dominated by an implicit set of rationales, a logical basis for a course of action or a particular belief. This creates the lens through which the world is perceived, the definitions and milestones of success, and the metrics that are chosen to measure progress. Table 15.1 describes the relevant metrics of innovation based on predominant paradigms underpinning each scenario.

Technological and social norms may also be different across future scenarios. In this respect, trust is both the glue that binds groups of people together and the lubricant that enables them to undertake collective action without transaction costs or a thicket of inflexible rules and regulations. It is built upon three interrelated components: efficiency, fairness, and consistency. Without these components, coercion is required to get results. Table 15.2 compares scenarios in terms of technological and social aspects of trust.

In every scenario, there are internal tensions and power struggles. Open AIR research explores the ways that these tensions may affect open innovation. A scenario dominated by high-tech hubs may see interoperability among technological, economic, and legal standards emerge as the greatest tension. A scenario of informality may create tensions over rules and stability, and the value of tacit versus codified knowledge. Additionally, a scenario built around Indigenous entrepreneurship will involve tensions between holistic and individualized perspectives. Table 15.3 elaborates on this point.

As a result of tensions, there are different winners and losers in every scenario, as shown in table 15.4. With high-tech hubs, the winners are those persons who are

Table 15.1

Key metrics to indicate successful innovation.

High-tech hubs	Informal innovation	Indigenous entrepreneurship
The rationale of the interconnected market economy that underpins this world is based on efficiency and return on investment. Success depends on a combination of skill and opportunity, of which standardized education is the key determinant. The metrics that matter here focus on outputs and capture efficiency, accountability, transparency, and interoperability.	A vibrant, informal economy depends on networks that simultaneously promote self-interest and community opportunity. Many successful actors are likely to be invisible to observers looking at output related indicators, although some who scale their activities will gain in profile. Surveys of the formal sector, national statistics, and financial metrics underrepresent the richness of informality.	This paradigm involves stewardship of valuable resources by intergenerational communities, linked by space, time, and identity. Behaviors are coordinated, collectively monitored, and enforced by social norms that implicitly acknowledge the long-term nature of systemic interactions. Prosperity will be measured over time, considering whether an identified community can sustain a thriving, yet self-contained unit.

Table 15.2
Technological and social aspects of trust.

High-tech hubs	Informal innovation	Indigenous entrepreneurship
In a rule-based wireless world, online verification provides access to those with the same skill sets and interests, so enabling the emerging middle class and civil society to create a strong government. Trust is impersonal and facilitated via digital intermediaries, most likely transnational corporations. There will be a strong drive for interoperability that comes with shared standards, and there is likely to be a growing demand for open standards that are globally recognized. This creates an inclusive world, but only for a small minority with the potential, skills, and networks of access. The relative size of this *insider* minority depends on the size of the middle and the extent to which advancement is based on individual ability or achievement. What matters for society as a whole are relationships with the *outsiders* (i.e., the mass of excluded and disengaged Africans).	In an informal world based on interpersonal relations, trust is socially and economically determined—"because I know someone you know." A handshake is the main method of contract, and for the many Africans who are illiterate or lack formal education, tacit and social norms work well. There is no middle, and the formal and informal are separate, yet interdependent, systems. They exist in parallel universes until some mutual benefit becomes apparent, at which point a pragmatic symbiotic relationship materializes. Trust is personal but also intragroup, not interspersed across society at large. Reputation matters a great deal, as competition is fierce within groups and between groups. The size of the community of trust is constantly evolving in this world, and among the greatest uncertainties is whether and how interpersonal networks may be affected by impersonal ICTs.	There are no standardized responses in this world, as it is based on local context; every case is unique and geographically and socially determined. There is no right way to do things—simply ways that work within a given context. Trust here is a two-way street based on independent and interdependent cooperative associations of individuals voluntarily committed to meeting shared economic, social, and cultural needs and wants. They will have a set of values and norms determined collectively and in common for the benefit of the fair sharing of resources. Where the group is able, there will be strong sanctions against those that flout social norms. The group's size will depend on its ability to maintain a strong boundary and protect its assets. Where the group is large, it is likely to have a nested structure of rules within rules. Stigma and shame are likely to be used to enforce cooperative behavior.

highly skilled and economically interconnected. With informal innovation, winners are adaptable and socially networked. With Indigenous entrepreneurship, winners are trusted and well respected.

Implications for Knowledge Governance

The central purpose of Open AIR's scenario-building exercise was to better understand various modes of knowledge governance. The research shows that knowledge

Table 15.3
Core tensions affecting open innovation.

High-tech hubs	Informal innovation	Indigenous entrepreneurship
In a world of wireless engagement, tensions exist between the silos of knowledge embedded in the hierarchical industrial/bureaucratic, rule-based impersonal logic, and the faster, networked, and interdependent knowledge interactive modes of social production. The tensions are likely to be most marked along the interface between the individualized knowledge workers dealing with contextual specificity and the global, impersonal system, with stresses across dimensions of speed and geography. Multinationals may require interoperability to optimize global value chains. Knowledge interactive entrepreneurs may find ample opportunities in global value chains, if they can interoperate with dominant technological, economic and legal standards.	With informality being normal, tensions are likely to be most marked along the interface between the formal, rule-based bureaucracy and its fluid, informal counterpart. Stresses lie in the very nature of knowledge of value and its governance, and the polarized interdependent modes of production, each with its own tools, work roles, relationships, and organizations. For the formal-sector workers, employment provides certainty, rules are known, and knowledge is generally universally applicable and stable. For their counterparts in the informal sector, there is no certainty of employment, and everything is dynamic and constantly changing. Knowledge of value is immediate and tacit, based on individual intuition and hunches shared between the informal networks of trust.	Tensions may be less dramatic, as both craft-independent and knowledge-interactive modes of production are more individualized, sharing a learned logic based on experimentation and experience. This form of knowledge is likely to be anathema to the industrial-bureaucrat, as it emphasizes a holistic independent approach, often unstructured and fluid, responding to external stimuli and valuing independence of thought, rather than a discrete, rules-based, universalized solution attempting to command and control the situation. Modes of knowledge distribution are self-organized and context specific and dependent on natural and human resources, the needs and organization of the group, and the geographic scale in question.

governance is intertwined with the social, economic, political, and technological contexts shaping innovation systems, including dominant economic modes of production. As Open AIR researchers reflected on knowledge governance in each of our scenarios, we identified four dimensions to consider.

Figure 15.1 is a *knowledge appropriation matrix*. It shows the ways in which knowledge can be appropriated and, consequently, governed. The first dimension is the specificity of knowledge. Some knowledge is context specific, rooted to a particular place or subject, while other knowledge is generalizable, and therefore more easily scalable. A second lens is the object of knowledge: who, how, what, and why. We can also examine the extent of legal formality, which can range anywhere from extremely informal to semiformal to fully formal protection, the last of which is typically considered as IP.

Table 15.4
Future winners and losers.

High-tech hubs	Informal innovation	Indigenous entrepreneurship
Transnational standard-setting corporations, supported locally by favorable business and education policies, dominate the globally interconnected marketplace. The winners in the world of wireless engagement are international investors, national policymakers, and local entrepreneurs with the skills and connections necessary to access opportunities that arise in this open, networked, and digital world. The losers are those with insufficient education, skills, or access to affordable technology to interconnect, or those whose skills become obsolete overnight.	Power lies with people operating beyond the effective reach of state control. Although urban settings reflect the most vibrant kaleidoscope of relationships, traders circulate both goods and knowledge throughout rural communities and across borders. The winners are those who can use interpersonal networks to adapt to constantly shifting circumstances. They are relatively insulated from the instability of the formal economy around them. Those people who lack trusting interpersonal relationships, or who are ejected from a shrinking formal sector, lose opportunities.	Community-based social and economic systems, often with strong rural ties, are where most opportunities for sustainable development lie. Winners in this scenario have access to natural and social capital and are able to impose boundaries to protect and control their resources. Outsiders lacking community ties are marginalized. The same fate befalls people in communities without resources, perhaps due to the aftereffects of conflict, or those in temporarily successful enclaves who cannot protect their limited resources against exploitation by outsiders.

Fourth and finally, there are variations between more informal tacit knowledge, on one hand, and formalized, codified knowledge, on the other.

On each of these dimensions, Open AIR has plotted a place for various kinds of IPRs. For example, copyrights, patents, and utility models are highly formalized and typically codified modes of protection. "Know how," "know what," and "know why" are more relevant than "know who." These modes of appropriation tend to be generalizable rather than contextual. Contrast these formal IPRs with modes of appropriation such as first mover advantage, apprenticeship training, and customer loyalty, all of which are highly informal and based mostly on tacit, not codified knowledge. Value is highly contextual and depends more on *whom* than on *what* is being protected. There are formal types of IPRs that protect *who* more than *what* and are also contextual: moral rights (a subset of copyright) and trademarks are good examples.

The real value of Open AIR's knowledge appropriation matrix becomes apparent when the three scenarios are overlaid, as in figure 15.2. This reveals the kinds of knowledge appropriation mechanisms that are likely to be most important in each scenario. Those who can anticipate and exploit these strategies will likely do well in a particular scenario.

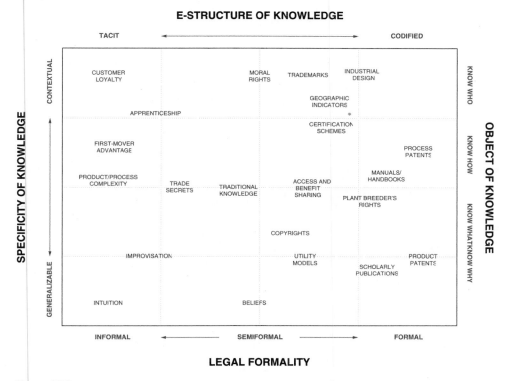

Figure 15.1
Knowledge appropriation matrix: modes of appropriation depend on the traits of knowledge.
Source: Elahi et al. (2013).

Figure 15.1 facilitated deep strategic insights into appropriate policies and practices for various future scenarios. Table 15.5 elaborates, in more specific detail, on the kinds of knowledge that will be most valuable in each of Open AIR's three future scenarios.

Summary Analysis of Future Scenarios

We cannot overemphasize the point that there is no single Africa and no single future. Countries, and even individuals and firms in the same geographic space, may find their particular future different from that of their neighbors. Our analysis has shown that conceptions of development, progress, and knowledge are all rooted in a particular context.

Open AIR's research demonstrates that innovation is one of the most fundamental processes underpinning economic growth, and it is also the basis for finding new

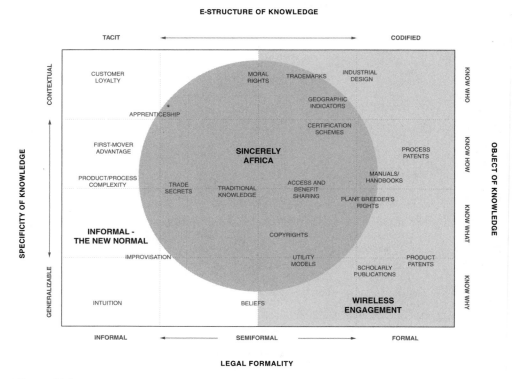

Figure 15.2
Scenarios for the future mapped over modes of appropriation.

solutions to key economic, social, and environmental problems for the future. For most African countries, it is important to examine local capacity and capabilities, as well as past causes of underdevelopment, before accepting well-meaning but potentially obsolete advice in a race to find new socioeconomic policies and incentives to support innovation.

Today's decisions create tomorrow's future. So, what might government policymakers, business leaders, scholarly researchers, civil society advocates, or other innovation system stakeholders do in response to indications that one or another of these scenarios is becoming their reality? The first action is to become attuned to the faint signals of change that might previously have passed by unnoticed. Armed with awareness of the key drivers of change identified in this document—those factors that will inevitably push or pull the African continent simultaneously in different directions—readers are likely to find themselves noticing patterns that were not apparent before.

Table 15.5
Knowledge of Value.

High-tech hubs	Informal innovation	Indigenous entrepreneurship
Here, valuable knowledge is globally generalizable and thus removed from its context. The emphasis is on knowledge that can be commoditized for commercial applications. Codified knowledge is valued over tacit knowledge, because the former is much easier to acquire and distribute online. There is growing convergence between local and imported knowledge. Digital learning resources are among the most valuable sources of codified, contexual knowledge. Without access to this knowledge, it is not possible to participate in this world.	Valuable knowledge is related to know-who highly contextualized, tacit knowledge. Know-what and know-why are of little use without crucial social networks and trusted relationships to exploit knowledge for social or economic gain. This knowledge is acquired by informal learning rather than formal education. Apprenticeships, or informal learning systems, are integral to the fabric of the informal sector and provide the primary avenue for gaining entry to that sector. Formal education does not equip graduates with the appropriate skills, knowledge, and attitudes.	The value of knowledge is judged by its ability to contribute to human social, economic, and environmental sustainability. A key focus is on slow variables: long-term variations that are difficult to quantify and discern. Knowledge is context specific, dependent on the physical and human resources available at a particular time and place, and also communal, serving the community from which it emerges. Intergenerational knowledge is woven together in novel ways and combined with contributions of global knowledge from a diaspora that values Africa's endowments.

Witnessing signals of a scenario dominated by high-tech hubs should lead stakeholders to worry about complex and controversial debates over the protection of codified knowledge through copyrights, patents, and similarly formal legal mechanisms. One must understand the global knowledge governance systems embedded within international law and administered via institutions such as the World Trade Organization and World Intellectual Property Organization. Tensions among those seeking maximum IP protection and others arguing for greater access to knowledge are unlikely to subside. Policymakers will be pressured by multinational firms to address persistent problems like patent thickets impeding efficiency in the information and communication technologies (ICT) sector. Meanwhile, business interests in creative industries like publishing, music and film, and webcasting will push for increasing minimum standards of protection, both online and off. Many people will resist this paradigm, cleverly making the best of the situation by adopting and promoting open-source licensing protocols if they are unable to change the system itself.

If this sounds like the status quo, it is not. The key difference is that African nations will have learned and embraced the rules of the global knowledge game. Key countries will have shifted from IP importers to exporters, at least in certain industries—Nollywood (the Nigerian film industry) is one plausible example—where promoting protection is or is perceived to be in their own domestic interests. Policymakers will need to appreciate that not everyone benefits equally in this world, and so mediating tensions among different interest groups will be needed. As the digital divide grows, governments that want to leave a positive legacy will have to find ways to ensure that formal IP systems (in particular, copyright and patent policies) function for the whole of society, not just for those who know what they need to conform to the standard economic, legal, and technological prerequisites for success.

If one sees signals of informal innovation becoming not just normal (as it already is) but embraced, then stakeholders might seriously reconsider whether investing scarce resources into building countries' capacity to process multinational patent applications or adjudicate formal copyright disputes is worthwhile. Formal modes of IP protection will be mostly irrelevant to local actors in innovative entrepreneurial communities and microenterprises. Even multinational businesses will need local knowhow and networks of trusted partners to succeed. The legal strength of formal IP protection will be irrelevant for firms focused more on adapting quickly to dynamic and diverse local opportunities. There will, however, be important roles for relatively less formal modes of protection to play. Trade secrets and confidentiality agreements are good examples. Whether these appropriation mechanisms are formally enforceable by contract law (doubtful) or bolstered by the risk of being ostracized for breaching community norms (likely), they are underpinned by trust.

Also, because tacit knowledge becomes far more important than codified knowledge, social networks are key to any IP-related outreach and training that is relevant on the ground. Policymakers should spend what little time and money they might have on building IP structures that facilitate symbiotic interactions. Perhaps there is a place for protecting utility models and industrial designs, which are easier to obtain, although no cheaper to enforce. Moral rights, such as the right to attribution and the protection of a work's integrity, may also be valuable. Branding, the trusted marks that certify the attributes of goods and services, will become increasingly important in this scenario. In particular, collective forms of protection, such as fair trade or organic certification schemes or geographic indications of origin, are probably most relevant.

If it seems that Open AIR's third scenario revolving around Indigenous entrepreneurship is emerging in the future, then stakeholders should focus on the formalized rules that govern traditional knowledge. Success will depend on understanding and embracing ecological, spiritual, social, and customary values. Legal frameworks, including IP frameworks, must reflect these values in order to be meaningful and legitimate.

International instruments like the Convention on Biological Diversity and its Nagoya Protocol on Access and Benefit Sharing will become profoundly important in this future. Local leaders will need to prioritize any potentially unfinished work on related issues of international protection for traditional cultural expressions and folklore.

Such formal instruments can help to prevent the misappropriation of traditional culture and knowledge by community outsiders seeking to exploit Africa's cultural and biologically rich heritage without fairly sharing the benefits. At the national and community levels, policymakers will need to engage with traditional leaders around policies and programs that help to codify tacit knowledge. The point, however, will not be to commodify and commercialize traditional knowledge, but to validate and preserve it. Digitization projects that identify, catalog, and communicate traditional knowledge can be useful, both to enhance access to a repository of African cultural, genetic, and ecological heritage and to ensure that financial and nonfinancial benefits that may be realized are shared fairly throughout the societies responsible for stewarding this knowledge into the future.

But what if the reality is a combination of these three scenarios, as so often is the case? The challenge will then be a policymaking environment that combines awareness and adaptability. There will have to be acceptance that in turbulent environments or times of disruptive change, the rules need to be regularly assessed and potentially recalibrated to find an acceptable balance that reflects the optimal outcome for the greatest number of stakeholders.

Our hope is that these scenarios, together with the research underpinning them, stimulate wider thinking about African innovation and creativity, and also that they enable policymakers and those interested parties to articulate a collective vision of innovation and creativity in Africa that is sustainably vibrant, properly valued, democratically participatory, collaboratively shared, widely accessible, and justly distributed throughout society.

A key insight from these scenarios is that the question is not whether knowledge governance policies and management practices will be relevant in the future, but rather which policies and practices will be most important in different scenarios. These scenarios are essential to understanding the structure of our proposed research around three thematic clusters. Our previous studies used robust research methods to identify the scenarios, sketch out their contours, and explore implications for IP. Our next project will dive much more deeply into particular aspects of each scenario—specifically, aspects around the use of open strategies and information communications technologies to scale up entrepreneurial innovative businesses in the networked economy.

Conclusion: Scaling Up African Innovation?

The Open AIR network's previous research showed that innovation is happening in Africa in ways that were previously overlooked. Our next step is to investigate whether that innovation is scalable, and if so, how. We previously showed that the role of IP is more nuanced than often portrayed. It can sometimes facilitate or frustrate innovation, or do both. Our next step is to expand on that analysis by focusing on the scalability of open and collaborative business models and their impacts on development. Our previous research identified three thematic areas that are local priorities, especially for marginalized communities, and reflect plausible scenarios for the future of knowledge and innovation. We now want to dig more deeply into particular dimensions of these scenarios—involving the informal economy, local communities, and high-tech hubs—specifically regarding scalable open and collaborative business models. Our previous activities created a new and unique interdisciplinary community of African researchers, adding a credible, independent, and distinctly African voice to global knowledge policy debates. Now we want to leverage this social capital to further enhance policy and practical influence and to position African leaders more centrally in global networks via cross-regional partnerships with Canada, as well as countries in the Global South.

The core goal of Open AIR moving forward is to help solve the scalability challenges facing knowledge-based businesses in the countries of Africa. Research is exploring how knowledge-based African enterprises grounded in collaborative innovation can scale up in a way that generates increased livelihood, entrepreneurship, business, and employment opportunities. Twinned with this core goal is an effort to compare the African research findings with findings and experiences elsewhere in the Global South and the Global North. This will ensure that the economic and social benefits of scaled-up, knowledge-based businesses can be harnessed in a manner that makes communities and societies, in both the developing and developed worlds, more prosperous and equitable.

Our previous research showed that old business models for scaling up entrepreneurial activity, based on tight, proprietary control over knowledge in closed innovation systems, will likely not work in most African settings. As a practical matter, many African countries lack the legal and economic infrastructure to support such models. Long-term institutional capacity building to support exclusive proprietary business models is perhaps possible, but not always advisable. Evidence from our recent research shows that one-size-fits-all models are not merely impractical, they are often incompatible with on the ground realities and local socioeconomic contexts. Moreover, many businesses in developed countries have already moved on to more open and collaborative approaches for generating jobs and economic growth. Promoting stale foreign business models in Africa may create an array of challenges that destabilize the collaborative dynamics of innovation in African settings.

There is the potential to avoid these risks by exploiting new, networked, open, and collaborative business models. Such models might harness rather than harm the informal sectors and local communities that dominate employment and economic activity in Africa. Collaborative innovation, supported by marketplace framework policies that recognize local realities and reflect strategic foresight, could help to foster entrepreneurship and scale businesses, thus alleviating poverty and promoting prosperity. By *collaborative innovation,* we mean the complex dynamics surrounding a blend of grounded theories about openness: a mixture of ideas about innovation across firm boundaries, and about consumer creativity, crowdsourcing, and peer production. The concept of collaborative innovation builds upon our previous empirical research and ongoing conceptual work tying that research with other literature in the field.

An important premise of Open AIR going forward is that we are not predefining what collaborative innovation is in developing countries before conducting on-the-ground research. Instead, we are building theory and definitions needed for policy impact from the ground up. Looking forward from the current realities of collaborative dynamics in African innovation, we have only just begun to grapple with the complex forces that will shape innovation and knowledge governance systems over the next several decades.

Notes

1. See www.OpenAIR.Africa/.

2. Open AIR's research has resulted in dozens of publications, including two scholarly books (Armstrong et al. 2010; de Beer et al. 2014), and a compendium of scenarios (Elahi et al. 2013). Parts of this chapter are abridged or derived from Open AIR's previous research outputs. While this chapter provides a high-level overview of activities and findings, readers seeking a more thorough discussion of the relevant literature, underlying data, and analyses of results should consult the original publications. Readers of this chapter may also be interested in publications that address Open AIR's findings on access to knowledge as a new conceptual paradigm for ICT research (Bannerman and de Beer 2013); training and capacity building on openness, innovation, and development (de Beer and Oguamanam 2013); monitoring and evaluating the impact of large-scale, multidisciplinary research (de Beer 2014); research partnership building to achieve inclusive, sustainable development (Oguamanam and de Beer 2018); and/or open innovation as a framework to link open science, open data, and open education for development (see chapter 3 in this volume and de Beer 2018). For a complete listing of relevant research by the Open AIR network, see http://www.openair.org.za/publication/.

3. One such brainstorming event was the IDRC Open Development Workshop in Ottawa (May 6–7, 2010).

References

Adewopo, Adebambo, Helen Chuma-Okoro, and Adejoke Oyewunmi. 2014. "A Consideration of Communal Trademarks for Nigerian Leather and Textile Products." In *Innovation and Intellectual Property: Collaborative Dynamics in Africa*, ed. Jeremy de Beer, Chris Armstrong, Chidi Oguamanam, and Tobias Schonwetter, 109–131. Cape Town: University of Cape Town Press. Cape Town, South Africa: IP Unit, Faculty of Law, University of Cape Town; Bonn, Germany: Deutsche Gesellschaft für Internationale Zusammenarbeit. https://open.uct.ac.za/bitstream/handle/11427/9759/Innovation%20%26%20Intellectual%20Property%20%20Collaborative%20Dynamics%20in%20Africa.pdf?sequence=1.

Ama, Njoku Ola. 2014. "Perspectives on Intellectual Property from Botswana's Publicly Funded Researchers." In *Innovation and Intellectual Property: Collaborative Dynamics in Africa*, ed. Jeremy de Beer, Chris Armstrong, Chidi Oguamanam, and Tobias Schonwetter, 335–372. Cape Town: University of Cape Town Press; Cape Town, South Africa: IP Unit, Faculty of Law, University of Cape Town; Bonn, Germany: Deutsche Gesellschaft für Internationale Zusammenarbeit. https://open.uct.ac.za/bitstream/handle/11427/9759/Innovation%20%26%20Intellectual%20Property%20%20Collaborative%20Dynamics%20in%20Africa.pdf?sequence=1.

Armstrong, Chris, Jeremy de Beer, Dick Kawooya, Achal Prabhala, and Tobias Schonwetter, eds. 2010. *Access to Knowledge in Africa: The Role of Copyright*. Cape Town: University of Cape Town Press.

Awad, Bassem, and Perihan Abou Zeid. 2014. "Reflections on the Lack of Biofuel Innovation in Egypt." In *Innovation and Intellectual Property: Collaborative Dynamics in Africa*, ed. Jeremy de Beer, Chris Armstrong, Chidi Oguamanam, and Tobias Schonwetter, 267–281. Cape Town: University of Cape Town Press; Cape Town, South Africa: IP Unit, Faculty of Law, University of Cape Town; Bonn, Germany: Deutsche Gesellschaft für Internationale Zusammenarbeit. https://open.uct.ac.za/bitstream/handle/11427/9759/Innovation%20%26%20Intellectual%20Property%20%20Collaborative%20Dynamics%20in%20Africa.pdf?sequence=1.

Bannerman, Sara, and Jeremy de Beer. 2013. "Access to Knowledge as a New Paradigm for Research on ICTs and Intellectual Property Rights." In *Connecting ICTs to Development: The IDRC Experience*, ed. Laurent Elder, Heloise Emdon, Richard Fuchs, and Ben Petrazzini, 75–90. London/Ottawa: Anthem Press/IDRC. https://idl-bnc-idrc.dspacedirect.org/bitstream/handle/10625/52228/IDL-52228.pdf?sequence=1&isAllowed=y.

Belete, Wondwossen. 2014. "Towards University–Industry Innovation Linkages in Ethiopia." In *Innovation and Intellectual Property: Collaborative Dynamics in Africa*, ed. Jeremy de Beer, Chris Armstrong, Chidi Oguamanam, and Tobias Schonwetter, 316–334. Cape Town: University of Cape Town Press; Cape Town, South Africa: IP Unit, Faculty of Law, University of Cape Town; Bonn, Germany: Deutsche Gesellschaft für Internationale Zusammenarbeit. https://open.uct.ac

.za/bitstream/handle/11427/9759/Innovation%20%26%20Intellectual%20Property%20%20Collaborative%20Dynamics%20in%20Africa.pdf?sequence=1.

Benkler, Yochai. 2005. *The Wealth of Networks: How Social Production Transforms Markets and Freedom*. New Haven, CT, and London: Yale University Press.

Cocchiaro, Gino, John Lorenzen, Bernard Maister, and Britta Rutert. 2014. "Consideration of a Legal 'Trust' Model for the Kukula Healers' TK Commons in South Africa." In *Innovation and Intellectual Property: Collaborative Dynamics in Africa*, ed. Jeremy de Beer, Chris Armstrong, Chidi Oguamanam, and Tobias Schonwetter, 151–170. Cape Town: University of Cape Town Press; Cape Town, South Africa: IP Unit, Faculty of Law, University of Cape Town; Bonn, Germany: Deutsche Gesellschaft für Internationale Zusammenarbeit. https://open.uct.ac.za/bitstream/handle/11427/9759/Innovation%20%26%20Intellectual%20Property%20%20Collaborative%20Dynamics%20in%20Africa.pdf?sequence=1.

De Beer, Jeremy, Chris Armstrong, Chidi Oguamanam, and Tobias Schonwetter, eds. 2014. *Innovation and Intellectual Property: Collaborative Dynamics in Africa*, Cape Town: University of Cape Town Press, 2014; Cape Town, South Africa: IP Unit, Faculty of Law, University of Cape Town; Bonn, Germany: Deutsche Gesellschaft für Internationale Zusammenarbeit. https://open.uct.ac.za/bitstream/handle/11427/9759/Innovation%20%26%20Intellectual%20Property%20%20Collaborative%20Dynamics%20in%20Africa.pdf?sequence=1.

De Beer, Jeremy, and Chidi Oguamanam. 2013. "Open Minds: Lessons on Intellectual Property, Innovation, and Development from Nigeria." In *Open Development: Networked Innovations in International Development*, ed. Matthew L. Smith and Katherine M. A. Reilly, 249–272. Cambridge, MA/Ottawa: MIT Press/IDRC. https://www.idrc.ca/en/book/open-development-networked-innovations-international-development.

Dos Santos, Fernando, and Simão Pelembe. 2014. "The State of Biofuel Innovation in Mozambique." In *Innovation and Intellectual Property: Collaborative Dynamics in Africa*, ed. Jeremy de Beer, Chris Armstrong, Chidi Oguamanam, and Tobias Schonwetter, 248–266. Cape Town: University of Cape Town Press. Cape Town, South Africa: IP Unit, Faculty of Law, University of Cape Town; Bonn, Germany: Deutsche Gesellschaft für Internationale Zusammenarbeit. https://open.uct.ac.za/bitstream/handle/11427/9759/Innovation%20%26%20Intellectual%20Property%20%20Collaborative%20Dynamics%20in%20Africa.pdf?sequence=1.

Elahi, Shirin, Jeremy de Beer, Dick Kawooya, Chidi Oguamanam, Nagla Rizk, and the Open AIR Network. 2013. *Knowledge and Innovation in Africa: Scenarios for the Future*. Open AIR Network. http://www.openair.org.za/images/Knowledge-Innovation-Africa-Scenarios-for-Future.pdf.

International Development Research Centre (IDRC). 2011. "Innovation for Inclusive Development, Program Prospectus for 2011–2016." http://www.slideshare.net/uniid-sea/october-2011-innovation-for-inclusive-development-program-prospectus-for-20112016.

Kawooya, Dick. 2014. "Informal–Formal Sector Interactions in Automotive Engineering, Kampala." In *Innovation and Intellectual Property: Collaborative Dynamics in Africa*, ed. Jeremy de Beer, Chris Armstrong, Chidi Oguamanam, and Tobias Schonwetter, 59–76. Cape Town: University of

Cape Town Press. Cape Town, South Africa: IP Unit, Faculty of Law, University of Cape Town; Bonn, Germany: Deutsche Gesellschaft für Internationale Zusammenarbeit. https://open.uct.ac .za/bitstream/handle/11427/9759/Innovation%20%26%20Intellectual%20Property%20%20Col laborative%20Dynamics%20in%20Africa.pdf?sequence=1.

Mandela, Nelson. 1995. *Long Walk to Freedom: The Autobiography of Nelson Mandela*. Boston: Little, Brown Book Group.

Mgbeoji, Ikechi. "African Patent Offices Not Fit for Purpose." 2014. In *Innovation and Intellectual Property: Collaborative Dynamics in Africa*, ed. Jeremy de Beer, Chris Armstrong, Chidi Oguamanam, and Tobias Schonwetter, 234–247. Cape Town: University of Cape Town Press; Cape Town, South Africa: IP Unit, Faculty of Law, University of Cape Town; Bonn, Germany: Deutsche Gesellschaft für Internationale Zusammenarbeit. https://open.uct.ac.za/bitstream/handle/11427 /9759/Innovation%20%26%20Intellectual%20Property%20%20Collaborative%20Dynamics%20 in%20Africa.pdf?sequence=1.

Ncube, Caroline B., Lucienne Abrahams, and Titilayo Akinsanmi. 2014. "Effects of the South African IP Regime on Generating Value from Publicly Funded Research: An Exploratory Study of Two Universities." 2014. In *Innovation and Intellectual Property: Collaborative Dynamics in Africa*, ed. Jeremy de Beer, Chris Armstrong, Chidi Oguamanam, and Tobias Schonwetter, 282–315. Cape Town: University of Cape Town Press. Cape Town, South Africa: IP Unit, Faculty of Law, University of Cape Town; Bonn, Germany: Deutsche Gesellschaft für Internationale Zusammenarbeit. https://open.uct.ac.za/bitstream/handle/11427/9759/Innovation%20%26%20Intellectual%20 Property%20%20Collaborative%20Dynamics%20in%20Africa.pdf?sequence=1.

Oguamanam, Chidi, and Teshager Dagne. 2014. "Geographical Indication (GI) Options for Ethiopian Coffee and Ghanaian Cocoa." In *Innovation and Intellectual Property: Collaborative Dynamics in Africa*, ed. Jeremy de Beer, Chris Armstrong, Chidi Oguamanam, and Tobias Schonwetter, 77–108. Cape Town: University of Cape Town Press. Cape Town, South Africa: IP Unit, Faculty of Law, University of Cape Town; Bonn, Germany: Deutsche Gesellschaft für Internationale Zusammenarbeit. https://open.uct.ac.za/bitstream/handle/11427/9759/Innovation%20%26%20 Intellectual%20Property%20%20Collaborative%20Dynamics%20in%20Africa.pdf?sequence=1.

Oguamanam, Chidi, and Jeremy de Beer. 2018. "Sustainable Development through a Cross-Regional Research Partnership." In *The Cambridge Handbook of Public-Private Partnerships, Intellectual Property Governance, and Sustainable Development*, ed. Margaret Chon, Pedro Roffe, and Ahmed Abdel-Latif, 376–397. Cambridge: Cambridge University Press. doi:10.1017/9781316809587.020.

Open AIR. 2014. *Briefing Note: Optimising Benefits from Publicly Funded Research*. Retrieved from https://openair.africa/2014/01/01/briefing-note-optimising-benefits-from-publicly-funded-research/.

Organisation for Economic Co-operation and Development (OECD). 2013. *Innovation and Inclusive Development: Discussion Report*. Paris: OECD. https://www.oecd.org/sti/inno/oecd-inclusive -innovation.pdf.

Ouma, Marisella. 2014. "The Policy Context for a Commons-Based Approach to Traditional Knowledge in Kenya." In *Innovation and Intellectual Property: Collaborative Dynamics in Africa*, ed.

Jeremy de Beer, Chris Armstrong, Chidi Oguamanam, and Tobias Schonwetter, 132–150. Cape Town: University of Cape Town Press. Cape Town, South Africa: IP Unit, Faculty of Law, University of Cape Town; Bonn, Germany: Deutsche Gesellschaft für Internationale Zusammenarbeit. https://open.uct.ac.za/bitstream/handle/11427/9759/Innovation%20%26%20Intellectual%20Property%20%20Collaborative%20Dynamics%20in%20Africa.pdf?sequence=1.

Rizk, Nagla. "From De Facto Commons to Digital Commons? The Case of Egypt's Independent Music Industry." 2014. In *Innovation and Intellectual Property: Collaborative Dynamics in Africa*, ed. Jeremy de Beer, Chris Armstrong, Chidi Oguamanam, and Tobias Schonwetter, 171–202. Cape Town: University of Cape Town Press. Cape Town, South Africa: IP Unit, Faculty of Law, University of Cape Town; Bonn, Germany: Deutsche Gesellschaft für Internationale Zusammenarbeit. https://open.uct.ac.za/bitstream/handle/11427/9759/Innovation%20%26%20Intellectual%20Property%20%20Collaborative%20Dynamics%20in%20Africa.pdf?sequence=1.

Sihanya, Ben. 2014. "Reflections on Open Scholarship Modalities and the Copyright Environment in Kenya." In *Innovation and Intellectual Property: Collaborative Dynamics in Africa*, ed. Jeremy de Beer, Chris Armstrong, Chidi Oguamanam, and Tobias Schonwetter, 203–233. Cape Town: University of Cape Town Press. Cape Town, South Africa: IP Unit, Faculty of Law, University of Cape Town; Bonn, Germany: Deutsche Gesellschaft für Internationale Zusammenarbeit. https://open.uct.ac.za/bitstream/handle/11427/9759/Innovation%20%26%20Intellectual%20Property%20%20Collaborative%20Dynamics%20in%20Africa.pdf?sequence=1.

Smith, Matthew L., Laurent Elder, and Heloise Emdon. 2011. "Open Development: A New Theory for ICT4D." *Information Technologies and International Development* 7:iii–ix.

Wunsch-Vincent, Sacha, and Graham Vickery. 2007. *Participative Web and User-Created Content: Web 2.0 Wikis and Social Networking*. Paris: OECD.

16 Conclusion: Understanding the Inclusive Potential of Open Development

Ruhiya Kristine Seward

Introduction

The driving aim of this volume is to understand and improve inclusion in open development practice. This concluding chapter is an attempt to draw out the key discussions, definitions, and lessons, in order to build an understanding of how inclusion matters for open practices. The first section explores the normative assumptions undergirding open practices, and the different ways that the authors of this volume frame inclusion in relation to open practices. The second section explores what matters for inclusion and open practices, providing nuance to the assumptions of open development. Finally, we offer some key takeaways and potential work going forward.

Assumptions and Ways of Seeing Inclusion

To draw out lessons on inclusion and open practices, it is important to understand the implicit normative assumptions behind open development practices. These assumptions are: first, knowledge is central to open development. The acquisition of knowledge is empowering, and its equitable distribution is, in turn, a public good. Second, the practices associated with openness—producing/creating, distributing/sharing, and using/reusing knowledge resources—contribute to the global knowledge commons by supporting the creation, sharing, management, and meaningful use of knowledge resources. Third, by offering cost-effective means for people and institutions to do so, open practices in education, science, governance, data, and innovation can facilitate inclusion. Fourth, over time, the distribution of knowledge, the broadening of information, and the flattening of hierarchies preventing access and use may just be able to help tackle the issue of inequality. These four assumptions show how inclusion undergirds open development; in fact, open development *is* a process of inclusion. These foundational ideas [and ideals] of open development offer a new imaginary for development practice, grounded in knowledge production, distribution, and use—and in the knowledge commons.

Yet these ideals also challenge us to understand and evaluate how, for whom, and under what conditions open practices *actualize* inclusion and when they do not. As we have seen throughout this volume, inclusion is complex, and the purposes behind open activities are, in the end, what condition the inclusion. From innovation to education, the authors in this volume explored and contested inclusion in the context of the practices associated with their particular areas, revealing important framing issues in complex and layered territory.

How are the core values and norms of inclusion engendered in open practices? The "action orientation" of open development—its production, distribution, and use—speaks to empowerment (or at least the empowering potential). It happens through the user's *participation* in the practices, when she exercises her *agency* to do so. In this sense, **inclusion builds around and is actualized by participation and agency.**

As people become engaged in activities, and because they have agency in that engagement, **inclusion develops and deepens over time as a process in, and an outcome of, open activities.** For example, with open educational resources (OER) and practices (OEP), inclusion develops through progressively deeper levels of engagement, from basic access (being able to access an open book) to participation (where users begin to engage and leverage content) to empowerment (where users are able to create and remix educational content) (chapter 12). As users increase their participation in OER activities, they are more included—and more empowered by that deeper engagement. This undergirds the "social" part of inclusion (World Bank 2013).[1]

Inclusion is also defined by its relation to *exclusion* and how this affects gaps in participation: gaps in who is counted, who gets named, who shows up on the map, and who even is allowed to do the counting, mapping, and naming are all critical variables of inclusion in the distribution of information online (chapter 5). Exclusion is how we know the inclusive potential of an activity. It is not just the number of people participating, but also *who is represented*. For example, many online platforms are considered "inclusive" by default because of the numbers of people who get involved, even though this approach suffers from considerable imbalances in gender, socioeconomic status, age, or geolocation in terms of those who choose or are able to participate (chapter 14). Therefore, engaging marginalized populations such as Indigenous, rural, or poor people—even if they are not represented in large numbers—strengthens the inclusive outcome because of the structural and epistemological barriers that have conditioned participation in the past. Diversity matters for inclusion.

Inclusion is understood by its relation to inequality because of the implicit assumption that it can generate greater *equality* (and/or equity) in general, and equality of access, use, and reuse of information in particular. Digitally mediated participation and representation promise equality by "circumventing traditional mediators of information" and by allowing people "a more significant role in shaping the content" (chapter 5); this is part of the empowering potential. "Open information is equally accessible and usable by all, and therefore portends more equality with respect to the meaningful use of this information" (Lessig 2003; chapter 5). This speaks to the promise of tools that "equalize the opportunity that people have to access and participate in the construction of knowledge and culture, regardless of their geographic placing" (chapter 5). According to chapter 7, the "critical element of peer production is that the open practices that it entails can spawn cycles of knowledge growth, reuse, and sharing, which lead to increasing returns and knowledge spillovers" (chapter 7; Garzarelli et al. 2008).

Yet we are seeing more and more how legitimate evidence and facts are competing with vast amounts of information garbage, including mis- and disinformation. Not all information is equal, and discerning fact from misinformation and propaganda is increasingly posing a challenge online. This is why the normative grounding of open development matters, because ideally **inclusion signals an individual's *capability*, with the skills, access, and genuine discernment, to exercise agency toward optimal *knowledge equity***. Undergirded by equitable knowledge, democratized knowledge production and dissemination in the commons offer both the challenge and the new imaginary of open development (chapter 2).

Furthermore, **inclusion is also an *outcome or consequence of actions by others* who have *capabilities* as intermediaries**. For example, open data democratize access to informational resources and offer a kind of inherent inclusivity, but the meaningful use of that data depends on the individual and communal capacity to leverage it as a resource, as well as the drive for, and interest in, using it for public, communal benefit (rather than to accrue additional benefits to the already privileged) (chapters 10 and 11). This approach to open data use as a public good in turn requires meaningful access to a digital ecosystem, with the skills and abilities to analyze and use that data, and the sociopolitical agency to apply the data to situations where there is a gap or need, and, furthermore, to use this concern to benefit the greatest number of people. Because these can be large barriers for genuine participation, intermediaries who leverage open data for public benefit offer a means to optimize the benefits of data. So, in some instances, open processes contribute to inclusion even if the leveraging of an open resource is done by an intermediary on behalf of an otherwise excluded population.

Even with the layers and complexities of inclusion that signal tensions in open development, inclusion is inseparable from openness. But a key emphasis from this volume is that **purpose conditions the inclusion that is realized**.

Lessons for Openness and Inclusion

Building on the different ways of understanding inclusion in open development, the following section draws out the lessons emerging from the chapters.

Digital Drives Open Practices

Even though a key piece of our revised definition of open development is that it does not necessarily have to be digital—for instance, the way educational data is "open" when it is publicly displayed/written on the walls of the school—most arguments made in this book imply that open resources have a digital component.[2] It follows that if a majority of open resources are digital, then poor telecom and electrical infrastructure are going to be barriers to the use and reuse of open resources. Indeed, a lack of electricity was cited as a barrier to OER adoption (chapter 12).

This suggests that the benefits that can be derived from open activities when they are digital are not evenly distributed; many people are excluded from benefits because of barriers having to do with costs to access and skills needed to leverage digital tools. Yet as we will discuss further, it is more complicated than simply an *access or no access* dichotomy. While there are many challenges with basic access to the technology infrastructure (to mobile phones and the online ecosystem), it is also about different levels of use when there is online access and having the capacity to use data and enjoy the benefits of that use (access, participation, voice, contribution, not just use-as-is, but remixing).

Benefits of Open Resources Are Conditioned by Diversity of Access

The types of devices (e.g., mobile phone versus a tablet) and locations through which someone has access (home versus school) condition the benefits of open resources. For example, in Latin America, being able to access the Internet from different places and on different devices affects the number and type of tasks performed online by the individual (chapter 9). This affects the open activities being realized, but also the capacity to benefit from these activities. This is because limited access signifies other kinds of inequalities having to do with location, age, and the educational and socioeconomic status of the user. Even though "smartphones are touted as the solution to Internet access issues, a large part of the population does not take advantage of this access" to participate and engage in open activities (chapter 9). Participation and use (which are further conditioned by the sex, age, and education level of the user) are affected by whether people can access the Internet from home, work, or an educational or public space, and use a computer, mobile phone, or tablet, and this in turn influences the kinds and number of open activities from which a user may benefit.

Knowledge Creation and Adaptation Support Agency

The power (or empowerment) of openness emerges from using (remixing) and engaging in production and sharing; this is the key to agency and the transformative potential of open practices. Inclusion actualized as participation in knowledge creation supports empowerment. In the OER space, maximal levels of participation allow contributors to engage in "sustained collaboration, or the development of communities of practice where creating, sharing, and peer reviewing of OER is a focal practice" (chapter 12). Moreover, the research suggests that exposure to OER and openness ideas more generally can change pedagogical practices—and facilitate a change in mindset. For instance, in a community water testing project in Lebanon, "not only did these citizen scientists feel more informed about water issues in their respective areas, they felt empowered to begin making demands on the government to pay attention to water-quality issues" (chapter 13).

Indeed, open practices support a change in the control of information and who can produce it; the remixing potential in open practices can actually overturn traditional knowledge hierarchies and epistemologies. Open resources not only reduce costs, they can offer potential tools for decolonizing curricula by allowing people to question and reflect (chapter 13), create and share information locally, and incorporate many nontraditional authors and voices (chapter 12). Deeper engagement, where users are active participants in knowledge creation, can produce a change in power relations. "Information and power thus became intimately intertwined as people capitalized on the value associated with epistemic control: information represented *this* and not *that*" (chapter 5). The creator of information is the creator of worlds.

Creation and Adaptation Lag Where They Could Have the Most Potential

Many openness activities are not quite there yet. The chapters of this volume show that the majority of people in developing countries are still on the earlier end of the use spectrum—meaning *use-as-is* rather than *use-as-remix* (chapters 4, 5, 12, 13, and 14). Most open activities outlined in the survey of Latin America are not done, and only 12 percent of the sampled population engages in open government activities like accessing e-services (chapter 9).

Moreover, chapter 5 provides the following examples. Activity emerging from the entire Middle East and Africa on open platforms like GitHub ("home to less than 1 percent of GitHub users and commits") compares to the level of activity in Switzerland. People living in these regions also contribute to platforms at lower rates, with Africans constituting less than 2 percent of edits on Wikipedia: "only 16 percent of content about Nigeria and 9 percent of content about Kenya are created by locals." Though some of this can be explained by poor Internet penetration, this explains only about "one-third of the variability in the number of GitHub users per country." So a driving question remains: "What sort of global information society are we building if large groups of people rarely participate in it as producers?"

Barriers to Open Resources Are Structured and Socially Embedded

The agency needed to engage in open practices is conditioned by the social structures that underlie gender discrimination, socioeconomic hierarchies, historical epistemological divisions, and even the infrastructural challenges associated with geolocation (chapters 4, 5, 6, and 13). This is because the discrimination and social biases that already exist in society easily move, and can be amplified, online. As the examples of gender biases within open-source software and Wikipedia suggest in the volume, certain types of participation are valued more highly than others, and this is often gendered. Women contributing on platforms such as Wikipedia reported a range of issues with the dominant masculine culture that had a cooling effect on their contributions and highlighted a need for safer or less stereotypically driven spaces (chapter 4).[3]

Furthermore, status and education also condition participation. The evidence from Latin America suggests that having an education above secondary school, higher socioeconomic status, and being able to access the Internet in a variety of ways allows people to engage in, and benefit from, open activities (chapter 9). In other words, because the socially embedded hierarchies and asymmetries associated with gender, history, geolocation, and socioeconomics that control knowledge production and dissemination affect agency, they in turn affect the inclusive potential of open resources and practices.

But there are ways to structure open spaces to decrease some forms of discrimination and to improve certain kinds of equitable inclusion. For instance, the Open and Collaborative Science in Development Network (OCSDNet) found that changing language around a project helped to improve female participation, overcoming some gendered barriers (chapter 13). Also, allowing men and women to have separate hours at computer labs in Afghanistan improved women's participation in an OER initiative (chapter 4). Furthermore, even though global asymmetries tend to reify historical barriers, open education research showed that OER use appears to be higher, or at least just as high, in the countries with lower gross domestic product (GDP) than in those with higher GDP. This suggests that the availability of OER is supportive in the locations that may need them the most (chapter 12), although the authors are cautious about this conclusion.

Informational Asymmetries Are Structured by Global North Dominance...

Increasingly, if knowledge cannot be located online, it effectively does not exist (chapter 6). Thus mapping, naming, and being counted are all critical in the twenty-first century because of the growing prevalence of the online environment and its increasing importance for brokering knowledge. This is where open practices and open resources have a role to play in the knowledge commons. Yet, as the authors argued, being recognized as a subject or as an actor with agency online is conditioned not only by the barriers outlined here—but significantly also by *proximity to Global North concerns*.

Inclusion in the informational ecosystem means having agency in being recognized and counted in information creation—whether through advocating for recognition (as an informational subject) or by creating the information/facilitating information development (as the user/creator)—and requires overturning informational asymmetries (for instance, ensuring participation is deconditioned by Global North interests alone). This speaks to the cognitive justice undergirding efforts to make science open, collaborative, and accessible to everyone as both participant and user (chapter 13). In fact, upending informational imbalances "'demands recognition of *knowledges*, not only as methods but as ways of life' (Visvanathan 2009), to ensure that all people have the right to access and create locally relevant knowledge with epistemologies, tools, and modes of collaboration of their choice" (chapter 13). It also means questioning the standard *determinants of legitimacy of content* (chapter 6) that have thus far structured knowledge development, creation, and reputational metrics. The lack of attention to the embedded hierarchies in information geographies undermines the promises of open, accessible information and knowledge.

Local platforms might be one way of countering these dynamics, particularly when they offer content in local/national languages. The example of Darakht-e Danesh in Afghanistan offers a glimpse into the possibilities of this idea, with localized content developed for teachers in the top three languages used in schools in Afghanistan. This helps to counter the problems that arise for OER that are only in dominant global languages (chapter 12). Local platforms can draw on global resources while encouraging local content creation.

...And Condition Discoverability

How open resources are found, or are "discoverable," in online searches (chapter 6)—conditioned by popularity, by language, by being known in the Global North, or by capabilities to leverage information—all reflect the underlying structure of global communicative dynamics. The 10 Cs[4] developed by ROER4D as an elaboration of the earlier 5 Rs[5] has loCate as an important precondition to other consumption practices; the knowledge commons ecosystem plays a critical role in the ease of locating the desired or appropriate content (chapters 6 and 12). Historical power dynamics and hierarchies support uneven *geographies of information* (chapter 5), which are not only fostered through platform idiosyncrasies, but are actually embedded in search algorithms. For example, an awkward consequence of Global North open access research systems is the tendency to exclude lesser-known researchers and their studies. Open access research policy mandates from the North (which are contributing to public goods) help to flood the Internet with content developed by and for scholars from privileged locales, and the algorithms for discoverability further privilege this abundant content (chapter 6).

Rather than supporting the removal of North-South barriers, open access research sometimes may unwittingly entrench them. Global South knowledge—already marginalized by historical power (and knowledge) relations between Northern and Southern scholars—then continues to have its legitimacy determined by Global North norms and practices, as well as epistemological hurdles (chapters 6 and 13). This is not to argue that open access is a bad thing, but rather to understand how better to support scholars on the margins "to curate their scholarship in ways that make it openly visible and discoverable" (chapter 6).

Global Platforms Shape Discourse and Act as *De Facto* Information Intermediaries

A key issue is that commercial platforms based and moderated in the Global North act as de facto intermediaries in informational intermediation and undergird exclusion because of their main focus on Global North markets and issues (chapters 4, 5, and 6). Knowledge itself is not neutral, and, in the global online marketplace, certain types of knowledge are devalued by their position in the North-South exchange of ideas. As delivery mechanisms for open goods and services, many online platforms can intensify this type of knowledge devaluation, particularly if they are global in scope and driven by Northern concerns.

In combination with the challenges of solving uneven Internet access (and establishing the diversity of access required for real engagement), platforms often lack content from marginalized locations (or else it is crowded out by the issues of discoverability, as just discussed). With the current reality of online platform business models, it can feel like issues from the margins do not matter, as marginal populations do not live in areas that drive commerce in the Global North and do not have the luxury of income to drive advertising revenue.

There are alternative platforms operating outside of Global North advertising models, particularly supporting some of the open practices around education and science discussed in this volume. These tend to be supported by governments (national governments, or more often, foreign governments) or by nongovernmental organizations (NGOs). The knowledge generated in these venues constitutes the public goods described in chapter 7 as "knowledge resources." And open provision can spread beyond borders (chapter 7) and allow materials to be reproduced and repurposed regionally. For example, open educational content developed in a regionally popular language, that is otherwise not common can dominate a region (and speaks to the importance of local engagement too).

The challenge of the public goods approach is that support, particularly funding, for those goods can be tenuous. NGOs, for instance, depend on funding from governments, either the national government or foreign aid. In these instances, while the inclusive potential exists, there must be accountability to the people who are meant to be served. This highlights a tension with the inclusive potential of public platforms. Decisions are sometimes made with the intent to secure further investments and funding for the model, and the sustainability of open platforms remains in question.

This tension between the public (both governmental organizations and NGOs) and private sectors in the generation and curation of open resources also shows up when trying to scale openness initiatives. For instance, when open science platforms connect to the private sector, those partnerships "tend to value the protection of data and forms of collaboration that offer value for money" (chapter 13). Given resource constraints (not just money, but also the time commitment required), it can be very hard for research institutions to prioritize openness, as well as open practices more generally (chapter 13).

Knowledge Commons Need New Governance Models

Knowledge and the digital commons that support the dissemination and use of that knowledge constitute public goods (chapter 7). Knowledge flows through innovation systems and influences how science, education, and data support positive development outcomes (chapter 3). Open innovation, integral to the informal sectors of many economies in the Global South, is supported by people's ability to unlock access to knowledge (chapter 3). There are many emerging models for the production and provision of digital public goods, but, as this volume shows, most of them struggle to be truly inclusive (for the reasons discussed previously)—and in the absence of successful alternative models, governments play a critical role in ensuring that openness is inclusive.

Governing these public goods requires the rethinking of laws—for instance, around intellectual property rights. Contrary to the way that intellectual property (IP) is often framed—as a key to innovation—there is evidence that stronger IP regimes do *not* play a significant role in spurring innovation (chapter 7). Moreover, IP is not critical to the informal economy, and the informal economy is what dominates much of the developing world—for instance, nearly two-thirds of the GDP in sub-Saharan Africa and half of the GDP of India. Open practices dominate the informal economy (chapter 3), and this drives some types of innovation.[6] Therefore, governing the digital commons requires rethinking copyright and reframing the governmental, private-sector, and not-for-profit roles in this process in order to mediate the tensions among openness, access, and the appropriation of knowledge.

Governments and Digital Public Goods

Though not always explicit in this volume, governments are the key players in the production, distribution, and use of digital public goods. Through legal and regulatory regimes, governments help shape the ecosystem in which openness plays out and incentivize open access policies. Governments shape social and economic progress by supporting development policies that allow inclusion and political economic participation through legal regimes, regulations, policies, and agenda setting. Sustainable and equitable human progress is shaped by knowledge and supported by a flourishing, accessible knowledge commons—and governments, as the institutions through which public goods are held, play a critical role in supporting the digital commons and knowledge as public goods. This is complicated, as governments in the abstract are the institutions that hold the social contract with society—but, in reality, this contract is failing in so many instances around the globe that it is tough to speak about the role of the state in terms of normative principles that are not evident in reality. Collectively, through governments or other mechanisms, we need to tackle the governance of digital public goods (chapters 3, 7, and 15).

Figure 16.1 shows the constituting ideas of open development in relation to inclusion and the knowledge commons, updated from figure 2.1 in chapter 2.

Key Takeaways on Facilitating Inclusion in Open Practices

Inclusion occurs when institutional and hierarchical barriers to knowledge and participation are removed or lessened, as well as when diversity is enhanced. Over time, distributing

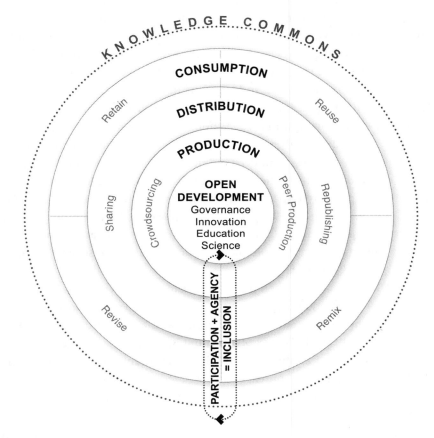

Figure 16.1

Reconsidering open development-as-inclusion in the knowledge commons: using, sharing, and producing knowledge are participatory practices, which in turn help one to recognize one's own agency in the production of knowledge. Participation and agency support inclusion and together shape the contours of the knowledge commons.

knowledge and disrupting hierarchies that prevent access and use can help tackle inequality and support pro-poor human development; these are the underlying norms of open development. What follows are some key takeaways in facilitating these shifts.

Reclaim the digital knowledge commons for development. The digital commons and knowledge itself are public goods, and it is time to reclaim this space. The relationship between knowledge and human development undergirds sustainable and equitable human progress, and it is facilitated by broadening inclusion. Knowledge equity and the growth and barrier-free sharing of knowledge requires investing in and facilitating the knowledge commons. This means reframing the business model for open initiatives from a knowledge economy, where knowledge is primarily commodified for profit, to a knowledge society, where knowledge is primarily treated as a public good. It also means rethinking the role of government in the open provision of goods and services, revamping IP policies, and investing in knowledge.

Make inclusion the goal. Inclusion must be an explicit goal if it is to be actualized in an open development initiative. Although inclusion is defined in a multitude of ways, it is exercised through broad, meaningful, and diverse participation. Facilitating that inclusion requires an understanding of structural inequality because how openness is operationalized and the contexts in which it is embedded determine who benefits. Without properly unpacking the contexts, and instituting safeguards, the availability of information may empower the empowered. "While openness implies a normative principle of inclusion, if we do not explicitly populate it with inclusion principles, it will only reflect the dominant paradigms existing in society" (chapter 4). We must design for equity from the start.

Start local. If you want to be inclusive, you have to be sufficiently local in your scope to be able to address structural impediments to inclusion and ensure open resources are relevant. The example of Darakht-e Danesh in Afghanistan is instructive. It is through local interaction that the challenges of structural inequality can be addressed. Large-scale open development initiatives cannot always sufficiently understand or unpack the multitude of challenging contexts—and will struggle to be inclusive, given the realities of our world. Contextual, local initiatives can directly target and overcome these challenges.

Focus on who is involved. Who has voice and agency? To reclaim the digital commons and ensure that it is inclusive, we have to advance, expand, and diversify who is able to produce, distribute, and use knowledge resources. Open development is about human agency in these open practices and the governance of the commons.

Aim for equitable governance. Maximize access, equity, and sustainability in governing the knowledge commons. This places a clear focus on institutional and technical arrangements and their link to equity, but it also requires tackling at least some of the underlying systemic inequalities that shape how open practices play out.

Prioritize gender equality. Making inclusion an explicit goal means ensuring gender equality because there are differences in how women and men leverage open resources. This is supported by gender-sensitive policymaking, gender parity in representation and participation, and by engaging women's civil society organizations. It also translates into facilitating equitable and safe spaces that allow women's equal participation, whether that means engaging men and women separately to participate in discussions, offering separate hours in computer labs, or offering childcare so that women can take part in workshops.

Develop an engagement strategy. Research and practice need to focus on the *engagement* connecting the supply of open informational resources with their uses, and to understand how it is used by or benefits marginalized communities. For example, from the OER work, we know that educators based in the Global South "would not have participated in OER creation activities without the intervention of an outside organization that had the capacity to help them develop materials and demonstrate what OEP looks like" (chapter 12). In most instances, without that concerted effort, open development initiatives undertaken in contexts of severely unequal distributions of access and skills will tend to entrench existing inequalities, if not actually make them worse. Facilitating inclusion in open practices is about developing a quality engagement strategy.

Leverage intermediaries. In a world of unequal access/skills and unequal power within information networks, intermediaries can be the critical links in the inclusive potential of open practices. They can be established knowledge brokers who are able to access opportunities—and decision-making venues—in order to act on behalf of excluded communities. Intermediation is really about having a model for engagement, facilitating participation, and supporting capacity development.

Incentivize openness. Institutional support for open practices makes a difference for their use. Currently, there are few examples of institutional support across the Global South (chapter 12), but policy frameworks incentivizing open education, science, and data support the knowledge commons. For instance, at the university level, institutions can encourage academics and authors as agents and owners of knowledge, protect the autonomy at the heart of commons-based structures for knowledge, and develop and support collaborative initiatives in knowledge dissemination (chapter 6). It could also include supporting marginalized scholars to curate their scholarship in ways that ensure that it can be discovered, contributing to the richness of the knowledge commons.

Focus on quality use and capabilities. For optimal inclusion, people need to not just have affordable and diverse access to the Internet, they also need to know how to use multiple devices and have the skills and capabilities to benefit from the resources they find. This represents a shift toward quality engagement and use, focusing not just on use-as-is, but rather on broader consumption practices, such as use-as-remix. This is not just the provision of goods but rather the capability to use. So, to tackle inclusion challenges, the delivery mechanism of open provision is what matters.

Final Thoughts: Rethinking Development?

We started this volume hoping to find that the practices of openness tend toward inclusion, tackling inequality, and helping to realize a new imaginary for development. What we learned, though, is that achieving inclusion is a bit like swimming upstream; any open initiative in the production, distribution, and use of knowledge must fight strong exclusionary currents. Sometimes these are structural and epistemological barriers—gender, socioeconomic status, historical positionality, and physical location barriers. And sometimes these are market barriers, where open practices get coopted by the bottom-line interests of bigger fish. Either way, on the whole, openness continues to be shaped by institutional, structural, and market arrangements rather than the other way around. At least that's been the case so far. Thus, in inequitable contexts, without a well-defined, targeted engagement element, openness initiatives may struggle with inclusive challenges.

Yet less equitable outcomes are not inevitable, and how we construct and govern open practices in our knowledge domains shapes equitability. This issue requires a healthy amount of pragmatism: figuring out the institutional arrangements for open practices and their link to equity, addressing underlying systemic inequalities that shape open practices, and, furthermore, understanding that governments play a critical role in facilitating and incentivizing openness. Concerted, pragmatic efforts, typically done locally, tend to be the most promising in terms of inclusive outcomes. As this volume shows, efforts can be made to promote inclusion within openness initiatives at all scales and levels. And as openness initiatives achieve success—for instance, demonstrating efficient use of resources (think of cost-saving for OER in public education) and bringing greater accountability into the public sphere (think of open and participatory budgeting)—the potential impact will cumulatively grow.

The extent to which open activities can truly offer an alternative or augmented approach to development, and ultimately their ability to do so, remain to be seen. Yet the redefinition of open development as a series of knowledge production, distribution, and use practices introduces a critical piece for human agency in terms of actualizing inclusion and improving knowledge governance, even if we happen to be witnessing a phase of "closure." Putting these knowledge tools at the core of human development helps us contextualize and rethink a range of challenges for development and openness activities moving forward. The hope is that if knowledge is recognized as the core of development (including the institutional shifts that this implies), then development policies, practices, and actions at all levels will be able to continue to actualize the open development imaginary.

Notes

1. Social inclusion, as represented by the World Bank, is about improving the terms for people and communities to participate in society—such as giving people a voice in decisions affecting their lives and equal access to markets, services, and political, social, and physical spaces.

2. This is not that surprising, given that the programming on open development at IDRC is emerging from the "Technology and Innovation" program area. The prevalence of digital open resources does not mean that we are going to change the definition of *open development*, but rather we will continue to interrogate the challenges of what the digital piece of open practices means for development.

3. Other gender-related issues include that women preferred to avoid "conflict during discussions, were worried about being wrong, and were willing to go along with their male colleagues" (as noted in chapter 4). Similarly, in the open science network, women said they were not comfortable going to meetings, and even if they did go, the men preferred to be the ones expressing their views (also noted in chapter 4).

4. Conceptualize, create, curate, circulate, certify, critique, loCate, customize, combine, and copy.

5. Reuse, revise, remix, redistribute, and retain.

6. However, as chapter 8 shows, the promises of novel innovations to spread access tend to fall short of expectations. Sophisticated open access arrangements require institutional expertise to control or manage resources, and this kind of expertise is often absent.

References

De Sousa Santos, Boaventura. 2014. *Epistemologies of the South: Justice against Epistemicide.* New York: Routledge.

Garzarelli, Giampaolo, Yamina R. Limam, and Bjørn Thomassen. 2008. "Open-Source Software and Economic Growth: A Classical Division of Labor Perspective." *Information Technology for Development* 14 (2): 116–135.

Visvanathan, Shiv. 2009. "The Search for Cognitive Justice." In *Knowledge in Question: A Symposium on Interrogating Knowledge and Questioning Science* no. 597, ed. Shiv Visvanathan. http://www .india-seminar.com/2009/597/597_shiv_visvanathan.htm.

World Bank. 2013. *Inclusion Matters: The Foundation for Shared Prosperity.* New Frontiers of Social Policy. Washington, DC. https://openknowledge.worldbank.org/handle/10986/16195?locale-attribute=en.

Contributors

Editors

Matthew L. Smith

Matthew Smith, a busy father of three and husband of one, also happens to be senior program specialist in the Technology and Innovation program at Canada's International Development Research Centre (IDRC), where he supports research and innovations to address pressing global challenges. During his decade-plus at IDRC, he has supported a wide range of research for development projects across the information and communication technologies for development (ICT4D) spectrum, a central focus being on deepening our understanding of the potential and perils of openness in development. Before IDRC, Matthew received a PhD in information systems from the London School of Economics and Political Science (LSE), focused on the interaction between technology and society. Matthew also has an MSc in development studies from the LSE, as well as an MSc in artificial intelligence from the University of Edinburgh. He is the coeditor of the book *Open Development: Networked Innovations for International Development* [MIT Press and International Development Research Centre (IDRC), 2013], which preceded this volume. Matthew has written on a variety of topics, including critical realism, e-government, trust, digital learning innovations, the capabilities approach, and artificial intelligence and human development.

Ruhiya Kristine Seward

Ruhiya has worked in international development at both the policy and community levels for twenty years, focusing on issues of inclusion, participation, and digital technologies. As a senior program officer with the Networked Economies team at the International Development Research Centre (IDRC), she oversees a broad research portfolio on gender equality, cyber policy and governance, digital rights, and innovation in the Global South. Before joining IDRC in March 2015, Ruhiya worked with the United Nations Development Programme (UNDP) in New York on international issues related to information and communication technologies for development (ICT4D). Ruhiya has a PhD in comparative politics from the New School for Social Research and an MSc in international relations from the London School of Economics and Political Science (LSE).

Chapter Authors

Denisse Albornoz

Denisse Albornoz was a research associate at the Open and Collaborative Science in Development Network (OCSDNet) from 2015 to 2018. She holds a BA in international development and sociology from the University of Toronto. Her research and advocacy work in India, Canada, and Peru has looked at questions of power and inequality in knowledge production, science, technology, and education. In the past, she has worked with the Centre for Internet and Society in Bangalore, and she is currently working for Hiperderecho, a digital rights organization in Peru, where she investigates gender and technology, data justice, and feminist digital culture.

Chris Armstrong

Chris Armstrong is a senior research associate with the Open African Innovation Research (Open AIR) project at the University of Ottawa's Centre for Law, Technology and Society (CLTS). He is also a research associate at the LINK Centre, University of the Witwatersrand, Johannesburg. He has been part of Open AIR since its inception in 2010, and he served as research manager for Open AIR's precursor network, African Copyright and Access to Knowledge (ACA2K), from 2007 to 2010. Armstrong was one of the editors of the books *Access to Knowledge in Africa: The Role of Copyright* (University of Cape Town Press and IDRC, 2010) and *Innovation and Intellectual Property: Collaborative Dynamics in Africa* (University of Cape Town Press, 2014). He is Publishing Editor of the LINK Centre journal, *African Journal of Information and Communication*, and holds a PhD in media studies (University of the Witwatersrand), a master's in journalism (Carleton), and a Bachelor of Arts in political science and English literature (Queen's).

Savita Bailur

Savita is a research director at Caribou Digital, managing multicountry research on user experiences of digital technology in low-income environments. She has worked with organizations including UNICEF, UN Women, the World Wide Web Foundation (on an open data research project funded by the International Development Research Centre [IDRC]), mySociety, the World Bank (Global Governance Practice), Microsoft Research India, Commonwealth Secretariat, and the US Agency for International Development (USAID). Savita is an adjunct professor at the School of Public and International Affairs, Columbia University, where she teaches the course "Policies and Practices in Digital Development"; a visiting fellow at the Digital Life Institute, Cornell Tech; and a visiting fellow at the Media and Communications Department of the London School of Economics and Political Science (LSE). She had a previous academic career at LSE and the Global Development Institute, University of Manchester, and has a PhD and MSc in information systems from the LSE, as well as degrees from the University of London and University of Cambridge. She has several publications, including two World Bank publications: *Evaluating Digital Citizen Engagement: A Practical Guide* (2016) and *Closing the Feedback Loop: Can Technology Bridge the Accountability Gap?* (2014), and peer-reviewed papers in the *International Journal of Communication, Government Information Quarterly, Information Technology and International Development,* and *Gender, Technology, and Development,* among others.

Roxana Barrantes

Roxana is an economist, holding a PhD (1992) and MS (1989) from the University of Illinois at Urbana-Champaign and a Bachelor of Social Sciences (1984) from the Pontificia Universidad Católica del Perú. She is a professor with the Department of Economics at the Pontifical Catholic University of Peru (PUCP) and director of its Master's Program. Previously a researcher at Instituto de Estudios Peruanos, she was also on the steering committee of the Regional Dialogue on the Information Society (DIRSI), leading research on information and communication technologies (ICTs) use and appropriation in the Americas. Currently, she serves as member of two dispute resolution administrative courts: the Division with Jurisdiction over Consumer Protection of the National Consumer Protection and Competition Enforcement Public Agency (Indecopi), and at Ositran, the National Transport Infrastructure Regulator. Recently, she was a board member of Petroperú (the national petroleum company), and the chief advisor to the minister of energy and mining. During her career, Barrantes has served on the staff and as a member of the board of directors of the Peruvian Telecommunications Regulatory Authority (OSIPTEL), as well as being a consultant to the Transport Regulatory commission in Peru (OSITRAN) and OSIPTEL, the National Superintendent of Sanitation (SUNASS), the Ministry of Transport and Communication, the National Ombudsman Office, and the Inter-American Development Bank.

Carla Bonina

Carla Bonina is an assistant professor of entrepreneurship and innovation at Surrey Business School in the UK and senior researcher at the Latin American Open Data Initiative (ILDA). Carla has fifteen years of experience conducting research work on digital innovation, entrepreneurship, and policy in international development. Her work has been published in leading academic journals such as *Government Information Quarterly* and *Information Systems Journal*, and she has contributed to previous edited volumes published by MIT Press. She provides regular strategic advice on digital transformation, open data, and value creation in the digital economy to governments, international organizations, and start-ups, including Avina Americas, the Organisation for Economic Co-operation and Development (OECD), International Development Research Centre (IDRC), and the World Bank. She is considered a Latin American expert. Carla holds a PhD in management from the London School of Economics and Political Science (LSE) in the UK. She is a member of Sandbox, a global network of young entrepreneurs, and shares a passion for social entrepreneurship.

Michael Cañares

Michael Cañares is an independent researcher and is currently strategy advisor at StepUp Consulting, based in the Philippines. He was recently the senior research manager for digital citizenship at the World Wide Web Foundation and once led the design and implementation of open data experiments in Southeast Asia for the foundation's Open Data Lab in Jakarta. His previous research has focused on local governance and local development issues, including public financial management, infrastructure governance, poverty issues, and open government.

Leslie Chan

Leslie Chan is an associate professor at the Centre for Critical Development Studies, University of Toronto Scarborough (UTSC). He is cross-appointed to the Department of Arts, Culture, and Media at UTSC. His teaching and professional practice center on the role of openness in the design of inclusive knowledge infrastructure and the implications for the production and flow of knowledge and their impact on local and international development. An original signatory of the Budapest Open Access Initiative, Leslie has been active in the experimentation and implementation of scholarly communication initiatives of varying scales around the world. He has served as director of Bioline International, an international collaborative open access platform, since 2000. Leslie was the Principal Investigator (PI) for the Open and Collaborative Science in Development Network (OCSDNet), funded by Canada's International Development Research Centre (IDRC) and the UK's Department for International Development (DFID), and the PI of the Knowledge G.A.P. (Geopolitics of Academic Production) project. He serves on the advisory board of the Directory of Open Access Journals and the San Francisco Declaration on Research Assessment (DORA). Recently, he became a member of an international working group on investing in open infrastructure. Leslie has published broadly on open access and scholarly communications.

Laura Czerniewicz

Laura Czerniewicz is the director of the Centre for Innovation in Learning and Teaching (CILT) at the University of Cape Town, and she was CILT's first director when it was formed in 2014. She has worked in education in a number of roles, with a continuous focus on inequality, access, and digital inequality. These have permeated her research interests, which include the changing nature of higher education in a digitally mediated society, as well as student and academic technological practices. She is currently the South African lead on a project funded by the Economic and Social Research Council National Research Foundation (ESRC NRF) on the Unbundled University, researching emerging models of teaching and learning provision. She has played a key strategic and scholarly role in the areas of blended and online learning, as well as open education. An NRF-rated researcher, Laura has published widely, both formally and informally. Her research outputs can be found at http://uct.academia.edu/LauraCzerniewicz and many of her presentations at https://www.slideshare.net/laura_Cz. She can be followed on Twitter at @czernie. For an interview with Laura Czerniewicz, listen to her podcast with Mark Nicols at http://onlinelearninglegends.com/podcast/007-professor-laura-czerniewicz/.

Jeremy de Beer

Jeremy de Beer creates and shapes ideas about innovation, intellectual property (IP), and international trade and development. He is an award-winning Professor of Law at the University of Ottawa and a member of the Centre for Law, Technology, and Society. He is a cofounding director of the Open African Innovation Research (Open AIR) network, www.OpenAIR.Africa; a senior fellow at the Centre for International Governance Innovation (CIGI); and a senior research associate at the University of Cape Town. His work has led to policy breakthroughs in digital communications, health sciences, food and agriculture, and clean energy. Jeremy has written over 100 refereed journal articles, book chapters, and other publications, and he is an author and editor of several books, including *Innovation and Intellectual Property: Collaborative Dynamics in Africa, Access to Knowledge in Africa: The Role of Copyright* (University of Cape Town Press, 2014), and *Implementing the WIPO Development Agenda* [Wilfrid Laurier University Press, Centre for International Governance Innovation (CIGI), International Development Research Centre (IDRC), 2009]. As a practicing lawyer and expert consultant, he has argued a dozen cases before the Supreme Court of Canada, advised businesses and law firms both large and small, and consulted for agencies from national governments, global think tanks, and the United Nations. Read more about how he is pioneering international, interdisciplinary research partnerships to transform complex legal concepts into real-world solutions at www.JeremydeBeer.com.

Stefano De Sabbata

Stefano De Sabbata is a lecturer in Quantitative Geography at the School of Geography, Geology, and the Environment of the University of Leicester and a Research Associate of the Oxford Internet Institute at the University of Oxford. He completed his undergraduate and master's studies at the Department of Mathematics and Computer Science of the University of Udine and then continued his studies at the Department of Geography of the University of Zurich, where he was awarded a PhD in geographic information science in 2013. He was a researcher at the Oxford Internet Institute of the University of Oxford and junior research fellow at the Wolfson College of the University of Oxford. His research focuses on geographic information science (GIS), critical GIS, and quantitative human geography. Stefano is part of the steering committee of GIScience Research UK (GISRUK) and was chair of the GISRUK 2018 conference. He is a member of the Commission on Location-Based Services of the International Cartographic Association and a Fellow of the Royal Geographical Society.

Shirin Elahi

Shirin Elahi is a scenario architect, working with organizations to help them imagine the future in order to grasp opportunities for growth and change. Shirin draws on her architectural expertise, using ideas rather than physical materials as the building blocks with which to imagine and build scenarios for the future—and then plans strategically. She has been involved in scenarios and strategic planning on the future of many global issues, including AIDS in Africa for UNAIDS, aviation for the Royal Aeronautical Society (RAeS), knowledge and innovation in Africa for the International Development Research Centre (IDRC), intellectual property and patenting for the European Patent Office, mobility and the motorcar for the Regional Airline Association (RAA), and nuclear safeguards for the International Atomic Energy Agency (IAEA). Shirin's interests lie in finding innovative ways to use scenarios to build common ground between different groups of stakeholders and to improve the quality of thinking and action around the future. Shirin lives in London.

Alison Gillwald

Alison Gillwald (PhD) is the executive director of Research ICT Africa (RIA) and holds an adjunct professorship at the Nelson Mandela School of Public Governance at the University of Cape

Town, where she convenes the Digital Economy and Society in Africa doctoral program. A former regulator, she was appointed to the founding Council of the South African Telecommunications Regulatory Authority (SATRA) in 1997 after setting up the Policy Department for the Independent Broadcasting Authority (IBA), which was established in the wake of the first democratic elections in South Africa in 1994. She has also served as chairperson of the South African National Digital Advisory Body, on the board of the public broadcaster SABC, and as the Deputy Chairperson of the SA National Broadband Advisory Council. Alison served on the Internet Corporation for Assigned Names and Numbers (ICANN) President's Strategy Panel on Multistakeholder Innovation, and she advised the Ministry of Communication on South Africa's Broadband Plan: SA Connect and the Government of Mauritius on the i-Mauritius broadband policy. She sits on the board of the South African Tertiary Education Networks (TENET). She is an Associate Editor of the International Telecommunication Union (ITU) journal, *Discoveries*, and sits on the editorial board of *Digital Policy*. She was appointed deputy chairperson of Giganet in 2019, having served as chairperson of the Communication Policy Research South conference.

Mark Graham

Mark Graham is the Professor of Internet Geography at the Oxford Internet Institute, a senior research fellow at Green Templeton College, and a faculty fellow at the Alan Turing Institute. He also holds visiting positions at the University of Cape Town, Wissenschaftszentrum Berlin für Sozialforschung, and Technische Universität Berlin. His research focuses on who benefits most and least from the world's increasing connectivity. Most recently, he was the coauthor (with Jamie Woodcock) of *The Gig Economy* (Polity Press, 2019) and is the editor of *Digital Economies at Global Margins* [MIT Press and International Development Research Centre (IDRC), 2019]. His full list of publications is available at www.markgraham.space.

Rebecca Hillyer

Rebecca Hillyer was the monitoring and evaluation coordinator with Open and Collaborative Science in Development Network (OCSDNet) from 2015 to 2018. She holds an MA in participation, power, and social change from the Institute of Development Studies in the UK, and an MPhil in urban and regional planning from Stellenbosch University in South Africa. She has worked for various community-based research and advocacy organizations across Canada, Ghana, South Africa, and the UK, with a focus on using participatory models to promote locally driven change. Prior to her work with OCSDNet, Rebecca was actively involved in coordinating another transnational research network, the Collaboration for Research on Democracy (CORD). Since 2017, Rebecca has focused her attention on understanding how individuals and communities can be involved in shaping urban life through her work with local municipalities in South Africa and, most recently, in her hometown of Owen Sound, Canada.

Cheryl Hodgkinson-Williams

Cheryl Hodgkinson-Williams is an associate professor, teaching online learning design and advanced research design courses to postgraduate students and supervising masters and PhD students in educational technology, open education, and higher-education studies. She holds a PhD in computer-assisted learning and has taught and supervised in the field of information communication technologies (ICTs) in education since 1994, first at the University of Pretoria, then at Rhodes University in Grahamstown, and now at the University of Cape Town. In addition, she was the Principal Investigator (PI) of the Research in Open Educational Resources for Development (ROER4D) project, funded by the International Development Research Centre (IDRC), which investigated the adoption and impact of the use of open educational resources in twenty-one countries in the Global South. She is an advisor on the Digital Open Textbooks for Development (DOT4D) project and the PI of the Cases on Open Learning (COOL) project, which is investigating the readiness toward open learning of Technical and Vocational Education and Training (TVET) and Higher Education (HE) institutions in South Africa. She was recently appointed as the United Nations Educational, Scientific, and Cultural Organization (UNESCO) Chair of Open Education and Social Justice.

Dick Kawooya

Dick Kawooya is an associate professor at the University of South Carolina's School of Library and Information Science (SLIS). Kawooya holds a PhD in Communication and Information from the University of Tennessee. His doctoral research explored Ugandan traditional musicians' construction of ownership. Kawooya held an Open Society Institute (OSI) Fellowship in 2006–2007 at the Center for Policy Studies, Central European University, Budapest, conducting research on the impact of copyright on representation of and access to African knowledge. Most recently, he was part of the Open African Innovation Research (Open AIR) and Training Project and network, under which he studied the role of intellectual property (IP) in the exchange and interactions between informal and formal sectors in Africa's emerging automotive industry. He was the Lead Researcher for the African Copyright and Access to Knowledge (ACA2K) Project (2007–2010). Kawooya has served as a member of the Commonwealth of Learning (CoL) Copyright Expert Group, and as Uganda's national copyright expert (representing the Consortium of Ugandan University Libraries) for the international Electronic Information for Libraries (eIFL). Kawooya has attended, and presented at, several meetings of the World Intellectual Property Organisation (WIPO), including the June 2005 Intersessional Intergovernmental Meeting (IIM) on a Development Agenda for WIPO.

Erika Kramer-Mbula

Erika Kraemer-Mbula is a professor of economics at the University of Johannesburg (South Africa) and holds the DST/NRF/Newton Fund Trilateral Research Chair in Transformative Innovation, the Fourth Industrial Revolution and Sustainable Development. She specializes in science, technology, and innovation policy analysis and innovation systems in connection with equitable and inclusive development. In her work, she has explored incremental and disruptive innovations by and for disadvantaged communities, including the informal sector.

Paulo Matos

Paulo Matos holds a BA in economics from Pontificia Universidad Católica del Perú (PUCP) and currently is a research associate at Innovations for Poverty Action. He was previously with Instituto de Estudios Peruanos (IEP, Institute of Peruvian Studies) and the Department of Economics at PUCP. His major interests are development economics, social studies, computer science, and mathematics.

Caroline Ncube

Caroline Ncube is a professor in the Department of Commercial Law at the University of Cape Town (UCT), where she teaches and supervises masters and doctoral students in intellectual property law. She holds the Department of Science and Technology/National Research Foundation Research Chair in Intellectual Property, Innovation, and Development under the auspices of the South African Research Chairs Initiative. She holds a PhD from UCT, an LLM from the University of Cambridge, and an LLB degree from the University of Zimbabwe. Caroline is a Fellow of the Cambridge Commonwealth Society and a Shell Centenary Fund Scholar. Before joining UCT, she lectured at the University of Limpopo (formerly University of the North) and the University of Zimbabwe. Prior to embarking on an academic career, she briefly practiced as an attorney. She has been engaged in several international intellectual property (IP) law research projects, such as the Open African Innovation Research (Open AIR) network project, of which she is a coleader. She has published widely on IP law on aspects including traditional knowledge, regional integration, patents, and copyright law. She is an associate member of the Centre for Law, Technology, and Society at the University of Ottawa. A founding coeditor of the *South African Intellectual Property Law Journal*, Caroline serves on the editorial boards of the *Journal of Corporate and Commercial Law and Practice*, the *African Journal of Intellectual Property*, and the *African Journal of Information and Communication*.

Chidi Oguamanam

Chidi Oguamanam is a professor in the Faculty of Law (Common Law Section) at the University of Ottawa, where he is affiliated with three Centres of Excellence: the Centre for Law, Technology, and Society; the Centre for Environmental Law and Global Sustainability; and the Centre for Health Law Policy and Ethics. He holds numerous research fellowships and affiliations with leading organizations, including the Centre for International Governance Innovation, the Centre for International Sustainable Development Law at McGill University, and the Intellectual Property Law Unit at the University of Cape Town. An author of several books that reflect a wide range of interdisciplinary research, Oguamanam leads and is affiliated with many research consortia, including ABS Canada and the Open Africa Innovation Research (Open AIR) partnership. He is a sought-after speaker and public intellectual committed to justice and fairness in global knowledge governance paradigms, with an emphasis on IP's interface with Indigenous knowledge systems. In 2016, he was named to the Royal Society of Canada College of New Scholars. Please visit https://www.oguamanam.com/.

Angela Okune

Angela Okune is a doctoral candidate in the Anthropology Department at the University of California, Irvine. She studies data-sharing cultures and infrastructures of qualitative research groups working in and on Kenya in order to explore broader questions of equity, knowledge production, and socioeconomic development in Africa. Angela is a recipient of a Wenner-Gren Foundation fieldwork grant and a 2016 Graduate Research Fellowship from the National Science Foundation, and she was a 2018 Fellow at the UC Berkeley Center for Technology, Society, and Policy. From 2010–2015, as cofounder of the research department at iHub, Nairobi's innovation hub for the tech community, Angela provided strategic guidance for the growth of tech research in Kenya. Angela has been involved with Open and Collaborative Science in Development Network (OCSDNet) as a Network Coordinator since the network's inception in 2014.

Alejandro Posada

Alejandro Posada was a research associate with Open and Collaborative Science in Development Network (OCSDNet) and a project director with the Knowledge G.A.P. (Geopolitics of Academic Production), based in Bogotá, Colombia. He graduated with high distinction from the International Development and Economics programs at the University of Toronto Scarborough (2016) and is interested in the political economy and financialization of the publishing industry. Alejandro has international work experience (in Guatemala, India, Colombia, and Canada) with nongovernmental organizations (NGOs), international cooperation agencies, and research networks; and in research areas including rural and agrarian development, agricultural financial markets, knowledge production, and open access. With the Knowledge G.A.P., he is investigating the inequality implications of academic publishers' transition into data analytics and the vertical integration of scholarly infrastructure. He currently works as a research analyst for Econometria Consultores, a policy evaluation firm based in Bogotá, Colombia, and has an ongoing research project on the impact of agricultural insurance on farmer risk management in Guatemala.

Nagla Rizk

Nagla Rizk is professor of economics and founding director of the Access to Knowledge for Development Center (A2K4D) at the American University in Cairo's School of Business. Her research area is the economics of knowledge, technology, and development, with a focus on digital platforms, entrepreneurship, innovation, data, knowledge governance, business models, and inclusion in the digital economy in the Middle East and Africa. She leads the Open Data for Development Node for the Middle East and North Africa and is a Steering Committee member of the Open African Innovation Research Partnership. She authored Egypt's National Strategy for Free and Open Source Software (2014), served as a member of Egypt's Ministerial Committee on the Right to Information law (2013), and is a member of the Academy of Scientific Research and Technology's Committee on Alternative Innovation Assessment in Egypt. Rizk is a faculty associate at Harvard's Berkman Klein Center for Internet and Society and Affiliated Faculty at Harvard Law School's Copyrightx course. She is also an affiliated fellow of Yale Law School's Information

Society Project; associate member of the University of Ottawa's Centre for Law, Technology, and Society; and a member of the Executive Committee of the International Economic Association. She received her PhD in Economics from McMaster University in 1995. She taught at the University of Toronto (2006), Yale Law School (2010), and Columbia University (2014).

Isaac Rutenberg

Isaac Rutenberg is an academic and lawyer based in Nairobi, Kenya. He is currently the director of the Centre for Intellectual Property and Information Technology Law (CIPIT) at the Strathmore Law School, Strathmore University in Nairobi, where he is also a senior lecturer. Isaac holds a JD (degree in law), a PhD in chemistry, and BSc degrees in chemistry and in mathematics/computer science. He has been admitted to practice law in California, patent law by the US Patent and Trademark Office, and patent/trademark law in the Kenya Industrial Property Institute. He is a member of the Chartered Institute of Arbitrators (Kenya branch) and the American Chemical Society.

Tobias Schonwetter

Tobias Schonwetter is director of the Intellectual Property (IP) Unit (www.ip-unit.org) and an associate professor in the University of Cape Town's law department. He is a Principal Investigator (PI) for various IP–related research and capacity-building projects, including Open African Innovation Research (Open AIR; www.openair.africa). Previously, Tobias was a senior manager, Technology and Innovation Law, at PwC South Africa, as well as the regional coordinator for Africa and Legal Lead South Africa for Creative Commons (CC). He also served as an editor for the *African Journal of Information and Communication* and its Thematic Issue on Knowledge Governance for Development, and was a postdoctoral fellow at the University of Cape Town's IP Unit. Tobias specializes in and teaches IP, particularly the relationship between IP, innovation, and development, as well as cyberlaw. Tobias studied and practiced law in Germany and holds PhD and LLM degrees from the University of Cape Town. Since 2017, Tobias has been an associate member of the Centre for Law, Technology, and Society at the University of Ottawa. Tobias has written numerous articles on IP law and has spoken at various national and international conferences.

Fabrizio Scrollini

Fabrizio Scrollini is the executive director of the Open Data Latin American Initiative (ILDA), and member of the Open Data Network for Development (OD4D). He cofounded and was the chairman of DATA Uruguay, a civic association that builds civic technology to promote human development. Fabrizio is also a cofounder of Abrelatam and the Open Data Regional Conference for Latin America and the Caribbean, and is one of the Lead Stewards of the International Charter of Open Data. He worked with governments, regulators, and civil society at international and regional levels on transparency, access to public information, open data projects, and public-sector reform. He holds a PhD in Government from the London School of Economics and Political Science (LSE).

Raed Sharif

With nearly two decades of experience as a researcher, practitioner, and educator, Raed makes sure that his knowledge and experience contribute to creating the enabling conditions for individuals and communities to improve and realize their potential, especially in the Global South. Throughout this journey, he has been a strong advocate for concepts such as inclusion, openness, and local innovation. He has worked and collaborated with a variety of organizations, including the SecDev Foundation, International Development Research Centre (IDRC), the Web Foundation, the US National Academy of Sciences, CODATA International, and the United Nations Development Programme (UNDP). He also taught at the University of Toronto and Syracuse University. He holds a PhD in Information Science and Technology from Syracuse University, and an MBA and a Bachelor in Economics and Political Science, both from Birzeit University in Palestine.

William Randall Spence

William Randall Spence currently heads Economic and Social Development Affiliates. Assignments include ICT policy and regulation, poverty and economic policy, human development and capability initiatives, intellectual property (IP), and innovation systems. From 1990–2005, he worked with International Development Research Centre (IDRC) as senior program specialist in economics and as Director of IDRC's Regional Office for Southeast and East Asia in Singapore. Prior to joining IDRC, he was a senior economist with the Canadian Departments of External Affairs, Finance, and EMR (Energy, Mines, and Resources), as well as the Ottawa-based North-South Institute. He has worked on a long-range planning project in Kenya (World Bank), as an economic advisor in the Tanzanian Ministry of Planning (CIDA), and has taught economics at McMaster and Guelph universities in Canada. He has a PhD in economics from the University of Toronto. He is a Fellow of the Human Development and Capability Association and a member of the International Advisory Board of LIRNEasia.

Henry Trotter

Henry Trotter works as a researcher with the Centre for Innovation in Learning and Teaching (CILT) at the University of Cape Town (UCT). He focuses on open access, open learning, and open educational resources (OER) and open educational practices (OEP), especially as they relate to the desire for greater social inclusion and social justice in the African higher education sector. The lead author of *Seeking Impact and Visibility: Scholarly Communication in Southern Africa* (African Minds, 2014), he has also coauthored a number of articles and book chapters on these openness themes. In addition to his work in higher education, Trotter has published widely in the field of South African history and culture, including an ethnography titled *Sugar Girls & Seamen: A Journey into the World of Dockside Prostitution in South Africa* (Jacana Media (Pty) Ltd, 2008) and an upcoming work of narrative nonfiction titled *Cape Town: A Place Between* (Catalyst Press, 2020).

François van Schalkwyk

François van Schalkwyk is a research fellow at the Centre for Research on Evaluation, Science and Technology (CREST) at Stellenbosch University. He holds a PhD in science and technology studies, as well as masters' degrees in education and publishing. His main research interests are in the areas of higher-education studies, data, and science communication. For more information on François's current research projects and a list of recent publications, please visit https://www .researchgate.net/profile/Francois_Van_Schalkwyk3.

Sonal Zaveri

Sonal Zaveri is an experienced evaluator, founder member, and Vice President of the Community of Evaluators South Asia; Coordinator of GENSA, the Gender and Equity Network South Asia; a member of the EvalGender+ global management group; cochair of the Tools and Approaches task group for gender-sensitive and equity-responsive evaluation; a member of the working group on the South2South Evaluation initiative; and course design and facilitator for the first online gender and evaluation course in India. Sonal's interests relate to how culture, rights, participation, and gender intersect with various evaluation approaches, such as outcome mapping and utilization-focused, feminist, and developmental evaluation. Since 2009, she has been involved with Developing Evaluation Capacity in ICT4D (DECI) to train existing information and communication technologies (ICT) researchers and evaluators in utility-outcome-ownership-based evaluation as applied to information and communication technology for development (ICT4D) projects in Asia, and she continues to do so with DECI-3, Designing Evaluation and Communication for Impact. Having worked previously in academia, her current work experience includes government, nongovernmental organizations (NGOs), international governmental organizations (INGOs), foundations, the United Nations, and bilaterals and multilaterals. She lives in India and has worked in more than twenty countries across Asia, East and West Africa, Asia-Pacific, Central Asia, Middle East, and Eastern Europe.

Index